Hc

EUROPEAN CUPS

Who won which where when
by Ron Hockings

EUROPEAN CUP · CUP WINNERS CUP · UEFA CUP

KENNETH MASON

Front cover pictures from left to right
- Stefano Tacconi, Juventus, UEFA
- Luca Pellegrini, Sampdoria, Cup Winners Cup
- Franco Baresi, Milan, European Cup

Photos Allsport

Published by Kenneth Mason
12a North Street, Emsworth, Hampshire PO10 7DQ

© Ron Hockings 1990

British Library Cataloguing in Publication Data
Hockings, Ron
Hockings' European cups: who won which where when - 2nd ed
1. Europe. Association football. Championships. Winners, history
I. Title
796.33464094

ISBN 0-85937-351-7

Printed and bound in Great Britain by Hartnolls Ltd, Bodmin, Cornwall
Typesetting and artwork by Articulate Studio, Hampshire 0243 374523

CONTENTS

FOREWORD

There have been many difficulties with names of the competing teams, particularly with countries like Austria, Bulgaria, East Germany and Romania who seem to change names of teams consistently, with Belgium and Holland having many amalgamations. I am grateful to the purchasers of the first edition for helping me to get names, amalgamations, colours, stadium names and capacities accurately described. Please let me know of any changes for updating in the next edition. Where I have been unable to find appropriate facts, such as names of teams, telephone numbers *etc*, I have simply left gaps. If you can provide answers I will include them in the third edition.

The political changes in Eastern Europe mean the face of European football will alter, many teams will revert to their old names or change them completely, some because names were forced on them by the political climate and others for more sinister reasons. The first of these was made on January 9 1990 when Dinamo Bucharest reverted to an earlier name of Unirea Tricolour.

ACKNOWLEDGEMENTS

I am greatly indebted to the following for help in compiling this edition: Keir Radnedge of *World Soccer*; Peter Cresswell of London; Sean Creedon of Dublin; Manuel Falmhaupt of Graz, Austria; Peter Kungler of Binningen, Switzerland; Jean-Pierre Meyer of Brussels, Belgium; Jorgen Nielsen of Randers, Denmark; Adalberto Sousa of Vila Mea, Portugal; Hakan Sjokvist of Gothenburg, Sweden; David Toole of Liverpool, England and Stefan Welte of Hard, Austria.

THE THREE CUPS

EUROPEAN CHAMPION CLUBS CUP

Commonly known as the European Cup, this is the top club trophy played for in Europe. Over many years people had favoured a genuine European competition. An organising body was set up by Gabriel Hanot, then editor of *L'Equipe*, a famous French sports paper. But FIFA, the world rulers and UEFA, the European rulers at first showed little interest. Nevertheless Hanot set up a first meeting in Paris in the spring of 1955 when delegates from 18 countries were asked to attend. The meeting went well and after a few hours' discussion, the idea of a tournament was accepted with the first matches arranged for the autumn of 1955. To the surprise of many FIFA promptly recognised the new competition provided that the participating clubs had the permission of their national associations. UEFA eventually agreed to take responsibility for the organisation. The competition was open to each league champion of the competing countries, although the country of the holders, who defended the trophy the following season, were allowed to enter a second team. Up to the Final, to take place on a neutral ground, the matches would be played on a home and away basis. If the aggregate scores were level then a third and deciding match would be played. This has changed over the years. After it was decided not to play a third match (possibly because of fixture congestion) a toss of a coin decided the winner after the second match had gone through extra time. What happens now if the aggregate scores are level after the second match and extra time, the team scoring the most away goals goes through. If the away goals by both sides are the same, a penalty shoot out decides the winners. Of the first 18 invitations sent out by Hanot and *L'Equipe* 12 countries took part in the first European Cup in the 1955-56 season. There would have been 13 but following bad advice by the English Football Association Chelsea withdrew and were replaced by Gwardia Warsaw, while Eindhoven of Holland and Aarhus of Denmark took over from the original Holland Sport and KB Copenhagen. Every European country now enters a team although the English entry has been suspended until further notice owing to the behaviour of some supporters at the 1985 Final in Brussels. Thirty-two countries plus the holders are entitled to enter a team, the exception being Wales who do not have a recognised national League.

EUROPEAN CUP WINNERS CUP

The institution of this cup for winning clubs of a national knock out competition took place in the 1960-61 season with ten entries. Since then the cup has truly established itself with entries from every European country including Wales (which has had a cup competition since 1878). The rules of the European Champion Clubs Cup apply to this competition in every respect.

INTER CITIES FAIRS CUP COMPETITION

The Inter Cities Fairs Cup was designed originally to give a competitive edge to friendly matches played between cities which held trade fairs, its name later changing to European Fairs Cup then to the UEFA Cup, as it is now known. It was the brainchild of Ernst Thommen, a Swiss vice-president of FIFA. The setting up of UEFA in 1954 gave him the chance to formulate his ideas and he invited officials from 12 cities holding trade fairs to endorse his plans.

The competition was to be held over two seasons for fear of disrupting domestic fixtures. The first entries represented cities that held trade fairs, in some cases a selection of several clubs making up the team (*ie* those in London, *etc*). The first competition over-ran to a third year. The second was completed in two years, but from thereon it was played annually.

By 1971, when it was renamed the UEFA Cup, it had become firmly established and was proving to be a lucrative third European competition for which a set number of clubs from each country, but only one per town or city, could qualify. Entry was based on league position after the Champions and Cup winners were entered for the two senior trophies. Any connection now with trade fairs is purely coincidental.

Entry Rules for the UEFA Cup. The merit table for a country's permitted club entries is based on the results of all three competitions over five years. A win counts for 2 points, a draw 1 point, a tie decided on penalties stands as a draw. In addition bonus points are awarded for teams reaching the last eight; every finalist receives 3 points, semi finalists 2 points and quarter finalists 1 point. The total points are divided by the number of participants to form a merit table of averages. The first three places have four teams, the next five have three teams, the next thirteen two teams, and the rest one team. When England returns to European Competition they will have only one team in the UEFA Cup.

RULES OF THE COMPETITIONS. From 1955-56 if two teams were level on aggregate after the two 90-minute legs of the tie, a play off was arranged on a neutral ground, with extra time and then a toss of a coin or disc if necessary. From the 1967-68 season if two teams were level on aggregate after two legs, then away goals goals should count double. If teams were still level, then a play-off should take place. From 1969-70 it was decided that teams level after extra time at the end of the second leg should spin a coin to decide who went through. From the start of the 1970-71 season a penalty competition was introduced. If this was not resolved after five penalties, each side would continue with a penalty each until one was missed, that team being the losers. Two substitutes from five rule was implemented at the start of the 1968-69 season.

TRANSLATIONS

English	French	German	Italian	Spanish
Colours	Couleurs	Farben	Colori	Colores
National Colours	Coluleurs Nationales	Landesfarben	Colori Nazionali	Colores Nacionales
Black	Noir	Schwarz	Nero	Negro
Blue	Bleu	Blau	Blu	Azul
Claret	Bordeaux	Weinrot	Rosso-Violetto	Rojo Purpura
Green	Vert	Grün	Verde	Verde
Lilac	Lilas	Lila	Lilla	Lila
Maroon	Pourpre	Kastonienbraun	Castano	Castaño
Navy Blue	Bleu Marine	Dunkelblau	Blu Scuro	Azul Marino
Old Gold	Vieil Or	Altgold	Color Oro Antico	Oro Viejo (Dorado)
Red	Rouge	Rot	Rosso	Rojo
Sky Blue	Bleu Ciel	Hellblau	Celeste	Azul Claro
Violet	Violet	Violett	Viola	Violeta
White	Blanc	Weiss	Bianco	Blanco
Yellow	Jaune	Gelb	Giallo	Amarillo
Shirts	Maillots	Trikots	Maglietta	Camisetas
Shorts	Shorts	Shorts	Calzoncini	Shorts (Pantalones Cortos)
Socks	Chaussettes	Stutzen	Calzettoni	Calcetines
Collars	Cols	Kragen	Colletto	Cuellos
Striped	À Rayures	Gestreift	Rigato	De rayas
Trim	Liseret	Rand	Bordo	Colores del equipo
Horizontal	Horizontal	Quer	Orrizzontale	Horizontal
Vertical	Vertical	Senkrecht	Verticale	Verticales
Hooped	À Rayures Horizontal	Geringelt	Strisce Sulla Maglietta	Horizontales
Withdrew	S'est Retiré	Richt Angetreten	Ritirato	Retiró
Played	Joué	Gespielt	Partita Giocata	Jugado
Stadium	Stade	Stadion	Stadio	Estadio
Amalgamated	Fusionné	Fusioniert	Club Amalgamati	Amalgamado
Halved	Bicolore	Halb-halb	Tenuta a due Colori	Dividido en dos
Founded	Fondé	Gegründet	Fondato	Fundado
League Champions	Vainqueurs du Championnat	Ligameister	Vincitore di Campionato	Campeones de Liga
Cup Winners	Vainqueurs de la Coupe	Pokalsieger	Vincitori di Coppa	Ganadores de la Copa
Super Cup	Super Coupe	Superpokal	Super Coppa	Super Copa
European Cups Record	Record des Coupes Européenes	Europapokalrekord	Record Coppa UEFA	Record de las Copas Europeas

English	French	German	Italian	Spanish
Combination	Coupe des Équipes Réserves	Reservoliga	Associazione	Combinación
Selection	Sélection	Auswahl	Selezione	Secleccíon
Formerly	Autrefois	Früher	Precedentemente	Anteriormente
Void	Abandonné	Ungültig	Partita Abbandonata	Anulado/Invalidado
Light	Clair	Hell	Chiaro (colore)	Luz/Lijero
Finalist	Finaliste	Finalist	Finalista	Finalista
Bye	Exempt	Freilos	Non Presentarsi dell'altra squadra	Un equipo que queda de nou
Previously	Auparavant	Früher	Precedentemente	Previamente
Band	Bande	Streifen	Striscia di Colore	Banda
Seats	Fauteuils	Sitzplätze	Posti	Asientos
Goals	Buts	Tore	Gol	Goles
p/pens: Penalties	Penalties	Elfm (Elfmeter)	Rigori	Penaltis
wot: won on toss of coin	Gagné à la pièce	gnM: Gewonnen nach Münzenwurf	Eliminatoria vinta per sorteggio	Ganó al "Cara y cruz"
lot: lost on toss of coin	Perdu à la pièce	vnM: Verloren nach Münzenwurf	Eliminatoria persa per sorteggio	Perdió al "Cara y cruz"
wop: won on penalty shoot out, 5 penalties each	Gagné aux penalties, 5 penalties chacun	gnE: Gewonnen nach Elfmeterschiesen, je 5 Elfmeter pro Mannschaft	Eliminatoria vinta ai rigori, 5 per ciascuna squadra	Ganó por penalties - 5 penalties cada uno
lop: lost on penalty shootout	Perdu aux penalties, 5 penalties chacun	vnE: Verloren nach Elfmeterschiessen	Eliminatoria persa ai rigori, 5 per ciascuna squadra	Perdiò por penalts
wag: won on away goals	Gagné sur buts à l'extérieur	gdA: Gewonnen durch Auswärtstore	Eliminatoria vinta per i gol segnati fuori casa	Ganó por goles fuera de casa
lag: lost on away goals	Perdu sur buts à	vdA: Verloren durch	Eliminatoria persa per i gol segnati fuori casa	Perdió por goles fuera de casa
pr: preliminaries	Eliminatoires	Vrd: Vorrunden	Preliminari	Preliminares

Please send amendments or suggestions for improvements to the author, Ron Hockings, 36 Lockier Walk, Wembley, Middlesex HA9 7TW, UK. Tel 081 904 7294

Veuillez adresser toutes modifications ou suggestions à l'auteur, Ron Hockings, 36 Lockier Walk, Wembley, Middlesex HA9 7TW, UK. Tel 081 904 7294

Schicken sie bitte dem Autor Vorschläge zur Abänderung oder Verbesserung; und zwar an Ron Hockings, 36 Lockier Walk, Wembley, Middlesex HA9 7TW, UK. Tel 081 904 7294

Per piacere mandi correzioni o suggerimenti all autore para el perfeccionamiento del libro Ron Hockings, 36 Lockier Walk, Wembley, Middlesex HA9 7TW, UK. Tel 081 904 7294

Per piacere mandi correzione o suggerimenti al autore, Ron Hockings, 36 Lockier Walk, Wembley, Middlesex HA9 7TW, UK. Tel 081 904 7294

THE WINNERS

EUROPEAN CUP FINAL RESULTS

Date	Winner		Runner-up	Score	Venue	Attendance
13-6-56	**Real Madrid, Spain** *Di Stefano, Rial 2, Marquitos*	v	Stade de Reims, France *Leblond, Hidalgo, Templin*	4-3	Paris	38,000
30-5-57	**Real Madrid, Spain** *Di Stefano penalty, Gento*	v	Fiorentina, Italy	2-0	Madrid	124,000
28-5-58	**Real Madrid, Spain** *Di Stefano, Rial, Gento*	v	AC Milan, Italy *Schaffino, Grillo*	3-2 aet	Brussels	67,000
3-6-59	**Real Madrid, Spain** *Mateos, Di Stefano*	v	Stade de Reims, France	2-0	Stuttgart	80,000
18-5-60	**Real Madrid, Spain** *Di Stefano 3, Puskas 4, 1 penalty*	v	Eintracht Frankfurt, Germany *Kress, Stein 2*	7-3	Glasgow	127,621
31-5-61	**Benfica, Portugal** *Aguas, Gensana own goal, Coluna*	v	CF Barcelona, Spain *Kocsis, Czibor*	3-2	Berne	33,000
2-5-62	**Benfica, Portugal** *Eusebio 2, 1 penalty, Aguas, Cavem, Coluna*	v	Real Madrid, Spain *Puskas 3*	5-3	Amsterdam	68,000
22-5-63	**AC Milan, Italy** *Altafini 2*	v	Benfica, Portugal *Eusebio*	2-1	Wembley, London	45,000
27-5-64	**Inter Milan, Italy** *Mazzola 2, Milani*	v	Real Madrid, Spain *Felo*	3-1	Vienna	72,000
27-5-65	**Inter Milan, Italy** *Jair*	v	Benfica, Portugal	1-0	Milan	80,000
11-5-66	**Real Madrid, Spain** *Amancio, Serena*	v	Partizan Belgrade, Yugoslavia *Vasovic*	2-1	Brussels	55,000
25-5-67	**Glasgow Celtic, Scotland** *Gemmell, Chalmers*	v	Inter Milan, Italy *Mazzola penalty*	2-1	Lisbon	55,000
29-5-68	**Manchester United, England** *Charlton 2, Best, Kidd*	v	Benfica, Portugal *Graca*	4-1 aet	Wembley, London	100,000
28-5-69	**AC Milan, Italy** *Prati 3, Sormani*	v	Ajax Amsterdam, Holland *Vasovic penalty*	4-1	Madrid	50,000
6-5-70	**Feyenoord Rotterdam, Holland** *Israel, Kindvall*	v	Glasgow Celtic, Scotland *Gemmell*	2-1 aet	Milan	53,187
2-6-71	**Ajax Amsterdam, Holland** *Van Dijk, Haan*	v	Panathinaikos, Greece	2-0	Wembley, London	90,000
31-5-72	**Ajax Amsterdam, Holland** *Cruyff 2*	v	Inter Milan, Italy	2-0	Rotterdam	61,000
30-5-73	**Ajax Amsterdam, Holland** *Rep*	v	Juventus, Italy	1-0	Belgrade	93,500
15-5-74	**Bayern Munich, Germany** *Schwarzenbeck*	v	Atletico Madrid, Spain *Luis*	1-1 aet	Brussels	65,000
17-5-74	**Bayern Munich, Germany** *Hoeness 2, Muller 2*	v	Atletico Madrid, Spain	4-0	Brussels	23,000
28-5-75	**Bayern Munich, Germany** *Roth, Muller*	v	Leeds United, England	2-0	Paris	48,000
12-5-76	**Bayern Munich, Germany** *Roth*	v	St Etienne, France	1-0	Glasgow	54,684
25-5-77	**Liverpool, England** *Mcdermott, Smith, Neal penalty*	v	Borussia Monchengladbach, Germany *Simonsen*	3-1	Rome	57,000
10-5-78	**Liverpool, England** *Dalglish*	v	Clube Bruges, Belgium	1-0	Wembley, London	92,000
30-5-79	**Nottingham Forest, England** *Francis*	v	Malmo FF, Sweden	1-0	Munich	57,500
28-5-80	**Nottingham Forest, England** *Robertson*	v	Hamburger SV, Germany	1-0	Madrid	51,000
27-5-81	**Liverpool, England** *Kennedy*	v	Real Madrid, Spain	1-0	Paris	48,360

Date	Team 1		Team 2	Score	Venue	Attendance
26-5-82	Aston Villa, England *Withe*	v	Bayern Munich, Germany	1-0	Rotterdam	46,000
25-5-83	Hamburger SV, Germany *Magath*	v	Juventus, Italy	1-0	Athens	80,000
30-5-84	Liverpool, England *Neal*	v	AS Roma, Italy *Pruzzo*	1-1 4-2 pens	Rome	69,693
29-5-85	Juventus, Italy *Platini penalty*	v	Liverpool, England	1-0	Brussels	58,000
7-5-86	Steaua Bucharest, Rumania	v	FC Barcelona, Spain	0-0 2-0 pens	Seville	70,000
27-5-87	FC Porto, Portugal *Madjer, Juary*	v	Bayern Munich, Germany *Kogl*	2-1	Vienna	56,000
25-5-88	PSV Eindhoven, Holland	v	Benfica, Portugal	0-0 6-5 pens	Stuttgart	55,000
24-5-89	AC Milan, Italy *Marco Van Basten 2, Ruud Gullit 2*	v	Steaua Bucharest, Rumania	4-0	Barcelona	97,000
23-5-90	AC Milan, Italy *F Rijkaard*	v	Benfica, Portugal	1-0	Vienna	56,000

CUP WINNERS CUP FINAL RESULTS

Date	Team 1		Team 2	Score	Venue	Attendance
17-5-61	Glasgow Rangers, Scotland	v	Fiorentina, Italy *Milan 2*	0-2 2 leg final	Glasgow	80,000
23-5-61	Fiorentina, Italy *Milan, Hamrin*	v	Glasgow Rangers, Scotland *Scott*	2-1	Florence	40,000
10-5-62	Atletico Madrid, Spain *Peiro*	v	Fiorentina, Italy *Hamrin*	1-1 aet	Glasgow	30,000
5-9-62	Atletico Madrid, Spain *Jones, Mendonca, Peiro*	v	Fiorentina, Italy	3-0	replay in Stuttgart	39,000
15-5-63	Tottenham Hotspur, England *Greaves 2, White, Dyson 2*	v	Atletico Madrid, Spain *Collar penalty*	5-1	Rotterdam	50,000
13-5-64	Sporting Lisbon, Portugal *Figueiredo 2, Dansky own goal*	v	MTK Budapest, Hungary *Sandor 2, Kuti*	3-3 aet	Brussels	4,000
15-5-64	Sporting Lisbon, Portugal *Mendes*	v	MTK Budapest, Hungary	1-0	Antwerp	14,000
19-5-65	West Ham United, England *Sealey 2*	v	TSV 1860 Munich, Germany	2-0	Wembley, London	98,000
5-5-66	Borussia Dortmund, Germany *Held, Yeats own goal*	v	Liverpool, England *Hunt*	2-1 aet	Glasgow	42,000
31-5-67	Bayern Munich, Germany *Roth*	v	Glasgow Rangers, Scotland	1-0 aet	Nurnburg	70,000
23-5-68	AC Milan, Italy *Hamrin 2*	v	Hamburger SV, Germany	2-0	Rotterdam	54,000
21-5-69	Slovan Bratislava, Czechoslovakia *Cvetler, Hrivnak, Jan Capkovic*	v	CF Barcelona, Spain *Zaluda, Rexach*	3-2	Basle	40,000
20-4-70	Manchester City, England *Young, Lee penalty*	v	Gornik Zabrze, Poland *Ozlizlo*	2-1	Vienna	10,000
19-5-71	Chelsea, England *Osgood*	v	Real Madrid, Spain *Zoco*	1-1 aet	Athens	42,000
21-5-71	Chelsea, England *Dempsey, Osgood*	v	Real Madrid, Spain *Fleitas*	2-1	Athens	24,000
24-5-72	Glasgow Rangers, Scotland *Stein, Johnston 2*	v	Dynamo Moscow, USSR *Estrekov, Makovikov*	3-2	Barcelona	35,000
16-5-73	AC Milan, Italy *Chiarugi*	v	Leeds United, England	1-0	Salonika	45,000
8-5-74	1.FC Magdeburg, Germany *Lanzi own goal, Seguin*	v	AC Milan, Italy	2-0	Rotterdam	5,000
14-5-75	Dynamo Kiev, U.S.S.R. *Onischenko 2, Blokhin*	v	Ferencvarosi TC, Hungary	3-0	Basle	13,000
5-5-76	RSC Anderlecht, Belgium *Rensenrink 2, 1 penalty, Van der Elst 2*	v	West Ham United, England *Holland, Robson*	4-2	Brussels	58,000
11-5-77	Hamburger SV, Germany *Volkert penalty, Magath*	v	RSC Anderlecht, Belgium	2-0	Amsterdam	65,000
3-5-78	RSC Anderlecht, Belgium *Rensenrink 2, Van Binst 2*	v	FK Austria/WAC, Austria	4-0	Paris	48,679

11

16-5-79	**FC Barcelona, Spain** *Sanchez, Asensi, Rexach, Krankl*	v	Fortuna Dusseldorf, Germany *Klaus Allofs, Seel 2*	4-3 aet	Basle	58,000
14-5-80	**Valencia, Spain**	v	Arsenal, England	0-0 0-5-4p	Brussels	40,000
13-5-81	**Dynamo Tbilisi, USSR** *Gutsayev, Daraselia*	v	Carl Zeiss Jena, East Germany *Hoppe*	2-1	Dusseldorf	9,000
12-5-82	**FC Barcelona, Spain** *Simonsen, Quini*	v	Standard Liege, Belgium *Vandermissen*	2-1	Barcelona	100,000
11-5-83	**Aberdeen, Scotland** *Black, Hewitt*	v	Real Madrid, Spain *Juanito penalty*	2-1	Gothenburg	17,804
16-5-84	**Juventus, Italy** *Vignola, Boniek*	v	FC Porto, Portugal *Sousa*	2-1	Basle	60,000
15-5-85	**Everton, England** *Gray, Steven, Sheedy*	v	Rapid Vienna, Austria *Krankl*	3-1	Rotterdam	50,000
2-5-86	**Dynamo Kiev, USSR** *Zavarov, Blokhin, Yevtushenko*	v	Atletico Madrid, Spain	3-0	Lyon	39,300
13-5-87	**Ajax Amsterdam, Holland** *Van Basten*	v	1FC Lokomotive Leipzig, East Germany	1-0	Athens	35,000
11-5-88	**KV Mechelen, Belgium** *Den Boer*	v	Ajax Amsterdam, Holland	1-0	Strasbourg	39,446
10-5-89	**FC Barcelona, Spain** *Salinas, Recarte*	v	Sampdoria, Italy	2-0	Bern	45,000
9-5-90	**Sampdoria, Italy** *G Vialli 2*		RSV Anderlecht, Belgium	2-0 aet	Gothenbourg	20,103

INTER CITIES FAIRS CUP FINAL RESULTS

1955-58

5-3-58	London XI, England *Greaves, Langley penalty*	v	**CF Barcelona, Spain** *Tejada, Martinez*	2-2	at Chelsea	45,466
1-5-58	**CF Barcelona, Spain** *Suarez 2, Martinez, Evaristo 2, Verges*	v	London XI, England	6-0	Barcelona	62,000

1958-60

29-3-60	Birmingham City, England	v	**CF Barcelona, Spain**	0-0		40,500
4-5-60	**CF Barcelona, Spain** *Martinez, Czibor 2, Coll*	v	Birmingham City, England *Hooper*	4-1		70,000
27-9-61	Birmingham City, England *Hellawell, Orritt*	v	**AS Roma, Italy** *Manfredini 2*	2-2		21,005
11-10-61	**AS Roma, Italy 1** *Farmer own goal, Pestrin*	v	Birmingham City, England	2-0		60,000
8-9-62	**Valencia CF, Spain** *Yosu 2, Guillot 3, Nunez*	v	CF Barcelona, Spain *Kocsis 2*	6-2		65,000
12-9-62	CF Barcelona, Spain *Kocsis*	v	**Valencia CF, Spain** *Guillot*	1-1		60,000
12-6-63	Dinamo Zagreb, Yugoslavia *Zambata*	v	**Valencia CF, Spain** *Waldo, Urtiaga*	1-2		40,000
26-6-63	**Valencia CF, Spain** *Mano, Nunez*	v	Dinamo Zagreb, Yugoslavia	2-0		55,000
24-6-64	**Real Zaragoza, Spain** *Villa, Marcellino*	v	Valencia CF, Spain *Urtiaga*	2-1	Barcelona	50,000
23-6-65	**Ferencvarosi TC, Hungary** *M.Fenyvesi*	v	Juventus, Italy	1-0	Turin	25,000
15-9-66	**CF Barcelona, Spain** *Canario*	v	Real Zaragoza, Spain	0-1		70,000
21-9-66	Real Zaragoza, Spain *Marcellino 2*	v	**CF Barcelona, Spain** *Pujol 3, Zaballa*	2-4 aet		70,000
30-8-67	**Dinamo Zagreb, Yugoslavia** *Cercer 2*	v	Leeds United, England	2-0		40,000
6-9-67	Leeds United, England	v	**Dinamo Zagreb, Yugoslavia**	0-0		35,604
7-8-68	**Leeds United, England** *Jones*	v	Ferencvarosi TC, Hungary	1-0		25,368
11-9-68	Ferencvarosi TC, Hungary	v	**Leeds United, England**	0-0		76,000
29-5-69	**Newcastle United, England** *Moncur 2, Scott*	v	Ujpest Dozsa, Hungary	3-0		59,234
11-6-69	Ujpest Dozsa, Hungary *Bene, Gorocs*	v	**Newcastle United, England** *Arentoft, Foggon, Moncur*	2-3		37,000
22-4-70	RSC Anderlecht, Belgium *Devrindt, Mulder 2*	v	**Arsenal, England** *Kennedy*	3-1		37,000
28-4-70	**Arsenal, England** *Kelly, Radford, Sammels*	v	RSC Anderlecht, Belgium	3-0		51,612
26-5-71	Juventus, Italy	v	**Leeds United, England**	0-0		65,000

Game abandoned after 65 minutes

| 29-5-71 | Juventus, Italy
Bettega, Capello | v | **Leeds United, England**
Madeley, Bates | 2-2 on away
goals | | 65,000 |
| 2-6-71 | **Leeds United, England**
Clarke | v | Juventus, Italy
Anastasi | 1-1 | Leeds United | 42,483 |

Changed to UEFA Cup

UEFA CUP FINAL RESULTS

Union of European Football Associations, PO Box 16, CH 3000, Bern 15, Switzerland · 010 41-31 321735

3-5-72	Wolverhampton Wanderers, England *McCalliog*	v	**Tottenham Hotspur, England** *Chivers 2*	1-2		45,000
17-5-72	**Tottenham Hotspur, England** *Mullery*	v	Wolverhampton Wanderers, England *Wagstaffe*	1-1		54,303
10-5-73	**Liverpool, England** *Keegan 2, Lloyd*	v	Borussia Monchengladbach, Germany	3-0		41,169
23-5-73	Borussia Monchengladbach, Germany *Heynckes 2*	v	**Liverpool, England**	2-0		35,000
21-5-74	Tottenham Hotspur, England *England, Van Daele own goal*	v	**Feyenoord Rotterdam, Holland** *Van Hanegem, De Jong*	2-2		46,281
29-5-74	**Feyenoord Rotterdam, Holland** *Rijsbergen, Ressel*	v	Tottenham Hotspur, England	2-0		59,317
7-5-75	**Borussia Monchengladbach, Germany**	v	Twente Enschede, Holland	0-0	in Dusseldorf	42,368
21-5-75	Twente Enschede, Holland *Drost*	v	**Borussia Monchengladbach, Germany** *Heynckes 3, Simonsen 2, 1 pen*	1-5		22,767
28-4-76	**Liverpool, England** *Kennedy, Case, Keegan penalty*	v	Clube Bruges, Belgium *Lambert, Cools*	3-2		49,981
19-5-76	Clube Bruges, Belgium *Lambert penalty*	v	**Liverpool, England** *Keegan*	1-1		32,000
4-5-77	**Juventus, Italy** *Tardelli*	v	Athletic Bilbao, Spain	1-0 on away goals	in Juventus	75,000
18-5-77	Athletic Bilbao, Spain *Irureta, Carlos*	v	**Juventus, Italy** *Bettega*	2-1		43,000
26-4-78	SEC Bastia Corsica, France	v	**PSV Eindhoven, Holland**	0-0		15,000
9-5-78	**PSV Eindhoven, Holland** *Van der Kerkhoff, Van der Kuylen*	v	SEC Bastia Corsica, France	3-0		27,000
9-5-79	Red Star Belgrade, Yugoslavia *Sestic*	v	**Borussia Monchengladbach, Germany** *Juristic own goal*	1-1		87,500
23-5-79	**Borussia Monchengladbach, Germany** *Simonsen penalty*	v	Red Star Belgrade, Yugoslavia	1-0	in Dusseldorf	45,000
7-5-80	Borussia Monchengladbach, Germany *Kulik 2, Matthaus*	v	**Eintracht Frankfurt, Germany** *Karger, Holzenbein*	3-2		25,000
21-5-80	**Eintracht Frankfurt, Germany** *Schaub*	v	Borussia Monchengladbach,	1-0 on away goals	in Eintracht	60,000
6-5-81	**Ipswich Town, England** *Wark penalty, Thijssen, Mariner*	v	AZ 67 Alkmaar, Holland	3-0		27,532
20-5-81	AZ 67 Alkmaar, Holland *Welzl, Metgod, Tol, Jonker*	v	**Ipswich Town, England** *Thijssen, Wark*	4-2		28,500
5-5-82	**IFK Gothenburg, Sweden** *Tord Holmgren*	v	Hamburger SV, Germany	1-0		42,548
19-5-82	Hamburger SV, Germany *Corneliussen, Nilsson, Fredriksson pen*	v	**IFK Gothenburg, Sweden**	0-3		60,000
4-5-83	**RSC Anderlecht, Belgium** *Brylle*	v	Benfica, Portugal	1-0		45,000
18-5-83	Benfica, Portugal *Sheu*	v	**RSC Anderlecht, Belgium** *Lozano*	1-1		80,000
9-5-84	RSC Anderlecht, Belgium *Olsen*	v	**Tottenham Hotspur, England** *Miller*	1-1		40,000
23-5-84	**Tottenham Hotspur, England** *Roberts*	v	RSC Anderlecht, Belgium *Czerniatynski*	1-1 aet 4-3 pens		46,258
8-5-85	Videoton Sekesfeheruar, Hungary *Michel, Santillana, Juanito*	v	**Real Madrid, Spain**	0-3		40,000
22-5-85	**Real Madrid, Spain** *Majer*	v	Videoton Sekesfeheruar, Hungary	0-1		98,300
30-4-86	**Real Madrid, Spain** *Sanchez, Gordillo, Valdano 2, Santillana*	v	1.FC Koln, Germany *Klaus Allofs*	5-1		85,000

13

Date	Home		Away	Score	Venue	Attendance
6-5-86	1.FC Koln, Germany	v	**Real Madrid, Spain**	2-0		15,000
	Bein, Geilenkirchen					
6-5-87	**IFK Gothenburg, Sweden**	v	Dundee United, Scotland	1-0		50,053
	Pettersson					
20-5-87	Dundee United, Scotland	v	**IFK Gothenburg, Sweden**	1-1		20,911
	Clark		*L.Nilsson*			
4-5-88	Espanol Barcelona, Spain	v	**Bayer Leverkusen, Germany**	3-0		45,000
	Losada 2, Soler					
18-5-88	**Bayer Leverkusen, Germany**	v	Espanol Barcelona, Spain	3-0 aet		22,000
	Tita, Cotz, Cha			3-2 pens		
3-5-89	**Napoli, Italy**	v	VfB Stuttgart, Germany	2-1		83,000
	Maradona penalty, Careca		*Gaudino*			
17-5-89	VfB Stuttgart, Germany	v	**Napoli, Italy**	3-3		67,000
	Klinsmann, De Napoli own goal, Schmaler		*Alemao, Ferrara, Careca*			
2-5-90	**Juventus, Italy**	v	Fiorentina, Italy	3-1	Turin	60,000
	R galia, P Casiraghi, L De Agostini		*R Buso*			
16-5-90	Fiorentian, Italy	v	**Juventus, Italy**	0-0	Avellino	41,000

EUROPEAN SUPER CUP

For the winners of the European Cup and the Cup Winners Cup

Date	Home		Away	Score	Venue	Attendance
16-1-73	Glasgow Rangers, Scotland	v	**Ajax Amsterdam, Holland**	1-3		57,000
	MacDonald		*Rep, Cruyff, Haan*			
24-1-73	**Ajax Amsterdam, Holland**	v	Glasgow Rangers, Scotland	3-2		37,000
	Haan, Muhren, Cruyff		*MacDonald, Young*			
9-1-74	AC Milan, Italy	v	**Ajax Amsterdam, Holland**	1-0		15,000
	Chiarugi					
16-1-74	**Ajax Amsterdam, Holland**	v	AC Milan, Italy	6-0		40,000
	Mulder, Keizer, Neeskens, Rep, G Muhren penalty, Haan					
1974	not played					
9-9-75	Bayern Munich, Germany	v	**Dynamo Kiev, USSR**	0-1		30,000
	Blokhin					
6-10-75	**Dynamo Kiev, USSR**	v	Bayern Munich, Germany	2-0		100,000
	Blokhin 2					
17-8-76	Bayern Munich, Germany	v	**RSC Anderlecht, Belgium**	2-1		41,000
	Muller 2		*Haan*			
30-8-76	**RSC Anderlecht, Belgium**	v	Bayern Munich, Germany	4-1		35,000
	Rensenbrink 2, Haan, Van der Elst		*Muller*			
22-11-77	Hamburger SV, Germany	v	**Liverpool, England**	1-1		16,000
	Keller		*Fairclough*			
6-12-77	**Liverpool, England**	v	Hamburger SV, Germany	6-0		34,931
	Thompson, McDermott 3, Fairclough, Dalglish					
4-12-78	**RSC Anderlecht, Belgium**	v	Liverpool, England	3-1		35,000
	Vercauteren, Van der Elst, Rensenbrink		*Case*			
19-12-78	Liverpool, England	v	**RSC Anderlecht, Belgium**	2-1		23,598
	Hughes, Fairclough		*Van der Elst*			
30-1-80	**Nottingham Forest, England**	v	FC Barcelona, Spain	1-0		23,807
	George					
5-2-80	FC Barcelona, Spain	v	**Nottingham Forest, England**	1-1		80,000
	Roberto penalty		*Burns*			
25-11-80	Nottingham Forest, England	v	**Valencia CF, Spain**	2-1 on away	in Valencia	12,463
	Bowyer 2		*Felman*	goals		
17-12-80	**Valencia CF, Spain**	v	Nottingham Forest, England	1-0		45,000
	Morena					
1981	not played					
19-1-83	FC Barcelona, Spain	v	**Aston Villa, England**	1-0		50,000
	Marcos					
26-1-83	**Aston Villa, England**	v	FC Barcelona, Spain	3-0 aet		32,570
	Shaw, Cowans penalty, McNaught					
22-11-83	Hamburger SV, Germany	v	**Aberdeen, Scotland**	0-0		12,000
20-12-83	**Aberdeen, Scotland**	v	Hamburger SV, Germany	2-0		24,000
	Simpson, McGhee					
16-1-85	**Juventus, Italy**	v	Liverpool, England	2-0	in Turin	60,000
	Boniek 2					

14

Date	Home Team		Away Team	Score	Venue	Attendance
1987	Juventus, Italy	v	Everton, England			
	Not played as English Clubs were banned					
24-2-87	Steaua Bucharest, Rumania	v	Dynamo Kiev, USSR	1-0	in Monaco	8,456
	Hagi					
24-11-87	Ajax Amsterdam, Holland	v	FC Porto, Portugal	0-1		27,000
			Rui Barros			
13-1-88	FC Porto, Portugal	v	Ajax Amsterdam, Holland	1-0		50,000
	Sousa					
1-2-89	KV Mechelen, Belgium	v	PSV Eindhoven, Holland	3-0		7,000
	John Bosman 2, Pascal De Wilde					
8-2-89	PSV Eindhoven, Holland	v	KV Mechelen, Belgium	1-0		17,100
	Gilhaus					
23-11-89	FC Barcelona Spain	v	AC Milan, Italy	1-1		70,000
7-12-89	AC Milan, Italy	v	FC Barcelona, Spain	1-0		50,000

WORLD CLUB CHAMPIONSHIP FINALS

Date	Home Team		Away Team	Venue	Score	Attendance
3-7-60	Penarol, Uruguay	v	Real Madrid, Spain	Montevideo	0-0	71,872
4-9-60	Real Madrid, Spain	v	Penarol, Uruguay	Madrid	(4-0) 5-1	125,000
	Puskas 2, Di Stefano, Herrera, Gento					
4-9-61	Benfica, Portugal	v	Penarol, Uruguay	Lisbon	(0-0) 1-0	55,000
	Coluna					
17-9-61	Penarol, Uruguay	v	Benfica, Portugal	Montevideo	(4-0) 5-0	56,358
	Sasia penalty, Joya 2, Spencer 2					
19-9-61	Penarol, Uruguay	v	Benfica, Portugal	Montevideo	(2-1) 2-1	60,241
	Sasia 2, 1 penalty		*Eusebio*			
19-9-62	Santos, Brazil	v	Benfica, Portugal	Rio	(1-0) 3-2	90,000
	Pele 2, Coutinho		*Santana 2*			
11-10-62	Benfica, Portugal	v	Santos, Brazil	Lisbon	(0-2) 2-5	75,000
	Eusebio, Santana		*Pele 3, Coutinho, Pepe*			
16-10-63	AC Milan, Italy	v	Santos, Brazil	Milan	(2-0) 4-2	80,000
	Trapattoni, Amarildo 2, Mora		*Pele 2, 1 penalty*			
14-11-63	Santos, Brazil	v	AC Milan, Italy	Rio	(0-2) 4-2	135,000
	Pepe 2, Almir, Amarildo, Lima		*Altafini, Mora*			
16-11-63	Santos, Brazil	v	AC Milan, Italy	Rio	(1-0) 1-0	121,000
	Dalmo penalty			play off		
9-9-64	Independiente, Argentina	v	Inter Milan, Italy	Buenos Aires	(0-0) 1-0	70,000
	Rodriguez					
23-9-64	Inter Milan, Italy	v	Independiente, Argentina	Milan	(2-0) 2-0	70,000
	Mazzola, Corso					
26-9-64	Inter Milan, Italy	v	Independiente, Argentina	Madrid	(0-0) 1-0 aet	45,000
	Corso					
8-9-65	Inter Milan, Italy	v	Independiente, Argentina	Milan	(2-0) 3-0	70,000
	Peiro, Mazzola 2					
15-9-65	Independiente, Argentina	v	Inter Milan, Italy	Buenos Aires	0-0	70,000
12-10-66	Penarol, Uruguay	v	Real Madrid, Spain	Montevideo	(1-0) 2-0	58,324
	Spencer 2					
26-10-66	Real Madrid, Spain	v	Penarol, Uruguay	Madrid	(0-2) 0-2	70,000
			Rocha penalty, Spencer			
18-10-67	Glasgow Celtic, Scotland	v	Racing Clube BA, Argentina	Glasgow	(0-0) 1-0	103,000
	McNeill					
1-11-67	Racing Clube BA, Argentina	v	Glasgow Celtic, Scotland	Buenos Aires	(1-1) 2-1	80,000
	Raffo 2		*Gemmell penalty*			
4-11-67	Racing Clube BA, Argentina	v	Glasgow Celtic, Scotland	Montevideo	(0-0) 1-0	65,172
	Cardenas					
25-9-68	Estudiantes, Argentina	v	Manchester United, England	Buenos Aires	(1-0) 1-0	50,120
	Conigliaro					
16-10-68	Manchester United, England	v	Estudiantes, Argentina	Manchester	(0-1) 1-1	63,428
	Morgan		*Veron*			
8-10-69	AC Milan, Italy	v	Estudiantes, Argentina	Milan	(2-0) 3-0	60,675
	Sormani 2, Combin					
22-10-69	Estudiantes, Argentina	v	AC Milan, Italy	Buenos Aires	(2-1) 2-1	65,000
	Aguirre, Suarez, Conigliaro		*Rivera*			
26-8-70	Estudiantes, Argentina	v	Feyenoord Rotterdam, Holland	Buenos Aires	(2-1) 2-2	50,000
	Echecopar, Veron		*Kindvall, van Hanegem*			
9-9-70	Feyenoord Rotterdam, Holland	v	Estudiantes, Argentina	Rotterdam	(0-0) 1-0	67,000
	van Daele					
15-9-71	Panathinaikos, Greece *	v	Nacional, Uruguay	Athens	(0-0) 1-1	60,000
	Filakouris		*Artime*			

Date	Team 1		Team 2	Venue	Score	Attendance
29-12-71	**Nacional, Uruguay** *Artime 2*	v	Panathinaikos, Greece * *Filakouris*	Montevideo	(1-0) 2-1	70,000
					* replaced Ajax	
6-9-72	Independiente, Argentina *Sa*	v	**Ajax Amsterdam, Holland** *Cruyff*	Buenos Aires	(0-1) 1-1	65,000
28-9-72	**Ajax Amsterdam, Holland** *Neeskens, Rep 2*	v	Independiente, Argentina	Amsterdam	(1-0) 3-0	65,000
28-11-73	Juventus, Italy	v	**Independiente, Argentina** *Bochini*	Rome	(0-0) 0-1 one game	35,000
11-3-75	Independiente, Argentina *Balbuena*	v	**Atletico Madrid, Spain ***	Buenos Aires	(1-0) 1-0	60,000
10-4-75	Atletico Madrid, Spain * *Irureta, Ayala*	v	Independiente, Argentina	Madrid	(1-0) 2-0	45,000
					* Bayern Munich replaced	
1975	Independiente, Argentina	v	Bayern Munich, Germany		could not agree dates.	
23-11-76	**Bayern Munich, Germany** *Muller, Kapellmann*	v	Cruzeiro, Brazil	Munich	(0-0) 2-0	22,000
21-12-76	Cruzeiro, Brazil	v	**Bayern Munich, Germany**	Belo Horizonte	0-0	114,000
21-3-78	**Boca Juniors, Argentina** *Mastrangelo, Ribolzi*	v	Borussia Monchengladbach, Germany *Hannes, Bonhof*	Buenos Aires	(1-1) 2-2	50,000
6-9-78	Borussia Monchengladbach, Germany	v	**Boca Juniors, Argentina** *Felman, Mastrangelo, Salinas*	Karlsruhe	(0-3) 0-3	21,500
1978	not played					
18-11-79	Malmo FF, Sweden *	v	**Olimpia, Paraguay** *Isasi*		(0-1) 0-1	4,811
					* replaced Notts Forest	
3-3-80	**Olimpia, Paraguay** *Solalinde penalty, Michelagnoli*	v	Malmo FF, Sweden * *Earlandsson*	Asuncion	(1-0) 2-1	35,000
11-2-81	**Nacional, Uruguay** *Victorino*	v	Nottingham Forest, England	Tokyo	(1-0) 1-0	62,000
13-12-81	**Flamengo, Brazil** *Nunes 2, Adilio*	v	Liverpool, England	Tokyo	(3-0) 3-0	62,000
12-12-82	**Penarol, Uruguay** *Jair, Silva*	v	Aston Villa, England	Tokyo	(1-0) 2-0	62,000
11-12-83	**Gremio Porto Alegre, Brazil** *Renato Gaucho 2*	v	Hamburger SV, Germany *Schroder*	Tokyo	(1-0) 2-1	62,000
9-12-84	**Independiente, Argentina** *Percudani*	v	Liverpool, England	Tokyo	(1-0) 1-0	62,000
8-12-85	**Juventus, Italy** *Platini penalty, Laudrup*	v	Argentinos Juniors, Argentina *Ereros, Castro*	Tokyo	(0-0) 2-2 aet 4-3 pens	62,000
14-12-86	**River Plate, Argentina** *Alzamendi*	v	Steaua Bucharest, Rumania	Tokyo	(1-0) 1-0	62,000
13-12-87	**FC Porto, Portugal** *Gomes, Madjer*	v	Penarol, Uruguay *Viera*	Tokyo	(1-0) 2-1 aet	45,000
11-12-88	**Nacional, Uruguay** *Ostolaza 2*	v	PSV Eindhoven, Holland *Romario, Ron Koeman penalty*	Tokyo	(1-0) 2-2 aet 7-6 pens	62,000
17-12-89	**AC Milan, Italy** *A Evani*	v	Nacional Medellin, Columbia	Tokyo	(0-0) 1-0	62,000

MITROPA CUP FINALS

1927	Sparta Prague, Czechoslovakia v Rapid Vienna, Austria	6-2 1-2	
1928	Ferencvarosi, Hungary v Rapid Vienna, Austria	7-1 3-5	
1929	Ujpest Dozsa, Hungary v Slavia Prague, Czechoslovakia	5-1 2-2	
1930	Rapid Vienna, Austria v Sparta Prague, Czechoslovakia	3-2 2-0	
1931	1st Vienna, Austria v WAC Vienna, Austria	3-2 2-1	
1932	Bologna, Italy v Slavia Prague, Czechoslovakia	walk over	
1933	Austria FK, Austria v Ambrosiana, Italy	3-1 1-2	
1934	Bologna, Italy v Admira, Austria	4-1 2-3	
1935	Sparta Prague, Czechoslovakia v Ferencvarosi, Hungary	3-0 1-2	
1936	Sparta Prague, Czechoslovakia v FK Austria, Austria	1-0 0-0	
1937	Ferencvarosi, Hungary v Lazio Rome, Italy	4-2 5-4	
1938	Slavia Prague, Czechoslovakia v Ferencvarosi, Hungary	2-2 2-0	
1939	Ujpest Dozsa, Hungary v Ferencvarosi, Hungary	4-1 2-2	
1955	Voros Lobago (MTK), Hungary v UDA (Dukla) Prague, Czechoslovakia	6-0 2-1	
1956	Vasas Budapest, Hungary v Rapid Vienna, Austria	3-3 1-1 9-2 pens	
1957	Vasas Budapest, Hungary v Vojvodina, Yugoslavia	4-0 1-2	
1958	no competition		
1959	Honved Budapest, Hungary v MTK Budapest, Hungary	4-3 2-2	
1960	new format, 5 nations, 6 teams each total league basis Hungary winners		
1961	Bologna, Italy v Slovan Nitra, Czechoslovakia		
1962	Vasas Budapest, Hungary v Bologna, Italy	5-1 1-2	
1963	MTK Budapest, Hungary v Vasas Budapest, Hungary	2-1 1-1	
1964	Sparta Prague, Czechoslovakia v Slovan Bratislava, Czechoslovakia	0-0 2-0	

1965	Vasas Budapest, Hungary v Fiorentina, Italy	1-0	
1966	Fiorentina, Italy v Jednota Trencin, Czechoslovakia	1-0	
1967	Spartak Trnava, Czechoslovakia v Ujpest Dozsa, Hungary	3-1 2-3	
1968	Red Star Belgrade, Yugoslavia v Spartak Trnava, Czechoslovakia	4-1 0-1	
1969	Inter Bratislava, Czechoslovakia v Union Teplice, Czechoslovakia	4-1 0-0	
1970	Vasas Budapest, Hungary v Inter Milan, Italy	4-1 1-2	
1971	Celik Zenica, Yugoslavia v Austria Salzburg, Austria	3-1	
1972	Celik Zenica, Yugoslavia v Fiorentina, Italy	0-0 1-0	
1973	Tatabanya Banyasz, Hungary v Celik Zenica, Yugoslavia	2-1 2-1	
1974	Tatabanya Banyasz, Hungary v Jednota Zilina, Czechoslovakia	3-2 2-0	
1975	SWW Innsbruck, Austria v Honved Budapest, Hungary	3-1 2-1	

1976	SWW Innsbruck, Austria v Velez Mostar, Yugoslavia	3-1 3-1
1977	Vojvodina Novi Sad, Yugoslavia (on league basis)	
1978	Partizan Belgrade, Yugoslavia v Honved Budapest, Hungary	1-0
1979	no competition	
1980	Udinese, Italy (on league basis)	
1981	Tatran Presov, Czechoslovakia (on league basis)	
1982	AC Milan, Italy (on league basis)	
1983	Vasas Budapest, Hungary (on league basis)	
1984	Banik Ostrava, Czechoslovakia (on league basis)	
1985	Iskra Busejno, Yugoslavia (on league basis)	
1986	Pisa, Italy v Debrecen, Hungary	2-0
1987	Ascoli, Italy v Bohemians, Czechoslovakia	2-0 1-0
1988	Pisa, Italy v Vaci Izzo, Hungary	3-0
1989	Banik Ostrava, Czechoslovakia v Bologna, Italy	3-1

CUP OF THE ALPS

1960	Italy (overall)	
1961	Italy (overall)	
1962	Genoa, Italy v Grenoble, France	1-0
1963	Juventus, Italy v Atalanta Bergamo, Italy	3-2
1964	Genoa, Italy v Catania, Italy	2-0
1966	Napoli, Italy (League)	
1967	Eintracht Frankfurt, Germany (League)	
1968	FC Schalke 04 Gelsenkirchen, Germany	
1969	FC Basle, Switzerland v Bologna,Italy	3-1
1970	FC Basle, Switzerland	
1971	Lazio Rome, Italy v FC Basel, Switzerland	3-1
1972	Nimes, France v Girondins Bordeaux, France	7-2
1973	Servette Geneva, Switzerland v Lausanne Sport, Switzerland	1-0
1974	Young Boys Bern, Switzerland	
1975	Servette Geneva, Switzerland	

1976	Servette Geneva, Switzerland	
1977	Stade de Reims, France v SEC Bastia, France	3-1
1978	FC Basle. Switzerland	
1979	AS Monaco, France v FC Metz, France	3-1
1980	Girondins Bordeaux, France v Nimes, France	3-1
1981	FC Basle, Switzerland v Sochaux, France	2-2 5-3 pens
1982	FC Nantes, France v FC Neuchatel Xamax, Switzerland	1-0
1983	AS Monaco, France v AJ Auxerre, France	2-1
1984	AS Monaco, France v Grasshoppers Zurich, Switzerland	2-0
1985	AJ Auxerre, France v AS Monaco, France	1-0
1986	not held	
1987	AJ Auxerre, France v Grasshoppers Zurich, Switzerland	3-1

BALKAN CUP WINNERS

1961-3	Steagul Rosu Brasov, Rumania on League basis	
1963-4	Olympiakos Piraeus, Greece v Levski Sofia, Bulgaria	1-0 0-1 1-0 playoff
1964-5	Rapid Bucharest, Rumania v Spartak Plovdiv, Bulgaria	2-0 1-1
1965-6	Rapid Bucharest, Rumania v Farul Konstanca, Rumania	2-0 3-3
1966-7	Fenerbahce Istanbul, Turkey v AEK Athens, Greece	1-2 1-0 3-1 playoff
1967-8	Beroe Stara Zagora, Bulgaria v Spartak Sofia, Bulgaria	3-0 3-4
1968-9	Beroe Stara Zagora, Bulgaria v Dinamo Tirana, Albania	0-1 3-0
1969-70	Partizani Tirana, Albania v Beroe Stara Zagora, Bulgaria	3-0 1-1
1970-1	Panionios Athens, Greece v Besa Kavaja, Albania	2-1 1-1
1971-2	Trakia Plovdiv, Bulgaria v Vardar Skopje, Yugoslavia	5-0 0-4
1972-3	Lokomotiv Sofia, Bulgaria v AS Armata Trgu Mures, Rumania	1-1 2-0

1973-4	Akademik Sofia, Bulgaria v Vardar Skopje, Yugoslavia	2-1 0-0
1975	Radnicki Nis, Yugoslavia v Eskisehirspor Eskisehir, Turkey	1-0 2-1
1976-7	Dinamo Zagreb, Yugoslavia v Sportul Studentesc Bucharest, Rumania	3-1 2-3
1977	Panathinaikos, Greece v Slavia Sofia, Bulgaria	2-1 0-0
1977-8	NK Rijeka, Yugoslavia - No Final	
1979	NK Rijeka, Yugoslavia - No Final	
1980	Sportul Studentesc Bucharest, Rumania v NK Rijeka, Yugoslavia	2-0 1-1
1981	Velez Mostar, Yugoslavia v Trakia Plovdiv, Bulgaria	6-5 6-2
1982		
1983	Beroe Stara Zagora, Bulgaria v 17 Nentori Tirana, Albania	3-0 3-1
1984		
1985		
1986	Slavia Sofia, Bulgaria v Panionios, Greece	3-0
1987		
1988	Slavia Sofia, Bulgaria v Arges Pitesti, Rumania	5-0 1-0

17

ALBANIA

Founded 1932, re-organised 1949
Federation Albanaise de Football, Rrunga, Kongresi I Permetit, 41 Tirana 2 Telex 2228 bfssh ab
National colours red shirts, black shorts, red socks. Season September to May

LEAGUE CHAMPIONS

1930	SK Tirana	**1950**	Dinamo Tirana	**1964**	Partizani Tirana	**1976**	Dinamo Tirana
1931	Teuta	**1951**	Dinamo Tirana	**1965**	17 Nentori Tirana	**1977**	Dinamo Tirana
1932	SK Tirana	**1952**	Dinamo Tirana	**1966**	17 Nentori Tirana†	**1978**	VLaznia Shkodar
1933	Skenderbeu Korce	**1953**	Dinamo Tirana	**1967**	Dinamo Titana	**1979**	Partizani Tirana
1934	SK Tirana	**1954**	Partizani Tirana	**1968**	17 Nentori Tirana		
1935	not held	**1955**	Dinamo Tirana		spring-autumn season*	**1980**	Dinamo Tirana
1936	SK Tirana	**1956**	Dinamo Tirana	**1969/70**	17 Nentori Tirana	**1981**	Partizani Tirana
1937	Sk Tirana	**1957**	Partizani Tirana†		autumn-spring season*	**1982**	17 Nentori Tirana
		1958	Partizani Tirana†			**1983**	Vlaznia Shkodar
1945	Vlaznia Shkodar	**1959**	Partizani Tirana	**1970**	17 Nentori Tirana	**1984**	Labinoti Elbasan
1946	Vlaznia Shkodar			**1971**	Partizani Tirana	**1985**	17 Nentori Tirana
1947	Partizani Tirana	**1960**	Dinamo Tirana	**1972**	Vlaznia Shkodar	**1986**	Dinamo Tirana
1948	Partizani Tirana	**1961**	Partizani Tirana†	**1973**	Dinamo Tirana	**1987**	Partizani Tirana
1949	Partizani Tirana	**1962/63**	Partizani Tirana	**1974**	Vlaznia Shkodar	**1988**	17 Nentori Tirana
			autumn-spring season*	**1975**	Dinamo Tirana	**1989**	17 Nentori Tirana

* note change of season
† Play off results for championships: 1957 Partizani v Dinamo 3-1, 1958 Partizani v Dinamo 3-1
1961 Partizani v Dinamo 1-1, 1-0, 1966 Nentori v Partizani 2-1

CUP WINNERS

1948	Partizani Tirana v 17 Nentori Tirana	5-2	**1962**	overlap season* changed to aut-sprg		
1949	Partizani Tirana v 17 Nentori Tirana	1-0	**1963**	17 Nentori Tirana v Besa Kavaja	wop 2-3 1-0	
1950	Dinamo Tirana v Partizani Tirana	2-1	**1964**	Partizani Tirana v Tomori	3-0	
1951	Dinamo Tirana v Partizani Tirana	3-2	**1965**	Vlaznia Shkodar v Skenderbeu	1-0	
1952	Dinamo Tirana v 17 Nentori Tirana	4-1	**1967**	no competition		
1953	Dinamo Tirana v Partizani Tirana	2-0	**1968**	Partizani Tirana v Vlaznia Shkodar	4-1	
1954	Dinamo Tirana v Partizani Tirana	2-1	**1969**	no competition		
1955	no competition		**1970**	Partizani Tirana v Vlaznia Shkodar	4-0 0-1	
1956	no competition		**1972**	Vlaznia Shkodar v Besa Kavaja	wop 2-0 0-2	
1957	Partizani Tirana v Lokomotiva Durrus	2-0	**1973**	Partizani Tirana v Dinamo Tirana	1-0	
1958	Partizani Tirana v Skenderbeu	4-0	**1974**	Dinamo Tirana v Partizani Tirana	1-0	
1959	no competition		**1975**	Labinoti Elbasan v Lokomotiva Durrus	1-0 1-0	
1960	Dinamo Tirana v Flamarturi Vlore	1-0 1-0	**1976**	17 Nentori Tirana v Skenderbeu	3-1 1-0	
1961	Partizani Tirana v Besa Kavaja	1-0 1-1	**1977**	17 Nentori Tirana v Dinamo Tirana	wop 1-2 2-1	

1978	Dinamo Tirana v Traktori	1-0 0-0
1979	Vlaznia Shkodar v Dinamo Tirana	2-1 1-1
1980	Partizani Tirana v Labinoti Elbasan	1-0 1-1
1981	Vlaznia Shkodar v Besa Kavaja	1-2 5-1
1982	Dinamo Tirana v 17 Nentori Tirana	1-0 2-3
1983	17 Nentori Tirana v Flamurtari Vlore	1-0
1984	17 Nentori Tirana v Flamurtari Vlore	2-1

1985	Flamarturi Vlore v Partizani Tirana	2-1
1966	Partizani Tirana v Vlaznia Shkodar	2-1 4-3
1986	17 Nentori Tirana v Vlaznia Shkodar	3-1
1987	Vlaznia Shkodar v Flamartuari Vlore	3-0 1-3
1988	Flamurtari Vlore v Partizani Tirana	1-0
1989	Dinamo Tirana v Partizani Tirana	3-1

SPARTACHIADES

Albanian "Olympic" Games

1959	Dinamo Tirana v Beas Kavaja	1-0
	Dinamo Tirana v Labinoti Elbasan	4-1
	Dinamo Tirana v Skenderbeu Korce	3-1
	Winners Dinamo Tirana	
1969	17 Nentori Tirana v Dinamo Tirana	0-0 5-1 penalties

1974	Dinamo Tirana v Vlaznia Shkodar	1-1 5-3 penalties
1979	Dinamo Tirana v 17 Nentori Tirana	1-0
1984	17 Nentori Tirana v Labinoti Elbasan	1-0

ALBANIAN SUPER CUP

1989 17 Nentori Tirana v Dinamo Tirana

FEATURED CLUBS IN EUROPEAN COMPETITION

Partizani Tirana	17 Nentori Tirana	Besa Kavaja	Vlaznia Shkodar
Dinamo Tirana	Labinoti Elbasan	Flamurtari Vlore	Appollonia Fier

PARTIZANI TIRANA

Founded 1946   Colours All Red with White on sleeves and shorts
Stadium Kambetar "Qemel Stafa" (19,923)   ☎ 3133
Champions 1947, 1948, 1949, 1954, 1957, 1958, 1959, 1961, 1964, 1971, 1979, 1981, 1987
Cup Winners 1948, 1949, 1957, 1958, 1961, 1964, 1966, 1968, 1970, 1973, 1980

Season	Opponent	Home	Result	Away	Rnd	Cup
1962-63	IFK Norrkoping, Sweden	1-1		0-2	1	ECC
1963-64	Spartak Plovdiv, Bulgaria	1-0		1-3	1	ECC
1964-65	1.FC Koln, Germany	0-0		0-2	pr	ECC
1968-69	Torino, Italy	1-0		1-3	1	CWC
1970-71	Atvidaberg FF, Sweden	2-0		1-1	1	CWC
	Wacker Innsbruck, Austria	1-2		2-3	2	CWC
1971-72	CSKA Sofia, Bulgaria	0-1		0-3	1	ECC
1979-80	Glasgow Celtic, Scotland	1-0		1-4	1	ECC
1980-81	Malmo FF, Sweden	0-0		0-1	1	CWC
1981-82	FK Austria, Austria	1-0		1-3	1	ECC
1987-88	Benfica, Portugal	disqualified		0-4	1	ECC

ALBANIA

17 NENTORI TIRANA

Founded 1920 as Agimi, 1927 SK Tirane, 1939 Shprefeja, 1945 17 Nentori, 1950 Tirana, 1951 Puma Tirana, 1958 17 Nentori
Colours blue and white striped shirts, white shorts
Stadium Qemel Stafa (19,293) or Dinamo (12,500) ☎ 7006
Champions 1965, 1966, 1968, 1970, 1982, 1985, 1988, 1989
Cup Winners 1963, 1976, 1977, 1983, 1984, 1986

Season	Opponent	Home	Result	Away	Rnd	Cup
1965-66	Kilmarnock, Scotland	0-0		0-1	pr	ECC
1966-67	Valerengens IF Oslo, Norway	withdrew			1	ECC
1969-70	Standard Liege, Belgium	1-1		0-3	1	ECC
1970-71	Ajax Amsterdam, Holland	2-2		0-2	1	ECC
1982-83	Linfield, Ireland	1-0	wag	1-2	1	ECC
	Dynamo Kiev, USSR	withdrew			2	ECC
1983-84	Hammarby IF Stockholm, Sweden	2-1		0-4	1	CWC
1986-87	Dinamo Bucharest, Romania	1-0		2-1	1	CWC
	Malmö FF, Sweden	0-3		0-0	2	CWC
1988-89	Hamrun Spartans, Malta	2-0		2-1	1	ECC
	IFK Gothenburg, Sweden	0-3		0-1	2	ECC
1989-90	Sliema Wanderers, Malta	5-0		0-1	1	ECC
	Bayern Munich, Germany	0-3		1-3	2	ECC

BESA KAVAJA

Founded 1930 as SC Kavaje, 1935 Besa, 1949-50 Kavaje, 1951 Puna Kavaje, 1957 Besa
Colours yellow shirts with two black stripes, black shorts
Stadium Besa (10,000) ☎ 341
Cup Winners 1972

Season	Opponent	Home	Result	Away	Rnd	Cup
1972-73	Fremad Amager, Denmark	0-0	wag	1-1	1	CWC
	Hibernian, Scotland	1-1		1-6	2	CWC

VLAZNIA SHKODAR

Founded 1919 as Bashkimi, 1935 Vlaznia, 1949 Shkodar, 1951 Puna Shkodar, 1957 Vlaznia
Colours all blue with red front panel and red trim on shorts
Stadium Vlaznim (13,000) ☎ 2045
Champions 1945, 1946, 1972, 1974, 1983
Cup Winners 1965, 1972, 1979, 1981, 1987

Season	Opponent	Home	Result	Away	Rnd	Cup
1971-72	Rapid Vienna, Austria	withdrew			1	UEFA
1978-79	FK Austria Vienna, Austria	2-0		1-4	1	ECC
1979-80	Moscow Dynamo, USSR	withdrew			1	CWC
1987-88	Sliema Wanderers, Malta	2-0		4-0	1	CWC
	RoPs Rovaniemen, Finland	0-1		0-1	2	CWC

DINAMO TIRANA

Founded 1950   Colours All White
Stadium Dinamo (12,000) or Qemel Stafa (19,293) ☎ 3000
Champions 1950, 1951, 1952, 1953, 1955, 1956, 1960, 1967, 1973, 1975, 1976, 1977, 1980, 1986
Cup Winners 1950, 1951, 1952, 1953, 1954, 1960, 1971, 1974, 1978, 1982, 1989

Season	Opponent	Home	Result	Away	Rnd	Cup
1967-68	Eintracht Braunschweig, Germany	withdrew			1	ECC
1971-72	FK Austria Vienna, Austria	1-1		0-1	1	CWC
1980-81	Ajax Amsterdam, Holland	0-2		0-1	1	ECC
1981-82	Carl Zeiss Jena, East Germany	1-0		0-4	1	UEFA
1982-83	Aberdeen, Scotland	0-0		0-1	1	CWC
1985-86	Hamrun Spartans, Malta	1-0		0-0	1	UEFA
	Sporting Lisbon, Portugal	0-0		0-1	2	UEFA
1986-87	Besiktas, Turkey	0-1		0-2	1	ECC
1989-90	Chernomoretz Bourgas, Bulgaria	4-0		1-3	pre	CWC
	Dinamo Bucharest, Romania	1-0		0-2	1	CWC

LABINOTI ELBASAN

Founded 1923 as Urani, 1934 Bashkimi Labinoti, 1949 Elbasani, 1950 Puna Elbasan, 1956 Labinoti
Colours white shirts, black shorts
Stadium Labinoti (12,000)   ☎ 2146
Champions 1984
Cup Winners 1975

Season	Opponent	Home	Result	Away	Rnd	Cup
1984-85	Lyngby BK, Denmark	0-3		0-3	1	ECC

FLAMURTARI VLORE

Founded in 1923 as Vlore, 1935 Ismail Qemali, 1949 Vlore, 1950 Puna Vlore, 1957 Flamurtari
Colours all orange with thin black stripes on shirt
Stadium Flamurtari (10,000) ☎ 3064
Cup Winners 1985, 1988

Season	Opponent	Home	Result	Away	Rnd	Cup
1985-86	HJK Helsinki, Finland	1-2		2-3	1	CWC
1986-87	CF Barcelona, Spain	1-1	lag	0-0	1	UEFA
1987-88	Partizan Belgrade, Yugoslavia	2-0		1-2	1	UEFA
	Wismut Aue, East Germany	2-0		0-1	2	UEFA
	FC Barcelona, Spain	1-0		1-4	3	UEFA
1988-89	Lech Poznan, Poland	2-3		0-1	1	CWC

APOLLONIA FIER

Founded in 1930 as Apollonia, 1949 Fier, 1950 Puna Fier, 1957 Apollonia Fier
Colours green and white striped shirts, white shorts
Stadium Apollonia Fier (10,000) ☎ 393

Season	Opponent	Home	Result	Away	Rnd	Cup
1989-90	AJ Auxerre, France	0-3*		0-5	1	UEFA

* in Vlora

21

AUSTRIA

Founded 1904
Osterreichischer Fussball-Bund, Praterstadion, Sector A/F, Meiereistrasse, PO Box 430, A-1021 Vienna ☎ 1-21718 Fax
1-218 16 32
National colours white shirts, black shorts and socks
Season August to December; February to June

LEAGUE CHAMPIONS

1912	SK Rapid Vienna	1931	First Vienna FC 1894	1950	FK Austria	1970	FK Austria
1913	SK Rapid Vienna	1932	Admira Vienna	1951	SK Rapid Vienna	1971	Wacker Innsbruck
1914	WAF Vienna	1933	First Vienna FC 1894	1952	SK Rapid Vienna	1972	Wacker Innsbruck
1915	WAC Vienna	1934	Admira Vienna	1953	FK Austria	1973	Wacker Innsbruck
1916	SK Rapid Vienna	1935	SK Rapid Vienna	1954	SK Rapid Vienna	1974	SK VoEST Linz
1917	SK Rapid Vienna	1936	Admira Vienna	1955	First Vienna FC 1894	1975	Wacker Innsbruck
1918	Floridsdorfer AC	1937	Admira Vienna	1956	SK Rapid Vienna	1976	FK Austria
1919	SK Rapid Vienna	1938	SK Rapid Vienna	1957	SK Rapid Vienna	1977	Wacker Innsbruck
		1939	Admira Vienna	1958	Wiener Sport-Club	1978	FK Austria
1920	SK Rapid Vienna			1959	Wiener Sport-Club	1979	FK Austria
1921	SK Rapid Vienna	1940	SK Rapid Vienna				
1922	Wiener Sport-Club	1941	SK Rapid Vienna	1960	SK Rapid Vienna	1980	FK Austria
1923	SK Rapid Vienna	1942	First Vienna FC 1894	1961	FK Austria	1981	FK Austria
1924	Amateure (FK Austria)	1943	First Vienna FC 1894	1962	FK Austria	1982	SK Rapid Vienna
1925	Hakoah Vienna	1944	First Vienna FC 1984	1963	FK Austria	1983	SK Rapid Vienna
1926	Amateure (FK Austria)	1945	SK Rapid Vienna	1964	SK Rapid Vienna	1984	FK Austria
Now Professional		1946	SK Rapid Vienna	1965	Linzer ASK	1985	FK Austria
1927	Admira Vienna	1947	Wacker Wien	1966	Admira Vienna	1986	FK Austria
1928	Admira Vienna	1948	SK Rapid Vienna	1967	SK Rapid Vienna	1987	FK Austria
1929	SK Rapid Vienna	1949	FK Austria	1968	SK Rapid Vienna	1988	SK Rapid Vienna
				1969	FK Austria	1989	FC Tirol Innsbruck
1930	SK Rapid Vienna						

VIENNESE CUP WINNERS

Only Viennese clubs played in the Cup until 1948 when a National Cup was started

1919	SK Rapid Vienna v Wiener Sport Club	3-0	1926	FK Austria v First Vienna FC 1894	4-3
			1927	SK Rapid Vienna v FK Austria (Ex Amateure)	3-0
1920	SK Rapid Vienna v Amateure (FK Austria)	5-2	1928	Admira Vienna v WAC Vienna	2-1
1921	Amateure (FK Austria) v Wiener Sport-Club	2-1	1929	First Vienna FC 1894 v SK Rapid Vienna	3-2
1922	WAG Vienna v Amateure (FK Austria)	2-1	1930	First Vienna FC 1894 v FK Austria	1-0
1923	Wiener Sport-Club v Wacker Vienna	3-1	1931	WAC Vienna winners of mini league	
1924	Amateure (FK Austria) v Slovan Vienna	8-6 aet	1932	Admira Vienna v WAC Vienna	2-1
1925	FK Austria v First Vienna FC 1894	3-1	1933	FK Austria v Brigittanauer AC	1-0

1934	Admira Vienna v SK Rapid Vienna	8-0
1935	FK Austria v WAC Vienna	5-1
1936	FK Austria v First Vienna FC 1894	3-0
1937	First Vienna FC 1894 v Wiener Sport-Club	2-0

1938	Schwarz-Rot (WAC) Vienna v Wiener Sport-Club	1-0
1939 until 1948 no competition		
1948	FK Austria v Admira Vienna	2-1
1949	FK Austria v First Vienna FC 1894	3-1

NATIONAL CUP WINNERS

Since 1985 the Final is played in one game if the teams come from the same city

1946	SK Rapid Vienna v First Vienna FC 1894	2-1
1947	Wacker Wien v FK Austria	4-3
1948	FK Austria v SK Sturm Graz	2-0
1949	FK Austria v SK Vorwaerts Steyr	5-2
1950 to 1958 not held		
1959	WAC Vienna v SK Rapid Vienna	2-0
1960	FK Austria v SK Rapid Vienna	4-2
1961	SK Rapid Vienna v First Vienna FC 1894	3-1
1962	FK Austria v Grazer AK	4-1
1963	FK Austria v Linzer ASK	1-0
1964	Admira Vienna v SC Rapid Vienna	1-0
1965	Linzer ASK v 1 Weiner Neustadter SC	1-0
1966	Admira Vienna v SK Rapid Vienna	1-0
1967	FK Austria v Linzer ASK	1-0
1968	SK Rapid Vienna v Grazer AK	2-0
1969	SK Rapid Vienna v Wiener Sport-Club	2-1
1970	FC Wacker Innsbruck v Linzer ASK	1-0

1971	FK Austria v SK Rapid Vienna	2-1 aet
1972	SK Rapid Vienna v Wiener Sport-Club	3-1 1-2
1973	Wacker Innsbruck v SK Rapid Vienna	1-0 1-2 wag
1974	FK Austria v SV Austria Salzburg	2-1 1-1
1975	Wacker Innsbruck v SK Sturm Graz	3-0 0-2
1976	SK Rapid Vienna v Wacker Innsbruck	1-0 1-2 wag
1977	Austria WAC v Wiener Sport-Club	1-0 3-0
1978	Wacker Innsbruck v SK VoEST Linz	2-1 1-1
1979	Wacker Innsbruck v FC Admira/WAC	1-0 1-1
1980	FK Austria v SV Austria Salzburg	2-0 0-1
1981	Grazer AK v SV Austria Salzburg	0-1 2-0 aet
1982	FK Austria v Wacker Innsbruck	1-0 3-1
1983	SK Rapid Vienna v Wacker Innsbruck	3-0 5-0
1984	FK Austria v SK Rapid Vienna	2-0 1-3 wag
1985	SK Rapid Vienna v FK Austria	3-3 aet 6-5p
1986	FK Austria v SC Rapid Vienna	6-4 aet
1987	SK Rapid Vienna v FC Tirol Innsbruck	2-0 2-2
1988	Kremser SC v FC Tirol Innsbruck	2-0 1-3 wag
1989	FC Tirol Innsbruk v Admira Wacker Vienna	6-2 0-2

SUPER CUP

1986	SK Rapid Vienna v FK Austria	3-1
1987	SK Rapid Vienna v FC Tirol Innsbruck	2-1
1988	SK Rapid Vienna v Kremser SC	1-1 3-1p
1989	not held FC Tirol won both competitions	

FEATURED CLUBS IN EUROPEAN COMPETITION

Please note that names in club titles eg Swarovski etc are the clubs sponsors and are not in general use within the countries' football fraternity, it is mentioned here as a guide and information only

FC Tirol Innsbruck	**Admira/Wacker**	**FK Austria**	**SK Rapid Vienna**
Linzer ASK	**First Vienna FC 1894**	**1.Wiener Neustadter SC**	**SK VoEST Linz**
Sport-Club Sturm Graz	**Grazer AK**	**SV Austria Salzburg**	**Wiener Sport-Club**
Kremser SC			

AUSTRIA

FC SWAROVSKI TIROL (INNSBRUCK)

Founded 1913 as Wacker Innsbruck, FC Wat- tens amalgamated on 3-7-71, 1978 clubs separated, 1986 FC Tirol
Colour dark blue shirts, white shorts or all dark blue with white trim or all white with dark blue trim
Stadium Tivoli (17,200) ☎ 05222-47880/47980
Champions 1971, 1972, 1973, 1975, 1977, 1989
Cup Winners 1970, 1973, 1975, 1978, 1979, 1989
Mitropa Cup Winners 1975, 1976

Season	Opponents	Home	Result	Away	Rnd	Cup
as WACKER INNSBRUCK						
1968-69	Eintracht Frankfurt, Germany	2-2		0-3	1	Fairs
1970-71	Partizan Tirana, Albania	3-2		2-1	1	CWC
	Real Madrid, Spain	0-2		1-0	2	CWC
1971-72	Benfica, Portugal	0-4		1-3	1	ECC
1972-73	Dynamo Kiev, USSR	0-1		0-2	1	ECC
1973-74	CSKA Sofia, Bulgaria	0-1		0-3	1	ECC
1974-75	Borussia Monchengladbach, Germany	2-1		0-3	1	UEFA
1975-76	Borussia Monchengladbach, Germany	1-6		1-1	1	ECC
1976-77	Start Kristiansand, Norway	2-1		5-0	1	UEFA
	Videoton Szekesfehervar, Hungary	1-1		0-1	2	UEFA
1977-78	FC Basle, Switzerland	0-1		3-1	1	ECC
	Glasgow Celtic, Scotland	3-0		1-2	2	ECC
	Borussia Monchengladbach, Germany	3-1	lag	0-2	qf	ECC
1978-79	Zaglebie Sosnowiecz, Poland	1-1		3-2	1	CWC
	Ipswich Town, England	1-1		0-1	2	CWC
1979-80	Lokomotiva Kosice, Czechoslovakia	1-2		0-1	1	CWC
1983-84	1.FC Koln, Germany	1-0		1-7	1	CWC
1984-85	Real Madrid, Spain	2-0		0-5	1	UEFA
1985-86	RFC Liege, Belgium	1-3		0-1	1	UEFA
as FC TIROL						
1986-87	Sredets Sofia, Bulgaria	0-1 abd	3-0	0-2	1	UEFA
	Standard Liege, Belgium	2-1		2-3	2	UEFA
	Spartak Moscow, USSR	2-0		0-1	3	UEFA
	Torino, Italy	2-1		0-0	qf	UEFA
	IFK Gothenburg, Sweden	0-1		1-4	sf	UEFA
1987-88	Sporting Lisbon, Portugal	4-2		0-4	1	CWC
1989-90	Omonia Nicosia, Cyprus	6-0		3-2	1	ECC
	Dnepr Dnepropetrovsk, USSR	2-2		0-2	2	ECC

FC ADMIRA-WACKER (VIENNA)

Founded 1905 as Admira, 1972 amalgamated with Wacker Vienna under Admira
Stadium Sudstadt (18,800) ☎ 02239-23479
Colours black shirts, white shorts or all white with black trim or all blue with white trim
Champions as Admira 1927, 1928, 1932, 1934, 1936, 1937, 1939, 1966 as Wacker 1947
Viennese Cup Winners 1928, 1932, 1934
Cup Winners as Admira 1964, 1966 as Wacker 1947

Season	Opponent	Home	Result	Away	Rnd	Cup
1964-65	Legia Warsaw, Poland	1-3		0-1	pr	CWC
1966-67	Vojvodina Novi Sad, Yugoslavia	0-1		0-0	pr	ECC
1973-74	Inter Milan, Italy	1-0	wag	1-2	1	UEFA
	Fortuna Dusseldorf, Germany	2-1		0-3	2	UEFA
1982-83	Bohemians Prague, Czechoslovakia	1-2		0-5	1	UEFA
1987-88	TPS Turun Palloseura Turku, Finland	0-2		1-0	1	UEFA
1989-90	AE Limmassol, Cyprus	3-0		0-1	1	CWC
	Ferenevaros, TC Hungary	1-0		1-0*	2	CWC
				*in Szeged		
	RSC Anderlecht, Belgium	1-1		0-2	qf	CWC

FK AUSTRIA MEMPHIS (VIENNA)

Founded 1911 as Amateure changed to FK Austria 1927, 1973 amalgamated with WAC Vienna
Colours violet and white or violet shirts, white shorts or all white with violet trim
Stadium Prater Stadion (62,958) for big games Franz Horr Stadion (10,000) ☎ 0222-218 64 91
Champions as Amateure 1924, 1926, as FK Austria 1949, 1950, 1953, 1961, 1962, 1963, 1969, 1970, 1976, 1978, 1979, 1980, 1981, 1984, 1985, 1986, 1987
Viennese Cup Winners as Amateure 1921, 1924
Cup Winners as FK Austria 1925, 1926, 1933, 1935, 1936, 1948, 1949, 1960, 1962, 1963, 1967, 1971, 1974, 1977, 1980, 1982, 1984, 1986
Mitropa Cup Winners as FK Austria 1933
CWC Finalists 1978

Season	Opponents	Home	Play-off Result	Away	Rd	Cup
1960-61	Wolverhampton Wanderers, England	2-0		0-5	1	CWC
1961-62	CCA Bucharest, Romania	2-0		0-0	1	ECC
	Benfica Lisbon, Portugal	1-1		1-5	2	ECC
1962-63	HIFK Helsinki, Finland	5-3		2-0	1	ECC
	Stade de Reims, France	3-2		0-5* *in Paris	2	ECC
1963-64	Gornik Zabrze, Poland	1-0	1-2* *in Vienna	0-1	1	ECC
1967-68	Steaua Bucharest, Romania	0-2		1-2	1	CWC
1969-70	Dynamo Kiev, USSR	1-2		1-3	1	ECC
1970-71	Levski Spartak Sofia, Bulgaria	3-0		1-3	pr	ECC
	Atletico Madrid, Spain	1-2		0-2	1	ECC
1971-72	B1909 Odense, Denmark	2-0	wag	2-4	pr	CWC
	Dinamo Tirana, Albania	1-0		1-1	1	CWC
	Torino, Italy	0-0		0-1	2	CWC
1972-73	Beroe Stara Zagora, Bulgaria	1-3		0-7	1	UEFA
1974-75	Waregem KSV, Belgium	4-1		1-2	1	CWC
	Real Madrid, Spain	2-2		0-3	2	CWC
1976-77	Borussia Monchengladbach, Germany	1-0		0-3	1	ECC
1977-78	Cardiff City, Wales	1-0		0-0	1	CWC
	Lokomotiva Kosice, Czechoslovakia	0-0	wag	1-1	2	CWC
	Hajduk Split, Yugoslavia	1-1	3-0p	1-1	3	CWC
	Dynamo Moscow, USSR	2-1	5-4p	1-2* *in Tbilisi	sf	CWC
	RSC Anderlecht, Belgium	0-4	in Paris		FINAL	CWC
1978-79	Vlaznia Shkodar, Albania	4-1		0-2	1	ECC
	Lillestrom SK, Norway	4-1		0-0	2	ECC
	Dynamo Dresden, East Germany	3-1		0-1	3	ECC
	Malmo FF, Sweden	0-0		0-1	sf	ECC
1979-80	Vejle BK, Denmark	1-1		2-3	1	ECC
1980-81	Aberdeen, Scotland	0-0		0-1	1	ECC
1981-82	Partizani Tirana, Albania	3-1		0-1	1	ECC
	Dynamo Kiev, USSR	0-1		1-1	2	ECC
1982-83	Panathinaikos, Greece	2-0		1-2	1	CWC
	Galatasaray, Turkey	0-1		4-2	2	CWC
	FC Barcelona, Spain	0-0	wag	1-1	3	CWC
	Real Madrid, Spain	2-2		1-3	sf	CWC
1983-84	Aris Bonnevoie, Luxembourg	10-0		5-0	1	UEFA
	Lavallois, France	2-0		3-3	2	UEFA
	Inter Milan, Italy	2-1		1-1	3	UEFA
	Tottenham Hotspur, England	2-2		0-2	4	UEFA
1984-85	Valletta, Malta	4-0		4-0	1	ECC
	FC Dynamo Berlin, East Germany	2-1		3-3	2	ECC
	Liverpool, England	1-1		1-4	3	ECC
1985-86	BFC Dynamo Berlin, East Germany	2-1		2-0	1	ECC
	Bayern Munich, Germany	3-3		2-4	2	ECC
1986-87	Avenir Beggen, Luxembourg	3-0		3-0	1	ECC
	Bayern Munich, Germany	1-1		0-1	2	ECC

25

AUSTRIA

1987-88	Bayer Leverkusen, Germany	0-0		1-5	1	UEFA
1988-89	Zhalgiris Vilnius, USSR	5-2		0-2	1	UEFA
	Heart of Midlothian, Scotland	0-1		0-0	2	UEFA
1989-90	Ajax Amsterdam, Holland	1-0		1-1*	1	UEFA

*abandoned 102 minutes, awarded to FK Austria

	Werder Bremen, Germany	2-0		0-5	2	UEFA

SK RAPID VIENNA

Founded 1899   Colours green and white striped shirts, black shorts
Stadium Gerhard Hanappi Stadion (19,300) ☎ 0222-94 76 70
Colours green and white striped shirts, white shorts or all green with white trim (Euro competitions) or all white with green
Champions 1912, 1913, 1916, 1917, 1919, 1920, 1921, 1923, 1929, 1930, 1935, 1938, 1940, 1941, 1945, 1946, 1948, 1951, 1952, 1954, 1956, 1957, 1960, 1964, 1967, 1968, 1982, 1983, 1988
Viennese Cup Winners 1919, 1920, 1927
Cup Winners 1946, 1961, 1968, 1969, 1972, 1976, 1983, 1985, 1987
Austrian Super Cup Winners 1986, 1987, 1988
Mitropa Cup Winners 1930
CWC Finalists 1985

Season	Opponents	Home	Play-off Result	Away	Rnd	Cup
1955-56	PSV Eindhoven, Holland	6-1		0-1	2	ECC
	AC Milan, Italy	1-1		2-7	3	ECC
1956-57	Real Madrid, Spain	3-1	0-2*	2-4	1	ECC
			*in Madrid			
1957-58	AC Milan, Italy	5-2	2-4*	1-4	pr	ECC
			*in Zurich			
1960-61	Besiktas, Turkey	4-0		0-1	1	ECC
	Wismut Karl Marx Stadt, East Germany	3-1	1-0*	0-2	2	ECC
			*in Basel			
	IFK Malmo, Sweden	2-0		2-0	3	ECC
	Benfica, Portugal	1-1		0-3	sf	ECC
1961-62	Spartak Varna, Bulgaria	5-2		0-0	1	CWC
	Fiorentina, Italy	2-6		1-3	2	CWC
1962-63	Red Star Belgrade, Yugoslavia	0-1		1-1	1	Fairs
1963-64	Racing Club de Paris, France	1-0		3-2	1	Fairs
	Valencia CF, Spain	0-0		2-3	2	Fairs
1964-65	Shamrock Rovers, Eire	3-0		2-0	pr	ECC
	Glasgow Rangers, Scotland	0-2		0-1	1	ECC
1966-67	Galatasaray, Turkey	4-0		5-3	1	CWC
	Spartak Moscow, USSR	1-0		1-1	2	CWC
	Bayern Munich, Germany	1-0		0-2	3	CWC
1967-68	Besiktas, Turkey	3-0		1-0	1	ECC
	Eintracht Braunschweig, Germany	1-0		0-2	2	ECC
1968-69	Rosenborg Trondheim, Norway	3-3		3-1	1	ECC
	Real Madrid, Spain	1-0	wag	1-2	2	ECC
	Manchester United, England	0-0		0-3	3	ECC
1969-70	Torpedo Moscow, USSR	0-0	wag	1-1	pr	CWC
	PSV Eindhoven, Holland	1-2		2-4	1	CWC
1971-72	Vlaznia Shkodar, Albania	withdrew			1	UEFA
	Dinamo Zagreb, Yugoslavia	0-0	wag	2-2	2	UEFA
	Juventus, Italy	0-1		1-4	3	UEFA
1972-73	PAOK Salonika, Greece	0-0	wag	2-2	1	CWC
	Rapid Bucharest, Romania	1-1		1-3	2	CWC
1973-74	Randers Freja, Denmark	2-1		0-0	1	CWC
	AC Milan, Italy	0-2		0-0	2	CWC
1974-75	Aris Salonika, Greece	3-1		0-1	1	UEFA
	Velez Mostar, Yugoslavia	1-1		0-1	2	UEFA
1975-76	Galatasaray, Turkey	1-0		1-3	1	UEFA
1976-77	Atletico Madrid, Spain	1-2		1-1	1	CWC
1977-78	Internacional Bratislava, Czechoslovakia	1-0		0-3	1	UEFA

1978-79	Hajduk Split, Yugoslavia	2-1		0-2	1	UEFA
1979-80	Diosgyoer, Hungary	0-1		2-3	1	UEFA
1981-82	Videoton Sekesfehervar, Hungary	2-2		2-0	1	UEFA
	PSV Eindhoven, Holland	1-0		1-2	2	UEFA
	Real Madrid, Spain	0-1		0-0	3	UEFA
1982-83	Avenir Beggen, Luxembourg	8-0		5-0	1	ECC
	Widzew Lodz, Poland	2-1		3-5	2	ECC
1983-84	FC Nantes, France	3-0		1-3	1	ECC
	Bohemians Prague, Czechoslovakia	1-0	wag	1-2	2	ECC
	Dundee United, Scotland	2-1	lag	0-1	qf	ECC
1984-85	Besiktas, Turkey	4-1		1-1	1	CWC
	Glasgow Celtic, Scotland	3-1	0-3 void	1-0*	2	CWC
				*in Manchester		
	Dynamo Dresden, East Germany	5-0		0-3	qf	CWC
	Dynamo Moscow, USSR	3-1		1-1	sf	CWC
	Everton, England	1-3	in Rotterdam		FINAL	CWC
1985-86	Tatabanya Banyasz, Hungary	5-0		1-1	1	CWC
	Fram Reykjavik, Iceland	3-0		1-2	2	CWC
	Dynamo Kiev, USSR	1-4		1-5	qf	CWC
1986-87	Clube Bruges, Belgium	4-3		3-3	1	CWC
	1.FC Lokomotive Leipzig, East Germany	1-1		1-2	2	CWC
1987-88	Hamrun Spartans, Malta	6-0		1-0	1	ECC
	PSV Eindhoven, Holland	1-2		0-2	2	ECC
1988-89	Galatasaray, Turkey	2-1		0-2	1	ECC
	Aberdeen, Scotland	1-0	wag	1-2	1	UEFA
	Club Bruges, Belgium	4-3		2-1	2	UEFA
	RFC Liege, Belgium	1-0		1-3	3	UEFA

LINZER ATHLETIK SPORTTCLUB 'LASK'

Founded 1908 as LSK Linz, 1912 Linzer ASK
Stadium Linzer Stadion (22,000) ☎ 0732-238241
Colours black and white striped shirts, black shorts or yellow shirts, blue shorts
Champions 1965
Cup Winners 1965

Season	Opponents	Home	Playoff Result	Away	Rnd	Cup
1963-64	Dinamo Zagreb, Yugoslavia	1-0	1-1 lot* *in Zagreb	0-1	1	CWC
1965-66	Gornik Zabrze, Poland	1-3		1-2* *in Krakow	pr	ECC
1969-70	Sporting Lisbon, Portugal	2-2		0-4	1	UEFA
1977-78	Ujpest Dozsa, Hungary	3-2		0-7	1	UEFA
1980-81	Radnicki Nis, Yugoslavia	1-2		1-4	1	UEFA
1984-85	Osters IF Vaxjo, Sweden	1-0		1-0	1	UEFA
	Dundee United, Scotland	1-2		1-5	2	UEFA
1985-86	Banik Ostrava, Czechoslovakia	2-0		1-0	1	UEFA
	Inter Milan, Italy	1-0		0-4	2	UEFA
1986-87	Widzew Lodz, Poland	1-1		0-1	1	UEFA
1987-88	FC Utrecht, Holland	0-0		0-2	1	UEFA

FIRST VIENNA FC 1894 FOTO NETTIG

Founded 1894   Colours yellow shirts, blue shorts
Stadium Hohe Warte (9,600) ☎ 0222-366136
Champions 1931, 1933, 1942,1943, 1944, 1955
Mitropa Cup Winners 1931
Viennese Cup Winners 1929, 1930, 1937
German Cup Winners 1943

AUSTRIA

Season	Opponents	Home	Result	Away	Rnd	Cup
1988-89	Ikast FS, Denmark	1-0	wag	1-2	1	UEFA
	TPS Turun Palloseaura Turku, Finland	2-1	lag	0-1	2	UEFA
1989-90	Valletta FC Malta	3-0		4-1	1	UEFA
	Olympiakos Piraeus, Greece	2-2	lag	1-1	2	UEFA

1.WIENER NEUSTADTER

Founded 1908   Colours all blue
Stadium Wiener Neustadt

Season	Opponent	Home	Result	Away	Rnd	Cup
1965-66	Universitatea Stiinta Cluj, Romania	0-1		0-2	pr	CWC

SPORTKLUB SALESIANER MIETTEX VoEST LINZ

VoEST = Vereinigte Oster- reichische Eisenund Stahlwerke

Founded 1949   Colours all white with blue trim or all blue with white trim
Stadium Linzer Stadion (22,000) ☎ 0732-585 83 98/0064
Champions 1974

Season	Opponents	Home	Result	Away	Rnd	Cup
1972-73	Dynamo Dresden, East Germany	2-2		0-2	1	UEFA
1974-75	FC Barcelona, Spain	0-0		0-5	1	ECC
1975-76	Vasas Budapest, Hungary	2-0		0-4	1	UEFA
1980-81	Zbrojovka Brno, Czechoslovakia	0-2		1-3	1	UEFA

SPORTKLUB RAIKA STURM GRAZ

Founded 1909
Stadium Sturm-Platz (12,000) or Liebenau (20,000) for important matches ☎ 0316-33168/37655
Colours all white with black trim or white shirts, black shorts or green shirts, black shorts

Season	Opponents	Home	Result	Away	Rnd	Cup
1970-71	Ilves Kissat Tampere, Finland	3-0		2-4	1	Fairs
	Arsenal, England	1-0		0-2	2	Fairs
1974-75	Royal Antwerp, Belgium	2-1	lag	0-1	1	UEFA
1975-76	Slavia Sofia, Bulgaria	3-1		0-1	1	CWC
	Haladas Vasutas Szombathely, Hungary	2-0		1-1	2	CWC
	Eintracht Frankfurt, Germany	0-2		0-1	3	CWC
1978-79	Borussia Monchengladbach, Germany	1-2		1-5	1	UEFA
1981-82	CSKA Moscow, USSR	1-0	wag	1-2	1	UEFA
	IFK Gothenburg, Sweden	2-2		2-3	2	UEFA
1983-84	Sportul Studentesc Bucharest, Romania	0-0		2-1	1	UEFA
	Verona Hellas, Italy	0-0	wag	2-2	2	UEFA
	1.FC Lokomotive Leipzig, East Germany	2-0		0-1	3	UEFA
	Nottingham Forest, England	1-1		0-1	4	UEFA
1988-89	Servette Geneva, Switzerland	0-0		0-1	1	UEFA

GRAZER ATHLETIK-KLUB RINGSCHUH (GAK)

Founded 1902
Stadium Casino-Stadion (10,000) or Liebenau (20,000) for important matches ☎ 0316-61201
Colours all red with white trim or all white with red trim
Cup Winners 1981

Season	Opponent	Home	Result	Away	Rnd	Cup
1962-63			bye		1	CWC
	B1909 Odense, Denmark	1-1		3-5	2	CWC
1964-65	ZNK Zagreb, Yugoslavia	0-6		2-3	pr	UEFA
1968-69	ADO The Hague, Holland	0-2		1-4	1	CWC
1973-74	Panachaiki Patras, Greece	0-1		1-2	1	UEFA
1981-82	Dynamo Tbilisi, USSR	2-2		0-2	1	CWC
1982-83	Corvinul Hunedoara, Romania	1-1		0-3	1	UEFA

SV AUSTRIA CASINO SALZBURG

formerly SV Austria Salzburg changed in 1978
Founded 1933   Colours all white with violet trim
Stadium Salzburg-Lehen (18,000) ☎ 0662-33332

Season	Opponent	Home	Result	Away	Rnd	Cup
1971-72	U T Flamurarosie Arad, Romania	3-1		1-4	1	UEFA
1976-77	Adanaspor, Turkey	5-0		0-2	1	UEFA
	Red Star Belgrade, Yugoslavia	2-1	lag	0-1	2	UEFA
1980-81	Fortuna Dusseldorf, Germany	0-3		0-5	1	CWC

WIENER SPORT-CLUB

Founded 1883, 1907 Soccer section started, 1975-76 only became Sportklub Post (1 season)
Stadium Sport-Club-Platz (9,600) ☎ 0222-456900
Colours all white with black trim or all red
Champions 1922, 1958, 1959
Viennese Cup Winners 1923
Amalgamation Wiener Sportclub with Post Sportclub Wien in 1976

Season	Opponents	Home	Result	Away	Rnd	Cup
1958-59	Juventus, Italy	7-0		1-3	1	ECC
	Dukla Prague, Czechoslovakia	3-1		0-1	2	ECC
	Real Madrid, Spain	0-0		1-7	qf	ECC
1959-60	Petrolul Ploesti, Romania	0-0		2-1	pr	ECC
	B1909 Odense, Denmark	2-2		3-0	1	ECC
	Eintracht Frankfurt, Germany	1-1		1-2	2	ECC
1964-65	SC Leipzig, East Germany	2-1		1-0	1	Fairs
	Ferencvarosi TC, Hungary	1-0	0-2*	1-2	2	airs
			*in Budapest			
1965-66	PAOK Salonica, Greece	6-0		1-2	1	Fairs
	Chelsea, England	1-0		0-2	2	Fairs
1966-67	Napoli, Italy	1-2		1-3	1	Fairs
1966-67	Napoli, Italy	1-2		1-3	1	Fairs
1967-68	Atletico Madrid, Spain	2-5		1-2	1	Fairs
1968-69	Slavia Prague,Czechoslovakia	1-0		0-5	1	Fairs
1969-70	Ruch Chorzow, Poland	4-2		1-4	1	Fairs
1970-71	SK Beveren Waas, Belgium	0-2		0-3	1	Fairs
1979-80	Universitatea Craiova, Romania	0-0		1-3	1	UEFA

AUSTRIA

KREMSER SC

Founded 1919   Colours all red with white trim
Stadium Kremser (10,000) ☎ 02732-5614
Cup Winners 1988

Season	Opponents	Home	Result	Away	Rnd	Cup
1988-89	Carl Zeiss Jena, East Germany	1-0		0-5	1	CWC

30 • Varendsvallen, Vaxjo, Sweden. Osters Vaxjo, Sweden

BELGIUM

Founded 1895
Union Royale Belge Des Societes de Football Association, Avenue Houbade Strooper 145.1020 ☎ 02-4771211
Fax 02-478 23 91
National colours all white or all red
Season September to May

LEAGUE CHAMPIONS

1896	FC Liege	1922	Beerschot	1947	RSC Anderlecht	1969	Standard Liege
1897	RC Brussels	1923	Union St Gilloise	1948	Malines	1970	Standard Liege
1898	FC Liege	1924	Beerschot	1949	RSC Anderlecht	1971	Standard Liege
1899	FC Liege	1925	Beerschot			1972	RSC Anderlecht
		1926	Beerschot	1950	RSC Anderlecht	1973	Clube Bruges
1900	RC Brussels	1927	CS Bruges	1951	RSC Anderlecht	1974	RSC Anderlecht
1901	RC Brussels	1928	Beerschot	1952	FC Liege	1975	RW Molenbeck
1902	RC Brussels	1929	RFC Antwerp	1953	FC Liege	1976	Clube Bruges
1903	RC Brussels			1954	RSC Anderlecht	1977	Clube Bruges
1904	Union St Gilloise	1930	CS Bruges	1955	RSC Anderlecht	1978	Clube Bruges
1905	Union St Gilloise	1931	RFC Antwerp	1956	RSC Anderlecht	1979	Beveren Waas
1906	Union St Gilloise	1932	Lierse	1957	RFC Antwerp		
1907	Union St Gilloise	1933	Union St Gilloise	1958	Standard Liege	1980	Clube Bruges
1908	RC Brussels	1934	Union St Gilloise	1959	RSC Anderlecht	1981	RSC Anderlecht
1909	Union St Gilloise	1935	Union St Gilloise			1982	Standard Liege
		1936	Daring	1960	Lierse	1983	Standard Liege
1910	Union St Gilloise	1937	Daring	1961	Standard Liege	1984	Beveren Waas
1911	CS Bruges	1938	Beerschot	1962	RSC Anderlecht	1985	RSC Anderlecht
1912	Daring	1939	Beerschot	1963	Standard Liege	1986	RSC Anderlecht
1913	Union St Gilloise			1964	RSC Anderlecht	1987	RSC Anderlecht
1914	Daring	1942	Lierse	1965	RSC Anderlecht	1988	Clube Bruges
		1943	Malines	1966	RSC Anderlecht	1989	KV Mechelen
1920	Clube Bruges	1944	RFC Antwerp	1967	RSC Anderlecht		
1921	Daring	1946	Malines	1968	RSC Anderlecht		

CUP WINNERS

1912	RC Brussels v RC Ghent	1-0	1927	CS Bruges v FC Subantia	2-1
1913	Union St Gilloise v CS Bruges	3-2			
1914	Union St Gilloise v Clube Bruges	4-1	1954	Standard Liege v R C Mechelen	3-1

BELGIUM

1955	RFC Antwerp v Waterschei Thor	4-0
1956	RRC Tournai v CS Verviers	2-1
1957 to 1963 no competition		
1964	La Ghantoise v Diest	4-2
1965	RSC Anderlecht v Standard Liege	3-2
1966	Standard Liege v RSC Anderlecht	1-0
1967	Standard Liege v K V Mechelen	3-1
1968	F C Bruges v Beerschot	1-1 4-4 4-2 pen
1969	Lierse v Racing White	2-0
1970	F C Bruges v Daring	6-1
1971	Beerschot v St Trond	2-1
1972	RSC Anderlecht v Standard Liege	1-0
1973	RSC Anderlecht v Standard Liege	2-1
1974	Waregem KSV v Tongeren	4-1
1975	RFC Anderlecht v RFC Antwerp	1-0
1976	RFC Anderlecht v Lierse	4-0

1977	Clube Bruges v RSC Anderlecht	4-3
1978	Beveren Waas v Sporting Charleroi	2-0
1979	Beerschot v Clube Bruges	1-0
1980	Waterschei Thor Genk v Beveren Waas	2-1
1981	Standard Liege v KSC Lokeren	4-0
1982	Waterschei Thor Genk v Waregem KSV	2-0
1983	Beveren Waas v Clube Bruges	3-1
1984	AA Ghent v Standard Liege	2-0
1985	Cercle Bruges v Beveren Waas	1-1 5-4 pen
1986	Clube Bruges v Cercle Bruges	3-0
1987	KV Mechelen v RFC Liege	1-0
1988	RSC Anderlecht v Standard Liege	2-0
1989	RSC Anderlecht v Standard Liege	2-0
1990	Standard Liege v RFC Leige	

SUPER CUP WINNERS

1979	SK Beveren Waas v K Beerschot V.A.V.	1-1 3-2 pens
1980	Club Bruges v SK Beveren Waas	1-1 4-3 pens
1981	Standard Liege v RSC Anderlecht	0-0 3-1 pens
1982	SV Waregem v Standard Liege	3-2
1983	Standard Liege v SK Beveren Waas	1-1 5-4 pens

1984	SK Beveren Waas v AA Gent	5-1
1985	RSC Anderlecht v Cercle Bruges	2-1
1986	Clube Bruges v RSC Anderlecht	1-0
1987	RSC Anderlecht v KV Mechelen	1-1 2-0
1988	Clube Bruges v RSC Anderlecht	1-0
1989	KV Mechelen v RSC Anderlecht	

FEATURED CLUBS IN EUROPEAN COMPETITION

RSC Anderlecht	Clube Bruges	Union St Gilloise	Lierse SK
Standard Liege	Royal Antwerp	RWD Molenbeeck	K Beerschot V.A.V
AA Ghent	RFC Liege	Sporting Charleroi SC	Waregem KSV
SK Beveren Waas	Waterschei Thor Genk	SV Cercle Bruges	KSC Lokeren
KFC Winterslag	KV Mechelen		

ROYALE CLUBE ANDERLECHT

Founded 1908   Colours mauve with white sleeves, mauve shorts
Stadium Parc Astrid (34,000). European Cup Games played at the Heysel Stadium (63,000) ☎ 02-522 15 39
Champions 1947, 1949, 1950, 1951, 1954, 1955, 1956, 1959, 1962, 1964, 1965, 1966, 1967, 1968, 1972, 1974 1981, 1985, 1986, 1987
Cup Winners 1965, 1972, 1973, 1975, 1976, 1988, 1989
CWC Winners 1976, 1978
CWC Finalists 1977
UEFA Cup Winners 1983
UEFA Cup Finalists 1984
UEFA Cup Finalists 1970
European Super Cup Winners 1976, 1978

Season	Opponent	Home	Playoff Result	Away	Rnd	Cup
1955-56	Voros Lobago(MTK), Hungary	1-4		3-6	1	ECC
1956-57	Manchester United, England	0-2		0-10	1	ECC
1959-60	Glasgow Rangers, Scotland	0-2		2-5	1	ECC
1962-63	Real Madrid, Spain	1-0		3-3	1	ECC
	CDNA Sofia, Bulgaria	2-0		2-2	2	ECC
	Dundee, Scotland	1-4		1-2	3	ECC

1964-65	Bologna, Italy	1-0	0-0 wot*	1-2	pr	ECC
			*in Barcelona aet			
	Liverpool, England	0-1		0-3	1	ECC
1965-66	Fenerbahce, Turkey	5-1		0-0	1	ECC
	Derry City, Ireland	9-0		not played	2	ECC
	Real Madrid, Spain	1-0		2-4	3	ECC
1966-67	Haka Valkeakoski, Finland	2-0		10-1	pr	ECC
	Dukla Prague, Czechoslovakia	1-2		1-4	1	ECC
1967-68	FC Karl Marx Stadt, East Germany	2-1		3-1	1	ECC
	Sparta Prague, Czechoslovakia	3-3		2-3	2	ECC
1968-69	Glentoran, Ireland	3-0		2-2	1	ECC
	Manchester United, England	3-1		0-3	2	ECC
1969-70	Valur Reykjavik, Iceland	6-0		2-0*	1	Fairs
				*in Ghent		
	Coleraine, Ireland	6-1		7-3	2	Fairs
	Dunfermline Athletic, Scotland	1-0	wag	2-3	3	Fairs
	Newcastle United, England	2-0	ʳ wag	1-3	qf	Fairs
	Inter Milan, Italy	0-1		2-0	sf	Fairs
	Arsenal, England	3-1		0-3	FINAL	Fairs
1970-71	Zeljeznicar Sarajevo, Yugoslavia	5-4		4-3	1	UEFA
	AB Copenhagen, Denmark	4-0		3-1	2	UEFA
	Vitoria Setubal, Portugal	2-1		1-3	3	UEFA
1971-72	Bologna, Italy	0-2		1-1	1	UEFA
1972-73	Vejle BK, Denmark	4-2		3-0	1	ECC
	Spartak Trnava, Czechoslovakia	0-1		0-1	2	ECC
1973-74	FC Zurich, Switzerland	3-2	lag	0-1	1	CWC
1974-75	Slovan Bratislava, Czechslovakia	3-1	wag	2-4	1	ECC
	Olympiakos Piraeus, Greece	5-1		0-3	2	ECC
	Leeds United, England	0-1		0-3	3	ECC
1975-76	Rapid Bucharest, Romania	2-0		0-1	1	CWC
	Borac Banja Luka, Yugoslavia	3-0		0-1	2	CWC
	Wrexham, Wales	1-0		1-1	qf	CWC
	Saschenring Zwickau, East Germany	2-0		3-0	sf	CWC
	West Ham United, England	4-2	in Brussels		FINAL	CWC
1976-77	Roda JC Kerkrade, Holland	2-1		3-2	1	CWC
	Galatasaray, Turkey	5-1		5-1	2	CWC
	Southampton, England	2-0		1-2	qf	CWC
	Napoli, Italy	2-0		0-1	sf	CWC
	Hamburger SV, Germany	0-2	in Amsterdam		FINAL	CWC
1977-78	Lokomotiv Sofia, Bulgaria	2-0		6-1	1	CWC
	Hamburger SV, Germany	1-1		2-1	2	CWC
	FC Porto, Portugal	3-0		0-1	qf	CWC
	Twente Enschede, Holland	2-0		1-0	sf	CWC
	Austria Wien, Austria	4-0	in Paris		FINAL	CWC
1978-79	bye				1	bye
	FC Barcelona, Spain	3-0	1-4p	0-3	2	CWC
1979-80	Dundee United, Scotland	1-1	lag	0-0	1	UEFA
1980-81	1.FC Kaiserslautern, Germany	3-2	lag	0-1	1	UEFA
1981-82	Widzew Lodz, Poland	2-1		4-1	1	ECC
	Juventus, Italy	3-1		1-1	2	ECC
	Red Star Belgrade, Yugoslavia	2-1		2-1	qf	ECC
	Aston Villa, England	0-0		0-1	sf	ECC
1982-83	KPT Kuopio Pallotovert, Finland	3-0		3-1	1	UEFA
	FC Porto, Portugal	4-0		2-3	2	UEFA
	FK Sarajevo, Yugoslavia	6-1		0-1	3	UEFA
	Valencia, Spain	3-1		2-1	qf	UEFA
	Bohemians Prague, Czechoslovakia	3-1		1-0	sf	UEFA
	Benfica, Portugal	1-0		1-1	FINAL	UEFA
1983-84	Bryne, Norway	1-1		3-0	1	UEFA
	Banik Ostrava, Czechoslovakia	2-0		2-2	2	UEFA
	RC Lens, France	1-0		1-1	3	UEFA
	Spartak Moscow, USSR	4-2		0-1	qf	UEFA
	Nottingham Forest, England	3-0		0-2	sf	UEFA
	Tottenham Hotspur, England	1-1	3-4p	1-1	FINAL	UEFA

BELGIUM

1984-85	Werder Bremen, Germany	1-0	wag	1-2	1	UEFA
	Fiorentina, Italy	6-2		1-1	2	UEFA
	Real Madrid, Spain	3-0		1-6	3	UEFA
1985-86	bye				1	ECC
	Omonia Nicosia, Cyprus	1-0		3-1	2	ECC
	Bayern Munich, Germany	2-0		1-2	qf	ECC
	Steaua Bucharest, Romania	1-0		0-3	sf	ECC
1986-87	Gornik Zabrze, Poland	2-0		1-1	1	ECC
	Steaua Bucharest, Romania	3-0		0-1	2	ECC
	Bayern Munich, Germany	2-2		0-5	qf	ECC
1987-88	Malmo FF, Sweden	1-1		1-0	1	ECC
	Sparta Prague, Czechoslovakia	1-0		2-1	2	ECC
	Benfica, Portugal	1-0		0-2	qf	ECC
1988-89	FC Metz, France	2-0		3-1	1	CWC
	KV Mechelen, Belgium	0-2		0-1	2	CWC
1989-90	Ballymena United, Eire	6-0		4-0	1	CWC
	FC Barcelona, Spain	2-0	wag	1-2 aet	2	CWC
	Admira Wacker Vienna, Austria	2-0		1-1	qf	CWC
	Dinamo Bucharest, Romania	1-0			sf	CWC
	Sampdoria, Italy	0-2 aet			FINAL	CWC
					in Gothenburg	

CLUBE BRUGES

Founded 1891   Colours light and dark blue shirts, sky blue shorts
Stadium Olympic (32,000) ☎ 050- 318155
Champions 1920, 1973, 1976, 1977, 1978, 1980, 1988
Cup Winners 1968, 1970, 1977, 1986
European Cup Finalists 1978
UEFA Cup Finalists 1976

Season	Opponents	Home	Result	Away	Rnd	Cup
1967-68	Sporting Lisbon, Portugal	0-0		1-2	1	Fairs
1968-69	West Bromwich Albion, England	3-1	lag	0-2	1	CWC
1969-70	CD Sabadell, Spain	5-1		0-2	1	Fairs
	Ujpest Dozsa, Hungary	5-2	lag	0-3	2	Fairs
1970-71	Kickers Offenbach, Germany	2-0		1-2	1	CWC
	FC Zurich, Switzerland	2-0		2-3	2	CWC
	Chelsea, England	2-0		0-4	3	CWC
1971-72	Zeljeznicar Sarajevo, Yugoslavia	3-1		0-3	1	UEFA
1972-73	Atvidaberg FF, Sweden	1-2		5-3	1	UEFA
	FC Porto, Portugal	3-2		0-3	2	UEFA
1973-74	Floriana, Malta	8-0		2-0	1	ECC
	FC Basle, Switzerland	2-1		4-6	2	ECC
1975-76	Olympique Lyon, France	3-0		3-4	1	UEFA
	Ipswich Town, England	4-0		0-3	2	UEFA
	AS Roma, Italy	1-0		1-0	3	UEFA
	AC Milan, Italy	2-0		1-2	qf	UEFA
	Hamburger SV, Germany	1-0		1-1	sf	UEFA
	Liverpool, England	1-1		2-3	FINAL	UEFA
1976-77	Steaua Bucharest, Romania	2-1		1-1	1	ECC
	Real Madrid, Spain	2-0		0-0*	2	ECC
				*in Malaga		
	Borussia Monchengladbach, Germany	0-1		2-2*	qf	ECC
				*in Dusseldorf		
1977-78	KuPS Kuopion Palloseura, Finland	5-2		4-0	1	ECC
	Panathinaikos, Greece	2-0		0-1	2	ECC
	Atletico Madrid, Spain	2-0		2-3	qf	ECC
	Juventus, Italy	2-0		0-1	sf	ECC
	Liverpool, England	0-1	in Wembley		FINAL	ECC
1978-79	Wisla Cracow, Poland	2-1		1-3	1	ECC
1980-81	FC Basle, Switzerland	0-1		1-4	1	ECC
1981-82	Spartak Moscow, USSR	1-3		1-3	1	UEFA
1984-85	Nottingham Forest, England	1-0		0-0	1	UEFA
	Tottenham Hotspur, England	2-1		0-3	2	UEFA

1985-86	Boavista, Portugal	3-1		3-4	1	UEFA
	Spartak Moscow, USSR	1-3		0-1	2	UEFA
1986-87	Rapid Vienna, Austria	3-3		3-4	1	CWC
1987-88	Zenit Leningrad, USSR	5-0		0-2	1	UEFA
	Red Star Belgrade, Yugoslavia	4-0		1-3	2	UEFA
	Borussia Dortmund, Germany	5-0		0-3	3	UEFA
	Panathinaikos, Greece	1-0		2-2	qf	UEFA
	Espanol Barcelona, Spain	2-0		0-3	sf	UEFA
1988-89	Brondbyernes, Denmark	1-0	wag	1-2	1	ECC
	AS Monaco, France	1-0		1-6	2	ECC
1989-90	Twente Enschede, Holland	4-1		0-0	1	UEFA
	Rapid Vienna, Austria	1-2		3-4	2	UEFA

ROYALE UNION GILLOISE (BRUSSELS)

Formerly Union St Gilloise
Founded 1897   Colours blue shirts, yellow shorts
Stadium Joseph Marien La Butte (30,000) ☎ 02-3441656
Champions 1904, 1905, 1906, 1907, 1909, 1910, 1913, 1923, 1933, 1934, 1935
Cup Winners 1913, 1914

Season	Opponent	Home	Playoff Result	Away	Rnd	Cup
1958-60	Leipzig Selection, East Germany	6-1		0-1	1	Fairs
	AS Roma, Italy	2-0		1-1	2	Fairs
	Birmingham City, England	2-4		2-4	3	Fairs
1960-61	AS Roma, Italy	0-0		1-4	1	Fairs
1961-62	Heart of Midlothian, Scotland	1-3		0-2	pr	Fairs
1962-63	Olympique Marseille, France	4-2		0-1	1	Fairs
	Dinamo Zagreb, Yugoslavia	1-0	2-3*	1-2	2	Fairs
			*in Linz			
1964-65	Juventus, Italy	0-1		0-1	1	Fairs

LIERSE SK

Founded 1980 as Lierse Sport Klub, 1972 amalgamated with TSV Lyra under Lierse SK
Colours white shirts with black sleeves, black shorts
Stadium Lisperstadion (20,000) ☎ 03-480 13 70
Champions 1932, 1942, 1960
Cup Winners 1969

Season	Opponent	Home	Result	Away	Rnd	Cup
1960-61	FC Barcelona, Spain	0-3		0-2	1	ECC
1969-70	Apoel Nicosia, Cyprus	10-1		1-0	1	CWC
	Manchester City, England	0-3		0-5	2	CWC
1971-72	Leeds United, England	0-2		4-0	1	UEFA
	Rosenborg Trondheim, Norway	3-0	wag	1-4	2	UEFA
	PSV Eindhoven, Holland	4-0		0-1	3	UEFA
	AC Milan, Italy	1-1		0-2	qf	UEFA
1976-77	Hajduk Split, Yugoslavia	1-0		0-3	1	CWC
1978-79	Carl Zeiss Jena, East Germany	2-2		0-1	1	UEFA

BELGIUM

STANDARD LIEGE

Founded 1898 Colours all white
Stadium Stade de Sclessin (43,000) ☎ 041-52 21 22/36 16 65
Champions 1958, 1961, 1963, 1969, 1970, 1971, 1982, 1983
Cup Winners 1966, 1967, 1981
CWC Finalists 1982

Season	Opponent	Home	Play off Result	Away	Rnd	Cup
1958-59	Heart of Midlothian, Scotland	5-1		1-2	1	ECC
	Sporting Lisbon, Portugal	3-0		3-2	2	ECC
	Stade de Reims, France	2-0		0-3*	qf	ECC
				*in Paris		
1961-62	Fredrikstad FK, Norway	2-1		2-0	1	ECC
	Valkeakoski Haka, Finland	5-1		2-0*	2	ECC
				*in Helsinki		
	Glasgow Rangers, Scotland	4-1		0-2	qf	ECC
	Real Madrid, Spain	0-2		0-4	sf	ECC
1963-64	IFK Norrkoping, Sweden	1-0		0-2	pr	ECC
1965-66	Cardiff City, Wales	1-0		2-1	1	CWC
	Liverpool, England	1-2		1-3	2	CWC
1966-67	Valur Reykjavik, Iceland	8-1		1-1	pr	CWC
	Apollon Limassol, Cyprus	5-1		1-0*	1	CWC
				*in Belgium		
	Chemie Leipzig, East Germany	1-0	wag	1-2	2	CWC
	Vasas Gyoer Eto, Hungary	2-0		1-2	qf	CWC
	Bayern Munich, Germany	1-3		0-2	sf	CWC
1967-68	Altay Izmir Gencik, Turkey	0-0		3-2	1	CWC
	Aberdeen, Scotland	3-0		0-2	2	CWC
	AC Milan, Italy	1-1	0-2*	1-1	qf	CWC
			*in Milan			
1968-69	Leeds United, England	0-0		2-3	1	Fairs
1969-70	17 Nentori Tirana, Albania	3-0		1-1	1	ECC
	Real Madrid, Spain	1-0		3-2	2	ECC
	Leeds United, England	0-1		0-1	qf	ECC
1970-71	Rosenborg Trondheim, Norway	5-0		2-0	1	ECC
	Legia Warsaw, Poland	1-0		0-2	2	ECC
1971-72	Linfield, Ireland	2-0		3-2	1	ECC
	CSKA Moscow, USSR	2-0		0-1	2	ECC
	Inter Milan, Italy	2-1	lag	0-1	qf	ECC
1972-73	Sparta Prague, Czechoslovakia	1-0		2-4	1	CWC
1973-74	Ards, Ireland	6-1		2-3	1	UEFA
	Universitatea Craiova, Romania	2-0		1-1	2	UEFA
	Feyenoord Rotterdam, Holland	3-1	lag	0-2	3	UEFA
1977-78	Slavia Prague, Czechoslovakia	1-0	wag	2-3	1	UEFA
	AEK Athens, Greece	4-1		2-2	2	UEFA
	Carl Zeiss Jena, East Germany	1-2		0-2	3	UEFA
1978-79	Dundee United, Scotland	1-0*		0-0	1	UEFA
			*in Ghent			
	Manchester City, England	2-0		0-4	2	UEFA
1979-80	Glenavon, Ireland	1-0		1-0	1	UEFA
	Napoli, Italy	2-1		1-1	2	UEFA
	Zbrojovka Brno, Czechoslovakia	1-2		2-3	3	UEFA
1980-81	Steaua Bucharest, Romania	1-1		2-1	1	UEFA
	1.FC Kaiserslautern, Germany	2-1		2-1	2	UEFA
	Dynamo Dresden, East Germany	1-1		4-1	3	UEFA
	1.FC Koln, Germany	0-0		2-3	qf	UEFA
1981-82	Floriana, Malta	9-0		3-1	1	CWC
	Vasas Budapest, Hungary	2-1		2-0	2	CWC
	FC Porto, Portugal	2-0		2-2	qf	CWC
	Dynamo Tbilisi, USSR	1-0		1-0	sf	CWC
	FC Barcelona, Spain	1-2	in Barcelona		FINAL	CWC
1982-83	Raba Vasas Eto, Hungary	5-0		0-3	1	ECC
	Juventus, Italy	1-1		0-2	2	ECC

1983-84	Athlone Town, Eire	8-2		3-2	1	ECC
	Dundee United, Scotland	0-0		0-4	2	ECC
1984-85	Glentoran, Ireland	2-0		1-1	1	UEFA
	1.FC Koln, Germany	0-2		1-2	2	UEFA
1986-87	NK Rijeka, Yugoslavia	1-1		1-0	1	UEFA
	FC Tirol, Austria	3-2	lag	1-2	2	UEFA

ROYAL FOOTBALL CLUB ANTWERP

Founded 1880 Colours white shirts, red shorts
Stadium Bosuilstadion (60,000) ☎ 03-324 64 06
Champions 1929, 1931, 1944, 1957
Cup Winners 1955

Season	Opponent	Home	Result	Away	Rnd	Cup
1957-58	Real Madrid, Spain	1-2		0-6	1	ECC
1964-65	Hertha BSC Berlin, Germany	2-0		1-2	pr	Fairs
	Atletico Bilbao, Spain	0-1		0-2	1	Fairs
1965-66	Glentoran, Ireland	1-0		3-3	1	Fairs
	CF Barcelona, Spain	2-1		0-2	2	Fairs
1966-67	Union Spora, Luxembourg	1-0		1-0	1	Fairs
	Kilmarnock, Scotland	0-1		2-7	2	Fairs
1967-68	Goztepe Izmir, Turkey	1-2		0-0	1	Fairs
1974-75	Sturm Graz, Austria	1-0	wag	1-2	1	UEFA
	Ajax Amsterdam, Holland	2-1	lag	0-1	2	UEFA
1975-76	Aston Villa, England	4-1		1-0	1	UEFA
	Slask Wroclaw, Poland	1-2		1-1	2	UEFA
1983-84	FC Zurich, Switzerland	4-2		4-1	1	UEFA
	RC Lens, France	2-3		2-2	2	UEFA
1988-89	1.FC Koln, Germany	2-4		1-2	1	UEFA
1989-90	Vitosha Sofia, Bulgaria	4-3		0-0	1	UEFA
	Dundee United, Scotland	4-0		2-3	2	UEFA
	VfB Stuttgart, Germany	1-0		1-1	3	UEFA
	1.FC Koln, Germany	0-0		0-2	qf	UEFA

RWD MOLENBEECK

Founded 1973 by amalgamation of Racing White, Daring, Molenbeck Brussels to form RWD Molenbeek
Colours white and red shirts, black shorts
Stadium Edmond Machtens, Brussels (31,750) ☎ 02-426 52 97
Champions as Daring 1912, 1914, 1921, 1936, 1937, as RWD Molenbeeck 1975

Season	Opponent	Home	Result	Away	Rnd	Cup
as DARING						
1965-66	AIK Stockholm, Sweden	1-3		0-0	1	Fairs
1968-69	Panathiniakos, Greece	2-1		0-2	1	Fairs
as RACING WHITE						
1972-73	CUF Barreiro, Portugal	0-1		0-2	1	UEFA
as RWD MOLENBEECK						
1973-74	Espanol Barcelona, Spain	1-2		3-0	1	UEFA
	Vitoria Setubal, Portugal	2-1	lag	0-1	2	UEFA
1974-75	Dundee, Scotland	1-0		4-2	1	UEFA
	Twente Enschede, Holland	0-1		1-2	2	UEFA
1975-76	Viking Stavanger, Norway	3-2		1-0	1	ECC
	Hajduk Split, Yugoslavia	2-3		0-4	2	ECC
1976-77	Naestved IF, Denmark	4-0		3-0	1	UEFA
	Wisla Krakow, Poland	1-1	5-4 pen	1-1	2	UEFA
	FC Schalke 04 Gelsenkirchen, Germany	1-0		1-1	3	UEFA
	Feyenoord Rotterdam, Holland	2-1		0-0	qf	UEFA
	Athletic Bilbao, Spain	1-1	lag	0-0	sf	UEFA
1977-78	Aberdeen, Scotland	0-0		2-1	1	UEFA
	Carl Zeiss Jena, East Germany	1-1	5-6 pen	1-1	2	UEFA
1980-81	Torino, Italy	1-2		2-2	1	UEFA

BELGIUM

K BEERSCHOT V A V (ANTWERP)

Founded 1899 Colours mauve and white shirts, mauve shorts
Stadium Stade du Kiel, Antwerp (25,000) ☎ 03-237 54 67
Champions 1922, 1924, 1925, 1926, 1928, 1938, 1939
Cup Winners 1971, 1979

Season	Opponent	Home	Result	Away	Rnd	Cup
1968-69	DWS Amsterdam, Holland	1-1		1-2	1	Fairs
1971-72	Anorthosis Famagusta, Cyprus	7-0		1-0	1	CWC
	BFC Dynamo Berlin, East Germany	1-3		1-3	2	CWC
1973-74	Vitoria Setubal, Portugal	0-2		0-2	1	UEFA
1979-80	NK Rijeka, Yugoslavia	0-0		1-2	1	CWC

A A GHENT (LA GHANTOISE)

Founded 1896 Colours white and blue striped shirts, blue shorts
Stadium Ottenstadion (25,000) ☎ 091-30 66 10
Cup Winners 1964, 1984

Season	Opponent	Home	Result	Away	Rnd	Cup
as LA GHANTOISE						
1963-64	1.FC Koln, Germany	1-1		1-3	1	Fairs
1964-65	West Ham United, England	0-1		1-1	pr	CWC
1966-67	Bye				1	Fairs
	Girondins Bordeaux, France	1-0		0-0	2	Fairs
	Kilmarnock, Scotland	1-2		0-1	3	Fairs
1970-71	Hamburger SV, Germany	0-1		1-7	1	Fairs
1982-83	Haarlem, Holland	3-3		1-2	1	UEFA
as AA GHENT						
1983-84	RC Lens, France	1-1		1-2	1	UEFA
1984-85	Glasgow Celtic, Scotland	1-0		0-3	1	CWC
1986-87	Jeunesse Esch, Luxembourg	1-1		2-1	1	UEFA
	Sportul Studentesc Bucharest, Romania	1-1		3-0	2	UEFA
	IFK Gothenburg, Sweden	0-1		0-4	3	UEFA

RFC LIEGE

Founded 1892 Colours red and blue shirts, blue shorts
Stadium Stade Recourt (40,000) ☎ 041-26 12 16
Champions 1896, 1898, 1899, 1952, 1953

Season	Opponent	Home	playoff Result	Away	Rnd	Cup
1963-64	Aris Bonneweg, Luxembourg	0-0		2-0	1	Fairs
	Arsenal, England	3-1		1-1	2	Fairs
	Spartak Brno, Czechoslovakia	2-0	1-0*	0-2	qf	Fairs
			*in Liege			
	Real Zaragoza, Spain	1-0	0-2**	1-2	sf	Fairs
			**in Zaragoza			
1964-65	Valencia CF, Spain	3-1		1-1	1	Fairs
	DOS Utrecht, Holland	2-0		2-0	2	Fairs
	Atletico Madrid, Spain	1-0		0-2	3	Fairs
1965-66	ZNK Zagreb, Yugoslavia	1-0		0-2	1	Fairs
1966-67	1.FC Lokomotive Leipzig, East Germany	1-2		0-0	2	Fairs
1967-68	PAOK Salonika, Greece	3-2		2-0	1	Fairs
	Dundee, Scotland	1-4		1-3	2	Fairs
1985-86	Wacker Innsbruck, Austria	1-0		3-1	1	UEFA
	Athletic Bilbao, Spain	0-1		1-3	2	UEFA

1988-89	Union Spora, Luxembourg	4-0		7-1	1	UEFA
	Benfica, Portugal	2-1		1-1	2	UEFA
	Juventus, Italy	0-1		0-1	3	UEFA
1989-90	IA Akranes, Iceland	4-1		2-0	1	UEFA
	Hibernian, Scotland	1-0		0-0	2	UEFA
	Rapid Vianna, Austria	3-1		0-1	3	UEFA
	Werder Bremen, Germany	1-4		2-0	qf	UEFA

SPORTING CLUB CHARLEROI SC

Founded 1904   Colours black and white striped shirts, white shorts
Stadium Stade Comunale (24,000) ☎ 071-32 87 34

Season	Opponent	Home	Result	Away	Rnd	Cup
1969-70	ZNK Zagreb, Yugoslavia	2-1		3-1	1	Fairs
	Rouen, France	3-1	lag	0-2	2	Fairs

WAREGEM KSV

Founded 1946 by amalgamation of Red Star and Sportief
Colours red and white shirts, red shorts
Stadium Stade Arc-en-Ciel (23,000) ☎ 056-60 19 89
Cup Winners 1974

Season	Opponent	Home	Result	Away	Rnd	Cup
1968-69	Atletico Madrid, Spain	1-0	wag	1-2	1	Fairs
	Legia Warsaw, Poland	1-0		0-2	2	Fairs
1974-75	Austra/WAC, Austria	2-1		1-4	1	CWC
1985-86	AGF Aarhus, Denmark	5-2		1-0	1	UEFA
	CA Osasuna, Spain	2-0		1-2	2	UEFA
	AC Milan, Italy	1-1		2-1	3	UEFA
	Hajduk Split, Yugoslvia	1-0	5-4 pen	0-1	qf	UEFA
	1.FC Koln, Germany	3-3		0-4	sf	UEFA
1988-89	Molde FK, Norway	5-1		0-0	1	UEFA
	Dynamo Dresden, East Germany	2-1		1-4	2	UEFA

SK BEVEREN WAAS

Founded 1935 by amalgamation of Amical and Standaard
Colours yellow and blue shirts, blue shorts
Stadium Freetheil (22,500) ☎ 03-775 90 00
Champions 1979, 1984
Cup Winners 1978, 1983

Season	Opponent	Home	Result	Away	Rnd	Cup
1970-71	Wiener Sport Club, Austria	3-0		2-0	1	Fairs
	Valencia CF, Spain	1-1		1-0	2	Fairs
	Arsenal, England	0-0		0-4	3	Fairs
1978-79	Ballymena United, Eire	3-0		3-0	1	CWC
	NK Rijeka, Yugoslavia	2-0		0-0	2	CWC
	Inter Milan, Italy	1-0		0-0	qf	CWC
	FC Barcelona, Spain	0-1		0-1	sf	CWC
1979-80	Servette Geneva, Switzerland	1-1		1-3	1	ECC
1981-82	Linfield, Ireland	3-0		5-0	1	UEFA
	Hajduk Split, Yugoslavia	2-3	lag	2-1	2	UEFA
1983-84	Paralimni Famagusta, Cyprus	3-1		4-2	1	CWC
	Aberdeen, Scotland	0-0		1-4	2	CWC

39

BELGIUM

1984-85	IA Akranes, Iceland	5-0		2-2*	1	ECC
				*in Reykjavik		
	IFK Gothenburg, Sweden	2-1	lag	0-1	2	ECC
1986-87	Valerengens IF Oslo, Norway	1-0		0-0	1	UEFA
	Atletico Bilbao, Spain	3-1		1-2	2	UEFA
	Torino, Italy	0-1		1-2	3	UEFA
1987-88	Bohemians Prague, Czechoslovakia	2-0		0-1	1	UEFA
	Vitoria Guimaraes, Portugal	1-0	4-5 pen	0-1	2	UEFA

WATERSCHEI THOR GENK

Merged with KFC Winterslag June 1988 to form RC Genk and play in Division One 1988-89 season Founded 1925
Colours yellow shirts, black shorts
Stadium Andre Dumontstadion (22,700)
Cup Winners 1980, 1982

Season	Opponent	Home	Result	Away	Rnd	Cup
1980-81	Omonia Nicosia, Cyprus	4-0		3-1	1	CWC
	Fortuna Dusseldorf, Germany	0-0		0-1	2	CWC
1982-83	Red Boys Differdange, Luxembourg	7-1		1-0	1	CWC
	B93 Copenhagen, Denmark	4-1		2-0	2	CWC
	Paris St Germain, France	3-0		0-2	qf	CWC
	Aberdeen, Scotland	1-0		1-5	sf	CWC

SV CERCLE SPORT BRUGES

Founded 1899   Colours green shirts with white trim, black shorts
Stadium Olympique (32,000) ☎ 050-31 81 93
Champions 1911, 1927, 1930
Cup Winners 1927, 1985

Season	Opponent	Home	Result	Away	Rnd	Cup
1985-86	Dynamo Dresden, East Germany	3-2	lag	1-2	1	CWC

KSC LOKEREN

Founded 1970 by amalgamation of Racing and Standaard Lokeren
Colours white shirts, black shorts
Stadium Stade de Daknam (18,000) ☎ 091-48 39 05

Season	Opponent	Home	Result	Away	Rnd	Cup
1976-77	Red Boys Differdange, Luxembourg	3-1		3-0	1	UEFA
	FC Barcelona, Spain	2-1		0-2	2	UEFA
1980-81	Dynamo Moscow, USSR	1-1		1-0	1	UEFA
	Dundee United, Scotland	0-0	wag	1-1	2	UEFA
	Real Sociedad San Sebastian, Spain	1-0		2-2	3	UEFA
	AZ 67 Alkmaar, Holland	1-0		0-2	qf	UEFA
1981-82	FC Nantes, France	4-2		1-1	1	UEFA
	Aris Salonika, Greece	4-0		1-1	2	UEFA
	1.FC Kaiserslautern, Germany	1-0		1-4	3	UEFA
1982-83	Stal Mielec, Poland	0-0	wag	1-1	1	UEFA
	Benfica, Portugal	1-2		0-2	2	UEFA
1987-88	Honved Budapest, Hungary	0-0		0-1	1	UEFA

KFC WINTERSLAG

Merged with Waterschei Thor Genk in June 1988 to form RC Genk and play in Division One 1988-89 season
Founded 1923   Colours red and white
Stadium Winterslag Stadion (15,000) ☎ 011-35 01 47

Season	Opponent	Home	Result	Away	Rnd	Cup
1981-82	Bryne IL, Norway	1-2		2-0	1	UEFA
	Arsenal, England	1-0	wag	1-2	2	UEFA
	Dundee United, Scotland	0-0		0-5	3	UEFA

K VOETBALCLUB MECHELEN

Founded 1904   Colours red and yellow striped shirts, black shorts
Stadium Mechelen Stadion (18,000) ☎ 015-21 82 30
Champions 1943, 1946, 1948, 1989
Cup Winners 1987
CWC Winners 1988
European Super Cup Winners 1988

Season	Opponent	Home	Result	Away	Rnd	Cup
1987-88	Dinamo Bucharest, Romania	1-0		2-0	1	CWC
	St Mirren, Scotland	0-0		2-0	2	CWC
	Dynamo Minsk, USSR	1-0		1-1	qf	CWC
	Atalanta Bergamo, Italy	2-1		2-1	sf	CWC
	Ajax Amsterdam, Holland	1-0	in Strasbourg		FINAL	CWC
1988-89	Avenir Beggen, Luxembourg	5-0		3-1	1	CWC
	RSC Anderlecht, Belgium	1-0		2-0	2	CWC
	Eintracht Frankfurt, Germany	1-0		0-0	qf	CWC
	Sampdoria, Italy	2-1		0-3	sf	CWC
1989-90	Rosenborg Trondheim BK, Norway	5-0		0-0	1	ECC
	Malmo FF, Sweden	4-1		0-0	2	ECC
	AC Milan, Italy	0-0*		0-2 aet	qf	ECC
	*Heysel Stadium					

● Lille Olympique

BULGARIA

Founded 1923
Federation Bulgare de Football Boul, Tolboukhine 18, Sofia ☎877490/874725
National Colours white shirts, green shorts, red socks

LEAGUE CHAMPIONS

1925	Chernomorets	1942	Levski Sofia	1960	CDNA Sofia	1978	Lokomotiv Sofia
1926	Chernomorets	1943	Slavia Sofia	1961	CDNA Sofia	1979	Levski Spartak Sofia
1927	not held	1944	not held	1962	CDNA Sofia		
1928	Slavia Sofia	1945	Lokomotiv Sofia	1963	Spartak Plovdiv	1980	CSKA Sofia
1929	Botev Plovdiv	1946	Levski Sofia	1964	Lokomotiv Sofia	1981	CSKA Sofia
		1947	Levski Sofia	1965	Dynamo Levski Sofia	1982	CSKA Sofia
1930	Slavia Sofia	1948	Septembri Sofia	1966	CSKA Sofia	1983	CSKA Sofia
1931	AC Sofia	1949	Levski Sofia	1967	Botev Plovdiv	1984	Levski Spartak Sofia
1932	CSC Sokol Varna			1968	Levski Sofia	1985	Trakia Plovdiv
1933	Levski Sofia	1950	Dynamo Levski Sofia	1969	CSKA Sofia	1986	Beroe Stara Zagora
1934	Vladislav Varna	1951	CDNA Sofia			1987	Sredets CSKA Sofia
1935	SC Varna	1952	CDNA Sofia			1988	Vitosha Sofia
1936	Slavia Sofia	1953	Dynamo Levski Sofia	1970	Levski Spartak Sofia	1989	Sredets CFKA Sofia
1937	Levski Sofia	1954	CDNA Sofia	1971	CSKA Sofia		
1938	Titschka Varna	1955	CDNA Sofia	1972	CSKA Sofia		
1939	Slavia Sofia	1956	CDNA Sofia	1973	CSKA Sofia		
		1957	CDNA Sofia	1974	Levski Spartak Sofia		
1940	JSK Sofia	1958	CDNA Sofia	1975	CSKA Sofia		
1941	Slavia Sofia	1959	CDNA Sofia	1976	CSKA Sofia		
				1977	Levski Spartak Sofia		

CUP WINNERS

1946	Levski Sofia v Chernolometz Popova	4-1
1947	Levski Sofia v Botev Plovdiv	1-0
1948	Lokomotiv Sofia v Slavia Plovdiv	1-0
1949	Levski Sofia v CDNA Sofia	1-1 2-2 aet 2-1
1950	Dinamo Levski Sofia v CDNA Sofia	1-1 1-1 aet 1-0
1951	CDNA Sofia v Akademik Sofia	1-0 aet
1952	Slavia Sofia v Spartak Sofia	3-1
1953	Lokomotiv Sofia v Levski Sofia	2-1
1954	CDNA Sofia v Slavia Sofia	2-1
1955	CDNA Sofia v Spartak Plovdiv	5-2 aet
1956	Levski Sofia v Botev Plovdiv	5-2

1957	Levski Sofia v Spartak Plovdiv	2-1
1958	Spartak Plovdiv v Mineur Pernik	1-0
1959	Levski Sofia v Spartak Plovdiv	1-0
1960	September Sofia v Lokomotiv Plovdiv	4-3 aet
1961	CDNA Sofia v Spartak Varna	3-0
1962	Botev Plovdiv v Dunav Russe	3-0
1963	Slavia Sofia v Botev Plovdiv	2-0
1964	Slavia Sofia v Botev Plovdiv	3-2
1965	CSKA Sofia v Levski Spartak	3-2
1966	Slavia Sofia v CSKA Sofia	1-0
1967	Levski Sofia v Spartak Sofia	3-0

1968	Spartak Sofia v Beroe Stara Zagora	3-2		1979	Levski Spartak Sofia v Beroe Stara Zagora	4-1
1969	CSKA Sofia v Levski Spartak	2-1				
				1980	Slavia Sofia v Beroe Stara Zagora	3-1
1970	Levski Spartak Sofia v CSKA Sofia	2-1		1981	Trakia Plovdiv v Pirin Blagojevgrad	1-0
1971	Levski Spartak Sofia v Lokomotiv Plovdiv	3-0		1982	Lokomotiv Sofia v Lokomotiv Plovdiv	2-1 aet
1972	CSKA Sofia v Levski Spartak, Sofia	3-0		1983	CSKA Sofia v JSK Spartak Varna	3-1
1973	CSKA Sofia v Beroe Stara Zagora	2-1		1984	Levski Spartak Sofia v Dorostol SS	4-0
1974	CSKA Sofia v Levski Spartak Sofia	2-1 aet		1985	CSKA Sofia v Levski Spartak Sofia	2-1 *
1975	Slavia Sofia v Lokomotiv Sofia	3-2		1986	Vitosha Sofia v Sredets Sofia	2-1
1976	Levski Spartak Sofia v CSKA Sofia	4-3 aet		1987	Sredets CSKA Sofia v Vitosha Sofia	2-1
1977	Levski Spartak Sofia v Lokomotiv Sofia	2-1		1988	Sredets CSKA Sofia v Vitosha Sofia	2-1
1978	Marek Stanke Dimitrov v CSKA Sofia	1-0		1989	Sredets CFKA Sofia v Chernomorets	3-0

*Cup withheld for violence among players and intimidating the referee. Both clubs disbanded and re-formed as Sredets and Vitosha

FEATURED CLUBS IN EUROPEAN COMPETITION

Vitosha Sofia (Levski Spartak Sofia)		Sredets CFKA Sofia (CSKA)	Beroe Stara Zagora
Lokomotiv Sofia	Lokomotiv Plovdiv	Spartak Plovdiv	Trakia Plovdiv
Spartak Varna	Dunav Russe	Etar Tirnovo	Spartak Sofia
FC Rila (Marek Stanke Dimitrov)	Akademic Sofia	Vratza Botev	FC Sliven Dimitrov
Slavia Sofia ESK	Pirin Blagojevgrad	Chernomeretz Bourgas	

VITOSHA

Founded 1914 as Levski, name changes to 1949 were Levskiego, Spartaka, Sportista, Levski, 1949 Dinamo, 1957 Levski, 1969 amalgamted with Spartak Sofia to become Levski-Spartak, 1985 dissolved and reformed as Vitosha
Colours all blue
Stadium Levsky Gerena (60,000) or National (70,000) ☎ 453071/457013/453074
Champions as Levski 1933, 1937, 1943, 1946, 1947, 1949, as Dinamo Levski 1950, 1953, as Levski 1965, 1968, as Levski Spartak 1970, 1974, 1977, 1979, 1984, as Vitosha 1988
Cup Winners as Levski 1946, 1947, 1949, as Dinamo Levski 1950, 1956, as Levski 1957, 1959, 1967, as Levski Spartak 1970, 1971, 1976, 1977, 1979, 1984 as Vitosha 1986

Season	Opponent	Home	Result	Away	Rnd	Cup
as LEVSKI SOFIA						
1965-66	Djurgarden IF Stockholm, Sweden	6-0		1-2	pr	ECC
	Benfica, Portugal	2-2		2-3	1	ECC
1967-68	AC Milan, Italy	1-1		1-5	1	CWC
1968-69	withdrew Czech crisis					
as LEVSKI SPARTAK SOFIA						
1969-70	IBV Reykjavik, Iceland	4-0		4-0*	1	CWC
				*in Reykjavik		
	St Gallen, Switzerland	4-0		0-0	2	CWC
	Gornik Zabrze, Poland	3-2	lag	1-2	3	CWC
1970-71	FK Austria Vienna, Austria	3-1		0-3	1	ECC
1971-72	Sparta Rotterdam, Holland	1-1		0-2	1	CWC
1972-73	Universitatea Stintza Cluj, Romania	5-1		1-4	1	UEFA
	BFC Dynamo Berlin, East Germany	2-0		0-3	2	UEFA
1974-75	Ujpest Dozsa, Hungary	0-3		1-4	1	ECC
1975-76	Eskisehirspor, Turkey	3-0		4-1	1	UEFA
	MSV Duisberg, Germany	2-1	wag	2-3	2	UEFA
	Ajax Amsterdam, Holland	2-1	5-3 pens	1-2	3	UEFA
	FC Barcelona, Spain	5-4		0-4	4	UEFA
1976-77	Reipas Lahti, Finland	12-2		7-1	1	CWC
	Boavista, Portugal	2-0	wag	1-3	2	CWC
	Atletico Madrid, Spain	2-1		0-2	3	CWC
1977-78	Slask Wroclaw, Poland	3-0		2-2	1	ECC
	Ajax Amsterdam, Holland	1-2		1-2	2	ECC
1978-79	Olympiakos Piraeus, Greece	3-1		1-2	1	UEFA
	AC Milan, Italy	1-1		0-3	2	UEFA
1979-80	Real Madrid, Spain	0-1		0-2	1	ECC
1980-81	Dynamo Kiev, USSR	0-0	wag	1-1	1	UEFA
	AZ 67 Alkmaar, Holland	1-1		0-5	2	UEFA
1981-82	Dinamo Bucharest, Romania	2-1		0-3	1	UEFA

43

BULGARIA

1982-83	Sevilla FC, Spain	0-3		1-3	1	UEFA
1983-84	VfB Stuttgart, Germany	1-0		1-1	1	UEFA
	Watford, England	1-3		1-1	2	UEFA
1984-85	VfB Stuttgart, Germany	1-1	wag	2-2	1	ECC
	Dnepr Dnepropetrovsk, USSR	3-1	lag	0-2	2	ECC
as VITOSHA						
1986-87	B 1903 Copenhagen, Denmark	2-0		0-1	1	CWC
	Velez Mostar, Yugoslavia	2-0		3-4	2	CWC
	Real Zaragoza, Spain	0-2		0-2	qf	CWC
1987-88	OFI Crete, Greece	1-0		1-3	1	CWC
1988-89	AC Milan, Italy	0-2		2-5	1	ECC
1989-90	Royal Antwerp, Belgium	0-0		3-4	1	UEFA

SREDETS CFKA (SOFIA)

Founded 1919 as Botev, 1948 Septemvri, 1951 Narodna Voiska, 1951 CDNA, 1953 Sofiaski Garnizon, 1953 amalgamated with Cerweno Zname to become CSKA-Cerweno Zname, 1969 amalgamated with Septemvri-CDW to become CSKA-Septemvri Zname, dissolved in 1985 and reformed to become CSKA Sredets, 1988 Sredets CFKA
Colours all white or red
Stadium Norodna Armia Stadion, Sofia (35,000) or Septemvri (20,000) ☎ 877329/873152
Champions as Septemvri 1948, as CDNA 1951, 1952, 1954, 1955, 1956, 1957, 1958, 1959, 1960, 1961, 1962, as CSKA 1966, 1969, 1971, 1972, 1973, 1975, 1976, 1980, 1981, 1982, 1983, as CFKA 1987, 1989
Cup Winners as CDNA 1951, 1954, 1955, as Septemvri 1960, as CDNA 1961, as Sredets CSKA 1965, 1969, 1972, 1973, 1974, 1983, 1985, 1987, 1988 as Sredets CFKA 1989

Season	Opponent	Home	Result	Away	Rnd	Cup
as CDNA RED BANNER						
1956-57	Dinamo Bucharest, Romania	8-1		1-3	1	ECC
	Red Star Belgrade, Yugoslavia	2-1		1-3	2	ECC
1957-58	Vasas Budapest, Hungary	2-1		1-6	pr	ECC
1958-59	Atletico Madrid, Spain	1-0	1-3*	1-2	1	ECC
			*in Geneva			
1959-60	CF Barcelona, Spain	2-2		2-6	pr	ECC
1960-61	Juventus, Italy	4-1		0-2	pr	ECC
	Malmo FF, Sweden	1-1		0-1	1	ECC
1961-62	Dukla Prague, Czechoslovakia	4-4		1-2	pr	ECC
1962-63	Partizan Belgrade, Yugoslavia	2-1		4-1	pr	ECC
	RSC Anderlecht, Belgium	2-2		0-2	1	ECC
1965-66	Limerick, Eire	2-0		2-1*	1	CWC
				*in Dublin		
	Borussia Dortmund, Germany	4-2		0-3	2	CWC
1966-67	Sliema Wanderers, Malta	4-0		2-1	pr	ECC
	Olympiakos Piraeus, Greece	3-1		0-1	1	ECC
	Gornik Zabrze, Poland	4-0		0-3	2	ECC
	Linfield, Ireland	1-0		2-2	3	ECC
	Inter Milan, Italy	1-1	0-1*	1-1	sf	ECC
			*in Bologna			
as CSKA						
1969-70	Ferencvarosi TC, Hungary	2-1		1-4	1	ECC
1970-71	Haka Valkeakoski, Finland	9-0		2-1	1	CWC
	Chelsea, England	0-1		0-1	2	CWC
1971-72	Partizani Tirana, Albania	3-0		1-0	1	ECC
	Benfica, Portugal	0-0		1-2	2	ECC
1972-73	Panathinaikos, Greece	2-1	2-0	1-2*	1	ECC
			*match void for infringement of rules			
	Ajax Amsterdam, Holland	1-3		0-3	2	ECC
1973-74	Wacker Innsbruck, Austria	3-0		1-0	1	ECC
	Ajax Amsterdam, Holland	2-0		0-1	2	ECC
	Bayern Munich, Germany	2-1		1-4	3	ECC
1974-75	Dynamo Kiev, USSR	0-1		0-1	1	CWC
1975-76	Juventus, Italy	2-1		0-2	1	ECC
1976-77	St Etienne, France	0-0		0-1	1	ECC
1977-78	FC Zurich, Switzerland	1-1		0-1	1	UEFA

1978-79	Valencia CF, Spain	2-1		1-4	1	UEFA
1979-80	Dynamo Kiev, USSR	1-1		1-2	1	UEFA
1980-81	Nottingham Forest, England	1-0		1-0	1	ECC
	GKS Szombierki Bytom, Poland	4-0		1-0	2	ECC
	Liverpool, England	0-1		1-5	3	ECC
1981-82	Real Sociedad San Sebastian, Spain	1-0		0-0	1	ECC
	Glentoran, Ireland	2-0		1-2	2	ECC
	Liverpool, England	2-0		0-1	3	ECC
	Bayern Munich, Germany	4-3		0-4	sf	ECC
1982-83	AS Monaco, France	2-0		0-0	1	ECC
	Sporting Lisbon, Portugal	2-2	lag	0-0	2	ECC
1983-84	Omonia Nicosia, Cyprus	3-0	wag	1-4	1	ECC
	AS Roma, Italy	0-1		0-1	2	ECC
1984-85	AS Monaco, France	2-1		2-2	1	UEFA
	Hamburger SV, Germany	1-2		0-4	2	UEFA
as SREDETS CSKA						
1986-87	FC Tirol, Austria	1-0 abd	2-0	0-3	1	UEFA
1987-88	Bayern Munich, Germany	0-1		0-4	1	ECC
as SREDETS CFKA						
1988-89	Internacional Bratislava, Czechoslovakia	5-0		3-2	1	CWC
	Panathinaikos, Greece	2-0		1-0	2	CWC
	Roda JC Kerkrade, Holland	2-1	4-3p	1-2 aet	qf	CWC
	FC Barcelona, Spain	1-3		2-4	sf	CWC
1989-90	Ruch Chorzow, Poland	5-1		1-1	1	EEC
	Sparta Prague, Czechoslovakia	3-0		2-2*	2	EEC
				*in Trnava		
	Olympique Marseille, France	0-1		1-3	qf	EEC

BEROE STARA ZAGORA

Founded 1958 by merger GLokomotiv and Botev
Colours green shirts, white shorts or white shirts, green shorts
Stadium Beroe (20,000) ☎ 042-39888
Champions 1986

Season	Opponent	Home	Result	Away	Rnd	Cup
1972-73	FK Austria Vienna, Austria	7-0		3-1	1	UEFA
	Honved Budapest, Hungary	3-0		0-1	2	UEFA
	OFK Belgrade, Yugoslavia	1-3		0-0	3	UEFA
1973-74	Fola Esch, Luxembourg	7-0		4-1	1	CWC
	Athletic Bilbao, Spain	3-0		0-1	2	CWC
	1.FC Magdeburg, East Germany	1-1		0-2	3	CWC
1979-80	Arka Gdynia, Poland	2-0		2-3	1	CWC
	Juventus, Italy	1-0		0-3	2	CWC
1980-81	Fenerbahce, Turkey	2-1		1-0	1	UEFA
	Radnicki Nis, Yugoslavia	0-1		1-2	2	UEFA
1986-87	Dynamo Kiev, USSR	1-1		0-2	1	EEC

45

BULGARIA

LOKOMOTIV SOFIA

Founded 1929 as JSK Sofia name changes to Energia, Lokomotiv, 1949 Torpedo, 1950 Lokomotiv, 1969 amalgamated with Slavia to become Slavia JSK, 1971 separated
Colours red and black striped shirts, black shorts
Stadium Lokomotiv (50,000) ☎ 02-38 80 10
Champions as JSK 1940, as Lokomotiv 1945, 1964, 1978
Cup Winners 1948, 1953, 1982

Season	Opponent	Home	Result	Away	Rnd	Cup
1964-65	Malmo FF, Sweden	8-3		0-2	pr	ECC
	Vasas Gyoer, Hungary	4-3		3-5	1	ECC
1977-78	RSC Anderlecht, Belgium	1-6		0-2	1	CWC
1978-79	B 1913 Odense, Denmark	2-1		2-2	1	ECC
	1.FC Koln, Germany	0-1		0-4	2	ECC
1979-80	Ferencvarosi TC, Hungary	3-0		0-2	1	UEFA
	AS Monaco, France	4-2		1-2	2	UEFA
	Dynamo Kiev, USSR	1-0	wag	1-2	3	UEFA
	VfB Stuttgart, Germany	0-1		1-3	4	UEFA
1982-83	Paris St Germain, France	1-0		1-5	1	CWC
1985-86	Apoel Nicosia, Cyprus	4-2		2-2	1	UEFA
	FC Neuchatel Xamax, Switzerland	1-1	lag	0-0	2	UEFA
1987-88	Dynamo Tbilisi, USSR	3-1		0-3	1	UEFA

LOKOMOTIV PLOVDIV

Founded 1936 as JSK Plovdiv name changes JSK Levski, Slavia Cengelov, Slavia, Torpedo, 1950 Lokomotiv
Colours black and blue or black and red striped shirts, red or white shorts
Stadium Deveti Septemuri (50,000) or Lokomotiv (20,000) ☎ 032-62551
Cup Winners 1983

Season	Opponent	Home	Playoff Result	Away	Rnd	Cup
1963-64	Red Star Brasov, Romania	3-1		2-1	1	Fairs
	Ujpest Dozsa, Hungary	0-0		1-3	2	Fairs
1964-65	Vojvodina Novi Sad, Yugoslavia	1-1	2-0	1-1	1	Fairs
	Petrolul Ploesti, Romania	2-0		0-1	2	Fairs
	Juventus, Italy	1-1	1-2*	1-1	3	Fairs
			*in Turin			
1965-66	Spartak Brno, Czechoslovakia	1-0		0-2	1	Fairs
1967-68	Partizan Belgrade, Yugoslavia	1-1		1-5	1	Fairs
1969-70	Juventus, Italy	1-2		1-3	1	Fairs
1971-72	Carl Zeiss Jena, East Germany	3-1		0-3	1	UEFA
1973-74	Sliema Wanderers, Malta	1-0		2-0	1	UEFA
	Honved Budapest, Hungary	3-4		2-3	2	UEFA
1974-75	Vasas Gyoer Eto, Hungary	3-1	4-5 pen	1-3	1	UEFA
1976-77	Red Star Belgrade, Yugoslavia	2-1		1-4	1	UEFA
1983-84	Aris Salonika, Greece	1-2		1-3	1	UEFA

SPARTAK PLOVDIV

Founded 1947 as Levski-Udarnik, Spartak, 1967 amalgamated with Akademik and Botev to become Trakia, 1982 separated
Colours blue and white striped shirts, blue shorts
Stadium Spartak (12,000)
Champions 1963
Cup Winners 1958

Season	Opponent	Home	Result	Away	Rnd	Cup
1963-64	Partizani Tirana, Albania	3-1		0-1	1	ECC
	PSV Eindhoven, Holland	0-1		0-0	2	ECC
1966-67	bye				1	Fairs
	Benfica, Portugal	1-1		0-3	2	Fairs

TRAKIA PLOVDIV

Founded 1912 as Botev, 1944 Chipka, 1947 Stefan Kiradchevs, 1950 Botev, merger of Botev, Academic and Spartak in 1967 to form Trakia separated 1982
Colours yellow and red stripes or yellow shirts, blue shorts
Stadium Hristo Botev (35,000) or Deveti (9th) Septembri (50,000) ☎ 032-23773
Champions 1929, 1967 Botev, 1985 Trakia Cup
Winners 1962 Botev, 1981 Trakia

Season	Opponent	Home	Result	Away	Rnd	Cup
as BOTEV PLODIV						
1962-63	Steaua Bucharest, Romania	2-3		5-1	1	CWC
	Shamrock Rovers, Eire	1-0*		4-0	2	CWC
		*in Sofia				
	Atletico Madrid, Spain	0-4		1-1	3	CWC
1967-68	Rapid Bucharest, Romania	2-0		0-3	1	ECC
as TRAKIA PLOVDIV						
1968-69	Real Zaragoza, Spain	3-1	lag	0-2	1	Fairs
1970-71	Coventry City, England	1-4		0-2	1	Fairs
1978-79	Hertha BSC Berlin, Germany	1-2		0-0	1	UEFA
1981-82	FC Barcelona, Spain	1-0		1-4	1	CWC
1984-85	Union Spora, Luxembourg	4-0		1-1	1	CWC
	Bayern Munich, Germany	2-0		1-4	2	CWC
1985-86	IFK Gothenburg, Sweden	1-2		2-3	1	ECC
1986-87	Hibernians, Malta	8-0		2-0	1	UEFA
	Hajduk Split, Yugoslavia	2-2		1-3	2	UEFA
1987-88	Red Star Belgrade, Yugoslavia	2-2		0-3	1	UEFA
1988-89	Dynamo Minsk, USSR	1-2		0-0	1	UEFA

SPARTAK VARNA

Founded 1919 Chipchenski Sokol, 1945 Radetskr-Levski, 1948 Spartak Varna
Colours white and blue shirts with white band, white shorts
Stadium Spartak (15,000) or Yuri Gagrin (55,000) ☎ 052-237541
Champions 1932 as CSC Sokol Varna

Season	Opponent	Home	Result	Away	Rnd	Cup
1961-62	Rapid Vienna, Austria	2-5		0-0	pr	CWC
1983-84	Mersin Idmanyurdu, Turkey	1-0		0-0	1	CWC
	Manchester United, England	1-2		0-2	2	CWC

BULGARIA

DUNAV RUSSE

Founded 1919 as Sava, Napredak, Levski, 1928 Varutz, Kantzev, Rakovski, Ruzenetz, Spartak, Partizani, 1957 Dunav
Russe
Colours blue shirts, white shorts
Stadium Sdradetz Dunav (12,000) or Gradskiya (25,000) ☎ 082-50776

Season	Opponent	Home	Result	Away	Rnd	Cup
1975-76	AS Roma, Italy	1-0		0-2	1	UEFA

ETAR TIRNOVO

Founded 1924 (former names Trapezitza, Udarnik, Cerweno Zname, Spartak, DNA)
Colours violet shirts, black or white shorts
Stadium Ivailo (20,000) ☎ 062-21849

Season	Opponent	Home	Result	Away	Rnd	Cup
1974-75	Inter Milan, Italy	0-0		0-3	1	UEFA

SPARTAK SOFIA

Founded 1907 as Iskra, 1911 Rakovski, 1913 FK '13, 1945 Rakovski, 1947 Spartak, 1969 merged with Levski to
become Levski-Spartak Sofia
Cup Winners 1968

Season	Opponent	Home	Result	Away	Rnd	Cup
1968-69	Gornik Zabrze, Poland	withdrew			1	CWC

FC RILA

Founded 1919 as Slavia, name changes Levski, Atletik, JSK, Pobeda, BP '24, Pod Botev, Vihar, Razwiti, Muzala, Lav,
Marek, 1949 Cerw Zname, 1953 Lokomotiv, DNA, Spartak, Septemvri, 1956 Marek, 1986 FC Rila
Colours white shirts, blue shorts
Stadium Bontzuk (30,000) ☎ 0701-3440
Cup Winners 1978

Season	Opponent	Home	Result	Away	Rnd	Cup
as Marek Stanke Dimitrov						
1977-78	Ferencvarosi TC, Hungary	3-0		0-2	1	UEFA
	Bayern Munich, Germany	2-0		0-3	2	UEFA
1978-79	Aberdeen, Scotland	3-2		0-3	1	CWC

AKADEMIC SOFIA

Founded 1959   Colours blue shirts, white shorts
Stadium Akademic Sports Complex (20,000) ☎ 0631-22665

Season	Opponent	Home	Result	Away	Rnd	Cup
1976-77	Slavia Prague, Czechoslovakia	3-0		0-2	1	UEFA
	AC Milan, Italy	4-3		0-2	2	UEFA
1981-82	1.FC Kaiserslautern, Germany	1-2		0-1	1	UEFA

48

VRATZA BOTEV

Founded 1921 as Vratza Botev, 1986 FC Vratza   Colours red shirts, black or white shorts
Stadium Hristo Botev (30,000) ☎ 092-22368/27265

Season	Opponent	Home	Result	Away	Rnd	Cup
1971-72	Dinamo Zagreb, Yugoslavia	1-2		1-6	1	UEFA

FC SLIVEN

Founded 1914 as Sportist, name changes Boris- Iav, Asenovetz, Trakijetz, Hadzji, Dimitar, Angel Dimitrov, Sabi
Dimitrov, DNA, SKNA, Mlada Gwardia, Slivenski Tekstiltez, Zaimov, 1963 Sliven Dimitrov, 1972 FC Sliven
Colours orange or red shirts, white shorts
Stadium Dimitrov Hadzhi (18,000) ☎ 044-84127

Season	Opponent	Home	Result	Away	Rnd	Cup
1984-85	Zeljeznicar Sarajevo, Yugoslavia	1-0		1-5	1	UEFA

SLAVIA SOFIA ESK

Founded 1913 by amalgamation of Botev and Raswita, 1920 Slavia, 1949 Stroutel, 1951 Udarnik, 1957 Slavia, 1969
amalgamated with Lokomotiv, 1971 separated
Colours all white
Stadium Slavia (32,000) ☎ 551137/550075
Champions 1928, 1930, 1936, 1939, 1941, 1943
Cup Winners 1952 as Udarnik, 1963, 1964, 1966, 1975, 1980

Season	Opponent	Home	Playoff Result	Away	Rnd	Cup
1963-64	MTK Budapest, Hungary	1-1		0-1	pr	CWC
1964-65	Cork Celtic, Eire	2-0		1-1	1	CWC
	Lausanne Sports, Switzerland	1-0	2-3	1-2	2	WC
1966-67	Swansea Town, Wales	4-0		1-1	1	CWC
	RC Strasbourg, France	2-0		0-1	2	CWC
	Servette Geneva, Switzerland	3-0		0-1	qf	CWC
	Glasgow Rangers, Scotland	0-1		0-1	sf	CWC
1968-69	Aberdeen, Scotland	0-0		0-2	1	Fairs
1969-70	Valencia CF, Spain	2-0		1-1	1	Fairs
	Kilmarnock, Scotland	2-0		1-4	2	Fairs
1970-71	Hajduk Split, Yugoslavia	3-0		0-1	1	Fairs
1972-73	FC Schalke 04 Gelsenkirchen, Germany	1-3		1-2	1	CWC
1973-74	Dynamo Tbilisi, USSR	2-0		1-4	1	UEFA
1975-76	Sturm Graz, Austria	1-0		1-3	1	CWC
1980-81	Legia Warsaw, Poland	3-1		0-1	1	CWC
	Sparta Prague, Czechoslovakia	3-0		0-2	2	CWC
	Feyenoord Rotterdam, Holland	3-2		0-4	3	CWC
1982-83	FK Sarajevo, Yugoslavia	2-2		2-4	1	UEFA
1988-89	Partizan Belgrade, Yugoslavia	0-5		0-5	1	UEFA

BULGARIA

PIRIN BLAGOJEVGRAD

Founded 1924 as Makedonia, 1934 merger of Makedonia and Botev to form Pirin Blagojevgrad
Colours green or red shirts, white shorts
Stadium Hristo Botev (20,000) ☎ 073-23090

Season	Opponent	Home	Result	Away	Rnd	Cup
1985-86	Hammarby IF Stockholm, Sweden	1-3		0-4	1	UEFA

CHERNOMORETZ BOURGAS

Founded 1919 as Chernomoretz, name changed to Lubislav, amalgamated 1969 with Lokomotiv and Botev Bourgas
to become Chernomoretz Bourgas
Colours all blue
Stadium 9th Setpemvri (24,000) ☎ 056-47787

Season	Opponent	Home	Result	Away	Rnd	Cup
1989-90	Dinamo Tirana, Albania	3-1		0-4	Pre	CWC

CYPRUS

Founded 1934
Cyprus Football Association, Stasinos Street 1, Engomi 114, PO Box 5071, Nicosia ☎ 45341/2 Fax 2-472 544
National Colours sky blue shirts, white shorts, blue and white socks
Season October to June

LEAGUE CHAMPIONS

1935 Trust Larnaca	1952 Apoel Nicosia	1967 Olympiakos Nicosia	1980 Apoel Nicosia
1936 Apoel Nicosia	1953 AE Limassol	1968 Apollon Limassol	1981 Omonia Nicosia
1937 Apoel Nicosia	1954 Pezoporikos Larnaca	1969 Olympiakos Nicosia	1982 Omonia Nicosia
1938 Apoel Nicosia	1955 AE Limassol		1983 Omonia Nicosia
1939 Apoel Nicosia	1956 AE Limassol	1970 EPA Larnaca	1984 Omonia Nicosia
	1957 Anorthosis Famagusta	1971 Olympiakos Nicosia	1985 Omonia Nicosia
1940 Apoel Nicosia	1958 Anorthosis Famagusta	1972 Omonia Nicosia	1986 Apoel Nicosia
1941 AE Limassol	1959 Anorthosis Famagusta	1973 Apoel Nicosia	1987 Omonia Nicosia
1945 EPA Larnaca		1974 Omonia Nicosia	1988 Pezoporikos Larnaca
1946 EPA Larnaca	1960 Anorthosis Famagusta	1975 Omonia Nicosia	1989 Omonia Nicosia
1947 Apoel Nicosia	1961 Omonia Nicosia	1976 Omonia Nicosia	
1948 Apoel Nicosia	1962 Anorthosis Famagusta	1977 Omonia Nicosia	
1949 Apoel Nicosia	1963 Anorthosis Famagusta	1978 Omonia Nicosia	
	1964 not held	1979 Omonia Nicosia	
1950 Anorthosis Famagusta	1965 Apoel Nicosia		
1951 Tsettin Kayia	1966 Omonia Nicosia		

CUP WINNERS

1935 Trust v Apoel Nicosia	0-0 1-0	1949 Anorthosis Famagusta v Apoel Nicosia	3-0
1936 Trust v a Turkish Club ?	4-1		
1937 Apoel Nicosia v Trust	2-1	1950 EPA Larnaca v Anorthosis Famagusta	2-0
1938 Trust v a Turkish Club ?	1-0	1951 Apoel Nicosia v EPA Larnax	7-0
1939 AE Limassol v Apoel Nicosia	3-1	1952 Tsettin Kayia v Pezoporikos Larnaca	4-1
		1953 EPA Larnaca v Tsettin Kayia	2-1
1940 AE Limassol v Pezoporikos Larnaca	3-1	1954 Tsettin Kayia v Pezoporikos Larnaca	2-1
1941 Apoel Nicosia v		1955 EPA Larnaca v Pezoporikos Larnaca	2-1
1945 EPA Larnaca v Apoel Nicosia	3-1	1956 no competition	
1946 EPA Larnaca v Apoel Nicosia	2-1	1957 no competition	
1947 Apoel Nicosia v Anorthosis Famagusta	4-1	1958 no competition	
1948 AEL Limassol v Apoel Nicosia	2-0	1959 Anorthosis Famagusta v AEL Limassol	1-0

51

CYPRUS

1960	no competition	
1961	no competition	
1962	Anorthosis Famagusta v Olympiakos Nicosia	5-2
1963	Apoel Nicosia v Anorthosis Famagusta	1-1 2-0
1964	Anorthosis Famagusta v Apoel Nicosia	3-0
1965	Omonia Nicosia v Apollon Limassol	5-1
1966	Apollon Limassol v New Salamis	4-2
1967	Apollon Limassol v Alke	1-0
1968	Apoel Nicosia v EPA Larnaca	2-1
1969	Apoel Nicosia v Omonia Nicosia	1-0
1970	Pezoporikos Larnaca v Alke	2-1
1971	Anorthosis Famagusta v Omonia Nicosia	1-1 1-0
1972	Omonia Nicosia v Pezoporikos Larnaca	2-1 aet
1973	Apoel Nicosia v Pezoporikos Larnaca	1-0
1974	Omonia Nicosia v Enosis	2-0

1975	Anorthosis Famagusta v Enosis	3-2
1976	Apoel Nicosia v Alke	6-0
1977	Olympiakos Nicosia v Alke	2-0
1978	Apoel Nicosia v Olympiakos Nicosia	3-0
1979	Apoel Nicosia v AE Limassol	1-0
1980	Omonia Nicosia v Alke	3-1
1981	Omonia Nicosia v Enosis	1-1 3-0
1982	Omonia Nicosia v Apollon Limassol	2-2 4-1
1983	Omonia Nicosia v Enosis	2-1
1984	Apoel Nicosia v Pezoporikos Larnaca	1-1 3-1
1985	AE Limassol v EPA Larnaca	1-0
1986	Apollon Limassol v Apoel Nicosia	2-0
1987	AE Limassol v Apollon Limassol	1-0
1988	Omonia Nicosia v AE Limassol	2-1
1989	AE Limassol v Aris Lemesos	3-2 aet

FEATURED CLUBS IN EUROPEAN COMPETITION

Apoel Nicosia	Anorthosis Famagusta	Omonia Nicosia	Apollon Limassol
Olympiakos Nicosia	EPA Larnaca	Pezoporikos Larnaca	Dighenis Akritas Morphou
Paralimni Famagusta	AE Limassol	Alki Larnaca	

APOEL NICOSIA

Founded 1926   Colours blue shirts, yellow shorts
Stadium Makarion (20,000) ☎ 02-44999/445888
Champions 1936, 1937, 1938, 1939, 1940, 1941, 1947, 1948, 1949, 1952, 1965, 1973, 1980, 1986
Cup Winners 1937, 1947, 1951, 1963, 1969, 1973, 1976, 1978, 1979, 1984

Season	Opponent	Home	Result	Away	Rnd	Cup
1963-64	Gjovik Lyn, Norway	6-0		1-0	1	CWC
	Sporting Lisbon, Portugal	0-2*		1-16*	2	CWC
		*both in Lisbon				
1965-66	Werder Bremen, Germany	0-5*		0-5	pr	ECC
		*in Hamburg				
1968-69	Dunfermline Athletic, Scotland	0-2		1-10	1	CWC
1969-70	Lierse SK, Belgium	0-1		1-10	1	CWC
1973-74	Zarja Voroshilovgrad, USSR	0-1		0-2	1	ECC
1976-77	Iraklis Salonika, Greece	2-0		0-0	1	CWC
	Napoli, Italy	1-1		0-2	2	CWC
1977-78	Torino, Italy	1-1		0-3	1	UEFA
1978-79	Shamrock Rovers, Eire	0-1		0-2	1	CWC
1979-80	B 1903 Copenhagen, Denmark	0-1		0-6	pr	CWC
1980-81	BFC Dynamo Berlin, East Germany	2-1		0-3	1	ECC
1981-82	FC Arges Pitesti, Romania	1-1		0-4	1	UEFA
1984-85	Servette Geneva, Switzerland	0-3		1-3	1	CWC
1985-86	Lokomotiv Sofia, Bulgaria	2-2		2-4	1	UEFA
1986-87	HJK Helsinki, Finland	1-0	wag	2-3	1	ECC
	Besiktas, Turkey	withdrew political				ECC
1988-89	Velez Mostar, Yugoslavia	2-5		0-1	1	UEFA

CYPRUS

ANORTHOSIS FAMAGUSTA

Founded 1911   Colours blue shirts, white shorts
Stadium GSE (10,000) ☎ 041-53117
Champions 1950, 1957, 1958, 1959, 1960, 1962, 1963
Cup Winners 1949, 1959, 1964, 1971, 1975

Season	Opponent	Home	Result	Away	Rnd	Cup
1963-64	Partizan Belgrade, Yugoslavia	1-3		0-3	1	ECC
1964-65	Sparta Prague, Czechoslovakia	0-6		0-10	pr	CWC
1971-72	K Beerschot VAV, Belgium	0-1		0-7	1	CWC
1975-76	Ararat Yerevan, USSR	1-1		0-9	1	CWC

OMONIA NICOSIA

Founded 1948   Colours green shirts, white shorts
Stadium Makarion (20,000) ☎ 02-444544/441677
Champions 1961, 1966, 1974, 1975, 1976, 1977, 1978, 1979, 1981, 1982, 1983, 1984, 1985, 1987, 1989
Cup Winners 1965, 1972, 1974, 1980, 1981, 1982, 1983, 1988

Season	Opponent	Home	Result	Away	Rnd	Cup
1965-66	Olympiakos Piraeus, Greece	0-1		1-1	pr	CWC
1966-67	TSV 1860 Munich, Germany	1-2*		0-8	pr	ECC
		*in Pocking, Bavaria				
1972-73	Waterford, Eire	2-0		1-2	1	ECC
	Bayern Munich, Germany	0-4*		0-9	2	ECC
		*in Augsburg				
1975-76	IA Akranes, Iceland	2-1		0-4*	1	ECC
				*in Reykjavik		
1976-77	PAOK Salonika, Greece	0-2		1-1	1	ECC
1977-78	Juventus, Italy	0-3		0-2	1	ECC
1978-79	Bohemians Dublin, Eire	2-1	lag	0-1*	1	ECC
				*in Cork (previous crowd trouble)		
1979-80	Red Boys Differdange, Luxembourg	6-1		1-2	1	ECC
	Ajax Amsterdam, Holland	4-0		0-10	2	ECC
1980-81	Waterschei Thor Genk, Belgium	1-3		0-4	1	CWC
1981-82	Benfica, Portugal	0-1		0-3	1	ECC
1982-83	HJK Helsinki, Finland	2-0		0-3	1	ECC
1983-84	CSKA Sofia, Bulgaria	4-1	lag	0-3	1	ECC
1984-85	Dinamo Bucharest, Romania	2-1		1-4	1	ECC
1985-86	Rabat Ajax, Malta	5-0		5-0	1	ECC
	RSC Anderlecht, Belgium	1-3		0-1	2	ECC
1986-87	Sportul Studentesc Bucharest, Romania	1-		0-1	1	UEFA
1987-88	Shamrock Rovers, Eire	0-0		1-0	1	ECC
	Steaua Bucharest, Romania	0-2		1-3	2	ECC
1988-89	Panathinaikos, Greece	0-1		0-2	1	CWC
1989-90	FC Tirol, Austria	2-3		0-6	1	ECC

CYPRUS

APOLLON LIMASSOL

Founded 1954   Colours blue shirts, white shorts
Stadium Tsirion (20,000) ☎ 051-63702
Champions 1968
Cup Winners 1966, 1967, 1986

Season	Opponent	Home	Result	Away	Rnd	Cup
1966-67	Standard Liege, Belgium	0-1*		1-5	pr	CWC
		*in Belgium				
1967-68	Vasas Gyoer Eto, Hungary	0-4		0-5	1	CWC
1968-69	Real Madrid, Spain	0-6		0-6	1	ECC
1982-83	FC Barcelona, Spain	1-1		0-8	1	CWC
1984-85	Bohemians Prague, Czechoslovakia	2-2		1-6	1	UEFA
1986-87	Malmo FF, Sweden	2-1		0-6	1	CWC
1989-90	Real Zaragoza, Spain	0-3		1-1	1	UEFA

OLYMPIAKOS NICOSIA

Founded 1931   Colours green shirts, black shorts
Stadium Makarion (20,000) for important games ☎ 02-430096/430405
Champions 1967, 1969, 1971
Cup Winners 1977

Season	Opponent	Home	Result	Away	Rnd	Cup
1967-68	FK Sarajevo, Yugoslavia	2-2		1-3	1	ECC
1969-70	Real Madrid, Spain	0-8		1-6	1	ECC
1971-72	Feyenoord Rotterdam, Holland	0-9*		0-8	1	ECC
		*in Rotterdam				
1973-74	VfB Stuttgart, Germany	0-4		0-9	1	UEFA
1977-78	Universitatea Craiova, Romania	1-6		0-2	1	CWC

EPA LARNACA

Founded 1932   Colours yellow shirts, black shorts
Stadium GSZ (10,000) ☎ 041- 53090/53615
Champions 1945, 1946, 1970
Cup Winners 1945, 1946, 1950, 1953, 1955

Season	Opponent	Home	Result	Away	Rnd	Cup
1970-71	Borussia Monchengladbach, Germany	0-10		0-6*	1	ECC
				*in Augsburg		
1972-73	Ararat Yerevan, USSR	0-1		0-1	1	UEFA

PEZOPORIKOS LARNACA

Founded 1927   Colours green shirts, white shorts
Stadium GSZ (10,000) ☎ 041- 52464
Champions 1954, 1988
Cup Winners 1970

Season	Opponent	Home	Result	Away	Rnd	Cup
1970-71	Cardiff City, Wales	0-0		0-8	1	CWC
1972-73	Cork Hibernians, Eire	1-2		1-4	1	CWC
1973-74	Malmo FF, Sweden	0-0		0-11	1	CWC

1978-79	Slask Wroclaw, Poland	2-2		1-5	1	UEFA
1980-81	VFB Stuttgart, Germany	1-4		0-6	1	UEFA
1982-83	FC Zurich, Switzerland	2-2		0-1	1	UEFA
1983-84	Bayern Munich, Germany	0-1		0-10	1	UEFA
1987-88	Victoria Bucharest, Romania	0-1		0-3	1	UEFA
1988-89	IFK Gothenburg, Sweden	1-2		1-5	1	ECC

DIGHENIS AKRITAS MORPHOU

Founded 1957 Colours green shirts, white shorts
Stadium Korivos until 1974, moved to Praxandros Nicosia after the Turkish invasion

Season	Opponent	Home	Result	Away	Rnd	Cup
1971-72	AC Milan, Italy	0-3		0-4	1	UEFA

PARALIMNI FAMAGUSTA

Founded 1936 Colours red shirts, white shorts
Stadium GSE (10,000) ☎ 031- 21352

Season	Opponent	Home	Result	Away	Rnd	Cup
1975-76	MSV Duisberg, Germany	2-3*		1-7	1	UEFA
		*in Oberhausen				
1976-77	1.FC Kaiserslautern, Germany	1-3		0-8	1	UEFA
1981-82	Vasas Budapest, Hungary	1-0		0-8	1	CWC
1983-84	SK Beveren Waas, Belgium	2-4		1-3	1	CWC

AE LIMASSOL

Founded 1933 Colours blue shirts, yellow shorts
Stadium Tsirion (20,000) ☎ 051-62598
Champions 1941, 1953, 1955, 1956
Cup Winners 1939, 1940, 1948, 1985, 1987, 1989

Season	Opponent	Home	Result	Away	Rnd	Cup
1985-86	Dukla Prague, Czechoslovakia	2-2		0-4	1	CWC
1987-88	DAC Dunajska Streda, Czechoslovakia	0-1		1-5	pr	CWC
1989-90	Admira Wacker Vienna, Austria	1-0		0-3	1	CWC

ALKI (LARNACA)

Founded 1948 Colours red shirts, blue shorts
Stadium Gynastiko Stadion (10,000) ☎041-54099/52955

Season	Opponent	Home	Result	Away	Rnd	Cup
1979-80	Dinamo Bucharest, Romania	0-9		0-3	1	UEFA

CZECHOSLOVAKIA

Association founded 1906, reorganised 1949
Ceskoslovenska Fotbalovy Svaz Na Porici 12, 115 30 Prague 1 ☎ 24 98 41,22 58 36 Fax 2-434 605
National Colours red shirts, white shorts, blue socks
Season August to November; February to June

LEAGUE CHAMPIONS

1912	AC Sparta Prague	**War Time League Winners**	1945-46	AC Sparta Prague	1967 Sparta CKD Prague
1913	SK Slavia Prague	1938-39 AC Sparta Prague	1946-47	SK Slavia Prague	1968 Spartak TAZ Trnava
1919	AC Sparta Prague	(Czecho-Moravska)	1947-48	AC Sparta Prague	1969 Spartak TAZ Trnava
		1938-39 Sparta Povazska	1948	Dynamo Slavia Prague	
1920	AC Sparta Prague	Bystrica (Slovenska)	1949	Sokol NV Bratislavia	1970 Slovan ChZJD Bratislava
1921	AC Sparta Prague	1939-40 SK Slavia Prague			1971 Spartak TAZ Trnava
1922	AC Sparta Prague	(Czech-Moravska)	1950	Sokol NV Bratislava	1972 Spartak TAZ Trnava
1923	AC Sparta Prague	1939-40 SK Bratislava	1951	Sokol NV Bratislava	1973 Spartak TAZ Trnava
1924	SK Slavia Prague	(Slovenska)	1952	Sparta CKD Sokolovo	1974 Slovan ChZJD Bratislava
1925	SK Slavia Prague	1940-41 SK Slavia Prague		Prague	1975 Slovan ChZJD Bratislava
1926	AC Sparta Prague	(Czecho-Moravska)	1953	UDA Prague	1976 Banik OKD Ostrava
1927	AC Sparta Prague	1940-41 SK Bratislava	1954	Spartak Sokolovo Prague	1977 Dukla Prague
1928	Viktoria Zizkov Prague	(Slovenska)	1955	Slovan UNV Bratislava	1978 Zbrojovka Brno
1929	SK Slavia Prague	1941-42 SK Slavia Prague	1956	Dukla Prague	1979 Dukla Prague
		(Czecho-Moravska)	1958	Dukla Prague	
1930	SK Slavia Prague	1941-42 SK Bratislava	1959	CH Bratislava	1980 Banik OKD Ostrava
1931	SK Slavia Prague	(Slovenska)			1981 Banik OKD Ostrava
1932	AC Sparta Prague	1942-43 SK Slavia Prague	1960	Spartak Hradec Kralove	1982 Dukla Prague
1933	SK Slavia Prague	(Czecho-Moravska)	1961	Dukla Prague	1983 Bohemians CKD Prague
1934	SK Slavia Prague	1942-43 OAP Bratislava	1962	Dukla Prague	1984 Sparta CKD Prague
1935	SK Slavia Prague	(Slovenska)	1963	Dukla Prague	1985 Sparta CKD Prague
1936	AC Sparta Prague	1943-44 AC Sparta Prague	1964	Dukla Prague	1986 TJ Vitkovice
1937	SK Slavia Prague	(Czecho-Moravska)	1965	Sparta CKD Prague	1987 Sparta CKD Prague
1938	AC Sparta Prague	1943-44 SK Bratislava	1966	Dukla Prague	1988 Sparta CKD Prague
1939	AC Sparta Prague	(Slovenska)			1989 Sparta CKD Prague
		1945 not held			

CUP WINNERS

1961	Dukla Prague v Dynamo Zilina	3-0
1962	Slovan Bratislava v Dukla Prague	1-1 4-1
1963	Slovan Bratislava v Dynamo Prague	0-0 9-0
1964	Sparta CKD Prague v VSS Kosice	4-1
1965	Dukla Prague v Slovan Bratislava	0-0 5-3 pens
1966	Dukla Prague v Tatran Presov	2-1 4-0
1967	Spartak Trnava v Sparta CKD Prague	2-4 2-0 5-4 pens

1968	Slovan Braislava v Dukla Prague	0-1 2-0
1969	Dukla Prague v VCHZ Pardubice	1-1 1-0
1970	TJ Gottwaldov v Slovan Bratislava	3-3 0-0 4-3 pens
1971	Spartak Trnava v Skoda Pilzen	5-1 2-1
1972	Sparta CKD Prague v Slovan Bratislava	4-3 0-1 4-2 pens
1973	Banik Ostrava v VSS Kosice	3-1 1-2

1974	Slovan Bratislava v Slavia Prague	1-0 0-1 4-3 pens	1982	Slovan Bratislava v Bohemians Prague	0-0 4-2 pens
1975	Spartak Trnava v Sparta CKD Prague	3-1 1-0	1983	Dukla Prague v Slovan Bratislava	2-1
1976	Sparta CKD Prague v Slovan Bratislava	1-0 3-2	1984	Sparta CKD Prague v Inter Bratislava	4-2
1977	Lokomotiva Kosice v Union Teplice	2-1	1985	Dukla Prague v Lokomotiva Kosice	3-2
1978	Banik Ostrava v Jednota Trencin	1-0	1986	Spartak Trnava v Sparta Prague	1-1 4-3 pens
1979	Lokomotiva Kosice v Banik Ostrava	2-1	1987	DAC Dunajska Streda v Sparta Prague	0-0 3-2 pens
			1988	Sparta CKD Prague v Inter Bratislava	2-0
1980	Sparta CKD Prague v ZTS Kosice	2-0	1989	Sparta CKD Prague v Slovan Bratislava	3-0
1981	Dukla Prague v Dukla Banska Bysrtica	4-1			

Since 1969-70 the Czechs and the Slovakians have had their own Cup, the winners of each play-off for the National Cup Title

CZECH CUP WINNERS

1970	TJ Gottwaldov v LIAZ Jablonec	2-2 4-0	1980	Sparta CKD Prague v Bohemians Prague	1-1 4-2
1971	Skoda Plzen v Sparta CKD Prague B	1-1 3-3 5-5 pens	1981	Dukla Prague v Bohemians Prague	3-1 2-3
1972	Sparta CKD Prague v Dukla Prague	2-1 2-1	1982	Bohemians Prague v Dukla Prague	4-0
1973	Banik Ostrava v Sklo Union Teplice	2-1 0-1 5-4 pens	1983	Dukla Prague	
1974	Slavia Prague v Sparta CKD Prague	1-1 3-1	1984	Sparta CKD Prague	
1975	Sparta CKD Prague v Banik Ostrava	1-0 2-1	1985	Dukla Prague v Dynamo JCE Ceske Budejovice	3-1
1976	Sparta CKD Prague v SONP Kladno	4-1 1-0	1986	Sparta CKD Prague v Dukla Prague	4-2
1977	Union Teplice v Sparta CKD Prague	1-0 2-1	1987	Sparta CKD Prague v Slavia Prague	1-1 4-3 pens
1978	Banik Ostrava v Skoda Mlada Bolesav	0-1 2-0	1988	Sparta CKD Prague v TJ Vitkovice	3-0
1979	Banik Ostrava v Skoda Plzen	1-0 2-0	1989	Sparta CKD Prague v	

SLOVAKIA CUP FINALS

1970	Slovan Bratislava v Dukla Banska Bystrica	2-2 1-0	1980	ZTS Kosice v ZVL Zilina	2-4 5-0
1971	Spartak Trnava v Slovan Bratislava	2-0 0-1	1981	Dukla Bandka Bystrica v ZTS Kosice	1-1 1-0
1972	Slovan Bratislava v Spartak Trnava	1-2 4-1	1982	Slovan Bratislava v ZTS Petrzalka	0-0 3-1
1973	VSS Kosice v Tatran Presov	3-0 3-3	1983	Slovan Bratislava v Plastica Nitra	0-0 wag 1-1
1974	Slovan Bratislava v Spartak Trnava	0-0 2-2 6-5 pens	1984	Inter Bratislava v Dukla Banska Bystrica	1-0 2-0
1975	Spartak Trnava v AC Nitra	2-0 1-2	1985	Lokomotiva Kosice v Tatran Presov	1-1 1-0
1976	Slovan Bratislava v Inter Bratislava	0-0 2-1	1986	Spartak Trnava v ZVL Zilina	1-0
1977	Lokomotiva Kosice v ZVL Zilina	0-2 4-0	1987	DAC Dunajska Streda v Plastica Nitra	0-0 6-5 pens
1978	Jednota Trencin v Slovan Bratislava	1-0 3-1	1988	Inter Bratislava v Spartak Trnava	1-0
1979	Lokomotiva Kosice v Inter Bratislava	2-2 3-0	1989	Slovan Bratislava v Povazska Bystrica	2-1

CZECHOSLOVAKIA

FEATURED CLUBS IN EUROPEAN COMPETITION

Dukla Prague	Slovan Bratislava	Inter Bratislava	Zbrojovka Brno
Sparta Prague	Spartak Trnava	Banik Ostrava	Slavia Prague
ZVL Zilina	Lokomotiva Kosice	ZTS Kosice	Bohemians Prague
Sklo Union Teplice	Skoda Plzen	Gottwaldov TJ	Tatran Presov
Dukla Banska Bystrica	TJ Vitkovice	Sigma Olumouc	DAC Dunajska Streda
Spartak Hradec Kralove	Plastika Nitra		

DUKLA PRAGUE

Founded 1948 as ATK Prague, 1952 UDA Prague, 1956 Dukla Prague
Colours red shirts, yellow sleeves, white shorts
Stadium Strahov, named changed 1960 to Juliska (28,000) situated in the Dejvice area of Prague The Army Club of Czechoslovakia ☎ 02-35 58 65
Champions as UDA 1953, as Dukla 1956, 1957, 1958, 1961, 1962, 1963, 1964, 1966, 1977, 1979, 1982
Cup Winners 1961, 1965, 1966, 1969, 1981, 1983, 1985

Season	Opponent	Home	Playoff Result	Away	Rnd	Cup
1957-58	Manchester United, England	1-0		0-3	1	ECC
1958-59	Dinamo Zagreb, Yugoslavia	2-1		2-2	pr	ECC
	Wiener Sports Club, Austria	1-0		1-3	1	ECC
1961-62	CDNA Sofia, Bulgaria	2-1		4-4	1	ECC
	Servette Geneva, Switzerland	2-0		3-4	2	ECC
	Tottenham Hotspur, England	1-0		1-4	qf	ECC
1962-63	ASK Vorwaerts Berlin, East Germany	1-0		3-0	1	ECC
	Esbjerg fB, Denmark	5-0		0-0	2	ECC
	Benfica, Portugal	0-0		1-2	qf	ECC
1963-64	Valletta, Malta	6-0		2-0	1	ECC
	Gornik Zabrze, Poland	4-1		0-2	2	ECC
	Borussia Dortmund, Germany	0-4		3-1	qf	ECC
1964-65	Gornik Zabrze, Poland	4-1	0-0* wot	0-3**	pr	ECC
			* in Duisberg aet, ** in Warsaw			
	Real Madrid, Spain	2-2		0-4	1	ECC
1965-66	Rennes, France	2-0		0-0	1	CWC
	Honved Budapest, Hungary	2-3	lag	2-1	2	CWC
1966-67	Esbjerg fB, Denmark	4-0		2-0	1	ECC
	RSC Anderlecht, Belgium	4-1		2-1	2	ECC
	Ajax Amsterdam, Holland	2-1		1-1	qf	ECC
	Glasgow Celtic, Scotland	0-0		1-3	sf	ECC
1969-70	Olympique Marseille, France	1-0		0-2	1	CWC
1972-73	OFK Belgrade, Yugoslavia	2-2		1-3	1	UEFA
1974-75	Pezoporikos Larnaca, Cyprus	walk over			1	UEFA
	Djurgarden IF Stockholm, Sweden	3-1		2-0	2	UEFA
	Twente Enschede, Holland	3-1		0-5	3	UEFA
1977-78	FC Nantes, France	1-1	lag	0-0	1	ECC
1978-79	Lanerossi Vicenza, Italy	1-0		1-1	1	UEFA
	Everton, England	1-0	wag	1-2	2	UEFA
	VfB Stuttgart, Germany	4-0		1-4	3	UEFA
	Hertha BSC Berlin, Germany	1-2		1-1	qf	UEFA
1979-80	Ujpest Dozsa, Hungary	2-0		2-3	1	ECC
	RC Strasbourg, France	1-0		0-2	2	ECC
1981-82	Glasgow Rangers, Scotland	3-0		1-2	1	CWC
	FC Barcelona, Spain	1-0		0-4	2	CWC
1982-83	Dinamo Bucharest, Romania	2-1		0-2	1	ECC
1983-84	Manchester United, England	2-2	lag	1-1	1	CWC
1984-85	Videoton Sekesfehervar, Hungary	0-0		0-1	1	UEFA
1985-86	AE Limassol, Cyprus	4-0		2-2	1	CWC
	AIK Stockholm, Sweden	1-0		2-2	2	CWC
	Benfica, Portugal	1-0	wag	1-2	qf	CWC
	Dynamo Kiev, USSR	1-1		0-3	sf	CWC

1986-87	Heart of Midlothian, Scotland	1-0	wag	2-3	1	UEFA
	Bayer Leverkusen, Germany	0-0	wag	1-1	2	UEFA
	Inter Milan, Italy	0-1		0-0	3	UEFA
1988-89	Real Sociadad San Sebastian, Spain	3-2	lag	1-2	1	UEFA

SLOVAN ChZJD BRATISLAVA

Founded 1919 ICSSK Bratislava, 1940 SK Bratislava, 1949 Sokol NV Bratislava, 1953 Slovan UNV Bratislava, 1961 merger of Slovan UNV and TJ Dimitrov to form Slovan ChZJD
Colours all blue
Stadium Tehelne Pole (48,000)
Champions as NV 1949, 1950, 1951 as Slovan 1955, 1970, 1974, 1975
Cup Winners 1962, 1963, 1968, 1982
CWC Winners 1969

Season	Opponent	Home	Result	Away	Rnd	Cup
1956-57	CKSW Warsaw, Poland	4-0		0-2	pr	ECC
	Grasshoppers Zurich, Switzerland	1-0		0-2*	1	ECC
				*in Munich		
1962-63	bye				1	CWC
	Lausanne Sports, Switzerland	1-1		1-0	2	CWC
	Tottenham Hotspur, England	2-0		0-6	qf	CWC
1963-64	KuPS Kuopion Palloseura, Finland	8-1		4-1	1	CWC
	Borough United, Wales	3-0		1-0	2	CWC
	Glasgow Celtic, Scotland	0-1		0-1	qf	CWC
1968-69	Borovo, Yugoslavia	3-0		0-2	1	CWC
	FC Porto, Portugal	4-0		0-1	2	CWC
	Torino, Italy	2-1		1-0	qf	CWC
	Dunfermline Athletic, Scotland	1-0		1-1	sf	CWC
	CF Barcelona, Spain	3-2	in Basle		FINAL	CWC
1969-70	Dinamo Zagreb, Yugoslavia	0-0		0-3	1	CWC
1970-71	BK 1903 Copenhagen, Denmark	2-1		2-2	1	ECC
	Panathinaikos, Greece	2-1		0-3	2	ECC
1972-73	Vojvodina Novi Sad, Yugoslavia	6-0		2-1	1	UEFA
	Las Palmas, Spain	0-1		2-2	2	UEFA
1974-75	RSC Anderlecht, Belgium	4-2	lag	1-3	1	ECC
1975-76	Derby County, England	1-0		0-3	1	ECC
1976-77	Fram Reykjavik, Iceland	5-0		3-0	1	UEFA
	Queens Park Rangers, England	3-3		2-5	2	UEFA
1982-83	Inter Milan, Italy	2-1		0-2	1	CWC
1989-90	Grasshoppers Zurich, Switzerland	3-0		0-4aet	1	CWC

CZECHOSLOVAKIA

TJ INTERNACIONAL SLOVNAFT ZTS BRATISLAVA-PETRZALKA

Founded 1940 as Cervena Hviezda (Red Star), amalgamated with Apollo in 1965 and became Slovnaft
TJ Internacional Slovnaft ZTS Bratislava-Petrzalka founded 1942 became Slovnaft 1965,
amalgamated with Petrzalka in 1986
Colours white shirts with black sleeves, black shorts
Stadium Patrzalke (12,000) ☎ 07-514 53
Champions 1959 Mitropa Cup Winners 1969

Season	Opponent	Home	Result	Away	Rnd	Cup
as RED STAR BRATISLAVA						
1959-60	FC Porto, Portugal	2-1		2-0	pr	ECC
	Glasgow Rangers, Scotland	1-1		3-4	1	ECC
as INTERNACIONAL BRATISLAVA						
1975-76	Real Zaragoza, Spain	5-0		3-2	1	UEFA
	AEK Athens, Greece	2-0	wag	1-3	2	UEFA
	Stal Mielec, Poland	1-0		0-2	3	UEFA
1977-78	Rapid Vienna, Austria	3-0		0-1	1	UEFA
	Grasshoppers Zurich, Switzerland	1-0		1-5	2	UEFA
1983-84	Rabat Ajax, Malta	6-0		10-0	1	UEFA
	Radnicki Nis, Yugoslavia	3-2		0-4	2	UEFA
1984-85	Kuusysi Lahti, Finland	2-1		0-0	1	CWC
	Everton, England	0-1		0-3	2	CWC
1988-89	Sredets CFKA Sofia, Bulgaria	2-3		0-5	1	CWC

ZBROJOVKA BRNO

Founded 1913 as Zidenice, 1949 Zbrojovka Zidenice, 1952 Mez Zidenice, 1953 Ruda Hvezda, 1961 Spartak Brno,
1965 Spartal ZJS, 1970 Zbrojovka Brno
Colours red shirts, white shorts
Stadium Luzankani (55,000) ☎ 05-740 111
Champions 1978

Season	Opponent	Home	Playoff Result	Away	Rnd	Cup
as RUDA HVEZDA BRNO (RED STAR)						
1960-61	ASK Vorwaerts Berlin, East Germany	2-0		1-2	1	CWC
	Dinamo Zagreb, Yugoslavia	0-0		0-2	qf	CWC
as SPARTAK BRNO						
1961-62	SC Chemie Halle, East Germany	2-2		1-4	1	Fairs
1962-63	Petrolui Ploesti, Romania	0-1		2-4	pr	Fairs
1963-64	Servette Geneva, Switzerland	5-0		2-1	1	Fairs
	Partick Thistle, Scotland	4-0		2-3	2	Fairs
	RFC Liege, Belgium	2-0	0-1 *	0-2	qf	Fairs
			*in Liege			
1964-65	Ferencvarosi TC, Hungary	1-0		0-2	pr	Fairs
1965-66	Lokomotiv Plovdiv, Bulgaria	2-0		0-1	1	Fairs
	Fiorentina, Italy	4-0		0-2	2	Fairs
	Dunfermline Athletic, Scotland	0-0		0-2	3	Fairs
1966-67	Dinamo Zagreb, Yugoslavia	2-0	lot	0-2	1	Fairs
as ZBROJOVKA BRNO						
1978-79	Ujpest Dozsa, Hungary	2-2		2-0	1	ECC
	Wisla Krakow, Poland	2-2	lag	1-1	2	ECC
1979-80	Esbjerg fB, Denmark	6-0		1-1	1	UEFA
	IBK Keflavik, Iceland	3-1		2-1	2	UEFA
	Standard Liege, Belgium	3-2		2-1	3	UEFA
	Eintracht Frankfurt, Germany	3-2		1-4	qf	UEFA
1980-81	SK VoEST Linz, Austria	3-1		2-0	1	UEFA
	Real Sociedad San Sebastian, Spain	1-1		1-2	2	UEFA

SPARTA CKD PRAGUE

Founded 1893 as AC Kralovske Vinohrady, 1894 AC Sparta, 1948 Sokol Sparta, 1949 Sparta Bratrstvi,
1951 Sparta Sokolovo, 1953 Spartak Sokolovo, 1964 Sparta
Colours red shirts, white shorts
Stadium Letnej (36,000) ☎ 02 37 21 19/38 24 41
Champions 1912, 1919, 1920, 1921, 1922, 1923, 1925, 1926, 1927, 1932, 1936, 1938, 1939, 1944, 1946, 1948, 1965,
1967, 1984, 1985, 1987, 1988, 1989
Cup Winners 1964, 1972, 1976, 1980, 1988, 1989
Mitropa Cup Winners 1927, 1935, 1936, 1964

Season	Opponent	Home	Result	Away	Rnd	Cup
1964-65	Anorthosis Famagusta, Cyprus	10-0		6-0	pr	CWC
	West Ham United, England	2-1		0-2	1	CWC
1965-66	Lausanne Sport, Switzerland	4-0		0-0	1	ECC
	Gornik Zabrze, Poland	3-0		2-1	2	ECC
	Partizan Belgrade, Yugoslavia	4-1		0-5	qf	ECC
1966-67	bye				1	Fairs
	Bologna, Italy	2-2		1-2	2	Fairs
1967-68	Skeid Oslo, Norway	1-1		1-0	1	ECC
	RSC Anderlecht, Belgium	3-2		3-3	2	ECC
	Real Madrid, Spain	2-1		0-3	qf	ECC
1969-70	Inter Milan, Italy	0-1		0-3	1	Fairs
1970-71	Atletico Bilbao, Spain	2-0		1-1	1	Fairs
	Dundee United, Scotland	3-1		0-1	2	Fairs
	Leeds United, England	2-3		0-6	3	Fairs
1972-73	Standard Liege, Belgium	4-2		0-1	1	CWC
	Ferencvarosi TC, Hungary	4-1		0-2	2	CWC
	FC Schalke 04, Gelsenkirchen, Germany	3-0		1-2	qf	CWC
	AC Milan, Italy	0-1		0-1	sf	CWC
1976-77	MTK Budapest, Hungary	1-1		1-3	1	CWC
1980-81	CA Spora, Luxembourg	6-0		6-0	1	CWC
	Slavia Sofia, Bulgaria	2-0		0-3	2	CWC
1981-82	FC Neuchatel Xamax, Switzerland	3-2		0-4	1	UEFA
1983-84	Real Madrid, Spain	3-2		1-1	1	UEFA
	Widzew Lodz, Poland	3-0		0-1	2	UEFA
	Watford, England	4-0		3-2	3	UEFA
	Hajduk Split, Yugoslavia	1-0		0-2	qf	UEFA
1984-85	Valerengens IF Oslo, Norway	2-0		3-3	1	ECC
	Lyngby BK, Denmark	0-0		2-1	2	ECC
	Juventus, Italy	1-0		0-3	qf	ECC
1985-86	FC Barcelona, Spain	1-2	lag	1-0	1	ECC
1986-87	Vitoria Guimaraes, Portugal	1-1		1-2	1	UEFA
1987-88	Fram Reykjavik, Iceland	8-0		2-0	1	ECC
	RSC Anderlecht, Belgium	1-2		0-1	2	ECC
1988-89	Steaua Bucharest, Romania	1-5		2-2	1	ECC
1989-90	Fenerbahce, Turkey	3-1		2-1	1	ECC
	Sredets CFKA Sofia, Bulgaria	2-2*		0-3	2	ECC
		*in Trnava				

61

CZECHOSLOVAKIA

SPARTAK ZTS TRNAVA

Founded 1925 as SK Rapid, 1939 merger with SK Trnava and SK Rapid and became TSS Trnava, 1948 Sokol NV Trnava, merger of Sokol NV and Kovosmalt to form ZTJ Kovosmalt, 1953 Spartak Trnava, 1967 Spartak TAZ Trnava, 1988 Spartak ZTS
Colours red shirts, black shorts
Stadium TAZ Stadion (28,000) ☎ 242 10
Champions 1968, 1969, 1971, 1972, 1973 Cup Winners 1967, 1970, 1971, 1975, 1986
Mitropa Cup Winners 1967

Season	Opponent	Home	Result	Away	Rnd	Cup
1967-68	Lausanne Sports, Switzerland	2-0		2-3	1	CWC
	Torpedo Moscow, USSR	1-3		0-3*	2	CWC
				*in Tashkent		
1968-69	Steaua Bucharest, Romania	4-0		1-3	1	ECC
	Reipas Lahti, Finland	7-1		9-1*	2	ECC
				*in Vienna		
	AEK Athens, Greece	2-1		1-1	qf	ECC
	Ajax Amsterdam, Holland	2-0		0-3	sf	ECC
1969-70	Hibernians, Malta	4-0		2-2	1	ECC
	Galatasaray, Turkey	1-0	lot*	0-1	2	ECC
				*last time toss of coin was used		
1970-71	Olympique Marseille, France	2-0	4-3p	0-2	1	Fairs
	Hertha BSC Berlin, Germany	3-1		0-1	2	Fairs
	1.FC Koln, Germany	0-1		0-3	3	Fairs
1971-72	Dinamo Bucharest, Romania	2-2	lag	0-0	1	ECC
1972-73	bye				1	ECC
	RSC Anderlecht, Belgium	1-0		1-0	2	ECC
	Derby County, England	1-0		0-2	qf	ECC
1973-74	Viking Stavanger, Norway	1-0		2-1	1	ECC
	Zarja Voroshilovgrad, USSR	0-0		1-0	2	ECC
	Ujpest Dozsa, Hungary	1-1	3-4p	1-1	qf	ECC
1975-76	Boavista, Portugal	0-0		0-3	1	CWC
1986-87	VfB Stuttgart, Germany	0-0		0-1	1	CWC

BANIK OKD OSTRAVA

Founded 1922 as SK Slezka Ostrava, 1948 Sokol Trojice Slezska Ostrava, 1951 Sokol OKD Ostrava, 1952 Banik OKD Ostrava
Colours white shirts, blue shorts
Stadium Bazalech (35,000) ☎ 0969-22 30 23/ 22 49 81
Champions 1976, 1980, 1981
Cup Winners 1973, 1978

Season	Opponent	Home	Result	Away	Rnd	Cup
1969-70	Vitoria Guimaraes, Portugal	1-1		0-1	1	Fairs
1973-74	Cork Hibernians, Eire	1-0		2-1	1	CWC
	1.FC Magdeburg, East Germany	2-0		0-3	2	CWC
1974-75	Real Sociedad San Sebastian, Spain	4-0		1-0	1	UEFA
	FC Nantes, France	2-0	aet	0-1	2	UEFA
	Napoli, Italy	1-1		2-0	3	UEFA
	Borussia Monchengladbach, Germany	0-1		1-3	qf	UEFA
1976-77	Viking Stavanger, Norway	2-0		1-2	1	ECC
	Bayern Munich, Germany	2-1		0-5	2	ECC
1978-79	Sporting Lisbon, Portugal	1-0		1-0	1	CWC
	Shamrock Rovers, Eire	3-0		3-1	2	CWC
	1.FC Magdeburg, East Germany	4-2		1-2	qf	CWC
	Fortuna Dusseldorf, Germany	2-1		1-3	sf	CWC
1979-80	Orduspor, Turkey	6-0		0-2	1	UEFA
	Dynamo Kiev, USSR	1-0		0-2	2	UEFA

1980-81	IBV Vestmannaeyjar, Iceland	1-0		1-1	1	ECC
	BFC Dynamo Berlin, East Germany	0-0	wag	1-1	2	ECC
	Bayern Munich, Germany	2-4		0-2	qf	ECC
1981-82	Ferencvarosi TC, Hungary	3-0		2-3	1	ECC
	Red Star Belgrade, Yugoslavia	3-1		0-3	2	ECC
1982-83	Glentoran, Ireland	1-0		3-1	1	UEFA
	Valencia CF, Spain	0-0		0-1	2	UEFA
1983-84	B1903 Copenhagen, Denmark	5-0		1-1	1	UEFA
	RSC Anderlecht, Belgium	2-2		0-2	2	UEFA
1985-86	Linzer ASK, Austria	0-1		0-2	1	UEFA
1989-90	Hansa Rostock, East Germany	4-0		3-2	1	UEFA
	Dynamo Kiev, USSR	1-1		0-3	2	UEFA

SLAVIA IPS PRAGUE

Founded 1892 as Acos Prague, 1895 SK Slavia, 1949 Sokol Dynamo Slavia, 1953 Dynamo, 1965 Slavia, 1977 Slavia IPS
Colours red and white halved shirts, white shorts
Stadium Novy (Vrsovicich) (46,200) ☎ 02-74 37 25/74 65 19
Champions 1929, 1930, 1931, 1933, 1934, 1935, 1937, 1940, 1941, 1942, 1943, 1947
Mitropa Cup Winners 1938

Season	Opponent	Home	Result	Away	Rnd	Cup
1967-68	1.FC Koln, Germany	2-2		0-2	1	Fairs
1968-69	Wiener SportClub, Austria	5-0		0-1	1	Fairs
	Hamburger SV, Germany	3-1		1-4	2	Fairs
1974-75	Carl Zeiss Jena, East Germany	1-0	2-3p	0-1	1	CWC
1976-77	Akademik Sofia, Bulgaria	2-0		0-3	1	UEFA
1977-78	Standard Liege, Belgium	3-2	lag	0-1	1	UEFA
1985-86	St Mirren, Scotland	1-0		0-3	1	UEFA

ZVL ZILINA

Founded 1908 as ZTK Zilina, 1919 SK Zilina, 1948 Slovena Zilina, 1953 Iskra Zilina, 1956 Dynamo Zilina,
1963 Jednota Zilina, 1967 ZVL Zilina
Colours green shirts with white sleeves, blue shorts
Stadium Zilinsky (15,000) ☎ 0989-23194

Season	Opponent	Home	Result	Away	Rnd	Cup
as DYNAMO ZILINA						
1961-62	bye				1	CWC
	Olympiakos Piraeus, Greece	1-0		3-2	2	CWC
	Fiorentina, Italy	3-2		0-2	qf	CWC

LOKOMOTIVA KOSICE

Founded 1946 as Zeleznicar, 1948 Zeleznicar-Sparta, 1949 Dynamo, 1952 amalgamated with VSZ Kosice,
1963 Lokomotiva Kosice
Colours blue shirts, white shorts
Stadium Jeho Cermell (28,000) ☎ 095-322 80
Cup Winners 1977, 1979

Season	Opponent	Home	Playoff Result	Away	Rnd	Cup
1977-78	Osters IF Vaxjo, Sweden	0-0	wag	2-2	1	CWC
	FK Austria/WAC, Austria	1-1	lag	0-0	2	CWC
1978-79	AC Milan, Italy	1-0	6-7 pen	0-1	1	UEFA
1979-80	Wacker Innsbruck, Austria	1-0		2-1	1	CWC
	NK Rijeka, Yugoslavia	2-0		0-3	2	CWC

CZECHOSLOVAKIA

ZTS KOSICE

Founded 1952 as Spartak Kosice, 1956 Jednota Kosice, 1962 VSS Kosice, 1979 ZTS Kosice
Colours yellow shirts, blue shorts
Stadium VSE Sportovni Stadion (40,000) ☎ 095-26225

Season	Opponent	Home	Result	Away	Rnd	Cup
as VSS KOSICE						
1971-72	Spartak Moscow, USSR	2-1		0-2	1	UEFA
1973-74	Honved Budapest, Hungary	1-0		2-5	1	UEFA

BOHEMIANS CKD PRAGUE

Founded 1903 as Kotva Vrsovice, 1905 AFK Vrsovice 1927 AFK Bohemians, 1939 AFK Bohemia, 1949 AFK Zeleznicar,
1951 Sokol Zeleznicari, 1952 Spartak Stalingrad, 1962 TJ CKD Bohemians, 1965 Bohemians CKD
Colours green shirts with white sleeves, white shorts
Stadium Vrsovice (20,000) and Dolicku (17,500) ☎ 02-72 21 80
Champions 1983

Season	Opponent	Home	Result	Away	Rnd	Cup
1975-76	Honved Budapest, Hungary	1-2		1-1	1	UEFA
1979-80	Bayern Munich, Germany	0-2		2-2	1	UEFA
1980-81	Real Sporting Gijon, Spain	3-1		1-2	1	UEFA
	Ipswich Town, England	2-0		0-3	2	UEFA
1981-82	Valencia CF, Spain	0-1		0-1	1	UEFA
1982-83	Admira Vienna, Austria	5-0		2-1	1	UEFA
	St Etienne, France	4-0		0-0	2	UEFA
	Servette Geneva, Switzerland	2-1		2-2	3	UEFA
	Dundee United, Scotland	1-0		0-0	qf	UEFA
	RSC Anderlecht, Belgium	0-1		1-3	sf	UEFA
1983-84	Fenerbahce, Turkey	4-0		1-0	1	ECC
	Rapid Vienna, Austria	2-1	lag	0-1	2	ECC
1984-85	Apollon Limassol, Cyprus	6-1		2-2	1	UEFA
	Ajax Amsterdam, Holland	1-0	4-2 pen	0-1	2	UEFA
	Tottenham Hotspur, England	1-1		0-2	3	UEFA
1985-86	Raba Vasas Eto, Hungary	4-1		1-3	1	UEFA
	1.FC Koln, Germany	2-4		0-4	2	UEFA
1987-88	SK Beveren Waas, Belgium	1-0		0-2	1	UEFA

SKLO UNION TEPLICE

Founded 1945 as SK Teplice, 1953 Slovan Teplice, 1966 Union
Colours yellow shirts, blue shorts
Stadium Sklo Union (20,000) ☎ 0417-3334

Season	Opponent	Home	Result	Away	Rnd	Cup
1971-72	Zaglebie Walbrzych, Poland	2-3		0-1	1	UEFA

SKODA PLZEN

Founded 1911 as SK Viktoria Plzen, 1948 Sokol Skoda Plzen, 1952 Zvil Plzen, 1953 Spartak Plzen IZ, 1965 Skoda Plzen
formerly Spartak Plzen and SK Viktoria Plzen
Colours white shirts, blue shorts
Stadium Struncove Sady (33,000) ☎ 019-35180/36038

Season	Opponent	Home	Result	Away	Rnd	Cup
1971-72	Bayern Munich, Germany	0-1		1-6	1	CWC

TJ GOTTWALDOV

Founded 1919 as FK Zlin, 1924 Bata Zlin, 1948 Botostroj Zlin, 1949 Svit Gottwaldov, 1953 Iskra Gottwaldov,
1958 TJ Gottwaldov
Colours blue shirts, yellow shorts
Stadium Stadion (15,000) ☎ 067-24252
Cup Winners 1970

Season	Opponent	Home	Result	Away	Rnd	Cup
1970-71	Bohemians Dublin, Eire	2-2		2-1	1	CWC
	PSV Eindhoven, Holland	2-1	lag	0-1	2	CWC

TATRAN PRESOV

Founded 1931 as Slavia Presov, 1945 PTS Presov, 1947 Sparta Presov, 1950 Dukla Presov, 1953 Tatran Presov
Colours green shirts, white shorts
Stadium Comunale (20,000) ☎ 091-325 66/335 53
Mitropa Cup Winners 1981

Season	Opponent	Home	Result	Away	Rnd	Cup
1966-67	Bayern Munich, Germany	1-1		2-3	pr	CWC
1973-74	Velez Mostar, Yugoslavia	4-2		1-1	1	UEFA
	VfB Stuttgart, Germany	3-5		1-3	2	UEFA

ASVS DUKLA BANSKA BYSTRICA

Founded 1965 as VTJ Dukla, 1967 AS Dukla, 1975 ASVS Dukla
Colours white shirts with red sleeves, white shorts
Stadium Stiavnickov (13,600) ☎ 088-325 93

Season	Opponent	Home	Result	Away	Rnd	Cup
1984-85	Borussia Monchengladbach, Germany	2-3		1-4	1	UEFA

TJ VITKOVICE (OSTRAVA)

Founded 1922 as SK Vitkovice, 1923 SSK Vitkovice, 1934 SK Vitkovice Zelezarny, 1939 CSK Vitkovice, 1945 SK Vit-
kovice Zelezarny, 1948 Vitkovice Zeleznicary, 1951 Sokol Vitkovice VZKA, 1952 Banik Vitkovice, 1957 Vitkovice,
1979 TJ Vitkovice
Colours all blue
Stadium Vitkovice (14,000) ☎ 0969- 356787
Champions 1986

Season	Opponent	Home	Result	Away	Rnd	Cup
1986-87	Paris St Germain, France	1-0		2-2	1	ECC
	FC Porto, Portugal	1-0		0-3	2	ECC
1987-88	AIK Stockholm, Sweden	1-1		2-0	1	UEFA
	Dundee United, Scotland	1-1		2-1	2	UEFA
	Vitoria Guimaraes, Portugal	2-0	5-4 pen	0-2	3	UEFA
	Espanol Barcelona, Spain	0-0		0-2	qf	UEFA

CZECHOSLOVAKIA

TJ SIGMA ZTS OLUMOUC

Founded 1919 as FK Hejcin, 1920 SK Hejcin, 1949 Sokol Mahrische Eisenwerke, 1953 Banik Sigma, 1956 Spartak,
1961 TJ moravske Zelezarny, 1966 TJ Sigma MZ, 1979 TJ Sigma ZTS Olomouc
Colours white shirts with blue sleeves, black shorts
Stadium Miru (14,000) ☎ 068-270 49/229 56

Season	Opponent	Home	Result	Away	Rnd	Cup
1986-87	IFK Gothenburg, Sweden	1-1		0-4	1	UEFA

DAC DUNAJSKA STREDA

Founded 1905 as DAC, 1974 DAC Dunajska Streda
Colours gold shirts, blue shorts
Stadium Dunajska (Corn Island) (9,300) ☎ 0709-24650
Cup Winners 1987

Season	Opponents	Home	Result	Away	Rnd	Cup
1987-88	AE Limassol, Cyprus	5-1		1-0	pre	CWC
	Young Boys Bern, Switzerland	2-1		1-3	1	CWC
1988-89	Osters IF Vaxjo, Sweden	6-0		0-2	1	UEFA
	Bayern Munich, Germany	0-2		1-2	2	UEFA

SPARTAK ZVU HRADEC KRALOVE

Founded 1905 as SK Hradec Kralove, 1948 Sokol Skoda, 1953 Spartak Hradec Kralove,
1976 Spartak ZVU Hradec Kralove
Colours white shirts, black shorts
Stadium Vsesportouni (20,000) ☎ 949-236 50/251 33
Champions 1960

Season	Opponent	Home	Result	Away	Rnd	Cup
1960-61	CCA Bucharest, Romania	withdrew			1	ECC
	Panathinaikos, Greece	1-0		0-0	2	ECC
	CF Barcelona, Spain	1-1		0-4	qf	ECC

PLASTIKA NITRA

Founded 1909 as NTVE Nitra, 1919 NSE Nitra, 1923 AC Nitra, 1948 Sokol Nitra, 1953 Slavoj Nitra, 1956 Slovan Nitra,
1966 AC Nitra, 1976 Plastika Nitra
Colours blued shirts, white shorts
Stadium Pod Zoborom (11,384) ☎ 98729133/28117

Season	Opponent	Home	Result	Away	Rnd	Cup
1989-90	1.FC Koln, Germany	0-1		1-4	1	UEFA

DENMARK

Founded 1899
Dansk Boldspil Union, ved Amagerbanen 15, 2300, Copenhagen ☎ 01 95 05 11 Fax 01 95 05 88
National Colours red shirts, white shorts, red socks. Season April to November

LEAGUE CHAMPIONS

1913	KB Copenhagen	1932	KB Copenhagen
1914	KB Copenhagen	1933	Frem Copenhagen
1915	not held	1934	B93 Copenhagen
1916	B93 Copenhagen	1935	B93 Copenhagen
1917	KB Copenhagen	1936	Frem Copenhagen
1918	KB Copenhagen	1937	AB Akademisk Boldklub
1919	AB Akademosl Boldklub	1938	B 1903 Copenhagen
		1939	B93 Copenhagen
1920	B 1903 Copenhagen		
1921	AB Akademisk Boldklub	1940	KB Copenhagen
1922	KB Copenhagen	1941	Frem Copenhagen
1923	Frem Copenhagen	1942	B93 Copenhagen
1924	B 1903 Copenhagen	1943	AB Akademisk Boldklub
1925	KB Copenhagen	1944	Frem Copenhagen
1926	B 1903 Copenhagen	1945	AB Akademisk Boldklub
1927	B93 Copenhagen	1946	B93 Copenhagen
1928	* 3 teams tied	1947	AB Akademisk Boldklub
1929	B93 Copenhagen	1948	KB Copenhagen
		1949	KB Copenhagen
1930	B93 Copenhagen		
1931	Frem Copenhagen	1950	KB Copenhagen

1951	AB Akademisk Boldklub	1970	B 1903 Copenhagen
1952	AB Akademisk Boldklub	1971	Vejle BK
1953	KB Copenhagen	1972	Vejle BK
1954	Koge BK	1973	Hvidovre IF
1955	AGF Aarhus	1974	KB Copenhagen
1956	AGF Aarhus	1975	Koge BK
1957	AGF Aarhus	1976	B 1903 Copenhagen
1958	Vejle BK	1977	OB Odense
1959	B 1909 Odense	1978	Vejle BK
		1979	Esbjerg FB
1960	AGF Aarhus		
1961	Esbjerg FB	1980	KB Copenhagen
1962	Esbjerg FB	1981	Hvidovre IF
1963	Esbjerg FB	1982	OB Odense
1964	B 1909 Odense	1983	Lyngby BK
1965	Esbjerg FB	1984	Vejle BK
1966	Hvidovre IF	1985	Brondbyernes IF
1967	AB Akademisk Boldklub	1986	AGF Aarhus
1968	KB Copenhagen	1987	Brondbyernes IF
1969	B 1903 Copenhagen	1988	Brondbyernes IF
		1989	OB Odense

*B 1903 Hellerup, B 1893 Copenhagen and BK Frem tied, no rule to decide who should be champions

CUP WINNERS

1955	AGF Aarhus v Aalborg Chang	4-0
1956	Frem Copenhagen v AB Akademisk Boldklub	1-0
1957	AGF Aarhus v Esbjerg FB	2-0
1958	Vejle BK v AGF Aarhus	3-2
1959	Vejle BK v AGF Aarhus	1-1 1-0
1960	AGF Aarhus v Frem Sakskobing	2-0
1961	AGF Aarhus v KB Copenhagen	2-0
1962	B 1909 Odense v Esbjerg FB	1-0
1963	B 1913 Odense v Koge BK	2-1
1964	Esbjerg FB v Odense KFUM	2-1
1965	AGF Aarhus v KB Copenhagen	1-0
1966	AaB Aalborg v KB Copenhagen	1-1 2-0
1967	Randers Freja v Aab Aalborg	1-0
1968	Randers Freja v Vejle BK	1-1 3-1
1969	KB Copenhagen v Frem Copenhagen	3-0
1970	Aab Aalborg v Lyngby BK	2-1
1971	B 1909 Odense v Frem Copenhagen	^-0
1972	Vejle BK v Fremad Amager	2-0

DENMARK

1973	Randers Freja v B 1901 Nykobing	2-0	1982	B93 Copenhagen v B 1903 Hellerup	3-3 1-0
1974	Vanlose IF Copenhagen v OB Odense	5-2	1983	OB Odense v B 1901 Nykobing	3-0
1975	Vejle BK v Holbaek IF	2-1	1984	Lyngby BK v KB Copenhagen	2-1
1976	Esbjerg FB v Holbaek IF	2-1	1985	Lyngby BK v Esbjerg FB	3-2
1977	Vejle v B 1909 Odense	2-1	1986	B 1903 Copenhagen v Ikast FS	2-1
1978	Frem Copenhagen v Esbjerg	1-1 1-1 1-1 4-3 pens	1987	AGF Aarhus v AaB Aalborg	3-0
1979	B 1903 Hellerup v Koge BK	1-0	1988	AGF Aarhus v Brondbyernes IF	2-1 aet
1980	Hvidovre IF v Lyngby BK	5-3	1989	Brondbyernes IF v Ikast FS	6-3 aet
1981	Vejle BK v Frem Copenhagen	2-1			

FEATURED CLUBS IN EUROPEAN COMPETITION

AGF Aarhus	**B93 Copenhagen**	**B 1903 Copenhagen**	**Brondbyernes IF**
Esbjeg FB	**Frem Copenhagen**	**Hvidovre IF**	**Koge BK**
Lyngby BK	**Naestved IF**	**OB Odense**	**Vejle BK**
AaB Aalborg	**AB Akademisk Boldklub**	**B 1909 Odense**	**B 1913 Odense**
KB Copenhagen	**Randers Freja**	**Fremad Amager Copenhagen**	**Vanlose IF Copenhagen**
Holbaek BI	**B 1901 Nykobing**	**F Copenhagen XI**	**Staevnet**
Odense Combination XI	**Ikast FS**		

AGF (Aarhus Gymnastik Forening)

Founded 1880   Colours white shirts, blue shorts
Stadium Aarhus (25,000) ☎ 06-14 10 70/14 55 60
Champions 1955, 1956, 1957, 1960, 1986
Cup Winners 1955, 1957, 1960, 1961, 1965, 1987, 1988

Season	Opponent	Home	Result	Away	Rnd	Cup
1955-56	Stade de Reims, France	0-2*		2-2	1	ECC
		*in Copenhagen				
1956-57	OGC Nice, France	1-1*		1-5	pr	ECC
		*in Copenhagen				
1957-58	Glenavon, Ireland	0-0		3-0	pr	ECC
	Sevilla CF, Spain	2-0		0-4	1	ECC
1960-61	Legia Warsaw, Poland	3-0		0-1	1	ECC
	Fredrikstad FK, Norway	3-0		1-0	2	ECC
	Benfica, Portugal	1-4		1-3	qf	ECC
1961-62			bye		1	CWC
	Werder Bremen, Germany	2-3		0-2	2	CWC
1965-66	Vitoria Setubal, Portugal	2-1		2-1	1	CWC
	Glasgow Celtic, Scotland	0-1		0-2	2	CWC
1979-80	Stal Meilec, Poland	1-1		1-0	1	UEFA
	Bayern Munich, Germany	1-2		1-3	2	UEFA
1983-84	Glasgow Celtic, Scotland	1-4		0-1	1	UEFA
1984-85	Widzew Lodz, Poland	1-0		0-2	1	UEFA
1985-86	Waregem KSV, Belgium	0-1		2-5	1	UEFA
1987-88	Juenesse Esch, Luxembourg	4-1		0-1	1	ECC
	Benfica, Portugal	0-0		0-1	2	ECC
1988-89	Glenavon, Ireland	3-1		4-1	1	CWC
	Cardiff City, Wales	4-0		2-1	2	CWC
	FC Barcelona, Spain	0-1		0-0	qf	CWC

B93 (Boldklubben Af 1893) COPENHAGEN

Founded 1893   Colours white shirts, blue shorts
Stadium Osterbro Stadion (7,000) ☎ 01-38 18 90/38 18 93
Champions 1916, 1927, 1929, 1930, 1934, 1935, 1939, 1942, 1946
Cup Winners 1982

Season	Opponent	Home	Result	Away	Rnd	Cup
1982-83	Dynamo Dresden, East Germany	2-1	wag	2-3	1	CWC
	Waterschei Thor Genk, Belgium	0-2		1-4	2	CWC

B 1903 HELLERUP (Boldklubben AF 1903)

Founded 1903   Colours white shirts, black shorts
Stadium Gentofte Stadion (18,000) ☎ 01-65 19 03
Champions 1920, 1924, 1926, 1938, 1969, 1970, 1976
Cup Winners 1979, 1986

Season	Opponent	Home	result	Away	Rnd	Cup
1970-71	Slovan Bratislava, Czechoslovakia	2-2		1-2	1	ECC
1971-72	Glasgow Celtic, Scotland	2-1		0-3	1	ECC
1973-74	AIK Stockholm, Sweden	2-1		1-1	1	UEFA
	Dynamo Kiev, USSR	1-2		0-1	2	UEFA
1975-76	1.FC Koln, Germany	2-3		0-2	1	UEFA
1977-78	Trabzonspor, Turkey	2-0		0-1	1	ECC
	Benfica, Portugal	0-1		0-1	2	ECC
1978-79	KuPS Kuopion Palloseura, Finland	4-4		1-2	1	UEFA
1979-80	Apoel Nicosia, Cyprus	6-0		1-0	pr	CWC
	Valencia CF, Spain	2-2		0-4	1	CWC
1983-84	Banik Ostrava, Czechoslovakia	1-1		0-5	1	UEFA
1986-87	Vitosha Sofia, Bulgaria	1-0		0-2	1	CWC

BRONDBYERNES (Brondbyernes Idraetsforening)

Founded 1964   Colours yellow shirts, white shorts
Stadium Brondby Stadion (10,000) ☎ 02-63 08 10/45 93 94
Champions 1985, 1987, 1988
Cup Winners 1989

Season	Opponent	Home	result	Away	Rnd	Cup
1986-87	Honved Budapest, Hungary	4-1		2-2	1	ECC
	BFC Dynamo Berlin, East Germany	2-1		1-1	2	ECC
	FC Porto, Portugal	1-1		0-1	qf	ECC
1987-88	IFK Gothenburg, Sweden	2-1		0-0	1	UEFA
	Sportul Studentesc Bucharest, Romania	3-0	0-3p	0-3	2	UEFA
1988-89	Club Bruges, Belgium	2-1	lag	0-1	1	ECC
1989-90	Olmpique Marseille, France	1-1		0-3	1	ECC

ESBJERG (Forenede Boldklubber)

Founded 1924   Colours white shirts, blue shorts
Stadium Esbjerg Idraetspark (20,000) ☎ 05-12 37 19
Champions 1961, 1962, 1963, 1965, 1979
Cup Winners 1964, 1976

Season	Opponent	Home	Result	Away	Rnd	Cup
1962-63	Linfield, Ireland	0-0		2-1	1	ECC
	Dukla Prague, Czechoslovakia	0-0		0-5	2	ECC
1963-64	PSV Eindhoven, Holland	3-4		1-7	pr	ECC
1964-65	Cardiff City, Wales	0-0		0-1	pr	CWC
1966-67	Dukla Prague, Czechoslovakia	0-2		0-4	pr	ECC
1976-77	Bohemians Dublin, Eire	0-1		1-2	1	CWC
1978-79	IFK Start Kristiansand, Norway	1-0		0-0	1	UEFA
	KuPS Kuopion Palloseura, Finland	4-1		2-0	2	UEFA
	Hertha BSC Berlin, Germany	2-1		0-4	3	UEFA
1979-80	Zbrojovka Brno, Czechoslovakia	1-1		0-6	1	UEFA
1980-81	Halmstad BK, Sweden	3-2		0-0	1	ECC
	Spartak Moscow, USSR	2-0		0-3	2	ECC

DENMARK

FREM (Copenhagen)

Founded 1886   Colours red and blue hooped shirts, white shorts
Stadium Valby Idraetspark (12,000) ☎ 01-17 13 17
Champions 1923, 1931, 1933, 1936, 1941, 1944
Cup Winners 1956, 1978

Season	Opponent	Home	Result	Away	Rnd	Cup
1958-60	Chelsea, England	1-3		1-4	1	Fairs
1967-68	Atletico Bilbao, Spain	0-1		2-3	1	Fairs
1969-70	St Gallen, Switzerland	2-1	lag	0-1	1	CWC
1972-73	Sochaux, France	2-1		3-1	1	UEFA
	Twente Enschede, Holland	0-5		0-4	abd	UEFA
1977-78	Grasshoppers Zurich, Switzerland	0-2		1-6	1	UEFA
1978-79	Nancy, France	2-0		0-4	1	CWC

HVIDOVRE IDRAETSFORENING

Founded 1925   Colours red shirts, blue shorts
Stadium Hvidovre Stadion (15,000) ☎ 01-78 11 33
Champions 1966, 1973, 1981
Cup Winners 1980

Season	Opponent	Home	Result	Away	Rnd	Cup
1967-68	FC Basle, Switzerland	3-3		2-1	1	ECC
	Real Madrid, Spain	2-2		1-4	2	ECC
1969-70	FC Porto, Portugal	1-2		0-2	1	Fairs
1972-73	HIFK Helsinki, Finland	walk over			1	UEFA
	Borussia Monchengladbach, Germany	1-3		0-3	2	UEFA
1974-75	Ruch Chorzow, Poland	0-0		1-2	1	ECC
1980-81	Fram Reykjavik, Iceland	1-0		2-0	1	CWC
	Feyenoord Rotterdam, Holland	1-2		0-1	2	CWC
1982-83	Juventus, Italy	1-4		3-3	1	ECC

KOGE BOLDKLUB

Founded 1927   Colours black and white striped shirts, black shorts
Stadium Koge Stadion (14,500) ☎ 03-65 12 56
Champions 1954, 1975

Season	Opponent	Home	Result	Away	Rnd	Cup
1976-77	Bayern Munich, Germany	0-5		1-2	1	ECC

LYNGBY BOLDKLUB 1921

Founded 1921   Colours blue shirts, white shorts
Stadium Lyngby Stadion (15,000) ☎ 02-88 46 00
Champions 1983
Cup Winners 1984, 1985

Season	Opponent	Home	Result	Away	Rnd	Cup
1982-83	IK Brage, Sweden	1-2		2-2	1	UEFA
1984-85	Labinoti Elbasan, Albania	3-0		3-0	1	ECC
	Sparta Prague, Czechoslovakia	1-2		0-0	2	ECC
1985-86	Galway United, Eire	1-0		3-2	1	CWC
	Red Star Belgrade, Yugoslavia	2-2		1-3	2	CWC
1986-87	FC Neuchatel Xamax, Switzerland	1-3		0-2	1	UEFA

NAESTVED IDRAETS FORENING

Founded 1939   Colours green shirts, white shorts
Stadium Naestved Stadion (20,000) ☎ 03-72 98 78/72 08 22

Season	Opponent	Home	Result	Away	Rnd	Cup
1973-74	Fortuna Dusseldorf, Germany	2-2		0-1	1	UEFA
1976-77	RWD Molenbeeck, Belgium	0-		0-4	1	UEFA
1981-82	PSV Eindhoven, Holland	2-1		0-7	1	UEFA
1989-90	Zenit Leningrad, USSR	0-0		1-3	1	UEFA

OB (Odense Boldklub)

Founded 1887   Colours blue and white striped shirts, blue shorts
Stadium Odense Stadion (30,000) ☎09-12 17 03
Champions 1977, 1982, 1989
Cup Winners 1983

Season	Opponent	Home	Result	Away	Rnd	Cup
1978-79	Lokomotiv Sofia, Bulgaria	2-2		1-2	1	ECC
1983-84	Liverpool, England	0-1		0-5	1	ECC
1984-85	Spartak Moscow, USSR	1-5		1-2	1	UEFA

VEJLE BOLDKLUB

Founded 1981   Colours red shirts, white shorts
Stadium Vejle Stadion (18,500) ☎ 05-82 20 91
Champions 1958, 1971, 1978, 1984
Cup Winners 1958, 1959, 1972, 1975, 1977, 1981

Season	Opponent	Home	Result	Away	Rnd	Cup
1972-73	RSC Anderlecht, Belgium	0-3		2-4	1	ECC
1973-74	FC Nantes, France	2-2		1-0	1	ECC
	Glasgow Celtic, Scotland	0-1		0-0	2	ECC
1975-76	FC Den Haag, Holland	0-2		0-2	1	CWC
1977-78	Progres Niedercorn, Luxembourg	9-0		1-0	1	CWC
	PAOK Salonika, Greece	3-0		1-2	2	CWC
	Twente Enschede, Holland	0-3		0-4	qf	CWC
1979-80	FK Austria Vienna, Austria	3-2		1-1	1	ECC
	Hajduk Split, Yugoslavia	0-3		2-1	2	ECC
1981-82	FC Porto, Portugal	2-1		0-3	1	CWC
1985-86	Steaua Bucharest, Romania	1-1		1-4	1	ECC

AaB (Aalborg Boldspilklub)

Founded 1885   Colours red and white striped shirts, white shorts
Stadium Aalborg Stadion (22,000) ☎ 08-15 72 22
Cup Winners 1966, 1970

Season	Opponent	Home	Result	Away	Rnd	Cup
1966-67	Everton, England	0-0		1-2	pr	CWC
1970-71	Gornik Zabrze, Poland	0-1		1-8	1	CWC
1987-88	Hadjuk Split, Yugoslavia	1-0	2-4p	0-1	1	CWC

DENMARK

AB AKADEMISK BOLDKLUB BAGS VAERD

Founded 1889   Colours green shirts, white shorts
Stadium Gladsaxe Idraetspark (10,000) ☎ 02-98 75 33
Champions 1919, 1921, 1937, 1943, 1945, 1947, 1951, 1952, 1967

Season	Opponent	Home	Result	Away	Rnd	Cup
1968-69	FC Zurich, Switzerland	1-2		3-1	1	EC
	AEK Athens, Greece	0-2		0-0	2	ECC
1970-71	Sliema Wanderers, Malta	7-0		3-2	1	Fairs
	RSC Anderlecht, Belgium	1-3		0-4	2	Fairs
1971-72	Dundee, Scotland	0-1		2-4	1	UEFA

B 1909 (Boldklubben AF 1909 Odense)

Founded 1909   Colours red shirts, white shorts
Stadium Odense Stadion (30,000) ☎ 09-10 29 09
Champions 1959, 1964
Cup Winners 1962, 1971

Season	Opponent	Home	Result	Away	Rnd	Cup
1959-60	Wiener Sport Club, Austria	0-3		2-2	1	ECC
1962-63	Alliance Dudelange, Luxembourg	8-1		1-1	1	CWC
	Grazer AK (GAK), Austria	5-3		1-1	2	CWC
	1.FC Nurnburg, Germany	0-1		0-6	qf	CWC
1964-65	Real Madrid, Spain	2-5		0-4	1	ECC
1965-66	Dinamo Bucharest, Romania	2-3		0-4	pr	ECC
1966-67	bye				1	Fairs
	Napoli, Italy	1-4		1-2	2	Fairs
1968-69	Hannover 96, Germany	2-3		0-1	1	Fairs
1969-70	CF Barcelona, Spain	0-2		0-4	1	Fairs
1971-72	FK Austria Vienna, Austria	4-2	lag	0-2	pr	CWC

B 1913 (Boldklubben Af 1913 Odense)

Founded 1913   Colours blue shirts, white shorts
Stadium Odense Stadion (30,000) ☎ 09-15 68 13
Cup Winners 1963

Season	Opponent	Home	Result	Away	Rnd	Cup
1961-62	CA Spora, Luxembourg	9-2		6-0	pr	ECC
	Real Madrid, Spain	0-3		0-9	1	ECC
1963-64	Olympique Lyon, France	1-3		1-3	1	CWC
1964-65	VfB Stuttgart, Germany	1-3		0-1	pr	Fairs

KB (Kjobenhavns Boldklub)

Founded 1876   Colours blue and white stripped shirts, blue shorts
Stadium Idraetspark (43,000) ☎ 01-71 41 50
Champions 1913, 1914, 1917, 1918, 1922, 1925, 1932, 1940, 1948, 1949, 1950, 1953, 1968, 1974, 1980
Cup Winners 1969

Season	Opponent	Home	Result	Away	Rnd	Cup
1958-59	FC Schalke 04 Gelsenkirchen, Germany	3-0	1-3*	2-5	pr	ECC
			*in Enschede			
1960-61	Basel City XI, Switzerland	8-1		3-3	1	Fairs
	Birmingham City, England	4-4		0-5	2	Fairs
1964-65	DOS Utrecht, Holland	3-4		1-2	pr	Fairs
1965-66			bye		1	Fairs
	Dunfermline Athletic, Scotland	2-4		0-5	2	Fairs
1968-69	1.FC Lokomotive Leipzig, East Germany	withdrew				Fairs
1969-70	TPS Turun Palloseura Turku, Finland	4-0		1-0	pr	ECC
	Benfica, Portugal	2-3		0-2	1	ECC
1974-75	Atletico Madrid, Spain	3-2		0-4	1	UEFA
1975-76	St Etienne, France	0-2		1-3	1	ECC
1977-78	Dundee United, Scotland	3-0		0-1	1	UEFA
	Dynamo Tbilisi, USSR	1-4		1-2	2	UEFA
1980-81	Grasshoppers Zurich, Switzerland	2-5		1-3	1	UEFA
1981-82	Athlone Town, Eire	1-1	wag	2-2	1	ECC
	Universitatea Craiova, Romania	1-0		1-4	2	ECC
1984-85	Fortuna Sittard, Holland	0-0		0-3	1	CWC

RANDERS SPORTSKLUB FREJA

Founded 1898   Colours blue and white striped shirts, blue shorts
Stadium Randers Stadion (20,000) ☎ 06-42 46 86
Cup Winners 1967, 1968, 1973

Season	Opponent	Home	Result	Away	Rnd	Cup
1967-68	Hamburger SV, Germany	0-2		3-5	1	CWC
1968-69	Shamrock Rovers, Eire	1-0		2-1	1	CWC
	Sliema Wanderers, Malta	6-0		2-0	2	CWC
	1.FC Koln, Germany	0-3		1-2	qf	CWC
1973-74	Rapid Vienna, Austria	0-0		1-2	1	CWC
1974-75	Dynamo Dresden, East Germany	1-1	lag	0-0	1	UEFA

FREMAD AMAGER (Copenhagen)

Founded 1910   Colours blue shirts, white shorts
Stadium Sundby Idraetspark (9,000) ☎ 01-55 52 81

Season	Opponent	Home	Result	Away	Rnd	Cup
1972-73	FC Besa Kavaja, Albania	1-1	lag	0-0	1	CWC

VANLOSE IDRAETS FORENING

Founded 1921   Colours white shirts, blue shorts
Stadium Vanlose Idraetspark (10,000) ☎ 01-71 10 70
Cup Winners 1974

Season	Opponent	Home	Result	Away	Rnd	Cup
1974-75	Benfica, Portugal	1-4		0-4	1	CWC

DENMARK

HOLBAEK BOLD & IDRAETSFORENING

Founded 1931   Colours blue shirts, white shorts
Stadium Holbaek Stadion (10,500) ☎ 03-43 33 10/43 23 40

Season	Opponent	Home	Result	Away	Rnd	Cup
1975-76	Stal Mielec, Poland	0-1		1-2	1	UEFA
1976-77	Eintracht Braunschweig, Germany	1-0		0-7	1	UEFA

B 1901 (Nykobing Falster Boldklub Af 1901)

Founded 1901   Colours blue and white striped shirts, blue shorts
Stadium Nykobing Idraetspark (8,500) ☎03-8 19 01

Season	Opponent	Home	Result	Away	Rnd	Cup
1970-71	Hertha BSC Berlin, Germany	2-4		1-4	1	Fairs
1983-84	Shakhtyor Donetsk, USSR	1-5		2-4	1	CWC

COPENHAGEN XI

Season	Opponent	Home	Result	Away	Rnd	Cup
1955-58	CF Barcelona, Spain	1-1		2-6	pr	Fairs

STAEVNET

Combination of B93 and KB, the original members, which was formed in 1904, AB and Frem joined together in 1911, then all four teams amalgamated in 1912 to play top teams from abroad, B 1903 joined the rest in 1923.

Season	Opponent	Home	Result	Away	Rnd	Cup
1961-62	Dinamo Zagreb, Yugoslavia	2-2		2-7	1	Fairs
1962-63	Hibernian, Scotland	2-3		0-4	1	Fairs
1963-64	Arsenal, England	1-7		3-2	1	Fairs

ODENSE COMBINED XI

Season	Opponent	Home	Result	Away	Rnd	Cup
1962-63	Drumcondra, Eire	4-2		1-4	pr	Fairs

IKAST FS

Founded 1935   Colours yellow shirts, blue shorts
Stadium Ikast Stadion (15,000) ☎ 07-15 12 43

Season	Opponent	Home	result	Away	Rnd	Cup
1988-89	First Vienna FC 1894, Austria	2-1	lag	0-1	1	UEFA
1989-90	FC Groningen, Holland	1-2		0-1	1	CWC

EAST GERMANY

Founded 1948 Deutscher Fussball-Verband, StorkowerStrasse 118, 1055 Berlin ☎ 4384 250/43286 690 Fax 2-436 53 51
National Colours white shirts, blue shorts, white socks
Season August to June (with Winter break)
Founded 1899

LEAGUE CHAMPIONS

SPRING-AUTUMN SEASON		**SPRING-AUTUMN SEASON**		**SPRING-AUTUMN SEASON**	**1978**	Dynamo Dresden
Russian Zone		**1956**	SC Wismut Karl Marx	**1966** FC Vorwaerts Berlin	**1979**	BFC Dynamo Berlin
1948	SG Planitz v		Stadt	**1967** FC Karl Marx Stadt		
	Freiimfelde Halle 1-0	**1957**	SC Wismut Karl Marx	**1968** FC Carl Zeiss Jena	**1980**	BFC Dynamo Berlin
1949	ZSG Halle v		Stadt	**1969** FC Vorwaerts Berlin	**1981**	BFC Dynamo Berlin
	Fortuna Erfurt 4-1	**1958**	ASK Vorwaerts Berlin		**1982**	BFC Dynamo Berlin
		1959	SC Wismut Karl Marx	**1970** FC Carl Zeiss Jena	**1983**	BFC Dynamo Berlin
AUTUMN-SPRING SEASON			Stadt	**1971** Dynamo Dresden	**1984**	BFC Dynamo Berlin
1950	Horch Zwickau	**1960**	ASK Vorwaerts Berlin	**1972** 1.FC Magdeburg	**1985**	BFC Dynamo Berlin
1951	Chemie Leipzig	**AUTUMN-SPRING SEASON**		**1973** Dynamo Dresden	**1986**	BFC Dynamo Berlin
1952	Turbine Halle	**1962**	ASK Vorwaerts Berlin	**1974** 1.FC Magdeburg	**1987**	BFC Dynamo Berlin
1953	Dynamo Dresden	**1963**	SC Motor Jena	**1975** 1.FC Magdeburg	**1988**	BFC Dynamo Berlin
1954	Turbine Erfurt	**1964**	Chemie Leipzig	**1976** Dynamo Dresden	**1989**	Dynamo Dresden
1955	Turbine Erfurt	**1965**	ASK Vorwaerts Berlin	**1977** Dynamo Dresden		

CUP WINNERS

1949	Dessau Waggon v Gera Sud	1-0	**1961**	not held	
			1962	SC Chemie Halle Leuno v SC Dynamo Berlin	3-1
1950	Thale EHW v KWU Erfurt	4-0	**1963**	Motor Zwickau v Chemie Zeitz	3-0
1951	not held		**1964**	SC Aufbau Magdeburg v SC Leipzig	3-2
1952	Dresden VP v Einheit Pankow	3-0	**1965**	SC Aufbau Magdeburg v SC Motor Jena	2-1
1953	not held		**1966**	Chemie Leipzig v Lokomotiv Stendal	1-0
1954	ASK Vorwaerts Berlin v Motor Zwickau	2-1	**1967**	Motor Zwickau v Hansa Rostock	3-0
1955	Wismut Karl Marx v Empor Rostock	3-2	**1968**	1.FC Union Berlin v FC Carl Zeiss Jena	2-1
1956	SC Chemie Halle Leuno v ASK Vorwaerts Berlin	2-1	**1969**	1.FC Magdeburg v FC Karl Marx Stadt	4-0
1957	SC Lokomotiv Leipzig v Empor Rostock	2-1			
1958	Dresden Einheit v SC Lokomotive Leipzig	2-1	**1970**	FC Vorwaerts Berlin v 1.FC Lokomotive Leipzig	4-2
1959	SC Dynamo Berlin v SC Wismut Karl Marx Stadt	3-2	**1971**	Dynamo Dresden v BFC Dynamo Berlin	2-1
1960	SC Motor Jena v Empor Rostock	3-2	**1972**	FC Carl Zeiss Jena v Dynamo Dresden	2-1

75

EAST GERMANY

1973	1.FC Magdeburg v 1.FC Lokomotive Leipzig	3-2
1974	FC Carl Zeiss Jena v Dynamo Dresden	3-1
1975	Sachsenring Zwickau v Dynamo Dresden	2-2 4-3
1976	1.FC Lokomotive Leipzig v FC Vorwaerts Frankfurt	3-0
1977	Dynamo Dresden v 1.FC Lokomotive Leipzig	3-2
1978	1.FC Magdeburg v Dynamo Dresden	1-0
1979	1.FC Magdeburg v BFC Dynamo Berlin	1-0
1980	FC Carl Zeiss Jena v FC Rot Weiss Erfurt	3-1

1981	1.FC Lokomotive Leipzig v FC Vorwaerts Frankfurt	4-1
1982	Dynamo Dresden v BFC Dynamo Berlin	1-1 5-4 pens
1983	1.FC Magdeburg v FC Karl Marx Stadt	4-0
1984	Dynamo Dresden v BFC Dynamo Berlin	2-1
1985	Dynamo Dresden v BFC Dynamo Berlin	3-2
1986	1.FC Lokomotive Leipzig v 1.FC Union Berlin	5-1
1987	1.FC Lokomotive Leipzig v FC Hansa Rostock	4-1
1988	BFC Dynamo Berlin v FC Carl Zeiss Jena	2-0 aet
1989	BFC Dynamo Berlin v FC Karl Marx Stadt	1-0

EAST GERMAN SUPER CUP

1989	BFC Dynamo Berlin v Dynamo Dresden	4-1

FEATURED CLUBS IN EUROPEAN COMPETITION

FC Carl Zeiss Jena	**Chemie Leipzig**	**FC Vorwaerts Berlin/Frankfurt**	**1FC Magdeburg**
1FC Lokomotiv Leipzig	**FC Karl Marx Stadt**	**SC Wismut Aue**	**Sachsenring Zwickau**
BFC Dynamo Berlin	**Dynamo Dresden**	**1FC Union Berlin**	**FC Hansa Rostock**
Stahl Brandenburg	**HFC Chemie (Halle)**	**Leipzig Selection**	

FC CARL ZEISS JENA

Founded 1945 as Motor Jena, 1957 as SC Motor Jena, 1.1.1966 as FC Carl Zeiss Jena
Colours blue and white shirts, white shorts
Stadium Ernst Abbe Sportfield (18,000) ☎ 078-83 33 66
Champions 1963 as SC Motor Jena, 1968, 1970
Cup Winners 1961 as SC Motor Jena, 1972, 1974, 1980
CWC Final ists 1981

Season	Opponents	Home	Result	Away	Rnd	Cup
as SC MOTOR JENA						
1961-62	Swansea Town, Wales	5-1	in Linz	2-2	1	CWC
	Alliance Dudelingen, Luxembourg	7-0	Erfurt	2-2	2	CWC
	Leixoes Sport Club, Portugal	1-1*		3-1**	qf	CWC
		* in Jena		** in Gera		
	Atletico Madrid, Spain	0-1	Malmo	0-4	sf	CWC
1963-64	Dinamo Bucharest, Romania	0-1		0-2	1	ECC
as FC CARL ZEISS JENA						
1968-69	Withdrew					ECC
1969-70	Altay Izmir, Turkey	1-0		0-0	1	Fairs
	Cagliari Sardinia, Italy	2-0		1-0	2	Fairs
	Ujpest Dozsa, Hungary	1-0		3-0	3	Fairs
	Ajax Amsterdam, Holland	3-1		1-5	qf	Fairs
1970-71	Fenerbahce, Turkey	1-0		4-0	1	ECC
	Sporting Lisbon, Portugal	2-1		2-1	2	ECC
	Red Star Belgrade, Yugoslavia	3-2		0-4	qf	ECC
1971-72	Lokomotiv Plovdiv, Bulgaria	3-0		1-3	1	UEFA
	OFK Belgrade, Yugoslavia	4-0		1-1	2	UEFA
	Wolverhampton Wanderers, England	0-1		0-3	3	UEFA
1972-73	MP Mikkeli, Finland	6-1		2-3	1	CWC
	Leeds United, England	0-0		0-2	2	CWC
1973-74	MP Mikkeli, Finland	3-0		3-0	1	UEFA
	Ruch Chorzow, Poland	1-0		0-3	2	UEFA
1974-75	Slavia Prague, Czechoslovakia	1-0	3-2p	0-1	1	CWC
	Benfica, Portugal	1-1	lag	0-0	2	CWC

1975-76	Olympique Marseille, France	3-0		1-0	1	UEFA
	Stal Mielec, Poland	1-0	2-3p	0-1	2	UEFA
1977-78	Altay Izmir, Turkey	5-1		1-4	1	UEFA
	RWD Molenbeeck, Belgium	1-1	6-5p	1-1	2	UEFA
	Standard Liege, Belgium	2-0		2-1	3	UEFA
	SEC Bastia Corsica, France	4-2		2-7	qf	UEFA
1978-79	Lierse SK, Belgium	1-0		2-2	1	UEFA
	MSV Duisberg, Germany	0-0		0-3	2	UEFA
1979-80	West Bromwich Albion, England	2-0		2-1	1	UEFA
	Red Star Belgrade, Yugoslavia	2-3		2-3	2	UEFA
1980-81	AS Roma, Italy	4-0		0-3	1	CWC
	Valencia CF, Spain	3-1		0-1	2	CWC
	Newport County, Wales	2-2		1-0	qf	CWC
	Benfica, Portugal	2-0		0-1	sf	CWC
	Dynamo Tbilisi, USSR	1-2	in Dusseldorf		FINAL	CWC
1981-82	Dinamo Tirana, Albania	4-0		0-1	1	UEFA
	Real Madrid, Spain	0-0		2-3	2	UEFA
1982-83	Girondins Bordeaux, France	3-1		0-5	1	UEFA
1983-84	IBV Vestmannaeyjar, Iceland	3-0		0-0	1	UEFA
	Sparta Rotterdam, Holland	1-1		2-3	2	UEFA
1986-87	Bayer Uerdingen, Germany	0-4		0-3	1	UEFA
1988-89	FC Kremser, Austria	5-0		0-1	1	CWC
	Sampdoria, Italy	1-1		1-3	2	CWC

CHEMIE LEIPZIG

Founded 1945 as Industrie Leipzig, 1950 as Chemie Leipzig, 1954 as Rotation Leipzig, 1963 as Chemie Leipzig
Colours white shirts, green shorts
Stadium Georg Schwarz Sportpark (22,000) ☎ 2-51 13 95
Champions 1951, 1964
Cup Winners 1966

Season	Opponent	Home	Result	Away	Rnd	Cup
1964-65	Vasas Gyoer Eto, Hungary	0-2		2-4	pr	ECC
1966-67	Legia Warsaw, Poland	3-0		2-2	1	CWC
	Standard Liege, Belgium	2-1	lag	0-1	2	CWC

FC VORWAERTS FRANKFURT ON ODER

Founded 1946 as Vorwaerts Leipzig, 1952 as KVP Vorwaerts Leipzig, 1954 promoted and moved to Berlin as ASK Vorwaerts Berlin, 1965 as FC Vorwaerts Berlin, 1971 moved to and became FC Vorwaerts on Oder
Colours yellow shirts, white shorts
Stadium Stadion der Freundschaft (18,000) ☎ 030-23 614
Champions 1958, 1960, 1962, 1965 as ASK Vorwaerts Berlin, 1966, 1969 as FC Vorwaerts Berlin
Cup Winners 1960, 1970
Cup Winners 1954 as ASK Vorwaerts Berlin, 1970 as FC Vorwaerts Berlin

			Playoff			
Season	Opponent	Home	Result	Away	Rnd	Cup
1959-60	Wolverhampton Wanderers, England	2-1		0-2	pr	ECC
1960-61	Red Star Brno, Czechoslovakia	2-1		0-2	pr	CWC
1961-62	Linfield, Ireland	3-0		no 2nd leg	1	ECC
	Glasgow Rangers, Scotland	1-2		1-4*	2	ECC
				* in Malmo		
1962-63	Dukla Prague, Czechoslovakia	0-3		0-1	pr	ECC
1965-66	Drumcondra, Eire	3-0		0-1	1	ECC
	Manchester United, England	0-2		1-3	2	ECC
1966-67	Waterford, Eire	6-0		6-1*	pr	ECC
				* in Dublin		
	Gornik Zabrze, Poland	2-1	1-3*	1-2	1	ECC
				* in Budapest		

EAST GERMANY

as FC VORWAERTS BERLIN

1969-70	Panathinaikos, Greece	2-0		1-1	1	ECC
	Red Star Belgrade, Yugoslavia	2-1	wag	2-3	2	ECC
	Feyenoord Rotterdam, Holland	1-0		0-2	qf	ECC
1970-71	Bologna, Italy	0-0	wag	1-1	1	CWC
	Benfica, Portugal	2-0 aet	4-3p	0-2	2	CWC
	PSV Eindhoven, Holland	1-0		0-2	qf	CWC

as FC VORWAERTS FRANKFURT ON ODER

1974-75	Juventus, Italy	2-1		0-3	1	UEFA
1980-81	Ballymena United, Ireland	3-0		1-2	1	UEFA
	VfB Stuttgart, Germany	1-2		1-5	2	UEFA
1982-83	Werder Bremen, Germany	1-3	lag	2-0	1	UEFA
1983-84	Nottingham Forest, England	0-1		0-2	1	UEFA
1984-85	PSV Eindhoven, Holland	2-0		0-3	1	UEFA

1.FC MAGDEBURG

Founded 1950 as Aufbau Magdeburg, 22.12.1965 as 1FC Magdeburg
Colours white shirts, blue shorts
Stadium Heinrich Gerner Stadion (22,000) 091-57 322
Champions 1972, 1974, 1975
Cup Winners 1964, 1965, 1969, 1973, 1978, 1979, 1983
CWC Winners 1974

Season	Opponent	Home	Playoff Result	Away	Rnd	Cup
as AUFBAU MAGDEBURG						
1964-65	Galatasaray, Turkey	1-1	1-1*lot	1-1	pr	CWC
						* in Vienna
as 1.FC MAGDEBURG						
1965-66	Spora CA, Luxembourg	1-0		2-0	1	CWC
	FC Sion, Switzerland	8-1		2-2	2	CWC
	West Ham United, England	1-1		0-1	qf	CWC
1969-70	MTK Budapest, Hungary	1-0		1-1	1	CWC
	Academica Coimbra, Portugal	1-0		0-2	2	CWC
1972-73	TPS Turun Palloseura Turku, Finland	6-0		3-1	1	ECC
	Juventus, Italy	0-1		0-1	2	ECC
1973-74	NAC Breda, Holland	2-0		0-0	1	CWC
	Banik Ostrava, Czechoslovakia	3-0		0-2	2	CWC
	Beroe Stara Zagora, Bulgaria	2-0		1-1	qf	CWC
	Sporting Lisbon, Portugal	2-1		1-1	sf	CWC
	AC Milan, Italy	2-0	in Rotterdam		FINAL	CWC
1974-75	bye				1	ECC
	Bayern Munich, Germany	1-2		2-3	2	ECC
1975-76	Malmo FF, Sweden	2-1	1-2 pens	1-2	1	ECC
1976-77	Cesena, Italy	3-0		1-3	1	UEFA
	Dinamo Zagreb, Yugoslavia	2-0		2-2	2	UEFA
	Videoton Sekesfehurvar, Hungary	5-0		0-1	3	UEFA
	Juventus, Italy	1-3		0-1	qf	UEFA
1977-78	Odra Opole, Poland	1-1		2-1	1	UEFA
	FC Schalke 04 Gelsenkirchen, Germany	4-2		3-1	2	UEFA
	RC Lens, France	4-0		0-2	3	UEFA
	PSV Eindhoven, Holland	1-0		2-4	qf	UEFA
1978-79	Valur Reykjavik, Iceland	4-0		1-1	1	CWC
	Ferencvarosi TC, Hungary	1-0	wag	1-2	2	CWC
	Banik Ostrava, Czechoslovakia	2-1		2-4	qf	CWC
1979-80	Wrexham, Wales	5-2		2-3	1	CWC
	Arsenal, England	2-2		1-2	2	CWC
1980-81	Moss FK, Norway	2-1		3-2	1	UEFA
	Torino, Italy	1-0		1-3	2	UEFA
1981-82	Borussia Monchengladbach, Germany	3-1	lag	0-2	1	UEFA
1983-84	Swansea City, Wales	1-0		1-1	pr	CWC
	FC Barcelona, Spain	1-5		0-2	1	CWC
1986-87	Athletic Bilbao, Spain	1-0		0-2	1	UEFA

1.FC LOKOMOTIVE LEIPZIG

Founded 1949 ZSG Industrie Leipzig, 1951 split into SC Lokomotive and BSG Chemie who folded in 1970,
1954 as SC Leipzig, as Einheit Ost Leipzig, 1963 as SC Leipzig, 1966 1.FC Lokomotive Leipzig
Colours yellow shirts, blue shorts
Stadium Bruno Plache Stadion (35,000) ☎ 041-85747
Cup Winners 1957, 1976, 1981, 1986, 1987
CWC Finalists 1987

Season	Opponent	Home	Playoff Result	Away	Rnd	Cup
as SC LEIPZIG						
1963-64	Ujpest Dozsa, Hungary	0-0		2-3	1	Fairs
1964-65	Wiener SportClub, Austria	0-1		1-2	pr	Fairs
as 1.FC LOKOMOTIVE LEIPZIG						
1965-66	bye				1	Fairs
	Leeds United, England	1-2		0-0	2	Fairs
1966-67	Djurgarden IF Stockholm, Sweden	2-1		3-1	1	Fairs
	RFC Liege, Belgium	0-0		2-1	2	Fairs
	Benfica, Portugal	3-1		1-2	3	Fairs
	Kilmarnock, Scotland	1-0		0-2	qf	Fairs
1967-68	Linfield, Ireland	5-1		0-1	1	Fairs
	Vojvodina Novi Sad, Yugoslavia	0-2		0-0	2	Fairs
1968-69	KB Copenhagen, Denmark KB		withdrew		1	Fairs
	Hibernian, Scotland	0-1		1-3	2	Fairs
1973-74	Torino, Italy	2-1		2-1	1	UEFA
	Wolverhampton Wanderers, England	3-0	wag	1-4	2	UEFA
	Fortuna Dusseldorf, Germany	3-0		1-2	3	UEFA
	Ipswich Town, England	1-0	4-3 pen	0-1	qf	UEFA
	Tottenham Hotspur, England	1-2		0-2	sf	UEFA
1976-77	Heart of Midlothian, Scotland	2-0		1-5	1	CWC
1977-78	Coleraine, Ireland	2-2		4-1	1	CWC
	Real Betis, Spain	1-1		1-2	2	CWC
1978-79	Arsenal, England	1-4		0-3	1	UEFA
1981-82	Politechnica Timisoara, Romania	5-0		0-2	pr	CWC
	Swansea City, Wales	2-1		1-0	1	CWC
	Velez Mostar, Yugoslavia	1-1	3-0 pen	1-1	2	CWC
	FC Barcelona, Spain	0-3		2-1	qf	CWC
1982-83	Viking Stavanger, Norway	3-2		0-1	1	UEFA
1983-84	Girondins Bordeaux, France	4-0		3-2	1	UEFA
	Werder Bremen, Germany	1-0		1-1	2	UEFA
	Sturm Graz, Austria	1-0		0-2	3	UEFA
1984-85	Lillestrom SK, Norway	7-0		0-3	1	UEFA
	Spartak Moscow, USSR	1-1		0-2	2	UEFA
1985-86	Coleraine, Ireland	5-0		1-1	1	UEFA
	AC Milan, Italy	3-1	lag	0-2	2	UEFA
1986-87	Glentoran, Ireland	2-0		1-1	1	CWC
	Rapid Vienna, Austria	2-1		1-1	2	CWC
	FC Sion, Switzerland	2-0		0-0	qf	CWC
	Girondins Bordeaux, France	0-1	6-5 pens	1-0	sf	CWC
	Ajax Amsterdam, Holland	0-1	in Athens		FINAL	CWC
1987-88	Olympique Marseille, France	0-0		0-1	1	CWC
1988-89	FC Aarau, Switzerland	4-0		3-0	1	UEFA
	Napoli, Italy	1-1		0-2	2	UEFA

EAST GERMANY

FC KARL MARX STADT

Founded 1950 as Chemie Karl Marx Stadt, 1956 as SC Motor Karl Marx Stadt, 1963 as SC Karl Marx Stadt,
1965 as FC Karl Marx Stadt
Colours sky blue shirts, white shorts
Stadium Dr Kurt Fischer (22,000) ☎ 071-58 941
Champions as Karl Marx Stadt 1967

Season	Opponent	Home	Playoff Result	Away	Rnd	Cup
1967-68	RSC Anderlecht, Belgium	1-3		1-2	1	ECC
1989-90	Boavista, Portugal	1-0		2-2 aet	1	UEFA
	FC Sion, Switzerland	4-1		1-2	2	UEFA
	Juventus, Italy	0-1		1-2	3	UEFA

WISMUT AUE

Founded 1948 as Zentrag Wismut, 1951 as Wismut Aue, 1954 moved to and became SC Wismut Karl Marx Stadt,
1963 returned to and became Wismut Aue Founded 1951
Colours violet shirts, white shorts
Stadium Otto Grotewohl (25,000) ☎ 0761-2920
Champions as SC Wismut Karl Marx Stadt 1956, 1957, 1959

Season	Opponent	Home	Playoff Result	Away	Rnd	Cup
1957-58	Gwardia Warsaw, Poland	3-1**	1-1*wot	1-3	pr	ECC
		** in Aue	* in East Berlin			
	Ajax Amsterdam, Holland	1-3*		0-1	1	ECC
		* in Aue				
1958-59	Petrolul Ploesti, Romania	4-2	4-0*	0-2	1	ECC
			* in Kiev			
	IFK Gothenburg, Sweden	4-0*		2-2	2	ECC
		* in Aue				
	Young Boys Bern, Switzerland	0-0**	1-2*	2-2	qf	ECC
		** in Aue	* in Amsterdam			
1960-61	Glenavon, Ireland		withdrew		1	ECC
	Rapid Vienna, Austria	2-0	0-1*	1-3	2	ECC
			* in Basle			
1985-86	Dnepr Dnepropetrovsk, USSR	1-3		1-2*	1	UEFA
				* in Krivoy Rog		
1987-88	Valur Reykjavik, Iceland	0-0		1-1	1	UEFA
	Flamutari Vlora, Albania	1-0		0-2	2	UEFA

SACHSENRING ZWICKAU

Founded 1948 as SG Planitz, 1949 as Horch Zwichau, 1950 as Motor Zwickau, 1967 as Sachsenring Zwickau
Colours white shirts, red shorts
Stadium Georgi Dimitroff (45,000) ☎ 03290-702268
Champions 1950 as Horch Zwickau Cup Winners 1963, 1967 as Sachsenring 1975

Season	Opponent	Home	Result	Away	Rnd	Cup
as MOTOR ZWICKAU						
1963-64	MTK Budapest, Hungary	1-0		0-2	1	CWC
1967-68	Torpedo Moscow, USSR	0-1		0-0	1	CWC
as SACHSENRING ZWICKAU						
1975-76	Panathinaikos, Greece	2-0		0-0*	1	CWC
				* in Patras		
	Fiorentina, Italy	1-0	5-4 pen	0-1	2	CWC
	Glasgow Celtic, Scotland	1-0		1-1	qf	CWC
	RSC Anderlecht, Belgium	0-3		0-2	sf	CWC

BERLINER FC DYNAMO

Founded 1.10.54 as SC Dynamo Berlin, 15.1.1966 as Berliner FC (BFC) Dynamo
Colours claret shirts, white shorts
Stadium Sportforum Berlin (30,000) 02-378 122 52
Champions 1979, 1980, 1981, 1982, 1983, 1984, 1985, 1986, 1987, 1988
Cup Winners 1959, 1988, 1989
East German Super Cup Winners 1989

Season	Opponent	Home	Result	Away	Rnd	Cup
1971-72	Cardiff City, Wales	1-1	5-4p	1-1	1	CWC
	K Beerschot V.A.V, Belgium	3-1		3-1	2	CWC
	Atvidabergs FF, Sweden	2-2		2-0	qf	CWC
	Dynamo Moscow, USSR	1-1	1-4p	1-1	sf	CWC
1972-73	Angers, France	2-1		1-1	1	UEFA
	Levski Spartak Sofia, Bulgaria	3-0		0-2	2	UEFA
	Liverpool, England	0-0		1-3	3	UEFA
1976-77	Shakhtyor Donetsk, USSR	1-1		0-3	1	UEFA
1978-79	Red Star Belgrade, Yugoslavia	5-2	lag	1-4	1	UEFA
1979-80	Ruch Chorzow, Poland	4-1		0-0	1	ECC
	Servette Geneva, Switzerland	2-1		2-2	2	ECC
	Nottingham Forest, England	1-3		1-0	qf	ECC
1980-81	Apoel Nicosia, Cyprus	3-0		1-2	1	ECC
	Banik Ostrava, Czechoslovakia	1-1	lag	0-0	2	ECC
1981-82	St Etienne, France	2-0		1-1	pr	ECC
	FC Zurich, Switzerland	2-0	wag	1-3	1	ECC
	Aston Villa, England	1-2	lag	1-0	2	ECC
1982-83	Hamburger SV, Germany	1-1		0-2	1	ECC
1983-84	Jeunesse Esch, Luxembourg	4-1		2-0	1	ECC
	Partizan Belgrade, Yugoslavia	2-0		0-1	2	ECC
	AS Roma, Italy	2-1		0-3	qf	ECC
1984-85	Aberdeen, Scotland	2-1	5-4p	1-2	1	ECC
	FK Austria Vienna, Austria	3-3		1-2	2	ECC
1985-86	FK Austria Vienna, Austria	0-2		1-2	1	ECC
1986-87	Orgryte IS Gothenburg, Sweden	4-1		3-2	1	ECC
	Brondbyernes IF, Denmark	1-1		1-2	2	ECC
1987-88	Girondins Bordeaux, France	0-2		0-2	1	ECC
1988-89	Werder Bremen, Germany	3-0		0-5	1	ECC
1989-90	Valur Reykjavik, Iceland	2-1		2-1	1	CWC
	AS Monaco, France	1-1 aet	lag	0-0	2	CWC

81

EAST GERMANY

DYNAMO DRESDEN

Founded 1945 as SG Dresden Friedrichstadt, 1950 as Volkspolizei Dresden, 1952 as Dynamo Dresden
Colours yellow shirts, black shorts
Stadium Dynamo Stadion (40,000) ☎ 051-496 60 46
Champions 1953, 1971, 1973, 1976, 1977, 1978, 1989
Cup Winners 1971, 1977, 1982, 1984, 1985

Season	Opponent	Home	Result	Away	Rnd	Cup
1967-68	Glasgow Rangers, Scotland	1-1		1-2	1	Fairs
1970-71	Partizan Belgrade, Yugoslavia	6-0		0-0	1	Fairs
	Leeds United, England	2-1	lag	0-1	2	Fairs
1971-72	Ajax Amsterdam, Holland	0-0		0-2	1	ECC
1972-73	VoEST Linz, Austria	2-0		2-2	1	UEFA
	Ruch Chorzow, Poland	3-0		1-0	2	UEFA
	FC Porto, Portugal	1-0		2-1	3	UEFA
	Liverpool, England	0-1		0-2	qf	UEFA
1973-74	Juventus, Italy	2-0		2-3	1	ECC
	Bayern Munich, Germany	3-3		3-4	2	ECC
1974-75	Randers Freja, Denmark	0-0	wag	1-1	1	UEFA
	Dynamo Moscow, USSR	1-0	4-3p	0-1	2	UEFA
	Hamburger SV, Germany	2-2		1-4	3	UEFA
1975-76	AS Armata Tirgu, Romania	4-1		2-2	1	UEFA
	Honved Budapest, Hungary	1-0		2-2	2	UEFA
	Torpedo Moscow, USSR	3-0		1-3	3	UEFA
	Liverpool, England	0-0		1-2	qf	UEFA
1976-77	Benfica, Portugal	2-0		0-0	1	ECC
	Ferencvarosi TC, Hungary	4-0		0-1	2	ECC
	FC Zurich, Switzerland	3-2	lag	1-2	qf	ECC
1977-78	Halmstads BK, Sweden	2-0		1-2	1	ECC
	Liverpool, England	2-1		1-5	2	ECC
1978-79	Partizan Belgrade, Yugoslavia	2-0	5-4p	0-2	1	ECC
	Bohemians Dublin, Eire	6-0		0-0*	2	ECC
				* in Dundalk		
				(previous crowd trouble)		
	FK Austria/WAC Vienna, Austria	1-0		1-3	qf	ECC
1979-80	Atletico Madrid, Spain	3-0		2-1	1	UEFA
	VfB Stuttgart, Germany	1-1	lag	0-0	2	UEFA
1980-81	Napredak Krusevac, Yugoslavia	1-0		1-0	1	UEFA
	Twente Enschede, Holland	0-0	wag	1-1	2	UEFA
	Standard Liege, Belgium	1-4		1-1	3	UEFA
1981-82	Zenit Leningrad, USSR	4-1		2-1	1	UEFA
	Feyenoord Rotterdam, Holland	1-1		1-2	2	UEFA
1982-83	B 93 Copenhagen, Denmark	3-2	lag	1-2	1	CWC
1984-85	Malmo FF, Sweden	4-1		0-2	1	CWC
	FC Metz, France	3-1		0-0	2	CWC
	Rapid Vienna, Austria	3-0		0-5	qf	CWC
1985-86	SV Cercle Bruges, Belgium	2-1	wag	2-1	1	CWC
	HJK Helsinki, Finland	7-2		0-1	2	CWC
	Bayer Uerdingen, Germany	2-0		3-7	qf	CWC
1987-88	Spartak Moscow, USSR	1-0		0-3	1	UEFA
1988-89	Aberdeen, Scotland	2-0		0-0	1	UEFA
	KSV Waregem, Belgium	4-1		1-2	2	UEFA
	AS Roma, Italy	2-0		2-0	3	UEFA
	Victoria Bucharest, Romania	4-0		1-1	qf	UEFA
	VfB Stuttgarf, Germany	1-1		0-1	sf	UEFA
1989-90	AEK Athens, Greece	1-0		3-5	1	ECC
Fe						

1.FC UNION BERLIN

Founded 1945 as Union Oberschoneweide, 1951 as Motor Oberschoneweide, 1966 as 1.FC Union Berlin
Colours red shirts, white shorts
Stadium Alte Forsterei (18,000) ☎ 02-657 25 85
Cup Winners 1968

Season	Opponent	Home	Result	Away	Rnd	Cup
1968-69	withdrew				1	CWC

HANSA ROSTOCK

Founded 1950 as Empor Rostock, 1965 as Hansa Rostock
Colours sky blue shirts, white shorts
Stadium Osteestadion (25,000) ☎ 081-34204
Champions 1961

Season	Opponent	Home	Result	Away	Rnd	Cup
1968-69	OGC Nice, France	3-0		1-2	1	Fairs
	Fiorentina, Italy	3-2	lag	1-2	2	Fairs
1969-70	Panionios, Greece	3-0		0-2	1	Fairs
	Inter Milan, Italy	2-1		0-3	2	Fairs
	Banik Ostrava, Czechoslovakia	2-3		0-4	1	UEFA

BSG STAHL BRANDENBURG

Founded 1949
Colours white shirts with thin blue hoops, blue shorts
Stadium Der Stahlwerker (15,000) ☎ 038-55 35 55

Season	Opponent	Home	Result	Away	Rnd	Cup
1986-87	Coleraine, Ireland	1-0		1-1	1	UEFA
	IFK Gothenburg, Sweden	1-1		0-2	2	UEFA

HFC CHEMIE HALLE

Founded 1947 as Freimfelde Halle, 1948 as ZSG Union Halle, 1950 as Turbine Halle, 1954 as SC Chemie Halle,
1965 as Hallischer FC Chemie
Colours red and white hooped shirts, red shorts
Stadium Kurt Wabbel (30,000) ☎ 046-24638
Champions 1949 as ZSG Halle, 1952 as Turbine Halle
Cup Winners 1956, 1962

Season	Opponent	Home	Playoff Result	Away	Rnd	Cup
as SC CHEMIE HALLE						
1961-62	Spartak Brno, Czechoslovakia	4-1		2-2	1	Fairs
	MTK Budapest, Hungary	3-0	0-2*	0-3	2	Fairs
			* in Bratislava			
1962-63	OFK Belgrade, Yugoslavia	3-3		0-2	pr	CWC
as HFC CHEMIE HALLE						
1971-72	PSV Eindhoven, Holland	0-0	withdrew		1	UEFA

EAST GERMANY

LEIPZIG SELECTION

Season	Opponent	Home	Playoff Result	Away	Rnd	Cup
1955-58	FC Lausanne, Switzerland	6-3		3-7	pr	Fairs
1958-60	Union St Gilloise, Belgium	1-0		0-6	1	Fairs
1960-61	Belgrade City XI, Yugoslavia	5-2	0-2*	1-4	1	Fairs
			* in Budapest			
1962-63	Vojvodina Novi Sad, Yugoslavia	0-1		2-0	1	Fairs
	Petrolul Ploesti, Romania	1-0	0-1*	0-1	2	Fairs
			* in Budapest			

84 • Olympia Stadion, Berlin Hertha Berlin

EIRE

Founded 1921 The Football Association of Ireland, 80 Merrion Square, Dublin 2. ☎ 765120 Fax 1-610931
National Colours green shirts with white collars, white shorts
Season August to May

LEAGUE CHAMPIONS

1922	St James's Gate	1940	St James's Gate	1958	Drumcondra	1975	Bohemians
1923	Shamrock Rovers	1941	Cork United	1959	Shamrock Rovers	1976	Dundalk
1924	Bohemians	1942	Cork United			1977	Sligo Rovers
1925	Shamrock Rovers	1943	Cork United	1960	Limerick	1978	Bohemians
1926	Shelbourne	1944	Shelbourne	1961	Drumcondra	1979	Dundalk
1927	Shamrock Rovers	1945	Cork United	1962	Shelbourne		
1928	Bohemians	1946	Cork United	1963	Dundalk	1980	Limerick
1929	Shelbourne	1947	Shelbourne	1964	Shamrock Rovers	1981	Athlone Town
		1948	Dumcondra	1965	Drumcondra	1982	Dundalk
1930	Bohemians	1949	Drumcondra	1966	Waterford	1983	Athlone Town
1931	Shelbourne			1967	Dundalk	1984	Shamrock Rovers
1932	Shamrock Rovers	1950	Cork Athletic	1968	Waterford	1985	Shamrock Rovers
1933	Dundalk	1951	Cork Athletic	1969	Waterford	1986	Shamrock Rovers
1934	Bohemians	1952	St Patrick's Athletic			1987	Shamrock Rovers
1935	Dolphin	1953	Shelbourne	1970	Waterford	1988	Dundalk
1936	Bohemians	1954	Shamrock Rovers	1971	Cork Hibernians	1989	Derry City
1937	Sligo Rovers	1955	St Patrick's Athletic	1972	Waterford		
1938	Shamrock Rovers	1956	St Patrick's Athletic	1973	Waterford		
1939	Shamrock Rovers	1957	Shamrock Rovers	1974	Cork Celtic		

CUP WINNERS

1922	St James's Gate v Shamrock Rovers	1-1 1-0	1934	Cork v St James's Gate	2-1
1923	Alton United v Shelbourne	1-0	1935	Bohemians v Dundalk	4-3
1924	Athlone Town v Fordsons	1-0	1936	Shamrock Rovers v Cork	2-1
1925	Shamrock Rovers v Shelbourne	2-1	1937	Waterford v St James's Gate	2-1
1926	Fordsons v Shamrock Rovers	3-2	1938	St James's Gate v Dundalk	2-1
1927	Drumcondra v Brideville	1-1 1-0	1939	Shelbourne v Sligo Rovers	1-1 1-0
1928	Bohemians v Drumcondra	2-1			
1929	Shamrock Rovers v Bohemians	0-0 3-0	1940	Shamrock Rovers v Sligo Rovers	3-0
			1941	Cork United v Waterford	2-2 3-1
1930	Shamrock Rovers v Brideville	1-0	1942	Dundalk v Cork United	3-1
1931	Shamrock Rovers v Dundalk	1-1 1-0	1943	Drumcondra v Cork United	2-1
1932	Shamrock Rovers v Dolphin	1-0	1944	Shamrock Rovers v Shelbourne	3-2
1933	Shamrock Rovers v Dolphin	3-3 3-0	1945	Shamrock Rovers v Bohemians	1-0

85

1946	Drumcondra v Shamrock Rovers	2-1
1947	Cork United v Bohemians	2-2 2-0
1948	Shamrock Rovers v Drumcondra	2-1
1949	Dundalk v Shelbourne	3-0
1950	Transport v Cork Athletic	2-2 2-2 3-1
1951	Cork Athletic v Shelbourne	1-1 1-0
1952	Dundalk v Cork Athletic	1-1 3-0
1953	Cork Athletic v Evergreen United	2-2 2-1
1954	Drumcondra v St Patrick's Athletic	1-0
1955	Shamrock Rovers v Drumcondra	1-0
1956	Shamrock Rovers v Cork Athletic	3-2
1957	Drumcondra v Shamrock Rovers	2-0
1958	Dundalk v Shamrock Rovers	1-0
1959	St Patrick's Athletic v Waterford	2-2 2-1
1960	Shelbourne v Cork Hibernians	2-0
1961	St Patrick's Athletic v Drumcondra	2-1
1962	Shamrock Rovers v Shelbourne	4-1
1963	Shelbourne v Cork Hibernians	2-0
1964	Shamrock Rovers v Cork Celtic	1-1 2-1
1965	Shamrock Rovers v Limerick	1-1 1-0
1966	Shamrock Rovers v Limerick	2-0
1967	Shamrock Rovers v St Patrick's Athletic	3-2
1968	Shamrock Rovers v Waterford	3-0
1969	Shamrock Rovers v Cork Celtic	1-1 4-1

1970	Bohemians v Sligo Rovers	0-0 0-0 2-1
1971	Limerick v Drogheda	0-0 3-0
1972	Cork Hibernians v Waterford	3-0
1973	Cork Hibernians v Shelbourne	0-0 1-0
1974	Finn Harps v St Patrick's Athletic	3-1
1975	Home Farm v Shelbourne	1-0
1976	Bohemians v Drogheda	1-0
1977	Dundalk v Limerick	2-0
1978	Shamrock Rovers v Sligo Rovers	1-0
1979	Dundalk v Waterford	2-0
1980	Waterford v St Patrick's Athletic	1-0
1981	Dundalk v Sligo Rovers	2-0
1982	Limerick v Bohemians	1-0
1983	Sligo Rovers v Bohemians	2-1
1984	University College v Shamrock Rovers	2-1
1985	Shamrock Rovers v Galway United	1-0
1986	Shamrock Rovers v Waterford	2-0
1987	Shamrock Rovers v Dundalk	3-0
1988	Dundalk v Derry City	1-0
1989	Derry City v Cork City	0-0 1-0
1990	Bray Wanderers v St Francis	

FEATURED CLUBS IN EUROPEAN COMPETITION

Bohemians Dublin	**Cork Hibernians**	**Cork Celtic**	**Athlone Town**
Drumcondra Dublin	**Dundalk**	**Finn Harps Ballybofey**	**Home Farm Dublin**
Limerick City	**Shamrock Rovers Dublin**	**Shelbourne Dublin**	**St Patrick's Athletic Dublin**
Sligo Rovers	**Drogheda United**	**Waterford United**	**Galway United**
University College Dublin	**Derry City**	**Cork City**	

BOHEMIANS (DUBLIN)

Founded 1890 Colours red and black striped shirts, black shorts
Stadium Dalymount Park (40,000) ☎ 01-300923
Champions 1924, 1928, 1930, 1934, 1936, 1975, 1978
Cup Winners 1928, 1935, 1970, 1976

Season	Opponent	Home	Result	Away	Rnd	Cup
1970-71	Gottwaldov TJ, Czechoslovakia	1-2		2-2	1	CWC
1972-73	1.FC Koln, Germany	0-3		1-2	1	UEFA
1974-75	Hamburger SV, Germany	0-1		0-3	1	UEFA
1975-76	Glasgow Rangers, Scotland	1-1		1-4	1	ECC
1976-77	Esbjerg fB, Denmark	2-1		1-0	1	CWC
	Slask Wroclaw, Poland	0-1		0-3	2	CWC
1977-78	Newcastle United, England	0-0		0-4	1	UEFA
1978-79	Omonia Nicosia, Cyprus	1-0*	wag	1-2	1	ECC
	*in Cork (previous crowd trouble)					
	Dynamo Dresden, East Germany	0-0*		0-6	2	ECC
	*in Dundalk (previous crowd trouble)					
1979-80	Sporting Lisbon, Portugal	0-0		0-2	1	UEFA
1984-85	Glasgow Rangers, Scotland	3-2		0-2	1	UEFA
1985-86	Dundee United, Scotland	2-5		2-2	1	UEFA
1987-88	Aberdeen, Scotland	0-0		0-1	1	UEFA

CORK HIBERNIANS

Club became defunct in 1976 previous name AOH (Ancient Order of Hibernians)
Founded 1957   Colours white shirts, green shorts
Stadium Flower Lodge (25,000)
Champions 1971
Cup Winners 1972, 1973

Season	Opponent	Home	Result	Away	Rnd	Cup
1970-71	Valencia CF, Spain	0-3		1-3	1	Fairs
1971-72	Borussia Monchengladbach, Germany	0-5		1-2	1	ECC
1972-73	Pezoporikos Larnaca, Cyprus	4-1		2-1	1	CWC
	FC Schalke 04 Gelsenkirchen, Germany	0-0		0-3	2	CWC
1973-74	Banik Ostrava, Czechoslovakia	1-2		0-1	1	CWC

CORK CELTIC

Founded 1959 as Evergreen United, 1959 Cork Celtic, 1979 dissolved
Colours all white
Stadium Turner's Cross (20,000)
Champions 1974

Season	Opponent	Home	Result	Away	Rnd	Cup
1964-65	Slavia Sofia, Bulgaria	0-2		1-1	1	CWC
1974-75	Omonia Nicosia, Cyprus	walk over			1	ECC
	Ararat Yerevan, USSR	1-2		0-5	2	ECC

ATHLONE TOWN

Founded 1892   Colours black and sky blue striped shirts, black shorts
Stadium St Mels Park (15,000) ☎ 0902-4088
Champions 1981, 1983
Cup Winners 1924

Season	Opponent	Home	Result	Away	Rnd	Cup
1975-76	Valerengen IF Oslo, Norway	3-1		1-1	1	UEFA
	AC Milan, Italy	0-0		0-3	2	UEFA
1981-82	KB Copenhagen, Denmark	2-2	lag	1-1	1	ECC
1983-84	Standard Liege, Belgium	2-3		2-8	1	EEC

DRUMCONDRA

Founded 1923, 1972 amalgamated with Home Farm under Home Farm
Colours gold shirts, blue shorts
Stadium Tolka Park,Dublin (20,000)
Champions 1948, 1949, 1958, 1961, 1965
Cup Winners 1927, 1943, 1946, 1954, 1957

Season	Opponent	Home	Result	Away	Rnd	Cup
1958-59	Atletico Madrid, Spain	1-5		0-8	pr	ECC
1961-62	1.FC Nurnburg, Germany	1-4		0-5	pr	ECC
1962-63	Odense City XI, Denmark	4-1		2-4	pr	Fairs
	Bayern Munich, Germany	1-0		0-6	1	Fairs
1965-66	FC Vorwaerts Berlin, East Germany	1-0		0-3	pr	ECC
1966-67	Eintracht Frankfurt, Germany	0-2		1-6	1	Fairs

DUNDALK

Founded 1919   Colours white shirts, black shorts
Stadium Oriel Park (18,000) ☎ 042-35398
Champions 1933, 1963, 1967, 1976, 1979, 1982, 1988
Cup Winners 1942, 1949, 1952, 1958, 1977, 1979, 1981, 1988

Season	Opponent	Home	Result	Away	Rnd	Cup
1963-64	FC Zurich, Switzerland	0-3*		2-1	1	ECC
		*in Dublin				
1967-68	Vasas Budapest, Hungary	0-1		1-8	1	ECC
1968-69	DOS Utrecht, Holland	2-1		1-1	1	Fairs
	Glasgow Rangers, Scotland	0-3		1-6	2	Fairs
1969-70	Liverpool, England	0-4		0-10	1	Fairs
1976-77	PSV Eindhoven, Holland	1-1		0-6	1	ECC
1977-78	Hajduk Split, Yugoslavia	1-0		0-4	1	CWC
1979-80	Linfield, Ireland	1-1		2-0*	pr	ECC
				*in Haarlem, Holland		
	Hibernians, Malta	2-0		0-1	1	ECC
	Glasgow Celtic, Scotland	0-0		2-3	2	ECC
1980-81	FC Porto, Portugal	0-0		0-1	1	UEFA
1981-82	Fram Reykjavik, Iceland	4-0		1-2	1	CWC
	Tottenham Hotspur, England	1-1		0-1	2	CWC
1982-83	Liverpool, England	1-4		0-1	1	ECC
1987-88	Ajax Amsterdam, Holland	0-2		0-4	1	CWC
1988-89	Red Star Belgrade, Yugoslavia	0-5		0-3	1	ECC
1989-90	FC Wettingen, Holland	0-2		0-3	1	UEFA

FINN HARPS (BALLYBOFEY)

Founded 1954   Colours blue shirts, white shorts
Stadium Finn Park, Ballybofey, Donegal (10,000) ☎ 074-31228
Cup Winners 1974

Season	Opponent	Home	Result	Away	Rnd	Cup
1973-74	Aberdeen, Scotland	1-3		1-4	1	UEFA
1974-75	Bursaspor, Turkey	0-0		2-4	1	CWC
1976-77	Derby County, England	1-4		0-12	1	UEFA
1978-79	Everton, England	0-5		0-5	1	UEFA

HOME FARM (DUBLIN)

Founded 1928, amalgamated with Drumcondra under Home Farm
Colours blue and white hooped shirts, white shorts
Stadium Tolka Park, Dublin (20,000) ☎ 01-373091/600311
Cup Winners 1975

Season	Opponent	Home	Result	Away	Rnd	Cup
1975-76	RC Lens, France	1-1		0-6	1	CWC

LIMERICK CITY

Founded 1937 as Limerick FC, 1979 Limerick United, 1983 Limerick City. A new club has been formed and named
Limerick United and will play at Markets Field (10,000) not elected to the League
Colours blue shirts, white shorts
Stadium Rathbane (10,000) ☎ 061-47874
Champions 1960, 1980
Cup Winners 1971, 1982

Season	Opponent	Home	Result	Away	Rnd	Cup
1960-61	Young Boys Bern, Switzerland	0-5		2-4	1	ECC
1965-66	Red Banner(CSKA) Sofia, Bulgaria	1-2*		0-2	1	CWC
		*in Dublin				
1971-72	Torino, Italy	0-1		0-4	1	CWC
1980-81	Real Madrid, Spain	1-2*		1-5	1	ECC
		*in Dublin				
1981-82	Southampton, England	0-3		1-1	1	UEFA
1982-83	AZ Alkmaar 67, Holland	1-1		0-1	1	CWC

SHAMROCK ROVERS (DUBLIN)

Founded 1899 Colours green & white hooped shirts, white shorts
Stadium Milltown has been sold to developers, played at Home Farms Tolka Park 1987-88, now play at Glenmalure Park
(20,000) ☎ 01-698252/698424/767437
Champions 1923, 1925, 1927, 1932, 1938, 1939, 1954, 1957, 1959, 1964, 1984, 1985, 1986, 1987
Cup Winners 1925, 1929, 1930, 1931, 1932, 1933, 1936, 1940, 1944, 1945, 1948, 1955, 1956, 1962, 1964, 1965, 1966,
1967, 1968, 1969, 1978, 1985, 1986, 1987

Season	Opponent	Home	Result	Away	Rnd	Cup
1957-58	Manchester United, England	0-6		2-3	pr	ECC
1959-60	OGC Nice, France	1-1		2-3	pr	ECC
1962-63	bye				1	CWC
	Botev Plovdiv, Bulgaria	0-4		0-1*	2	CWC
				*in Sofia		
1963-64	Valencia CF, Spain	0-1		2-2	pr	Fairs
1964-65	Rapid Vienna, Austria	0-2		0-3	pr	ECC
1965-66	bye				1	Fairs
	Real Zaragoza, Spain	1-1		1-2	2	Fairs
1966-67	Spora CA, Luxembourg	4-1		4-1	pr	CWC
	Bayern Munich, Germany	1-1		2-3	1	CWC
1967-68	Cardiff City, Wales	1-1		0-2	1	CWC
1968-69	Randers Freja, Denmark	1-2		0-1	1	CWC
1969-70	FC Schalke 04, Gelsenkirchen, Germany	2-1		0-3	1	CWC
1978-79	Apoel Nicosia, Cyprus	2-0		1-0	1	CWC
	Banik Ostrava, Czechoslovakia	1-3		0-3	2	CWC
1982-83	Fram Reykjavik, Iceland	4-0		3-0	1	UEFA
	Universitatea Craiova, Romania	0-2		0-3	2	UEFA
1984-85	Linfield, Ireland	1-1	lag	0-0	1	ECC

89

1985-86	Honved Budapest, Hungary	1-3		0-2	1	ECC
1986-87	Glasgow Celtic, Scotland	0-1		0-2	1	ECC
1987-88	Omonia Nicosia, Cyprus	0-1		0-0	1	ECC

SHELBOURNE (DUBLIN)

Founded 1895 as Shelbourne FC, 1934 Reds United, 1936 Shelbourne FC
Colours red shirts, white shorts
Stadium Harold's Cross (18,000) ☎ 01-741811
Champions 1926, 1929, 1931, 1944, 1947, 1953, 1962
Cup Winners 1939, 1960, 1963

Season	Opponent	Home	playoff Result	Away	Rnd	Cup
1962-63	Sporting Lisbon, Portugal	0-2		1-5	1	ECC
1963-64	CF Barcelona, Spain	0-2		1-3	1	CWC
1964-65	Belenenses, Portugal	0-0	2-1* *in Dublin	1-1	pr	Fairs
	Atletico Madrid, Spain	0-1		0-1	1	Fairs
1971-72	Vasas Budapest, Hungary	1-1		0-1	1	UEFA

ST PATRICK'S ATHLETIC (DUBLIN)

Founded 1929   Colours red & white shirts, white shorts
Stadium Richmond Park, Inchicore, Dublin (15,000) ☎ 01-755582
Champions 1952, 1955, 1956
Cup Winners 1959, 1961

Season	Opponent	Home	Result	Away	Rnd	Cup
1961-62	Dunfermline Athletic, Scotland	0-4		1-4	pr	CWC
1967-68	Girondins Bordeaux, France	1-3		3-6	1	Fairs
1988-89	Heart of Midlothian, Scotland	0-2		0-2	1	UEFA

SLIGO ROVERS

Founded 1908   Colours red and white striped shirts, white shorts
Stadium Sligo Showgrounds (6,000) ☎ 071-6041
Champions 1937, 1977
Cup Winners 1983

Season	Opponent	Home	Result	Away	Rnd	Cup
1977-78	Red Star Belgrade, Yugoslavia	0-3		0-3	1	ECC
1983-84	Haka Valkeakoski, Finland	0-1		0-3	1	CWC

DROGHEDA UNITED

Founded 1932 as Drogheda, 1975 Drogheda United
Colours blue shirts, white shorts
Stadium United Park (20,000) ☎ 041-36127

Season	Opponent	Home	Result	Away	Rnd	Cup
1983-84	Tottenham Hotspur, England	0-6		0-8	1	UEFA

WATERFORD UNITED

Founded 1921 as Waterford, 1982 Waterford United
Colours blue shirts, white shorts
Stadium Kilcohan Park (15,000) ☎ 051-81255
Champions 1966, 1968, 1969, 1970, 1972, 1973
Cup Winners 1937, 1980

Season	Opponent	Home	Result	Away	Rnd	Cup
1966-67	FC Vorwaerts Berlin, East Germany	1-6*		0-6	pr	ECC
		*in Dublin				
1968-69	Manchester United, England	1-3*		1-7	1	ECC
		*in Dublin				
1969-70	Galatasaray, Turkey	2-3*		0-2	1	ECC
		*in Dublin				
1970-71	Glentoran, Ireland	1-0		3-1	1	ECC
	Glasgow Celtic, Scotland	0-7*		2-3	2	ECC
		*in Dublin				
1972-73	Omonia Nicosia, Cyprus	2-1		0-2	1	ECC
1973-74	Ujpest Dozsa, Hungary	2-3*		0-3	1	ECC
		*in Dublin				
1979-80	IFK Gothenburg, Sweden	1-1		0-1	1	CWC
1980-81	Hibernians, Malta	4-0		0-1	1	CWC
	Dynamo Tbilisi, USSR	0-1		0-4	2	CWC
1986-87	Girondins Bordeaux, France	1-2*		0-4	1	CWC
		*in Dublin				

GALWAY UNITED

Founded 1977 as Galway Rovers, 1981 Galway United
Colours all maroon
Stadium Terryland Park (15,000) ☎ 091-67951

Season	Opponent	Home	Result	Away	Rnd	Cup
1985-86	Lyngby BK, Denmark	2-3		0-1	1	CWC
1986-87	FC Groningen, Holland	1-3		1-5	1	UEFA

UNIVERSITY COLLEGE DUBLIN

Founded 1895 Colours red shirts, black shorts
Stadium Belfield Sports Complex, Stillorgan, Dublin (10,000) ☎ 01-694684/693244

Season	Opponent	Home	Result	Away	Rnd	Cup
1984-85	Everton, England	0-0		0-1	1	CWC

DERRY CITY

Founded 1928 Colours red and white striped shirts, black shorts
Stadium Brandywell Park (11,500) ☎ 080504-262276
Reformed in after playing in Ireland (Northern) Champions in Ireland 1965 Irish Cup Winners 1949, 1954, 1964
Champions 1989
Cup Winners 1989

Season	Opponent	Home	Result	Away	Rnd	Cup
1988-89	Cardiff City, Wales	0-0		0-4	1	CWC
1989-90	Benfica, Portugal	1-2		0-4	1	ECC

91

CORK CITY

Founded 1984   Colours red and white hooped shirts, red shorts
Stadium Turner's Cross (20,000) ☎ 021-885715

Season	Opponent	Home	Result	Away	Rnd	Cup
1989-1990	Torpedo Moscow, USSR	0-1		0-5	1	CWC

● Parc Des Princes, Paris, Paris St Germain, ECC Finals 1956, 1975, 1981, CWC 1978

ENGLAND

Founded 1872 The Football Association, 22 Lancaster Gate, London W2 3LW ☎ 01-262 4542
National Colours white shirts, navy blue shorts
Season August to May

LEAGUE CHAMPIONS

1889 Preston North End	**1912** Blackburn Rovers	**1947** Liverpool	**1968** Manchester City
	1913 Sunderland	**1948** Arsenal	**1969** Leeds United
1890 Preston North End	**1914** Blackburn Rovers	**1949** Portsmouth	
1891 Everton	**1915** Everton		**1970** Everton
1892 Sunderland		**1950** Portsmouth	**1971** Arsenal
1893 Sunderland	**1920** West Bromwich Albion	**1951** Tottenham Hotspur	**1972** Derby County
1894 Aston Villa	**1921** Burnley	**1952** Manchester United	**1973** Liverpool
1895 Sunderland	**1922** Liverpool	**1953** Arsenal	**1974** Leeds United
1896 Aston Villa	**1923** Liverpool	**1954** Wolverhampton	**1975** Derby County
1897 Aston Villa	**1924** Huddersfield Town	Wanderers	**1976** Liverpool
1898 Sheffield United	**1925** Huddersfield Town	**1955** Chelsea	**1977** Liverpool
1899 Aston Villa	**1926** Huddersfield Town	**1956** Manchester United	**1978** Nottingham Forest
	1927 Newcastle United	**1957** Manchester United	**1979** Liverpool
1900 Aston Villa	**1928** Everton	**1958** Wolverhampton	
1901 Liverpool	**1929** Sheffield Wednesday	Wanderers	**1980** Liverpool
1902 Sunderland		**1959** Wolverhampton	**1981** Aston Villa
1903 The Wednesday	**1930** Sheffield Wednesday	Wanderers	**1982** Liverpool
1904 The Wednesday	**1931** Arsenal		**1983** Liverpool
1905 Newcastle United	**1932** Everton	**1960** Burnley	**1984** Liverpool
1906 Liverpool	**1933** Arsenal	**1961** Tottenham Hotspur	**1985** Everton
1907 Newcastle United	**1934** Arsenal	**1962** Ipswich Town	**1986** Liverpool
1908 Manchester United	**1935** Arsenal	**1963** Everton	**1987** Everton
1909 Newcastle United	**1936** Sunderland	**1964** Liverpool	**1988** Liverpool
	1937 Manchester City	**1965** Manchester United	**1989** Arsenal
1910 Aston Villa	**1938** Arsenal	**1966** Liverpool	
1911 Manchester United	**1939** Everton	**1967** Manchester United	**1990** Liverpool

ENGLAND

FA CUP WINNERS

Year	Match	Score
1872	Wanderers v Royal Engineers	1-0
1873	Wanderers v Oxford University	2-0
1874	Oxford University v Royal Engineers	2-0
1875	Royal Engineers v Old Etonians	1-1 2-0
1876	Wanderers v Old Etonians	1-1 3-0
1877	Wanderers v Oxford University	2-1
1878	Wanderers v Royal Engineers	3-1
1879	Old Etonians v Clapham Rovers	1-0
1880	Clapham Rovers v Oxford University	1-0
1881	Old Carthusians v Old Etonians	3-0
1882	Old Etonians v Blackburn Rovers	1-0
1883	Blackburn Olympic v Old Etonians	2-1
1884	Blackburn Rovers v Queen's Park Glasgow	2-1
1885	Blackburn Rovers v Queen's Park Glasgow	2-0
1886	Blackburn Rovers v West Bromwich Albion	0-0 2-0
1887	Aston Villa v West Bromwich Albion	2-0
1888	West Bromwich Albion v Preston North End	2-1
1889	Preston North End v Wolverhampton Wanderer	3-0
1890	Blackburn Rovers v Sheffield Wednesday	6-1
1891	Blackburn Rovers v Notts County	3-1
1892	West Bromwich Albion v Aston Villa	3-0
1893	Wolverhampton Wanderers v Everton	1-0
1894	Notts County v Bolton Wanderers	4-1
1895	Aston Villa v West Bromwich Albion	1-0
1896	Sheffield Wednesday v Wolverhampton Wanderer	2-1
1897	Aston Villa v Everton	3-2
1898	Nottingham Forest v Derby County	3-1
1899	Sheffield United v Derby County	4-1
1900	Bury v Southampton	4-0
1901	Tottenham Hotspur v Sheffield United	2-2 3-1
1902	Sheffield United v Southampton	1-1 2-1
1903	Bury v Derby County	6-0
1904	Manchester City v Bolton Wanderers	1-0
1905	Aston Villa v Newcastle United	2-0
1906	Everton v Newcastle United	1-0
1907	Sheffield Wednesday v Everton	2-1
1908	Wolverhampton Wanderers v Newcastle United	3-1
1909	Manchester United v Bristol City	1-0
1910	Newcastle United v Barnsley	1-1 2-0
1911	Bradford City v Newcastle United	0-0 1-0
1912	Barnsley v West Bromwich Albion	0-0 1-0
1913	Aston Villa v Sunderland	1-0
1914	Burnley v Liverpool	1-0
1915	Sheffield United v Chelsea	3-0
1920	Aston Villa v Huddersfield Town	1-0
1921	Tottenham Hotspur v Wolverhampton Wanderers	1-0
1922	Huddersfield Town v Preston North End	1-0
1923	Bolton Wanderers v West Ham United	2-0
1924	Newcastle United v Aston Villa	2-0
1925	Sheffield United v Cardiff City	1-0
1926	Bolton Wanderers v Manchester City	1-0
1927	Cardiff City v Arsenal	1-0
1928	Blackburn Rovers v Huddersfield Town	3-1
1929	Bolton Wanderers v Portsmouth	2-0
1930	Arsenal v Huddersfield Town	2-0
1931	West Bromwich Albion v Birmingham City	2-1
1932	Newcastle United v Arsenal	2-1
1933	Everton v Manchester City	3-0
1934	Manchester City v Portsmouth	2-1
1935	Sheffield Wednesday v West Bromwich Albion	4-2
1936	Arsenal v Sheffield United	1-0
1937	Sunderland v Preston North End	3-1
1938	Preston North End v Huddersfield Town	1-0
1939	Portsmouth v Wolverhampton Wanderers	4-1
1946	Derby County v Charlton Athletic	4-1
1947	Charlton Athletic v Burnley	1-0
1948	Manchester United v Blackpool	4-2
1949	Wolverhampton Wanderers v Leicester City	3-1
1950	Arsenal v Liverpool	2-0
1951	Newcastle United v Blackpool	2-0
1952	Newcastle United v Arsenal	1-0
1953	Blackpool v Bolton Wanderers	4-3
1954	West Bromwich Albion v Preston North End	3-2
1955	Newcastle United v Manchester City	3-1
1956	Manchester City v Birmingham City	3-1
1957	Aston Villa v Manchester United	2-1
1958	Bolton Wanderers v Manchester United	2-0
1959	Nottingham Forset v Luton Town	2-1
1960	Wolverhampton Wanderers v Blackburn Rovers	3-0
1961	Tottenham Hotspur v Leicester City	2-0
1962	Tottenham Hotspur v Burnley	3-1
1963	Manchester United v Leicester City	3-1
1964	West Ham United v Preston North End	3-2
1965	Liverpool v Leeds United	2-1
1966	Everton v Sheffield Wednesday	3-2
1967	Tottenham Hotspur v Chelsea	2-1
1968	West Bromwich Albion v Everton	1-0
1969	Manchester City v Leicester City	1-0
1970	Chelsea v Leeds United	2-2 2-1
1971	Arsenal v Liverpool	2-1
1972	Leeds United v Arsenal	1-0
1973	Sunderland v Leeds United	1-0
1974	Liverpool v Newcastle United	3-0
1975	West Ham United v Fulham	2-0
1976	Southampton v Manchester United	1-0
1977	Manchester United v Liverpool	2-1
1978	Ipswich Town v Arsenal	1-0
1979	Arsenal v Manchester United	3-2
1980	West Ham United v Arsenal	1-0
1981	Tottenham Hotspur v Manchester City	1-1 3-2
1982	Tottenham Hotspur v Queens Park Rangers	1-1 1-0
1983	Manchester United v Brighton & Hove	2-2 4-0
1984	Everton v Watford	2-0
1985	Manchester United v Everton	1-0
1986	Liverpool v Everton	3-1
1987	Coventry City v Tottenham Hotspur	3-2 aet
1988	Wimbledon v Liverpool	1-0
1989	Liverpool v Everton	3-2 aet
1990	Manchester United v Crystal Palace	

LEAGUE CUP

Two legs
1961	Aston Villa v Rotherham United	0-2 3-0
1962	Norwich City v Rochdale	1-0 3-0
1963	Birmingham City v Aston Villa	3-1 0-0
1964	Leicester City v Stoke City	3-2 1-1
1965	Chelsea v Leicester City	3-2 0-0
1966	West Bromwich Albion v West Ham United	4-1 1-2

FINAL PLAYED AT WEMBLEY STADIUM
1967	Queens Park Rangers v West Bromwich Albion	3-2
1968	Leeds United v Arsenal	1-0
1969	Swindon Town v Arsenal	3-1
1970	Manchester City v West Bromwich Albion	2-1
1971	Tottenham Hotspur v Aston Villa	2-0
1972	Stoke City v Chelsea	2-1
1973	Tottenham Hotspur v Norwich City	1-0
1974	Wolverhampton Wanderers v Manchester City	2-1
1975	Aston Villa v Norwich City	1-0
1976	Manchester City v Newcastle United	2-1
1977	Aston Villa v Everton	0-0 1-1 3-2
1978	Nottingham Forest v Liverpool	0-0 1-0
1979	Nottingham Forest v Southampton	3-2
1980	Wolverhampton Wanderer v Nottingham Forset	1-0
1981	Liverpool v West Ham United	1-1 2-1
1982	Liverpool v Tottenham Hotspur	3-1 aet
1983	Liverpool v Manchester United	2-1 aet
1984	Liverpool v Everton	0-0 1-0
1985	Norwich City v Sunderland	1-0
1986	Oxford United v Queens Park Rangers	3-0
1987	Arsenal v Liverpool	2-1
1988	Luton Town v Arsenal	3-2
1989	Nottingham Forest v Luton Town	3-1
1990	Nottingham Forest v Oldham Athletic	1-0

FA CHARITY SHIELD

1908	Manchester United v Queens Park Rangers	1-1 4-0
1909	Newcastle United v Northampton Town	2-0
1910	Brighton v Aston Villa	1-0
1911	Manchester United v Swindon Town	8-4
1912	Blackburn Rovers v Queens Park Rangers	2-1
1913	Professionals v Amateurs	7-2
1919	West Bromwich Albion v Tottenham Hotspur	2-0
1920	Tottenham Hotspur v Burnley	2-0
1921	Huddersfield Town v Liverpool	1-0
1922	not played	
1923	Professionals v Amateurs	2-0
1924	Professionals v Amateurs	3-1
1925	Amateurs v Professionals	6-1
1926	Amateurs v Professionals	6-3
1927	Cardiff City v Corinthians	2-1
1928	Everton v Blackburn Rovers	2-1
1929	Professionals v Amateurs	3-0
1930	Arsenal v Sheffield Wednesday	2-1
1931	Arsenal v West Bromwich Albion	1-0
1932	Everton v Newcastle United	5-3
1933	Arsenal v Everton	3-0
1934	Arsenal v Manchester City	4-0
1935	Sheffield Wednesday v Arsenal	1-0
1936	Sunderland v Arsenal	2-1
1937	Manchester City v Sunderland	2-0
1938	Arsenal v Preston North End	2-1
1948	Arsenal v Manchester United	4-3
1949	Portsmouth v Wolverhampton Wanderers	1-1*
1950	World Cup Team v Canadian Touring Team	4-2
1951	Tottenham Hotspur v Newcastle United	2-1
1952	Manchester Unted v Newcastle United	4-2
1953	Arsenal v Blackpool	3-1
1954	Wolverhampton Wanderers v West Bromwich Albion	4-4*
1955	Chelsea v Newcastle United	3-0
1956	Manchester United v Manchester City	1-0
1957	Manchester United v Aston Villa	4-0
1958	Bolton Wanderers v Wolverhampton Wanderers	4-1
1959	Wolverhampton Wanderers v Nottingham Forest	3-1
1960	Burnley v Wolverhampton Wanderers	2-2*
1961	Tottenham Hotspur v FA XI	3-2
1962	Tottenham Hotspur v Ipswich Town	5-1
1963	Everton v Manchester United	4-0
1964	Liverpool v West Ham United	2-2*
1965	Manchester United v Liverpool	2-2*
1966	Liverpool v Everton	1-0
1967	Manchester United v Tottenham Hotspur	3-3*
1968	Manchester City v West Bromwich Albion	6-1
1969	Leeds United v Manchester City	2-1
1970	Everton v Chelsea	2-1
1971	Leicester City v Liverpool	1-0
1972	Manchester City v Aston Villa	1-0
1973	Burnley v Manchester City	1-0

*Each club retained shield for six months. All played at Wembley since 1974

ENGLAND

1974	Liverpool v Leeds United	1-1 6-5 pens	**1982**	Liverpool v Tottenham Hotspur	1-0
1975	Derby County v West Ham United	2-0	**1983**	Manchester United v Liverpool	2-0
1976	Liverpool v Southampton	1-0	**1984**	Everton v Liverpool	1-0
1977	Liverpool v Manchester United	0-0*	**1985**	Everton v Manchester United	2-0
1978	Nottingham Forest v Ipswich Town	5-0	**1986**	Everton v Liverpool	1-1*
1979	Liverpool v Arsenal	3-1	**1987**	Everton v Coventry City	1-0
			1988	Liverpool v Wimbledon	2-1
1980	Liverpool v West Ham United	1-0	**1989**	Liverpool v Arsenal	1-0
1981	Aston Villa v Tottenham Hotspur	2-2*			

FULL MEMBERS CUP

First played in the 1985-86 season for full members of the Football League, played at Wembley Stadium.

1986	Chelsea v Manchester City	5-4	**1988**	Reading v Luton Town	4-1
1987	Blackburn Rovers v Charlton Athletic	1-0	**1989**	Nottingham Forest v Everton	4-3 aet

BRITISH CHAMPIONSHIP (UNOFFICIAL)

1989	Arsenal v Glasgow (Glasgow)	2-1

● Wembley Stadium, England. ECC Finals 1963, 1968, 1971, 1978, CWC Final 1965

FEATURED CLUBS IN EUROPEAN COMPETITION

Arsenal	Aston Villa	Birmingham City	Burnley
Chelsea	Coventry City	Derby County	Everton
Ipswich Town	Leeds United	Leicester City	Liverpool
Manchester City	Manchester United	Newcastle United	Nottingham Forest
Queens Park Rangers	Sheffield Wednesday	Southampton	Stoke City
Sunderland	Tottenham Hotspur	Watford	West Bromwich Albion
West Ham United	Wolverhampton Wanderers	London XI	

ARSENAL

Founded 1886 as Dial Square, Royal Arsenal in December 1886, Woolwich Arsenal in 1892, The Arsenal in 1913, Arsenal in 1919
Colours red shirts with white sleeves, white shorts
Stadium Highbury, London (60,000) ☎ 01-226 0304
Champions 1931, 1933, 1934, 1935, 1938, 1948, 1953, 1971, 1989
Cup Winners 1930, 1936, 1950, 1971, 1979
League Cup Winners 1987
Fairs Cup Winners 1970
Charity Shield Winners 1930, 1931, 1933, 1934, 1938, 1948, 1953
CWC Finalists 1980

Season	Opponent	Home	Result	Away	Rnd	Cup
1963-64	Staevnet Copenhagen, Denmark	2-3		7-1	1	Fairs
	RFC Liege, Belgium	1-1		1-3	2	Fairs
1969-70	Glentoran, Ireland	3-0		0-1	1	Fairs
	Sporting Lisbon, Portugal	3-0		0-0	2	Fairs
	Rouen, France	1-0		0-0	3	Fairs
	Dinamo Bacau, Romania	7-1		2-0	qf	Fairs
	Ajax Amsterdam, Holland	3-0		0-1	sf	Fairs
	RSC Anderlecht, Belgium	3-0		1-3	FINAL	Fairs
1970-71	Lazio Rome, Italy	2-0		2-2	1	Fairs
	Sturm Graz, Austria	2-0		0-1	2	Fairs
	SK Beveren Waas, Belgium	4-0		0-0	3	Fairs
	1.FC Koln, Germany	2-1	lag	0-1	qf	Fairs
1971-72	Stroemgodset Drammen, Norway	4-0		3-1	1	ECC
	Grasshoppers Zurich, Switzerland	3-0		2-0	2	ECC
	Ajax Amsterdam, Holland	0-1		1-2	qf	ECC
1978-79	1.FC Lokomotive Leipzig, East Germany	3-0		4-1	1	UEFA
	Hajduk Split, Yugoslavia	1-0	wag	1-2	2	UEFA
	Red Star Belgrade, Yugoslavia	1-1		0-1	3	UEFA
1979-80	Fenerbahce, Turkey	2-0		0-0	1	CWC
	1.FC Magdeburg, East Germany	2-1		2-2	2	CWC
	IFK Gothenburg, Sweden	5-1		0-0	qf	CWC
	Juventus, Italy	1-1		1-0	sf	CWC
	Valencia CF, Spain	0-0	4-5 pen	in Brussels	FINAL	CWC
1981-82	Panathinaikos, Greece	1-0		2-0	1	UEFA
	KFC Winterslag, Belgium	2-1	lag	0-1	2	UEFA
1982-83	Moscow Spartak, USSR	2-5		2-3	1	UEFA

ENGLAND

ASTON VILLA

Founded 1874   Colours claret and light blue shirts, white shorts
Stadium Villa Park, Birmingham (48,000) ☎ 021-328 1722
Champions 1984, 1896, 1897, 1899, 1900, 1910, 1981
Cup Winners 1887, 1895, 1897, 1905, 1913, 1920, 1957
League Cup Winners 1961, 1975, 1977
European Cup Winners 1982
European Super Cup Winners 1983
World Club Champions Finalists 1982
FA Charity Shield 1981 (shared)

Season	Opponent	Home	Result	Away	Rnd	Cup
1975-76	Royal Antwerp, Belgium	0-1		1-4	1	UEFA
1977-78	Fenerbahce, Turkey	4-0		2-0	1	UEFA
	Gornik Zabrze, Poland	2-0		1-1	2	UEFA
	Athletic Bilbao, Spain	2-0		1-1	3	UEFA
	FC Barcelona, Spain	2-2		1-2	qf	UEFA
1981-82	Valur Reykjavik, Iceland	5-0		2-0	1	ECC
	BFC Dynamo Berlin, East Germany	0-1	wag	2-1	2	ECC
	Dynamo Kiev, USSR	2-0		0-0*	qf	ECC
				*in Simferopol		
	RSC Anderlecht, Belgium	1-0		0-0	sf	ECC
	Bayern Munich, Germany	1-0	in Rotterdam		FINAL	ECC
1982-83	Besiktas, Turkey	3-1*		0-0	1	ECC
		*behind closed doors				
	Dinamo Bucharest, Romania	4-2		2-0	2	ECC
	Juventus, Italy	1-2		1-3	qf	ECC
1983-84	Vitoria Guimaraes, Portugal	5-0		0-1	1	UEFA
	Spartak Moscow, USSR	1-2		2-2	2	UEFA

BIRMINGHAM CITY

Founded 1875 as Small Heath Alliance, 1888 as Small Heath FC Ltd, 1904 as Birmingham FC, 1946 as Birmingham City
Colours blue shirts, white shorts
Stadium St Andrews (45,000) ☎ 021-772 0101/2689
League Cup Winners 1963
Fairs Cup Finalists 1958-60, 1961

Season	Opponent	Home	Playoff Result	Away	Rnd	Cup
1955-58	Inter Milan, Italy	2-1		0-0	1	Fairs
	Zagreb City XI, Yugoslavia	3-0		1-0	2	Fairs
	CF Barcelona, Spain	4-3	1-2*	0-1	sf	Fairs
			*in Basel			
1958-60	1.FC Koln, Germany	2-0		2-2	1	Fairs
	Zagreb City XI, Yugoslavia	1-0		3-3	2	Fairs
	Union St Gilloise, Belgium	4-2		4-2	sf	Fairs
	CF Barcelona, Spain	0-0		1-4	FINAL	Fairs
1960-61	Ujpest Dozsa, Hungary	3-2		2-1	1	Fairs
	KB Copenhagen, Denmark	5-0		4-4	2	Fairs
	Inter Milan, Italy	2-1		2-1	sf	Fairs
	AS Roma, Italy	2-2		0-2	FINAL	Fairs
1961-62	Espanol Barcelona, Spain	1-0		2-5	1	Fairs

BURNLEY

Founded 1881 as Burnley Rovers, 1882 as Burnley
Colours claret and light blue shirts, white shorts
Stadium Turf Moor (25,000) ☎ 0282-27777/38021
Champions 1921, 1960
Cup Winners 1914
FA Charity Shield Winners 1960, 1973

Season	Opponent	Home	Result	Away	Rnd	Cup
1960-61	Stade de Reims, France	2-0		2-3*	1	ECC
				*in Paris		
	Hamburger SV, Germany	3-1		1-4	2	ECC
1966-67	VfB Stuttgart, Germany	2-0		1-1	1	Fairs
	Lausanne Sport, Switzerland	5-0		3-1	2	Fairs
	Napoli, Italy	3-0		0-0	3	Fairs
	Eintracht Frankfurt, Germany	1-2		1-1	qf	Fairs

CHELSEA

Founded 1905   Colours all blue
Stadium Stamford Bridge, London (44,200) ☎ 01-325 5545
Champions 1955
Cup Winners 1970
League Cup Winners 1965
CWC Winners 1971
Full Members Cup Winners 1986
FA Charity Shield Winners 1955

Season	Opponent	Home	Playoff Result	Away	Rnd	Cup
1958-60	Frem Copenhagen, Denmark	4-1		3-1	1	Fairs
	Belgrade City XI, Yugoslavia	1-0		1-4	2	Fairs
1965-66	AS Roma, Italy	4-1		0-0	1	Fairs
	Wiener SportClub, Austria	2-0		0-1	2	Fairs
	AC Milan, Italy	2-1	1-1* wot	1-2	3	Fairs
			*in Milan			
	TSV 1860 Munich, Germany	1-0		2-2	qf	Fairs
	CF Barcelona, Spain	2-0	0-5*	0-2	sf	Fairs
			*in Barcelona			
1968-69	Greenock Morton, Scotland	5-0		4-3	1	Fairs
	DWS Amsterdam, Holland	0-0	lot	0-0	2	Fairs
1970-71	Aris Salonika, Greece	5-1		1-1	1	CWC
	CSKA Sofia, Bulgaria	1-0		1-0	2	CWC
	Clube Bruges, Belgium	4-0		0-2	qf	CWC
	Manchester City, England	1-0		1-0	sf	CWC
	Real Madrid, Spain	1-1		2-1	FINAL	CWC
					both in Athens	
1971-72	Jeunesse Hautacharage, Luxembourg	13-0		8-0	1	CWC
	Atvidaberg FF, Sweden	1-1	lag	0-0	2	CWC

ENGLAND

COVENTRY CITY

Founded 1883 as Singers FC, 1888 as Coventry City
Colours all sky blue
Stadium Highfield Road (22,500) ☎ 0203-57171
Cup Winners 1987

Season	Opponent	Home	Result	Away	Rnd	Cup
1970-71	Trakia Plovdiv, Bulgaria	4-1		2-0	1	Fairs
	Bayern Munich, Germany	2-1		1-6	2	Fairs

DERBY COUNTY

Founded 1884 Colours white shirts, black shorts
Stadium Baseball Ground (33,300) ☎ 0332-40105
Champions 1972, 1975
Cup Winners 1946
FA Charity Shield Winners 1975

Season	Opponent	Home	Result	Away	Rnd	Cup
1972-73	Zeljeznicar Sarajevo, Yugoslavia	2-0		2-1	1	ECC
	Benfica, Portugal	3-0		0-0	2	ECC
	Spartak Trnava, Czechoslovakia	2-0		0-1	qf	ECC
	Juventus, Italy	0-0		1-3	sf	ECC
1974-75	Servette Geneva, Switzerland	4-1		2-1	1	UEFA
	Atletico Madrid, Spain	2-2	7-6 pen	2-2	2	UEFA
	Velez Mostar, Yugoslavia	3-1		1-4	3	UEFA
1975-76	Slovan Bratislava, Czechoslovakia	3-0		0-1	1	ECC
	Real Madrid, Spain	4-1		1-5	2	ECC
1976-77	Finn Harps, Eire	12-0		4-1	1	UEFA

EVERTON

Founded 1878 as St Domingo, 1879 as Everton
Colours blue shirts, white shorts
Stadium Goodison Park, Liverpool (53,091)
Champions 1891, 1915, 1928, 1932, 1939, 1963, 1970, 1985, 1987
Cup Winners 1906, 1933, 1966, 1984
CWC Winners 1984
FA Charity Shield Winners 1932, 1963, 1970, 1984, 1985, 1986 (shared), 1987

Season	Opponent	Home	Result	Away	Rnd	Cup
1962-63	Dunfermline Athletic, Scotland	1-0		0-2	1	Fairs
1963-64	Inter Milan, Italy	0-0		0-1	1	ECC
1964-65	Valerengen IF Oslo, Norway	4-2		5-2	1	Fairs
	Kilmarnock, Scotland	4-1		2-0	2	Fairs
	Manchester United, England	1-2		1-1	3	Fairs
1965-66	1.FC Nurnburg, Germany	1-0		1-1	1	Fairs
	Ujpest Dozsa, Hungary	2-1		0-3	2	Fairs
1966-67	AaB Aalborg, Denmark	2-1		0-0	pr	CWC
	Real Zaragoza, Spain	1-0		0-2	1	CWC
1970-71	IBK Keflavik, Iceland	6-2		3-0*	1	ECC
				*in Reykjavik		
	Borussia Monchengladbach, Germany	1-1	4-3 pen	1-1	2	ECC
	Panathinaikos, Greece	1-1	lag	0-0	qf	ECC
1975-76	AC Milan, Italy	0-0		0-1	1	UEFA

100

1978-79	Finn Harps, Eire	5-0		5-0	1	UEFA
	Dukla Prague, Czechoslovakia	2-1	lag	0-1	2	UEFA
1979-80	Feyenoord Rotterdam, Holland	0-1		0-1	1	UEFA
1984-85	University College Dublin, Eire	1-0		0-0	1	CWC
	Internacional Bratislava, Czechoslovakia	3-0		1-0	2	CWC
	Fortuna Sittard, Holland	3-0		2-0	qf	CWC
	Bayern Munich, Germany	3-1		0-0	sf	CWC
	Rapid Vienna, Austria	3-1	in Rotterdam		FINAL	CWC

IPSWICH TOWN

Founded 1880   Colours blue shirts, white shorts
Stadium Portman Road (37,000) ☎ 0473-219211
Champions 1962
Cup Winners 1978
UEFA Cup Winners 1981

Season	Opponent	Home	Result	Away	Rnd	Cup
1962-63	Floriana, Malta	10-0		4-1	1	ECC
	AC Milan, Italy	2-1		0-3	2	ECC
1973-74	Real Madrid, Spain	1-0		0-0	1	UEFA
	Lazio Rome, Italy	4-0		2-4	2	UEFA
	Twente Enschede, Holland	1-0		2-1	3	UEFA
	1.FC Lokomotive Leipzig, East Germany	1-0	3-4p	0-1	qf	UEFA
1974-75	Twente Enschede, Holland	2-2		1-1	1	UEFA
1975-76	Feyenoord Rotterdam, Holland	2-0		2-1	1	UEFA
	Clube Bruges, Belgium	3-0		0-4	2	UEFA
1977-78	Landskrona BoIS, Sweden	5-0		1-0	1	UEFA
	Las Palmas, Spain	1-0		3-3	2	UEFA
	FC Barcelona, Spain	3-0	1-3p	0-3	3	UEFA
1978-79	AZ 67 Alkmaar, Holland	2-0		0-0	1	CWC
	Wacker Innsbruck, Austria	1-0		1-1	2	CWC
	FC Barcelona, Spain	2-1	1-3 pen	0-1	qf	CWC
1979-80	Skeid Oslo, Norway	7-0		3-1	1	UEFA
	Grasshoppers Zurich, Switzerland	1-1	lag	0-0	2	UEFA
1980-81	Aris Salonika, Greece	5-1		1-3	1	UEFA
	Bohemians Prague, Czechoslovakia	3-0		0-2	2	UEFA
	RTS Widzew Lodz, Poland	5-0		0-1	3	UEFA
	St Etienne, France	3-1		4-1	qf	UEFA
	1.FC Koln, Germany	1-0		1-0	sf	UEFA
	AZ 67 Alkmaar, Holland	3-0		2-4*	FINAL	UEFA
				*in Amsterdam		
1981-82	Aberdeen, Scotland	1-1		1-3	1	UEFA
1982-83	AS Roma, Italy	3-1		0-3	1	UEFA

ENGLAND

LEEDS UNITED

Founded 1919 as Leeds United after disbandment (by FA Order) of Leeds City founded in 1904
Colours all white
Stadium Elland Road (39,423) ☎ 0532-716037
Champions 1969, 1974
Cup Winners 1972
League Cup Winners 1968
Fairs Cup Winners 1968, 1971
Finalists 1967
ECC Finalists 1975
FA Charity Shield Winners 1969

Season	Opponent	Home	Playoff Result	Away	Rnd	Cup
1965-66	Torino, Italy	2-1		0-0	pr	Fairs
	1.FC Lokomotive Leipzig, East Germany	0-0		2-1	1	Fairs
	Valencia CF, Spain	1-1		1-0	2	Fairs
	Ujpest Dozsa, Hungary	4-1		1-1	qf	Fairs
	Real Zaragoza, Spain	2-1	1-3*	0-1	sf	Fairs
			*in Zaragoza			
1966-67	bye				1	Fairs
	DWS Amsterdam, Holland	5-1		3-1	2	Fairs
	Valencia CF, Spain	1-1		2-0	3	Fairs
	Bologna, Italy	1-0	wot	0-1	qf	Fairs
	Kilmarnock, Scotland	4-2		0-0	sf	Fairs
	Dinamo Zagreb, Yugoslavia	0-0		0-2	FINAL	Fairs
1967-68	Spora CA, Luxembourg	7-0		9-0	1	Fairs
	Partizan Belgrade, Yugoslavia	1-1		2-1	2	Fairs
	Hibernian, Scotland	1-0		1-1	3	Fairs
	Glasgow Rangers, Scotland	2-0		0-0	qf	Fairs
	Dundee, Scotland	1-0		1-1	sf	Fairs
	Ferencvarosi TC, Hungary	1-0		0-0	FINAL	Fairs
1968-69	Standard Liege, Belgium	3-2		0-0	1	Fairs
	Napoli, Italy	2-0	wot	0-2	2	Fairs
	Hannover 96, Germany	5-1		2-1	3	Fairs
	Ujpest Dozsa, Hungary	0-1		0-2	qf	Fairs
1969-70	Lyn Oslo, Norway	10-0		6-0	1	ECC
	Ferencvarosi FC, Hungary	3-0		3-0	2	ECC
	Standard Liege, Belgium	1-0		1-0	qf	ECC
	Glasgow Celtic, Scotland	0-1		1-2*	sf	ECC
			*Hampden Park, Glasgow			
1970-71	Sarpsborg FK, Norway	5-0		1-0	1	Fairs
	Dynamo Dresden, East Germany	1-0	wag	1-2	2	Fairs
	Sparta Prague, Czechoslovakia	6-0		3-2	3	Fairs
	Vitoria Setubal, Portugal	2-1		1-1	qf	Fairs
	Liverpool, England	0-0		1-0	sf	Fairs
	Juventus, Italy	1-1	wag	2-2	FINAL	Fairs
			0-0 in Turin abd 55 mins pitch water-logged			
1971-72	Lierse SK, Belgium	0-4		2-0	1	UEFA
1972-73	Ankaragucu, Turkey	1-0		1-1	1	CWC
	Carl Zeiss Jena, East Germany	2-0		0-0	2	CWC
	Rapid Bucharest, Romania	5-0		3-1	qf	CWC
	Hajduk Split, Yugoslavia	1-0		0-0	sf	CWC
	AC Milan, Italy	0-1	in Salonika		FINAL	CWC
1973-74	Stroemgodset Drammen, Norway	6-1		1-1	1	UEFA
	Hibernian, Scotland	0-0	5-4 pen	0-0	2	UEFA
	Vitoria Setubal, Portugal	1-0		1-3	3	UEFA
1974-75	FC Zurich, Switzerland	4-1		1-2	1	ECC
	Ujpest Dozsa, Hungary	3-0		2-1	2	ECC
	RSC Anderlecht, Belgium	3-0		1-0	qf	ECC
	CF Barcelona, Spain	2-1		1-1	sf	ECC
	Bayern Munich, Germany	0-2	in Paris		FINAL	ECC

1979-80	Valletta, Malta	3-0		4-0	1	UEFA
	Universitatea Craiova, Romania	0-2		0-2	2	UEFA

LEICESTER CITY

Founded 1884 as Leicester Fosse, 1919 as Leicester City
Colours blue shirts, white shorts
Stadium Filbert Street (31,000) ☎ 0533-555000
League Cup Winners 1964
FA Charity Shield Winners 1971

Season	Opponent	Home	Result	Away	Rnd	Cup
1961-62	Glenavon, Ireland	3-1		4-1	pr	CWC
	Atletico Madrid, Spain	1-1		0-2	1	CWC

LIVERPOOL

Founded 1892   Colours all red
Stadium Anfield (45,600) ☎ 051-263 2361
Champions 1901, 1906, 1922, 1923, 1947, 1964, 1966, 1973, 1976, 1977, 1979, 1980, 1982, 1983, 1984, 1986, 1988, 1990
Cup Winners 1965, 1974, 1986, 1989
League Cup Winners 1981, 1982, 1983, 1984
European Cup Winners 1977, 1978, 1981, 1984
European Cup Finalists 1985
CWC Finalists 1966
UEFA Cup Winners 1973, 1976
Super Cup Winners 1977
Finalists 1978, 1984
World Club Championship Finalists 1981, 1984
FA Charity Shield Winners 1964 (Shared), 1966, 1974, 1976, 1977 (Shared), 1979, 1980, 1982, 1986 (Shared), 1988, 1989

Season	Opponent	Home	Playoff Result	Away	Rnd	Cup
1964-65	KR Reykjavik, Iceland	6-1		5-0	pr	ECC
	RSC Anderlecht, Belgium	3-0		1-0	1	ECC
	1.FC Koln, Germany	0-0	2-2* wot	0-0	qf	ECC
			*in Rotterdam aet			
	Inter Milan, Italy	3-1		0-3	sf	ECC
1965-66	Juventus, Italy	2-0		0-1	1	CWC
	Standard Liege, Belgium	3-1		2-1	2	CWC
	Honved Budapest, Hungary	2-0		0-0	qf	CWC
	Glasgow Celtic, Scotland	2-0		0-1	sf	CWC
	Borussia Dortmund, Germany	1-2	in Glasgow		FINAL	CWC
1966-67	Petrolul Ploesti, Romania	2-0	2-0*	1-3	pr	ECC
			*in Brussels			
	Ajax Amsterdam, Holland	2-2		1-5	1	ECC
1967-68	Malmo FF, Sweden	2-1		2-0	1	Fairs
	TSV 1860 Munich, Germany	8-0		1-2	2	Fairs
	Ferencvarosi TC, Hungary	0-1		0-1	3	Fairs
1968-69	Atletico Bilbao, Spain	2-1	lot	1-2	1	Fairs
1969-70	Dundalk, Eire	10-0		4-0	1	Fairs
	Vitoria Setubal, Portugal	3-2	lag	0-1	2	Fairs
1970-71	Fernecvarosi TC, Hungary	1-0		1-1	1	Fairs
	Dinamo Bucharest, Romania	3-0		1-1	2	Fairs
	Hibernian, Scotland	2-0		1-0	3	Fairs
	Bayern Munich, Germany	3-0		1-1	qf	Fairs
	Leeds United, England	0-1		0-0	sf	Fairs
1971-72	Servette Geneva, Switzerland	2-0		1-2	1	CWC
	Bayern Munich, Germany	0-0		1-3	2	CWC

103

ENGLAND

Year	Opponent				Round	Comp
1972-73	Eintracht Frankfurt, Germany	2-0		0-0	1	UEFA
	AEK Athens, Greece	3-0		3-1	2	UEFA
	BFC Dynamo Berlin, East Germany	3-1		0-0	3	UEFA
	Dynamo Dresden, East Germany	2-0		1-0	qf	UEFA
	Tottenham Hotspur, England	1-0	wag	1-2	sf	UEFA
	Borussia Monchengladbach, Germany	3-0	0-0*	0-2	FINAL	UEFA
			*abd 28 mins in Liverpool waterlogged pitch			
1973-74	Jeunesse Esch, Luxembourg	2-0		1-1	1	ECC
	Red Star Belgrade, Yugoslavia	1-2		1-2	2	ECC
1974-75	Stroemgodset Drammen, Norway	11-0		1-0	1	CWC
	Ferencvarosi TC, Hungary	1-1	lag	0-0	2	CWC
1975-76	Hibernian, Scotland	3-1		0-1	1	UEFA
	Real Sociedad San Sebastian, Spain	6-0		3-1	2	UEFA
	Slask Wroclaw, Poland	3-0		2-1	3	UEFA
	Dynamo Dresden, East Germany	2-1		0-0	qf	UEFA
	FC Barcelona, Spain	1-1		1-0	sf	UEFA
	Clube Bruges, Belgium	3-2		1-1	FINAL	UEFA
1976-77	Crusaders, Ireland	2-0		5-0	1	ECC
	Trabzonspor, Turkey	3-0		0-1	2	ECC
	St Etienne, France	3-1		0-1	qf	ECC
	FC Zurich, Switzerland	3-0		3-1	sf	ECC
	Borussia Monchengladbach, Germany	3-1	in Rome		FINAL	ECC
1977-78	bye				1	ECC
	Dynamo Dresden, East Germany	5-1		1-2	2	ECC
	Benfica, Portugal	4-1		2-1	qf	ECC
	Borussia Monchengladbach, Germany	3-0		1-2	sf	ECC
	Clube Bruges, Belgium	1-0	at Wembley		FINAL	ECC
1978-79	Nottingham Forest, England	0-0		0-2	1	ECC
1979-80	Dynamo Tbilisi, USSR	2-1		0-3	1	ECC
1980-81	Oulun Palloseura (OPS), Finland	10-1		1-1	1	ECC
	Aberdeen, Scotland	4-0		1-0	2	ECC
	CSKA Sofia, Bulgaria	5-1		1-0	qf	ECC
	Bayern Munich, Germany	0-0	wag	1-1	sf	ECC
	Real Madrid, Spain	1-0	in Paris		FINAL	ECC
1981-82	Oulun Palloseura (OPS), Finland	7-0		1-0	1	ECC
	AZ 67 Alkmaar, Holland	3-2		2-2*	2	ECC
			*in Amsterdam			
	CSKA Sofia, Bulgaria	1-0		0-2	qf	ECC
1982-83	Dundalk, Eire	1-0		4-1	1	ECC
	HJK Helsinki, Finland	5-0		0-1	2	ECC
	Widzew Lodz, Poland	3-2		0-2	qf	ECC
1983-84	Odense BK, Denmark	5-0		1-0	1	ECC
	Atletico Bilbao, Spain	0-0		1-0	2	ECC
	Benfica, Portugal	1-0		4-1	qf	ECC
	Dinamo Bucharest, Romania	1-0		2-1	sf	ECC
	AS Roma, Italy	1-1	4-2 pen Rome		FINAL	ECC
1984-85	Lech Poznan, Poland	4-0		1-0	1	ECC
	Benfica, Portugal	3-1		0-1	2	ECC
	FK Austria Vienna, Austria	4-1		1-1	qf	ECC
	Panathinaikos, Greece	4-0		1-0	sf	ECC
	Juventus, Italy	0-1	in Brussels		FINAL	ECC

MANCHESTER CITY

Founded 1887 as Ardwick by merger of West Gorton (1880) and Gorton Athletic (1884), 1894 as Manchester City
Colours sky blue shirts, white shorts
Stadium Maine Road (52,600) ☎ 061-226 1191/2
Champions 1937, 1968
Cup Winners 1904, 1934, 1956, 1969
League Cup Winners 1970, 1976
CWC Winners 1970
FA Charity Shield Winners 1937, 1968, 1972

Season	Opponent	Home	Playoff Result	Away	Rnd	Cup
1968-69	Fenerbahce, Turkey	0-0		1-2	1	ECC
1969-70	Atletico Bilbao, Spain	3-0		3-3	1	CWC
	Lierse SK, Belgium	5-0		3-0	2	CWC
	Academica Coimbra, Portugal	1-0		0-0	qf	CWC
	FC Schalke 04 Gelsenkirchen, Germany	5-1		0-1	sf	CWC
	Gornik Zabrze, Poland	2-1	in Vienna		FINAL	CWC
1970-71	Linfield, Ireland	1-0	wag	1-2	1	CWC
	Honved Budapest, Hungary	2-0		1-0	2	CWC
	Gornik Zabrze, Poland	2-0	3-1*	0-2	qf	CWC
			*in Copenhagen			
	Chelsea, England	0-1		0-1	sf	CWC
1972-73	Valencia CF, Spain	2-2		1-2	1	UEFA
1976-77	Juventus, Italy	1-0		0-2	1	UEFA
1977-78	Widzew Lodz, Poland	2-2	lag	0-0	1	UEFA
1978-79	Twente Enschede, Holland	3-2		1-1	1	UEFA
	Standard Liege, Belgium	4-0		0-2	2	UEFA
	AC Milan, Italy	3-0		2-2	3	UEFA
	Borussia Monchengladbach, Germany	1-1		1-3	qf	UEFA

MANCHESTER UNITED

Founded 1878 as Newton Heath Lancashire and Yorkshire Railway FC, 1892 reconstituted as Newton Heath,
1902 as Manchester United
Colours red shirts, white shorts
Stadium Old Trafford (56,925) ☎ 061-872 1661/2
Champions 1908, 1911, 1952, 1956, 1957, 1965, 1967
Cup Winners 1909, 1948, 1963, 1977, 1983, 1985
European Cup Winners 1968
FA Charity Shield Winners 1908, 1911, 1952, 1956, 1957, 1965, 1967, 1977 (Shared), 1983

Season	Opponent	Home	Result	Away	Rnd	Cup
1956-57	RSC Anderlecht, Belgium	10-0*		2-0	pr	ECC
		*All played				
	Borussia Dortmund, Germany	3-2*		0-0	1	ECC
		*at Maine Road				
	Atletico Bilbao, Spain	3-0*		3-5	2	ECC
		*Manchester City Stadium				
	Real Madrid, Spain	2-2		1-3	sf	ECC
1957-58	Shamrock Rovers, Eire	3-2		6-0	1	ECC
	Dukla Prague, Czechoslovakia	3-0		0-1	2	ECC
	Red Star Belgrade, Yugoslavia	2-1		3-3	qf	ECC
	AC Milan, Italy	2-1		0-4	sf	ECC
1958-59	Invited by UEFA to take part following the Munich air disaster, FA made United decline					
1963-64	Willem II Tilburg, Holland	6-1		1-1	1	CWC
	Tottenham Hotspur, England	4-1		0-2	2	CWC
	Sporting Lisbon, Portugal	4-1		0-5	qf	CWC

Season	Opponent	Home	Result	Away	Rnd	Cup
1964-65	Djurgarden IF Stockholm, Sweden	6-1		1-1	pr	Fairs
	Borussia Dortmund, Germany	4-0		6-1	1	Fairs
	Everton, England	1-1		2-1	2	Fairs
	RC Strasbourg, France	0-0		5-0	qf	Fairs
	Ferencvarosi TC, Hungary	3-2	1-2*	0-1	sf	Fairs
	*in Budapest					
1965-66	HJK Helsinki, Finland	6-0		3-2	pr	ECC
	FC Vorwaerts Berlin, East Germany	3-1		2-0	1	ECC
	Benfica, Portugal	3-2		5-1	2	ECC
	Partizan Belgrade, Yugoslavia	1-0		0-2	sf	ECC
1967-68	Hibernians, Malta	4-0		0-0	1	ECC
	FK Sarajevo, Yugoslavia	2-1		0-0	2	ECC
	Gornik Zabrze, Poland	2-0		0-1	qf	ECC
	Real Madrid, Spain	1-0		3-3	sf	ECC
	Benfica, Portugal	4-1	at Wembley		FINAL	ECC
1968-69	Waterford, Eire	7-1		3-1*	1	ECC
	*in Dublin					
	RSC Anderlecht, Belgium	3-0		1-3	2	ECC
	Rapid Vienna, Austria	3-0		0-0	qf	ECC
	AC Milan, Italy	1-0		0-2	sf	ECC
1976-77	Ajax Amsterdam, Holland	2-0		0-1	1	UEFA
	Juventus, Italy	1-0		0-3	2	UEFA
1977-78	St Etienne, France	2-0*		1-1	1	CWC
	*in Plymouth					
	FC Porto, Portugal	5-2		0-4	2	CWC
1980-81	RTS Widzew Lodz, Poland	1-1	lag	0-0	1	UEFA
1982-83	Valencia CF, Spain	0-0		1-2	1	UEFA
1983-84	Dukla Prague, Czechoslovakia	1-1	wag	2-2	1	CWC
	Spartak Varna, Bulgaria	2-0		2-1	2	CWC
	FC Barcelona, Spain	3-0		0-2	qf	CWC
	Juventus, Italy	1-1		1-2	sf	CWC
1984-85	Raba Vasas Eto, Hungary	3-0		2-2	1	UEFA
	PSV Eindhoven, Holland	1-0		0-0	2	UEFA
	Dundee United, Scotland	2-2		3-2	3	UEFA
	Videoton Sekesfehervar, Hungary	1-0	4-5	0-1	qf	UEFA

NEWCASTLE UNITED

Founded 1882 as Newcastle East End, 1892 became Newcastle United after merger with Newcastle West End
Colours black and white striped shirts, black shorts
Stadium St James's!Park (37,718) ☎ 0632-328 361
Champions 1905, 1907, 1909, 1927
Cup Winners 1910, 1924, 1932, 1951, 1952, 1955
Fairs Cup Winners 1969
FA Charity Shield Winners 1909

Season	Opponent	Home	Result	Away	Rnd	Cup
1968-69	Feyenoord Rotterdam, Holland	4-0		0-2	1	Fairs
	Sporting Lisbon, Portugal	1-0		1-1	2	Fairs
	Real Zaragoza, Spain	2-1	wag	2-3	3	Fairs
	Vitoria Setubal, Portugal	5-1		1-3*	qf	Fairs
	*in Lisbon, ground reconstruction					
	Glasgow Rangers, Scotland	2-0		0-0	sf	Fairs
	Ujpest Dozsa, Hungary	3-0		3-2	FINAL	Fairs
1969-70	Dundee United, Scotland	1-0		2-1	1	Fairs
	FC Porto, Portugal	1-0		0-0	2	Fairs
	Southampton, England	0-0	wag	1-1	3	Fairs
	RSC Anderlecht, Belgium	3-1	lag	0-2	qf	Fairs
1970-71	Inter Milan, Italy	2-0		1-1	1	Fairs
	Pecsi Dozsa, Hungary	2-0	0-3p	0-2 aet	2	Fairs
1977-78	Bohemians Dublin, Eire	4-0		0-0	1	UEFA
	SEC Bastia Corsica, France	1-3		1-2	2	UEFA

NOTTINGHAM FOREST

Founded 1865 Colours red shirts, white shorts
Stadium City Ground (35,000) ☎ 0602-822202
Champions 1978
Cup Winners 1898, 1959
League Cup Winners 1978, 1979, 1989, 1990
European Cup Winners 1979, 1980
Full Members Cup Winners 1989
Super Cup Winners 1979 Finalists 1980
FA Charity Shield Winners 1978
World Club Championship Finalists 1980

Season	Opponent	Home	Result	Away	Rnd	Cup
1961-62	Valencia CF, Spain	0-2		1-5	pr	Fairs
1967-68	Eintracht Frankfurt, Germany	4-0		1-0	1	Fairs
	FC Zurich, Switzerland	2-1	lag	0-11	2	Fairs
1978-79	Liverpool, England	2-0		0-0	1	ECC
	AEK Athens, Greece	5-1		2-1	2	ECC
	Grasshoppers Zurich, Switzerland	4-1		1-1	qf	ECC
	1.FC Koln, Germany	3-3		1-0	sf	ECC
	Malmo FF, Sweden	1-0	in Munich		FINAL	ECC
1979-80	Osters IF Vaxjo, Sweden	2-0		1-1	1	ECC
	FC Arges Pitesti, Romania	2-0		2-1	2	ECC
	BFC Dynamo Berlin, East Germany	0-1		3-1	qf	ECC
	Ajax Amsterdam, Holland	2-0		0-1	sf	ECC
	Hamburger SV, Germany	1-0	in Madrid		FINAL	ECC
1980-81	CSKA Sofia, Bulgaria	0-1		0-1	1	ECC
1983-84	FC Vorwaerts on Oder, East Germany	2-0		1-0	1	UEFA
	PSV Eindhoven, Holland	1-0		2-1	2	UEFA
	Glasgow Celtic, Scotland	0-0		2-1	3	UEFA
	Sturm Graz, Austria	1-0		1-1	4	UEFA
	RSC Anderlecht, Belgium	2-0		0-3	sf	UEFA
1984-85	Clube Bruges, Belgium	0-0		0-1	1	UEFA

QUEENS PARK RANGERS

Founded 1885 as St Judes, 1887 as QPR
Colours blue and white hooped shirts, white shorts
Stadium Loftus Road (27,500) ☎ 01-743 0262/5
League Cup Winners 1967

Season	Opponent	Home	Playoff Result	Away	Rnd	Cup
1976-77	Brann Bergen, Norway	4-0		7-0	1	UEFA
	Slovan Bratislava, Czechoslovakia	5-2		3-3	2	UEFA
	1.FC Koln, Germany	3-0	wag	1-4	3	UEFA
	AEK Athens, Greece	3-0	6-7p	0-3	qf	UEFA
1984-85	KR Reykjavik, Iceland	4-0*		3-0	1	UEFA
		*at Arsenal				
	Partizan Belgrade, Yugoslavia	6-2*	lag	0-4	2	UEFA
		*Astro Turf banned				

ENGLAND

SHEFFIELD WEDNESDAY

Founded 1867   Colours blue and white striped shirts, black shorts
Stadium Hillsborough (50,174) ☎ 0742-343123
Champions 1903, 1904, 1929, 1930
Cup Winners 1896, 1907, 1935
FA Charity Shield Winners 1935

Season	Opponent	Home	Result	Away	Rnd	Cup
1961-62	Olympique Lyon, France	5-2		2-4	pr	Fairs
	AS Roma, Italy	4-0		0-1	1	Fairs
	CF Barcelona, Spain	3-2		0-2	2	Fairs
1963-64	DOS Utrecht, Holland	4-1		4-1	1	Fairs
	1.FC Koln, Germany	1-2		2-3	2	Fairs

SOUTHAMPTON

Founded 1885 as Southampton St Mary's, 1897 as Southampton FC
Colours red and white striped shirts, black shorts
Stadium The Dell (25,175) ☎ 0703-39444/39633
Cup Winners 1976

Season	Opponent	Home	Result	Away	Rnd	Cup
1969-70	Rosenborg Trondheim, Norway	2-0		0-1	1	Fairs
	Vitoria Guimaraes, Portugal	5-1		3-3	2	Fairs
	Newcastle United, England	1-1	lag	0-0	3	Fairs
1971-72	Athletic Bilbao, Spain	2-1		0-2	1	UEFA
1976-77	Olympique Marseille, France	4-0		1-2	1	CWC
	Carrick Rangers, Eire	4-1		5-2	2	CWC
	RSC Anderlecht, Belgium	2-1		0-2	qf	CWC
1981-82	Limerick, Eire	1-1		3-0	1	UEFA
	Sporting Lisbon, Portugal	2-4		0-0	2	UEFA
1982-83	IFK Norrkoping, Sweden	2-2	lag	0-0	1	UEFA
1984-85	Hamburger SV, Germany	0-0		0-2	1	UEFA

STOKE CITY

Founded 1863 as Stoke FC, 1885 as Stoke City
Colours red and white striped shirt, black shorts
Stadium Victoria Ground (31,718) ☎ 0782- 413511
League Cup Winners 1972

Season	Opponent	Home	Result	Away	Rnd	Cup
1972-73	1.FC Kaiserslautern, Germany	3-1		0-4	1	UEFA
1974-75	Ajax Amsterdam, Holland	1-1	lag	0-0	1	UEFA

SUNDERLAND

Founded 1879 as Sunderland and District Teachers AFC, 1881 as Sunderland
Colours red and white striped shirts, black shorts
Stadium Roker Park (37,683) ☎ 0783-40332
Champions 1892, 1893, 1895, 1902, 1913, 1936
Cup Winners 1937, 1973
FA Charity Shield Winners 1936

Season	Opponent	Home	Result	Away	Rnd	Cup
1973-74	Vasas Budapest, Hungary	1-0		2-0	1	CWC
	Sporting Lisbon, Portugal	2-1		0-2	2	CWC

TOTTENHAM HOTSPUR

Founded 1882   Colours white shirts, navy blue shorts
Stadium White Hart Lane (48,200) ☎ 01-801 3411
Champions 1951, 1961
Cup Winners 1901, 1921, 1961, 1962, 1967, 1981, 1982
League Cup Winners 1971, 1973
CWC Winners 1963
UEFA Cup Winners 1972, 1984 Finalists 1974
FA Charity Shield Winners 1920, 1951, 1961, 1962, 1967 (Shared), 1981 (Shared)

Season	Opponent	Home	Result	Away	Rnd	Cup
1961-62	Gornik Zabrze, Poland	8-1		2-4	pr	ECC
	Feyenoord Rotterdam, Holland	1-1		3-1	1	ECC
	Dukla Prague, Czechoslovakia	4-1		0-1	qf	ECC
	Benfica, Portugal	2-1		1-3	sf	ECC
1962-63	Glasgow Rangers, Scotland	5-2		3-2	1	CWC
	Slovan Bratislava, Czechoslovakia	6-0		0-2	qf	CWC
	OFK Belgrade, Yugoslavia	3-1		2-1	sf	CWC
	Atletico Madrid, Spain	5-1	in Amsterdam		FINAL	CWC
1963-64	bye				1	CWC
	Manchester United, England	2-0		1-4	2	CWC
1967-68	Hajduk Split, Yugoslavia	4-3		2-0	1	CWC
	Olympique Lyon, France	4-3	lag	0-1	2	CWC
1971-72	IBK Keflavik, Iceland	9-0		6-1*	1	UEFA
				*in Reykjavik		
	FC Nantes, France	1-0		0-0	2	UEFA
	Rapid Bucharest, Romania	3-0		2-0	3	UEFA
	UT Arad Flamurarosie, Romania	1-1		2-0	qf	UEFA
	AC Milan, Italy	2-1		1-1	sf	UEFA
	Wolverhampton Wanderers, England	1-1		2-1	FINAL	UEFA
1972-73	Lyn Oslo, Norway	6-0		6-3	1	UEFA
	Olympiakos Piraeus, Greece	4-0		0-1	2	UEFA
	Red Star Belgrade, Yugoslavia	2-0		0-1	3	UEFA
	Vitoria Setubal, Portugal	1-0	wag	1-2	qf	UEFA
	Liverpool, England	2-1	lag	0-1	sf	UEFA
1973-74	Grasshoppers Zurich, Switzerland	4-1		5-1	1	UEFA
	Aberdeen, Scotland	4-1		1-1	2	UEFA
	Dynamo Tbilisi, USSR	5-1		1-1	3	UEFA
	1.FC Koln, Germany	3-0		2-1	qf	UEFA
	1.FC Lokomotive Leipzig, East Germany	2-0		2-1	sf	UEFA
	Feyenoord Rotterdam, Holland	2-2		0-2	FINAL	UEFA
1981-82	Ajax Amsterdam, Holland	3-0		3-1	1	CWC
	Dundalk, Eire	1-0		1-1	2	CWC
	Eintracht Frankfurt, Germany	2-0		1-2	qf	CWC
	FC Barcelona, Spain	1-1		0-1	sf	CWC

109

ENGLAND

1982-83	Coleraine, Ireland	4-0		3-0	1	CWC
	Bayern Munich, Germany	1-1		1-4	2	CWC
1983-84	Drogheda, Eire	8-0		6-0	1	UEFA
	Feyenoord Rotterdam, Holland	4-2		2-0	2	UEFA
	Bayern Munich, Germany	2-0		0-1	3	UEFA
	FK Austria Vienna, Austria	2-0		2-2	qf	UEFA
	Hajduk Split, Yugoslavia	1-0	wag	1-2	sf	UEFA
	RSC Anderlecht, Belgium	1-1	4-3p	1-1	FINAL	UEFA
1984-85	Sporting Braga, Portugal	6-0		3-0	1	UEFA
	Clube Bruges, Belgium	3-0		1-2	2	UEFA
	Bohemians Prague, Czechoslovakia	2-0		1-1	3	UEFA
	Real Madrid, Spain	0-1		0-0	qf	UEFA

WATFORD

Founded 1891 Colours yellow shirts with black and red trim, red shorts
Stadium Vicarage Road (28,500) ☎ 0923-30933

Season	Opponent	Home	Result	Away	Rnd	Cup
1983-84	1.FC Kaiserslautern, Germany	3-0		1-3	1	UEFA
	Levski Spartak Sofia, Bulgaria	1-1		3-1	2	UEFA
	Sparta Prague, Czechoslovakia	2-3		0-4	3	UEFA

WEST BROMWICH ALBION

Founded 1879 as WB Strollers, 1880 as Albion
Colours blue and white striped shirts, white shorts
Stadium The Hawthorns (39,159) ☎ 021- 525 8888
FA Charity Shield Winners 1919
Champions 1920
Cup Winners 1888, 1892, 1931, 1954, 1968
League Cup Winners 1966

Season	Opponent	Home	Result	Away	Rnd	Cup
1966-67	bye				1	Fairs
	DOS Utrecht, Holland	5-2		1-1	2	Fairs
	Bologna, Italy	1-3		0-3	3	Fairs
1968-69	Clube Bruges, Belgium	2-0	wag	1-3	1	CWC
	Dinamo Bucharest, Romania	4-0		1-1	2	CWC
	Dunfermline Athletic, Scotland	0-1		0-0	qf	CWC
1978-79	Galatasaray, Turkey	3-1		3-1*	1	UEFA
				*in Izmir		
	Sporting Braga, Portugal	1-0		2-0	2	UEFA
	Valencia CF, Spain	2-0		1-1	3	UEFA
	Red Star Belgrade, Yugoslavia	1-1		0-1	qf	UEFA
1979-80	Carl Zeiss Jena, East Germany	1-2		0-2	1	UEFA
1981-82	Grasshoppers Zurich, Switzerland	1-3		0-1	1	UEFA

WEST HAM UNITED

Founded 1895 as Thames Ironworks FC, 1900 as West Ham United
Colours claret and blue shirts, white shorts
Stadium Upton Park (35,237) ☎ 01-472 2740
Cup Winners 1964, 1975, 1980
CWC Winners 1965
Finalists 1976

Season	Opponent	Home	Result	Away	Rnd	Cup
1964-65	La Ghantoise, Belgium	1-1		1-0	pr	CWC
	Sparta Prague, Czechoslovakia	2-0		1-2	1	CWC
	Lausanne Sport, Switzerland	4-3		2-1	2	CWC
	Real Zaragoza, Spain	2-1		1-1	sf	CWC
	TSV 1860 Munich, Germany	2-0	at Wembley		FINAL	CWC
1965-66	bye				1	CWC
	Olympiakos Piraeus, Greece	4-0		2-2	2	CWC
	1.FC Magdeburg, East Germany	1-0		1-1	qf	CWC
	Borussia Dortmund, Germany	1-2		1-3	sf	CWC
1975-76	Reipas Lahti, Finland	3-0		2-2	1	CWC
	Ararat Yerevan, USSR	3-1		1-1	2	CWC
	FC Den Haag, Holland	3-1	wag	2-4	qf	CWC
	Eintracht Frankfurt, Germany	3-1		1-2	sf	CWC
	RSC Anderlecht, Belgium	2-4	in Brussels		FINAL	CWC
1980-81	Castilia Madrid, Spain	5-1*		1-3	1	CWC
		*behind closed doors				
	Timisoara Politechnico, Romania	4-0		0-1	2	CWC
	Dynamo Tbilisi, USSR	1-4		1-0	qf	CWC

WOLVERHAMPTON WANDERERS

Founded 1877 as St Luke's, 1880 as Wolves
Colours old gold shirts, black shorts
Stadium Molineaux (39,000) ☎ 0902-711457/711422
Champions 1954, 1958, 1959
Cup Winners 1893, 1908, 1949, 1960
FA Charity Shield Winners 1949 (Shared), 1954 (Shared), 1959, 1960 (Shared)

Season	Opponent	Home	Result	Away	Rnd	Cup
1958-59	FC Schalke 04 Gelsenkirchen, Germany	2-2		1-2	1	ECC
1959-60	ASK Vorwaerts Berlin, East Germany	2-0		1-2	pr	ECC
	Red Star Belgrade, Yugoslavia	3-0		1-1	1	ECC
	CF Barcelona, Spain	2-5		0-4	2	ECC
1960-61	FK Austria Vienna, Austria	5-0		0-2	1	CWC
	Glasgow Rangers, Scotland	1-1		0-2	2	CWC
1971-72	Academica Coimbra, Portugal	3-0		4-1	1	UEFA
	FC Den Haag, Holland	4-0		3-1	2	UEFA
	Carl Zeiss Jena, East Germany	3-0		1-0	3	UEFA
	Juventus, Italy	2-1		1-1	qf	UEFA
	Ferencvarosi TC, Hungary	2-1		2-2	sf	UEFA
	Tottenham Hotspur, England	1-2		1-1	FINAL	UEFA
1973-74	Belenenses, Portugal	2-1		2-0	1	UEFA
	1.FC Lokomotive Leipzig, East Germany	4-1	lag	0-3	2	UEFA
1974-75	FC Porto, Portugal	3-1		1-4	1	UEFA
1980-81	PSV Eindhoven, Holland	1-0		1-3	1	UEFA

ENGLAND

LONDON XI

Colours white shirts, black shorts
Players from Arsenal, Chelsea, Charlton Athletic, Crystal Palace, Fulham, Leyton Orient, Millwall, QPR, Tottenham Hotspur and West Ham United

Season	Opponent	Home	Result	Away	Rnd	Cup
1955-58	Basel City XI, Switzerland	1-0		5-0	pr	Fairs
	Frankfurt City XI, Germany	3-2		0-1	1	Fairs
	Lausanne Sport, Switzerland	2-0		1-2	sf	Fairs
	CF Barcelona, Spain	2-2		0-6	FINAL	Fairs

112 ● Rhein Stadion, Dusseldorf, Germany. Fortuna Dusseldorf, CWC Final 1981

FAROE ISLANDS

Founded 1979, FIFA 1988
Football Association, PO Box 128, FR110 TORSHAVN ☎ 12606 Telefax 298 19079

LEAGUE CHAMPIONS

1942	KI Klaksvik	1955	HB Torshavn	1967	KI Klaksvik	1980	TB Tvoroyri
1943	TB Tvoroyri	1956	KI Klaksvik	1968	KI Klaksvik	1981	HB Torshavn
1944	not held	1957	KI Klaksvik	1969	KI Klaksvik	1982	HB Torshavn
1945	TB Tvoroyri	1958	KI Klaksvik			1983	GI Gotu
1946	B'36 Torshavn	1959	B'36 Torshavn	1970	KI Klaksvik	1984	B'68 Toftir
1947	SI Sorvag			1971	HB Torshavn	1985	B'68 Toftir
1948	B'36 Torshavn	1960	HB Torshavn	1972	KI Klaksvik	1986	GI Gotu
1949	TB Tvoroyri	1961	KI Klaksvik	1973	HB Torshavn	1987	GI Gotu
		1962	B'36 Torshavn	1974	HB Torshavn	1988	HB Torshavn
1950	B'36 Torshavn	1963	HB Torshavn	1975	HB Torshavn	1989	B'71
1951	TB Tvoroyri	1964	HB Torshavn	1976	TB Tvoroyri		
1952	KI Klaksvik	1965	HB Torshavn	1977	TB Tvoroyri		
1953	KI Klaksvik	1966	KI Klaksvik	1978	HB Torshavn		
1954	KI Klaksvik			1979	IF Fuglafjordur		

CUP WINNERS

1967	KI Klaksvik v B'36 Torshavn	6-2	1980	TB Tvoroyri v NSI Runavik	2-1
1968	HB Torshavn v B'36 Torshavn	2-1	1981	HB Torshavn v TB Tvoroyri	5-2
			1982	HB Torshavn v IF Fuglafjordur	2-1
1973	HB Torshavn v KI Klaksvik	2-1	1983	GI Gotu v Royn Valba	5-1
1974	VB Vagur v HB Torshavn	7-5	1984	HB Torshavn v GI Gotu	2-0
1975	HB Torshavn v IF Fuglafjordur	7-2	1985	GI Gotu v NSI Runavik	4-2
1976	HB Torshavn v TB Tvoroyri	3-1	1986	NSI Runavik v LIF Lorvik	3-1
1977	TB Tvoroyri v VB Vagur	4-3	1987	HB Torshavn v IF Fuglafjordur	2-2 3-0
1978	TB Tvoroyri v HB Torshavn	5-2	1988	HB Torshavn v NSI Runavik	1-0
1979	TB Tvoroyri v KI Klaksvik	5-0			

FINLAND

Founded 1907
Suomen Palloliito Finlands Bollforbund, Stadium 00250 Helsinki 25 ☎ 90-5626233
National Colours blue shirts with white collars and cuffs, white shorts.   Season April to October

LEAGUE CHAMPIONS

Played as Final to decide the Champions up until 1929

1908	Unitas Helsinki v US Helsingissa	4-1
1909	Pus Helsinki v HIFK Helsinki	4-0
1910	IFK Abo v Reipas Viipuri	4-2
1911	HJK Helsinki v AIFK Abo	7-1
1912	HJK Helsinki v HIFK Helsinki	7-1
1913	KIF Kronohagens v AIFK Abo	5-3
1914	not held	
1915	KIF Kronohagens v AIFK Abo	1-0
1916	KIF Kronohagens v AIFK Abo	3-2
1917	HJK Helsinki v AIFK Abo	4-2
1918	HJK Helsinki v Reipas Viipuri	3-0
1919	HJK Helsinki v Reipas Lahti	1-0
1920	AIFK Abo v HPS	2-1
1921	HPS Helsinki v HJK Helsinki	2-1
1922	HPS Helsinki v Reipas Lahti	4-2
1923	HJK Helsinki v TPS Turku	3-1
1924	AIFK Abo v HPS	4-3
1925	HJK Helsinki v TPS Turku	3-2
1926	PSH v TPS Turku	5-2
1927	HPS Helsinki v Reipas Lahti	6-0
1928	TPS Turku v HIFK	3-2
1929	HPS Helsinki v HIFK	4-0

NATIONAL LEAGUE CHAMPIONSHIP

1930 HIFK Helsinki	1946 VIFK Vaasa	1960 Haka Valkeakoski	1975 TPS Turku
1931 HIFK Helsinki	1947 HIFK Helsinki	1961 HIFK Helsinki	1976 KuPS Kuopio
1932 HPS Helsinki	1947-48 VIFK Vaasa†	1962 Haka Valkeakoski	1977 Haka Valkeakoski
1933 HIFK Helsinki	1948 VPS Vaasa	1963 Reipas Lahti	1978 HJK Helsinki
1934 HPS Helsinki	1949 TPS Turku	1964 HJK Helsinki	1979 Oulu Palloseura
1935 HPS Helsinki		1965 Haka Valkeakoski	
1936 HJK Helsinki	1950 Ilves Kissat	1966 KuPS Kuopio	1980 OPS Oulun
1937 HIFK Helsinki	1951 KTP Kotka	1967 Reipas Lahti	1981 HJK Helsinki
1938 HJK Helsinki	1952 KTP Kotka	1968 TPS Turku	1982 Kuusysi Lahti
1939 TPS Turku	1953 VIFK Vaasa	1969 KPV Kokkola	1983 Ilves Kissat
	1954 TuPY Pyrkiva		1984 Kuusysi Lahti
1940 Sudet Viipuri*	1955 KIF Kvonohagens	1970 Reipas Lahti	1985 HJK Helsinki
1941 TPS Turku	1956 KuPS Kuopio	1971 TPS Turku	1986 Kuuysyi Lahti
1942 Pallo Toverit Helsinki (HT)	1957 HPS Helsinki	1972 TPS Turku	1987 HJK Helsinki
1943 not held	1958 KuPS Kuopio	1973 HJK Helsinki	1988 HJK Helsinki
1944 VIFK Vaasa	1959 HIFK Helsinki	1974 KuPS Kuopio	1989 Kuusysi Lahti
1945 VPS Vaasa			

* team now situated in the USSR   † (Summer to Autumn)

CUP WINNERS

1955	Haka Valkeakoski v HPS Helsinki	5-1	**1972**	Reipas Lahti v VPS Vaasa	2-0
1956	PP Pallo Pojat Helsinki TkT Tampere Kisatoverit	2-1	**1973**	Reipas Lahti v SePs Seinajoen	1-0
1957	Drott v KPT Kuopio	2-1	**1974**	Reipas Lahti v OTP Oulu	1-0
1958	KTP Kotka v KIF Kvonohagens	4-1	**1975**	Reipas Lahti v HJK Helsinki	6-2
1959	Haka Valkeakoski v HIFK Helsinki	2-1	**1976**	Reipas Lahti v Ilves Kissat	2-0
			1977	Haka Valkeakoski v SePs Seinajoen	3-1
1960	Haka Valkeakoski v RU 38 Porin Assat	3-1	**1978**	Reipas Lahti v KPT Kuopio	3-1
1961	KTP Kotka v PP Pallo Pojat Helsinki	5-2	**1979**	Ilves Kissat v TPS Turku	2-0
1962	HPS Helsinki v RoPS Rovaniemi	5-0			
1963	Haka Valkeakoski v Reipas Lahti	1-0	**1980**	KTP Kotka v Haka Valkeakoski	3-2
1964	Reipas Lahti v LaPa Lappenranta	1-0	**1981**	HJK Helsinki v Kuusysi Lahti	4-0
1965	AIFK Abo v TPS Turku	1-0	**1982**	Haka Valkeakoski v KPV Kokkolan	3-2
1966	HJK Helsinki v KTP Kotka	6-1	**1983**	Kuusysi Lahti v Haka Valkeakoski	2-0
1967	KTP Kotka v Reipas Lahti	2-0	**1984**	HJK Helsinki v Kuusysi Lahti	2-1
1968	KuPS Kuopio v KTP Kotka	2-1	**1985**	Haka Valkeakoski v HJK Helsinki	2-2 2-1
1969	Haka Valkeakoski v Honka	2-0	**1986**	RoPs Rovaniemen v KePS Kemin,Kemi	2-0
			1987	Kuuysyi Lahti v OTP Oulu	5-4
1970	Mikkelin Palloilijat v Reipas Lahti	2-0	**1988**	Haka Valkeakoski v OTP Oulu	1-0
1971	MP Mikkelin Palloilijat v Sport Vasa	4-1	**1989**	Kups Kuopio v Haka Valkeakoski	3-2

FEATURED CLUBS IN EUROPEAN COMPETITION

Haka Valkeakoski	**Reipas Lahti**	**HJK Helsinki**	**HPS Helsinki**
KuPS Kuopio	**TPS Turku**	**HIFK Helsinki**	**MP Mikkelin**
Ilves Tampere	**KPV Kokkolan**	**AIFK Abo**	**Kuusysi Lahti**
OPS Oulu	**KTP Kotkan Tyovaen Palloilijat**		**KPT Kuopion Pallotoverit**
RoPs Rovaniemen Palloseura			

HAKA VALKEAKOSKI (HAKA)

Founded 1932
Colours white shirts with black collars, black shorts. Stadium Tehtaan Kentta (6,000). ☎ 937-41194
Champions 1960, 1962, 1965, 1977
Cup Winners 1955, 1593 1960, 1963, 1969, 1977, 1980, 1982, 1985, 1988

Season	Opponent	Home	Result	Away	Rnd	Cup
1961-62	Standard Liege, Belgium	0-2*		1-5	1	ECC
		*in Helsinki				
1963-64	Jeunesse Esch, Luxembourg	4-1		0-4	pr	ECC
1964-65	Skeid Oslo, Norway	2-0		0-1	pr	CWC
	Torino, Italy	0-1		0-5	1	CWC
1966-67	RSC Anderlecht, Belgium	1-10		0-2	pr	ECC
1970-71	CSKA Sofia, Bulgaria	1-2		0-9	1	CWC
1977-78	Gornik Zabrze, Poland	0-0		3-5	1	UEFA
1978-79	Dynamo Kiev, USSR	0-1		1-3*	1	ECC
				*in Kharkov		
1981-82	IFK Gothenburg, Sweden	2-3		0-4	1	UEFA
1983-84	Sligo Rovers, Eire	3-0		1-0	1	CWC
	Hammarby IF Stockholm, Sweden	2-1		1-1	2	CWC
	Juventus, Italy	0-1*		0-1	qf	CWC
		*in Strasbourg				
1986-87	Torpedo Moscow, USSR	2-2		1-3	1	CWC
1989-90	Ferebevarisu TC, Hungary	1-1		1-5	1	CWC

FINLAND

REIPAS LAHTI

Founded 1891
Colours orange and black striped shirts, black shorts.   Stadium Kisapuisto (8,000). ☎ 918-520200
Champions 1963, 1967, 1970, 1971
Cup Winners 1964, 1972, 1973, 1974, 1976, 1977, 1978

Season	Opponent	Home	Result	Away	Rnd	Cup
1964-65	Gjovik Lyn, Norway	2-1		0-3	pr	ECC
1965-66	Honved Budapest, Hungary	2-10		0-6	1	CWC
1968-69	Floriana, Malta	2-0		1-1	1	ECC
	Spartak Trnava, Czechoslovakia	1-9*		1-7	2	ECC
		*in Vienna				
1971-72	Grasshoppers Zurich, Switzerland	1-1		0-8	1	ECC
1973-74	Olympique Lyon, France	0-0		0-2	1	CWC
1974-75	Sliema Wanderers, Malta	4-1		0-2	1	CWC
	Malmo FF, Sweden	0-0		1-3	2	CWC
1975-76	West Ham United, England	2-2		0-3	1	CWC
1976-77	Levski Spartak Sofia, Bulgaria	1-7		2-12	1	CWC
1977-78	Hamburger SV, Germany	2-5		1-8	1	CWC
1979-80	Aris Bonnevoie, Luxembourg	0-1		0-1	1	CWC

HELSINGEN JALKA-PALLOKLUBI (HJK)

Founded 1907
Colours all blue.   Stadium Olympique (40,000). ☎ 90-448693/448612
Champions 1911, 1912, 1917, 1918, 1919, 1923, 1925, 1936, 1938, 1964, 1973, 1978, 1981, 1987, 1988
Cup Winners 1966, 1981, 1984

Season	Opponent	Home	Result	Away	Rnd	Cup
1965-66	Manchester United, England	2-3		0-6	pr	ECC
1967-68	Wisla Krakow, Poland	1-4		0-4	1	CWC
1974-75	Valletta, Malta	4-1		0-1	1	ECC
	Atvidaberg FF, Sweden	0-3		0-1	2	ECC
1975-76	Hertha BSC Berlin, Germany	1-2		1-4	1	UEFA
1979-80	Ajax Amsterdam, Holland	1-8		1-8	1	ECC
1982-83	Omonia Nicosia, Cyprus	3-0		0-2	1	ECC
	Liverpool, England	1-0		0-5	2	ECC
1983-84	Spartak Moscow, USSR	0-5		0-2	1	UEFA
1984-85	Dynamo Minsk, USSR	0-6		0-4	1	UEFA
1985-86	Flamurtari Vlore, Albania	3-2		2-1	1	CWC
	Dynamo Dresden, East Germany	1-0		2-7	2	CWC
1986-87	Apoel Nicosia, Cyprus	3-2	lag	0-1	1	ECC
1988-89	FC Porto, Portugal	2-0		0-3	1	ECC
1989-90	AC Milan, Italy	0-1		0-4	1	ECC

HELSINGIN PALLOSEURA (HPS)

Founded 1917
Colours all green.   Stadium Helsingin Pallokentta (7,000). ☎ 119925
Champions 1921, 1922, 1927, 1929, 1932, 1934, 1935, 1957
Cup Winners 1962

Season	Opponent	Home	Result	Away	Rnd	Cup
1958-59	Stade de Reims, France	0-3*		0-4	1	ECC
		*in Rouen				
1963-64	Slovan Bratislava, Czechoslovakia	1-4		1-8	1	CWC

KUOPION PALLOSEURA (KuPS)

Founded 1923
Colours yellow shirts, black shorts. Stadium Vainolanniemi (12,000). ☎ 971-119925
Champions 1956, 1958, 1966, 1974, 1976
Cup Winners 1968, 1989

Season	Opponent	Home	Result	Away	Rnd	Cup
1959-60	Eintracht Frankfurt, Germany	withdrew			pr	ECC
1967-68	St Etienne, France	0-3		0-2	1	ECC
1969-70	Academica Coimbra, Portugal	0-1		0-0	1	CWC
1975-76	Ruch Chorzow, Poland	2-2		0-5	1	ECC
1976-77	Osters IF Vaxjo, Sweden	3-2		0-2	1	UEFA
1977-78	Clube Bruges, Belgium	0-4		2-5	1	ECC
1978-79	B 1903 Copenhagen, Denmark	2-1		4-4	1	UEFA
	Esbjerg fB, Denmark	0-2*		1-4	2	UEFA
		*in Mikkeli				
1979-80	Malmo FF, Sweden	1-2		0-2	1	UEFA
1980-81	St Etienne, France	0-7		0-7	1	UEFA

TURUN PALLOSEURA (TPS),TURKU

Founded 1922
Colours black and white striped shirts, white shorts.
Stadium Kupittaan Jalkapallostadion (10,000). ☎ 921-360625/500000
Champions 1928, 1939, 1941, 1949, 1968, 1971, 1972, 1975

Season	Opponent	Home	Result	Away	Rnd	Cup
1969-70	KB Copenhagen, Denmark	0-1		0-4	pr	ECC
1972-73	1.FC Magdeburg, East Germany	1-3		0-6	1	ECC
1973-74	Glasgow Celtic, Scotland	1-6		0-3	1	ECC
1976-77	Sliema Wanderers, Malta	1-0	wag	1-2	1	ECC
	FC Zurich, Switzerland	0-1		0-2	2	ECC
1985-86	Spartak Moscow, USSR	1-3		0-1	1	UEFA
1987-88	Admira Wacker, Austria	0-1		2-0	1	UEFA
	Inter Milan, Italy	0-2		1-0	2	UEFA
1988-89	Linfield, Ireland	0-0	wag	1-1*	1	UEFA
				*in Wrexham, Wales		
	First Vienna FC 1894, Austria	1-0aet	wag	1-2	2	UEFA
	Victoria Bucharest, Romania	3-2	lag	0-1	3	UEFA

HELSINGIN IDROTTSFORENINGEN KAMRATERNA (HIFK)

Founded 1897
Colours red shirts, white shorts. Stadium Helsingin Pallokentta (7,000). ☎ only private number listed
Champions 1930, 1931, 1933, 1937, 1959, 1961

Season	Opponent	Home	Result	Away	Rnd	Cup
1960-61	IFK Malmo, Sweden	1-3		1-2	1	ECC
1962-63	FK Austria Vienna, Austria	0-2		3-5	1	ECC
1971-72	Rosenborg Trondheim, Norway	0-1		0-3	1	UEFA
1972-73	Hvidovre IF, Denmark	withdrew			1	UEFA

117

FINLAND

MIKKELIN PALLOILIJAT (MP)

Founded 1929
Colours blue shirts, white shorts. Stadium Urheilupuisto (10,000). ☎ 955-369122
Cup Winners 1970, 1971

Season	Opponent	Home	Result	Away	Rnd	Cup
1971-72	Eskisehirspor, Turkey	0-0		0-4	1	CWC
1972-73	Carl Zeiss Jena, East Germany	3-2		1-6	1	CWC
1973-74	Carl Zeiss Jena, East Germany	0-3		0-3	1	UEFA

ILVES TAMPERE

Founded 1931 as Ilves Kissat Tampere, 1970 Ilves
Colours yellow shirts, green shorts. Stadium Ratina Stadion (25,000). ☎ 931-559960
Champions 1950, 1983
Cup Winners 1979

Season	Opponent	Home	Result	Away	Rnd	Cup
1970-71	Sturm Graz, Austria	4-2		0-3	1	Fairs
1980-81	Feyenoord Rotterdam, Holland	1-3		2-4	1	CWC
1984-85	Juventus, Italy	0-4		1-2	1	ECC
1986-87	Glasgow Rangers, Scotland	2-0		0-4	1	UEFA

KOKKOLAN PALLO-VEIKOT (KPV)

Founded 1930
Colours all green. Stadium Keskusurheilukentta (10,000). ☎ 13368
Champions 1969

Season	Opponent	Home	Result	Away	Rnd	Cup
1970-71	Glasgow Celtic, Scotland	0-5		0-9	1	ECC
1974-75	1.FC Koln, Germany	1-4		1-5	1	UEFA

IF KAMRATERNA, ABO (AIFK)

Founded 1908
Colours yellow shirts, black shorts. Stadium Kupittaan Jalkapallostadion (10,000). ☎ only private number listed
Champions 1910, 1920, 1924
Cup Winners 1965

Season	Opponent	Home	Result	Away	Rnd	Cup
1966-67	Servette Geneva, Switzerland	1-2		1-1	pr	CWC

KUUSYSI LAHTI

Founded 1934 as U.P., 1969 Lahti '69, 1974 Kuusysi
Colours all white. Stadium Keskusurheilukentta (10,000). ☎ 918-512505
Champions 1982, 1984, 1986, 1989
Cup Winners 1983

Season	Opponent	Home	Result	Away	Rnd	Cup
1982-83	Galatasaray, Turkey	1-1		1-2	1	CWC

1983-84	Dinamo Bucharest, Romania	0-1		0-3	1	ECC
1984-85	Internacional Bratislava, Czechoslovakia	0-0		1-2	1	CWC
1985-86	FK Sarajevo, Yugoslavia	2-1		2-1	1	ECC
	Zenit Leningrad, USSR	3-1		1-2	2	ECC
	Steaua Bucharest, Romania	0-1*		0-0	qf	ECC
	*in Helsinki					
1987-88	FC Neuchatel Xamax, Switzerland	2-1		0-5	1	ECC
1988-89	Dinamo Bucharest, Romania	0-3		0-3	1	CWC
1989-90	Paris St Germain, France	0-0		2-3	1	UEFA

OULUN PALLOSEURA (OPS) OULU

Founded 1925
Colours yellow shirts, blue shorts.   Stadium Raatti (10,000). ☎ 14391
Champions 1979, 1980

Season	Opponent	Home	Result	Away	Rnd	Cup
1980-81	Liverpool, England	1-1		1-10	1	ECC
1981-82	Liverpool, England	0-1		0-7	1	ECC

KOTKAN TYOVAEN PALLOILIJAT (KTP) KOTKA

Founded 1927
Colours green and white striped shirts, white shorts.   Stadium Urheilukeskus (6,000). ☎ 11631
Cup Winners 1980

Season	Opponent	Home	Result	Away	Rnd	Cup
1981-82	SEC Bastia Corsica, France	0-0		0-5	1	CWC

KUOPION PALLOTOVERIT (KPT) (Koparit)

Founded 1931
Colours green shirts, white shorts.   Stadium Vainolanniemi (12,000). ☎ 971-123601/121066

Season	Opponent	Home	Result	Away	Rnd	Cup
1982-83	RSC Anderlecht, Belgium	1-3		0-3	1	UEFA

RoPs ROVANIEMEN PALLOSEURA

Founded 1950
Colours blue shirts, white shorts.   Stadium Keskuskentta (4,000). ☎ 960-291349
Cup Winners 1986

Season	Opponent	Home	Result	Away	Rnd	Cup
1987-88	Glentoran, Ireland	0-0	wag	1-1	1	CWC
	Vlaznia Shkodar, Albania	1-0		1-0	2	CWC
	Olympique Marseille, France	0-1		0-3	qf	CWC
1989-90	GKS Katowice, Poland	1-1		1-0	1	UEFA
	AJ Auxerre, France	0-5		0-3	2	UEFA

FRANCE

Founded 1919
Federation Francaise De Football, 60 Bis Avenue, Diena, Paris 16e ☎ 7206540
National Colours blue shirts, white shorts, red socks
Season August to June

LEAGUE CHAMPIONS

1933 Lille Olympique	1950 Bordeaux	1965 FC Nantes	1980 FC Nantes
1934 Sete	1951 OGC Nice	1966 FC Nantes	1981 St Etienne
1935 Sochaux	1952 OGC Nice	1967 St Etienne	1982 AS Monaco
1936 Racing Club Paris	1953 Stade de Reims	1968 St Etienne	1983 FC Nantes
1937 Olympique Marseille	1954 Lille OSC	1969 St Etienne	1984 Girondins Bordeaux
1938 Sochaux	1955 Stade de Reims		1985 Girondins Bordeaux
1939 Sete	1956 OGC Nice	1970 St Etienne	1986 Paris St Germain
	1957 St Etienne	1971 Olympique Marseille	1987 Girondins Bordeaux
1946 Lille OSC	1958 Stade de Reims	1972 Olympique Marseille	1988 AS Monaco
1947 CO Roubaix-Tourcoing	1959 OGC Nice	1973 FC Nantes	1989 Olympique Marseille
1948 Olympique Marseille		1974 St Etienne	
1949 Stade de Reims	1960 Stade de Reims	1975 St Etienne	
	1961 AS Monaco	1976 St Etienne	
	1962 Stade de Reims	1977 FC Nantes	
	1963 AS Monaco	1978 AS Monaco	
	1964 St Etienne	1979 RC Strasbourg	

CUP WINNERS

1918 Olympique de Pantin v FC Lyon	3-0	
1919 CAS Generaux Paris v Olympique de Paris	3-2	
1920 CA Paris v Le Havre AC	2-1	
1921 Red Star v Olympique de Paris	2-1	
1922 Red Star v Stade Rennes	2-0	
1923 Red Star v Sete	4-2	
1924 Olympique Marseille v Sete	3-2	
1925 CAS Generaux Paris v Rouen	1-1 3-2	
1926 Olympique Marseille v Valentigny	4-1	
1927 Olympique Marseille v US Quevilloise	3-0	
1928 Red Star Olympique v CA Paris	3-1	
1929 SO Montpellierains v Sete 2-0		
1930 Sete v RC France	3-1	
1931 Club Francaise v SO Montpellierains	3-0	

1932 AS Cannes v RC Roubaix	1-0	
1933 Excelsior v RC Roubaix	3-1	
1934 Sete v Olympique Marseille	2-1	
1935 Olympique Marseille v Rennes	3-0	
1936 Racing Club Paris v FCO Charleville	1-0	
1937 Sochaux v RC Strasbourg	2-1	
1938 Olympique Marseille v Metz	2-1	
1939 Racing Club Paris v Lille Olympique	3-1	
1940 Racing Club Paris v Olympique Marseille	2-1	
1941* Girondins Bordeaux v Fives	2-0	
1942* Red Star Olympique v Sete	2-0	
1943* Olympique Marseille v Girondins Bordeaux	2-2 4-0	
* 3 teams in finals, country divided into 3 zones		
1945 Racing Club Paris v Lille OSC	3-0	
1946 Lille OSC v Red Star Olympique	4-1	

120

1947	Lille OSC v RC Strasbourg	2-0
1948	Lille OSC v RC Lens	3-2
1949	Racing Club Paris v Lille OSC	5-2
1950	Stade de Reims v Racing Club Paris	2-0
1951	RC Strasbourg v US Valenciennes	3-0
1952	OGC Nice v Girondins Bordeaux	5-3
1953	Lille OSC v Nancy	2-1
1954	OGC Nice v Olympique Marseille	2-1
1955	Lille OSC v Girondins Bordeaux	5-2
1956	Sedan v Troyes	3-1
1957	Toulouse v Angers	6-3
1958	Stade de Reims v Nimes Olympique	3-1
1959	Le Havre v Sochaux	2-2 3-0
1960	AS Monaco v St Etienne	4-2
1961	Sedan v Nimes Olympique	3-1
1962	St Etienne v Nancy	1-0
1963	AS Monaco v Olympique Lyon	0-0 2-0
1964	Olympique Lyon v Girondins Bordeaux	2-0
1965	Rennes v Sedan	2-2 3-1
1966	RC Strasbourg v FC Nantes	1-0
1967	Olympique Lyon v Sochaux	3-1
1968	St Etienne v Girondins Bordeaux	2-1

1969	Olympique Marseille v Girondins Bordeaux	2-0
1970	St Etienne v FC Nantes	5-0
1971	Rennes v Olympique Lyon	1-0
1972	Olympique Marseille v Bastia Corsica	2-1
1973	Olympique Lyon v FC Nantes	2-1
1974	St Etienne v AS Monaco	2-1
1975	St Etienne v RC Lens	2-0
1976	Olympique Marseille v Olympique Lyon	2-0
1977	St Etienne v Stade de Reims	2-1
1978	Nancy v OGC Nice	1-0
1979	FC Nantes v Auxerre	4-1
1980	AS Monaco v Orleans	3-1
1981	Bastia Corsica v St Etienne	2-1
1982	Paris St Germain v St Etienne	2-2 6-5 pens
1983	Paris St Germain v FC Nantes	3-2
1984	FC Metz v AS Monaco	2-0
1985	AS Monaco v Paris St Germain	1-0
1986	Girondins Bordeaux v Olympique Marseille	2-1
1987	Girondins Bordeaux v Olympique Marseille	2-0
1988	FC Metz v Sochaux	1-1 5-4 pens
1989	Olympique Marseille v AS Monaco	4-3

FRENCH SUPER CUP

1955	Stade de Reims v Lille OSC	7-1
1956	Sedan v OGC Nice	1-0
1957	St Etienne v Toulouse	2-1
1958	Stade de Reims v Nimes Olympique	2-1
1959	Le Havre v OGC Nice	2-0
1960	Stade de Reims v AS Monaco	6-2
1961	AS Monaco v Sedan	1-1
	Monaco won on toss of coin	
1962	St Etienne v Stade de Reims	3-2
1963	AS Monaco won league and cup	
1964	not held	
1965	FC Nantes v Rennes	4-2

1966	Stade de Reims v FC Nantes	2-0
1967	St Etienne v Olympique Lyon	2-0
1968	St Etienne v Girondins Bordeaux	5-3
1969	St Etienne v Olympique Marseille	3-2
1970	not held	
1971	Olympique Marseille v Rennes	2-2
1985	AS Monaco v Girondins Bordeaux	1-1 8-7 pens

FRANCE

FEATURED CLUBS IN EUROPEAN COMPETITION

St Etienne	Olympique Lyon	FC Nantes	Olympique Marseille
Stade de Reims	AS Monaco	Girondins Bordeaux	RC Strasbourg
OGC Nice	Rennes	CS Sedan-Ardennes	Matra Racing Paris
Nimes Olympique	Toulouse FC	RC Lens	SC Angers
Sochaux	Nancy	Rouen	FC Metz
SEC Bastia Corsica	Angouleme	AJ Auxerre	Paris St Germain
Laval	Stade Francais	Montpellier-Paillade SC	

AS SAINT ETIENNE

Founded 1920
Colours green shirts, white shorts
Stadium Stade Geoffrey-Guichard (42,000) ☎ 77-74 63 55
Champions 1957, 1964, 1967, 1968, 1969, 1970, 1974, 1975, 1976, 1981
Cup Winners 1962, 1968, 1970, 1974, 1975, 1977
French Super Cup Winners 1957, 1962, 1967, 1968, 1969
European Cup Finalist 1976

Season	Opponent	Home	Result	Away	Rnd	Cup
1957-58	Glasgow Rangers, Scotland	2-1		1-3	pr	ECC
1962-63	Vitoria Setubal, Portugal	1-1		3-0	1	CWC
	1.FC Nurnburg, Germany	0-3		0-0	2	CWC
1964-65	FC La Chaux de Fonds, Switzerland	2-2		1-2	pr	ECC
1967-68	KuPS Kuopio Palloseura, Finland	2-0		3-0	1	ECC
	Benfica, Portugal	1-0		0-2	2	ECC
1968-69	Glasgow Celtic, Scotland	2-0		0-4	1	ECC
1969-70	Bayern Munich, Germany	3-0		0-2	1	ECC
	Legia Warsaw, Poland	0-1		1-2	2	ECC
1970-71	Cagliari Sardinia, Italy	1-0		0-3	1	ECC
1971-72	1.FC Koln, Germany	1-1		1-2	1	UEFA
1974-75	Sporting Lisbon, Portugal	2-0		1-1	1	ECC
	Hajduk Split, Yugoslavia	5-1		1-4	2	ECC
	Ruch Chorzow, Poland	2-0		2-3	qf	ECC
	Bayern Munich, Germany	0-0		0-2	sf	ECC
1975-76	KB Copenhagen, Denmark	3-1		2-0	1	ECC
	Glasgow Rangers, Scotland	2-0		2-1	2	ECC
	Dynamo Kiev, USSR	3-0		0-2*	qf	ECC
				* in Simferopol		
	PSV Eindhoven, Holland	1-0		0-0	sf	ECC
	Bayern Munich, Germany	0-1	in Glasgow	FINAL		ECC
1976-77	CSKA Sofia, Bulgaria	1-0		0-0	1	ECC
	PSV Eindhoven, Holland	1-0		0-0	2	ECC
	Liverpool, England	1-0		1-3	qf	ECC
1977-78	Manchester United, England	1-1		0-2*	1	CWC
				* in Plymouth		
1979-80	Widzew Lodz, Poland	3-0		1-2	1	UEFA
	PSV Eindhoven, Holland	6-0		0-2	2	UEFA
	Aris Salonika, Greece	4-1		3-3	3	UEFA
	Borussia Monchengladbach, Germany	1-4		0-2	qf	UEFA
1980-81	KuPS Kuopion Palloseura, Finland	7-0		7-0	1	UEFA
	St Mirren, Scotland	2-0		0-0	2	UEFA
	Hamburger SV, Germany	1-0		5-0	3	UEFA
	Ipswich Town, England	1-4		1-3	qf	UEFA
1981-82	BFC Dynamo Berlin, East Germany	1-1		0-2	pr	ECC
1982-83	Tatabanya Banyasz, Hungary	4-1		0-0	1	UEFA
	Bohemians Prague, Czechoslovakia	0-0		0-4	2	UEFA

OLYMPIQUE LYON

Founded 1945 by merger of Villeurbanne and FC Lyon
Colours all red
Stadium Stade de Gerland (50,000) ☎ 78-58 64 22
Cup Winners 1964, 1967, 1973

Season	Opponent	Home	Playoff Result	Away	Rnd	Cup
1958-60	Inter Milan, Italy	1-1		0-7	1	Fairs
1960-61	1.FC Koln, Germany	2-1		1-3	1	Fairs
1961-62	Sheffield Wednesday, England	4-2		2-5	pr	Fairs
1963-64	B 1909 Odense, Denmark	3-1		3-1	pr	CWC
	Olympiakos Piraeus, Greece	4-1		1-2	1	CWC
	Hamburger SV, Germany	2-0		1-1	2	CWC
	Sporting Lisbon, Portugal	0-0	0-1* * in Madrid	1-1	qf	CWC
1964-65	FC Porto, Portugal	0-1		0-3	pr	CWC
1967-68	Aris Bonneweg, Luxembourg	2-1		3-0	1	CWC
	Tottenham Hotspur, England	1-0	wag	3-4	2	CWC
	Hamburger SV, Germany	2-0	0-2* * in Hamburg	0-2	qf	CWC
1968-69	Academica Coimbra, Portugal	1-0	wot	0-1	1	Fairs
	Vitoria Setubal, Portugal	1-2		0-5	2	Fairs
1973-74	Reipas Lahti, Finland	2-0		0-0	1	CWC
	PAOK Salonika, Greece	3-3		0-4	2	CWC
1974-75	Red Boys Differdange, Luxembourg	7-0		4-1	1	UEFA
	Borussia Monchengladbach, Germany	2-5		0-1	2	UEFA
1975-76	Clube Bruges, Belgium	4-3		0-3	1	UEFA

FC NANTES

Founded 21-4-1943 by merger of St Pierre, Mellinet, Loire, ASO Nantes and Stade Nantes
Colours yellow and green striped shirts, Green shorts
Stadium La Beaujoire (44,927) ☎ 50-93 17 07/ 40-29 15 59
Champions 1965, 1966, 1973, 1977, 1980, 1983
Cup Winners 1979
French Super Cup Winners 1965

Season	Opponent	Home	Result	Away	Rnd	Cup
1965-66	Partizan Belgrade, Yugoslavia	2-2		0-2	1	ECC
1966-67	KR Reykjavik, Iceland	5-2		3-2	1	ECC
	Glasgow Celtic, Scotland	1-3		1-3	2	ECC
1970-71	Stroemgodset Drammen, Norway	2-3		5-0	1	CWC
	Cardiff City, Wales	1-2		1-5	2	CWC
1971-72	FC Porto, Portugal	1-1		2-0	1	UEFA
	Tottenham Hotspur, England	0-0		0-1	2	UEFA
1973-74	Vejle BK, Denmark	0-1		2-2	1	ECC
1974-75	Legia Warsaw, Poland	2-2		1-0	1	UEFA
	Banik Ostrava, Czechoslovakia	1-0		0-2 aet	2	UEFA
1977-78	Dukla Prague, Czechoslovakia	0-0	wag	1-1	1	ECC
	Atletico Madrid, Spain	1-1		1-2	2	ECC
1978-79	Benfica, Portugal	0-2		0-0	1	UEFA
1979-80	Cliftonville, Ireland	7-0		1-0	1	CWC
	Steaua Bucharest, Romania	3-2		2-1	2	CWC
	Dynamo Moscow, USSR	2-3		2-0	qf	CWC
	Valencia CF, Spain	2-1		0-4	sf	CWC
1980-81	Linfield, Ireland	2-0		1-0* * in Haarlem, Netherlands	1	ECC
	Inter Milan, Italy	1-2		1-1	2	ECC

123

1981-82	KSC Lokeren, Belgium	1-1		2-4	1	UEFA
1983-84	Rapid Vienna, Austria	3-1		0-3	1	ECC
1985-86	Valur Reykjavik, Iceland	3-0		1-2	1	UEFA
	Partizan Belgrade, Yugoslavia	4-0		1-1	2	UEFA
	Spartak Moscow, USSR	1-1		1-0*	3	UEFA
				* in Tbilisi		
	Inter Milan, Italy	3-3		0-3	qf	UEFA
1986-87	Torino, Italy	0-4		1-1	1	UEFA

OLYMPIQUE MARSEILLE

Founded 1899
Colours white shirts with blue facings, white shorts
Stadium Stade Velodrome (46,000) ☎ 91-76 56 09
Champions 1937, 1948, 1971, 1972, 1989
Cup Winners 1924, 1926, 1927, 1935, 1938, 1943, 1969, 1972, 1976, 1989
French Super Cup Winners 1971

Season	Opponent	Home	Result	Away	Rnd	Cup
1962-63	Union St Gilloise, Belgium	1-0		2-4	pr	Fairs
1968-69	Goztepe Izmir, Turkey	2-0	lot	0-2	1	Fairs
1969-70	Dukla Prague, Czechoslovakia	2-0		0-1	1	CWC
	Dinamo Zagreb, Yugoslavia	1-1		0-2	2	CWC
1970-71	Spartak Trnava, Czechoslovakia	2-0	3-4 pen	0-2	1	Fairs
1971-72	Gornik Zabrze, Poland	2-1		1-1	1	ECC
	Ajax Amsterdam, Holland	1-2		1-4	2	ECC
1972-73	Juventus, Italy	1-0*		0-3	1	ECC
		* in Lyon				
1973-74	US Spora, Luxembourg	7-1		5-0	1	UEFA
	1.FC Koln, Germany	2-0		0-6	2	UEFA
1975-76	Carl Zeiss Jena, East Germany	0-1		0-3	1	UEFA
1976-77	Southampton, England	2-1		0-4	1	CWC
1987-88	1.FC Lokomotive Leipzig, East Germany	1-0		0-0	1	CWC
	Hadjuk Split, Yugoslavia	4-0		0-2	2	CWC
	RoPs Rovaniemen, Finland	3-0		1-0	qf	CWC
	Ajax Amsterdam, Holland	0-3		2-1	sf	CWC
1989-90	Brondbyernes IF, Denmark	3-0		1-1	1	ECC
	AEK Athens, Greece	2-0		1-1	2	ECC
	Sredets CFKA Sofia, Bulgaria	3-1		1-0	qf	ECC
	Benfica, Portugal	2-1	lag	0-1	sf	ECC

STADE DE REIMS

Founded 1911 as Souck Sportive au Parc de Pommery, 1931 as Stade Remois, merged in 1938 with Sporting Club Remois to become Stade de Reims
Colours red shirts with white facings, white shorts
Stadium Auguste Delaune (18,000) ☎ 26-40 26 91 European matches played at the Parc De Princes Paris (49,700)
Champions 1949, 1953, 1955, 1958, 1960, 1962
Cup Winners 1950, 1958
French Super Cup Winners 1955, 1958, 1960, 1966
European Cup Finalists 1956, 1959

Season	Opponent	Home	Result	Away	Rnd	Cup
1955-56	AGF Aarhus, Denmark	2-2		2-0*	1	ECC
				* in Copenhagen		
	Voros Lobago, MTK, Hungary	4-2*		4-4	2	ECC
		* in Paris				
	Hibernian, Scotland	2-0*		1-0	sf	ECC
		* in Paris				
	Real Madrid, Spain	3-4	in Paris		FINAL	ECC

1958-59	Ards, Ireland	6-2*		4-1**	1	ECC
		* in Paris		** in Belfast		
	HPS Palloseura Helsinki, Finland	4-0*		3-0**	2	ECC
		* in Paris		** in Rouen		
	Standard Liege, Belgium	3-0*		0-2	qf	ECC
		* in Paris				
	Young Boys Bern, Switzerland	3-0*		0-1	sf	ECC
		* in Paris				
	Real Madrid, Spain	0-2	in Stuttgart		FINAL	ECC
1960-61	Jeunesse Esch, Luxembourg	6-1		5-0	1	ECC
	Burnley, England	3-2*		0-2	2	ECC
		* in Paris				
1962-63	FK Austria Vienna, Austria	5-0*		2-3	1	ECC
		* in Paris				
	Feyenoord Rotterdam, Holland	0-1*		1-1	2	ECC
		* in Paris				

AS MONACO

Founded 1924
Colours red and white diagonal halved shirts, white shorts and socks
Stadium Louis II Nou Veau (20,000) ☎ 93-30 45 29
Champions 1961, 1963, 1978, 1982, 1988
Cup Winners 1960, 1963, 1980, 1985
French Super Cup Winners 1961, 1963, 1985

Season	Opponent	Home	Result	Away	Rnd	Cup
1961-62	Glasgow Rangers, Scotland	2-3		2-3	1	ECC
1963-64	AEK Athens, Greece	7-2*		1-1	1	ECC
		* in Nice				
	Inter Milan, Italy	1-3*		0-1	2	ECC
		* in Marseille				
1974-75	Eintracht Frankfurt, Germany	2-2		0-3	1	CWC
1978-79	Steaua Bucharest, Romania	3-0		0-2	pr	ECC
	Malmo FF, Sweden	0-1		0-0	1	ECC
1979-80	Schackhtor Donetz, USSR	2-0		1-2	1	UEFA
	Lokomotiv Sofia, Bulgaria	2-1		2-4	2	UEFA
1980-81	Valencia CF, Spain	3-3		0-2	1	CWC
1981-82	Dundee United, Scotland	2-5		2-1	1	UEFA
1982-83	CSKA Sofia, Bulgaria	0-0*		0-2	1	ECC
		* in Nice				
1984-85	CSKA Sofia, Bulgaria	2-2		1-2	1	UEFA
1985-86	Universitatea Craiova, Romania	2-0		0-3	1	CWC
1988-89	Valur Reykjavik, Iceland	2-0		0-1	1	ECC
	Clube Bruges, Belgium	6-1		0-1	2	ECC
	Galatasaray, Turkey	0-1		0-0*	qf	ECC
				* in Koln		
1989-90	Belenenses, Portugal	3-0		1-1	1	CWC
	BFC Dynamo Berlin, East Germany	0-0	wag	1-1aet	2	CWC
	Real Valladolid, Spain	0-0aet	3-1p	0-0	qf	CWC
	Sampdoria, Italy	2-2		0-2	sf	CWC

FRANCE

GIRONDINS BORDEAUX

Founded 1881, Football section 1910 as Bordeaux FC, 1936 Bordeaux Port, 1945 Girondins Bordeaux
Colours all navy blue with white trim
Stadium Parc de Lescure (38,056) ☎ 56-08 63 63
Champions 1950, 1984, 1985, 1987
Cup Winners 1941, 1986, 1987

Season	Opponent	Home	Result	Away	Rnd	Cup
1964-65	Borussia Dortmund, Germany	2-0		1-4	pr	Fairs
1965-66	Sporting Lisbon, Portugal	0-4		1-6	1	Fairs
1966-67	FC Porto, Portugal	2-1	wot	1-2	1	Fairs
	La Ghantoise, Belgium	0-0		0-1	2	Fairs
1967-68	St Patrick's Athletic, Eire	6-3		3-1	1	Fairs
	Atletico Bilbao, Spain	1-3		0-1	2	Fairs
1968-69	1.FC Koln, Germany	2-1		0-3	1	CWC
1969-70	Dunfermline Athletic, Scotland	2-0		0-4	1	Fairs
1981-82	Vikingur Reykjavik, Iceland	4-0		4-0*	1	UEFA
				* in Reykjavik		
	Hamburger SV, Germany	2-1		0-2	2	UEFA
1982-83	Carl Zeiss Jena, East Germany	5-0		1-3	1	UEFA
	Hajduk Split, Yugoslavia	4-0		1-4	2	UEFA
	Universitatea Craiova, Romania	1-0		0-2	3	UEFA
1983-84	1.FC Lokomotive Leipzig, East Germany	2-3		0-4	1	UEFA
1984-85	Athletic Bilbao, Spain	3-2		0-0	1	ECC
	Dinamo Bucharest, Romania	1-0		1-1	2	ECC
	Dnepr Dnepropetrovsk, USSR	1-1	5-3p	1-1*	qf	ECC
				* in Krivoy Rog		
	Juventus, Italy	2-0		0-3	sf	ECC
1985-86	Fenerbahce, Turkey	2-3		0-0	1	ECC
1986-87	Waterford, Eire	4-0		2-1*	1	CWC
				* in Dublin		
	Benfica, Portugal	1-0		1-1	2	CWC
	Torpedo Moscow, USSR	1-0	wag	2-3*	qf	CWC
				* in Tbilisi		
	1.FC Lokomotive Leipzig, East Germany	0-1	5-6 pen	1-0	sf	CWC
1987-88	BFC Dynamo Berlin, East Germany	2-0		2-0	1	ECC
	Lillestrom SK, Norway	1-0		0-0	2	ECC
	PSV Eindhoven, Holland	1-1	lag	0-0	qf	ECC
1988-89	Dnepr Dnepropetrovsk, USSR	2-1		1-1	1	UEFA
	Ujest Dozsa, Hungary	1-0		1-0	2	UEFA
	Napoli, Italy	0-1		0-0	3	UEFA

RACING CLUB DE STRASBOURG

Founded 1906
Colours blue shirts, white shorts
Stadium De La Meinau (42,756) ☎88-34 12 18
Champions 1979
Cup Winners 1951, 1966

Season	Opponent	Home	Playoff Result	Away	Rnd	Cup
1961-62	MTK Budapest, Hungary	1-3		2-10	1	Fairs
1964-65	AC Milan, Italy	2-0		0-1	pr	Fairs
	AC Basle, Switzerland	5-2		1-0	1	Fairs
	CF Barcelona, Spain	0-0	0-0 wot*	2-2	2	Fairs
			* in Barcelona			
	Manchester United, England	0-5		0-0	3	Fairs

1965-66	AC Milan, Italy	2-1	1-1 lot*	0-1	pr	Fairs
			* in Milan			
1966-67	Steaua Bucharest, Romania	1-0		1-1	1	CWC
	Slavia Sofia, Bulgaria	1-0		0-2	2	CWC
1978-79	IF Elfsborg Boras, Sweden	4-1		0-2	1	UEFA
	Hibernian, Scotland	2-0		0-1	2	UEFA
	MSV Duisberg, Germany	0-0		0-4	3	UEFA
1979-80	IFK Start Kristiansand, Norway	4-0		2-1	1	ECC
	Dukla Prague, Czechoslovakia	2-0		0-1	2	ECC
	Ajax Amsterdam, Holland	0-0		0-4	qf	ECC

OLYMPIQUE GYMNASTE CLUB NICE

Founded 1904 as Gymnaste '04, 1924 amalgamation of FAC Nice and Gymneste '04
Colours red and black striped shirts, black shorts
Stadium Municipal de Ray (29,000) ☎ 93-83 22 60
Champions 1951, 1952, 1956, 1959
Cup Winners 1952, 1954

Season	Opponent	Home	Playoff Result	Away	Rnd	Cup
1956-57	AGF Aarhus, Denmark	5-1		1-1*	1	ECC
				* in Copenhagen		
	Glasgow Rangers, Scotland	1-2	3-1*	2-1	2	ECC
			* in Paris			
	Real Madrid, Spain	2-3		0-3	qf	ECC
1959-60	Shamrock Rovers, Eire	3-2		1-1	1	ECC
	Fenerbahce, Turkey	2-1	5-1*	1-2	2	ECC
			* in Geneva			
	Real Madrid, Spain	3-2		0-4	qf	ECC
1966-67	Orgryte IS Gothenborg, Sweden	2-2		1-2	1	Fairs
1967-68	Fiorentina, Italy	0-1		0-4	1	Fairs
1968-69	Hansa Rostock, East Germany	2-1		0-3	1	Fairs
1973-74	CF Barcelona, Spain	3-0		0-2	1	UEFA
	Fenerbahce, Turkey	4-0		0-2	2	UEFA
	1.FC Koln, Germany	1-0		0-4	3	UEFA
1976-77	Espanol Barcelona, Spain	2-1		1-3	1	UEFA

STADE RENNES

Founded 1901
Colours red shirts, black shorts
Stadium Stade de la route de Lorient (25,000) ☎ 99-59 62 03/54 25 25
Cup Winners 1965, 1971

Season	Opponent	Home	Result	Away	Rnd	Cup
1965-66	Dukla Prague, Czechoslovakia	0-0		0-2	1	CWC
1971-72	Glasgow Rangers, Scotland	1-1		0-1	1	CWC

FRANCE

SEDAN (CS SEDAN-ARDENNES)

Founded 1920 as Union Athletique Sedan- Tarcy, 1966 merged with Racing Club de Paris and played one season as
Racing Club Paris-Sedan. In 1967 club was reconstituted as CS Sedan-Ardennes
Colours green shirts, red shorts
Stadium Stade Emile Albeau (15,000) ☎ 24-27 00 59
Cup Winners 1956, 1961
French Super Cup Winners 1956

Season	Opponent	Home	Result	Away	Rnd	Cup
1961-62	Atletico Madrid, Spain	2-3		1-4	1	CWC
1970-71	1.FC Koln, Germany	1-0		1-5	1	Fairs

MATRA RACING DE PARIS

Founded 1882 as Racing Club de France, football section added in 1896 In 1932 became professional and became
independent as Racing Clube de Paris, from 1987 Matra Racing de Paris, Matra being the sponsors
Colours sky blue shirts, white shorts
Stadium Parc des Princes (49,700) ☎ 47- 86 19 61
Champions 1936
Cup Winners 1936, 1939, 1940, 1945, 1949

Season	Opponent	Home	Result	Away	Rnd	Cup
as RACING CLUB DE PARIS						
1963-64	Rapid Vienna, Austria	2-3		0-1	1	Fairs

NIMES OLYMPIQUE

Founded 1901 as SC Nimes, 1937 Nimes Olym pique
Colours red shirts, white shorts
Stadium Stade Jean Bouin (14,000) ☎ 66-67 8439

Season	Opponent	Home	Result	Away	Rnd	Cup
1971-72	Vitoria Setubal, Portugal	2-1	lag	0-1	1	UEFA
1972-73	Grasshoppers Zurich, Switzerland	1-2		1-2	1	UEFA

TOULOUSE FC

Founded 1937 as Toulouse, 1967 amalgamated with Red Star Paris under Toulouse FC
Colours violet shirts, white shorts
Stadium Stade Municipal (35,000) ☎ 61-55 11 11
Cup Winners 1957

Season	Opponent	Home	Result	Away	Rnd	Cup
1966-67	bye				1	Fairs
	Dinamo Pitesti, Romania	3-0		1-5	2	Fairs
1986-87	Napoli, Italy	1-0	4-3p	0-1	1	UEFA
	Spartak Moscow, USSR	3-1		1-5	2	UEFA
1987-88	Panionios, Greece	5-1		1-0	1	UEFA
	Bayer Leverkusen, Germany	1-1		0-1	2	UEFA

RACING CLUB DE LENS

Founded 1906
Colours gold shirts, red shorts
Stadium Felix Bollaert (51,000) ☎ **21-28 05 79**

Season	Opponent	Home	Result	Away	Rnd	Cup
1975-76	Home Farm, Eire	6-0		1-1	1	CWC
	FC Den Haag, Holland	1-3		2-3	2	CWC
1977-78	Malmo FF, Sweden	4-1		0-2	1	UEFA
	Lazio Rome, Italy	6-0		0-2	2	UEFA
	1.FC Magdeburg, East Germany	2-0		0-4	3	UEFA
1983-84	La Ghantoise, Belgium	2-1		1-1	1	UEFA
	Royal Antwerp, Belgium	2-2		3-2	2	UEFA
	RSC Anderlecht, Belgium	1-1		0-1	3	UEFA
1986-87	Dundee United, Scotland	1-0		0-2	1	UEFA

SPORTING CLUB ANGERS

Full name Sporting Club de l'Ouest Angers Founded 1917
Colours white shirts with black stripes on sleeves, black shorts
Stadium Stade Jean Bouin (20,000) ☎ **41-88 96 97**

Season	Opponent	Home	Result	Away	Rnd	Cup
1972-73	BFC Dynamo Berlin, East Germany	1-1		1-2	1	UEFA

SOCHAUX (FC SOCHAUX-MONTBELIARD)

Founded 1929
Colours yellow shirts, blue shorts
Stadium Stade Bonal (17,000) ☎ **81-94 53 46**
Champions 1935, 1938
Cup Winners 1937

Season	Opponent	Home	Result	Away	Rnd	Cup
1972-73	Frem Copenhagen, Denmark	1-3		1-2	1	UEFA
1976-77	Hibernian, Scotland	0-0		0-1	1	UEFA
1980-81	Servette Geneva, Switzerland	2-0		1-2	1	UEFA
	Boavista, Portugal	2-2		1-0	2	UEFA
	Eintracht Frankfurt, Germany	2-0	wag	2-4	3	UEFA
	Grasshoppers Zurich, Switzerland	2-1		0-0	qf	UEFA
	AZ 67 Alkmaar, Holland	1-1		2-3	sf	UEFA
1982-83	PAOK Salonika, Greece	2-1	lag	0-1	1	UEFA
1989-90	Jeunesse Esch, Luxembourg	7-0		5-0	1	UEFA
	Fiorentina, Italy	1-1	lag	0-0*	2	UEFA
				in Perugia		

FRANCE

NANCY (AS NANCY LORRAINE)

Founded 1967
Colours all white with red stripe on shirt
Stadium Stade Marcel Picot (37,000) ☎ 35-72 16 25
Cup Winners 1978

Season	Opponent	Home	Result	Away	Rnd	Cup
1978-79	Frem Copenhagen, Denmark	4-0		0-2	1	CWC
	Servette Geneva, Switzerland	2-2		1-2	2	CWC

ROUEN

Founded 1899
Colours red shirts with white V, red shorts
Stadium Stade Robert Diochan (21,000) ☎ 35-72 16 25

Season	Opponent	Home	Result	Away	Rnd	Cup
1969-70	Twente Enschede, Holland	2-0		0-1	1	Fairs
	Sporting Charleroi SC, Belgium	2-0	wag	1-3	2	Fairs
	Arsenal, England	0-0		0-1	3	Fairs

FC METZ

Founded 1932 by merger of CA Messin and AS Messine
Colours lilac shirts, white shorts
Stadium Saint Symphorien (30,000) ☎ 87-66 72 15
Cup Winners 1984, 1988

Season	Opponent	Home	Result	Away	Rnd	Cup
1968-69	Hamburger SV, Germany	1-4		2-3	1	Fairs
1969-70	Napoli, Italy	1-1		1-2	1	Fairs
1984-85	FC Barcelona, Spain	2-4		4-1	1	CWC
	Dynamo Dresden, East Germany	0-0		1-3	2	CWC
1985-86	Hajduk Split, Yugoslavia	2-2		1-5	1	UEFA
1988-89	RSC Anderlecht, Belgium	1-3		0-2	1	CWC

SEC BASTIA CORSICA

Founded 1962 by merger of Sporting Club and Etoile Filante Full name Sporting Etoile Club Bastia
Colours all blue
Stadium Armand Cesari (12,000) ☎ 95-33 56 54
Cup Winners 1981
UEFA Cup Finalists 1978

Season	Opponent	Home	Result	Away	Rnd	Cup
1972-73	Atletico Madrid, Spain	0-0		1-2	1	CWC
1977-78	Sporting Lisbon, Portugal	3-2		2-1	1	UEFA
	Newcastle United, England	2-1		3-1	2	UEFA
	Torino, Italy	2-1		3-2	3	UEFA
	Carl Zeiss Jena, East Germany	7-2		2-4	qf	UEFA
	Grasshoppers Zurich, Switzerland	1-0	wag	2-3	sf	UEFA
	PSV Eindhoven, Holland	0-0		0-3	FINAL	UEFA
1981-82	KTP Kotkan Tyovaen Palloilijat, Finland	5-0		0-0	1	CWC
	Dynamo Tbilisi, USSR	1-1		1-3	2	CWC

ANGOULEME CHARENTE

Founded 1914 as AS Charentes, 1925 Angouleme
Colours blue shirts, white shorts
Stadium Stade Chanzy (15,000) ☎ 45-95 14 20

Season	Opponent	Home	Result	Away	Rnd	Cup
1970-71	Vitoria Guimaraes, Portugal	3-1		0-3	1	Fairs

AJ AUXERRE

Founded 1905
Colours all white
Stadium Abbe Deschamps (22,000) ☎ 86-52 24 71

Season	Opponent	Home	Result	Away	Rnd	Cup
1984-85	Sporting Lisbon, Portugal	2-2		0-2	1	UEFA
1985-86	AC Milan, Italy	3-1		0-3	1	UEFA
1987-88	Panathinaikos Piraeus, Greece	3-2		0-2	1	UEFA
1989-90	Dinamo Sagreb, Yugoslavia	0-1		3-1	pre	UEFA
	Apollonia Fieri, Albania	5-0		3-0*	1	UEFA
	RoPs Rovaniemen, Finland	3-0		5-0	2	UEFA
	Olympiakos Piraeus, Greece	0-0	wag	1-1	3	UEFA
	Fiorentina, Italy	0-1		0-1	qf	UEFA

PARIS ST GERMAIN

Founded 1973
Colours white shirts with 1 red band 1 blue band, red shorts
Stadium Parc des Princes (49,700) ☎42-46 90 84/39-73 42 11
Champions 1986
Cup Winners 1982, 1983

Season	Opponent	Home	Result	Away	Rnd	Cup
1982-83	Lokomotiv Sofia, Bulgaria	5-1		0-1	1	CWC
	Swansea City, Wales	2-0		1-0	2	CWC
	Waterschei Thor Genk, Belgium	2-0		0-3	qf	CWC
1983-84	Glentoran, Ireland	2-1		2-1	1	CWC
	Juventus, Italy	2-2	lag	0-0	2	CWC
1984-85	Heart of Midlothian, Scotland	4-0		2-2	1	UEFA
	Videoton Sekesfehervar, Hungary	2-4		0-1*	2	UEFA
				* first game abandoned 0-2 fog		
1986-87	TJ Vitkovice, Czechoslovakia	2-2		0-1	1	ECC
1989-90	Kuusysi Lahti, Finland	3-2		0-0	1	UEFA
	Juventus, Italy	0-1		1-2	2	UEFA

LAVAL (STADE LAVALOIS)

Founded 1902
Colours all orange
Stadium Francis Le Basser (18,000) ☎ 43-53 97 05

Season	Opponent	Home	Result	Away	Rnd	Cup
1983-84	Dynamo Kiev, USSR	1-0		0-0	1	UEFA
	FK Austria Vienna, Austria	3-3		0-2	2	UEFA

131

FRANCE

STADE FRANCAIS

Founded 1888, Football section added before 1900
Colours blue shirts, red shorts
Stadium Stade Mathieu, Bobigny Club went out of existance in 1985

Season	Opponent	Home	Result	Away	Rnd	Cup
1964-65	Real Betis, Spain	2-0		1-1	1	Fairs
	Juventus, Italy	0-0		0-1	2	Fairs
1965-66	FC Porto, Portugal	0-0		0-1	1	Fairs

MONTPELLIER PAILLADE SPORTS-CLUB

Founded 1974 by merger of Paillade and Littard
Colours red shirts, white shorts
Stadium Stade de la Mosson (17,233) ☎ 67-65 54 64

Season	Opponent	Home	Result	Away	Rnd	Cup
1988-89	Benfica, Portugal	0-3		1-3	1	UEFA

● Stade De Gerland, Lyon, France. Olympique Lyon, CWC Final 1986

GERMANY

Federal Republic of Germany
Founded 1900 Deutscher Fussballbund, Otto-Fleck-Schneise 6, Frankfurt on Maine 71 ☎ 0611 67881
National Colours white shirts, black shorts, white socks
Season July to December; March to June

LEAGUE CHAMPIONS

play off each year

1903	VfB Leipzig v DFC Prague	7-2		**1940**	Schalke 04 v Dresdner SK	1-0
1905	FC Union Berlin v Karlsruher FV	2-0		**1941**	Rapid Vienna v Schalke 04	4-3
1906	VfB Leipzig v 1.FC Pforzheim	2-1		**1942**	Schalke 04 v Vienna Wien	2-0
1907	Frieburger FC v Viktoria 89 Berlin	3-1		**1943**	Dresdner SK v FV Saarbrucken	3-0
1908	Viktoria 89 Berlin v Stuttgart Kickers	3-0		**1944**	Dresdner SK v Luftwaffen SV Hamburg	4-0
1909	Phonix Karlsruhe v Viktoria 89 Berlin	4-2				

1910	Karlsruher FV v Holstein Kiel	1-0 aet
1911	Viktoria 89 Berlin v VfB Leipzig	3-1
1912	KSV Holstein Kiel v Karlsruher FV	1-0
1913	VfB Leipzig v Duisburger SpV	3-1
1914	SpVgg Furth v VfB Leipzig	3-2 aet

now WEST GERMANY
(Regional preliminaries, then final to determine champions)

1948	1.FC Nurnburg v 1.FC Kaiserslautern	2-1
1949	VfB Mannheim v Borussia Dortmund	3-2

1920	1.FC Nurnburg v SpVgg Furth	2-0
1921	1.FC Nurnburg v Vorwaerts Berlin	5-0
1922	Hamburger SV v 1.FC Nurnburg	2-2 1-1

DFB declared Hamburger SV Champions, but Hamburger
refused to accept after protest from 1.FC Nurnburg

1923	Hamburger SV v Union Oberschonweide Berlin	3-0
1924	1.FC Nurnburg v Hamburger SV	2-0
1925	1.FC Nurnburg v FSV Frankfurt	1-0 aet
1926	SpVgg Furth v Hertha BSC Berlin	4-1
1927	1.FC Nurnburg v Hertha BSC Berlin	2-0
1928	Hamburger SV v Hertha BSC Berlin	5-2
1929	SpVgg Furth v Hertha BSC Berlin	3-2

1930	Hertha BSC Berlin v Holstein Kiel	5-4
1931	Hertha BSC Berlin v TSV 1860 Munich	3-2
1932	Bayern Munich v Eintracht Frankfurt	2-0
1933	Fortuna Dusseldorf v Schalke 04	3-0
1934	Schalke 04 v 1.FC Nurnburg	2-1
1935	Schalke 04 v VfB Stuttgart	6-4
1936	1.FC Nurnburg v Fortuna Dusseldorf	2-1 aet
1937	Schalke 04 v 1.FC Nurnburg	2-0
1938	Hannover 96 v Schalke	04 3-3 4-3
1939	Schalke 04 v Admira Wien	9-0

1950	VfB Stuttgart v FC Offenbach Kickers	2-1
1951	1.FC Kaiserslautrn v Preussen Munster	2-1
1952	VfB Stuttgart v 1.FC Saarbrucken	3-2
1953	1.FC Kaiserslautern v VfB Stuttgart	4-1
1954	Hannover 96 v 1.FC Kaiserslautern	5-1
1955	Rot Weiss Essen v 1.FC Kaiserslautern	4-3
1956	Borussia Dortmund v Karlsruher SC	4-2
1957	Borussia Dortmund v Hamburger SV	4-1
1958	Schalke 04 v Hamburger SV	3-0
1959	Eintracht Frankfurt v Offenbach Kickers	5-3

1960	Hamburger SV v 1.FC Koln	3-2
1961	1.FC Nurnburg v Borussia Dortmund	3-0
1962	1.FC Koln v 1.FC Nurnburg	4-0
1963	Borussia Dortmund v 1.FC Koln	3-1

BUNDESLIGA (NATIONAL LEAGUE)

1964	1.FC Koln	**1970**	Borussia Monchengladbach
1965	Werder Bremen		
1966	TSV 1860 Munich	**1971**	Borussia Monchengladbach
1967	Eintracht Braunschweig	**1972**	Bayern Munich
1968	1.FC Nurnburg	**1973**	Bayern Munich
1969	Bayern Munich	**1974**	Bayern Munich

133

GERMANY

1975	Borussia Monchengladbach	1978	1.FC Koln	1982	Hamburger SV	1987	Bayern Munich
1976	Borussia Monchengladbach	1979	Hamburger SV	1983	Hamburger SV	1988	Werder Bremen
1977	Borussia Monchengladbach	1980	Bayern Munich	1984	VfB Stuttgart	1989	Bayern Munich
		1981	Bayern Munich	1985	Bayern Munich		
				1986	Bayern Munich		

CUP FINAL WINNERS

1935	1.FC Nurnburg v Schalke 04	2-0
1936	VfB Leipzig v Schalke 04	2-1
1937	Schalke 04 v Fortuna Dusseldorf	2-1
1938	Rapid Vienna v FSV Frankfurt	3-1
1939	1.FC Nurnburg v SV 07 Waldorf Mannheim	2-0
1940	Dresdner Sport-Club v 1.FC Nurnburg	2-1 aet
1941	Dresdner Sport-Club v Schalke 04	2-1
1942	TSV 1860 Munich v Schalke 04	2-0
1943	Vienna Wien v Luftwaffen SV Hamburg	3-2 aet
1953	Rot Weiss Essen v Alemannia Aachen	2-1
1954	VfB Stuttgart v 1.FC Koln	1-2
1955	Karlsruher Sport-Club v Schalke D4	3-2
1956	Karlsruher Sport-Club v Hamburger SV	3-1
1957	Bayern Munich v Fortuna Dusseldorf	1-0
1958	Stuttgart v Fortuna Dusseldorf	4-3 aet
1959	Schwarz Weiss Essen v Borussia Neunkirchen	5-2
1960	Borussia Monchengladbach v Karlsruher SC	3-2
1961	Werder Bremen v 1.FC Kaiserslautern	2-0
1962	1.FC Nuremburg v Fortuna Dusseldorf	2-1
1963	Hamburger SV v Borussia Dortmund	3-0
1964	TSV 1860 Munich v Eintracht Frankfurt	2-0
1965	Borussia Dortmund v Alemannia Aachen	2-0
1966	Bayern Munich v MSV Duisburg	4-2

1967	Bayern Munich v Hamburger SV	4-0
1968	1.FC Koln v VfL Bochum	4-1
1969	Bayern Munich v Schalke 04	2-1
1970	Kickers Offenbach v 1.FC Koln	2-1
1971	Bayern Munich v 1.FC Koln	2-1 aet
1972	Schalke 04 v 1.FC Kaiserslautern	5-0
1973	Borussia Monchengladbach v 1st FC Koln	2-1 aet
1974	Eintracht Frankfurt v Hamburger SV	3-1 aet
1975	Eintracht Frankfurt v MSV Duisburg	1-0
1976	Hamburger SV v 1.FC Kaiserslautern	2-0
1977	1.FC Koln v Hertha BSC Berlin	1-1* 1-0 *aet
1978	1.FC Koln v Fortuna Dusseldorf	2-0
1979	Fortuna Dusseldorf v Hertha BSC Berlin	1-0 aet
1980	Fortuna Dusseldorf v 1.FC Koln	2-1
1981	Eintracht Frankfurt v 1.FC Kaiserslautern	3-1
1982	Bayern Munich v 1.FC Nurnburg	4-2
1983	1.FC Koln v Fortuna Koln	1-0
1984	Bayern Munich v Borussia Monchengladbach	1-1 7-6 pen
1985	Bayer Uerdingen v Bayern Munich	2-1
1986	Bayern Munich v VfB Stuttgart	5-2
1987	Hamburger SV v Stuttgart Kickers	3-1
1988	Eintracht Frankfurt v VfL Bochum	1-0
1989	Borussia Dortmund v Werder Bremen	4-1
1990	Werder Bremen v 1.FC Kaiserslaitern	

LEAGUE CUP

1973	Hamburger SV v Borussia Monchengladbach	4-0

GERMAN SUPER CUP

1977	Borussia Monchengladbach v Hamburger SV	3-2 unofficial
1983	Bayern Munich v Hamburger SV	1-1 4-2 pen unofficial
1987	Bayern Munich v Hamburger SV	2-1
1988	Werder Bremen v Eintracht Frankfurt	2-0
1989	Borussia Dortmund v Bayern Munich	4-3

GERMANY

FEATURED CLUBS IN EUROPEAN COMPETITION

Eintracht Frankfurt	TSV 1860 Munich	Hamburger SV	1.FC Koln
Borussia Dortmund	Bayern Munich	1.FC Nurnberg	VfB Stuttgart
Hertha BSC Berlin	Hannover 96	Eintracht Braunschweig	Fortuna Dusseldorf
Borussia Monchengladbach	MSV Duisburg	Werder Bremen	1.FC Kaiserslautern
FC Schalke 04 Gelsenkirchen	Rot Weiss Essen	1.FC Saarbrucken	Viktoria Koln
Tasmania Berlin	Wuppertaler SV	Kickers Offenbach	Bayer Uerdingen
Bayer Leverkusen	Frankfurt City XI	West Berlin City XI	

SG EINTRACHT FRANKFURT

Founded 1-5-1899
Colours red and black diagonal striped shirts, black shorts
Stadium Waldstadion (61,146) ☎ 069-420 97 00
Champions 1959
Cup Winners 1974, 1975, 1981, 1988
ECC Finalists 1960
UEFA Cup Winners 1980

Season	Opponents	Home	Playoff Result	Away	Rnd	Cup
1959-60	Kuopion Palloseura (KuPS), Finland	withdrew			pr	ECC
	Young Boys Bern, Switzerland	1-1		4-1	1	ECC
	Wiener Sport Club, Austria	2-1		1-1	qf	ECC
	Glasgow Rangers, Scotland	6-1		6-3	sf	ECC
	Real Madrid, Spain	3-7	in Glasgow		FINAL	ECC
1964-65	Kilmarnock, Scotland	3-0		1-5	pr	Fairs
1966-67	Drumcondra, Eire	6-1		2-0	1	Fairs
	Hvidovre IF, Denmark	5-1		2-2	2	Fairs
	Ferencvarosi TC, Hungary	4-1		1-2	3	Fairs
	Burnley, England	1-1		2-1	qf	Fairs
	Dinamo Zagreb, Yugoslavia	3-0		0-4	sf	Fairs
1967-68	Nottingham Forest, England	0-1		0-4	1	Fairs
1968-69	Wacker Innsbruck, Austria	3-0		2-2	1	Fairs
	Juventus, Italy	1-0		0-0	2	Fairs
	Atletico Bilbao, Spain	1-1		0-1	3	Fairs
1972-73	Liverpool, England	0-0		0-2	1	UEFA
1974-75	AS Monaco, France	3-0		2-2	1	CWC
	Dynamo Kiev, USSR	2-3		1-2	2	CWC
1975-76	Coleraine, Ireland	5-1		6-2	1	CWC
	Atletico Madrid, Spain	1-0		2-1	2	CWC
	Sturm Graz, Austria	1-0		2-0	qf	CWC
	West Ham United, England	2-1		1-3	sf	CWC
1977-78	Sliema Wanderers, Malta	5-0		0-0	1	UEFA
	FC Zurich, Switzerland	4-3		3-0	2	UEFA
	Bayern Munich, Germany	4-0		2-1	3	UEFA
	Grasshoppers Zurich, Switzerland	3-2	lag	0-1	qf	UEFA
1979-80	Aberdeen, Scotland	1-0		1-1	1	UEFA
	Dinamo Bucharest, Romania	3-0		0-2	2	UEFA
	Feyenoord Rotterdam, Holland	4-1		0-1	3	UEFA
	Zbrojovka Brno, Czechoslovakia	4-1		2-3	qf	UEFA
	Bayern Munich, Germany	5-1		0-2	sf	UEFA
	Borussia Monchengladbach, Germany	1-0		2-3	FINAL	UEFA
1980-81	Shakhtyor Donetsk, USSR	3-0		0-1	1	UEFA
	FC Utrecht, Holland	3-1		1-2	2	UEFA
	Sochaux, France	4-2	lag	0-2	3	UEFA
1981-82	PAOK Salonika, Greece	2-0	5-4 pen	0-2	1	CWC
	SKA Rostov on Don, USSR	2-0		0-1	2	CWC
	Tottenham Hotspur, England	2-1		0-2	qf	CWC

GERMANY

1988-89	Grasshoppers Zurich, Switzerland	1-0		0-0	1	CWC
	Sakaryaspor, Turkey	3-1		3-0	2	CWC
	KV Mechelen, Belgium	0-0		0-1	qf	CWC

TSV 1860 MUNICH

(Turn Und Sportverein)
Founded 17-5-1860, Football section added on 25-4-1899
Colours sky blue shirts with 2 white bands, white shorts
Stadium Grunwalderstrasse (31,500) ☎ 089-64 30 48
Champions 1966
Cup Winners 1942, 1964
CWC Finalists 1965

Season	Opponent	Home	Playoff Result	Away	Rnd	Cup
1964-65	Union Spora, Luxembourg	6-0		4-0	1	CWC
	FC Porto, Portugal	1-1		1-0	2	CWC
	Legia Warsaw, Poland	4-0		0-0	qf	CWC
	Torino, Italy	3-1	2-0*	0-2	sf	CWC
			* in Zurich			
	West Ham United, England	0-2	at Wembley		FINAL	CWC
1965-66	Malmo FF, Sweden	4-1		3-0	1	Fairs
	Goztepe Izmir, Turkey	9-1		1-2	2	Fairs
	Servette Geneva, Switzerland	4-1		1-1	3	Fairs
	Chelsea, England	2-2		0-1	qf	Fairs
1966-67	Omonia Nicosia, Cyprus	8-0		2-1*	pr	ECC
				* in Pocking, Bavaria		
	Real Madrid, Spain	1-0		1-3	1	ECC
1967-68	Servette Geneva, Switzerland	4-0		2-2	1	Fairs
	Liverpool, England	2-1		0-8	2	Fairs
1968-69	Legia Warsaw, Poland	2-3		0-6	1	Fairs
1969-70	Skeid Oslo, Norway	2-2		1-2	1	Fairs

HAMBURGER SV (Sport Voren)

Founded 29-9-1887, then 1919 by merger of Germania (1887), Hamburger FC (1888) and FC Falke (1908)
Colours white shirts, red shorts
Stadium Volksparkstadion (61,418) ☎ 040-41 55 109
Champions 1923, 1928, 1960, 1979, 1982, 1983
Cup Winners 1963, 1976, 1987
ECC Finalists 1980
League Cup Winners 1973
CWC Winners 1977
Finalists 1968
UEFA Cup Finalists 1982
Super Cup Finalists 1984
World Club Championship Winners 1984

Season	Opponent	Home	Playoff Result	Away	Rnd	Cup
1960-61	Young Boys Bern, Switzerland	3-3		5-0	1	ECC
	Burnley, England	4-1		1-3	qf	ECC
	CF Barcelona, Spain	2-1	0-1*	0-1	sf	ECC
			* in Brussels			
1963-64	Union Spora, Luxembourg	4-0		3-2	1	CWC
	CF Barcelona, Spain	4-4	3-2*	0-0	2	CWC
			* in Lausanne			
	Olympique Lyon, France	1-1		0-2	qf	CWC
1967-68	Randers Freja, Denmark	5-3		2-0	1	CWC
	Wisla Cracow, Poland	4-0		1-0	2	CWC
	Olympique Lyon, France	2-0	2-0*	0-2	qf	CWC
			* in Hamburg			
	Cardiff City, Wales	1-1		3-2	sf	CWC
	AC Milan, Italy	0-2	in Rotterdam		FINAL	CWC
1968-69	FC Metz, France	3-2		4-1	1	Fairs
	Slavia Prague, Czechoslovakia	4-1		1-3	2	Fairs
	Hibernian, Scotland	1-0	wag	1-2	3	Fairs
	Goztepe Izmir, Turkey	withdrew			qf	Fairs
1970-71	La Ghantoise, Belgium	7-1		1-0	1	Fairs
	Dinamo Zagreb, Yugoslavia	1-0		0-4	2	Fairs
1971-72	St Johnstone, Scotland	2-1		0-3	1	UEFA
1974-75	Bohemians Dublin, Eire	3-0		1-0	1	UEFA
	Steagul Rosu Brasov, Romania	8-0		2-1	2	UEFA
	Dynamo Dresden, East Germany	4-1		2-2	3	UEFA
	Juventus, Italy	0-0		0-2	qf	UEFA
1975-76	Young Boys Bern, Switzerland	4-2		0-0	1	UEFA
	Red Star Belgrade, Yugoslavia	4-0		1-1	2	UEFA
	FC Porto, Portugal	2-0		1-2	3	UEFA
	Stal Mielec, Poland	1-1		1-0	qf	UEFA
	Clube Bruges, Belgium	1-1		0-1	sf	UEFA
1976-77	IBK Keflavik, Iceland	3-0		1-1*	1	CWC
			* in Reykjavik			
	Heart of Midlothian, Scotland	4-2		4-1	2	CWC
	MTK Budapest, Hungary	4-1		1-1	qf	CWC
	Atletico Madrid, Spain	3-0		1-3	sf	CWC
	RSC Anderlecht, Belgium	2-0	in Amsterdam		FINAL	CWC
1977-78	Reipas Lahti, Finland	8-1		5-2	1	CWC
	RSC Anderlecht, Belgium	1-2		1-1	2	CWC
1979-80	Valur Reykjavik, Iceland	2-1		3-0	1	ECC
	Dynamo Tbilisi, USSR	3-1		3-2	2	ECC
	Hajduk Split, Yugoslavia	1-0	wag	2-3	qf	ECC
	Real Madrid, Spain	5-1		0-2	sf	ECC
	Nottingham Forest, England	0-1	in Madrid		FINAL	ECC
1980-81	FK Sarajevo, Yugoslavia	4-2		3-3	1	UEFA
	PSV Eindhoven, Holland	2-1		1-1	2	UEFA
	St Etienne, France	0-5		0-1	3	UEFA

GERMANY

1981-82	FC Utrecht, Holland	0-1		6-3	1	UEFA
	Girondins Bordeaux, France	2-0		1-2	2	UEFA
	Aberdeen, Scotland	3-1		2-3	3	UEFA
	FC Neuchatal Xamax, Switzerland	3-2		0-0	qf	UEFA
	Radnicki Nis, Yugoslavia	5-1		1-2	sf	UEFA
	IFK Gothenburg, Sweden	0-3		0-1	FINAL	UEFA
1982-83	BFC Dynamo Berlin, East Germany	2-0		1-1	1	ECC
	Olympiakos Piraeus, Greece	1-0		4-0	2	ECC
	Dynamo Kiev, USSR	1-2		3-0	qf	ECC
	Real Sociedad San Sebastien, Spain	2-1		1-1	sf	ECC
	Juventus, Italy	1-0	in Athens		FINAL	ECC
1983-84	bye				1	ECC
	Dinamo Bucharest, Romania	3-2		0-3	2	ECC
1984-85	Southampton, England	2-0		0-0	1	UEFA
	CSKA Sofia, Bulgaria	4-0		2-1	2	UEFA
	Inter Milan, Italy	2-1	lag	0-1	3	UEFA
1985-86	Sparta Rotterdam, Holland	2-0	3-4 pen	0-2	1	UEFA
1987-88	Avenir Beggen, Luxembourg	3-0		5-0	1	CWC
	Ajax Amsterdam, Holland	0-1		0-2	2	CWC
1989-90	Orgryte IS Gothenburg, Sweden	5-1		2-1	1	UEFA
	Real Zaragoza, Spain	2-0 aet		0-1	2	UEFA
	FC Porto, Portugal	1-0	wag	1-2	3	UEFA
	Juventus, Italy	0-2		2-1	qf	UEFA

1.FC KOLN (Cologne)

Founded 13-2-1948 by merger of Kolner BC 01 and Sulz 07
Colours red shirts, white shorts
Stadium Mungersdorfer (61,118) ☎ 0221-43 44 31/43 28 93
Champions 1962, 1964, 1978
Cup Winners 1968, 1977, 1978, 1983
UEFA Cup Finalists 1986

Season	Opponent	Home	Playoff Result	Away	Rnd	Cup
1958-60	Birmingham City, England	2-2		0-2	1	Fairs
1960-61	Olympique Lyon, France	3-1		1-2	1	Fairs
	AS Roma, Italy	2-0	1-4*	0-2	2	Fairs
			* in Rome			
1961-62	Inter Milan, Italy	4-2	3-5*	0-2	pr	Fairs
			* in Milan			
1962-63	Dundee, Scotland	4-0		1-8	1	ECC
1963-64	La Ghantoise, Belgium	3-1		1-1	1	Fairs
	Sheffield Wednesday, England	3-2		2-1	2	Fairs
	AS Roma, Italy	4-0		1-3	3	Fairs
	Valencia CF, Spain	2-0		1-4	qf	Fairs
1964-65	Partizani Tirana, Albania	2-0		0-0	1	ECC
	Panathinaikos, Greece	2-1		1-1	2	ECC
	Liverpool, England	0-0	2-2* lot	0-0	qf	ECC
			* in Rotterdam			
1965-66	Union Spora, Luxembourg	13-0		4-0	1	Fairs
	Aris Salonika, Greece	2-0		1-2	2	Fairs
	Ujpest Dozsa, Hungary	3-2		0-4	3	Fairs
1967-68	Slavia Prague, Czechoslovakia	2-0		0-0	1	Fairs
	Glasgow Rangers, Scotland	3-1		0-3	2	Fairs
1968-69	Girondins Bordeaux, Belgium	3-0		1-2	1	CWC
	ADO Den Haag, Holland	3-0		1-0	2	CWC
	Randers Freja, Denmark	2-1		3-0	qf	CWC
	CF Barcelona, Spain	2-2		1-4	sf	CWC

1970-71	CS Sedan-Ardennes, France	5-1		0-1	1	Fairs
	Fiorentina, Italy	1-0		2-1	2	Fairs
	Spartak Trnava, Czechoslovakia	3-0		1-0	3	Fairs
	Arsenal, England	1-0	wag	1-2	qf	Fairs
	Juventus, Italy	1-1		0-2	sf	Fairs
1971-72	St Etienne, France	2-1		1-1	1	UEFA
	Dundee, Scotland	2-1		2-4	2	UEFA
1972-73	Bohemians Dublin, Eire	2-1		3-0	1	UEFA
	Viking Stavanger, Norway	9-1		0-1	2	UEFA
	Borussia MonchenGladbach, Germany	0-0		0-5	3	UEFA
1973-74	Eskisekirspor, Turkey	2-0		0-0	1	UEFA
	Olympique Marseille, France	6-0		0-2	2	UEFA
	OGC Nice, France	4-0		0-1	3	UEFA
	Tottenham Hotspur, England	1-2		0-3	qf	UEFA
1974-75	Kokkolan Pallo Veikot (KPV), Finland	5-1		4-1	1	UEFA
	Dinamo Bucharest, Romania	3-2		1-1	2	UEFA
	Partizan Belgrade, Yugoslavia	5-1		0-1	3	UEFA
	FC Amsterdam, Holland	5-1		3-2	qf	UEFA
	Borussia Monchengladbach, Germany	1-3		0-1	sf	UEFA
1975-76	BK 1903 Copenhagen, Denmark	2-0		3-2	1	UEFA
	Spartak Moscow, USSR	0-1		0-2	2	UEFA
1976-77	GKS Tichy, Poland	2-0		1-1	1	UEFA
	Grasshoppers Zurich, Switzerland	2-0		3-2	2	UEFA
	Queens Park Rangers, England	4-1	lag	0-3	3	UEFA
1977-78	FC Porto, Portugal	2-2		0-1*	1	CWC
				* in Coimbra		
1978-79	IA Akranes, Iceland	4-1		1-1*	1	ECC
				* in Reykjavik		
	Lokomotiv Sofia, Bulgaria	4-0		1-0	2	ECC
	Glasgow Rangers, Scotland	1-0		1-1	qf	ECC
	Nottingham Forest, England	0-1		3-3	sf	ECC
1980-81	IA Akranes, Iceland	6-0		4-0*	1	UEFA
				* in Reykjavik		
	FC Barcelona, Spain	0-1		4-0	2	UEFA
	VfB Stuttgart, Germany	4-1		1-3	3	UEFA
	Standard Liege. Belgium	3-2		0-0	qf	UEFA
	Ipswich Town, England	0-1		0-1	sf	UEFA
1982-83	AEK Athens, Greece	5-0	3-3*	1-0	1	UEFA
			* abandoned first leg			
	Glasgow Rangers, Scotland	5-0		1-2	2	UEFA
	AS Roma, Italy	1-0		0-2	3	UEFA
1983-84	Wacker Innsbruck, Austria	7-1		0-1	1	CWC
	Ujpest Dozsa, Hungary	4-2	lag	1-3	2	CWC
1984-85	Pogon Szczecin, Poland	2-1		1-0	1	UEFA
	Standard Liege, Belgium	2-1		2-0	2	UEFA
	Spartak Moscow, USSR	2-0		0-1*	3	UEFA
				* in Tbilisi		
	Inter Milan, Italy	1-3		0-1	qf	UEFA
1985-86	Real Sporting Gijon, Spain	0-0		2-1	1	UEFA
	Bohemians Prague, Czechoslovakia	4-0		4-2	2	UEFA
	Hammarby IF Stockholm, Sweden	3-1		1-2	3	UEFA
	Sporting Lisbon, Portugal	2-0		1-1	qf	UEFA
	KSV Waregem, Belgium	4-0		3-3	sf	UEFA
	Real Madrid, Spain	2-0*		1-5	FINAL	UEFA
		* in West Berlin				
1988-89	Royal Antwerp, Belgium	2-1		4-2	1	UEFA
	Glasgow Rangers, Scotland	2-0		1-1	2	UEFA
	Real Sociedad San Sebastien, Spain	2-2		0-1	3	UEFA
1989-90	Plastika Nitra, Czechoslovakia	4-1		1-0	1	UEFA
	Spartak Moscow, USSR	3-1		0-0	2	UEFA
	Red Star Belgrade, Yugoslavia	3-0		0-2	3	UEFA
	Royal Antwerp, Belgium	2-0		0-0	qf	UEFA
	Juventus, Italy	0-0		2-3	sf	UEFA

GERMANY

BV 09 BORUSSIA DORTMUND

Founded 19-12-1909
Colours yellow shirts, black shorts
Stadium Westfalenstadion (53,790) ☎ 0231-122083/4
Champions 1956, 1957, 1963
Cup Winners 1965, 1989
German Super Cup Winners 1989
CWC Winners 1966

Season	Opponent	Home	Playoff Result	Away	Rnd	Cup
1956-57	CA Spora, Luxembourg	4-3	7-0*	1-2	pr	ECC
			* in Dortmund			
	Manchester United, England	0-0		2-3	1	ECC
1957-58	CCA Bucharest, Romania	4-2	3-1*	1-3	1	ECC
			* in Bologna			
	AC Milan, Italy	1-1		1-4	qf	ECC
1963-64	Lyn Oslo, Norway	3-1		4-2	1	ECC
	Benfica, Portugal	5-0		1-2	2	ECC
	Dukla Prague, Czechoslovakia	1-3		4-0	qf	ECC
	Inter Milan, Italy	2-2		0-2	sf	ECC
1964-65	Girondins Bordeaux, Belgium	4-1		0-2	1	Fairs
	Manchester United, England	1-6		0-4	2	Fairs
1965-66	Floriana, Malta	8-0		5-1	1	CWC
	CSKA Sofia, Bulgaria	3-0		2-4	2	CWC
	Atletico Madrid, Spain	1-0		1-1	qf	CWC
	West Ham United, England	3-1		2-1	sf	CWC
	Liverpool, England	2-1	in Glasgow		FINAL	CWC
1966-67	Glasgow Rangers, Scotland	0-0		1-2	1	CWC
1982-83	Glasgow Rangers, Scotland	0-0		0-2	1	UEFA
1987-88	Glasgow Celtic, Scotland	2-0		1-2	1	UEFA
	Velez Mostar, Yugoslavia	2-0		1-2	2	UEFA
	Clube Bruges, Belgium	3-0		0-5	3	UEFA
1989-90	Besiktas Istanbul, Turkey	2-1		1-0	1	CWC
	Sampdoria, Italy	1-1		0-2	2	CWC

FC BAYERN MUNICH (Munchen)

Founded 27-2-1900
Colours all red
Stadium Olympiastadion (77,573) ☎ 089-69931/0
Champions 1932, 1969, 1972, 1973, 1974, 1980, 1981, 1985, 1986, 1987, 1989
Cup Winners 1957, 1966, 1967, 1969, 1971, 1982, 1984, 1986
German Super Cup Winners 1983, 1987
European Cup Winners 1974, 1975, 1976
Finalists 1982, 1987
CWC Winners 1967
World Club Champions 1976

Season	Opponent	Home	Result	Away	Rnd	Cup
1962-63	Basel City XI, Switzerland	3-0		not played	1	Fairs
	Drumcondra, Eire	6-0		0-1	2	Fairs
	Dinamo Zagreb, Yugoslavia	0-0		1-4	3	Fairs
1966-67	Tatran Presov, Czechoslovakia	3-2		1-1	1	CWC
	Shamrock Rovers, Eire	3-2		1-1	2	CWC
	Rapid Vienna, Austria	2-0		0-1	qf	CWC
	Standard Liege, Belgium	2-0		3-1	sf	CWC
	Glasgow Rangers, Scotland	1-0	in Nurnburg		FINAL	CWC

140

Season	Opponent				Round	Comp
1967-68	Panathinaikos, Greece	5-0		2-1*	1	CWC
	Vitoria Setubal, Portugal	6-2		1-1*	2	CWC
	* in Lisbon construction work at Setubal ground					
	Valencia CF, Spain	1-0		1-1	qf	CWC
	AC Milan, Italy	0-0		0-2	sf	CWC
1969-70	St Etienne, France	2-0		0-3	1	ECC
1970-71	Glasgow Rangers, Scotland	1-0		1-1	1	Fairs
	Coventry City, England	6-1		1-2	2	Fairs
	Sparta Rotterdam, Holland	2-1		3-1	3	Fairs
	Liverpool, England	1-1		0-3	qf	Fairs
1971-72	Skoda Plzen, Czechoslovakia	6-1		1-0	1	CWC
	Liverpool, England	3-1		0-0	2	CWC
	Steaua Bucharest, Romania	0-0	wag	1-1	qf	CWC
	Glasgow Rangers, Scotland	1-1		0-2	sf	CWC
1972-73	Galatasaray, Turkey	6-0		1-1	1	ECC
	Omonia Nicosia, Cyprus	9-0		4-0*	2	ECC
	* in Augsburg					
	Ajax Amsterdam, Holland	2-1		0-4	qf	ECC
1973-74	Atvidaberg FF, Sweden	3-1	4-3p	1-3	1	ECC
	Dynamo Dresden, East Germany	4-3		3-3	2	ECC
	CSKA Sofia, Bulgaria	4-1		1-2	qf	ECC
	Ujpest Dozsa, Hungary	3-0		1-1	sf	ECC
	Atletico Madrid, Spain	1-1*		4-0*	FINAL	ECC
	* both in Brussels					
1974-75	bye				1	ECC
	1.FC Magdeburg, East Germany	3-2		2-1	2	ECC
	Ararat Yerevan, USSR	2-0		0-1	qf	ECC
	St Etienne, France	2-0		0-0	sf	ECC
	Leeds United, England	2-0	in Paris		FINAL	ECC
1975-76	Jeunesse Esch, Luxembourg	3-1		5-0*	1	ECC
	* in Luxembourg					
	Malmo FF, Sweden	2-0		0-1	2	ECC
	Benfica, Portugal	5-1		0-0	qf	ECC
	Real Madrid, Spain	2-0		1-1	sf	ECC
	St Etienne, France	1-0	in Glasgow		FINAL	ECC
1976-77	Koge BK, Denmark	2-1		5-0	1	ECC
	Banik Ostrava, Czechoslovakia	5-0		1-2	2	ECC
	Dynamo Kiev, USSR	1-0		0-2	qf	ECC
1977-78	Mjondalen IF, Norway	8-0		4-0	1	UEFA
	Marek Stanke Dimitrov, Bulgaria	3-0		0-2	2	UEFA
	Eintracht Frankfurt, Germany	1-2		0-4	3	UEFA
1979-80	Bohemians Prague, Czechoslovakia	2-2		2-0	1	UEFA
	AGF Aarhus, Denmark	3-1		2-1	2	UEFA
	Red Star Belgrade, Yugoslavia	2-0		2-3	3	UEFA
	1.FC Kaiserslautern, Germany	4-1		0-1	qf	UEFA
	Eintracht Frankfurt, Germany	2-0		1-5	sf	UEFA
1980-81	Olympiakos Piraeus, Greece	3-0		4-2	1	ECC
	Ajax Amsterdam, Holland	5-1		1-2	2	ECC
	Banik Ostrava, Czechoslovakia	2-0		4-2	qf	ECC
	Liverpool, England	1-1	lag	0-0	sf	ECC
1981-82	Osters IF Vaxjo, Sweden	5-0		1-0	1	ECC
	Benfica, Portugal	4-1		0-0	2	ECC
	Universitatea Craiova, Romania	1-1		2-0	qf	ECC
	CSKA Sofia, Bulgaria	4-0		3-4	sf	ECC
	Aston Villa, England	0-1	in Rotterdam		FINAL	ECC
1982-83	Torpedo Moscow, USSR	0-0	wag	1-1	1	CWC
	Tottenham Hotspur, England	4-1		1-1	2	CWC
	Aberdeen, Scotland	0-0		2-3	qf	CWC
1983-84	Anorthosis Larnaca, Cyprus	10-0		1-0	1	UEFA
	PAOK Salonika, Greece	0-0	9-8p	0-0	2	UEFA
	Tottenham Hotspur, England	1-0		0-2	3	UEFA
1984-85	Moss FK, Norway	4-1		2-1	1	CWC
	Trakia Plovdiv, Bulgaria	4-1		0-2	2	CWC
	AS Roma, Italy	2-0		2-1	qf	CWC
	Everton, England	0-0		1-3	sf	CWC

1985-86	Gornik Zabrze, Poland	4-1		2-1*	1	ECC
				* in Chorzow		
	FK Austria Vienna, Austria	4-2		3-3	2	ECC
	RSC Anderlecht, Belgium	2-1		0-2	qf	ECC
1986-87	PSV Eindhoven, Holland	0-0		2-0	1	ECC
	FK Austria Vienna, Austria	2-0		1-1	2	ECC
	RSC Anderlecht, Belgium	5-0		2-2	qf	ECC
	Real Madrid, Spain	4-1		0-1	sf	ECC
	FC Porto, Portugal	1-2	in Vienna		FINAL	ECC
1987-88	Sredets CSKA Sofia, Bulgaria	4-0		1-0	1	ECC
	FC Neuchatel Xamax, Switzerland	2-0		1-2	2	ECC
	Real Madrid, Spain	3-2	lag	1-2	qf	ECC
1988-89	Legia Warsaw, Poland	3-1		7-3	1	UEFA
	DAC Dunajska Streda, Czechoslovakia	3-1		2-0	2	UEFA
	Inter Milan, Italy	0-2	wag	3-1	3	UEFA
	Heart of Midlothian, Scotland	2-0		0-1	qf	UEFA
	Napoli, Italy	2-2		0-2	sf	UEFA
1989-90	Glasgow Rangers, Scotland	0-0		3-1	1	ECC
	17 Nentori Tirana, Albania	3-1		3-0	2	ECC
	PSV Eindhoven, Holland	2-1		1-0	qf	ECC
	AC Milan, Italy	2-1	lag	0-1	sf	ECC

1. FC NURNBURG

Founded 4-5-1900
Colours white shirts with red sleeves, white shorts
Stadium Stadttisches Stadion (60,000) ☎ 0911-40 40 45/47
Champions 1920, 1921, 1924, 1925, 1927, 1936, 1948, 1961, 1968
Cup Winners 1935, 1939, 1962

Season	Opponent	Home	Result	Away	Rnd	Cup
1961-62	Drumcondra, Eire	5-0		4-1	1	ECC
	Fenerbahce, Turkey	1-0		2-1	2	ECC
	Benfica, Portugal	3-1		0-6	qf	ECC
1962-63	bye				1	CWC
	St Etienne, France	0-0		3-0	2	CWC
	B 1909 Odense, Denmark	6-0		1-0	qf	CWC
	Atletico Madrid, Spain	2-1		0-2	sf	CWC
1965-66	Everton, England	1-1		0-1	1	Fairs
1966-67	Valencia CF, Spain	1-2		0-2	1	Fairs
1968-69	Ajax Amsterdam, Holland	1-1		0-4	1	ECC
1988-89	AS Roma, Italy	1-3		2-1	1	UEFA

VfB STUTTGART

VfB=Verein fur Bewegungsspiele
Founded 9-9-1893
Colours all white with 1 red hoop on shirt
Stadium Neckarstadion (70,704) ☎ 0711-56 16 71/74
Champions 1950, 1952, 1984
Cup Winners 1954, 1958
UEFA Cup Finalists 1989

Season	Opponent	Home	Result	Away	Rnd	Cup
1964-65	BK 1913 Odense, Denmark	1-0		3-1	pr	Fairs
	Dunfermline Athletic, Scotland	0-0		0-1	1	Fairs
1966-67	Burnley, England	1-1		0-2	1	Fairs
1969-70	Malmo FF, Sweden	3-0		1-1	1	Fairs
	Napoli, Italy	0-0		0-1	2	Fairs

1973-74	Olympiakos Piraeus, Greece	4-0		9-0	1	UEFA
	Tatran Presov, Czechoslovakia	3-1		5-3	2	UEFA
	Dynamo Kiev, USSR	3-0		0-2	3	UEFA
	Vitoria Setubal, Portugal	1-0		2-2	qf	UEFA
	Feyenoord Rotterdam, Holland	2-2		1-2	sf	UEFA
1978-79	FC Basle, Switzerland	4-1		3-2	1	UEFA
	Torpedo Moscow, USSR	2-0		1-2	2	UEFA
	Dukla Prague, Czechoslovakia	4-1		0-4	3	UEFA
1979-80	Torino, Italy	1-0	wag	1-2	1	UEFA
	Dynamo Dresden, East Germany	0-0	wag	1-1	2	UEFA
	Grasshoppers Zurich, Switzerland	3-0		2-0	3	UEFA
	Lokomotiv Sofia, Bulgaria	3-1		1-0	qf	UEFA
	Borussia Monchengladbach, Germany	2-1		0-2	sf	UEFA
1980-81	Pezoporikos Larnaca, Cyprus	6-0		4-1	1	UEFA
	FC Vorwaerts Frankfurt on Oder, East Germany	5-1		2-1	2	UEFA
	1.FC Koln, Germany	3-1		1-4	3	UEFA
1981-82	Hajduk Split, Yugoslavia	2-2		1-3	1	UEFA
1983-84	Levski Spartak Sofia, Bulgaria	1-1		0-1	1	UEFA
1984-85	Levski Spartak Sofia, Bulgaria	2-2	lag	1-1	1	ECC
1986-87	Spartak Trnava, Czechoslovakia	1-0		0-0	1	CWC
	Torpedo Moscow, USSR	3-5		0-2	2	CWC
1988-89	Tatabanya Banyasz SC, Hungary	2-0		1-2	1	UEFA
	Dinamo Zagreb, Yugoslavia	1-1		3-1	2	UEFA
	FC Groningen, Holland	2-0		3-1	3	UEFA
	Real Sociedad San Sebastien, Spain	1-0	4-2p	0-1 aet	qf	UEFA
	Dynamo Dresden, East Germany	1-0		1-1	sf	UEFA
	Napoli, Italy	3-3		1-2	FINAL	UEFA
1989-90	Feyenoord Rotterdam, Holland	2-0		1-2	1	UEFA
	Zenit Leningrad, USSR	5-0		1-0	2	UEFA
	Royal Antwerp, Belgium	1-1		0-1	3	UEFA

HERTHA BSC BERLIN

Founded 25-7-1892 as Hertha '92, 1923 amalgamation of Hertha '92 and Berliner BC '99 to form Hertha BSC
Colours blue and white striped shirts, blue shorts
Stadium Olympiastadion (76,000) ☎ 030-305 5001/02
Champions 1930, 1931

Season	Opponent	Home	Result	Away	Rnd	Cup
1963-64	AS Roma, Italy	1-3		0-2	1	Fairs
1964-65	Royal Antwerp, Belgium	2-1		0-2	pr	Fairs
1969-70	Las Palmas, Spain	1-0		0-0	1	Fairs
	Juventus, Italy	3-1		0-0	2	Fairs
	Vitoria Setubal, Portugal	1-0		1-1	3	Fairs
	Inter Milan, Italy	1-0		0-2	qf	Fairs
1970-71	B 1901 Nykobing, Denmark	4-1		4-2	1	Fairs
	Spartak Trnava, Czechoslovakia	1-0		1-3	2	Fairs
1971-72	IFK Elfsborg Boras, Sweden	3-1		4-1	1	UEFA
	AC Milan, Italy	2-1		2-4	2	UEFA
1975-76	HJK Helsinki, Finland	4-1		2-1	1	UEFA
	Ajax Amsterdam, Holland	1-0		1-4	2	UEFA
1978-79	Trakia Plovdiv, Bulgaria	0-0		2-1	1	UEFA
	Dynamo Tbilisi, USSR	2-0		0-1	2	UEFA
	Esbjerg fB, Denmark	4-0		1-2	3	UEFA
	Dukla Prague, Czechoslovakia	1-1		2-1	qf	UEFA
	Red Star Belgrade, Yugoslavia	2-1	lag	0-1	sf	UEFA

GERMANY

HANNOVERSCHER SV 96

Founded 12-4-1896
Colours red shirts, black shorts
Stadium Niedersachsenstadion (60,449) ☎ 0511-28 20 96/97
Champions 1938, 1954

Season	Opponent	Home	Result	Away	Rnd	Cup
1958-60	AS Roma, Italy	1-3		1-1	1	Fairs
1960-61	Inter Milan, Italy	1-6		2-8	1	Fairs
1961-62	Espanol Barcelona, Spain	0-1		0-2	pr	Fairs
1965-66	bye				1	Fairs
	FC Porto, Portugal	5-0		1-2	2	Fairs
	CF Barcelona, Spain	2-1	1-1 lot*	0-1	3	Fairs
			* in Hannover aet			
1967-68	Napoli, Italy	1-1		0-4	1	Fairs
1968-69	B 1909 Odense, Denmark	3-2		1-0	1	Fairs
	AIK Stockholm, Sweden	5-2		2-4	2	Fairs
	Leeds United, England	1-2		1-5	3	Fairs
1969-70	Ajax Amsterdam, Holland	2-1		0-3	1	Fairs

EINTRACHT BRAUNSCHWEIG

Founded 15-12-1895
Colours yellow shirts with blue collar, blue shorts
Stadium Hamburger Strasse Stadion (35,000) ☎ 0531-328 56
Champions 1967

Season	Opponent	Home	Playoff Result	Away	Rnd	Cup
1967-68	Dinamo Tirana, Albania	withdrew			1	ECC
	Rapid Vienna, Austria	2-0		0-1	2	ECC
	Juventus, Italy	3-2	0-1*	0-1	qf	ECC
			* in Berne			
1971-72	Glentoran, Ireland	6-1		1-0	1	UEFA
	Athletic Bilbao, Spain	2-1		2-2	2	UEFA
	Ferencvarosi TC, Hungary	1-1		2-5	3	UEFA
1976-77	Holbaek BI, Denmark	7-0		0-1	1	UEFA
	Espanol Barcelona, Spain	2-1		0-2	2	UEFA
1977-78	Dynamo Kiev, USSR	0-0	wag	1-1	1	UEFA
	IFK Start Kristiansand, Norway	4-0		0-1	2	UEFA
	PSV Eindhoven, Holland	1-2		0-2	3	UEFA

FORTUNA DUSSELDORF

Founded 1-8-1895
Colours red shirts with white striped sleeve, white shorts
Stadium Rheinstadion (67,851) ☎ 0211-23 30 59
Champions 1933
Cup Winners 1979, 1980
CWC Finalists 1979

Season	Opponent	Home	Result	Away	Rnd	Cup
1973-74	Naestved IF, Denmark	1-0		2-2	1	UEFA
	Admira Wacker, Austria	3-0		1-2	2	UEFA
	1.FC Lokomotive Leipzig, East Germany	2-1		0-3	3	UEFA
1974-75	Torino, Italy	3-1		1-1	1	UEFA
	Raba Vasas Eto, Hungary	3-0		0-2	2	UEFA
	FC Amsterdam, Holland	1-2		0-3	3	UEFA
1978-79	Universitatea Craiova, Romania	1-1		4-3	1	CWC
	Aberdeen, Scotland	3-0		0-2	2	CWC
	Servette Geneva, Switzerland	0-0	wag	1-1	qf	CWC
	Banik Ostrava, Czechoslovakia	3-1		1-2	sf	CWC
	FC Barcelona, Spain	3-4	in Basle		FINAL	CWC
1979-80	Glasgow Rangers, Scotland	0-0		1-2	1	CWC
1980-81	SV Austria Salzburg, Austria	5-0		3-0	1	CWC
	Waterschei Thor Genk, Belgium	1-0		0-0	2	CWC
	Benfica, Portugal	2-2		0-1	qf	CWC

BORUSSIA MONCHENGLADBACH

Founded 1-8-1900
Colours white shirts with green and black sleeves, white shorts
Stadium Bokelberg (38,500) ☎ 02161-10031/34
Champions 1970, 1971, 1975, 1976, 1977
Cup Winners 1960, 1973
German Super Cup Winners 1977
UEFA Winners 1975, 1979 Finalists 1973, 1980

Season	Opponent	Home	Result	Away	Rnd	Cup
1960-61	Glasgow Rangers, Scotland	0-3		0-8	1	CWC
1970-71	EPA Larnaca, Cyprus	6-0*		10-0	1	ECC
		* in Augsburg				
	Everton, England	1-1	2-4 pen	1-1	2	ECC
1971-72	Cork Hibernians, Eire	2-1		5-0	1	ECC
	Inter Milan, Italy	0-0*	7-1**	2-4	2	ECC
		* in West Berlin, ** match void				
1972-73	Aberdeen, Scotland	6-3*		3-2	1	UEFA
		* in Nurnburg				
	Hvidovre IF, Denmark	3-0		3-1	2	UEFA
	1.FC Koln, Germany	5-0		0-0	3	UEFA
	1.FC Kaiserslautern, Germany	7-1		2-1	qf	UEFA
	Twente Enschede, Holland	3-0		2-1	sf	UEFA
	Liverpool, England	2-0		0-3*	FINAL	UEFA
		* 0-0 abd 28 mins waterlogged pitch				
1973-74	IBV Vestmannaeyja, Iceland	9-1		7-1*	1	CWC
		* in Reykjavik				
	Glasgow Rangers, Scotland	3-0		2-3	2	CWC
	Glentoran, Ireland	5-0		2-0	qf	CWC
	AC Milan, Italy	1-0		0-2	sf	CWC

145

GERMANY

	Home		Away	Rnd	Cup
1974-75 Wacker Innsbruck, Austria	3-0		1-2	1	UEFA
Olympique Lyon, France	1-0		5-2	2	UEFA
Real Zaragoza, Spain	5-0		4-2	3	UEFA
Banik Ostrava, Czechoslovakia	3-1		1-0	qf	UEFA
1.FC Koln, Germany	1-0		3-1	sf	UEFA
Twente Enschede, Holland	0-0*		5-1	FINAL	UEFA
* in Dusseldorf					
1975-76 Wacker Innsbruck, Austria	1-1		6-1	1	ECC
Juventus, Italy	2-0		2-2	2	ECC
Real Madrid, Spain	2-2	lag	1-1	qf	ECC
1976-77 FK Austria/WAC Vienna, Austria	3-0		0-1	1	ECC
Torino, Italy	0-0*		2-1	2	ECC
* in Dusseldorf					
Clube Bruges, Belgium	2-2*		1-0	qf	ECC
* in Dusseldorf					
Dynamo Kiev, USSR	2-0		0-1	sf	ECC
Liverpool, England	1-3	in Rome		FINAL	ECC
1977-78 Vasas Budapest, Hungary	1-1		3-0	1	ECC
Red Star Belgrade, Yugoslavia	5-1		3-0	2	ECC
Wacker Innsbruck, Austria	2-0	wag	1-3	qf	ECC
Liverpool, England	2-1		0-3	sf	ECC
1978-79 Sturm Graz, Austria	5-1		2-1	1	UEFA
Benfica, Portugal	2-0		0-0	2	UEFA
Slask Wroclaw, Poland	1-1		4-2	3	UEFA
Manchester City, England	3-1		1-1	qf	UEFA
MSV Duisburg, Germany	4-1		2-2	sf	UEFA
Red Star Belgrade, Yugoslavia	1-0*	wag	1-1	FINAL	UEFA
* in Dusseldorf					
1979-80 Viking Stavanger, Norway	3-0		1-1	1	UEFA
Inter Milan, Italy	1-1		3-2	2	UEFA
Universitatea Craiova, Romania	2-0		0-1	3	UEFA
St Etienne, France	2-0		4-1	qf	UEFA
VfB Stuttgart, Germany	2-0		1-2	sf	UEFA
Eintracht Frankfurt, Germany	3-2	lag	0-1	FINAL	UEFA
1981-82 1.FC Magdeburg, East Germany	2-0	wag	1-3	1	UEFA
Dundee United, Scotland	2-0		0-5	2	UEFA
1984-85 Dukla Banska Bystrica, Czechoslovakia	4-1		3-2	1	UEFA
Widzew Lodz, Poland	3-2	lag	0-1	2	UEFA
1985-86 Lech Poznan, Poland	1-1		2-0	1	UEFA
Sparta Rotterdam, Holland	5-1		1-1	2	UEFA
Real Madrid, Spain	5-1*	lag	0-4	3	UEFA
* in Dusseldorf					
1986-87 Partizan Belgrade, Yugoslavia	1-0		3-1	1	UEFA
Feyenoord Rotterdam, Holland	5-1		2-0	2	UEFA
Glasgow Rangers, Scotland	0-0	wag	1-1	3	UEFA
Vitoria Guimaraes, Portugal	3-0		2-2	qf	UEFA
Dundee United, Scotland	0-2		0-0	sf	UEFA
1987-88 Espanol Barcelona, Spain	0-1		1-4	1	UEFA

MSV DUISBURG

Founded 17-9-1902
Colours blue and white hooped shirts, white shorts
Stadium Wedaustadion (32,000) ☎ 0203-44 35 77/44 86 17

Season	Opponent	Home	Result	Away	Rnd	Cup
1975-76	Paralimni Famagusta, Cyprus	7-1		3-2*	1	UEFA
				* in Oberhausen		
	Levski Spartak Sofia, Bulgaria	3-2	lag	1-2	2	UEFA
1978-79	Lech Poznan, Poland	5-0		5-2	1	UEFA
	Carl Zeiss Jena, East Germany	3-0		0-0	2	UEFA
	RC Strasbourg, France	4-0		0-0	3	UEFA
	Honved Budapest, Hungary	1-2	wag	3-2	qf	UEFA
	Borussia Monchengladbach, Germany	2-2		1-4	sf	UEFA

SV WERDER BREMEN

Founded 1-2-1899
Colours green shirts, white shorts
Stadium Weserstadion (40,000) ☎ 0421-49 81 06
Champions 1965, 1988
Cup Winners 1961
German Super Cup Winners 1988

Season	Opponent	Home	Result	Away	Rnd	Cup
1961-62	bye				1	CWC
	AGF Aarhus, Denmark	2-0		3-2	2	CWC
	Atletico Madrid, Spain	1-1		1-3	qf	CWC
1965-66	Apoel Nicosia, Cyprus	5-0		5-0*	pr	ECC
				* in Hamburg		
	Partizan Belgrade, Yugoslavia	1-0		0-3	1	ECC
1982-83	FC Vorwaerts Frankfurt on Oder, East Germany	0-2	wag	3-1	1	UEFA
	IK Brage, Sweden	2-0		6-2	2	UEFA
	Dundee United, Scotland	1-1		1-2	3	UEFA
1983-84	Malmo FF, Sweden	1-1		2-1	1	UEFA
	1.FC Lokomotive Leipzig, East Germany	1-1		0-1	2	UEFA
1984-85	RSC Anderlecht, Belgium	2-1	lag	0-1	1	UEFA
1985-86	Chernmorets Odessa, USSR	3-2	lag	1-2	1	UEFA
1986-87	Atletico Madrid, Spain	2-1		0-2	1	UEFA
1987-88	Mjondalen IF, Norway	0-1		5-0	1	UEFA
	Spartak Moscow, USSR	6-2		1-4	2	UEFA
	Dynamo Tbilisi, USSR	2-1		1-1	3	UEFA
	Hellas-Verona, Italy	1-1		1-0	qf	UEFA
	Bayer Leverkusen, Germany	0-0		0-1	sf	UEFA
1988-89	BFC Dynamo Berlin, East Germany	5-0		0-3	1	ECC
	Glasgow Celtic, Scotland	0-0		1-0	2	ECC
	AC Milan, Italy	0-0		0-1	qf	ECC
1989-90	Lillestrom SK, Norway	2-0		3-1	1	UEFA
	FK Austria, Austria	5-0		0-2	2	UEFA
	Napoli, Italy	5-1		3-2	3	UEFA
	RFC Liege, Belgium	0-2		4-1	qf	UEFA
	Fiorentina, Italy	1-1	lag	0-0	sf	UEFA

1.FC KAISERSLAUTERN

Founded 2-6-1900
Colours all red
Stadium Fritz Walter Stadion (33,000) ☎ 0631-12005/7
Champions 1951, 1953

Season	Opponent	Home	Playoff Result	Away	Rnd	Cup
1972-73	Stoke City, England	4-0		1-3	1	UEFA
	CUF Barreiro, Portugal	0-1		3-1	2	UEFA
	Ararat Yerevan, USSR	2-0	5-4p	0-2	3	UEFA
	Borussia Monchengladbach, Germany	1-2		1-7	qf	UEFA
1976-77	Paralimni Famagusta, Cyprus	8-0		3-1	1	UEFA
	Feyenoord Rotterdam, Holland	2-2		0-5	2	UEFA
1979-80	FC Zurich, Switzerland	5-1		3-1	1	UEFA
	Sporting Lisbon, Portugal	2-0		1-1	2	UEFA
	Diosgyoer Miskolc, Hungary	6-1		2-0	3	UEFA
	Bayern Munich, Germany	1-0		1-4	qf	UEFA
1980-81	RSC Anderlecht, Belgium	1-0	wag	2-3	1	UEFA
	Standard Liege, Belgium	1-2		1-2	2	UEFA

147

GERMANY

1981-82	Akademik Sofia, Bulgaria	1-0		2-1	1	UEFA
	Spartak Moscow, USSR	4-0		1-2	2	UEFA
	KSV Lokeren, Belgium	4-1		0-1	3	UEFA
	Real Madrid, Spain	5-0		1-3	qf	UEFA
	IFK Gothenburg, Sweden	1-1		1-2	sf	UEFA
1982-83	Trabzonspor, Turkey	3-0		3-0	1	UEFA
	Napoli, Italy	2-0		2-1	2	UEFA
	Sevilla FC, Spain	4-0		0-1	3	UEFA
	Universitatea Craiova, Romania	3-2	lag	0-1	qf	UEFA
1983-84	Watford, England	3-1		0-3	1	UEFA

FC SCHALKE 04 (Gelsenkirchen)

Founded 4-5-1904
Colours blue shirts, white shorts
Stadium Parkstadion (72,139) ☎ 0209-72024/5
Champions 1934, 1935, 1937, 1939, 1940, 1942, 1958
Cup Winners 1937, 1972

Season	Opponent	Home	Playoff Result	Away	Rnd	Cup
1958-59	KB Copenhagen, Denmark	5-2	3-1*	0-3	1	ECC
			* in Enschede			
	Wolverhampton Wanderers, England	2-1		2-2	2	ECC
	Atletico Madrid, Spain	1-1		0-3	qf	ECC
1969-70	Shamrock Rovers, Eire	3-0		1-2	1	CWC
	IFK Norrkoping, Sweden	1-0		0-0	2	CWC
	Dinamo Zagreb, Yugoslavia	1-0		3-1	qf	CWC
	Manchester City, England	1-0		1-5	sf	CWC
1972-73	Slavia Sofia, Bulgaria	2-1	3-1	1-2*	1	CWC
				* abandoned		
	Cork Hibernians, Eire	3-0		0-0	2	CWC
	Sparta Prague, Czechoslovakia	2-1		0-3	qf	CWC
1976-77	FC Porto, Portugal	3-2		2-2*	1	UEFA
				* in Lisbon		
	Sportul Studentesc Bucharest, Romania	4-0		1-0	2	UEFA
	RWD Molenbeeck, Belgium	1-1		0-1	3	UEFA
1977-78	Fiorentina, Italy	2-1		3-0*	1	UEFA
				* awarded to Schalke		
	1.FC Magdeburg, East Germany	1-3		2-4	2	UEFA

ROT-WEISS ESSEN

Founded 1-2-1907
Colours white shirts with red sleeves, red shorts
Stadium Georg Melches Stadion (36,000) ☎ 0201-66 07 89
Champions 1955

Season	Opponent	Home	Result	Away	Rnd	Cup
1955-56	Hibernian, Scotland	0-4		1-1	1	ECC

1.FC SAARBRUCKEN

Founded 18-4-1903
Colours blue and black striped shirts, blue or white shorts
Stadium Ludwigspark (36,000) ☎ 0681-54341

Season	Opponent	Home	Result	Away	Rnd	Cup
1955-56	AC Milan, Italy	1-4		4-3	1	ECC

SC VIKTORIA KOLN 04

Founded 1904 merger of VfR Koln, Mulheimer SV 06, SC Rapid Koln and Prussen Dellbruck, Viktoria Koln 04 on 10-7-1957
Colours sky blue and white shirts, white shorts
Stadium Sportpark Hohenberg (15,000) ☎ 0221-89 69 91

Season	Opponent	Home	Result	Away	Rnd	Cup
1962-63	Ferencvarosi TC, Hungary	1-4		4-3	1	Fairs

TASMANIA 73 BERLIN

Founded 1900 disbanded 1973 as bankrupt, new club Tasmania 73, Berlin formed soon afterwards
Colours blue and white shirts, blue/white shorts
Stadium Neukolln (10,000) ☎ 687-4184

Season	Opponent	Home	Result	Away	Rnd	Cup
as TASMANIA 1900 BERLIN						
1962-63	Utrecht City XI, Holland	1-2		2-3	1	Fairs

WUPPERTALER SV

Founded 1954 by merger of SSV Wuppertal and Vohwinkel (1880)
Colours orange shirts, blue shorts
Stadium am Zoo (28,000) ☎ 0202-74 12 85

Season	Opponent	Home	Result	Away	Rnd	Cup
1973-74	Ruch Chorzow, Poland	5-4		1-4	1	UEFA

KICKERS OFFENBACH

Founded 27-5-1901
Colours red shirts, white shorts
Stadium Bieberer Berg (31,500) ☎ 069-30 441/85 3045
Cup Winners 1970

Season	Opponent	Home	Result	Away	Rnd	Cup
1970-71	Clube Bruges, Belgium	2-1		0-2	1	CWC

149

GERMANY

BAYER 05 UERDINGEN (Krefeld)

Founded 17-11-1905
Colours red and blue striped shirts, red or blue shorts
Stadium Grotenburg Kampfbahn (30,000) ☎ 02151-480188/88 56 32
Cup Winners 1985

Season	Opponent	Home	Result	Away	Rnd	Cup
1985-86	Zurrieq, Malta	9-0		3-0	1	CWC
	Galatasaray, Turkey	2-0		1-1	2	CWC
	Dynamo Dresden, East Germany	7-3		0-2	qf	CWC
	Atletico Madrid, Spain	2-3		0-1	sf	CWC
1986-87	Carl Zeiss Jena, East Germany	3-0		4-0	1	UEFA
	Widzew Lodz, Poland	2-0		0-0	2	UEFA
	FC Barcelona, Spain	0-2		0-2	3	UEFA

BAYER 04 LEVERKUSEN

Founded 15-6-1904
Colours white shirts, red shorts
Stadium Ulrich Haberland Stadion (28,000) ☎ 0214-6199/6299
UEFA Cup Winners 1988

Season	Opponent	Home	Result	Away	Rnd	Cup
1986-87	Kalmar FF, Sweden	3-0		4-1	1	UEFA
	Dukla Prague, Czechoslovakia	1-1	lag	0-0	2	UEFA
1987-88	FK Austria Vienna, Austria	5-1		0-0	1	UEFA
	Toulouse FC, France	1-0		1-1	2	UEFA
	Feyenoord Rotterdam, Holland			2-2	3	UEFA
	FC Barcelona, Spain	1-0*		1-0	qf	UEFA
		* in Koln				
	Werder Bremen, Germany	1-0		0-0	sf	UEFA
	Espanol Barcelona, Spain	3-0	3-2 pen	0-3	FINAL	UEFA
1988-89	Belenenses, Portugal	0-1		0-1	1	UEFA

FRANKFURT CITY XI

Season	Opponent	Home	Result	Away	Rnd	Cup
1955-58	Basel City XI, Switzerland	5-1	mini	2-6	pr	Fairs
	London XI, England	1-0	league	2-3	pr	Fairs

WEST BERLIN CITY XI

Season	Opponent	Home	Result	Away	Rnd	Cup
1961-62	CF Barcelona, Spain	1-0		0-3	1	Fairs

GREECE

Founded 1926 Federation Hellenique de Football Association, Singrou Avenue 137, Athens ☎Telephone 933 4922
National Colours white shirts, blue shorts, white socks
Season September to June

LEAGUE CHAMPIONS

1928	Aris Salonika	1948	Olympiakos Piraeus	1962	Panathinaikos	1976	PAOK Salonika
1930	Panathinaikos	1949	Panathinaikos	1963	AEK Athens	1977	Panathinaikos
1931	Olympiakos Piraeus	1950	not decided	1964	Panathinaikos	1978	AEK Athens
1932	Aris Salonika	1951	Olympiakos Piraeus	1965	Panathinaikos	1979	AEK Athens
1933	Olympiakos Piraeus	1952	no competition	1966	Olympiakos Piraeus	1980	Olympiakos Piraeus
1934	Olympiakos Piraeus	1953	Panathinaikos	1967	Olympiakos Piraeus	1981	Olympiakos Piraeus
1935	not decided	1954	Olympiakos Piraeus	1968	AEK Athens	1982	Olympiakos Piraeus
1936	Olympiakos Piraeus	1955	Olympiakos Piraeus	1969	Panathinaikos	1983	Olympiakos Piraeus
1937	Olympiakos Piraeus	1956	Olympiakos Piraeus	1970	Panathinaikos	1984	Panathinaikos
1938	Olympiakos Piraeus	1957	Olympiakos Piraeus	1971	AEK Athens	1985	PAOK Salonika
1939	AEK Athens	1958	Olympiakos Piraeus	1972	Panathinaikos	1986	Panathinaikos
1940	AEK Athens	1959	Olympiakos Piraeus	1973	Olympiakos Piraeus	1987	Olympiakos Piraeus
1946	Aris Salonika	1960	Panathinaikos	1974	Olympiakos Piraeus	1988	Larissa
1947	Olympiakos Piraeus	1961	Panathinaikos	1975	Olympiakos Piraeus	1989	AEK Athens

CUP WINNERS

1932	AEK Athens v Aris Salonika	5-3	1961	Olympiakos Piraeus v Panionios	3-0
1933	Ethnikos v Aris Salonika	2-2 2-1	1962	no Competition	
1939	AEK Athens v PAOK Salonika	2-1	1963	Olympiakos Piraeus v Pierikos	3-0
1940	Panathinaikos v Aris Salonika	3-1	1964	no competition	
1947	Olympiakos Piraeus v Iraklis Salonika	5-0	1965	Olympiakos Piraeus v Panathinaikos	1-0
1948	Panathinaikos v AEK Athens	2-1	1966	AEK Athens v Olympiakos Piraeus	2-0
1949	AEK Athens v Panathinaikos	0-0 2-1	1967	Panathinaikos v Panionios	1-0
1950	AEK Athens v Aris Salonika	4-0	1968	Olympiakos Piraeus v Panathinaikos	1-0
1951	Olympiakos Piraeus v PAOK Salonika	4-0	1969	Panathinaikos v Olympiakos Piraeus	1-1 wot
1952	Olympiakos Piraeus v Panionios	2-2 2-0	1970	Aris Salomika v PAOK Salonika	1-0
1953	Olympiakos Piraeus v AEK Athens	3-2	1971	Olympiakos Piraeus v PAOK Salonika	3-1
1954	Olympiakos Piraeus v Doksa Drama	2-0	1972	PAOK Salonika v Panathinaikos	2-1
1955	Panathinaikos v PAOK Salonika	2-0	1973	Olympiakos Piraeus v PAOK Salonika	1-0
1956	AEK Athens v Olympiakos Piraeus	2-1	1974	PAOK Salonika v Olympiakos Piraeus	2-2 4-3p
1957	Olympiakos Piraeus v Iraklis Salonika	2-0	1975	Olympiakos Piraeus v Panathinaikos	1-0
1958	Olympiakos Piraeus v Doksa Drama	5-1	1976	Heraklis Salonika v Olympiakos Piraeus	4-4 6-5p
1959	Olympiakos Piraeus v Doksa Drama	2-1	1977	Panathinaikos v PAOK Salonika	2-1
1960	Olympiakos Piraeus v Panathinaikos	1-1 3-0	1978	AEK Athens v PAOK Salonika	2-0

GREECE

1979	Panionios v AEK Athens	3-1
1980	Kastoria v Iraklis Salonika	5-2
1981	Olympiakos Piraeus v PAOK Salonika	3-1
1982	Panathinaikos v Larissa	1-0
1983	AEK Athens v PAOK Salonica	2-0
1984	Panathinaikos v Larissa	2-0

1985	Larissa v PAOK Salonika	4-1
1986	Panathinaikos v Olympiakos Piraeus	4-0
1987	OFI Crete v Iraklis Salonika	1-1 3-1p
1988	Panathinaikos v Olympiakos Piraeus	2-2 6-5p
1989	Panathinaikos v Panionios	3-1
1990	Olympiakos Piraeus v OFI Crete	

GREEK SUPER CUP

1989	AEK Athens v Panathinaikos	1-1 6-5p

FEATURED CLUBS IN EUROPEAN COMPETITION

Panathinaikos	Olympiakos Piraeus	AEK Athens	PAOK Salonika
Aris Salonika	Panionios	Iraklis Salonika	Panachaiki Patras
Kastoria	Larissa	OFI Crete	

PANATHINAIKOS (ATHENS)

Founded 1908 Colours green shirts, white shorts, green socks Stadium Panathinaikos (25,000)
Champions 1930, 1949, 1953, 1960, 1961, 1962, 1964, 1965, 1969, 1970, 1972, 1977, 1984, 1986
☎ Telephone 1-646 0469
Cup Winners 1940, 1948, 1955, 1967, 1969, 1977, 1982, 1984, 1986, 1988, 1989
ECC Finalists 1971

Season	Opponents	Home	Playoff Result	Away	Rnd	Cup
1960-61	bye				1	ECC
	Spartak Hradec Kralove, Czechoslovakia	0-0		0-1	2	ECC
1961-62	Juventus, Italy	1-1		1-2	pr	ECC
1962-63	Polonia Bytom, Poland	1-4		1-2	1	ECC
1964-64	Glentoran, Ireland	3-2		2-2	pr	ECC
	1.FC Koln, Germany	1-1		1-2	1	ECC
1965-66	Sliema Wanderers, Malta	4-1		0-1	pr	ECC
	Ferencvarosi TC, Hungary	1-3		0-0	1	ECC
1967-68	Bayern Munich, Germany	1-2		0-5	1	CWC
1968-69	Daring, Belgium	2-0		1-2	1	Fairs
	Atletico Bilbao, Spain	0-0		0-1	2	Fairs
1969-70	FC Vorwaerts Berlin, East Germany	1-1		0-2	1	ECC
1970-71	Jeunesse Esch, Luxembourg	5-0		2-1	1	ECC
	Slovan Bratislava, Czechoslovakia	3-0		1-2	2	ECC
	Everton, England	0-0	wag	1-1	qf	ECC
	Red Star Belgrade, Yugoslavia	3-0	wag	1-4	sf	ECC
	Ajax Amsterdam, Holland		0-2 at Wembley		FINAL	ECC
1972-73	CSKA September Flag, Bulgaria	2-1*	0-2	1-2	1	ECC
	* match void for rule infringement					
1973-74	OFK Belgrade, Yugoslavia	1-2	lag	1-0	1	UEFA
1974-75	Grasshoppers Zurich, Switzerland	2-1		0-2	1	UEFA
1975-76	Sachsenring Zwickau, East Germany	0-0*		0-2	1	CWC
	* in Patras					
1977-78	Floriana, Malta	4-0		1-1	1	ECC
	Clube Bruges, Belgium	1-0		0-2	2	ECC
1978-79	FC Arges Pitiesti, Romania	1-2		0-3	1	UEFA
1980-81	Juventus, Italy	4-2		0-4	1	UEFA
1981-82	Arsenal, England	0-2		0-1	1	UEFA
1982-83	FK Austria Vienna, Austria	2-1		0-2	1	CWC
1984-85	Feyenoord Rotterdam, Holland	2-1		0-0	1	ECC
	Linfield, Ireland	2-1		3-3	2	ECC

	IFK Gothenburg, Sweden	2-2		1-0	qf	ECC
	Liverpool, England	0-1		0-4	sf	ECC
1985-86	Torino, Italy	1-1		1-2	1	UEFA
1986-87	Red Star Belgrade, Yugoslavia	2-1		0-3	1	ECC
1987-88	AJ Auxerre, France	2-0		2-3	1	UEFA
	Juventus, Italy	1-0		2-3	2	UEFA
	Honved Budapest, Hungary	5-1		2-5	3	UEFA
	Clube Bruges, Belgium	2-2		0-1	qf	UEFA
1988-89	Omonia Nicosia, Cyprus	2-0		1-0	1	CWC
	Sredets CFKA Sofia, Bulgaria	0-1		0-2	2	CWC
1989-90	Swansea City, Wales	3-2		3-3	1	CWC
	Dinamo Bucharest, Romania	0-2		1-6	2	CWC

OLYMPIAKOS (PIRAEUS)

Founded 1925 Colours red and white striped shirts, white shorts
Stadium Karaiskaki (45,000) ☎ 1-412 8323
Champions 1931, 1933, 1934, 1936, 1937, 1938, 1947, 1948, 1951, 1954, 1955, 1956, 1957, 1958, 1959, 1966, 1967, 1973, 1974, 1975, 1980, 1981, 1982, 1983, 1987
Cup Winners 1947, 1951, 1952, 1953, 1954, 1957, 1958, 1959, 1960, 1961, 1963, 1965, 1968, 1971, 1973, 1975, 1981

Season	Opponents	Home	Playoff Result	Away	Rnd	Cup
1958-59	Besiktas, Turkey	withdrew			1	EEC
1959-60	AC Milan, Italy	2-2		1-3	pr	ECC
1961-62	bye				1	CWC
	Dynamo Zilina, Czechoslovakia	2-3		0-1	2	CWC
1962-63		withdrew			1	Fairs
1963-64	Zaglebie Sosnowice, Poland	2-1	2-0*	0-1	pr	CWC
			* in Piraeus			
	Olympique Lyon, France	2-1		1-4	1	CWC
1965-66	Omonia Nicosia, Cyprus	1-1		1-0	1	CWC
	West Ham United, England	2-2		0-4	2	CWC
1966-67	CSKA Sofia, Bulgaria	1-0		1-3	pr	ECC
1967-68	Juventus, Italy	0-0		0-2	1	ECC
1968-69	Fram Reykjavik, Finland	2-0		2-0*	1	CWC
				* in Greece		
	Dunfermline Athletic, Scotland	3-0		0-4	2	CWC
1969-70	Gornik Zabrze, Poland	2-2		0-5	1	CWC
1971-72	Dynamo Moscow, USSR	2-1		0-2	1	CWC
1972-73	Cagliari Sardinia, Italy	2-1		1-0	1	UEFA
	Tottenham Hotspur, England	1-0		0-4	2	UEFA
1973-74	Benfica, Portugal	0-1		0-1	1	ECC
1974-75	Glasgow Celtic, Scotland	2-0		1-1	1	ECC
	RSC Anderlecht, Belgium	3-0		1-5	2	ECC
1975-76	Dynamo Kiev, USSR	2-2		0-1	1	ECC
1976-77	Universitatea Craiova, Romania	2-1		0-3	1	UEFA
1977-78	Dinamo Zagreb, Yugoslavia	3-1		1-5	1	UEFA
1978-79	Levski Spartak Sofia, Bulgaria	2-1		1-3	1	UEFA
1979-80	Napoli, Italy	1-0		0-2	1	UEFA
1980-81	Bayern Munich, Germany	2-4		0-3	1	ECC
1981-82	Universitatea Craiova, Romania	2-0		0-3	1	ECC
1982-83	Osters IF Vaxjo, Sweden	2-0		0-1	1	ECC
	Hamburger SV, Germany	0-4		0-1	2	ECC
1983-84	Ajax Amsterdam, Holland	2-0		0-0	1	ECC
	Benfica, Portugal	1-0		0-3	2	ECC
1984-85	FC Neuchatal Xamax, Switzerland	1-0		2-2	1	UEFA
	Universitatea Craiova, Romania	0-1		0-1	2	UEFA
1986-87	Union Spora, Luxembourg	3-0		3-0	1	CWC
	Ajax Amsterdam, Holland	1-1		0-4	2	CWC
1987-88	Gornik Zabrze, Poland	1-1		1-2	1	ECC
1989-90	RAD Belgrade, Yugoslavia	2-0		1-2	1	UEFA
	First Vienna FC 1894, Austria	1-1	wag	2-2	2	UEFA
	AJ Auxerre, France	1-1	lag	0-0	3	UEFA

153

GREECE

AEK (ATHENS)

AEK = Athlitiki Enosis Konstantinopoleos
Founded 1924 Colours yellow shirts, black shorts Stadium AEK (35,000) ☎ 1-8224 666
Champions 1939, 1940, 1963, 1968, 1971, 1978, 1979, 1989
Cup Winners 1932, 1939, 1949, 1950, 1956, 1966, 1978, 1983
Greek Super Cup Winners 1989

Season	Opponents	Home	Result	Away	Rnd	Cup
1963-64	AS Monaco, France	1-1		2-7*	pr	ECC
				* in Nice		
1964-65	Dinamo Zagreb, Yugoslavia	2-0		0-3	pr	CWC
1966-67	Sporting Braga, Portugal	0-1		2-3	pr	CWC
1968-69	Jeunesse Esch, Luxembourg	3-0		2-3	1	ECC
	AB Copenhagen, Denmark	0-0		2-0	2	ECC
	Spartak Trnava, Czechoslovakia	1-1		1-2	qf	ECC
1970-71	Twente Enschede, Holland	0-1		0-3	1	Fairs
1971-72	Inter Milan, Italy	3-2		1-4	1	ECC
1972-73	Salgotaryan Banyasz, Hungary	3-1		1-1	1	UEFA
	Liverpool, England	1-3		0-3	2	UEFA
1975-76	Vojvodina Novi Sad, Yugoslavia	3-1		0-0	1	UEFA
	Internacional Bratislava, Czechoslovakia	3-1	lag	0-2	2	UEFA
1976-77	Dynamo Moscow, USSR	2-0		1-2	1	UEFA
	Derby County, England	2-0		3-2	2	UEFA
	Red Star Belgrade, Yugoslavia	2-0	wag	1-3	3	UEFA
	Queens Park Rangers, England	3-0	7-6p	0-3	qf	UEFA
	Juventus, Italy	0-1		1-4	sf	UEFA
1977-78	Tirgu Mures, Romania	3-0		0-1	1	UEFA
	Standard Liege, Belgium	2-2		1-4	2	UEFA
1978-79	FC Porto, Portugal	6-1		1-4	1	ECC
	Nottingham Forest, England	1-2		1-5	2	ECC
1979-80	FC Arges Pitesti, Romania	2-0		0-3	1	ECC
1982-83	1.FC Koln, Germany	0-1	3-3*	0-5	1	UEFA
			* abandoned			
1983-84	Ujpest Dozsa, Hungary	2-0		1-4	1	CWC
1985-86	Real Madrid, Spain	1-0		0-5	1	UEFA
1986-87	Inter Milan, Italy	0-1		0-2	1	UEFA
1988-89	Athletic Bilbao, Spain	1-0		0-2	1	UEFA
1989-90	Dynamo Dresden, East Germany	5-3		0-1	1	EEC
	Olympique Marseille, France	1-1		0-2	2	EEC

PAOK (SALONIKA)

PAOK = Panthessalonikeios Athlitikos Omilos Konstantinopoliton
Founded 1926 Colours black and white shirts, red shorts
Stadium Toumpas (40,000) ☎ 031-238 560
Champions 1976, 1985
Cup Winners 1972, 1974

Season	Opponents	Home	Result	Away	Rnd	Cup
1965-66	Wiener Sport Club, Austria	2-1		0-6	1	Fairs
1967-68	FC Leige, Belgium	0-2		2-3	1	Fairs
1970-71	Dinamo Bucharest, Romania	1-0		0-5	1	Fairs
1972-73	Rapid Vienna, Austria	2-2	lag	0-0	1	CWC
1973-74	Legia Warsaw, Poland	1-0		1-1	1	CWC
	Olympique Lyon, France	4-0		3-3	2	CWC
	AC Milan, Italy	2-2		0-3	qf	CWC
1974-75	Red Star Belgrade, Yugoslavia	1-0		0-2aet	1	CWC
1975-76	FC Barcelona, Spain	1-0		1-6	1	UEFA
1976-77	Omonia Nicosia, Cyprus	1-1		2-0	1	ECC
	Dynamo Kiev, USSR	0-2		0-4	2	ECC

154

1977-78	Zaglebie Sosnowice, Poland	2-0		2-0	1	CWC
	Vejle BK, Denmark	2-1		0-3	2	CWC
1978-79	Servette Geneva, Switzerland	2-0		0-4	1	CWC
1981-82	Eintracht Frankfurt, Germany	2-0	4-5p	0-2	1	CWC
1982-83	Sochaux, France	1-0	wag	1-2	1	UEFA
	Sevilla FC, Spain	2-0		0-4	2	UEFA
1983-84	Lokomotiv Plovdiv, Bulgaria	3-1		2-1	1	UEFA
	Bayern Munich, Germany	0-0	8-9 pen	0-0	2	UEFA
1985-86	Hellas-Verona, Italy	1-2		1-3	1	ECC
1988-89	Napoli, Italy	1-1		0-1	1	UEFA

ARIS SALONIKA

Founded 1914 Colours yellow shirts, black shorts Stadium Harilaon (30,000) ☎ 031-842 700
Champions 1928, 1932, 1946
Cup Winners 1970

Season	Opponents	Home	Result	Away	Rnd	Cup
1964-65	AS Roma, Italy	0-0		0-3	pr	Fairs
1965-66	bye				1	Fairs
	1.FC Koln, Germany	2-1		0-2	2	Fairs
1966-67	Juventus, Italy	0-2		0-5	1	Fairs
1968-69	Hibernians, Malta	1-0		6-0	1	Fairs
	Ujpest Dozsa, Hungary	1-2		1-9	2	Fairs
1969-70	Cagliari Sardinia, Italy	1-1		0-3*	1	Fairs

*abandoned after 80 mins; AEK players fought police

1970-71	Chelsea, England	1-1		1-5	1	CWC
1974-75	Rapid Vienna, Austria	1-0		1-3	1	UEFA
1979-80	Benfica, Portugal	3-1		1-2	1	UEFA
	Perugia, Italy	1-1		3-0	2	UEFA
	St Etienne, France	3-3		1-4	3	UEFA
1980-81	Ipswich Town, England	3-1		1-5	1	UEFA
1981-82	Sliema Wanderers, Malta	4-0		4-2	1	UEFA
	KSC Lokeren, Belgium	1-1		0-4	2	UEFA

PANIONIOS (ATHENS)

Founded 1890 Colours red shirts, blue shorts Stadium Neo Smurnis (25,000) ☎ 933 2036
Cup Winners 1979

Season	Opponents	Home	Result	Away	Rnd	Cup
1969-70	Hansa Rostock, East Germany	2-0		0-3	1	Fairs
1971-72	Atletico Madrid, Spain	1-0	wag	1-2	1	UEFA
	Ferencvarosi TC, Hungary		disqualified	0-6	2	UEFA
1979-80	Twente Enschede, Holland	4-0		1-3	1	CWC
	IFK Gothenburg, Sweden	1-0		0-2	2	CWC
1987-88	Toulouse FC, France	0-1		1-5	1	UEFA

IRAKLIS SALONIKA

Founded 1908 Colours sky blue and white striped shirts, sky blue shorts
Stadium Kautatzogleou (45,000) ☎ 031-275 089
Cup Winners 1976

Season	Opponents	Home	Result	Away	Rnd	Cup
1961-62	bye				1	Fairs
	Vojvodina Novi Sad, Yugoslavia	2-1		1-9	1	Fairs

GREECE

1963-64	Real Zaragoza, Spain	0-3	1-6	1	Fairs
1976-77	Apoel Nicosia, Cyprus	0-0	0-2	1	CWC
1989-90	FC Sion, Switzerland	1-0	0-2	1	UEFA

PANAHAIKI PATRAS

Founded 1891 as Gymnasik Club, 1923 as Panahaiki Patras
Colours red and black striped shirts, black shorts Stadium Panachaikis (20,000) ☎ 061-225 401/2

Season	Opponents	Home	Result	Away	Rnd	Cup
1973-74	Grazer AK Graz, Austria	2-1		1-0	1	UEFA
	Twente Enschede, Holland	1-1		0-7	2	UEFA

KASTORIA

Founded 1962 by amalgamation of Aris, Atromitos and Orestiade
Colours red and yellow striped shirts, red shorts Stadium Kastoria (6,000) ☎ 0467-22080
Cup Winners 1980

Season	Opponents	Home	Result	Away	Rnd	Cup
1980-81	Dynamo Tbilisi, USSR	0-0		0-2	1	CWC

LARISSA

Founded 1964 by amalgamation of Iraklis, Larissaikos, Aris and Toxotis
Colours maroon shirts, white shorts Stadium Alkazar (25,000) ☎ 041-257 960
Champions 1988 Cup Winners 1985

Season	Opponents	Home	Result	Away	Rnd	Cup
1983-84	Honved Budapest, Hungary	2-0		0-3	1	UEFA
1984-85	Siofoki Banyasz, Hungary	2-0		1-1	1	CWC
	Servette Geneva, Switzerland	2-1		1-0	2	CWC
	Dynamo Moscow, USSR	0-0		0-1*	qf	CWC
				* in Tbilisi		
1985-86	Sampdoria, Italy	1-1		0-1	1	CWC
1988-89	FC Neuchatel Xamax, Switzerland	2-1	0-3p	1-2	1	ECC

OFI CRETE

OFI = Omilos Filathlos Irakliou
Founded 1925 Colours black and white shirts, white shorts Stadium Demotikou (13,000) ☎ 081-283 920
Cup Winners 1987

Season	Opponents	Home	Result	Away	Rnd	Cup
1986-87	Hajduk Split, Yugoslavia	1-0		0-4	1	UEFA
1987-88	Vitosha Sofia, Bulgaria	3-1		0-1	1	CWC
	Atalanta Bergamo, Italy	1-0		0-2	1	CWC

HOLLAND

The Netherlands
Founded 1889 Koninklijke Nederlandsche Voetbalbond, (KNVB) Woudenbergseweg 56-58, Postbus 615, 3700 Am Zeist
☎ **(0031) 3439 1922**
National Colours orange shirts, white shorts, orange socks
Season August to June

LEAGUE CHAMPIONS

1898 RAP Amsterdam	1921 NAC Breda	1944 De Volewyckers Amsterdam	1967 Ajax Amsterdam
1899 RAP Amsterdam	1922 Go Ahead Deventer	1945 not held	1968 Ajax Amsterdam
	1923 RC Haarlem	1946 FC Haarlem	1969 Feyenoord Rotterdam
1900 VV The Hague	1924 Feyenoord Rotterdam	1947 Ajax Amsterdam	
1901 VV The Hague	1925 HBS The Hague	1948 VV Herzogogenbosch	1970 Ajax Amsterdam
1902 VV The Hague	1926 SC Enschede	1949 SSV Scheidam	1971 Feyenoord Rotterdam
1903 VV The Hague	1927 Heracles Almelo		1972 Ajax Amsterdam
1904 HBS The Hague	1928 Feyenoord Rotterdam	1950 Limburg Brunssum	1973 Ajax Amsterdam
1905 VV The Hague	1929 PSV Eindhoven	1951 PSV Eindhoven	1974 Feyenoord Rotterdam
1906 HBS The Hague		1952 Willem II Tilburg	1975 PSV Eindhoven
1907 VV The Hague	1930 Go Ahead Deventer	1953 RC Haarlem	1976 PSV Eindhoven
1908 Quick The Hague	1931 Ajax Amsterdam	1954 PSV Eindhoven	1977 Ajax Amsterdam
1909 Sparta Rotterdam	1932 Ajax Amsterdam	1955 Willem II Tilburg	1978 PSV Eindhoven
	1933 Go Ahead Deventer	1956 Rapid JC Haarlem	1979 Ajax Amsterdam
1910 VV The Hague	1934 Ajax Amsterdam	1957 Ajax Amsterdam	
1911 Sparta Rotterdam	1935 PSV Eindhoven	1958 DOS Utrecht	1980 Ajax Amsterdam
1912 Sparta Rotterdam	1936 Feyenoord Rotterdam	1959 Sparta Rotterdam	1981 AZ 67 Alkmaar
1913 Sparta Rotterdam	1937 Ajax Amsterdam		1982 Ajax Amsterdam
1914 VV The Hagueenter	1938 Feyenoord Rotterdam	1960 Ajax Amsterdam	1983 Ajax Amsterdam
1915 Sparta Rotterdam	1939 Ajax Amsterdam	1961 Feyenoord Rotterdam	1984 Feyenoord Rotterdam
1916 Willem II Tilburg		1962 Feyenoord Rotterdam	1985 Ajax Amsterdam
1917 Go Ahead Deventer	1940 Feyenoord Rotterdam	1963 PSV Eindhoven	1986 PSV Eindhoven
1918 Ajax Amsterdam	1941 Heracles Almelo	1964 DWS Amsterdam	1987 Ajax Amsterdam
1919 Ajax Amsterdam	1942 ADO Den Hague	1965 Feyenoord Rotterdam	1988 PSV Eindhoven
	1943 ADO Den Hague	1966 Ajax Amsterdam	1989 PSV Eindhoven
1920 Be Quick The Hague			

HOLLAND

CUP WINNERS

Year	Match	Score
1899	RAP v HVV The Hague	1-0
1900	Velocitas Breda v Ajax Leiden	3-1
1901	HBS The Hague v RAP	4-3
1902	Haarlem v HBS The Hague 2	2-1
1903	HVV The Hague v HBS The Hague	6-1
1904	HFC v HVV The Hague	3-1
1905	VOC v HBS 2	3-0
1906	Concordia Rotterdam v Volharding	3-2
1907	VOC v Voorwaarts	4-3
1908	HBS 2 v VOC	3-1
1909	Quick The Hague 2 v VOC	2-0
1910	Quick The Hague 2 v HVV The Hague 2	2-0
1911	Quick The Hague v Haarlem	1-0
1912	Haarlem v Vitesse	2-0
1913	HFC v DFC	4-1
1914	DFC v Haarlem	3-2
1915	HFC v HBS The Hague	1-0
1916	Quick The Hague v HBS The Hague	2-1
1917	Ajax Amsterdam v VSV	5-0
1918	RCH v VVA	2-1
1919	not held	
1920	CVV v Vuc	2-1
1921	Schoten v RFC	2-1
1922	not held	
1923	not held	
1924	not held	
1925	ZFC v Xerxes	5-1
1926	Longa v de Spartaan	5-2
1927	VUC v Vitesse	3-1
1928	RCH v PEC Zwolle	2-0
1929	not held	
1930	Feyenoord Rotterdam v Excelsior Rotterdam	1-0
1931	not held	
1932	DFC v PSV Eindhoven	5-4
1933	not held	
1934	Velocitas Groningen v Feyenoord Rotterdam	3-2
1935	Feyenoord Rotterdam v Helmond	5-2
1936	Roermond v KFC	4-2
1937	VV Eindhoven v De Spartaan Amsterdam	1-0
1938	VSV Ijminden v AGOVV Apeldoorn	4-1
1939	Wageningen v PSV Eindhoven	2-1
1940	not held	
1941	not held	
1942	not held	
1943	Ajax Amsterdam v DFC	3-2
1944	Willem II v Groene Star	9-2
1945	not held	
1946	not held	
1947	not held	
1948	Wageningen v DMV	0-0 wop
1949	Quick Nijmegan v Helmondia	1-1 wop
1950	PSV Eindhoven v Haarlem	4-3
1951	not held	
1952	not held	
1953	not held	
1954	not held	
1955	not held	
1956	not held	
1957	Fortuna 54 Geleen v Feyenoord Rotterdam	4-2
1958	Sparta Rotterdam v Volendam	4-3
1959	VVV Venlo v ADO Den Hague	4-1
1960	not held	
1961	Ajax Amsterdam v NAC Breda	3-0
1962	Sparta Rotterdam v DHC	1-0
1963	Willem II v ADO Den Hague	3-0
1964	Fortuna 54 Geleen v ADO Den Hague	0-0 wop
1965	Feyenoord Rotterdam v Go Ahead Deventer	1-0
1966	Sparta Rotterdam v ADO Den Hague	1-0
1967	Ajax Amsterdam v NAC Breda	2-1
1968	ADO Den Hague v Ajax Amsterdam	2-1
1969	Feyenoord Rotterdam v PSV Eindhoven	1-1 2-0
1970	Ajax Amsterdam v PSV Eindhoven	2-0
1971	Ajax Amsterdam v Sparta Rotterdam	2-2 2-1
1972	Ajax Amsterdam v FC Den Haag	3-2
1973	NAC Breda v NEC Nijmegan	2-0
1974	PSV Eindhoven v NAC Breda	6-0
1975	FC Den Haag v Twente Enschede	1-0
1976	PSV Eindhoven v Roda JC	1-0
1977	Twente Enschede v PEC Zwolle	3-0
1978	AZ 67 Alkmaar v Ajax Amsterdam	1-0
1979	Ajax Amsterdam v Twente Enschede	1-1 3-0
1980	Feyenoord Rotterdam v Ajax Amsterdam	3-1
1981	AZ 67 Alkmaar v Ajax Amsterdam	3-1
1982	AZ 67 Alkmaar v Utrecht	1-1 5-1
1983	Ajax Amsterdam v NEC Nijmegan	3-1 3-1
1984	Feyenoord Rotterdam v Fortuna Sittard	1-0
1985	Utecht v Helmond Sport	1-0
1986	Ajax Amsterdam v RBC Roosenoaal	3-0
1987	Ajax Amsterdam v Den Hague	4-2 aet
1988	PSV Eindhoven v Roda JC Kerkrade	3-2 aet
1989	PSV Eindhoven v FC Groningen	4-1
1990	PSV Eindhoven v Vitesse Arnheim	1-0

FEATURED CLUBS IN EUROPEAN COMPETITION

Ajax Amsterdam
Twente Enschede
Sparta Rotterdam
Roda JC Kirkrade (Rapid Heerlen)
NAC Breda
Utrecht City XI

Feyenoord Rotterdam
Den Haag (ADO The Hague)
FC Utrecht (DOS Utrecht)

Fortuna Sittard

PSV Eindhoven
FC Amsterdam (DWS, Bauw Wit)
AZ 67 Alkmnaar
HFC Haarlem
FC Groningen

Willem II, Tilburg

Go Ahead Eagles Deventer
NEC Nijmegen

AJAX AMSTERDAM

Founded 1900
Colours white shirts with one broad red stripe, white shorts
Stadium Derr Meer (29,380) ☎ 020-6654440
Champions 1918, 1919, 1931, 1932, 1934, 1937, 1939, 1947, 1957, 1960, 1966, 1967, 1968, 1970, 1972, 1973, 1977, 1979, 1980, 1982, 1983, 1985
Cup Winners 1917, 1943, 1961, 1967, 1970, 1971, 1972, 1979, 1983, 1986, 1987
ECC Winners 1971, 1972, 1973 Finalists 1969
CWC Winners 1987 Finalists 1988
European Super Cup Winners 1972, 1973 Finalists 1987
World Club Champions 1972

Season	Opponents	Home	Playoff Result	Away	Rnd	Cup
1957-58	bye				pr	ECC
	Wismut SC Karl Marx Stadt, East Germany	1-0		3-1	1	ECC
	Vasas Budapest, Hungary	2-2		0-4	qf	ECC
1960-61	Fredrikstad FK, Norway	0-0		3-4	pr	ECC
1961-62	bye				1	CWC
	Ujpest Dozsa, Hungary	2-1		1-3	2	CWC
1966-67	Besiktas, Turkey	2-0		2-1	1	ECC
	Liverpool, England	5-1		2-2	2	ECC
	Dukla Prague, Czechoslovakia	1-1		1-2	qf	ECC
1967-68	Real Madrid, Spain	1-1		1-2	1	ECC
1968-69	1.FC Nurnburg, Germany	4-0		1-1	1	ECC
	Fenerbahce, Turkey	2-0		2-0	2	ECC
	Benfica, Portugal	1-3	3-0aet* * in Paris	3-1	qf	ECC
	Spartak Trnava, Czechoslovakia	3-0		0-2	sf	ECC
	AC Milan, Italy		1-4 in Madrid		FINAL	EEC
1969-70	Hannover 96, Germany	3-0		1-2	1	Fairs
	Ruch Chorzow, Poland	7-0		2-1	2	Fairs
	Napoli, Italy	4-0		0-1	3	Fairs
	Carl Zeiss Jena, East Germany	5-1		1-3	qf	Fairs
	Arsenal, England	1-0		0-3	sf	Fairs
1970-71	17 Nentori Tirana, Albania	2-0		2-2	1	ECC
	FC Basle, Switzerland	3-0		2-1	2	ECC
	Glasgow Celtic, Scotland	3-0		0-1	qf	ECC
	Atletico Madrid, Spain	3-0		0-1	sf	ECC
	Panathinaikos, Greece		2-0 at Wembley		FINAL	ECC
1971-72	Dynamo Dresden, East Germany	2-0		0-0	1	ECC
	Olympique Marseille, France	4-1		2-1	2	ECC
	Arsenal, England	2-1		1-0	qf	ECC
	Benfica, Portugal	1-0		0-0	sf	ECC
	Inter Milan, Italy		2-0 in Rotterdam		FINAL	ECC
1972-73	bye				1	ECC
	CSKA Sofia, Bulgaria	3-0		3-1	2	ECC
	Bayern Munich, Germany	4-0		1-2	qf	ECC
	Real Madrid, Spain	2-1		1-0	qf	ECC
	Juventus, Italy		1-0 in Belgrade		FINAL	ECC
1973-74	bye				1	ECC
	CSKA Sofia, Bulgaria	1-0		0-2	2	ECC

159

HOLLAND

Season	Opponents	Home		Away	Rnd	Cup
1974-75	Stoke City, England	0-0	wag	1-1	1	UEFA
	Royal Antwerp, Belgium	1-0	wag	1-2	2	UEFA
	Juventus, Italy	2-1	lag	0-1	3	UEFA
1975-76	Glentoran, Ireland	8-0		6-1	1	UEFA
	Hertha BSC Berlin, Germany	4-1		0-1	2	UEFA
	Levski Spartak Sofia, Bulgaria	2-1	3-5p	1-2	3	UEFA
1976-77	Manchester United, England	1-0		0-2	1	UEFA
1977-78	Lillestrom SK, Norway	4-0		0-2	1	ECC
	Levski Spartak Sofia, Bulgaria	2-1		2-1	2	ECC
	Juventus, Italy	1-1	0-3 pen	1-1	qf	ECC
1978-79	Athletic Bilbao, Spain	3-0		0-2	1	UEFA
	Lausanne Sport, Switzerland	1-0		4-0	2	UEFA
	Honved Budapest, Hungary	2-0		1-4	3	UEFA
1979-80	HJK Helsinki, Finland	8-0		8-1	1	ECC
	Omonia Nicosia, Cyprus	10-0		0-4	2	ECC
	RC Strasbourg, France	4-0		0-0	qf	ECC
	Nottingham Forest, England	1-0		0-2	sf	ECC
1980-81	Dinamo Tirana, Albania	1-0		2-0	1	ECC
	Bayern Munich, Germany	2-1		1-5	2	ECC
1981-82	Tottenham Hotspur, England	1-3		0-3	1	CWC
1982-83	Glasgow Celtic, Scotland	1-2		2-2	1	ECC
1983-84	Olympiakos Piraeus, Greece	0-0		0-2	1	ECC
1984-85	Red Boys Differdange, Luxembourg	14-0		0-0	1	UEFA
	Bohemians Prague, Czechoslovakia	1-0	2-4 pen	0-1	2	UEFA
1985-86	FC Porto, Portugal	0-0		0-2	1	ECC
1986-87	Bursaspor, Turkey	5-0		2-0	1	CWC
	Olympiakos Piraeus, Greece	4-0		1-1	2	CWC
	Malmo FF, Sweden	3-1		0-1	qf	CWC
	Real Zaragoza, Spain	3-0		3-2	sf	CWC
	1.FC Lokomotive Leipzig, East Germany		1-0 in Athens		FINAL	CWC
1987-88	Dundalk, Eire	4-0		2-0	1	CWC
1989-90	FK Austria, Austria	*1-1aet		0-1	1	UEFA
		*abandoned, awarded to FK Austria				

FEYENOORD (ROTTERDAM)

Founded 1908
Colours red and white halved shirts, black shorts
Stadium Feyenoord (de Kuip) (62,215) ☎ 010-419 43 83
Champions 1924, 1928, 1936, 1938, 1940, 1961, 1962, 1965, 1969, 1971, 1974, 1984
Cup Winners 1930, 1935, 1965, 1969, 1980, 1984
ECC Winners 1970   UEFA Winners 1974   World Club Champions 1970

Season	Opponents	Home	Playoff Result	Away	Rnd	Cup
1961-62	IFK Gothenburg, Sweden	8-2		3-0	pr	ECC
	Tottenham Hotspur, England	1-3		1-1	1	ECC
1962-63	Servette Geneva, Switzerland	1-3	3-1*	3-1	1	ECC
			* in Dusseldorf			
	Vasas Budapest, Hungary	1-1	1-0*	2-2	2	ECC
			* in Anvers			
	Stade de Reims, France	1-1		1-0*	qf	ECC
				*in Paris		
	Benfica, Portugal	0-0		1-3	sf	ECC
1965-66	Real Madrid, Spain	2-1		0-5	pr	ECC
1968-69	Newcastle United, England	2-0		0-4	1	Fairs
1969-70	KR Reykjavik, Iceland	12-2*		4-0*	1	ECC
			* both in Rotterdam			
	AC Milan, Italy	2-0		0-1	2	ECC
	FC Vorwaerts Berlin, East Germany	2-0		0-1	qf	ECC
	Legia Warsaw, Poland	2-0		0-0	sf	ECC
	Glasgow Celtic, Scotland		2-1 in Milan		FINAL	ECC

HOLLAND

1970-71	UT Flamurarosie Arad, Romania	1-1	lag	0-0	1	ECC
1971-72	Olympiakos Nicosia, Cyprus	8-0		9-0*	1	ECC
				*in Rotterdam		
	Dinamo Bucharest, Romania	2-0		3-0	2	ECC
	Benfica, Portugal	1-0		1-5	qf	ECC
1972-73	US Rumelingen, Luxembourg	9-0		12-0	1	UEFA
	OFK Belgrade, Yugoslavia	4-3	lag	1-2	2	UEFA
1973-74	Osters IF Vaxjo, Sweden	2-1		3-1	1	UEFA
	Gwardia Warsaw, Poland	3-1		0-1	2	UEFA
	Standard Liege, Belgium	2-0		3-1	3	UEFA
	Ruch Chorzow, Poland	3-1		1-1	qf	UEFA
	VfB Stuttgart, Germany	2-1		2-2	sf	UEFA
	Tottenham Hotspur, England	2-0		2-2	FINAL	UEFA
1974-75	Coleraine, Ireland	7-0		4-1	1	ECC
	CF Barcelona, Spain	0-0		0-3	2	ECC
1975-76	Ipswich Town, England	1-2		0-2	1	UEFA
1976-77	Djurgarden IF Stockholm, Sweden	3-0		1-2	1	UEFA
	1.FC Kaiserslautern, Germany	5-0		2-2	2	UEFA
	Espanol Barcelona, Spain	2-0		1-0	3	UEFA
	RWD Molenbeeck, Belgium	0-0		1-2	qf	UEFA
1979-80	Everton, England	1-0		1-0	1	UEFA
	Malmo FF, Sweden	4-0		1-1	2	UEFA
	Eintracht Frankfurt, Germany	1-0		1-4	3	UEFA
1980-81	Ilves Tampere, Finland	4-2		3-1	1	CWC
	Hvidovre IF, Denmark	2-1		1-0	2	CWC
	Slavia Sofia, Bulgaria	4-0		2-3	qf	CWC
	Dynamo Tbilisi, USSR	2-0		0-3	sf	CWC
1981-82	Szombierki Bytom, Poland	2-0		1-1	1	UEFA
	Dynamo Dresden, East Germany	2-1		1-1	2	UEFA
	Radnicki Nis, Yugoslavia	1-0		0-2	3	UEFA
1983-84	St Mirren, Scotland	2-0		1-0	1	UEFA
	Tottenham Hotspur, England	0-2		2-4	2	UEFA
1984-85	Panathinaikos, Greece	0-0		1-2	1	ECC
1985-86	Sporting Lisbon, Portugal	2-1		1-3	1	ECC
1986-87	Pecsi Munkas, Hungary	2-0		0-1	1	UEFA
	Borussia Monchengladbach, Germany	0-2		1-5	2	UEFA
1987-88	CA Spora, Luxembourg	5-0		5-2	1	UEFA
	Aberdeen, Scotland	1-0		1-2	2	UEFA
	Bayer Leverkusen, Germany	2-2		0-1	3	UEFA
1989-90	VfB Stuttgart, Germany	2-1		0-2	1	UEFA

PSV EINDHOVEN

PSV = Philips Sports Vereniging
Founded 1913
Colours red and white striped shirts, black shorts
Stadium Philips Sportspark (22,000) ☎ 040-511917
Champions 1929, 1935, 1951, 1954, 1963, 1975, 1976, 1978, 1987, 1989
Cup Winners 1950, 1974, 1976, 1989, 1990
ECC Winners 1988
World Club Championship Finalists 1988
UEFA Cup Winners 1978

Season	Opponents	Home	Result	Away	Rnd	Cup
1955-56	Rapid Vienna, Austria	1-0		1-6	1	ECC
1963-64	Esbjerg fB, Denmark	7-1		4-3	1	ECC
	Spartak Plovdiv, Bulgaria	0-0		1-0	2	ECC
	FC Zurich, Switzerland	1-0		1-3	qf	ECC
1969-70	Rapid Vienna, Austria	4-2		2-1	1	CWC
	AS Roma, Italy	1-0	lot	0-1	2	CWC

Season	Opponents	Home	Result	Away	Rnd	Cup
1970-71	Gottwaldov TJ, Czechoslovakia	1-0	wag	1-2	1	CWC
	Steaua Bucharest, Romania	4-0		3-0	2	CWC
	FC Vorwaerts Berlin, East Germany	2-0		0-1	qf	CWC
	Real Madrid, Spain	0-0		1-2	sf	CWC
1971-72	HFC Chemie Halle, East Germany	withdrew		0-0	1	UEFA
	Real Madrid, Spain	2-0	wag	1-3	2	UEFA
	Lierse SK, Belgium	1-0		0-4	3	UEFA
1974-75	Ards, Ireland	10-0		4-1	1	CWC
	Gwardia Warsaw, Poland	3-0		5-1	2	CWC
	Benfica, Portugal	0-0		2-1	qf	CWC
	Dynamo Kiev, USSR	2-1		0-3	sf	CWC
1975-76	Linfield, Ireland	8-0		2-1	1	ECC
	Ruch Chorzow, Poland	4-0		3-1	2	ECC
	Hajduk Split, Yugoslavia	3-0		0-2	qf	ECC
	St Etienne, France	0-0		0-1	sf	ECC
1976-77	Dundalk, Eire	6-0		1-1	1	ECC
	St Etienne, France	0-0		0-1	2	ECC
1977-78	Glenavon, Ireland	5-0		6-2	1	UEFA
	Widzew Lodz, Poland	1-0		5-3	2	UEFA
	Eintracht Braunschweig, Germany	2-0		2-1	3	UEFA
	1.FC Magdeburg, East Germany	4-2		0-1	qf	UEFA
	FC Barcelona, Spain	3-0		1-3	sf	UEFA
	SEC Bastia Corsica, France	3-0		0-0	FINAL	UEFA
1978-79	Fenerbahce, Turkey	6-1		1-2	1	ECC
	Glasgow Rangers, Scotland	2-3		0-0	2	ECC
1980-81	Wolverhampton Wanderers, England	3-1		0-1	1	UEFA
	Hamburger SV, Germany	1-1		1-2	2	UEFA
1981-82	Naestved IF, Denmark	7-0		1-2	1	UEFA
	Rapid Vienna, Austria	2-1	lag	0-1	2	UEFA
1982-83	Dundee United, Scotland	0-2		1-1	1	UEFA
1983-84	Ferencvarosi TC, Hungary	4-2		2-0	1	UEFA
	Nottingham Forest, England	1-2		0-1	2	UEFA
1984-85	FC Vorwaerts Frankfurt, East Germany	3-0		0-2	1	UEFA
	Manchester United, England	0-0		0-1	2	UEFA
1985-86	Avenir Beggen, Luxembourg	4-0		2-0*	1	UEFA
	Dnepr Dnepropetrovsk, USSR	2-2		0-1*	2	UEFA
				* in Krivoy Rog		
1986-87	Bayern Munich, Germany	0-2		0-0	1	ECC
1987-88	Galatasaray, Turkey	3-0		0-2	1	ECC
	Rapid Vienna, Austria	2-0		2-1	2	ECC
	Girondin Bordeaux, France	0-0	wag	1-1	qf	ECC
	Real Madrid, Spain	0-0	wag	1-1	sf	ECC
	Benfica, Portugal			* 0-0 6-5pens	FINAL	ECC
				* in Stuttgart		
1988-89	bye				1	ECC
	FC Porto, Portugal	5-0		0-2	2	ECC
1989-90	FC Luzern, Switzerland	3-0		2-0	1	ECC
	Steaua Bucharest, Romania	5-1		0-1	2	ECC
	Bayern Munich, Germany	0-1		1-2	qf	ECC

WILLEM II, TILBURG

Founded 1896
Colours red and white shirts, blue shorts
Stadium Gemeentelijk Sportpark (22,000)
Champions 1916, 1952, 1955
Cup Winners 1944, 1963

Season	Opponents	Home	Result	Away	Rnd	Cup
1963-64	Manchester United, England	1-1		1-6	1	CWC

FC TWENTE (ENSCHEDE)

Founded 1965 by amalgamation of SC Enschede and Enschedese Boys
Colours all red
Stadium Diekman (24,500) ☎ 053-310080
Amalgamation of Sportsclub Enschede and Enschede Boys
Champions 1926   Cup Winners 1977   UEFA Finalists 1975

Season	Opponents	Home	Result	Away	Rnd	Cup
1969-70	Rouen, France	1-0		0-2	1	Fairs
1970-71	AEK Athens, Greece	3-0		1-0	1	Fairs
	Eskischirspor, Turkey	6-1		2-3	2	Fairs
	Dinamo Zagreb, Yugoslavia	1-0		2-2	3	Fairs
	Juventus, Italy	2-2		0-2	qf	Fairs
1972-73	Dynamo Tbilisi, USSR	2-0		2-3	1	UEFA
	Frem Copenhagen, Denmark	4-0 abd		5-0	2	UEFA
	Las Palmas, Spain	3-0		1-2	3	UEFA
	OFK Belgrade, Yugoslavia	2-0		2-3	qf	UEFA
	Borussia Monchengladbach, Germany	0-2		0-3	sf	UEFA
1973-74	Dundee, Scotland	4-2		3-1	1	UEFA
	Panchaiki Patras, Greece	7-0		1-1	2	UEFA
	Ipswich Town, England	1-2		0-1	3	UEFA
1974-75	Ipswich Town, England	1-1	wag	2-2	1	UEFA
	RWD Molenbeeck, Belgium	2-1		1-0	2	UEFA
	Dukla Prague, Czechoslovakia	5-0		1-3	3	UEFA
	Velez Mostar, Yugoslavia	2-0		0-1	qf	UEFA
	Juventus, Italy	3-1		1-0	sf	UEFA
	Borussia Monchengladbach, Germany	1-5		0-0	FINAL	UEFA
1977-78	Glasgow Rangers, Scotland	3-0		0-0	1	CWC
	Brann Bergen, Norway	2-0		2-1	2	CWC
	Vejle BK, Denmark	4-0		3-0	qf	CWC
	RSC Anderlecht, Belgium	0-1		0-2	sf	CWC
1978-79	Manchester City, England	1-1		2-3	1	UEFA
1979-80	Panionios, Greece	3-1		0-4	1	CWC
1980-81	IFK Gothenburg, Sweden	5-1		0-2	1	UEFA
	Dynamo Dresden, East Germany	1-1	lag	0-0	2	UEFA
1989-90	Club Bruges, Belgium	0-0		1-4	1	UEFA

FC DEN HAAG

Founded 1905 as ADO'S Gravenhage, 1971 amalgamated with Holland Sport to become FC Den Haag
Colours yellow shirts, green shorts
Stadium Zuiderpark (26,500) ☎ 070-804411
Champions 1942, 1943   Cup Winners 1968 as ADO, 1975

Season	Opponents	Home	Result	Away	Rnd	Cup
as ADO DEN HAAG						
1968-69	Grazer AK (GAK), Austria	4-1		2-0	1	CWC
	1.FC Koln, Germany	0-1		0-3	2	CWC
as FC DEN HAAG						
1971-72	Aris Bonnevoie, Luxembourg	5-0		2-2	1	UEFA
	Wolverhampton Wanderers, England	1-3		0-4	2	UEFA
1972-73	Spartak Moscow, USSR	0-0		0-1	1	CWC
1975-76	Velje BK, Denmark	2-0		2-0	1	CWC
	RC Lens, France	3-2		3-1	2	CWC
	West Ham United, England	4-2	lag	1-3	qf	CWC
1987-88	Ujpest Dozsa, Hungary	3-1		0-1	1	CWC
	Young Boys Bern, Switzerland	2-1		0-1	2	CWC

HOLLAND

FC AMSTERDAM

Founded 1907 as DWS Amsterdam, 1958 amalgamated with BVC Amsterdam to become DWS/A, 1962 became DWS, 1972 amalgamated with Blauw Wit to become FC Amsterdam. DWS = Door Wilskracht Sterk
Colours white shirts, red shorts
Stadium Olympic (61,500) ☎ 020-721480/711115
Champions 1964 as DWS

Season	Opponents	Home	Result	Away	Rnd	Cup
1964-65	Fenerbahce, Turkey	3-1		1-0	1	ECC
	Gjovik Lyn, Norway	5-0		3-1	2	ECC
	Vasas Gyoer Eto, Hungary	1-1		0-1	qf	ECC
1966-67	bye				1	Fairs
	Leeds United, England	1-3		1-5	2	Fairs
1967-68	Dundee, Scotland	2-1		0-3	1	Fairs
1968-69	K Beerschot VAV Belgium	2-1		1-1	1	Fairs
	Chelsea, England	0-0	wot	0-0	2	Fairs
	Glasgow Rangers, Scotland	0-2		1-2	3	Fairs
as FC AMSTERDAM						
1974-75	Hibernians, Malta	7-0*		5-0*	1	UEFA
			* both in Amsterdam			
	Inter Milan, Italy	0-0		2-1	2	UEFA
	Fortuna Dusseldorf, Germany	3-0		2-1	3	UEFA
	1.FC Koln, Germany	2-3		1-5	qf	UEFA

SPARTA (ROTTERDAM)

Founded 1888
Colours red and white striped shirts, white shorts
Stadium Spangen (29,687) ☎ 010-4152087
Champions 1909, 1911, 1912, 1913, 1959
Cup Winners 1958, 1962, 1966

Season	Opponents	Home	Playoff Result	Away	Rnd	Cup
1959-60	IFK Gothenburg, Sweden	3-1	3-1*	1-3	1	ECC
			*in Bremen			
	Glasgow Rangers, Scotland	2-3	2-3*	1-0	qf	ECC
			*at Arsenal			
1962-63	Lausanne Sport, Switzerland	4-2		0-3	1	CWC
1966-67	Floriana, Malta	6-0		1-1	1	CWC
	Servette Geneva, Switzerland	1-0		0-2	2	CWC
1970-71	IA Akranes, Iceland	9-0		6-0*	1	Fairs
				* in Holland		
	Coleraine, Ireland	2-0		2-1	2	Fairs
	Bayern Munich, Germany	1-3		1-2	3	Fairs
1971-72	Levski Spartak Sofia, Bulgaria	2-0		1-1	1	CWC
	Red Star Belgrade, Yugoslavia	1-1		1-2	2	CWC
1983-84	Coleraine, Ireland	4-0		1-1	1	UEFA
	Carl Zeiss Jena, East Germany	3-2		1-1	2	UEFA
	Spartak Moscow, USSR	1-1		0-2	3	UEFA
1985-86	Hamburger SV, Germany	2-0	4-3 pen	0-2	1	UEFA
	Borussia Monchengladbach, Germany	1-1		1-5	2	UEFA

HOLLAND

FC UTRECHT

Founded 1902 as DOS (Door Oefening Sterk), 1970 amalgamated with Elinkwijk and Velox to become FC Utrecht
Colours red and white shirts, white shorts
Stadium Galgenwaard (22,000) ☎ 030-512521
Champions 1958   Cup Winners 1985

Season	Opponents	Home	Result	Away	Rnd	Cup
as DOS UTRECHT						
1958-59	Sporting Lisbon, Portugal	3-4		1-2	pr	ECC
1963-64	Sheffield Wednesday, England	1-4		1-4	1	Fairs
1964-65	KB Copenhagen, Denmark	4-3		2-1	1	Fairs
	RFC Liege, Belgium	0-2		0-2	2	Fairs
1965-66	CF Barcelona, Spain	0-0		1-7	1	Fairs
1966-67	FC Basle, Switzerland	2-1		2-2	1	Fairs
	West Bromwich Albion, England	1-1		2-5	2	Fairs
1967-68	Real Zaragoza, Spain	3-2		1-3	1	Fairs
1968-69	Dundalk, Eire	1-1		1-2	1	Fairs
as FC UTRECHT						
1980-81	FC Arges Pitesti, Romania	2-0		0-0	1	UEFA
	Eintracht Frankfurt, Germany	2-1		1-3	2	UEFA
1981-82	Hamburger SV, Germany	3-6		1-0	1	UEFA
1982-83	FC Porto, Portugal	0-1*		0-2**	1	UEFA
		* in Groningen		** in Lisbon		
1985-86	Dynamo Kiev, USSR	2-1		1-4	1	CWC
1987-88	Linzer ASK, Austria	2-0		0-0	1	UEFA
	Hellas-Verona, Italy	1-1		1-2	2	UEFA

AZ 67 ALKMAAR

Founded 1954 as Alkmaar, 1967 amalgamation of Alkmaar and Zaanstreak to become A.Z.'67, 1986 became A.Z.
A.Z. = Alkmaar Zaanstreek
Colours red shirts, white shorts Stadium De Hout (18,500) ☎ 072-154744
Champions 1981   Cup Winners 1978, 1981, 1982   UEFA Cup Finalists 1981

Season	Opponents	Home	Result	Away	Rnd	Cup
1977-78	Red Boys Differdange, Luxembourg	11-1		5-0	1	UEFA
	FC Barcelona, Spain	1-1	4-5 pen	1-1	2	UEFA
1978-79	Ipswich Town, England	0-0		0-2	1	CWC
1980-81	Red Boys Differdange, Luxembourg	6-0		4-0	1	UEFA
	Levski Spartak Sofia, Bulgaria	5-0		1-1	2	UEFA
	Radnicki Nis, Yugoslavia	5-0		2-2	3	UEFA
	KSC Lokeren, Belgium	2-0		0-1	qf	UEFA
	Sochaux, France	3-2		1-1	sf	UEFA
	Ipswich Town, England	4-2*		0-3	FINAL	UEFA
		* in Amsterdam				
1981-82	IFK Start Kristiansand, Norway	1-0		3-1	1	ECC
	Liverpool, England	2-2*		2-3	2	ECC
		* in Amsterdam				
1982-83	Limerick, Eire	1-0		1-1	1	CWC
	Inter Milan, Italy	1-0		0-2	2	CWC

HOLLAND

RODA JC KERKRADE

Founded 1954 as Rapid JC, 1962 merged of Rapid JC Heerlen and Roda JC = Roda Juliana Combinatie
Roda Sport Kerkrade to become Roda JC Kerkrade
Colours blue shirts, red shorts
Stadium Sportspark Kaalheide (27,000) ☎ 045-411053
Champions 1956 as Rapid JC Heerlen

Season	Opponents	Home	Result	Away	Rnd	Cup
as RAPID JC HEERLEN						
1956-57	Red Star Belgrade, Yugoslavia	3-4		0-2	1	ECC
as Roda JC KIRKRADE						
1976-77	RSC Anderlecht, Belgium	2-3		1-2	1	CWC
1988-89	Vitoria SC Guimaraes, Portugal	2-0		0-1	1	CWC
	Metallist Kharkov, USSR	1-0		0-0	2	CWC
	Sredets CFKA Sofia, Bulgaria	2-1aet	3-4p	1-2	qf	CWC

HFC HAARLEM

Founded 1889
Colours blue shirts, red shorts
Stadium Haarlem (18,000) ☎ 023-252233
Champions 1946   Cup Winners 1902, 1912

Season	Opponents	Home	Result	Away	Rnd	Cup
1982-83	A A Ghent, Belgium	2-1		3-3	1	UEFA
	Spartak Moscow, USSR	1-3		0-2	2	UEFA

GO AHEAD EAGLES (DEVENTER)

Founded 1902 Re-formed 1971 to become Go Ahead Eagles
Colours red shirts, yellow shorts
Stadium De Adelaarshorst (17,000) ☎ 05700-21357
Champions 1917, 1922, 1930, 1933

Season	Opponents	Home	Result	Away	Rnd	Cup
1965-66	Glasgow Celtic, Scotland	0-6		0-1	1	CWC

NAC BREDA

NAC = Noad Advendo Combinatie
Founded 1912
Colours yellow shirts, black shorts
Stadium NAC (20,000) ☎ 076-214500
Champions 1921 Cup Winners 1973

Season	Opponents	Home	Result	Away	Rnd	Cup
1967-68	Floriana, Malta	1-0		2-1	1	CWC
	Cardiff City, Wales	1-1		1-4	2	CWC
1973-74	1.FC Magdeburg, East Germany	0-0		0-2	1	CWC

FORTUNA SITTARD

Founded 1954 as Fortuna '54, 1968 amalgamated with Sittardia to become F.S.C. (Fortuna Sittardia Combinatie),
1979 Fortuna Sittard
Colours green shirts, yellow shorts
Stadium De Baandert (20,100) ☎ 04490-13947/18777
Cup Winners as Fortuna Geleen 1964

Season	Opponents	Home	Result	Away	Rnd	Cup
as FORTUNA GELEEN						
1964-65	AS Torino, Italy	2-2		1-3	pr	CWC
as FORTUNA SITTARD						
1984-85	KB Copenhagen, Denmark	3-0		0-0	1	CWC
	Wisla Krakow, Poland	2-0		1-2	2	CWC
	Everton, England	0-2		0-3	qf	CWC

FC GRONINGEN

Founded 1921 as GVAV Rapichtas, changed name in 1971 to FC Groningen
Colours green shirts, white shorts
Stadium Osterpark (15,500) ☎ 050-180814/12707

Season	Opponents	Home	Result	Away	Rnd	Cup
1983-84	Atletico Madrid, Spain	3-0		1-2	1	UEFA
	Inter Milan, Italy	2-0		1-5*	2	UEFA
				*in Bari		
1986-87	Galway United, Eire	5-1		3-1	1	UEFA
	FC Neuchatel Xamax, Switzerland	0-0	wag	1-1	2	UEFA
	Vitoria SC Guimaraes, Portugal	1-0		0-3	3	UEFA
1988-89	Atletico Madrid, Spain	1-0	wag	1-2	1	UEFA
	Servette Geneva, Switzerland	2-0		1-1	2	UEFA
	VfB Stuttgart, Germany	1-3		0-2	3	UEFA
1989-90	Ikast FS, Denmark	1-0		2-1	1	CWC
	Partizan Belgrade, Yugoslavia	4-3		1-3	2-	CWC

NEC NIJMEGEN

NEC = Nijmegen Eeindracht Combinatie
Founded 1900 by merger of Eeindracht and Nijmegen
Colours red and green shirts, white shorts
Stadium De Goffert (29,000) ☎ 080-554564

Season	Opponents	Home	Result	Away	Rnd	Cup
1983-84	Brann Bergen, Norway	1-1		1-0	1	CWC
	FC Barcelona, Spain	2-3		0-2	2	CWC

UTRECHT CITY XI

Made up of players from DOS Utrecht, Velox Utrecht and Elinkwyk Utrecht

Season	Opponents	Home	Result	Away	Rnd	Cup
1962-63	Tasmania 1900 Berlin, Germany	3-2		2-1	1	Fairs
	Hibernian, Scotland	1-2		0-1	2	Fairs

HUNGARY

Founded 1901 Federation Hongroise de Football, Nepkoztarsasag utja 47, 1061 Budapest VI
☎ 1 12 25 817 Fax 36-114 25 103
National Colours red shirts, white shorts, green socks
Season September to December; March to June

LEAGUE CHAMPIONS

1901	BTC Budapest	1926	FTC Ferencvaros	1950	(spring)	1970	Ujpest Dozsa
1902	BTC Budapest	1927	Ferencvarosi TC		Honved Budapest	1971	Ujpest Dozsa
1903	FTC Ferencvaros	1928	Ferencvarosi TC	1950	(autumn)	1972	Ujpest Dozsa
1904	MTK Budapest	1929	Hungaria Budapest		Honved Budapest	1973	Ujpest Dozsa
1905	FTC Ferencvaros			1951	Bastya Budapest	1974	Ujpest Dozsa
1906	FTC Ferencvaros	1930	Ujpest Dozsa	1952	Honved Budapest	1975	Ujpest Dozsa
1907	FTC Ferencvaros	1931	Ujpest Dozsa	1953	Voros Lobago	1976	Ferencvarosi TC
1908	MTK Budapest	1932	Ferencvarosi TC	1954	Honved Budapest	1977	Vasas Budapest
1909	FTC Ferencvaros	1933	Ujpest Dozsa	1955	Honved Budapest	1978	Ujpest Dozsa
		1934	Ferencvarosi TC	1956	not finished	1979	Ujpest Dozsa
1910	FTC Ferencvaros	1935	Ujpest Dozsa	1957	Vasas Budapest		
1911	FTC Ferencvaros	1936	Hungaria Budapest	1958	MTK Budapest	1980	Honved Budapest
1912	FTC Ferencvaros	1937	Hungaria Budapest	1959	Csepel Budapest	1981	Ferencvarosi TC
1913	FTC Ferencvaros	1938	Ferencvarosi TC			1982	Raba Eto Gyoer
1914	MTK Budapest	1939	Ujpest Dozsa	1960	Ujpest Dozsa	1983	Raba Eto Gyoer
1917	MTK Budapest			1961	Vasas Budapest	1984	Honved Budapest
1918	MTK Budapest	1940	Ferencvarosi TC	1962	Vasas Budapest	1985	Honved Budapest
1919	MTK Budapest	1941	Ferencvarosi TC	1963	Ferencvarosi TC	1986	Honved Budapest
		1942	Csepel Budapest	1963	(short season)	1987	MTK/VM Budapest
1920	MTK Budapest	1943	Csepel Budapest		Vasas Gyoer	1988	Honved Budapest
1921	MTK Budapest	1944	Nagyvarad AC	1964	Ferencvarosi TC	1989	Honved Budapest
1922	MTK Budapest	1945	Ujpest Dozsa	1965	Vasas Budapest		
1923	MTK Budapest	1946	Ujpest Dozsa	1966	Vasas Budapest		
1924	MTK Budapest	1947	Ujpest Dozsa	1967	Ferencvarosi TC		
1925	MTK Budapest	1948	Csepel Budapest	1968	Ferencvarosi TC		
		1949	Csepel Budapest	1969	Ujpest Dozsa		

CUP WINNERS

1910	MTK Budapest v FTC	3-1	1913	FTC Ferencvaros v Budapest AK	2-1
1911	MTK Budapest v Magyar AC Budapest	1-0	1914	MTK Budapest v Magyar AC Budapest	4-1
1912	MTK Budapest v FTC Ferencvaros	walkover			

1922	FTC Ferencvaros v Ujpest TE	2-2 1-0
1923	MTK Budapest v Ujpest TE	4-1
1925	MTK Budapest v Ujpest TE	4-0
1926	Kispest AC v BEAC Budapest	1-1 3-2
1927	Ferencvarosi TC v Ujpest Dozsa	3-0
1928	Ferencvarosi TC v Attila Miskolc	5-1
1930	Bocskai Debrecan v Bastya Szeged	5-1
1931	III Kerulet v Ferencvarosi TC	4-1
1932	Hungaria Budapest v Ferencvarosi TC	1-1 4-3
1933	Ferencvarosi TC v Ujpest Dozsa	11-1
1934	Soroksar AC v BSZKRT	1-1 2-2 2-0
1935	Ferencvarosi TC v Hungaria Budapest	2-1
1941	Szolnoki MAV v SBTC Salgotarjan	3-0
1942	Ferencvarosi TC v VTK Diosgyor Miskolc	6-2
1943	Ferencvarosi TC v SBTC Salgotarjan	3-0
1944	Ferencvarosi TC v Kispesti AC	2-2 3-1
1952	Bastya Budapest v Dorog Banyasz	3-2
1955	Vasas Budapest v Honved Budapest	3-2
1958	Ferencvarosi TC v SBTC Salgotarjan	2-1
1960	Ferencvarosi TC CWC entry	
1961	Ujpest Dozsa CWC entry	
1962	Ujpest Dozsa CWC entry	
1963	MTK Budapest v Dorog Banyasz	3-2

1964	Honved Budapest v Vasas Gyoer ETO	1-0
1965	Vasas Gyoer ETO v Diosgyoer Miskolc	4-0
1966	Vasas Gyoer ETO v Ferencvarosi TC	1-1 2-1
1967	Vasas Gyoer ETO v SBTC Salgotarjan	1-0
1968	MTK Budapest v Honved Budapest	2-1
1969	Ujpest Dozsa v Honved Budapest	3-1
1970	Ujpest Dozsa v Komlo Banyasz	3-2
1971	Komlo Banyasz CWC entry	
1972	Ferencvarosi TC v Tatabanya Banyasz	2-1
1973	Vasas Budapest v Honved Budapest	4-3
1974	Ferencvarosi TC v Komlo Banyasz	3-1
1975	Ujpest Dozsa v Haladas Vasutas	3-2
1976	Ferencvarosi TC v MTK/VM Budapest	2-0
1977	Diosgyor Miskolc v Vasas Budapest	walkover
1978	Ferencvarosi TC v Pecs Munkas SC	4-2
1979	Raba Eto Gyoer v Ferencvarosi TC	1-0
1980	Diosgyor Miskolc v Vasas Budapest	3-1
1981	Vasas Budapest v Diosgyor Miskolc	1-0
1982	Ujpest Dozsa v Videoton Sekesfehervar	2-0
1983	Ujpest Dozsa v Honved Budapest	3-2
1984	Siofoik Banyasz v Raba Eto Gyoer	2-0
1985	Honved Budapest v Tatabanya Banyasz	5-0
1986	Vasas Budapest v Ferencvarosi TC	0-0 5-4 pens
1987	Ujpest Dozsa v Pecs Munkas SC	3-2
1988	Spartacus ESC Bekescsaba v Honved Budapest	3-2
1989	Honved Budapest v Ferencvarosi TC	1-0

FEATURED CLUBS IN EUROPEAN COMPETITION

Ujpest Dozsa	**Ferencvarosi TC**	**Raba Eto Gyoer**	**Honved Budapest**
MTK/VM Budapest	**Vasas Budapest**	**Csepel Budapest**	**Tatabanya Banyasz**
Salgotarjan Banyasz	**Komlo Banyasz**	**Pecsi Munkas SC**	**Diosgyor Miskolc**
Videoton Szekesfehervar	**Siofoki Banyasz**	**Haladas Vasutas**	**Spartacus ESC Bekescsaba**

UJPEST DOZSA SC

Founded 1885 as U.T.E. 1926 as Ujpest FC, 1946 as Ujpest Dozsa SC
Colours lilac and white shirts, white shorts
Stadium Ujpest Dosza, Budapest (30,000) ☎ 1-428 564/5/6
Champions 1930, 1931, 1933, 1935, 1939, 1945, 1946, 1947, 1960, 1969, 1970, 1971, 1972, 1973, 1974, 1975, 1978, 1979
Cup Winners 1969, 1970, 1971, 1975, 1982, 1983, 1987
Fairs Cup Finalists 1969
Mitropa Cup Winners 1929, 1939

Season	Opponent	Home	Playoff Result	Away	Rnd	Cup
1958-60	Zagreb City XI, Yugoslavia	1-0		2-4	1	Fairs
1960-61	Birmingham City, England	1-2		2-3	1	Fairs
1960-61	Red Star Belgrade, Yugoslavia	3-0		2-1	1	ECC
	Benfica, Portugal	2-1		2-6	2	ECC
1961-62	Floriana, Malta	10-2		5-2	1	CWC
	Ajax Amsterdam, Holland	3-1		1-2	2	CWC
	Dunfermline Athletic, Scotland	4-3		1-0	qf	CWC
	Fiorentina, Italy	0-1		0-2	sf	CWC
1962-63	Zaglebie Sosnowice, Poland	5-0		0-0	1	CWC
	Napoli, Italy	1-1	1-3*	1-1	2	CWC
			* in Lausanne			
1963-64	SC Leipzig, East Germany	3-2		0-0	1	Fairs
	Lokomotiv Plovdiv, Bulgaria	3-1		0-0	2	Fairs
	Valencia CF, Spain	3-1		2-5	qf	Fairs
1965-66	bye				1	Fairs
	Everton, England	3-0		1-2	2	Fairs
	1.FC Koln, Germany	4-0		2-3	3	Fairs
	Leeds United, England	1-1		1-4	qf	Fairs

HUNGARY

1968-69	Union Spora, Luxembourg		withdrew	1	Fairs
	Aris Salonika, Greece	9-1		2-1	2	Fairs
	Legia Warsaw, Poland	2-2		1-0	3	Fairs
	Leeds United, England	2-0		1-0	qf	Fairs
	Goztepe Izmir, Turkey	4-0		4-1	sf	Fairs
	Newcastle United, England	2-3		0-3	FINAL	Fairs
1969-70	Partizan Belgrade, Yugoslavia	2-0		1-2	1	Fairs
	Clube Bruges, Belgium	3-0	wag	2-5	2	Fairs
	Carl Zeiss Jena, East Germany	0-3		0-1	3	Fairs
1970-71	Red Star Belgrade, Yugoslavia	2-0		0-4	1	ECC
1971-72	Malmo FF, Sweden	4-0		0-1	1	ECC
	Valencia CF, Spain	2-1		1-0	2	ECC
	Glasgow Celtic, Scotland	1-2		1-1	qf	ECC
1972-73	FC Basle, Switzerland	2-0		2-3	1	ECC
	Glasgow Celtic, Scotland	3-0		1-2	2	ECC
	Juventus, Italy	2-2	lag	0-0	qf	ECC
1973-74	Waterford, Eire	3-0		3-2*	1	ECC
				* in Dublin		
	Benfica, Portugal	2-0		1-1	2	ECC
	Spartak Trnava, Czechoslovakia	1-1	4-3 pen	1-1	qf	ECC
	Bayern Munich, Germany	1-1		0-3	sf	ECC
1974-75	Levski Spartak Sofia, Bulgaria	4-1		3-0	1	ECC
	Leeds United, England	1-2		0-3	2	ECC
1975-76	FC Zurich, Switzerland	4-0	wag	1-5	1	ECC
	Benfica, Portugal	3-1		2-5	2	ECC
1976-77	Athletic Bilbao, Spain	1-0		0-5	1	UEFA
1977-78	Linzer ASK, Austria	7-0		2-3	1	UEFA
	Athletic Bilbao, Spain	2-0		0-3	2	UEFA
1978-79	Zborjovka Brno, Czechoslovakia	0-2		2-2	1	ECC
1979-80	Dukla Prague, Czechoslovakia	3-2		0-2	1	ECC
1980-81	Real Sociedad San Sebastien, Spain	1-1		0-1	1	UEFA
1982-83	IFK Gothenburg, Sweden	3-1		1-1	1	CWC
	Real Madrid, Spain	0-1		1-3	2	CWC
1983-84	AEK Athens, Greece	4-1		0-2	1	CWC
	1. FC Koln, Germany	3-1	wag	2-4	2	CWC
	Aberdeen, Scotland	2-0		0-3	qf	CWC
1987-88	FC Den Haag, Holland	1-0		1-3	1	CWC
1988-89	IA Akranes, Iceland	2-1		0-0	1	UEFA
	Girondins Bordeaux, France	0-1		0-1	2	UEFA

FERENCVAROSI TORNA CLUB

Founded 1899 as FTC, 1926 as Ferencvaros FC, 1937 as Ferencvarosi Torna Club, 1950 Edosz, 1951 Budapest Kinizsi, 1956 Ferencvarosi
Colours green and white hooped shirts, white shorts
Stadium Ulloi Ut, Budapest (27,906) ☎ 1-136 025
Champions 1903, 1905, 1906, 1907, 1909, 1910, 1911, 1912, 1913, 1926, 1927, 1928, 1932, 1934, 1938, 1940, 1941, 1949, 1964, 1967, 1968, 1976, 1981
Cup Winners 1913, 1922, 1927, 1928, 1933, 1935, 1942, 1943, 1944, 1958, 1972, 1974, 1976, 1978
Mitropa Cup Winners 1928, 1937
Fairs Cup Winners 1965. Finalists 1968
CWC Finalists 1975

Season	Opponent	Home	Playoff Result	Away	Rnd	Cup
1960-61	Glasgow Rangers, Scotland	2-1		2-4	pr	CWC
1962-63	Viktoria Koln 04, Germany	3-4		4-1	1	Fairs
	Sampdoria, Italy	6-0		0-1	2	Fairs
	Petrolui Ploesti, Romania	2-0		0-1	qf	Fairs
	Dinamo Zagreb, Yugoslavia	1-2		0-1	sf	Fairs
1963-64	Galatasaray, Turkey	2-0		0-4	1	ECC
1964-65	Spartak Brno, Czechoslovakia	2-0		0-1	1	Fairs
	Wiener Sport Club, Austria	2-1	2-0*	0-1	2	Fairs
			* in Budapest			
	AS Roma, Italy	1-0		2-1	3	Fairs
	Atletico Bilbao, Spain	1-0	3-0*	1-2	qf	Fairs
			* in Budapest			
	Manchester United, England	1-0	2-1*	2-3	sf	Fairs
			* in Budapest			
	Juventus, Italy	1-0	in Turin		FINAL	Fairs
1965-66	IBK Keflavik, Iceland	9-1		4-1*	1	ECC
				* in Reykjavik		
	Panathinaikos, Greece	0-0		3-1	2	ECC
	Inter Milan, Italy	1-1		0-4	qf	ECC
1966-67	Olimpia Ljubljana, Yugoslavia	3-0		3-3	1	Fairs
	Orgryte IS Gothenburg, Sweden	7-1		0-0	2	Fairs
	Eintracht Frankfurt, Germany	2-1		1-4	3	Fairs
1967-68	Argesul Pitesti, Romania	4-0		1-3	1	Fairs
	Real Zaragoza, Spain	3-0		1-2	2	Fairs
	Liverpool, England	1-0		1-0	3	Fairs
	Atletico Bilbao, Spain	2-1		2-1	qf	Fairs
	Bologna, Italy	3-2		2-2	sf	Fairs
	Leeds United, England	0-0		0-1	FINAL	Fairs
1968-69		withdrew			1	Fairs
1969-70	CSKA Sofia, Bulgaria	4-1		1-2	1	ECC
	Leeds United, England	0-3		0-3	2	ECC
1970-71	Liverpool, England	1-1		0-1	1	Fairs
1971-72	Fenerbahce, Turkey	3-1		1-1	1	UEFA
	Panionios, Greece	6-0	disqualified		2	UEFA
	Eintracht Braunschweig, Germany	5-2		1-1	3	UEFA
	Zeljeznicar Sarajevo, Yugoslavia	1-2	7-5p	2-1	qf	UEFA
	Wolverhampton Wanderers, England	2-2		1-2	sf	UEFA
1972-73	Floriana, Malta	6-0		0-1	1	CWC
	Sparta Prague, Czechoslovakia	2-0		1-4	2	CWC
1973-74	Gwardia Warsaw, Poland	0-1		1-2	1	UEFA
1974-75	Cardiff City, Wales	2-0		4-1	1	CWC
	Liverpool, England	0-0	wag	1-1	2	CWC
	Malmo FF, Sweden	1-1		3-1	qf	CWC
	Red Star Belgrade, Yugoslavia	2-1		2-2	sf	CWC
	Dynamo Kiev, USSR	0-3	in Basel		FINAL	CWC
1976-77	Jeunesse Esch, Luxembourg	5-1		6-2	1	ECC
	Dynamo Dresden, East Germany	1-0		0-4	2	ECC
1977-78	Marek Stanke Dimitrov, Bulgaria	2-0		0-3	1	UEFA

171

HUNGARY

1978-79	Kalmar FF, Sweden	2-0		2-2	1	CWC
	1.FC Magdeburg, East Germany	2-1	lag	0-1	2	CWC
1979-80	Lokomotiv Sofia, Bulgaria	2-0		0-3	1	UEFA
1981-82	Banik Ostrava, Czechoslovakia	3-2		0-3	1	ECC
1982-83	Athletic Bilbao, Spain	2-1		1-1	1	UEFA
	FC Zurich, Switzerland	1-1		0-1	2	UEFA
1983-84	PSV Eindhoven, Holland	0-2		2-4	1	UEFA
1989-90	Haka Valkeakoski, Finland	5-1		1-1	1	CWC
	Admira Wacker Vienna, Austria	0-1*		0-1	2	CWC
		* in Szeged				

RABA ETO

Founded 1904 as ETO Gyoer, 1946 Vasas ETO Gyoer, 1957 Magyar Vagon Es Gepgyar, 1958 Vasas ETO Gyoer, 1968 Raba ETO
Colours green and white
Stadium Gyoer (12,000) all seats ☎ 96-124 33
Champions 1963, 1982, 1983
Cup Winners 1965, 1966, 1967, 1979

Season	Opponent	Home	Result	Away	Rnd	Cup
as VASAS GYOER ETO						
1964-65	Chemie Leipzig, East Germany	4-2		2-0	1	ECC
	Lokomotiv Sofia, Bulgaria	5-3		3-4	2	ECC
	DWS Amsterdam, Holland	1-0		1-1	qf	ECC
	Benfica, Portugal	0-1		0-4	sf	ECC
1966-67	Fiorentina, Italy	4-2		0-1	1	CWC
	Sporting Braga, Portugal	3-0		0-2	2	CWC
	Standard Liege, Belgium	2-1		0-2	qf	CWC
1967-68	Apollon Limassol, Cyprus	5-0		4-0	1	CWC
	AC Milan, Italy	2-2	lag	1-1	2	CWC
1968-69	Dinamo Bucharest, Romania		withdrew		1	CWC
1969-70	Lausanne Sport, Switzerland	2-1		2-1	1	Fairs
	CF Barcelona, Spain	2-3		0-2	2	Fairs
as RABA VASAS ETO						
1974-75	Lokomotiv Plovdiv, Bulgaria	3-1	5-4p	1-3	1	UEFA
	Fortuna Dusseldorf, Germany	2-0		0-3	2	UEFA
1979-80	Juventus, Italy	2-1		0-2	1	CWC
1982-83	Standard Liege, Belgium	3-0		0-5	1	ECC
1983-84	Vikingur Reykjavik, Iceland	2-1		2-0*	1	ECC
				* in Reykjavik		
	Dynamo Minsk, USSR	3-6		1-3	2	ECC
1984-85	Manchester United, England	2-2		0-3	1	UEFA
1985-86	Bohemians Prague, Czechoslovakia	3-1		1-4	1	UEFA
1986-87	Dinamo Minsk, USSR	0-1		4-2	1	UEFA
	Torino, Italy	1-1		0-4	2	UEFA

HONVED BUDAPEST

Founded 1909 as Kispesti AC, 1926 as Kispest FC, 1949 as Honved
Colours white with red, white and green hoops, white shorts
Stadium Honved (30,000) ☎ 1-408 916
Champions 1950 (spring), 1950 (autumn), 1952, 1954, 1955, 1980, 1984, 1985, 1986, 1988, 1989
Cup Winners 1964, 1985, 1989
Mitropa Cup Winners 1959

Season	Opponent	Home	Result	Away	Rnd	Cup
1956-57	Atletico Bilbao, Spain	3-3*		2-3	1	ECC
		* in Brussels				
1964-65	Lausanne Sport, Switzerland	1-0		0-2	pr	CWC
1965-66	Reipas Lahti, Finland	6-0		10-2	1	CWC
	Dukla Prague, Czechoslovakia	1-2	wag	3-2	2	CWC
	Liverpool, England	0-0		0-2	qf	CWC
1970-71	Aberdeen, Scotland	3-1	5-4p	1-3 aet	1	CWC
	Manchester City, England	0-1		0-2	2	CWC
1972-73	Partick Thistle, Scotland	1-0		3-0	1	UEFA
	Beroe Stara Zagora, Bulgaria	1-0		0-3	2	UEFA
1973-74	VSS Kosice, Czechoslovakia	5-2		0-1	1	UEFA
	Lokomotiv Plovdiv, Bulgaria	3-2		4-3	2	UEFA
	Ruch Chorzow, Poland	2-0		0-5	3	UEFA
1975-76	Bohemians Prague, Czechoslovakia	1-1		2-1	1	UEFA
	Dynamo Dresden, East Germany	2-2		0-1	2	UEFA
1976-77	Inter Milan, Italy	1-1		1-0	1	UEFA
	Shakhtyor Donetsk, USSR	2-3		0-3	2	UEFA
1978-79	Adanaspor, Turkey	6-0		2-2	1	UEFA
	Politecnica Timisoara, Romania	4-0		0-2	2	UEFA
	Ajax Amsterdam, Holland	4-1		0-2	3	UEFA
	MSV Duisburg, Germany	2-3	lag	2-1	qf	UEFA
1980-81	Valletta, Malta	8-0		3-0	pr	ECC
	Sporting Lisbon, Portugal	1-0		2-0	1	ECC
	Real Madrid, Spain	0-2		0-1	2	ECC
1983-84	Larissa, Greece	3-0		0-2	1	UEFA
	Hajduk Split, Yugoslavia	3-2		0-3	2	UEFA
1984-85	Grasshoppers Zurich, Switzerland	2-1		1-3	1	ECC
1985-86	Shamrock Rovers, Eire	2-0		3-1	1.	ECC
	Steaua Bucharest, Romania	1-0		1-4	2	ECC
1986-87	Brondbyernes IF, Denmark	2-2		1-4	1	ECC
1987-88	KSC Lokeren, Belgium	1-0		0-0	1	UEFA
	Desportivo Chaves, Portugal	3-1		2-1	2	UEFA
	Panathinaikos, Greece	5-2		1-5	3	UEFA
1988-89	Glasgow Celtic, Scotland	1-0		0-4	1	ECC
1989-90	Vojvodina Novi Sad, Yugoslavia	1-0	wag	1-2	1	ECC
	Benfica, Portugal	0-2		0-7	2	ECC

HUNGARY

MTK/VM (MAGYAR TESTGYAKORLOK KOERE)

Founded 1888 as MTK, 1926 as Hungaria FC, 1948 as MTK, 1948 as Tekstiles, 1950 as Bastya, 1952 as Voros Lobogo,
1956 as MTK, 1975 merged with VM Egyeretes to become MTK/VM Budapest
Colours all blue
Stadium Nep, Budapest (97,000) ☎ 1-216 940/338 368
Champions 1904, 1908, 1914, 1917, 1918, 1919, 1920, 1921, 1922, 1923, 1924, 1925 all as MTK, 1929, 1936, 1937 as
Hungaria, 1953 as Voros Lobago, 1958 as MTK, as MTK/VM 1987
Cup Winners 1910, 1911, 1912, 1914, 1923, 1925 as MTK, 1932 as Hungaria, 1963, 1968 as MTK
Mitropa Cup Winners 1955, 1963
CWC Finalists 1964

Season	Opponent	Home	Playoff Result	Away	Rnd	Cup
as VOROS LOBOGO						
1955-56	RSC Anderlecht, Belgium	6-3		4-1	1	ECC
	Stade de Reims, France	4-4		2-4*	2	ECC
				* in Paris		
as MTK						
1958-59	Polonia Bytom, Poland	3-0		3-0	pr	ECC
	Young Boys Bern, Switzerland	1-2		1-4	1	ECC
1961-62	RC Strasbourg, France	10-2		3-1	1	Fairs
	SC Chemie Halle, East Germany	3-0	2-0*	0-3	2	Fairs
			* in Bratislava			
	Vojvodina Novi Sad, Yugoslavia	4-1		2-1	qf	Fairs
	Valencia CF, Spain	3-7		0-3	sf	Fairs
1963-64	Slavia Sofia, Bulgaria	1-0		1-1	1	CWC
	Motor Zwickau, East Germany	2-0		0-1	2	CWC
	Fenerbahce, Turkey	2-0	1-0*	1-3	qf	CWC
			* in Rome			
	Glasgow Celtic, Scotland	4-0		0-3	sf	CWC
	Sporting Lisbon, Portugal	3-3	in Glasgow		FINAL	CWC
	Sporting Lisbon, Portugal	0-1	in Brussels		replay	CWC
1969-70	1.FC Magdeburg, East Germany	1-1		0-1	1	CWC
as MTK/VM						
1976-77	Sparta Prague, Czechoslovakia	3-1		1-1	1	CWC
	Dynamo Tbilisi, USSR	1-0		4-1	2	CWC
	Hamburger SV, Germany	1-1		1-4	qf	CWC
1978-79	Politecnica Timisoara, Romania	2-1		0-2	1	UEFA
1987-88	Steaua Bucharest, Romania	2-0		0-4	1	ECC
1989-90	Dynamo Kiev, USSR	1-2		0-4	1	UEFA

VASAS

Founded 1911
Colours red and blue hooped shirts, blue shorts
Stadium Beke, Budapest (20,000). European games at Nep ☎ 1-294 075
Champions 1957, 1961, 1962, 1965, 1966, 1977
Cup Winners 1955, 1973, 1981, 1986
Mitropa Cup Winners 1956, 1957, 1962, 1965, 1970, 1983

Season	Opponent	Home	Playoff Result	Away	Rnd	Cup
1957-58	CDNA Sofia, Bulgaria	6-1		1-2	1	ECC
	Young Boys Bern, Switzerland	2-1		1-1*	2	ECC
				* in Geneva		
	Ajax Amsterdam, Holland	4-0		2-2	qf	ECC
	Real Madrid, Spain	2-0		0-4	sf	ECC
1961-62	Real Madrid, Spain	0-2		1-3	pr	ECC
1962-63	Fredrikstad FK, Norway	7-0		4-1	pr	ECC
	Feyenoord Rotterdam, Holland	2-2	0-1*	1-1	1	ECC
			* in Anvers			

1966-67	Sporting Lisbon, Portugal	5-0		2-0	pr	ECC
	Inter Milan, Italy	0-2		1-2	1	ECC
1967-68	Dundalk, Eire	8-1		1-0	1	ECC
	Valur Reykjavik, Iceland	6-0		5-1*	2	ECC
				* in Varpalota, Hungary		
	Benfica, Portugal	0-0		0-3	qf	ECC
1971-72	Shelbourne, Eire	1-0		1-1	1	UEFA
	St Johnstone, Scotland	1-0		0-2	2	UEFA
1973-74	Sunderland, England	0-2		0-1	1	CWC
1975-76	VoEST Linz, Austria	4-0		0-2	1	UEFA
	Sporting Lisbon, Portugal	3-1		1-2	2	UEFA
	FC Barcelona, Spain	0-1		1-3	3	UEFA
1977-78	Borussia Monchengladbach, Germany	0-3		1-1	1	ECC
1980-81	Boavista, Portugal	0-2		1-0	1	UEFA
1981-82	Paralimni Famagusta, Cyprus	8-0		0-1	1	CWC
	Standard Liege, Belgium	0-2		1-2	2	CWC
1986-87	Velez Mostar, Yugoslavia	2-2		2-3	1	CWC

CSEPEL SC

Founded 1912 as Csepel TK, 1932 Csepel FC, 1937 Csepel Weisz Manfred FC, 1942 Csepel GYTK, then Csepel MTK, then Csepel Vasas, 1957 Csepel
Colours red shirts, blue shorts
Stadium Beke Ter (15,000) ☎ 1-479 517/279 247/342 518
Champions 1942, 1943, 1948, 1959

Season	Opponent	Home	Result	Away	Rnd	Cup
1959-60	Fenerbahce, Turkey	2-3		1-1	pr	ECC

TATABANYA BANYASZ SC

Founded 1910 as Tatabanya SC, 1949 Tatabanya Tarna, 1950 Tatabanya Banyasz
Colours blue shirts, white shorts
Stadium Sagvary Endre U (21,530) ☎ 34-10 395/10 410
Mitropa Cup Winners 1973, 1974

Season	Opponent	Home	Result	Away	Rnd	Cup
1981-82	Real Madrid, Spain	2-1	lag	0-1	1	UEFA
1982-83	St Etienne, France	0-0		1-4	1	UEFA
1985-86	Rapid Vienna, Austria	1-1		0-5	1	CWC
1987-88	Vitoria SC Guimaraes, Portugal	1-1		0-1	1	UEFA
1988-89	VfB Stuttgart, Germany	2-1		0-2	1	UEFA

SALGOTARJAN BANYASZ TORNA CLUB

Founded 1920 as STC, 1925 Banyatelepi SC, 1977 amalgamated to become Salgotarjan TC, 1984 separated as Salgotarjan BTC
Colours white shirts, black shorts
Stadium Kohasz (15,000) ☎ 34-14 5050/14 243

Season	Opponent	Home	Result	Away	Rnd	Cup
1972-73	AEK Athens, Greece	1-1		1-3	1	UEFA

HUNGARY

KOMLO BANYASZ

Founded 1922 as Komlo SC, 1931 Komlo SE, 1949 Komlo Szakszervezeti, 1951 Komlo Banyasz
Colours blue shirts, white shorts
Stadium Komlo (10,000) ☎ 34-81 430

Season	Opponent	Home	Result	Away	Rnd	Cup
1971-72	Red Star Belgrade, Yugoslavia	2-7		2-1	1	CWC

PECSI MUNKAS SPORT CLUB

Founded 1950 as Pecsi Dozsa, 1973 amalgamated with Pecs Banyasz, Ercbanyasz, Helyipar and Pecs Epitok to
form Pecs MSC
Colours red shirts, black shorts
Stadium Szamuely (12,000) ☎ 72-124 94/128 80

Season	Opponent	Home	Result	Away	Rnd	Cup
as PECSI DOZSA						
1970-71	Universitatea Craiova, Romania	3-0		1-2	1	Fairs
	Newcastle United, England	2-0	3-0 pen	0-2	2	Fairs
	Juventus, Italy	0-1		0-2	3	Fairs
as PECSI MUNKAS SC						
1986-87	Feyenoord Rotterdam, Holland	1-0		0-2	1	UEFA

DIOSGYOR VSK (VASGYARAK TESTGYAKORLO KORE)

Founded 1910 by merger of DIK and DVLI, 1938 amalgamation with to become Dimavag, 1945 Diosgyor VTK
Colours red shirts, white shorts
Stadium Karoly Marx (33,100) ☎ 46-51 552
Cup Winners 1977

Season	Opponent	Home	Result	Away	Rnd	Cup
1977-78	Besiktas, Turkey	5-0		0-2	1	CWC
	Hajduk Split, Yugoslavia	2-1	3-4 pen	1-2	2	CWC
1979-80	Rapid Vienna, Austria	3-2		1-0	1	UEFA
	Dundee United, Scotland	3-1		1-0	2	UEFA
	1.FC Kaiserslautern, Germany	0-2		1-6	3	UEFA
1980-81	Glasgow Celtic, Scotland	2-1		0-6	pr	CWC

VIDEOTON (SZEKESFEHERVAR)

Founded 1941 as Vadasztol Tenygyar SK, 1948 Dolgozok, 1950 Vasas, 1968 Videoton
Colours red shirts, blue shorts
Stadium Sostoi (22,000) ☎ 22-14 123/12 730
UEFA Cup Finalists 1985

Season	Opponent	Home	Result	Away	Rnd	Cup
1974-75	Napoli, Italy	1-1		0-2	1	UEFA
1976-77	Fenerbahce, Turkey	4-0		1-2	1	UEFA
	Wacker Innsbruck, Austria	1-0		1-1	2	UEFA
	1.FC Magdeburg, East Germany	1-0		0-5	3	UEFA
1981-82	Rapid Vienna, Austria	0-2		2-2	1	UEFA

1984-85	Dukla Prague, Czechoslovakia	1-0		0-0	1	UEFA
	Paris St Germain, France	1-0*		4-2	2	UEFA
		* abandoned in fog after 67 mins at 2-0				
	Partizan Belgrade, Yugoslavia	5-0		0-2	3	UEFA
	Manchester United, England	1-0	5-4p	0-1	qf	UEFA
	Zeljeznicar Sarajevo, Yugoslavia	3-1		1-2	sf	UEFA
	Real Madrid, Spain	0-3		1-0	FINAL	UEFA
1985-86	Malmo FF, Sweden	1-0	wag	2-3	1	UEFA
	Legia Warsaw, Poland	0-1		1-1	2	UEFA
1989-90	Hibernian, Scotland	0-3		0-1	1	UEFA

SIOFOKI BANYASZ SE

Founded 1921 as Siofok SE, 1949 Dolgozok, 1950 Epitok, 1953 Spartacus, 1955 Voros Meteor, 1956 Banyasz,
1957 MAV, 1957 Olajmunkas,Olajbanyasz, 1963 Siofok Banyasz SE
Colours red shirts, black shorts
Stadium Siofok (12,000) ☎ 34-12 311/12 659
Cup Winners 1984

Season	Opponent	Home	Result	Away	Rnd	Cup
1984-85	Larissa, Greece	1-1		0-2	1	CWC

HALADAS VSE (VASUTAS SPORT EGYTEMI) SZOMBATHELY

Founded 1919 as Haladas, 1926 Szombathely MAV, 1936 Haladas, 1948 Szombathely VSE, 1949 Lokomotiv,
1954 Torekves, 1956 Haladas
Colours green shirts, white shorts
Stadium Szombathely (20,000) ☎ 94-14 966/11 494

Season	Opponent	Home	Result	Away	Rnd	Cup
1975-76	Valletta, Malta	7-0		1-1	1	CWC
	Sturm Graz, Austria	1-1		0-2	2	CWC

SPARTACUS ESC BEKESCSABA

Founded 1912 as Bekescsaba EMTE, 1950 Bekescsaba SE, 1970 Spartacus ESC (ESC=Elore SportClub)
Colours lilac shirts, white shorts
Stadium Bekescsaba (20,000) ☎ 66-21 577/21 229
Cup Winners 1988

Season	Opponent	Home	Result	Away	Rnd	Cup
1988-89	Bryne IL, Norway	3-0		1-2	1	CWC
	Sakaryaspor, Turkey	1-0		0-2	2	CWC

ICELAND

Founded 1912
Knattspyrnusamband Islands (KSL), Box 1011, Reykjavik ☎84 44
National Colours blue shirts, white shorts, blue socks. Season April to October

LEAGUE CHAMPIONS

1912 KR Reykjavik	1932 KR Reykjavik	1952 KR Reykjavik	1972 Fram Reykjavik
1913 Fram Reykjavik	1933 Valur Reykjavik	1953 IA Akranes	1973 IBK Keflavik
1914 Fram Reykjavik	1934 KR Reykjavik	1954 IA Akranes	1974 IA Akranes
1915 Fram Reykjavik	1935 Valur Reykjavik	1955 KR Reykjavik	1975 IA Akranes
1916 Fram Reykjavik	1936 Valur Reykjavik	1956 Valur Reykjavik	1976 Valur Reykjavik
1917 Fram Reykjavik	1937 Valur Reykjavik	1957 IA Akranes	1977 IA Akranes
1918 Fram Reykjavik	1938 Valur Reykjavik	1958 IA Akranes	1978 Valur Reykjavik
1919 KR Reykjavik	1939 Fram Reykjavik	1959 KR Reykjavik	1979 IBV Vestmannaeyjer
1920 Fram Reykjavik	1940 Valur Reykjavik	1960 IA Akranes	1980 Valur Reykjavik
1921 Fram Reykjavik	1941 KR Reykjavik	1961 KR Reykjavik	1981 Vikingur
1922 Fram Reykjavik	1942 Valur Reykjavik	1962 Fram Reykjavik	1982 Vikingur
1923 Fram Reykjavik	1943 Valur Reykjavik	1963 KR Reykjavik	1983 IA Akranes
1924 Vikingur	1944 Valur Reykjavik	1964 IBK Keflavik	1984 IA Akranes
1925 Fram Reykjavik	1945 Valur Reykjavik	1965 KR Reykjavik	1985 Valur Reykjavik
1926 KR Reykjavik	1946 Fram Reykjavik	1966 Valur Reykjavik	1986 Fram Reykjavik
1927 KR Reykjavik	1947 Fram Reykjavik	1967 Valur Reykjavik	1987 Valur Reykjavik
1928 KR Reykjavik	1948 KR Reykjavik	1968 KR Reykjavik	1988 Fram Reykjavik
1929 KR Reykjavik	1949 KR Reykjavik	1969 IBK Keflavik	1989 KA Akureyri
1930 Valur Reykjavik	1950 KR Reykjavik	1970 IA Akranes	
1931 KR Reykjavik	1951 IA Akranes	1971 IBK Keflavik	

CUP WINNERS

1960 KR Reykjavik v Fram Reykjavik	2-0	1970 Fram Reykjavik v IBV Vestmannaeyjer	2-1
1961 KR Reykjavik v IA Ak ranes	4-3	1971 Vikingur v UBK Kopavogur	1-0
1962 KR Reykjavik v Fram Reykjavik	3-0	1972 IBV Vestmannaeyjer v FH Hafnarfjaroar	2-0
1963 KR Reykjavik v IA Akranes	4-1	1973 Fram Reykjavik v IBK Keflavik	2-1
1964 KR Reykjavik v IA Akranes	4-0	1974 Valur Reykjavik v IA Akranes	4-1
1965 Valur Reykjavik v IA Akranes	5-3	1975 IBK Keflavik v IA Akranes	1-0
1966 KR Reykjavik v Valur Reykjavik	1-0	1976 Valur Reykjavik v IA Akranes	3-0
1967 KR Reykjavik v Vikingur	3-0	1977 Valur Reykjavik v Fram Reykjavik	2-1
1968 IBV Vestmannaeyjer v KR Reykjavik(reserves)	2-1	1978 IA Akranes v Valur Reykjavik	1-0
1969 IBA Akureyri v IA Akranes	3-2	1979 Fram Reykjavik v Valur Reykjavik	1-0

1980	Fram Reykjavik v IBV Vestmannaeyjer	2-1	1985	Fram Reykjavik v IBK Keflavik	3-1
1981	IBV Vestmannaeyjer v Fram Reykjavik	3-2	1986	IA Akranes v Fram Reykjavik	2-1
1982	IA Akranes v IBK Keflavik	2-1	1987	Fram Reykjavik v Vidar	5-0
1983	IA Akranes v IBV Vestmannaeyjer	2-1	1988	Valur Reykjavik v IBK Keflavik	1-0
1984	IA Akranes v Fram Reykjavik	2-1	1989	Fram Roykjavik v KR Reykjavik	3-1

FEATURED CLUBS IN EUROPEAN COMPETITION

KR Reykjavik	**IBK Keflavik**	**Valur Reykjavik**	**IA Akranes**
Fram Reykjavik	**IBV Vestmannaeyjer**	**Vikingur Reykjavik**	**IBA Akureyi**

KR REYKJAVIK (KNATTSPURNUFELAG REYKAVIKUR)

Founded 1899   Colours black and white striped shirts with white chest, black shorts
Stadium KR Vollur (14,800)   ☎ 96-27181
Champions 1912, 1919, 1926, 1927, 1928, 1929, 1931, 1932, 1934, 1941, 1948, 1949, 1950, 1952, 1955, 1959, 1961, 1963, 1965, 1968
Cup Winners 1960, 1961, 1962, 1963, 1964, 1966, 1967

Season	Opponent	Home	Result	Away	Rnd	Cup
1964-65	Liverpool, England	0-5		1-6	pr	ECC
1965-66	Rosenborg Trondheim, Norway	1-3		1-3	1	CWC
1966-67	FC Nantes, France	2-3		2-5	pr	ECC
1967-68	Aberdeen, Scotland	1-4		0-10	1	CWC
1969-70	Feyenoord Rotterdam, Holland	0-4*		2-12	1	ECC
		* in Rotterdam				
1978-79	1.FC Magdeburg, East Germany	1-1		0-4	1	CWC
1984-85	Queens Park Rangers, England	0-3		0-4	1	UEFA

IBK KEFLAVIK (ITHROTTABANDALAG KEFLAVIKUR)

Founded 1956   Colours yellow shirts, blue shorts
Stadium Keflavkurvollur (5,000) ☎92-4609
Champions 1964, 1969, 1971, 1973
Cup Winners 1975

Season	Opponent	Home	Result	Away	Rnd	Cup
1965-66	Ferencvarosi TC, Hungary	1-4		1-9	pr	ECC
1970-71	Everton, England	0-3		2-6	1	ECC
1971-72	Tottenham Hotspur, England	1-6		0-9	1	UEFA
1972-73	Real Madrid, Spain	0-1		0-3	1	ECC
1973-74	Hibernian, Scotland	1-1		0-2	1	UEFA
1974-75	Hajduk Split, Yugoslavia	1-7*		0-2	1	ECC
		* in Split				
1975-76	Dundee United, Scotland	0-2		0-4	1	UEFA
1976-77	Hamburger SV, Germany	1-1		0-3	1	CWC
1979-80	Kalmar FF, Sweden	1-0	wag	1-2	1	UEFA
	Zbrojovka Brno, Czechoslovakia	1-2		1-3	2	UEFA

* All home games in Reykjavik unless marked

ICELAND

VALUR REYKJAVIK

Founded 1911   Colours red shirts, white shorts
Stadium Hlioarenda Vollur (14,800) ☎91-45423
Champions 1930, 1933, 1935, 1936, 1937, 1938, 1940, 1942, 1943, 1944, 1945, 1956, 1966, 1967, 1976, 1978, 1980, 1985, 1987
Cup Winners 1965, 1974, 1976, 1977, 1988

Season	Opponent	Home	Result	Away	Rnd	Cup
1966-67	Standard Liege, Belgium	1-1		1-8	pr	CWC
1967-68	Jeunesse Esch, Luxembourg	1-1	wag	3-3	1	ECC
	Vasas Budapest, Hungary	1-5*		0-6	2	ECC
		* in Varpalota, Hungary				
1968-69	Benfica, Portugal	0-0		1-8	1	ECC
1969-70	RSC Anderlecht, Belgium	0-2*		0-6	1	Fairs
		* in Ghent				
1974-75	Portadown, Ireland	0-0		1-2	1	UEFA
1975-76	Glasgow Celtic, Scotland	0-2		0-7	1	CWC
1977-78	Glentoran, Ireland	1-0		0-2	1	ECC
1978-79	1.FC Magdeburg, East Germany	1-1		0-4	1	CWC
1979-80	Hamburger SV, Germany	0-3		1-2	1	ECC
1981-82	Aston Villa, England	0-2		0-5	1	ECC
1985-86	FC Nantes, France	2-1		0-3	1	UEFA
1986-87	Juventus, Italy	0-4		0-7	1	ECC
1987-88	SC Wismut Aue, East Germany	1-1	lag	0-0	1	UEFA
1988-89	AS Monaco, France	1-0		0-2	1	ECC
1989-90	BFC Dynamo Berlin, East Germany	1-2		1-2	1	CWC

IA AKRANES (ITHROTTABANDALAG AKRANES)

Founded 1946   Colours yellow shirts, black shorts
Stadium Akranesvollur (3,000) ☎93-1216
Champions 1951, 1953, 1954, 1957, 1958, 1960, 1970, 1974, 1975, 1977, 1983, 1984
Cup Winners 1978, 1982, 1983, 1984, 1986

Season	Opponent	Home	Result	Away	Rnd	Cup
1970-71	Sparta Rotterdam, Holland	0-6*		0-9	1	Fairs
		* in Holland				
1971-72	Sliema Wanderers, Malta	0-0*		0-4	1	ECC
		* in Malta				
1975-76	Omonia Nicosia, Cyprus	4-0		1-2	1	ECC
	Dynamo Kiev, USSR	0-2		0-3	2	ECC
1976-77	Trabzonspor, Turkey	1-3		2-3	1	ECC
1977-78	Brann Bergen, Norway	0-4*		0-1	1	CWC
		* in Akranes				
1978-79	1.FC Koln, Germany	1-1		1-4	1	ECC
1979-80	FC Barcelona, Spain	0-1		0-5	1	CWC
1980-81	1.FC Koln, Germany	0-4		0-6	1	UEFA
1983-84	Aberdeen, Scotland	1-2		1-1	1	CWC
1984-85	SK Beveren Waas, Belgium	2-2		0-5	1	ECC
1985-86	Aberdeen, Scotland	1-3		1-4	1	ECC
1986-87	Sporting Lisbon, Portugal	0-9		0-6	1	UEFA
1987-88	Kalmar FF, Sweden	0-0*		0-1	1	CWC
		* in Akranes				
1988-89	Ujpest Dozsa, Hungary	0-0		1-2	1	UEFA
1989-90	RFC Liege, Belgium	0-2*		1-4	1	UEFA
		* in Akranes				

FRAM REYKJAVIK

Founded 1908   Colours blue shirts, white shorts
Stadium Laugardalsvollur (14,800) ☎91-34792/35033
Champions 1913, 1914, 1915, 1916, 1917, 1918, 1921, 1922, 1923, 1925, 1939, 1946, 1947, 1962, 1972, 1986, 1988
Cup Winners 1970, 1973, 1979, 1980, 1985, 1987, 1989

Season	Opponent	Home	Result	Away	Rnd	Cup
1968-69	Olympiakos Piraeus, Greece	0-2*		0-2	1	CWC
		* in Greece				
1971-72	Hibernians, Malta	0-3*		2-0*	pr	CWC
				* in Malta		
1973-74	FC Basle, Switzerland	2-6*		0-5	1	ECC
		* in Olten, Switzerland				
1974-75	Real Madrid, Spain	0-2		0-6	1	CWC
1976-77	Slovan Bratislava, Czechoslovakia	0-3		0-5	1	UEFA
1977-78	IFK Start Kristiansand, Norway	0-2		0-6	1	UEFA
1980-81	Hvidovre IF, Denmark	0-2		0-1	1	CWC
1981-82	Dundalk, Eire	2-1		0-4	1	CWC
1982-83	Shamrock Rovers, Eire	0-3		0-4	1	UEFA
1985-86	Glentoran, Ireland	3-1		0-1	1	CWC
	Rapid Vienna, Austria	2-1		0-3	2	CWC
1986-87	GKS Katowice, Poland	0-3		0-1	1	CWC
1987-88	Sparta Prague, Czechoslovakia	0-2		0-8	1	ECC
1988-89	FC Barcelona, Spain	0-2		0-5	1	CWC
1989-90	Steaua Bucharest, Romania	0-1		0-4	1	ECC

IBV (ITHROTTABADALAG VESTMANNAEYJAR)

Founded 1950   Colours white shirts, green shorts
Stadium Akeryar (5,000) ☎
Champions 1979
Cup Winners 1968, 1971, 1972, 1981

Season	Opponent	Home	Result	Away	Rnd	Cup
1969-70	Levski Spartak Sofia, Bulgaria	0-4		0-4	1	CWC
1972-73	Viking Stavanger, Norway	0-0		0-1	1	UEFA
1973-74	Borussia Monchengladbach, Germany	0-7		1-9	1	CWC
1978-79	Glentoran, Ireland	0-0	wag	1-1	1	UEFA
	Slask Wroclaw, Poland	0-2		1-2	2	UEFA
1980-81	Banik Ostrava, Czechoslovakia	1-1		0-1	1	ECC
1982-83	Lech Poznan, Poland	0-1*		1-3	1	CWC
		* in Kopavogur				
1983-84	Carl Zeiss Jena, East Germany	0-0		0-3	1	UEFA
1984-85	Wisla Krakow, Poland	1-3		2-4	1	CWC

ICELAND

VIKINGUR REYKJAVIK

Founded 1908   Colours red and black striped shirts, black shorts
Stadium Laugardalsvollur (14,800) ☎ 91-36882
Champions 1920, 1924, 1981, 1982
Cup Winners 1971

Season	Opponent	Home	Result	Away	Rnd	Cup
1972-73	Legia Warsaw, Poland	0-2		0-9	1	CWC
1981-82	Girondins Bordeaux, France	0-4		0-4	1	UEFA
1982-83	Real Sociedad San Sebastian, Spain	0-1		2-3	1	ECC
1983-84	Raba Vasas Eto, Hungary	0-2		1-2	1	ECC

IBA (ITHROTTABANDALAG AKUREYRI)

Split into two clubs in 1974, Bor Akureyri and KA Akureyri
Cup Winners 1969

Season	Opponent	Home	Result	Away	Rnd	Cup
1970-71	FC Zurich, Switzerland	1-7*		0-7*	1	CWC

* both in Switzerland

IRELAND

Northern Ireland
Founded 1880 Irish Football Association, Ulster Chambers, 20 Windsor Avenue, Belfast ☎ 010 0232 669458. Irish League 87, University Street, Belfast BT7 1HP ☎ 010 0232 242888 Fax 0232-667620
National Colours green shirts, white shorts
Season August to May

LEAGUE CHAMPIONS

1891	Linfield	**1920**	Belfast Celtic	**1950**	Linfield	**1973**	Crusaders
1892	Linfield	**1921**	Glentoran	**1951**	Glentoran	**1974**	Coleraine
1893	Linfield	**1922**	Linfield	**1952**	Glenavon	**1975**	Linfield
1894	Glentoran	**1923**	Linfield	**1953**	Glentoran	**1976**	Crusaders
1895	Linfield	**1924**	Queen's Island	**1954**	Linfield	**1977**	Glentoran
1896	Distillery	**1925**	Glentoran	**1955**	Linfield	**1978**	Linfield
1897	Glentoran	**1926**	Belfast Celtic	**1956**	Linfield	**1979**	Linfield
1898	Glenfield	**1927**	Belfast Celtic	**1957**	Glentoran		
1899	Distillery	**1928**	Belfast Celtic	**1958**	Ards	**1980**	Linfield
		1929	Belfast Celtic	**1959**	Linfield	**1981**	Glentoran
1900	Belfast Celtic					**1982**	Linfield
1901	Distillery	**1930**	Linfield	**1960**	Glenavon	**1983**	Linfield
1902	Linfield	**1931**	Glentoran	**1961**	Linfield	**1984**	Linfield
1903	Distillery	**1932**	Linfield	**1962**	Linfield	**1985**	Linfield
1904	Linfield	**1933**	Belfast Celtic	**1963**	Distillery	**1986**	Linfield
1905	Glentoran	**1934**	Linfield	**1964**	Glentoran	**1987**	Linfield
1906	Cliftonville+Distillery	**1935**	Linfield	**1965**	Derry City	**1988**	Glentoran
1907	Linfield	**1936**	Belfast Celtic	**1966**	Linfield	**1989**	Linfield
1908	Linfield	**1937**	Belfast Celtic	**1967**	Glentoran		
1909	Linfield	**1938**	Belfast Celtic	**1968**	Glentoran		
		1939	Belfast Celtic	**1969**	Linfield		
1910	Cliftonville						
1911	Linfield	**1940**	Belfast Celtic	**1970**	Glentoran		
1912	Glentoran	**1948**	Belfast Celtic	**1971**	Linfield		
1913	Glentoran	**1949**	Linfield	**1972**	Glentoran		
1914	Linfield						
1915	Belfast Celtic						

IRELAND

IRISH CUP WINNERS 'BASS'

1881	Mayola Park v Cliftonville	1-0
1882	Queen's Island v Cliftonville	2-1
1883	Cliftonville v Ulster	5-0
1884	Distillery v Ulster	5-0
1885	Distillery v Limavady	2-0
1886	Distillery v Limavady	1-0
1887	Ulster v Cliftonville	3-1
1888	Cliftonville v Distillery	2-1
1889	Distillery v YMCA	5-4
1890	Gordon Highlanders v Cliftonville	2-2 3-0
1891	Linfield v Ulster	4-2
1892	Linfield v The Black Watch	7-0
1893	Linfield v Cliftonville	5-1
1894	Distillery v Linfield	2-2 3-2
1895	Linfield v Bohemians	10-1
1896	Distillery v Glentoran	3-1
1897	Cliftonville v Sherwood Foresters Curragh	3-1
1898	Linfield v St Columbs Hall Celtic Derry	2-0
1899	Linfield v Glentoran	1-0
1900	Cliftonville v Bohemians	2-1
1901	Cliftonville v Freebooters, Dublin	1-0
1902	Linfield v Distillery	5-1
1903	Distillery v Bohemians	3-1
1904	Linfield v Derry Celtic	5-0
1905	Distillery v Shelbourne	3-0
1906	Shelbourne v Belfast Celtic	2-0
1907	Cliftonville v Shelbourne	0-0 1-0
1908	Bohemians v Shelbourne	1-1 3-1
1909	Cliftonville v Bohemians	0-0 2-1
1910	Distillery v Cliftonville	1-0
1911	Shelbourne v Bohemians	0-0 2-1
1912	Linfield not played Linfield awarded cup	
1913	Linfield v Glentoran	2-0
1914	Glentoran v Linfield	3-1
1915	Linfield v Belfast Celtic	1-0
1916	Linfield v Glentoran	1-0
1917	Glentoran v Belfast Celtic	2-0
1918	Belfast Celtic v Linfield	0-0 0-0 2-0
1919	Linfield v Glentoran	1-1 0-0 2-1
1920	Shelbourne not played Shelbourne awarded cup	
1921	Glentoran v Glenavon	2-0
1922	Linfield v Glenavon	2-0
1923	Linfield v Glentoran	2-0
1924	Queen's Island v Willowfield	1-0
1925	Distillery v Glentoran	2-1
1926	Belfast Celtic v Linfield	3-2
1927	Ards v Cliftonville	3-2
1928	Willowfield v Larne	1-0
1929	Ballymena United v Belfast Celtic	2-1
1930	Linfield v Ballymena United	4-3
1931	Linfield v Ballymena United	3-0
1932	Glentoran v Linfield	2-1
1933	Glentoran v Distillery	1-1 1-1 3-1
1934	Linfield v Cliftonville	5-0
1935	Glentoran v Larne	0-0 0-0 1-0

1936	Linfield v Derry City	0-0 2-1
1937	Belfast Celtic v Linfield	3-0
1938	Belfast Celtic v Bangor	0-0 2-0
1939	Linfield v Ballymena United	2-0
1940	Ballymena United v Glenavon	2-0
1941	Belfast Celtic v Linfield	1-0
1942	Linfield v Glentoran	3-1
1943	Belfast Celtic v Glentoran	1-0
1944	Belfast Celtic v Linfield	3-1
1945	Linfield v Glentoran	4-2
1946	Linfield v Distillery	3-0
1947	Belfast Celtic v Glentoran	1-0
1948	Linfield v Coleraine	3-0
1949	Derry City v Glentoran	3-1
1950	Linfield v Distillery	2-1
1951	Glentoran v Ballymena United	3-1
1952	Ards v Glentoran	1-0
1953	Linfield v Coleraine	5-0
1954	Derry City v Glentoran	2-2 0-0 1-0
1955	Dundela v Glenavon	3-0
1956	Distillery v Glentoran	2-2 0-0 1-0
1957	Glenavon v Derry City	2-0
1958	Ballymena United v Linfield	2-0
1959	Glenavon v Ballymena United	1-1 2-0
1960	Linfield v Ards	5-1
1961	Glenavon v Linfield	5-1
1962	Linfield v Portadown	4-0
1963	Linfield v Distillery	2-1
1964	Derry City v Glentoran	2-0
1965	Coleraine v Glenavon	2-1
1966	Glentoran v Linfield	2-0
1967	Crusaders v Glentoran	3-1
1968	Crusaders v Linfield	2-0
1969	Ards v Distillery	0-0 4-2
1970	Linfield v Ballymena United	2-1
1971	Distillery v Derry City	3-0
1972	Coleraine v Portadown	2-1
1973	Glentoran v Linfield	3-2
1974	Ards v Ballymena United	2-1
1975	Coleraine v Linfield	1-1 0-0 1-0
1976	Carrick Rangers v Linfield	2-1
1977	Coleraine v Linfield	4-1
1978	Linfield v Ballymena United	3-1
1979	Cliftonville v Portadown	3-2
1980	Linfield v Crusaders	2-0
1981	Ballymena United v Glenavon	1-0
1982	Linfield v Coleraine	2-1
1983	Glentoran v Linfield	1-1 2-1
1984	Ballymena United v Carrick Rangers	4-1
1985	Glentoran v Linfield	1-1 1-0
1986	Glentoran v Coleraine	2-1
1987	Glentoran v Larne	1-0
1988	Glentoran v Glenavon	1-0
1989	Ballymena United	1-0

ULSTER CUP

The above competition is run on a mini league basis of four groups with the winners of each group going into semi finals then final.

1949 Linfield	1960 Linfield	1970 Linfield	1980 Ballymena United
	1961 Ballymena United	1971 Linfield	1981 Glentoran
1950 Larne	1962 Linfield	1972 Coleraine	1982 Glentoran
1951 Glentoran	1963 Crusaders	1973 Ards	1983 Glentoran
1952 no competition	1964 Linfield	1974 Linfield	1984 Linfield
1953 Glentoran	1965 Coleraine	1975 Coleraine	1985 Linfield
1954 Crusaders	1966 Glentoran	1976 Glentoran	1986 Coleraine
1955 Glenavon	1967 Linfield	1977 Linfield	1987 Glentoran
1956 Linfield	1968 Coleraine	1978 Linfield	1988 Larne
1957 Linfield	1969 Coleraine	1979 Linfield	1989 Glentoran
1958 Distillery			
1959 Glenavon			

THE GOLD CUP

1913 Belfast Celtic	1936 Belfast Celtic	1955 Glenavon	1974 Linfield
1914 not held	1937 Linfield	1956 Linfield	1975 Ballymena United
1915 Distillery	1938 Linfield	1957 Glenavon	1976 Coleraine
1916 Shelbourne	1939 Portadown	1958 Linfield	1977 Glentoran
		1959 Coleraine	1978 Glentoran
1921 Distillery	1940 Belfast Celtic		1979 Portadown
1922 Linfield	1941 Belfast Celtic	1960 Linfield	
1923 Linfield	1942 Belfast Celtic	1961 Glentoran	1980 Linfield
1924 Cliftonville	1943 Glentoran	1962 Linfield	1981 Cliftonville
1925 Linfield	1944 Linfield	1963 Glentoran	1982 Glentoran
1926 Distillery	1945 Belfast Celtic	1964 Linfield	1983 Glentoran
1927 Belfast Celtic	1946 Belfast Celtic	1965 Derry City	1984 Linfield
1928 Linfield	1947 Belfast Celtic	1966 Linfield	1985 Linfield
1929 Linfield	1948 Belfast Celtic	1967 Glentoran	1986 Crusaders
	1949 Linfield	1968 Linfield	1987 Glentoran
1930 Linfield		1969 Linfield	1988 Linfield
1931 Distillery	1950 Linfield		1989 Linfield
1932 Linfield	1951 Linfield	1970 Coleraine	
1933 Coleraine	1952 Glentoran	1971 Linfield	1990 Linfield
1934 Cliftonville	1953 Portadown	1972 Linfield	
1935 Portadown	1954 Ards	1973 Portadown	

CITY CUP

1896 Linfield	1910 Shelbourne	1928 Linfield	1940 Portadown
1897 Glentoran	1911 Linfield	1929 Belfast Celtic	1941 Belfast Celtic
1898 Glentoran	1912 Glentoran		1949 Belfast Celtic
1899 Linfield	1913 Glentoran	1930 Linfield	
	1914 Distillery	1931 Belfast Celtic	1950 Belfast Celtic
1900 Glentoran	1915 Glentoran	1932 Belfast Celtic	1951 Linfield
1901 Linfield	1916 Glentoran	1933 Glentoran	1952 Glentoran
1902 Linfield		1934 Belfast Celtic	1953 Linfield
1903 Linfield	1921 Linfield	1935 Distillery	1954 Glentoran
1904 not held	1922 Glenavon		1955 Coleraine
1905 Linfield	1923 Linfield	1936 Derry City	1956 Glenavon
1906 Distillery	1924 Queen's Island	1937 Linfield	1957 Glenavon
1907 Belfast Celtic	1925 Queen's Island	1938 Derry City	1958 Glentoran
1908 Belfast Celtic	1926 Queen's Island	1939 Linfield	1959 Linfield
1909 Linfield	1927 Belfast Celtic		1960 Linfield

185

IRELAND

1961 Distillery	1966 Glentoran	1970 Glentoran	1974 Linfield
1962 Glenavon	1967 Glenavon	1971 Bangor	1975 Glentoran
1963 Linfield	1968 Linfield	1972 Ballymena United	1976 Bangor
1964 Distillery	1969 Coleraine	1973 Glentoran	1977 discontinued
1965 Glentoran			

FEATURED CLUBS IN EUROPEAN COMPETITION

Linfield Belfast	Glentoran Belfast	Glenavon Lurgan	Ards Newtownards
Derry City (now play in Eire)	Distillery Ballyskeagh	Coleraine	Portadown
Cliftonville Belfast	Crusaders Belfast	Carrick Rangers Carrickfergus	Ballymena United

LINFIELD

Founded 1886
Colours blue shirts, white shorts
Stadium Windsor Park, Belfast (40,000) ☎ 0232-223703
Champions 1891, 1892, 1893, 1895, 1898, 1902, 1904, 1907, 1908, 1909, 1911, 1914, 1922, 1923, 1930, 1932, 1934, 1935, 1949, 1950, 1954, 1955, 1956, 1959, 1961, 1962, 1966, 1969, 1971, 1975, 1978, 1979, 1980, 1982, 1983, 1984, 1985, 1986, 1987, 1989
Irish Cup Winners 1891, 1892, 1893, 1895, 1898, 1899, 1902, 1904, 1912, 1913, 1915, 1916, 1919, 1922, 1923, 1930, 1931, 1934, 1936, 1939, 1942, 1945, 1946, 1948, 1950, 1953, 1960, 1962, 1963, 1970, 1978, 1980, 1982, 1989
Ulster Cup 1949, 1956, 1957, 1960, 1962, 1964, 1967, 1970, 1971, 1974, 1977, 1978, 1979, 1984
Gold Cup 1922, 1923, 1925, 1928, 1929, 1930, 1932, 1937, 1938, 1944, 1949, 1950, 1951, 1956, 1958, 1960, 1962, 1964, 1966, 1968 1969, 1971, 1972, 1974, 1980, 1982, 1984, 1985, 1988, 1989, 1990
City Cup 1896, 1899, 1901, 1902, 1903, 1905, 1909, 1911, 1921, 1923, 1928, 1930, 1937, 1939, 1951, 1953, 1959, 1960, 1963, 1968 1974

Season	Opponent	Home	Result	Away	Rnd	Cup
1959-60	IFK Gothenburg, Sweden	2-1		1-6	pr	ECC
1961-62	ASK Vorwaerts Berlin, East Germany	0-3	not played		pr	ECC
1962-63	Esbjerg fB, Denmark	1-2		0-0	pr	ECC
1963-64	Fenerbahce, Turkey	2-0		1-4	1	CWC
1966-67	Aris Bonneweg, Luxembourg	6-1		3-3	1	ECC
	Valerengen IF Oslo, Norway	1-1		4-1	2	ECC
	CSKA Sofia, Bulgaria	2-2		0-1	qf	ECC
1967-68	1.FC Lokomotive Leipzig, East Germany	1-0		1-5	1	Fairs
1968-69	Vitoria Setubal, Portugal	1-3		0-3	1	Fairs
1969-70	Red Star Belgrade, Yugoslavia	2-4		0-8	1	ECC
1970-71	Manchester City, England	2-1	lag	0-1	1	CWC
1971-72	Standard Liege, Belgium	2-3		0-2	1	ECC
1975-76	PSV Eindhoven, Holland	1-2		0-8	1	ECC
1978-79	Lillestrom SK, Norway	0-0		0-1	1	ECC
1979-80	Dundalk, Eire	0-2*		1-1	1	ECC
	* in Haarlem, Holland					
1980-81	FC Nantes, France	0-1*		0-2	1	ECC
	* in Haarlem, Holland					
1981-82	SK Beveren Waas, Belgium	0-5		0-3	1	UEFA
1982-83	17 Nentori Tirana, Albania	2-1	lag	0-1	1	ECC
1983-84	Benfica, Portugal	2-3		0-3	1	ECC
1984-85	Shamrock Rovers, Eire	0-0	wag	1-1	1	ECC
	Panathinaikos, Greece	3-3		1-2	2	ECC
1985-86	Servette Geneva, Switzerland	2-2		1-2	1	ECC
1986-87	Rosenborg Trondheim, Norway	1-1		0-1	1	ECC
1987-88	Lillestrom SK, Norway	2-4		1-1	1	ECC
1988-89	TPS Turun Palloseura Turku, Finland	1-1*	lag	0-0	1	UEFA
	* in Wrexham					
1989-90	Dnepr Dnepropetrovsk, USSR	1-2*		0-1	1	ECC
	* in Wrexham					

GLENTORAN

Founded 1883
Colours red and green striped shirts, white shorts
Stadium The Oval, Mersey Street, Belfast (40,000) ☎ 0232-56137/57670
Champions 1894, 1897, 1905, 1912, 1913, 1921, 1925, 1931, 1951, 1953, 1964, 1967, 1968, 1970, 1972, 1977, 1981, 1988
Irish Cup Winners 1914, 1917, 1921, 1932, 1933, 1935, 1951, 1966, 1973, 1983, 1985, 1986, 1987, 1988
Ulster Cup 1951, 1953, 1966, 1976, 1981, 1982, 1983, 1987, 1989 Gold Cup 1943, 1952, 1961, 1963, 1967, 1977, 1978, 1983, 1987
City Cup 1897, 1898, 1900, 1912, 1913, 1915, 1916, 1933, 1952, 1954, 1958, 1965, 1966, 1970, 1973, 1975

Season	Opponent	Home	Result	Away	Rnd	Cup
1962-63	Real Zaragoza, Spain	0-2		2-6	1	Fairs
1963-64	Partick Thistle, Scotland	1-4		0-3	pr	Fairs
1964-65	Panathinaikos, Greece	2-2		2-3	pr	ECC
1965-66	Royal Antwerp, Belgium	3-3		0-1	1	Fairs
1966-67	Glasgow Rangers, Scotland	1-1		0-4	pr	CWC
1967-68	Benfica, Portugal	1-1	lag	0-0	1	ECC
1968-69	RSC Anderlecht, Belgium	2-2		0-3	1	ECC
1969-70	Arsenal, England	1-0		0-3	1	Fairs
1970-71	Waterford, Eire	1-3		0-1	1	ECC
1971-72	Eintracht Braunschweg, Germany	0-1		1-6	1	UEFA
1973-74	Chemia Ramnicu Valcea, Romania	2-0		2-2	1	CWC
	Brann Bergen, Norway	3-1		1-1	2	CWC
	Borussia Monchengladbach, Germany	0-2		0-5	qf	CWC
1975-76	Ajax Amsterdam, Holland	1-6		0-8	1	UEFA
1976-77	FC Basle, Switzerland	3-2		0-3	1	UEFA
1977-78	Valur Reykjavik, Iceland	2-0		0-1	1	ECC
	Juventus, Italy	0-1		0-5	2	ECC
1978-79	IBV Vestmannaeyja, Iceland	1-1	lag	0-0*	1	UEFA
				* in Reykjavik, ground unfit		
1981-82	Progres Niedercorn, Luxembourg	4-0		1-1	1	ECC
	CSKA Sofia, Bulgaria	2-1		0-2	2	ECC
1982-83	Banik Ostrava, Czechoslovakia	1-3		0-1	1	UEFA
1983-84	Paris St Germain, France	1-2		1-2	1	CWC
1984-85	Standard Liege, Belgium	1-1		0-2	1	UEFA
1985-86	Fram Reykjavik, Iceland	1-0		1-3	1	CWC
1986-87	1.FC Lokomotive Leipzig, East Germany	1-1		0-2	1	CWC
1987-88	RoPs Rovaniemen, Finland	1-1		0-0	1	CWC
1988-89	Spartak Moscow, USSR	1-1		0-2	1	ECC
1989-90	Dundee United	1-3		0-2	1	UEFA

GLENAVON

Founded 1889
Colours blue shirts, white shorts
Stadium Mourneview Park, Lurgan (8,000) ☎ 07622-22472
Champions 1952, 1957, 1960
Irish Cup Winners 1957, 1959, 1961
Ulster Cup 1955, 1959
Gold Cup 1955, 1957
City Cup 1922, 1956, 1957, 1962, 1967

Season	Opponent	Home	Result	Away	Rnd	Cup
1957-58	AGF Aarhus, Denmark	0-3		0-0	pr	ECC
1960-61	SC Wismut Karl Marx Stadt, East Germany		withdrew			ECC
1961-62	Leicester City, England	1-4		1-3	pr	CWC
1977-78	PSV Eindhoven, Holland	2-6		0-5	1	UEFA
1979-80	Standard Liege, Belgium	0-1		0-1	1	UEFA
1988-89	AGF Aarhus, Denmark	1-4		1-3	1	CWC

187

IRELAND

ARDS

Founded 1902
Colours red and blue striped shirts, blue shorts
Stadium Castlereagh Park, Newtownards, Co Down (10,000) ☎ 0247-817562
Champions 1958
Irish Cup Winners 1927, 1952, 1969, 1974
Ulster Cup 1973
Gold Cup 1954

Season	Opponent	Home	Result	Away	Rnd	Cup
1958-59	Stade de Reims, France	1-4*		2-6**	pr	ECC
		* in Belfast		** in Paris		
1969-70	AS Roma, Italy	0-0		1-3	1	CWC
1973-74	Standard Liege, Belgium	3-2		1-6	1	UEFA
1974-75	PSV Eindhoven, Holland	1-4		0-10	1	CWC

DERRY CITY

disbanded, reformed in 1984 and joined The League of Ireland ☎ 080504-262276
Champions 1965
Irish Cup Winners 1949, 1954, 1964
Gold Cup 1965 City Cup 1936, 1938

Season	Opponent	Home	Result	Away	Rnd	Cup
1964-65	Steaua Bucharest, Romania	0-2		0-3	1	CWC
1965-66	Gjovik Lyn, Norway	5-1		3-5	1	ECC
	RSC Anderlecht, Belgium	not played*		0-9	2	ECC
		* ground unsuitable				

DISTILLERY

Founded 1880
Colours white shirts, blue shorts
Stadium Grosvenor Park, Ballyskeagh, Lampeg, Lisborn (14,000) ☎ 0232-629148
Champions 1896, 1899, 1901, 1903, 1906, 1963
Ulster Cup 1958
Irish Cup Winners 1884, 1885, 1886, 1889, 1894, 1896, 1903, 1905, 1910, 1925, 1956, 1971
Gold Cup 1915, 1921, 1926, 1931
City Cup 1906, 1914, 1935, 1961, 1964

Season	Opponent	Home	Result	Away	Rnd	Cup
1963-64	Benfica, Portugal	3-3		0-5	1	ECC
1971-72	CF Barcelona, Spain	1-3		0-4	1	CWC

COLERAINE

Founded 1927
Colours blue and white striped shirts, white shorts
Stadium The Showgrounds, Coleraine (8,000) ☎ 0265-53655
Champions 1974
Irish Cup Winners 1965, 1972, 1975, 1977
Ulster Cup 1965, 1968, 1969, 1972, 1975, 1985, 1986
Gold Cup 1933, 1959, 1970, 1976
City Cup 1955, 1969

Season	Opponent	Home	Result	Away	Rnd	Cup
1965-66	Dynamo Kiev, Russia	1-6		0-4	1	CWC
1969-70	Jeunesse Esch, Luxembourg	4-0		2-3	1	Fairs
	RSC Anderlecht, Belgium	3-7		1-6	2	Fairs
1970-71	Kilmarnock, Scotland	1-1		3-2	1	Fairs
	Sparta Rotterdam, Holland	1-2		0-2	2	Fairs
1974-75	Feyenoord Rotterdam, Holland	1-4		0-7	1	ECC
1975-76	Eintracht Frankfurt, Germany	2-6		1-5	1	CWC
1977-78	1.FC Lokomitive Leipzig, East Germany	1-4		2-2	1	CWC
1982-83	Tottenham Hotspur, England	0-3		0-4	1	CWC
1983-84	Sparta Rotterdam, Holland	1-1		0-4	1	UEFA
1985-86	1.FC Lokomotive Leipzig, East Germany	1-1		0-5	1	UEFA
1986-87	Stahl Brandenburg, East Germany	1-1		0-1	1	UEFA
1987-88	Dundee United, Scotland	0-1		1-3	1	UEFA

PORTADOWN

Founded 1924
Colours red shirts, white shorts
Stadium Shamrock Park, Portadown (20,000) ☎ 0762-332726
Gold Cup 1935, 1939, 1953, 1973, 1979
City Cup 1940

Season	Opponent	Home	Result	Away	Rnd	Cup
1962-63	bye				1	CWC
	OFK Belgrade, Yugoslavia	3-2*		1-5	2	CWC
		* in Belfast				
1974-75	Valur Reykjavik, Iceland	2-1		0-0	1	UEFA
	Partizan Belgrade, Yugoslavia	1-1		0-5	2	UEFA

CLIFTONVILLE

Founded 1879
Colours red shirts, white shorts
Stadium Solitude, Belfast (21,000) ☎ 0232-754628
Champions 1973, 1976
Irish Cup Winners 1883, 1888, 1897, 1900, 1901, 1907, 1909, 1979
Gold Cup 1924, 1934, 1981

Season	Opponent	Home	Result	Away	Rnd	Cup
1979-80	FC Nantes, France	0-1		0-7	1	CWC

IRELAND

CRUSADERS

Founded 1909
Colours red and black striped shirts, black shorts
Stadium Seaview, Belfast (10,000) ☎ 0232-778777
Champions 1973, 1976
Irish Cup Winners 1967, 1968
Ulster Cup 1954, 1963
Gold Cup 1986

Season	Opponent	Home	Result	Away	Rnd	Cup
1967-68	Valencia CF, Spain	2-4		0-4	1	CWC
1968-69	IFK Norrkoping, Sweden	2-2		1-4	1	CWC
1973-74	Dinamo Bucharest, Romania	0-1		0-11	1	ECC
1976-77	Liverpool, England	0-5		0-2	1	ECC
1980-81	Newport County, Wales	0-0		0-4	1	CWC

CARRICK RANGERS

Founded 1939
Colours yellow shirts, black shorts
Stadium Taylors Avenue, Carrickfergus (5,000) ☎ 09603-93 61009
Irish Cup Winners 1976

Season	Opponent	Home	Result	Away	Rnd	Cup
1976-77	Aris Bonnevoie, Luxembourg	3-1		1-2	1	CWC
	Southampton, England	2-5		1-4	2	CWC

BALLYMENA UNITED

Founded 1928
Colours all sky blue
Stadium The Showgrounds, Ballymena (8,000) ☎ 0266-2049
Irish Cup Winners 1940, 1929, 1958, 1981, 1989
Ulster Cup 1961, 1980
Gold Cup 1975
City Cup 1972

Season	Opponent	Home	Result	Away	Rnd	Cup
1978-79	SK Beveren Waas, Belgium	0-3		0-3	1	CWC
1980-81	FC Vorwaerts Frankfurt on Oder, East Germany	2-1		0-3	1	UEFA
1981-82	AS Roma, Italy	0-2		0-4	1	CWC
1984-85	Hamrun Spartans, Malta	0-1		1-2	1	CWC
1989-90	RSC Anderlecht, Belgium	0-4		0-6	1	CWC

ITALY

Founded 1898
Federazione Italiana Giuoco Calcio, Via Gregorio Allegri 14, CP 2450, 00198 Rome Phone 84 911
National Colours blue shirts, white shorts, blue socks
Season September to June

CHAMPIONSHIP PLAYOFF

1898	Genoa v Internazionale FC Torino	2-1
1899	Genoa v Internazionale FC Torino	2-0
1900	Genoa v FC Torinese	1-0
1901	Milan Cricket & FC v Genoa	1-0
1902	Genoa v Milan Cricket & FC	2-0
1903	Genoa v Juventus	3-0
1904	Genoa v Juventus	1-0
1905	Juventus mini league	
1906	AC Milan mini league	
1907	AC Milan mini league	
1908	Pro Vercelli mini league	
1909	Pro Vercelli v US Milanese	2-0 1-1
1910	Ambrosiana Inter v Pro Vercelli	10-3
1911	Pro Vercelli v Vicenza	3-0 2-1
1912	Pro Vercelli v Venezia	6-0 7-0

1913	Pro Vercelli v Lazio	6-0
1914	Casele v Lazio	7-1 2-0
1915	Genoa awarded title, Finals not played	
1920	Ambrosiana Inter v Livorno	3-2
1921	Pro Vercelli v Pisa	2-1
1922	US Novese v Sampierdarenese	0-0 0-0 2-1
	F.I.G.C. League	
1922	US Pro Vercelli v Fortitude Roma	3-0 5-2
	C.C.I. League	
1923	Genoa v Lazio	3-3 4-1
1924	Genoa v Savoia	3-1 1-1
1925	Bologna v Alba	4-0 2-0
1926	Juventus v Alba	7-1 5-0
1927	Torino mini League	
1928	Torino mini League	
1929	Bologna v Torino	3-1 0-1 1-0

NATIONAL LEAGUE CHAMPIONS

1930	Ambrosiana Inter	**1947**	Torino	**1960**	Juventus	**1975**	Juventus
1931	Juventus	**1948**	Torino	**1961**	Juventus	**1976**	Torino
1932	Juventus	**1949**	Torinoan	**1962**	AC Milan	**1977**	Juventus
1933	Juventus			**1963**	Inter Milan	**1978**	Juventus
1934	Juventus	**1950**	Juventus	**1964**	Bologna	**1979**	AC Milan
1935	Juventus	**1951**	AC Milan	**1965**	Inter Milan		
1936	Bologna	**1952**	Juventus	**1966**	Inter Milan	**1980**	Inter Milan
1937	Bologna	**1953**	Inter Milan	**1967**	Juventus	**1981**	Juventus
1938	Ambrosiana Inter	**1954**	Inter Milan	**1968**	AC Milan	**1982**	Juventus
1939	Bologna	**1955**	AC Milan	**1969**	Fiorentina	**1983**	AS Roma
		1956	Fiorentina			**1984**	Juventus
1940	Ambrosiana Inter	**1957**	AC Milan	**1970**	Cagliari	**1985**	Verona
1941	Bologna	**1958**	Juventus	**1971**	Inter Milan	**1986**	Juventus
1942	AS Roma	**1959**	AC Milan	**1972**	Juventus	**1987**	Napoli
1943	Torino			**1973**	Juventus	**1988**	AC Milan
1946	Torino			**1974**	Lazio Rome	**1989**	Inter Milan

ITALY

CUP WINNERS

Played on a league basis then quarter, semi and one- or two-legged final

1922	Vado v Polisportiva Libertas Firenze	1-0	**1970**	Bologna (mini league)	
1936	Torino v USC Alessandria	5-1	**1971**	Torino v AC Milan	0-0 5-3 pen
1937	Genoa '93 v AS Roma	1-0	**1972**	AC Milan v Napoli	2-1
1938	Juventus v Torino 3-1 2-1		**1973**	AC Milan v Juventus	1-1 5-2 pen
1939	Ambrosiana Inter v AC Novara	2-1	**1974**	Bologna v Palermo	1-1 4-3 pen
			1975	Fiorentina v AC Milan	3-2
1940	Fiorentina v Genoa '93	1-0	**1976**	Napoli v Hellas Verona	4-0
1941	Venezia v AS Roma	3-3 1-0	**1977**	AC Milan v Inter Milan	2-0
1942	Juventus v AC Milan	1-1 4-1	**1978**	Inter Milan v Napoli	2-1
1943	Torino v Venezia	4-0	**1979**	Juventus v Palermo	2-1
1958	Lazio Rome v Fiorentina	1-0	**1980**	AS Roma v Torino	0-0 3-2 pen
1959	Juventus v Inter Milan	4-1	**1981**	AS Roma v Torino	1-1 1-1 5-3 pen
			1982	Inter Milan v Torino	1-0 1-1
1960	Juventus v Fiorentina	3-2	**1983**	Juventus v Hellas Verona	3-0 0-2
1961	Fiorentina v Lazio	2-0	**1984**	AS Roma v Hellas Verona	1-1 1-0
1962	Napoli v Spal Ferrara	2-1	**1985**	Sampdoria v AC Milan	1-0 2-1
1963	Atalanta v Torino	3-1	**1986**	AS Roma v Sampdoria	2-0 1-2
1964	AS Roma v Torino	0-0 1-0	**1987**	Napoli v Atalanta Bergamo	4-0 0-1
1965	Juventus v Inter Milan	1-0	**1988**	Sampdoria v Torino	2-0 1-2
1966	Fiorentina v Catanzaro	2-1	**1989**	Sampdoria v Naples	4-0 0-1
1967	AC Milan v Padova	1-0			
1968	Torino (mini league)		**1990**	Juventus v AC Milan	0-0 1-0
1969	AS Roma (mini league)				

ITALIAN SUPER CUP

1988	AC Milan v Sampdoria	3-1
1989	Inter-Milan v Sampdoria	2-0

FEATURED CLUBS IN EUROPEAN COMPETITION

AC Milan	Inter Milan	Juventus Turin	Fiorentina Florence
Bologna	Torino	Napoli	AS Roma
Sampdoria Genoa	Atalanta Bergamo	Cagliari Sardinia	Cesna
Perugia	Verona Hellas	Lazio Rome	Lanerossi Vicenza

AC MILAN

Founded 1899 as Milan Cricket and Football Club, 1905 Milan FC, 1945 AC Milan
Colours red and black striped shirts, white shorts
Stadium Giuseppe Meazza (83,141) ☎ 02-65 59 016/7/8/9
Champions 1901, 1906, 1907, 1951, 1955, 1957, 1959, 1962, 1968, 1979, 1988
Cup Winners 1967, 1972, 1973, 1977
Italian Super Cup Winners 1988
Mitropa Cup Winners 1982
ECC Winners 1963, 1969, 1989, 1990 Finalists 1958
CWC Winners 1968, 1973 Finalists 1974
World Club Champions 1969, 1989 Finalists 1963
European Super Cup Winners 1989 Finalists 1973

Season	Opponent	Home	Playoff Result	Away	Rnd	Cup
1955-56	1.FC Saarbrucken, Germany	3-4		4-1	1	ECC
	Rapid Vienna, Austria	7-2		1-1	qf	ECC
	Real Madrid, Spain	2-1		2-4	sf	ECC
1957-58	Rapid Vienna, Austria	4-1	4-2* * in Zurich	2-5	pr	ECC
	Glasgow Rangers, Scotland	2-0		4-1	1	ECC
	Borussia Dortmund, Germany	4-1		1-1	qf	ECC
	Manchester United, England	4-0		1-2	sf	ECC
	Real Madrid, Spain	2-3	in Brussels		FINAL	ECC
1959-60	Olympiakos Piraeus, Greece	3-1		2-2	pr	ECC
	CF Barcelona, Spain	0-2		1-5	1	ECC
1961-62	Vojvodina Novi Sad, Yugoslavia	0-0		0-2	pr	Fairs
1962-63	Union Sportive, Luxembourg	8-0		6-0	1	ECC
	Ipswich Town, England	3-0		1-2	2	ECC
	Galatasaray, Turkey	5-0		3-1	qf	ECC
	Dundee, Scotland	5-1		0-1	sf	ECC
	Benfica, Portugal	2-1	at Wembley		FINAL	ECC
1963-64	IFK Norrkoping, Sweden	5-2		1-1	1	ECC
	Real Madrid, Spain	2-0		1-4	2	ECC
1964-65	RC Strasbourg, France	1-0		0-2	pr	Fairs
1965-66	RC Strasbourg, France	1-0	1-1* wot * in Milan	1-2	1	Fairs
	CUF Barreiro, Portugal	2-0	1-0* * in Milan	0-2	2	Fairs
	Chelsea, England	2-1	1-1* lot * in Milan	1-2	qf	Fairs
1967-68	Levski Spartak Sofia, Bulgaria	5-1		1-1	1	CWC
	Vasas Gyoer Eto, Hungary	1-1	wag	2-2	2	CWC
	Standard Liege, Belgium	1-1	2-0* * in Milan	1-1	qf	CWC
	Bayern Munich, Germany	2-0		0-0	sf	CWC
	Hamburger SV, Germany	2-0	in Rotterdam		FINAL	CWC
1968-69	Malmo FF, Sweden	4-1		1-2	1	ECC
	bye				2	ECC
	Glasgow Celtic, Scotland	0-0		1-0	qf	ECC
	Manchester United, England	2-0		0-1	sf	ECC
	Ajax Amsterdam, Holland	4-1	in Madrid		FINAL	ECC
1969-70	Avenir Beggen, Luxembourg	5-0		3-0	1	ECC
	Feyenoord Rotterdam, Holland	1-0		0-2	2	ECC
1971-72	Dighenis Akritas Morphou, Cyprus	4-0		3-0	1	UEFA
	Hertha BSC Berlin, Germany	4-2		1-2	2	UEFA
	Dundee, Scotland	3-0		0-2	3	UEFA
	Lierse SK, Belgium	2-0		1-1	qf	UEFA
	Tottenham Hotspur, England	1-1		1-2	sf	UEFA
1972-73	Red Boys Differdange, Luxembourg	3-0		4-1	1	CWC
	Legia Warsaw, Poland	2-1		1-1	2	CWC
	Spartak Moscow, USSR	1-1		1-0	qf	CWC
	Sparta Prague, Czechoslovakia	1-0		1-0	sf	CWC
	Leeds United, England	1-0	in Salonika		FINAL	CWC
1973-74	Dinamo Zagreb, Yugoslavia	3-1		1-0	1	CWC
	Rapid Vienna, Austria	0-0		2-0	2	CWC
	PAOK Salonika, Greece	3-0		2-2	qf	CWC
	Borussia Monchengladbach, Germany	2-0		0-1	sf	CWC
	1.FC Magdeburg, East Germany	0-2	in Rotterdam		FINAL	CWC
1975-76	Everton, England	1-0		0-0	1	UEFA
	Athlone Town, Eire	3-0		0-0	2	UEFA
	Spartak Moscow, USSR	4-0		0-2	3	UEFA
	Clube Bruges, Belgium	2-1		0-2	qf	UEFA
1976-77	Dinamo Bucharest, Romania	2-1		0-0	1	UEFA
	Akademik Sofia, Bulgaria	2-0		3-4	2	UEFA
	Athletic Bilbao, Spain	3-1		1-4	3	UEFA
1977-78	Real Betis, Spain	2-1		0-2	1	CWC
1978-79	Lokomotiva Kosice, Czechoslovakia	1-0	7-6p	0-1	1	UEFA
	Levski Spartak Sofia, Bulgaria	3-0		1-1	2	UEFA
	Manchester City, England	2-2		0-3	3	UEFA

193

1979-80	FC Porto, Portugal	0-1		0-0	1	ECC
1985-86	AJ Auxerre, France	3-0		1-3	1	UEFA
	1.FC Lokomotive Leipzig, East Germany	2-0		1-3	2	UEFA
	Waregem KSV, Belgium	1-2		1-1	3	UEFA
1987-88	Real Sporting Gijon, Spain	3-0		0-1	1	UEFA
	Espanol Barcelona, Spain	0-2*		0-0	2	UEFA
		* in Lecce				
1988-89	FC Vitosha Sofia, Bulgaria	5-2		2-0	1	ECC
	Red Star Belgrade, Yugoslavia	1-1	4-2p	1-1	2	ECC
		(0-1 abandoned in fog after 61 minutes)				
	Werder Bremen, Germany	1-0		0-0	qf	ECC
	Real Madrid, Spain	5-0		1-1	sf	ECC
	Steaua Bucharest, Romania	4-0	in Barcelona		FINAL	ECC
1989-90	HJK Helsinki, Finland	4-0		1-0	1	ECC
	Real Madrid, Spain	2-0		0-1	2	ECC
	KV Mechelen, Belgium	2-0aet		0-0	qf	ECC
	Bayern Munich, Germany	1-0	wag	1-2	sf	ECC
	Benfica, Portugal	1-0	in Vienna		FINAL	ECC

INTERNAZIONALE MILAN

Founded 1908 as Internazionale FC Milano, 1929 merged with US Milanese to become Ambrosiana Inter, 1945 renamed Internazionale FC
Colours black and pale blue striped shirts, black shorts
Stadium Giuseppe Meazza (83,141) ☎ 02-78 25 31
Champions 1910, 1920, 1930, 1938, 1940 all as Ambrosiana, 1953, 1954, 1963, 1965, 1966, 1971, 1980, 1989
Cup Winners 1939, 1978
Italian Super Cup Winners 1989
ECC Winners 1964, 1965
Finalists 1967, 1972
World Club Champions 1964, 1965

Season	Opponent	Home	Playoff Result	Away	Rnd	Cup
1955-58	Birmingham City, England	0-0		1-2	pr	Fairs
	Zagreb City XI, Yugoslavia	4-0		1-0	pr	Fairs
1958-60	Olympique Lyon, France	7-0		1-1	1	Fairs
	CF Barcelona, Spain	2-4		0-4	2	Fairs
1960-61	Hannover 96, Germany	8-2		6-1	1	Fairs
	Belgrade City XI, Yugoslavia	5-0		0-1	2	Fairs
	Birmingham City, England	1-2		1-2	qf	Fairs
1961-62	1.FC Koln, Germany	2-0	5-3*	2-4	1	Fairs
			* in Milan			
	Heart of Midlothian, Scotland	4-0		1-0	2	Fairs
	Valencia CF, Spain	0-2		3-3	qf	Fairs
1963-64	Everton, England	1-0		0-0	1	ECC
	AS Monaco, France	1-0		3-1*	2	ECC
				* in Marseille		
	Partizan Belgrade, Yugoslavia	2-1		2-0	qf	ECC
	Borussia Dortmund, Germany	2-0		2-2	sf	ECC
	Real Madrid, Spain	3-1	in Vienna		FINAL	ECC
1964-65	bye				1	ECC
	Dinamo Bucharest, Romania	6-0		1-0	2	ECC
	Glasgow Rangers, Scotland	3-1		0-1	qf	ECC
	Liverpool, England	3-0		1-3	sf	ECC
	Benfica, Portugal	1-0	in Milan		FINAL	ECC
1965-66	Dinamo Bucharest, Romania	2-0		1-2	1	ECC
	Ferencvarosi TC, Hungary	4-0		1-1	qf	ECC
	Real Madrid, Spain	1-1		0-1	sf	ECC

1966-67	Torpedo Moscow, USSR	1-0		0-0	1	ECC
	Vasas Budapest, Hungary	2-1		2-0	2	ECC
	Real Madrid, Spain	1-0		2-0	qf	ECC
	CSKA Sofia, Bulgaria	1-1	1-0*	1-1	sf	ECC
			* in Bologna			
	Glasgow Celtic, Scotland	1-2	in Lisbon		FINAL	ECC
1969-70	Sparta Prague, Czechoslovakia	3-0		1-0	1	Fairs
	Hansa Rostock, East Germany	3-0		1-2	2	Fairs
	CF Barcelona, Spain	1-1		2-1	3	Fairs
	Hertha BSC Berlin, Germany	2-0		0-1	qf	Fairs
	RSC Anderlecht, Belgium	0-2		1-0	sf	Fairs
1970-71	Newcastle United, England	1-1		0-2	1	Fairs
1971-72	AEK Athens, Greece	4-1		2-3	1	ECC
	Borussia Monchengladbach, Germany	4-2	0-0*	1-7 (void)		ECC
			* in West Berlin			
	Standard Liege, Belgium	1-0	wag	1-2	qf	ECC
	Glasgow Celtic, Scotland	0-0	5-4p	0-0	sf	ECC
	Ajax Amsterdam, Holland	0-2	in Rotterdam		FINAL	ECC
1972-73	Valletta, Malta	6-1		1-0	1	UEFA
	IFK Norrkoping, Sweden	2-2		2-0	2	UEFA
	Vitoria Setubal, Portugal	1-0		0-2	3	UEFA
1973-74	Admira Wacker Vienna, Austria	2-1	lag	0-1	1	UEFA
1974-75	Etar Tirnovo, Bulgaria	3-0		0-0	1	UEFA
	FC Amsterdam, Holland	1-2		0-0	2	UEFA
1976-77	Honved Budapest, Hungary	0-1		1-1	1	UEFA
1977-78	Dynamo Tbilisi, USSR	0-1		0-0	1	UEFA
1978-79	Floriana, Malta	5-0		3-1	1	CWC
	Bodo Glimt, Norway	5-0		2-1	2	CWC
	SK Beveren Waas, Belgium	0-0		0-1	qf	CWC
1979-80	Real Socided San Sebastien, Spain	3-0		0-2	1	UEFA
	Borussia Monchengladbach, Germany	2-3		1-1	2	UEFA
1980-81	Universitatea Craiova, Romania	2-0		1-1	1	ECC
	FC Nantes, France	1-1		2-1	2	ECC
	Red Star Belgrade, Yugoslavia	1-1		1-0	qf	ECC
	Real Madrid, Spain	1-0		0-2	sf	ECC
1981-82	Adanaspor, Turkey	4-1		3-1	1	UEFA
	Dinamo Bucharest, Romania	1-1		2-3	2	UEFA
1982-83	Slovan Bratislava, Czechoslovakia	2-0		1-2	1	CWC
	AZ 67 Alkmaar, Holland	2-0		0-1	2	CWC
	Real Madrid, Spain	1-1		1-2	qf	CWC
1983-84	Trabzonspor, Turkey	2-0*		0-1	1	UEFA
			* in Cesena			
	FC Groningen, Holland	5-1*		0-2	2	UEFA
			* in Bari			
	FK Austria Vienna, Austria	1-1		1-2	3	UEFA
1984-85	Sportul Studentesc Bucharest, Romania	2-0		0-1	1	UEFA
	Glasgow Rangers, Scotland	3-0		1-3	2	UEFA
	Hamburger SV, Germany	1-0	wag	1-2	3	UEFA
	1.FC Koln, Germany	1-0		3-1	qf	UEFA
	Real Madrid, Spain	2-0		0-3	sf	UEFA
1985-86	St Gallen, Switzerland	5-1		0-0	1	UEFA
	Linzer ASK, Austria	4-0		0-1	2	UEFA
	Legia Warsaw, Poland	0-0		1-0	3	UEFA
	FC Nantes, France	3-0		3-3	qf	UEFA
	Real Madrid, Spain	3-1		1-5	sf	UEFA
1986-87	AEK Athens, Greece	2-0		1-0	1	UEFA
	Legia Warsaw, Poland	1-0	wag	2-3	2	UEFA
	Dukla Prague, Czechoslovakia	0-0		1-0	3	UEFA
	IFK Gothenburg, Sweden	1-1	lag	0-0	qf	UEFA
1987-88	Besiktas, Turkey	3-1		0-0	1	UEFA
	TPS Turun Turku, Finland	0-1		2-0	2	UEFA
	Espanol Barcelona, Spain				3	UEFA
1988-89	IK Brage, Sweden	2-1		2-1	1	UEFA
	Malmo FF, Sweden	1-1		1-0	2	UEFA
	Bayern Munich, Germany	1-3	lag	2-0	3	UEFA
1989-90	Malmo FF, Sweden	1-1		0-1	1	ECC

ITALY

JUVENTUS

Founded 1897
Colours black and white striped shirts, white shorts
Stadium Stade Comunale, Turin (71,000) ☎ 011-6509 706/7/8/9
Champions 1905, 1926, 1931, 1932, 1933, 1934, 1935, 1950, 1952, 1958, 1960, 1961, 1967, 1972, 1973, 1975, 1977, 1978, 1981, 1982, 1984, 1986
Cup Winners 1938, 1942, 1959, 1960, 1965, 1979, 1990
ECC Winners 1985 Finalists 1973, 1983
CWC Winners 1984
Fairs Cup Finalists 1965, 1971
UEFA Cup Winners 1977, 1990
Super Cup Winners 1984, 1985
World Club Champions 1985 Finalists 1973

Season	Opponent	Home	Playoff Result	Away	Rnd	Cup
1958-59	Wiener Sport Club, Austria	3-1		0-7	1	ECC
1960-61	CDNA Sofia, Bulgaria	2-0		1-4	1	ECC
1961-62	Panathinaikos, Greece	2-1		1-1	1	ECC
	Partizan Belgrade, Yugoslavia	5-0		2-1	2	ECC
	Real Madrid, Spain	0-1	1-3* * in Paris	1-0	qf	ECC
1963-64	OFK Belgrade, Yugoslavia	2-1	1-0* * in Trieste	1-2	1	Fairs
	Atletico Madrid, Spain	1-0		2-1	2	Fairs
	Real Zaragoza, Spain	0-0		2-3	qf	Fairs
1964-65	Union St Gilliose, Belgium	1-0		1-0	1	Fairs
	Stade Francais, France	1-0		0-0	2	Fairs
	Lokomotiv Plovdiv, Bulgaria	1-1	2-1 *aet * in Turin	1-1	3	Fairs
	bye				qf	
	Atletico Madrid, Spain	3-1	3-1* * in Turin	1-3	sf	Fairs
	Ferencvarosi TC, Hungary	0-1	in Turin		FINAL	Fairs
1965-66	Liverpool, England	1-0		0-2	1	CWC
1966-67	Aris Salonika, Greece	5-0		2-0	1	Fairs
	Vitoria Setubal, Portugal	3-1		2-0	2	Fairs
	Dundee United, Scotland	3-0		0-1	3	Fairs
	Dinamo Zagreb, Yugoslavia	2-2		0-3	qf	Fairs
1967-68	Olympiakos Piraeus, Greece	2-0		0-0	1	ECC
	Rapid Bucharest, Romania	1-0		0-0	2	ECC
	Eintracht Braunschweig, Germany	1-0	1-0* * in Bern	2-3	qf	EEC
	Benfica, Portugal	0-1		0-2	sf	ECC
1968-69	Lausanne Sport, Switzerland	2-0		2-0	1	Fairs
	Eintracht Frankfurt, Germany	0-0		0-1	2	Fairs
1969-70	Lokomotiv Plovdiv, Bulgaria	3-1		2-1	1	Fairs
	Hertha BSC Berlin, Germany	0-0		1-3	2	Fairs
1970-71	US Rumelingen, Luxembourg	7-0		4-0	1	Fairs
	CF Barcelona, Spain	2-1		2-1	2	Fairs
	Pecsi Dozsa, Hungary	2-0		1-0	3	Fairs
	Twente Enschede, Holland	2-0		2-2	qf	Fairs
	1.FC Koln, Germany	2-0		1-1	sf	Fairs
	Leeds United, England	2-2*	lag	1-1	FINAL	Fairs
	* 0-0 abandoned after 55 minutes, waterlogged pitch					
1971-72	Marsa Valletta, Malta	5-0		6-0	1	UEFA
	Aberdeen, Scotland	2-0		1-1	2	UEFA
	Rapid Vienna, Austria	4-1		1-0	3	UEFA
	Wolverhampton Wanderers, England	1-1		1-2	qf	UEFA

196

1972-73	Olympique Marseille, France	3-0		0-1*	1	ECC
				* in Lyon		
	1.FC Magdeburg, East Germany	1-0		1-0	2	ECC
	Ujpest Dozsa, Hungary	0-0	wag	2-2	qf	ECC
	Derby County, England	3-1		0-0	sf	ECC
	Ajax Amsterdam, Holland	0-1	in Belgrade		FINAL	ECC
1973-74	Dynamo Dresden, East Germany	3-2		0-2	1	ECC
1974-75	FC Vorwaers Frankfurt on Oder, East Germany	3-0		1-2	1	UEFA
	Hibernian, Scotland	4-0		4-2	2	UEFA
	Ajax Amsterdam, Holland	1-0	wag	1-2	3	UEFA
	Hamburger SV, Germany	2-0		0-0	qf	UEFA
	Twente Enschede, Holland	0-1		1-3	sf	UEFA
1975-76	CSKA Sofia, Bulgaria	2-0		1-2	1	ECC
	Borussia Monchengladbach, Germany	2-2		0-2	2	ECC
1976-77	Manchester City, England	2-0		0-1	1	UEFA
	Manchester United, England	3-0		0-1	2	UEFA
	Shakhtyor Donetsk, USSR	3-0		0-1	3	UEFA
	1.FC Magdeburg, East Germany	1-0		3-1	qf	UEFA
	AEK Athens, Greece	4-1		1-0	sf	UEFA
	Athletic Bilbao, Spain	1-0	wag	1-2	FINAL	UEFA
1977-78	Omonia Nicosia, Cyprus	2-0		3-0	1	ECC
	Glentoran, Ireland	5-0		1-0	2	ECC
	Ajax Amsterdam, Holland	1-1	3-0p	1-1	qf	ECC
	Clube Bruges, Belgium	1-0		0-2	sf	ECC
1978-79	Glasgow Rangers, Scotland	1-0		0-2	1	ECC
1979-80	Raba Vasas Eto, Hungary	2-0		1-2	1	CWC
	Beroe Stara Zagora, Bulgaria	3-0		0-1	2	CWC
	NK Rijeka, Yugoslavia	2-0		0-0	qf	CWC
	Arsenal, England	0-1		1-1	sf	CWC
1980-81	Panathinaikos, Greece	4-0		2-4	1	UEFA
	RTS Widzew Lodz, Poland	3-1	1-4p	1-3	2	UEFA
1981-82	Glasgow Celtic, Scotland	2-0		0-1	1	ECC
	RSC Anderlecht, Belgium	1-1		1-3	2	ECC
1982-83	Hvidovre IF, Denmark	3-3		4-1	1	ECC
	Standard Liege, Belgium	2-0		1-1	2	ECC
	Aston Villa, England	3-1		2-1	qf	ECC
	RTS Widzew Lodz, Poland	2-0		2-2	sf	ECC
	Hamburger SV, Germany	0-1	in Athens		FINAL	ECC
1983-84	Gdansk Lechia, Poland	7-0		3-2	1	CWC
	Paris St Germain, France	0-0	wag	2-2	2	CWC
	Haka Valkeakosken, Finland	1-0		1-0*	qf	CWC
				* in Strasbourg		
	Manchester United, England	2-1		1-1	sf	CWC
	FC Porto, Portugal	2-1	in Basel		FINAL	CWC
1984-85	Ilves Tampere, Finland	2-1		4-0	1	ECC
	Grasshoppers Zurich, Switzerland	2-0		4-2	2	ECC
	Sparta Prague, Czechoslovakia	3-0		0-1	qf	ECC
	Girondins Bordeaux, France	3-0		0-2	sf	ECC
	Liverpool, England	1-0	in Brussels		FINAL	ECC
1985-86	Jeunesse Esch, Luxembourg	4-1		5-0	1	ECC
	Hellas-Verona, Italy	2-0		0-0	2	ECC
	FC Barcelona, Spain	1-1		0-1	qf	ECC
1986-87	Valur Reykjavik, Iceland	7-0		4-0	1	ECC
	Real Madrid, Spain	1-0	1-3p	0-1	2	ECC
1987-88	Valletta, Malta	3-0		4-0	1	UEFA
	Panathinaikos, Greece	3-2		0-1	2	UEFA
1988-89	Otelul Galati, Romania	5-0		0-1	1	UEFA
	Atletico Bilbao, Spain	5-1		2-3	2	UEFA
	FC Liege, Belgium	1-0		1-0	3	UEFA
	Napoli, Italy	2-0		0-3 aet	qf	UEFA
1989-90	Gornik Zabrze, Poland	4-2		1-0	1	UEFA
	Paris St Germain, France	2-1		1-0	2	UEFA
	Karl Marx Stadt, East Germany	2-1		1-0	3	UEFA
	Hamburger SV, Germany	1-2		2-0	qf	UEFA
	1.FC Koln, Germany	3-2			sf	UEFA
	Fiorentina, Italy	3-1		0-0	FINAL	UEFA

197

ITALY

FIORENTINA

Founded 1913
Colours violet shirts, white shorts
Stadium Stadio Comunale (52,000) ☎ 055-572625/6/7
Champions 1956, 1969
Cup Winners 1940, 1961, 1966, 1975
ECC Finalists 1957
CWC Winners 1961 Finalists 1962
Mitropa Cup Winners 1966

Season	Opponent	Home	Result	Away	Rnd	Cup
1956-57	IFK Norrkoping, Sweden	1-1		1-0*	1	ECC
				* in Rome		
	Grasshoppers Zurich, Switzerland	3-1		2-2	qf	ECC
	Red Star Belgrade, Yugoslavia	0-0		1-0	sf	ECC
	Real Madrid, Spain	0-2	in Madrid		FINAL	ECC
1960-61	FC Luzern, Switzerland	6-2		3-0	1	CWC
	Dinamo Zagreb, Yugoslavia	3-0		1-2	sf	CWC
	Glasgow Rangers, Scotland	2-1		2-0	FINAL	CWC
1961-62	bye				1	CWC
	Rapid Vienna, Austria	3-1		6-2	2	CWC
	Dynamo Zilina, Czchoslovakia	2-0		2-3	qf	CWC
	Ujpest Dozsa, Hungary	2-0		1-0	sf	CWC
	Atletico Madrid, Spain	1-1	in Glasgow		FINAL	CWC
	Atletico Madrid, Spain	0-3	in Stuttgart		Replay	CWC
1964-65	CF Barcelona, Spain	1-0		0-2	pr	Fairs
1965-66	Red Star Belgrade, Yugoslavia	3-1		4-0	1	Fairs
	Spartak Brno, Czechoslovakia	2-0		0-4	2	Fairs
1966-67	Vasas Gyoer Eto, Hungary	1-0		2-4	pr	CWC
1967-68	OGC Nice, France	4-0		1-0	1	Fairs
	Sporting Lisbon, Portugal	1-1		1-2	2	Fairs
1968-69	Dinamo Zagreb, Yugoslavia	2-1		1-1	1	Fairs
	Hansa Rostock, East Germany	2-1	wag	2-3	2	Fairs
	Vitoria Setubal, Portugal	2-1		0-3	3	Fairs
1969-70	Osters IF Vaxjo, Sweden	1-0		2-1	1	ECC
	Dynamo Kiev, USSR	0-0		2-1	2	ECC
	Glasgow Celtic, Scotland	1-0		0-3	qf	ECC
1970-71	Ruch Chorzow, Poland	2-0		1-1	1	Fairs
	1.FC Koln, Germany	1-2		0-1	2	Fairs
1972-73	Eskisehirspor, Turkey	3-0		2-1	1	UEFA
	Vitoria Setubal, Portugal	2-1	lag	0-1	2	UEFA
1973-74	Universitatea Craiova, Romania	0-0		0-1	1	UEFA
1975-76	Besiktas, Turkey	3-0		3-0	1	CWC
	Sachsenring Zwickau, East Germany	1-0	4-5p	0-1	2	CWC
1977-78	FC Schalke 04 Gelsenkirchen, Germany	0-0	0-3*	1-2	1	UEFA
			* awarded to Schalke for Fiorentina fielding an ineligible player			
1982-83	Universitatea Craiova, Romania	1-0		1-3	1	UEFA
1984-85	Fenerbahce, Turkey	2-0		1-0	1	UEFA
	RSC Anderlecht, Belgium	1-1		2-6	2	UEFA
1986-87	Boavista, Portugal	1-0	1-3 pen	0-1	1	UEFA
1989-90	Atletico Madrid, Spain	1-0aet*	3-1p	0-1	1	UEFA
		* in Perugia				
	Sochaux, France	0-0*	wag	1-1	2	UEFA
		* in Perugia				
	Dynamo Kiev, USSR	1-0*		0-0	3	UEFA
		* in Perugia				
	AJ Auxerre, France	1-0*		1-0	qf	UEFA
		* in Perugia				
	Werder Bremen, Germany	0-0	wag	1-1	sf	UEFA
	Juventus, Italy	0-0		1-3	FINAL	UEFA

BOLOGNA

Founded 1909
Colours red and blue striped shirts, white shorts
Stadium Stadio Comunale (46,000) ☎ 051-2235 54/5
Champions 1925, 1929, 1936, 1937, 1939, 1941, 1964
Cup Winners 1970, 1974
Mitropa Cup Winners 1932, 1934, 1961

Season	Opponent	Home	Playoff Result	Away	Rnd	Cup
1964-65	RSC Anderlecht, Belgium	2-1	0-0 lot*	0-1	pr	ECC
			* in Barcelona			
1966-67	Goztepe Izmir, Turkey	3-1		2-1	1	Fairs
	Sparta Prague, Czechoslovakia	2-1		2-2	2	Fairs
	West Bromwich Albion, England	3-0		3-1	3	Fairs
	Leeds United, England	1-0	lot	0-1	qf	Fairs
1967-68	Lyn Oslo, Norway	2-0		0-0	1	Fairs
	Dinamo Zagreb, Yugoslavia	0-0		2-1	2	Fairs
	bye				3	Fairs
	Vojvodina Novi Sad, Yugoslavia	0-0		2-0	qf	Fairs
	Ferencvarosi TC, Hungary	2-2		2-3	sf	Fairs
1968-69	FC Basle, Switzerland	4-1		2-1	1	Fairs
	OFK Belgrade, Yugoslavia	1-1		0-1	2	Fairs
1970-71	FC Vorwaerts Berlin, East Germany	1-1	lag	0-0	1	CWC
1971-72	RSC Anderlecht, Belgium	1-1		2-0	1	UEFA
	Zeljeznicar Sarajevo, Yugoslavia	2-2	lag	1-1	2	UEFA
1974-75	Gwardia Warsaw, Poland	2-1	3-5p	1-2	1	CWC

TORINO

Founded 1906
Colours red shirts, white shorts
Stadium Stadio Comunale, Turin (71,000) ☎ 011-51 39 41
Champions 1927, 1928, 1943, 1946, 1947, 1948, 1949, 1976
Cup Winners 1936, 1943, 1968, 1971

Season	Opponent	Home	Playoff Result	Away	Rnd	Cup
1964-65	Fortuna Geleen 54, Holland	3-1		2-2	1	CWC
	Valkeakosken Haka, Finland	5-0		1-0	2	CWC
	Dinamo Zagreb, Yugoslavia	2-1		1-1	qf	CWC
	TSV 1860 Munich, Germany	2-0	0-2*	1-3	sf	CWC
			* in Zurich			
1965-66	Leeds United, England	0-0		1-2	1	Fairs
1968-69	Partizan Tirana, Albania	3-1		0-1	1	CWC
	bye				2	CWC
	Slovan Bratislava, Czechoslovakia	0-1		1-2	qf	CWC
1971-72	Limerick, Eire	4-0		1-0	1	CWC
	FK Austria Vienna, Austria	1-0		0-0	2	CWC
	Glasgow Rangers, Scotland	1-1		0-1	qf	CWC
1972-73	Las Palmas, Spain	2-0		0-4	1	UEFA
1973-74	1.FC Lokomotive Leipzig, East Germany	1-2		1-2	1	UEFA
1974-75	Fortuna Dusseldorf, Germany	1-1		1-3	1	UEFA
1976-77	Malmo FF, Sweden	2-1		1-1	1	ECC
	Borussia Monchengladbach, Germany	1-2		0-0	2	ECC
1977-78	Apoel Nicosia, Cyprus	3-0		1-1	1	UEFA
	Dinamo Zagreb, Yugoslavia	3-1		0-1	2	UEFA
	SEC Bastia Corsica, France	2-3		1-2	3	UEFA

ITALY

1978-79	Real Sporting Gijon, Spain	1-0		0-3	1	UEFA
1979-80	VfB Stuttgart, Germany	2-1	lag	0-1	1	UEFA
1980-81	RWD Molenbeeck, Belgium	2-2		2-1	1	UEFA
	1.FC Magdeburg, East Germany	3-1		0-1	2	UEFA
	Grasshoppers Zurich, Switzerland	2-1	3-4 pen	1-2	3	UEFA
1985-86	Panathinaikos, Greece	2-1		1-1	1	UEFA
	Hajduk Split, Yugoslavia	1-1		1-3	2	UEFA
1986-87	FC Nantes, France	1-1		4-0	1	UEFA
	Raba Vasas Eto, Hungary	4-0		1-1	2	UEFA
	SK Beveren Waas, Belgium	2-1		1-0	3	UEFA
	FC Tirol, Austria	0-0		1-2	qf	UEFA

NAPOLI

Founded 1904 as Naples, 1912 Internazionale Napoli, 1926 Associazione Calcio Napoli
Colours blue shirts, white shorts
Stadium San Paolo (82,000) ☎ 081-40 74 77
Champions 1987
Cup Winners 1962, 1976, 1987
UEFA Cup Winners 1989

Season	Opponent	Home	Playoff Result	Away	Rnd	Cup
1962-63	Bangor City, Wales	3-1	2-1*	0-2	1	CWC
			* at Arsenal			
	Ujpest Dozsa, Hungary	1-1	3-1*	1-1	2	CWC
			* in Lausanne			
	OFK Belgrade, Yugoslavia	3-1	1-3*	0-2	qf	CWC
			* in Marseille			
1966-67	Wiener Sport Club, Austria	3-1		2-1	1	Fairs
	B 1909 Odense, Denmark	2-1		4-1	2	Fairs
	Burnley, England	0-0		0-3	3	Fairs
1967-68	Hannover 96, Germany	-0		1-1	1	Fairs
	Hibernian, Scotland	4-1		0-5	2	Fairs
1968-69	Grasshoppers Zurich, Switzerland	3-1		0-1	1	Fairs
	Leeds United, England	2-0	lot	0-2	2	Fairs
1969-70	FC Metz, France	2-1		1-1	1	Fairs
	VfB Stuttgart, Germany	1-0		0-0	2	Fairs
	Ajax Amsterdam, Holland	1-0		0-4	3	Fairs
1971-72	Rapid Bucharest, Romania	1-0		0-2	1	UEFA
1974-75	Videoton Szekesfehervar, Hungary	2-0		1-1	1	UEFA
	FC Porto, Portugal	1-0		1-0	1	UEFA
	Banik Ostrava, Czechoslovakia	0-2		1-1	3	UEFA
1975-76	Torpedo Moscow, USSR	1-1		1-4	1	UEFA
1976-77	Bodo Glimt, Norway	1-0		2-0	1	CWC
	Apoel Nicosia, Cyprus	2-0		1-1	2	CWC
	Slask Wroclaw, Poland	2-0		0-0	qf	CWC
	RSC Anderlecht, Belgium	1-0		0-2	sf	CWC
1978-79	Dynamo Tbilisi, USSR	1-1		0-2	1	UEFA
1979-80	Olympiakos Piraeus, Greece	2-0		0-1	1	UEFA
	Standard Liege, Belgium	1-1		1-2	2	UEFA
1981-82	Radnicki Nis, Yugoslavia	2-2	lag	0-0	1	UEFA
1982-83	Dynamo Tbilisi, USSR	1-0	wag	1-2	1	UEFA
	1.FC Kaiserslautern, Germany	1-2		0-2	2	UEFA
1986-87	Toulouse FC, France	1-0	3-4p	0-1	1	UEFA
1987-88	Real Madrid, Spain	1-1		0-2*	1	ECC
			* played behind closed doors			
1988-89	PAOK Salonika, Greece	1-0		1-1	1	UEFA
	1.FC Lokomotive Leipzig, East Germany	2-0		1-1	2	UEFA
	Girondins Bordeaux, France	0-0		1-0	3	UEFA
	Juventus, Italy	3-0	aet	0-2	qf	UEFA
	Bayern Munich, Germany	2-0		2-2	sf	UEFA
	VfB Stuttgart, Germany	2-1		3-3	FINAL	UEFA

1989-90	Sporting Lisbon, Portugal	0-0aet	4-3p	0-0	1	UEFA
	FC Wettingen, Swiss	2-1		0-0*	2	UEFA
				* in Zurich		
	Werder Bremen, Germany	2-3		1-5	3	UEFA

AS ROMA (ASSOCIAZIONE SPORTIV)

Founded 1927 an amalgamation of Roman 1903, SC Fortitudo 1906, Alba 1911
Colours maroon shirts with yellow collars and cuffs, white shorts
Stadium Olympic (66,341) ☎ 06-57 51 51
Champions 1942, 1983
Cup Winners 1964, 1969, 1980, 1981, 1984, 1986
Fairs Cup Winners 1961
ECC Finalists 1984

Season	Opponent	Home	Playoff Result	Away	Rnd	Cup
1958-60	Hannover 96, Germany	1-1		3-1	1	Fairs
	Union St Gilloise, Belgium	1-1		0-2	2	Fairs
1960-61	Union St Gilloise, Belgium	4-1		0-0	1	Fairs
	1.FC Koln, Germany	2-0	4-1*	0-2	qf	Fairs
			* in Rome			
	Hibernian, Scotland	3-3	6-0*	2-2	sf	Fairs
			* in Rome			
	Birmingham City, England	2-0		2-2	FINAL	Fairs
1961-62	bye				1	Fairs
	Sheffield Wednesday, England	1-0		0-4	2	Fairs
1962-63	Altay Izmir, Turkey	10-1*		3-2	1	Fairs
			* in Istanbul			
	Real Zaragoza, Spain	4-2		2-1	2	Fairs
	Red Star Belgrade, Yugoslavia	3-0		0-2	qf	Fairs
	Valencia CF, Spain	1-0		0-3	sf	Fairs
1963-64	Hertha BSC Berlin, Germany	2-0		3-1	1	Fairs
	Belenenses, Portugal	1-0		2-1	2	Fairs
	1.FC Koln, Germany	3-1		0-4	qf	Fairs
1964-65	Aris Salonika, Greece	3-0		0-0	1	Fairs
	ZNK Zagreb, Yugoslavia	1-0		1-1	2	Fairs
	Ferencvarosi TC, Hungary	1-2		0-1	3	Fairs
1965-66	Chelsea, England	0-0		1-4	1	Fairs
1969-70	Ards, Ireland	3-1		0-0	1	CWC
	PSV Eindhoven, Holland	1-0	wot	0-1	2	CWC
	Goztepe Izmir, Turkey	2-0		0-0	qf	CWC
	Gornik Zabrze, Poland	2-2	1-1 *lot	1-1	sf	CWC
			* in Strasbourg			
1975-76	Dunev Russe, Bulgaria	2-0		0-1	1	UEFA
	Osters IF Vaxjo, Sweden	2-0		0-1	2	UEFA
	Clube Bruges, Belgium	0-1		0-1	3	UEFA
1980-81	Carl Zeiss Jena, East Germany	3-0		0-4	1	CWC
1981-82	Ballymena United, Ireland	4-0		2-0	1	CWC
	FC Porto, Portugal	0-0		0-2	2	CWC
1982-83	Ipswich Town, England	3-0		1-3	1	UEFA
	IFK Norrkoping, Sweden	1-0	4-2p	0-1	2	UEFA
	1.FC Koln, Germany	2-0		0-1	3	UEFA
	Benfica, Portugal	1-2		1-1	qf	UEFA
1983-84	IFK Gothenburg, Sweden	3-0		1-2	1	ECC
	CSKA Sofia, Bulgaria	1-0		1-0	2	ECC
	BFC Dynamo Berlin, East Germany	3-0		1-2	qf	ECC
	Dundee United, Scotland	3-0		0-2	sf	ECC
	Liverpool, England	1-1	2-4p	in Rome		FINAL
1984-85	Steaua Bucharest, Romania	1-0		0-0	1	CWC
	Wrexham, Wales	2-0		1-0	2	CWC
	Bayern Munich, Germany	1-2		0-2	qf	CWC
1986-87	Real Zaragoza, Spain	2-0	3-4p	0-2	1	CWC

201

ITALY

1988-89	1.FC Nurnburg, Germany	1-2		3-1	1	UEFA
	Partizan Belgrade, Yugoslavia	2-0	wag	2-4	2	UEFA
	Dynamo Dresden, East Germany	0-2		0-2	3	UEFA

SAMPDORIA

Founded 1946
Colours blue shirts with red and white rings, white shorts
Stadium Luigi Ferraris, Genoa (64,000) ☎ 010-59 37 27/56 48 80
Cup Winners 1985, 1988, 1989
Cup Winners Cup 1990 Finalists 1989

Season	Opponent	Home	Result	Away	Rnd	Cup
1962-63	Aris Bonneweg, Luxembourg	1-0		2-0	1	Fairs
	Ferencvarosi TC, Hungary	1-0		0-6	2	Fairs
1985-86	Larissa, Greece	1-0		1-1	1	CWC
	Benfica, Portugal	1-0		0-2	2	CWC
1988-89	IFK Norrkoping, Sweden	2-0		1-2	1	CWC
	Carl Zeiss Jena, East Germany	3-1		1-1	2	CWC
	Dinamo Bucharest, Romania	0-0*	wag	1-1	qf	CWC
	* in Cremona, own ground being renovated					
	KV Mechelen, Belgium	3-0		1-2	sf	CWC
	FC Barcelona, Spain	0-2	in Bern		FINAL	CWC
1989-90	SK Brann Bergen, Norway	1-0		2-0	1	CWC
	Borussia Dortmund Germany	2-0		1-1	2	CWC
	Grasshoppers Zurich, Switzerland	2-0		2-1	qf	CWC
	AS Monaco, France	2-0		2-2	sf	CWC
	Anderlecht, Belgium	2-0 aet	in Gothenburg		FINAL	CWC

ATALANTA BERGAMO

Founded 1907
Colours black and blue striped shirts, black shorts
Stadium Stadio Comunale (34,000) ☎ 035-24 25 55
Cup Winners 1963

Season	Opponent	Home	Playoff Result	Away	Rnd	Cup
1963-64	Sporting Lisbon, Portugal	2-0	1-3	1-3	1	CWC
1987-88	Merthyr Tydfil, Wales	2-0		1-2	1	CWC
	OFI Crete, Greece	2-0		0-1	2	CWC
	Sporting Lisbon, Portugal	2-0		1-1	qf	CWC
	KV Mechelen, Belgium	1-2		1-2	sf	CWC
1989-90	Spartak Moscow, USSR	0-0		0-2	1	UEFA

CAGLIARI

Founded 1920
Colours red and blue shirts, white shorts
Stadium Stadio Ansicora, Sardinia (16,000) ☎ 070-48 93 75
Champions 1970

Season	Opponent	Home	Result	Away	Rnd	Cup
1969-70	Aris Salonika, Greece	3-0*		1-1	1	Fairs
	* abandoned after 80 minutes, Aris and police fighting					
	Carl Zeiss Jena, East Germany	0-1		0-2	2	Fairs
1970-71	St Etienne, France	3-0		0-1	1	ECC
	Atletico Madrid, Spain	2-1		0-3	2	ECC
1972-73	Olympiakos Piraeus, Greece	0-1		1-2	1	UEFA

ITALY

CESENA

Founded 1940
Colours white shirts, black shorts
Stadium Dino Manuzzi (30,000) ☎ 0547-21511

Season	Opponent	Home	Result	Away	Rnd	Cup
1976-77	1.FC Magdeburg, East Germany	3-1		0-3	1	UEFA

PERUGIA

Founded 1905
Colours red shirts, white shorts
Stadium Renato Curi (40,000) ☎ 075-71 641/2

Season	Opponent	Home	Result	Away	Rnd	Cup
1979-80	Dinamo Zagreb, Yugoslavia	1-0		0-0	1	UEFA
	Aris Salonika, Greece	0-3		1-1	2	UEFA

HELLAS VERONA

Founded 1903
Colours all sky blue
Stadium Marc'Antonio Bentegodi (36,000) ☎ 045-56 40 63
Champions 1985

Season	Opponent	Home	Result	Away	Rnd	Cup
1983-84	Red Star Belgrade, Yugoslavia	1-0		3-2	1	UEFA
	Sturm Graz, Austria	2-2	lag	0-0	2	UEFA
1985-86	PAOK Salonika, Greece	3-1		2-1	1	ECC
	Juventus, Italy	0-0		0-2	2	ECC
1987-88	Pogon Szezecin, Poland	3-1		1-1	1	UEFA
	FC Utrecht, Holland	2-1		1-1	2	UEFA
	Sportul Studentesc Bucharest, Romania	3-1		1-0	3	UEFA
	Werder Bremen, Germany	0-1		1-1	qf	UEFA

LAZIO

Founded 1900
Colours sky blue and white striped shirts, white shorts
Stadium Olympic (66,341) ☎ 06-67 81 843
Champions 1974
Cup Winners 1958

Season	Opponent	Home	Result	Away	Rnd	Cup
1970-71	Arsenal, England	2-2		0-2	1	Fairs
1973-74	FC Sion, Switzerland	3-0		1-3	1	UEFA
	Ipswich Town, England	4-2		0-4	2	UEFA
1975-76	Chernomoreiz Odessa, USSR	3-0		0-1	1	UEFA
	FC Barcelona, Spain	walk over*		0-4	2	UEFA
	* game awarded to Barcelona					
1977-78	Boavista, Portugal	5-0		0-1	1	UEFA
	RC Lens, France	2-0		0-6	2	UEFA

ITALY

LANEROSSI VICENZA

Founded 1902
Colours red and white striped shirts, white shorts
Stadium Romeo Menti (30,000) ☎ 0444-50 50 44

Season	Opponents	Home	Result	Away	Rnd	Cup
1978-79	Dukla Prague, Czechoslovakia	1-1		0-1	1	UEFA

Betzenberg, Kaiserslautern, Germany. 1st FC Kaiserlautern

LIECHTENSTEIN

Founded 1933
Liechtensteiner Fussballverband, Postfach 165, 9490 Vaduz ☎ 66 251
National colours blue shirts, red shorts, blue socks
Language German, English, French
The clubs play in the Swiss league

CUP WINNERS

1946	Triesen v Vaduz	3-1
1947	Triesen v Vaduz	2-0
1948	Triesen v Vaduz	4-2 aet
1949	Vaduz v Triesen	2-2 2-1 aet
1950	Triesen v Vaduz	3-2
1951	Triesen v Vaduz	3-1
1952	Vaduz v Triesen	2-0
1953	Vaduz v Triesen	4-2
1954	Vaduz v Triesen	1-0
1955	Schaan v Vaduz	1-0
1956	Vaduz v Schaan	4-1
1957	Vaduz v Schaan	4-0
1958	Vaduz v Triersen	2-0
1959	Vaduz v Triesen	3-0
1960	Vaduz v Schaan	3-2
1961	Vaduz v Schaan	3-0
1962	Vaduz v Schaan	4-0
1963	Schaan v Ruggell	3-1
1964	Balzers v Triesen	1-0
1965	Triesen v Schaan	4-3
1966	Vaduz v Schaan	7-0
1967	Vaduz v Triesen	2-1 aet
1968	Vaduz v Triesen	4-2
1969	Vaduz v Triesen	1-0

1970	Vaduz v Schaan	2-1
1971	Vaduz v Schaan	4-2
1972	Triesen v Vaduz	2-1
1973	Balzers v Ruggell	2-1
1974	Vaduz v Balzers	2-2 4-3p
1975	Triesen v Balzers	5-2
1976	USV Eschen/Mauren v Balzers	3-1
1977	USV Eschen/Mauren v Vaduz	0-0 4-2p
1978	USV Eschen/Mauren v Ruggell	3-1
1979	Balzers v USV Eschen/Mauren	3-1
1980	Vaduz v Balzers	1-1 4-2p
1981	Balzers v Ruggell	3-0 aet
1982	Balzers v USV Eschen/Mauren	5-0
1983	Balzers v USV Eschen/Mauren	1-1 5-3p
1984	Balzers v Vaduz	2-0
1985	Vaduz v USV Eschen/Mauren	5-0
1986	Vaduz v Balzers	2-0
1987	USV Eschen/Mauren v Vaduz	1-0
1988	Vaduz v USV Eschen/Mauren	2-0
1989	Balzers v USV Eschea/Mauren	4-2

LUXEMBOURG

Founded 1908
Federation Luxembourgeoise de Football, 50 Rue De Strasbourg, L-2560 Luxembourg ☎ 48 8665
National colours red shirts, white shorts, blue socks
Season August to June

LEAGUE CHAMPIONS

L=Luxembourg

1910 Racing L	1930 Fola Esch	1954 Jeunesse Esch	1973 Jeunesse Esch
1911 Sporting L	1931 Red Boys Differdange	1955 Stade Dudelingen	1974 Jeunesse Esch
1912 US Hollerich	1932 Red Boys Differdange	1956 Spora L	1975 Jeunesse Esch
1913 not held	1933 Red Boys Differdange	1957 Stade Dudelingen	1976 Jeunesse Esch
1914 US Hollerich	1934 Spora L	1958 Jeunesse Esch	1977 Jeunesse Esch
1915 US Hollerich	1935 Spora L	1959 Jeunesse Esch	1978 Progres Niedercorn
1916 US Hollerich	1936 Spora L		1979 Red Boys Differdange
1917 US Hollerich	1937 Jeunesse Esch	1960 Jeunesse Esch	
1918 Fola Esch	1938 Spora L	1961 Spora L	1980 Jeunesse Esch
1919 SCL	1939 Stade Dudelingen	1962 USL	1981 Progres Niedercorn
		1963 Jeunesse Esch	1982 Avenir Beggen
1920 Fola Esch	1940 Stade Dudelingen	1964 Aris Bonneweg	1983 Jeunesse Esch
1921 Jeunesse Esch	1946 Stade Dudelingen	1965 Stade Dudelingen	1984 Avenir Beggen
1922 Fola Esch	1947 Stade Dudelingen	1966 Aris Bonneweg	1985 Jeunesse Esch
1923 Red Boys Differdange	1948 Stade Dudelingen	1967 Jeunesse Esch	1986 Avenir Beggen
1924 Fola Esch	1949 Spora L	1968 Jeunesse Esch	1987 Jeunesse Esch
1925 Spora L		1969 Avenir Beggen	1988 Jeunesse Esch
1926 Red Boys Differdange	1950 Stade Dudelingen	1970 Jeunesse Esch	1989 Spora L
1927 US Hollerich	1951 Jeunesse Esch		
1928 Spora L	1952 The National	1971 Union L	
1929 Spora L	1953 Progres Niedercorn	1972 Aris Bonneweg	

CUP WINNERS

1922 Racing L v Jeunesse Esch	2-0	
1923 Fola Esch v US Hollerich	3-0	
1924 Fola Esch v Red Boys Differdange	2-0	
1925 Red Boys Differdange v Spora L	1-1 3-0	
1926 Red Boys Differdange v US Hollerich	5-2	
1927 Red Boys Differdange v Jeunesse Esch	3-2	
1928 Spora L v Stade Dudelingen	2-2 3-3 5-2	
1929 Red Boys Differdange v Spora L	5-3	
1930 Red Boys Differdange v Spora L	2-1	
1931 Red Boys Differdange v Spora L	5-3	

1932 Spora L v Red Boys Differdange	2-1	
1933 Progres Niedercorn v Union L	4-1	
1934 Red Boys Differdange v Spora L	5-2	
1935 Jeunesse Esch v Red Boys Differdange	4-2	
1936 Red Boys Differdange v Stade Dudelingen	2-0	
1937 Jeunesse Esch v Union L	3-0	
1938 Stade Dudelingen v The National	1-0	
1939 US Dudelingen v Stade Dudelingen	2-1	
1940 Spora L v Stade Dudelingen	6-2	
1945 Progres Niedercorn v Spora L	2-0	

Year	Match	Result		Year	Match	Result
1946	Jeunesse Esch v Progres Niedercorn	3-1		1968	US Rumelingen v Aris Bonneweg	0-0 1-0
1947	Union L v Stade Dudelingen	2-1		1969	Union L v Alliance Dudelingen	5-2
1948	Stade Dudelingen v Red Boys Differdange	1-0				
1949	Stade Dudelingen v Racing Rodange	1-0		1970	Union L v Red Boys Differdange	1-0
				1971	Jeunesse Hautcharage v Jeunesse Esch	4-1
1950	Spora L v Red Boys Differdange	5-1		1972	Red Boys Differdange v Aris Bonneweg	4-3
1951	Sport C Tetange v CS Grevenmacher	1-1 2-0		1973	Jeunesse Esch v Fola Esch	3-2
1952	Red Boys Differdange v Red Star Merl	1-0		1974	Jeunesse Esch v Avenir Beggen	4-1
1953	Red Boys Differdange v CS Grevenmacher	2-1		1975	US Rumelange v Jeunesse Esch	2-0
1954	Jeunesse Esch v CS Grevenmacher	5-0		1976	Jeunesse Esch v Aris Bonneweg	2-1
1955	Fola Esch v Red Boys Differdange	1-1 4-1		1977	Progres Niedercorn v Red Boys Diff	4-4 3-1
1956	Stade Dudelingen v Progres Niedercorn	3-1		1978	Progres Niedercorn v Union L	2-1
1957	Spora L v Stade Dudelingen	2-1		1979	Red Boys Differdange v Aris Bonneweg	4-1
1958	Red Boys Differdange v US Dudelingen	3-1				
1959	Union L v CS Grevenmacher	3-1		1980	Spora L v Progres Niedercorn	3-2
1960	The National v Stade Dudelange	3-0		1981	Jeunesse Esch v Eischen Olympique	5-0
1961	Alliance Dudelingen v Union L	3-2		1982	Red Boys Differdange v US Rumelange	2-1
1962	Alliance Dudelingen v Union L	1-0		1983	Avenir Beggen v US Luxembourg	4-2
1963	Union L v Spora L	2-1		1984	Avenir Beggen v US Rumelange	4-1
1964	Union L v Aris Bonneweg	1-0		1985	Red Boys Differdange v Jeunesse Esch	1-0
1965	Spora L v Jeunesse Esch	1-0		1986	US Luxembourg v Red Boys Differdange	4-1
1966	Spora L v Jeunesse Esch	2-0		1987	Avenir Beggen v Spora L	6-0
1967	Aris Bonneweg v Union L	1-0		1988	Jeunesse Esch v Avenir Beggen	1-0
				1989	US Luxembourg v Avenir Beggen	2-0

FEATURED CLUBS IN EUROPEAN COMPETITION

Union Sportive (USL)	**CA Spora**	**Stade Dudelingen**	**Alliance Dudelange**
Jeunesse Esch	**Aris Bonneweg**	**Red Boys Differdange**	**Union Sportive Rumelingen**
Progres Niedercorn	**Fola Esch**	**Avenir Beggen**	**Jeunesse Hautcharage**

USL (UNION SPORTIVE LUXEMBOURG)

Founded 1908 by merger of Juenesse Verlorenkost and US Hollerich
Colours white shirts with blue facings, blue shorts
Stadium Achille Hammerel (6,000) ☎ 49 35 48
Champions 1962, 1971
Cup Winners 1963, 1964, 1969, 1970, 1986, 1989

Season	Opponent	Home	Result	Away	Rnd	Cup
1962-63	AC Milan, Italy	0-6		0-8	1	ECC
1963-64	Hamburger SV, Germany	2-3		0-4	1	CWC
1964-65	TSV 1860 Munich, Germany	0-4		0-6	pr	CWC
1965-66	1.FC Koln, Germany	0-4		0-13	1	Fairs
1966-67	Royal Antwerp, Belgium	0-1		0-1	1	Fairs
1968-69	withdrew				1	Fairs
1969-70	Goztepe Izmir, Turkey	2-3		0-3	1	CWC
1970-71	Goztepe Izmir, Turkey	1-0		0-5	1	CWC
1971-72	Valencia CF, Spain	0-1		1-3	pr	ECC
1973-74	Olympique Marseille, France	0-5		1-7	1	UEFA
1978-79	Bodo Glimt, Norway	1-0		1-4	1	CWC
1984-85	Trakia Plovdiv, Bulgaria	1-1		0-4	1	CWC
1986-87	Olympiakos Piraeus, Greece	0-3		0-3	1	CWC
1988-89	RFC Liege, Belgium	1-7		0-4	1	UEFA
1989-90	Djurgarden IF Stockholm, Sweden	0-0		0-5	1	CWC

LUXEMBOURG

CA SPORA

Founded 1923 by merger of Sporting Club Luxembourg and Racing Club
Colours blue shirts with thick yellow band, yellow shorts
Stadium Municipal D'Arlon (14,000) ☎ 4993-292
Champions 1925, 1928, 1929, 1934, 1935, 1936, 1938, 1949, 1956, 1961, 1989
Cup Winners 1965, 1966, 1980

Season	Opponent	Home	Playoff Result	Away	Rnd	Cup
1956-57	Borussia Dortmund, Germany	2-1	0-7*	3-4	pr	ECC
			* in Dortmund			
1961-62	B 1913 Odense, Denmark	0-6		2-9	pr	ECC
1964-65	FC Basle, Switzerland	1-0		0-2	1	Fairs
1965-66	1.FC Magdeburg, East Germany	0-2		0-1	1	CWC
1966-67	Shamrock Rovers, Eire	1-4		1-4	pr	CWC
1967-68	Leeds United, England	0-9		0-7	1	Fairs
1980-81	Sparta Prague, Czechoslovakia	0-6		0-6	1	CWC
1987-88	Feyenoord Rotterdam, Holland	2-5		0-5	1	UEFA
	Real Madrid, Spain	0-3*		0-6	1	ECC
		in Saarbrucken				

STADE DUDELINGEN (CERCLE SPORTIF)

Founded 1913 by merger of Sparta and Fleurus Dudelange
Colours white shirts, black shorts
Stadium Aloyse-Meyer 51 51 51
Champions 1939, 1940, 1946, 1947, 1948, 1950, 1955, 1957, 1965

Season	Opponent	Home	Result	Away	Rnd	Cup
1957-58	Red Star Belgrade, Yugoslavia	0-5		1-9	pr	ECC
1965-66	Benfica, Portugal	0-8		0-10	pr	ECC

ALLIANCE DUDELANGE (CERCLE SPORTIF)

Founded 1916
Colours
Stadium Amadeo Barozzi (3,000) ☎ 51 81 86
Cup Winners 1961, 1962

Season	Opponent	Home	Result	Away	Rnd	Cup
1961-62	bye				1	
1961-62	Motor Jena, East Germany	2-2		0-7	2	CWC
1962-63	B 1909 Odense, Denmark	1-1		1-8	1	CWC

JEUNESSE ESCH

Founded 1907
Colours black and white striped shirts, white shorts
Stadium dela Frontiere (7,000) ☎ 547 383/260
Champions 1921, 1937, 1951, 1954, 1958, 1959, 1960, 1963, 1967, 1968, 1970, 1973, 1974, 1975, 1976, 1977, 1980, 1983, 1985, 1987, 1988
Cup Winners 1973, 1974, 1976, 1981, 1988

Season	Opponent	Home	Playoff Result	Away	Rnd	Cup
1958-59	IFK Gothenburg, Sweden	1-2	1-5*	1-0*	pr	ECC
			* both in Gothenburg			
1959-60	LKS Lodz, Poland	5-0		1-2	pr	ECC
	Real Madrid, Spain	2-5		0-7	1	ECC
1960-61	Stade de Reims, France	0-5		1-6	1	ECC
1963-64	Valkeakoski Haka, Finland	4-0		1-4	1	ECC
	Partizan Belgrade, Yugoslavia	2-1		2-6	2	ECC
1967-68	Valur Reykjavik, Iceland	3-3	lag	1-1	1	ECC
1968-69	AEK Athens, Greece	3-2		0-3	1	ECC
1969-70	Coleraine, Ireland	3-2		0-4	1	Fairs
1970-71	Panathinaikos, Greece	1-2		0-5	1	ECC
1973-74	Liverpool, England	1-1		0-2	1	ECC
1974-75	Fenerbahce, Turkey	2-3		0-2	1	ECC
1975-76	Bayern Munich, Germany	0-5*		0-3	1	ECC
		* in Luxembourg				
1976-77	Ferencvarosi TC, Hungary	2-6		1-5	1	ECC
1977-78	Glasgow Celtic, Scotland	1-6		0-5	1	ECC
1978-79	Lausanne Sport, Switzerland	0-0		0-2	1	UEFA
1980-81	Spartak Moscow, USSR	0-5		0-4	1	ECC
1981-82	Velez Mostar, Yugoslavia	1-1		1-6	1	CWC
1983-84	BFC Dynamo Berlin, East Germany	0-2		1-4	1	ECC
1985-86	Juventus, Italy	0-5		1-4	1	ECC
1986-87	AA Ghent, Belgium	1-2		1-1	1	UEFA
1987-88	AGF Aarhus, Denmark	1-0		1-4	1	ECC
1988-89	Gornik Zabrze, Poland	1-4		0-3	1	ECC
1989-90	Sochaux, France	0-5		0-7	1	UEFA

ARIS BONNEWEG (BONNEVOIE)

Founded 1922
Colours black shorts
Stadium Camille-Polfer (3,000) ☎ 43 10 14
Champions 1964, 1966, 1972
Cup Winners 1967

Season	Opponent	Home	Result	Away	Rnd	Cup
1962-63	Sampdoria, Italy	0-2		0-1	pr	Fairs
1963-64	RFC Liege, Belgium	0-2		0-0	1	Fairs
1964-65	Benfica, Portugal	1-5		1-5	pr	ECC
1966-67	Linfield, Ireland	3-3		1-6	pr	ECC
1967-68	Olympique Lyon, France	0-3		1-2	1	CWC
1971-72	FC Den Haag, Holland	2-2		0-5	1	UEFA
1972-73	FC Arges Pitiesti, Romania	0-2		0-4	1	ECC
1976-77	Carrick Rangers, Ireland	2-1		1-3	1	CWC
1979-80	Reipas Lahti, Finland	1-0		1-0	1	CWC
	FC Barcelona, Spain	1-4		1-7	2	CWC
1983-84	FK Austria Vienna, Austria	0-5		0-10	1	UEFA

LUXEMBOURG

RED BOYS DIFFERDANGE

Founded 1907
Colours red shirts, white shorts
Stadium Thillenburg (6,000) ☎ 586 648
Champions 1923, 1926, 1931, 1932, 1933, 1979
Cup Winners 1972, 1979, 1982, 1985

Season	Opponent	Home	Result	Away	Rnd	Cup
1972-73	AC Milan, Italy	1-4		0-3	1	CWC
1974-75	Olympique Lyon, France	1-4		0-7	1	UEFA
1976-77	KSC Lokeren, Belgium	0-3		1-3	1	UEFA
1977-78	AZ 67 Alkmaar, Holland	0-5		1-11	1	UEFA
1979-80	Omonia Nicosia, Cyprus	2-1		1-6	1	ECC
1980-81	AZ 67 Alkmaar, Holland	0-4		0-6	1	UEFA
1981-82	Sporting Lisbon, Portugal	0-7		0-4	1	UEFA
1982-83	Waterschei Thor Genk, Belgium	0-1		1-7	1	CWC
1984-85	Ajax Amsterdam, Holland	0-0		0-14	1	UEFA
1985-86	AIK Stockholm, Sweden	0-5		0-8	1	CWC

UNION SPORTIVE RUMELINGEN

Founded 1908
Colours blue shirts, white shorts
Stadium Municipal Kolscheid (3,000) ☎ 56 54 71
Cup Winners 1968, 1975

Season	Opponent	Home	Result	Away	Rnd	Cup
1968-69	Sliema Wanderers, Malta	2-1	lag	0-1	1	CWC
1970-71	Juventus, Italy	0-4		0-7	1	Fairs
1972-73	Feyenoord Rotterdam, Holland	0-12		0-9	1	UEFA
1975-76	Borac Banja Luka, Yugoslavia	1-5*		0-9	1	CWC
		* in Esch				

PROGRES NIEDERCORN

Founded 1919
Colours yellow shirts, black shorts
Stadium Jos-Hauport (3,200) ☎ 501 960
Champions 1953, 1978, 1981
Cup Winners 1977, 1978

Season	Opponent	Home	Result	Away	Rnd	Cup
1977-78	Vejle BK, Denmark	0-1		0-9	1	CWC
1978-79	Real Madrid, Spain	0-7		0-5	1	ECC
1979-80	Grasshoppers Zurich, Switzerland	0-2		0-4	1	UEFA
1981-82	Glentoran, Ireland	1-1		0-4	1	ECC
1982-83	Servette Geneva, Switzerland	0-1		0-3	1	UEFA

C.S. FOLA ESCH

Fola=Football and Lawntennis Club
Founded 1906
Colours red shirts, white shorts
Stadium Emile Mayrisch ☎ 5 25 97
Champions 1918, 1920, 1922, 1924, 1930

Season	Opponent	Home	Result	Away	Rnd	Cup
1973-74	Beroe Stara Zagora, Bulgaria	1-4		0-7	1	CWC

AVENIR BEGGEN

Founded 1915
Colours yellow shirts, black shorts
Stadium Emile Metz Taesch (4,800) ☎ 4794-473
Champions 1969, 1982, 1984, 1986
Cup Winners 1983, 1984, 1987

Season	Opponent	Home	Result	Away	Rnd	Cup
1969-70	AC Milan, Italy	0-3		0-5	1	ECC
1974-75	Paralimni Famagusta, Cyprus	walk over			pr	CWC
	Red Star Belgrade, Yugoslavia	1-6		1-5	1	CWC
1975-76	FC Porto, Portugal	0-3		0-7	1	UEFA
1982-83	Rapid Vienna, Austria	0-5		0-8	1	ECC
1983-84	Servette Geneva, Switzerland	1-5		0-4	1	CWC
1984-85	IFK Gothenburg, Sweden	0-8		0-9	1	ECC
1985-86	PSV Eindhoven, Holland	0-2		0-4	1	UEFA
1986-87	FK Austria Vienna, Austria	0-3		0-3	1	ECC
1987-88	Hamburger SV, Germany	0-5		0-3	1	CWC
1988-89	KV Mechelen, Belgium	1-3		0-5	1	CWC

FC JEUNESSE HAUTCHARAGE

Founded 1919
Colours white shirts, dark blue shorts
Stadium Stade du FC Jeunesse Hautcharage ☎ 50 05 32
Cup Winners 1971

Season	Opponent	Home	Result	Away	Rnd	Cup
1971-72	Chelsea, England	0-8		0-13	1	CWC

MALTA

Founded 1900
Malta Football Association, 280 St Paul's Street, Valletta ☎ 22697-605794 Fax 60 51 37
National colours red shirts, white shorts, red socks
Season August to June

LEAGUE CHAMPIONS

1910 Floriana	**1930** Sliema Wanderers	**1953** Floriana	**1970** Floriana
1911 not held	**1931** Floriana	**1954** Sliema Wanderers	**1971** Sliema Wanderers
1912 Floriana	**1932** Valletta United	**1955** Floriana	**1972** Sliema Wanderers
1913 Floriana	**1933** Sliema Wanderers	**1956** Sliema Wanderers	**1973** Floriana
1914 Hamrun Spartans	**1934** Sliema Wanderers	**1957** Sliema Wanderers	**1974** Valletta
1915 Valletta United	**1935** Floriana	**1958** Floriana	**1975** Floriana
1917 St Georges	**1936** Sliema Wanderers	**1959** Valletta	**1976** Sliema Wanderers
1918 Hamrun Spartans	**1937** Floriana		**1977** Floriana
1919 Komr Milizia	**1938** Sliema Wanderers	**1960** Valletta	**1978** Valletta
	1939 Sliema Wanderers	**1961** Hibernians	**1979** Hibernians
1920 Sliema Wanderers		**1962** Floriana	
1921 Floriana	**1940** Sliema Wanderers	**1963** Valletta	**1980** Valletta
1922 Floriana	**1945** Valletta	**1964** Sliema Wanderers	**1981** Hibernians
1923 Sliema Wanderers	**1946** Valletta	**1965** Sliema Wanderers	**1982** Hibernians
1924 Sliema Wanderers	**1947** Hamrun Spartan	**1966** Sliema Wanderers	**1983** Hamrun Spartans
1925 Floriana	**1948** Valletta	**1967** Hibernians	**1984** Valletta
1926 Sliema Wanderers	**1949** Sliema Wanderers	**1968** Floriana	**1985** Rabat Ajax
1927 Floriana		**1969** Hibernians	**1986** Rabat Ajax
1928 Floriana	**1950** Floriana		**1987** Hamrun Spartans
1929 Floriana	**1951** Floriana		**1988** Hamrun Spartans
	1952 Floriana		**1989** Sliema Wanderers

TROPHY WINNERS

1935 Sliema Wanderers v Floriana	4-0	
1936 Sliema Wanderers v Floriana	2-1	
1937 Sliema Wanderers v St Gerrge's	2-1	
1938 Floriana v Sliema Wanderers	2-1	
1939 Melita St Julians v Sliema Wanderers	4-0	
1940 Sliema Wanderers v Melita St Julions	3-2	
1945 Floriana v Sliema Wanderers	2-1	
1946 Sliema Wanderers v Hamrun Liberty	2-1	
1947 Floriana v Valletta	3-0	
1948 Sliema Wanderers v Hibernians	2-2 1-0	

1949 Floriana v Sliema Wanderers	5-1	
1950 Floriana v St George's	3-1	
1951 Sliema Wanderers v Hibernians	5-0	
1952 Sliema Wanderers v Hibernians	3-3 1-1 1-0	
1953 Floriana v Sliema Wanderers	1-0	
1954 Floriana v Rabat	5-1	
1955 Floriana v Sliema Wanderers	1-0	
1956 Sliema Wanderers v Floriana	1-0	
1957 Floriana v Valletta	2-0	
1958 Floriana v Sliema Wanderers	2-0	

1959	Sliema Wanderers v Valletta	1-1 1-0	**1974**	Sliema Wanderers v Floriana	1-0
			1975	Valletta v Hibernians	1-0
1960	Valletta v Floriana	3-0	**1976**	Floriana v Valletta	2-0 abd 86 mins
1961	Floriana v Hibernians	2-0	**1977**	Valletta v Floriana	1-0
1962	Hibernians v Valletta	1-0	**1978**	Valletta v Floriana	3-2
1963	Sliema Wanderers v Hibernians	2-0	**1979**	Sliema Wanderers v Floriana	2-1
1964	Valletta v Sliema Wanderers	1-0			
1965	Sliema Wanderers v Floriana	4-2	**1980**	Hibernians v Sliema Wanderers	2-1
1966	Floriana v Hibernians	2-1	**1981**	Floriana v Senglea	2-1
1967	Floriana v Hibernians	1-0	**1982**	Hibernians v Sliema Wanderers	2-0
1968	Sliema Wanderers v Hibernians	3-2 aet	**1983**	Hamrun Spartans v Valletta	2-0
1969	Sliema Wanderers v Hamrun Spartans	3-1	**1984**	Hamrun Spartans v Zurrieq	0-0 1-0 aet
			1985	Zurrieq v Valletta	0-0 2-1
1970	Hibernians v Valletta	1-1 2-1	**1986**	Rabat Ajax v Zurrieq	2-0
1971	Hibernians v Sliema Wanderers	1-1 2-0	**1987**	Hamrun Spartans v Sliema Wanderers	2-1
1972	Floriana v Sliema Wanderers	3-1	**1988**	Hamrun Spartans v Floriana	4-2
1973	Gzira United v Birkirkara	0-0 0-0 2-0 aet	**1989**	Hamrun Spartans v Floriana	1-0

INDEPENDENCE CUP

For League Champions & Trophy Winners

1965	Sliema Wanderers	**From here included UEFA**		**1974**	Sliema Wanderers	**1980**	Valletta
1966	not held	**Cup representative**		**1975**	Valletta	**1981**	Valletta & Hibernians
1967	Floriana	**1970**	Sliema Wanderers	**1976**	Floriana	**1982**	Sliema Wanderers
1968	Hibernians	**1971**	Hibernians	**1977**	Floriana		
1969	Floriana	**1972**	Sliema Wanderers	**1978**	Floriana		
		1973	Floriana	**1979**	Floriana		

EURO CUP WINNERS

Replaced Independence Cup

1983	Sliema Wanderers	1987	Rabat Ajax
1984	Valletta	1988	Sliema Wanderers &
1985	Rabat Ajax		Valletta
1986	Hamrun Spartans		

ROTHMANS SUPER CUP

1985	Rabat Ajax	
1986	Rabat Ajax	
1987	Hamrun Spartans	
1988	Hamrun Spartans v Sliema Wanderers	1-0 aet

MALTA

FEATURED CLUBS IN EUROPEAN COMPETITION

Floriana
Marsa
Rabat Ajax

Sliema Wanderers
Gzira United

Hibernians Paola
Hamrun Spartans

Valletta
Zurrieq

FLORIANA

Founded 1900
Colours green and white striped shirts
Stadium Ta 'Qali (40,000) all the islands teams play at this ground ☎ 228 664
Champions 1910, 1912, 1913, 1921, 1922, 1925, 1927, 1928, 1929, 1931, 1935, 1937, 1950, 1951, 1952, 1953, 1955, 1958, 1962, 1968, 1970, 1973, 1975, 1977
Trophy Winners 1938, 1945, 1947, 1949, 1950, 1953, 1954, 1955, 1957, 1958, 1961, 1966, 1967, 1972, 1976, 1981

Season	Opponent	Home	Result	Away	Rnd	Cup
1961-62	Ujpest Dozsa, Hungary	2-5		2-10	pr	CWC
1962-63	Ipswich Town, England	1-4		0-10	pr	ECC
1965-66	Borussia Dortmund, Germany	1-5		0-8	1	CWC
1966-67	Sparta Rotterdam, Holland	1-1		0-6	pr	CWC
1967-68	NAC Breda, Holland	1-2		0-1	1	CWC
1968-69	Reipas Lahti, Finland	1-1		0-2	1	ECC
1969-70	Dynamo Bacau, Romania	0-1		0-6	1	Fairs
1970-71	Sporting Lisbon, Portugal	0-4		0-5	1	ECC
1972-73	Ferencvarosi TC, Hungary	1-0		0-6	1	CWC
1973-74	Clube Bruges, Belgium	0-2		0-8	1	ECC
1975-76	Hajduk Split, Yugoslavia	0-5		0-3	1	ECC
1976-77	Slask Wroclaw, Poland	1-4		0-2	1	CWC
1977-78	Panathinaikos, Greece	1-1		0-4	1	ECC
1978-79	Inter Milan, Italy	1-3		0-5	1	CWC
1981-82	Standard Liege, Belgium	1-3		0-9	1	CWC
1988-89	Dundee United, Scotland	0-0		0-1	1	CWC

SLIEMA WANDERERS

Founded 1902, 1939 amalgamated with Sliema Rangers under Sliema Wanderers
Colours sky blue shirts, blue shorts
☎ 332 033
Champions 1920, 1923, 1924, 1926, 1930, 1933, 1934, 1936, 1938, 1939, 1940, 1949, 1954, 1956, 1957, 1964, 1965, 1966, 1971, 1972, 1976, 1989
Trophy Winners 1935, 1936, 1937, 1940, 1946, 1948, 1951, 1952, 1956, 1959, 1963, 1965, 1968, 1969, 1974, 1979

Season	Opponent	Home	Result	Away	Rnd	Cup
1963-64	Borough United, Wales	0-0		0-2	pr	CWC
1964-65	Dinamo Bucharest, Romania	0-2		0-5	1	ECC
1965-66	Panathinaikos, Greece	1-0		1-4	pr	ECC
1966-67	CSKA Sofia, Bulgaria	1-2		0-4	pr	ECC
1968-69	US Rumelingen, Luxembourg	1-0	wag	1-2	1	CWC
	Randers Freja, Denmark	0-2		0-6	2	CWC
1969-70	IFK Norrkoping, Sweden	1-0		1-5	1	CWC
1970-71	Akadamist Copenhagen, Denmark	2-3		0-7	1	Fairs
1971-72	IA Akranes, Iceland	4-0		0-0*	1	ECC
				* in Malta		
	Glasgow Celtic, Scotland	1-2		0-5	2	ECC
1972-73	Gornik Zabrze, Poland	0-5		0-5	1	ECC
1973-74	Lokomotiv Plovdiv, Bulgaria	0-2		0-1	1	UEFA
1974-75	Reipas Lahti, Finland	2-0		1-4	1	CWC
1975-76	Sporting Lisbon, Portugal	1-2		1-3	1	UEFA
1976-77	TPS Turun Palloseura Turku, Finland	2-1	lag	0-1	1	ECC

1977-78	Eintracht Frankfurt, Germany	0-0	0-5	1	UEFA
1979-80	Boavista, Portugal	2-1	0-8	1	CWC
1980-81	FC Barcelona, Spain	0-2	0-1	1	UEFA
1981-82	Aris Salonika, Greece	2-4	0-4	1	UEFA
1982-83	Swansea City, Wales	0-5	0-12	1	CWC
1987-88	Vlaznia Skhodar, Albania	0-4	0-2	1	CWC
1988-89	Victoria Bucharest, Romania	0-2	1-6	1	UEFA
1989-90	17 Nentori Tirana, Albania	1-0	0-5	1	ECC

HIBERNIANS Paola

Founded 1932
Colours white shirts, black shorts
☎ 828 416
Champions 1961, 1967, 1969, 1979, 1981, 1982
Trophy Winners 1962, 1970, 1971, 1980, 1982

Season	Opponent	Home	Result	Away	Rnd	Cup
1961-62	Servette Geneva, Switzerland	1-2		0-5	pr	ECC
1962-63	Olympiakos Piraeus, Greece	withdrew			1	CWC
	Atletico Madrid, Spain	0-1		0-4	2	CWC
1967-68	Manchester United, England	0-0		0-4	1	ECC
1968-69	Aris Salonika, Greece	0-6		0-1	1	Fairs
1969-70	Spartak Trnava, Czechoslovakia	2-2		0-4	1	ECC
1970-71	Real Madrid, Spain	0-0		0-5	1	CWC
1971-72	Fram Reykjavik, Iceland	0-2		*3-0	pr	CWC
				* in Malta		
	Steaua Bucharest, Romania	0-0		0-1	1	CWC
1974-75	FC Amsterdam, Holland	0-5*		0-7	1	UEFA
		* in Amsterdam				
1976-77	Grasshoppers Zurich, Switzerland	0-2		0-7	1	UEFA
1978-79	Sporting Braga, Portugal	3-2		0-5	1	UEFA
1979-80	Dundalk, Eire	1-0		0-2	1	ECC
1980-81	Waterford, Eire	1-0		0-4	1	CWC
1981-82	Red Star Belgrade, Yugoslavia	1-2		1-8	1	ECC
1982-83	Widzew Lodz, Poland	1-4		1-3	1	ECC
1986-87	Trakia Plovdiv, Bulgaria	0-2		0-8	1	UEFA

VALLETTA

Founded 1910
Colours all white
☎ 224 939
Champions 1915, 1932, 1945, 1946, 1948, 1959, 1960, 1963, 1974, 1978, 1980, 1984
Trophy Winners 1960, 1964, 1975, 1977, 1978

Season	Opponent	Home	Result	Away	Rnd	Cup
1963-64	Dukla Prague, Czechoslovakia	0-2		0-6	1	ECC
1964-65	Real Zaragoza, Spain	0-3		1-3	1	CWC
1972-73	Inter Milan, Italy	0-1		1-6	1	UEFA
1974-75	HJK Helsinki, Finland	1-0		1-4	1	ECC
1975-76	Haladas Vasutas, Hungary	1-1		0-7	1	CWC
1977-78	Dynamo Moscow, USSR	0-2		0-5	1	CWC
1978-79	Grasshoppers Zurich, Switzerland	3-5		0-8	1	ECC
1979-80	Leeds United, England	0-4		0-3	1	UEFA
1980-81	Honved Budapest, Hungary	0-3		0-8	pr	ECC
1983-84	Glasgow Rangers, Scotland	0-8		0-10	1	CWC
1984-85	FK Austria Vienna, Austria	0-4		0-4	1	ECC
1987-88	Juventus, Italy	0-4		0-3	1	UEFA
1989-90	First Vienna FC 1894, Austria	1-4		0-3	1	UEFA

215

MALTA

MARSA

Founded 1931
Colours blue and red striped shirts, white shorts
☎ 222 137

Season	Opponent	Home	Result	Away	Rnd	Cup
1971-72	Juventus, Italy	0-6		0-5	1	UEFA

GZIRA UNITED

Founded 1950
Colours claret and blue shirts, white shorts
☎ 338 708
Trophy Winner 1973

Season	Opponent	Home	Result	Away	Rnd	Cup
1973-74	Brann Bergen, Norway	0-2		0-7	1	CWC

HAMRUN SPARTANS

Founded 1906, amalgamated with Hamrun Lions under Hamrun Spartans
Colours red shirts, black shorts
☎ 496 829
Champions 1914, 1918, 1947, 1983, 1987, 1988
Trophy Winners 1983, 1984, 1987, 1988, 1989

Season	Opponent	Home	Result	Away	Rnd	Cup
1983-84	Dundee United, Scotland	0-3		0-3	1	ECC
1984-85	Ballymena United, Ireland	2-1		1-0	1	CWC
	Dynamo Moscow, USSR	0-1		0-5	2	CWC
1985-86	Dinamo Tirana, Albania	0-0		0-1	1	UEFA
1987-88	Rapid Vienna, Austria	0-1		0-6	1	ECC
1988-89	17 Nentori Tirana, Albania	2-1		0-2	1	ECC
1989-90	Real Vallidolid, Spain	0-1		0-5	1	CWC

ZURRIEQ

Founded 1948
Colours red shirts, white shorts
☎ 820 642
Trophy Winner 1985

Season	Opponent	Home	Result	Away	Rnd	Cup
1982-83	Hajduk Split, Yugoslavia	1-4		0-4	1	UEFA
1985-86	Bayer Uerdingen, Germany	0-3		0-9	1	CWC
1986-87	Wrexham, Wales	0-3		0-4	1	CWC

RABAT AJAX

Founded 1929 as Rabat Rovers, 1933 Rabat Rangers, 1938 Svanks FC, 1944 Rabat FC, 1981 Rabat Ajax
Colours black and white striped shirts, black shorts
☎ 674 244
Champions 1985, 1986
Trophy Winner 1986

Season	Opponent	Home	Result	Away	Rnd	Cup
1983-84	Internacional Bratislava, Czechoslovakia	0-10		0-6	1	UEFA
1984-85	Partizan Belgrade, Yugoslavia	0-2		0-2	1	UEFA
1985-86	Omonia Nicosia, Cyprus	0-5		0-5	1	ECC
1986-87	FC Porto, Portugal	0-1		0-9	1	ECC

● NYA Ullevi, Gothenburg, Sweden. IFK Gothenburg, CWC Final 1983

217

NORWAY

Founded 1902 Norges Fotballforbund, Ulleval
Stadium, Postboks 3823, Ulleval Hageby, Oslo 8 ☎ 46 98 30
National Colours red shirts, white shorts, blue and white socks
Season April to November (break in July)

LEAGUE CHAMPIONS

Playoff series

1938	Fredrikstad FK v SKF Lyn Oslo	0-0 4-0		1954	Fredrikstad FK v Skeid Oslo	2-1
1939	Fredrikstad FK v Skeid Oslo	2-1		1955	Larvik Turn v Fredrikstad FK	4-2
				1956	Larvik Turn v Fredrikstad FK	3-2
1948	SK Freidig v IL Sparta	2-1		1957	Fredrikstad FK v Odds BK	6-1
1949	Fredrikstad FK v Valerengens IF	3-1 3-0		1958	Viking Stavanger v Skeid Oslo	2-0
				1959	Lillestrom SK v Fredrikstad FK	2-0 4-1
1950	IF Fram Larvik v Fredrikstad FK	1-0 1-1				
1951	Fredrokstad FK v Odds BK	3-1 4-2		1960	Fredrikstad FK v Lillestrom SK	6-2
1952	Fredrikstad FK v Brann Bergen	3-1		1961	Fredrikstad FK v EiK IF	2-0
1953	Larvik Turn v Skeid Oslo	3-2				

NATIONAL LEAGUE CHAMPIONS

1962	Brann Bergen	1970	Stromgodset	1978	Start Kristiansand	1985	Rosenborg Trondheim
1963	Brann Bergen	1971	Rosenborg Trondheim	1979	Viking Stavanger	1986	Lillestrom SK
1964	SFK Lyn Oslo	1972	Viking Stavanger			1987	FK Moss
1965	Valerengens IF Oslo	1973	Viking Stavanger	1980	Start Kristiansand	1988	Rosenborg Trondheim
1966	Skeid Oslo	1974	Viking Stavanger	1981	Valerengens IF Oslo	1989	Lillestrom SK
1967	Rosenborg Trondheim	1975	Viking Stavanger	1982	Viking Stavanger		
1968	SFK Lyn Oslo	1976	Lillestrom SK	1983	Valerengens IF Oslo		
1969	Rosenborg Trondheim	1977	Lillestrom SK	1984	Valerengens IF Oslo		

CUP WINNERS

1902	Grane Nordstrand Arendel v Odds BK Skien	2-0		1909	Lyn Oslo v Odds BK Skien	4-3
1903	Odds BK Skien v Grane Nordstrand Arendal	1-0				
1904	Odds BK Skien v IF Uraedd	4-0		1910	Lyn Oslo v Odds BK Skien	4-2
1905	Odds BK Skien v Akademisk	2-1		1911	Lyn Oslo v IF Uraedd	5-2
1906	Odds BK Skien v Sarpsborg FK	1-0		1912	Mercantile Oslo v Fram Oslo	6-0
1907	Mercantile Oslo v Sarpsborg FK	3-0		1913	Odds BK Skien v Mercantile Oslo	2-1
1908	Lyn Oslo v Odds BK Skien	3-2		1914	Frigg Oslo v Gjovik/Lyn	4-2

1915 Odds BK Skien v Kvik Halden	2-1	
1916 Frigg Oslo v Orn Horten	2-0	
1917 Sarpsborg FK v Brann Bergen	4-1	
1918 Kvik Halden v Brann Bergen	4-0	
1919 Odds BK Skien v Frigg Oslo	1-0	
1920 Orn Horten v Frigg Oslo	1-0	
1921 Frigg Oslo v Odds BK Skien	2-0	
1922 Odds BK Skien v Kvik Halden	5-1	
1923 Brann Bergen v Lyn Oslo	2-1	
1924 Odds BK Skien v Mjondalen IF	3-0	
1925 Brann Bergen v Sarpsborg FK	3-0	
1926 Odds BK Skien v Orn Horten	3-0	
1927 Orn Horten v Drafn SK	4-0	
1928 Orn Horten v Lyn Oslo	2-1	
1929 Sarpsborg FK v Orn Horten	2-1	
1930 Orn Horten v Drammen BK	4-2	
1931 Odds BK Skien v Mjondalen IF	3-1	
1932 Fredrikstad FK v Orn Horten	6-1	
1933 Mjondalen IF v Viking Stavanger	3-1	
1934 Mjondalen IF v Sarpsborg FK	2-1	
1935 Fredrikstad FK v Sarpsborg FK	4-0	
1936 Fredrikstad FK v Mjondalen IF	2-0	
1937 Mjondalen IF v Odds BK Skien	4-2	
1938 Fredrikstad FK v Mjondalen IF	3-2	
1939 Sarpsborg FK v Skeid Oslo	2-1	
1940 Fredrikstad FK v Skeid Oslo	3-0	
1945 Lyn Oslo v Fredrikstad FK	1-1 1-1 4-0	
1946 Lyn Oslo v Fredrikstad FK	3-2	
1947 Skeid Oslo v Viking Stavanger	2-0	
1948 Sarpsborg FK v Fredrikstad FK	1-0	
1949 Sarpsborg FK v Skeid Oslo	3-1	
1950 Fredrikstad FK v Brann Bergen	3-0	
1951 Sarpsborg FK v Asker	3-2	
1952 Sparta Sarpsborg v Solberg	3-2	
1953 Viking Stavanger v Lillestrom SK	2-1	

1954 Skeid Oslo v Fredrikstad FK	3-0	
1955 Skeid Oslo v Lillestrom SK	5-0	
1956 Skeid Oslo v Larvik Turn	2-1	
1957 Fredrikstad FK v Sandefjord	4-0	
1958 Skeid Oslo v Lillestrom SK	1-0	
1959 Viking Stavanger v Sandefjord	2-1	
1960 Rosenborg Trondheim v Odds BK Skien	3-3	
1961 Fredrikstad FK v Haugar Haugesund	7-0	
1962 Gjovik/Lyn v Vard	2-0	
1963 Skeid Oslo v Fredrikstad FK	2-1	
1964 Rosenborg Trondheim v Sarpsborg FK	2-1	
1965 Skeid Oslo v Frigg Oslo	2-2 1-1 2-1	
1966 Fredrikstad FK v Lyn Oslo	3-2	
1967 Lyn Oslo v Rosenborg Trondheim	4-1	
1968 Lyn Oslo v Mjondalen IF	3-0	
1969 Stromgodset v Fredrikstad FK	2-2 5-3	
1970 Stromgodset v Lyn Oslo	4-2	
1971 Rosenborg Trondheim v Fredrikstad FK	4-1	
1972 Brann Bergen v Rosenborg Trondheim	1-0	
1973 Stromgodset v Rosenborg Trondheim	1-0	
1974 Skeid Oslo v Viking Stavanger	3-1	
1975 Bodo Glimt v Vard	2-0	
1976 Brann Bergen v Sogndal IF	2-1	
1977 Lillestrom SK v Bodo Glimt	1-0	
1978 Lillestrom SK v Brann Bergen	2-1	
1979 Viking Stavanger v Haugar Haugesund	2-1	
1980 Valerengens IF Oslo v Lillestrom SK	4-1	
1981 Lillestrom SK v FK Moss	3-1	
1982 Brann Bergen v Molde FK	3-2	
1983 FK Moss v Valerengens IF Oslo	2-0	
1984 Fredrikstad FK v Viking Stavanger	3-3 3-2	
1985 Lillestrom SK v Valerengens IF Oslo	4-1	
1986 Tromso IL v Lillestrom SK	4-0	
1987 Bryne IL v Brann Bergen	1-0 aet	
1988 Rosenborg Trondheim v Brann Bergen	2-2 2-0	
1989 Viking Stavanger v Molde FK	2-2 2-1	

FEATURED CLUBS IN EUROPEAN COMPETITION

Fredrikstad FK	**Valerengens IF Oslo**	**Lyn Oslo**	**Gjovik Lyn**
FK Skeid Oslo	**Lillestrom SK**	**Rosenborg Trondheim**	**Frigg Oslo**
Viking Stavanger	**SK Brann Bergen**	**IFK Start Kristiansand**	**IF Stromgodset Drammen**
Molde FK	**Mjondalen IF**	**Sarpsborg FK**	**SOFK Bodo Glimt**
FK Moss	**Hauger Haugesund**	**Bryne IL**	**Tromso IL**

FREDRIKSTAD FK

Founded 1903
Colours white shirts, red shorts
Stadium Fredrikstad (16,000) ☎ 032 13888
Champions 1938, 1939, 1949, 1951, 1952, 1954, 1957, 1960, 1961
Cup Winners 1932, 1935, 1936, 1938, 1940, 1950, 1957, 1961, 1966, 1984

Season	Opponent	Home	Result	Away	Rnd	Cup
1960-61	Ajax Amsterdam, Holland	4-3		0-0	1	ECC
	AGF Aarhus, Denmark	0-1		0-3	2	ECC
1961-62	Standard Liege, Belgium	0-2		1-2	pr	ECC
1962-63	Vasas Budapest, Hungary	1-4		0-7	pr	ECC
1967-68	Vitoria Setubal, Portugal	1-5		1-2	1	CWC
1972-73	Hajduk Split, Yugoslavia	0-1		0-1	1	CWC
1973-74	Dynamo Kiev, USSR	0-1		0-4	1	UEFA
1985-86	Bangor City, Wales	1-1	lag	0-0	1	CWC

219

NORWAY

VALERENGENS IF OSLO

Founded 1913
Colours blue shirts with one red hoop, white shorts
Stadium Bislett (28,000) ☎ 02-671743/657932
Champions 1965, 1981, 1983, 1984
Cup Winners 1980

Season	Opponent	Home	Result	Away	Rnd	Cup
1964-65	Everton, England	2-5		2-4	pr	Fairs
1965-66	bye				1	Fairs
	Heart of Midlothian, Scotland	1-3		0-1	2	Fairs
1966-67	17 Nentori Tirana, Albania	withdrew				
	Linfield, Ireland	1-4		1-1	1	ECC
1975-76	Athlone Town, Eire	1-1		1-3	1	UEFA
1981-82	Legia Warsaw, Poland	2-2		1-4	1	CWC
1982-83	Dinamo Bucharest, Romania	2-1		1-3	pr	ECC
1984-85	Sparta Prague, Czechoslovakia	3-3		0-2	1	ECC
1985-86	Zenit Leningrad, USSR	0-2		0-2	1	ECC
1986-87	SK Beveren Waas, Belgium	0-0		0-1	1	UEFA

LYN OSLO

Also known as Ski Og fk Lyn
Founded 1896
Colours red and white striped shirts, blue shorts
Stadium Ulleval (24,500) ☎ 02-465482/467862
Champions 1964, 1968
Cup Winners 1908, 1909, 1910, 1911, 1945, 1946, 1967, 1968

Season	Opponent	Home	Result	Away	Rnd	Cup
1963-64	Borussia Dortmund, Germany	2-4		1-3	1	ECC
1964-65	Reipas Lahti, Finland	3-0		1-2	pr	ECC
	DWS Amsterdam, Holland	1-3		0-5	1	ECC
1965-66	Derry City, Ireland	5-3		1-5	pr	ECC
1967-68	Bologna, Italy	0-0		0-2	1	Fairs
1968-69	Altay Izmir, Turkey	4-1		1-3	1	CWC
	IFK Norrkoping, Sweden	2-0		2-3	2	CWC
	CF Barcelona, Spain	2-2		2-3	qf	CWC
1969-70	Leeds United, England	0-6		0-10	1	ECC
1971-72	Sporting Lisbon, Portugal	0-3		0-4	1	CWC
1972-73	Tottenham Hotspur, England	3-6		0-6	1	UEFA

GJOVIK/LYN, GJOVIK

Founded 1902
Colours red shirts, white shorts
Stadium Gjovik (16,000) ☎ 061 71914
Cup Winners 1962

Season	Opponent	Home	Result	Away	Rnd	Cup
1963-64	Apoel Nicosia, Cyprus	0-1		0-6	1	CWC

FK SKEID OSLO

Founded 1915 merger of Frem '14 Oslo and Kristiania BK to form FK Skeid Oslo
Colours red shirts, blue shorts
Stadium Grefsen Bislett (25,000) for big matches ☎ 02-222882
Champions 1966
Cup Winners 1947, 1954, 1955, 1956, 1958, 1963, 1965, 1974

Season	Opponent	Home	Result	Away	Rnd	Cup
1964-65	Valkeaskosken Haka, Finland	1-0		0-2	pr	CWC
1966-67	Real Zaragoza, Spain	3-2		1-3	pr	CWC
1967-68	Sparta Prague, Czechoslovakia	0-1		1-1	1	ECC
1968-69	AIK Stockholm, Sweden	1-1		1-2	1	Fairs
1969-70	TSV 1860 Munich, Germany	2-1		2-2	1	Fairs
	Dinamo Bacau, Romania	0-0		0-2	2	Fairs
1975-76	Stal Rzeszow, Poland	1-4		0-4	1	CWC
1979-80	Ipswich Town, England	1-3		0-7	1	UEFA

LILLESTROM SK (SPORTSKLUBB)

Founded 1917
Colours yellow shirts, black shorts
Stadium Lillestrom (8,000) ☎ 02-712341
Champions 1959, 1976, 1977, 1986, 1989
Cup Winners 1977, 1978, 1981, 1985

Season	Opponent	Home	Result	Away	Rnd	Cup
1977-78	Ajax Amsterdam, Holland	2-0		0-4	1	ECC
1978-79	Linfield, Ireland	1-0		0-0	1	ECC
	FK Austria/WAC Vienna, Austria	0-0		1-4	2	ECC
1979-80	Glasgow Rangers, Scotland	0-2		0-1	pr	CWC
1982-83	Red Star Belgrade, Yugoslavia	0-4		0-3	1	CWC
1984-85	1.FC Lokomotive Leipzig, East Germany	3-0		0-7	1	UEFA
1986-87	Benfica, Portugal	1-2		0-2	1	CWC
1987-88	Linfield, Ireland	1-1		4-2	1	ECC
	Girondins Bordeaux, France	0-0		0-1	2	ECC
1989-90	Werder Bremen, Germany	1-3		0-2	1	UEFA

ROSENBORG TRONDHEIM

Founded 1917
Colours white shirts, black shorts
Stadium Lerkendal (30,000) ☎ 07-939300
Champions 1967, 1969, 1971, 1985, 1988
Cup Winners 1960, 1964, 1971, 1988

Season	Opponent	Home	Result	Away	Rnd	Cup
1965-66	KR Reykjavik, Iceland	3-1		3-1	1	CWC
	Dynamo Kiev, USSR	1-4		0-2	2	CWC
1968-69	Rapid Vienna, Austria	1-3		3-3	1	ECC
1969-70	Southampton, England	1-0		0-2	1	Fairs
1970-71	Standard Liege, Belgium	0-2		0-5	1	ECC
1971-72	HIFK Helsinki, Finland	3-0		1-0	1	UEFA
	Lierse SK, Belgium	4-1	lag	0-3	2	UEFA
1972-73	Glasgow Celtic, Scotland	1-3		1-2	1	ECC
1974-75	Hibernian, Scotland	2-3		1-9	1	UEFA
1986-87	Linfield, Ireland	1-0		1-1	1	ECC
	Red Star Belgrade, Yugoslavia	0-3		1-4	2	ECC
1989-90	KV Mechelen, Belgium	0-0		0-5	1	ECC

221

NORWAY

FRIGG OSLO

Founded 1904
Colours sky blue shirts, white shorts
Stadium Voldslokka (4,000) or Bislett (25,000) ☎ 02-605910
Cup Winners 1914, 1916, 1921

Season	Opponent	Home	Result	Away	Rnd	Cup
1966-67	Dunfermline Athletic, Scotland	1-3		1-3	1	Fairs

VIKING STAVANGER

Founded 1899
Colours blue shirts, white shorts
Stadium Stavanger (19,800) ☎ 045 28117
Champions 1958, 1972, 1973, 1974, 1975, 1979, 1982
Cup Winners 1953, 1959, 1979, 1989

Season	Opponent	Home	Result	Away	Rnd	Cup
1972-73	IBV Vestmannaeyja, Iceland	1-0		0-0*	1	UEFA
				* in Reykjavik		
	1.FC Koln, Germany	1-0		1-9	2	UEFA
1973-74	Spartak Trnava, Czechoslovakia	1-2		0-1	1	ECC
1974-75	Ararat Yerevan, USSR	0-2		2-4	1	ECC
1975-76	RWD Molenbeeck, Belgium	0-1		2-3	1	ECC
1976-77	Banik Ostrava, Czechoslovakia	2-1		0-2	1	ECC
1979-80	Borussia Monchengladbach, Germany	1-1		0-3	1	UEFA
1980-81	Red Star Belgrade, Yugoslavia	2-3		1-4	1	ECC
1982-83	1.FC Lokomotive Leipzig, East Germany	1-0	wag	2-3	1	UEFA
	Dundee United, Scotland	1-3		0-0	2	UEFA
1983-84	Partizan Belgrade, Yugoslavia	0-0		1-5	1	ECC
1985-86	Legia Warsaw, Poland	1-1		0-3	1	UEFA

SK BRANN BERGEN

Founded 1908
Colours red shirts, white shorts
Stadium Brann (25,200) ☎ 05-296944/299825
Champions 1962, 1963
Cup Winners 1923, 1925, 1972, 1976, 1982

Season	Opponent	Home	Result	Away	Rnd	Cup
1973-74	Gzira United, Malta	7-0		2-0	1	CWC
	Glentoran, Ireland	1-1		1-3	2	CWC
1976-77	Queens Park Rangers, England	0-7		0-4	1	UEFA
1977-78	IA Akranes, Iceland	1-0		4-0	1	CWC
	Twente Enschede, Holland	1-2		0-2	2	CWC
1983-84	NEC Nijmegen, Holland	0-1		1-1	1	CWC
1989-90	Sampdoria, Italy	0-2		0-1	1	CWC

IFK START KRISTIANSAND

Founded 1905
Colours yellow shirts, black shorts
Stadium Kristiansand (6,000) ☎ 042-21143/96091
Champions 1978, 1980

Season	Opponent	Home	Result	Away	Rnd	Cup
1974-75	Djurgardens IF Stockholm, Sweden	1-2		1-5	1	UEFA
1976-77	Swarovski Wacker Innsbruck, Austria	0-5		1-2	1	UEFA
1977-78	Fram Reykjavik, Iceland	6-0		2-0	1	UEFA
	Eintracht Braunschweig, Germany	1-0		0-4	2	UEFA
1978-79	Esbjerg fB, Denmark	0-0		0-1	1	UEFA
1979-80	RC Strasbourg, France	1-2		0-4	1	ECC
1981-82	AZ 67 Alkmaar, Holland	1-3		0-1	1	ECC

IF STROMGODSET DRAMMEN

Founded 1907
Colours blue shirts, white shorts
Stadium Idrettsparken (17,000) ☎ 03-834368/832203
Champions 1970
Cup Winners 1969, 1970, 1973

Season	Opponent	Home	Result	Away	Rnd	Cup
1970-71	FC Nantes, France	0-5		3-2	1	CWC
1971-72	Arsenal, England	1-3		0-4	1	ECC
1973-74	Leeds United, England	1-1		1-6	1	UEFA
1974-75	Liverpool, England	0-1		0-11	1	CWC

MOLDE FK

Founded 1911
Colours blue shirts, white shorts
Stadium Molde (15,000) ☎ 072-53297

Season	Opponent	Home	Result	Away	Rnd	Cup
1975-76	Osters IF Vaxjo, Sweden	1-0		0-6	1	UEFA
1978-79	Torpedo Moscow, USSR	3-3		0-4	1	UEFA
1988-89	KSV Waregem, Belgium	0-0		1-5	1	UEFA

MJONDALEN IF

Founded 1910
Colours brown shirts, white shorts
Stadium Nedre Eiker (12,000) ☎ 03-826092/871200
Cup Winners 1933, 1934, 1937

Season	Opponent	Home	Result	Away	Rnd	Cup
1969-70	Cardiff City, Wales	1-7		1-5	1	CWC
1977-78	Bayern Munich, Germany	0-4		0-8	1	UEFA
1987-88	Werder Bremen, Germany	0-5		1-0	1	UEFA

223

NORWAY

SARPSBORG FK

Founded 1903
Colours blue and white striped shirts, white shorts
Stadium Sarpsborg (20,000) ☎ 031-51975
Cup Winners 1917, 1929, 1939, 1948, 1949, 1951

Season	Opponent	Home	Result	Away	Rnd	Cup
1970-71	Leeds United, England	0-1		0-5	1	Fairs

SOFK BODO GLIMT

SOFK=Ski og Fotball Klub
Founded 1916
Colours yellow shirts, white shorts
Stadium Aspmyra (12,000) ☎ 081-22277
Cup Winners 1975

Season	Opponent	Home	Result	Away	Rnd	Cup
1976-77	Napoli, Italy	0-2		0-1	1	CWC
1978-79	Union Sportive, Luxembourg	4-1		0-1	1	CWC
	Inter Milan, Italy	1-2		0-5	2	CWC

FK MOSS

Founded 1906
Colours yellow shirts, black shorts
Stadium Mellos (8,000) ☎ 032-52277/52716
League Champions 1987
Cup Winners 1983

Season	Opponent	Home	Result	Away	Rnd	Cup
1980-81	1.FC Magdeburg, East Germany	2-3		1-2	1	UEFA
1984-85	Bayern Munich, Germany	1-2		1-4	1	CWC
1988-89	Real Madrid, Spain	0-1		0-3	1	ECC

HAUGAR (HAUGESUND)

Founded 1939
Colours grey and green shirts, black shorts
Stadium Haugersund (15,000) ☎ 047-29336/21424

Season	Opponent	Home	Result	Away	Rnd	Cup
1980-81	FC Sion, Switzerland	2-0		1-1	1	CWC
	Newport County, Wales	0-0		0-6	2	CWC

BRYNE IL

Founded 1926
Colours red shirts with white sleeves, white shorts
Stadium Bryne (15,000) ☎ 044-81756/483010
Cup Winners 1987

Season	Opponent	Home	Result	Away	Rnd	Cup
1981-82	KFC Winterslag, Belgium	0-2		2-1	1	UEFA
1983-84	RSC Anderlecht, Belgium	0-3		1-1	1	UEFA
1988-89	Bekescsaba Elore Spartacus, Hungary	2-1		0-3	pre	CWC

TROMSO IL

Founded 1920
Colours red and white striped shirts, white shorts
Stadium Nye Alfheim (9,000) ☎ 083-84724/57949
Cup Winners 1986

Season	Opponent	Home	Result	Away	Rnd	Cup
1987-88	St Mirren, Scotland	0-0		0-1	1	CWC

- Solna, Stockholm. AIK Stockholm

POLAND

Founded 1923
Polish Football Association, Al Ujazdowskie 22, 00-478 Warszawa ☎ 28 93 44/29 24 89/21 91 75
National colours white shirts, red shorts, white and red socks
Season August to November; March to June

LEAGUE CHAMPIONS

1921	Cracovia Krakow	1938	Ruch Chorzow	1960	Ruch Chorzow	1976	Stal Mielec
1922	Pogon Lwow	1939	not finished	1961	Gornik Zabrze	1977	Slask Wroclaw
1923	Pogon Lwow	1946	Polonia Warsaw	1962	Polonia Bytom	1978	Wisla Krakow
1924	not held	1947	Warta Poznan	1963	Gornik Zabrze	1979	Ruch Chorzow
1925	Pogon Lwow	1948	Cracovia Krakow	1964	Gornik Zabrze		
1926	Pogo Lwow	1949	Wisla Krakow	1965	Gornik Zabrze	1980	Szombierki Bytom
1927	Wisla Krakow			1966	Gornik Zabrze	1981	Widzew Lodz
1928	Wisla Krakow	1950	Wisla Krakow	1967	Gornik Zabrze	1982	Widzew Lodz
1929	Warta Poznan	1951	Ruch Chorzow	1968	Ruch Chorzow	1983	Lech Poznan
		1952	Ruch Chorzow	1969	Legia Warsaw	1984	Lech Poznan
1930	Cracovia Krakow	1953	Ruch Chorzow			1985	Gornik Zabrze
1931	Garbarnia Krakow	1954	Polonia Bytom	1970	Legia Warsaw	1986	Gornik Zabrze
1932	Cracovia Krakow	1955	CWKS Warsaw (Legia)	1971	Gornik Zabrze	1987	Gornik Zabrze
1933	Ruch Chorzow	1956	CWKS Warsaw (Legia)	1972	Gornik Zabrze	1988	Gornik Zabrze
1934	Ruch Chorzow	1957	Gornik Zabrze	1973	Stal Mielec	1989	Ruch Chorzow
1935	Ruch Chorzow	1958	LKS Lodz Bytom	1974	Ruch Chorzow		
1936	Ruch Chorzow	1959	Gornik Zabrze	1975	Ruch Chorzow		
1937	Cracovia Krakow						

CUP WINNERS

1926	Wisla Krakow v Sparta Lwow	2-1	1962	Zaglebie Sosnowiec v Gornik Zabrze	2-1
			1963	Zaglebie Sosnowiec v Ruch Chorzow	2-0
1951	Ruch Chorzow v Wisla Krakow	2-0	1964	Legia Warsaw v Polonia Bytom	2-1
1952	Polonia Bytom v CWKS Warsaw	1-0	1965	Gornik Zabrze v Czarni Zagan	4-0
1953	not held		1966	Legia Warsaw v Gornik Zabrze	2-1
1954	Gwardia Warsaw v Wisla Krakow	0-0 3-1	1967	Wisla Krakow v Rakow Czestochowa	2-0
1955	CWKS Warsaw v Lechia Gdansk	5-0	1968	Gornik Zabrze v Ruch Chorzow	3-0
1956	CWKS Warsaw v Gornik Zabrze	3-0	1969	Gornik Zabrze v Legia Warsaw	2-0
1957	LKS Lodz v Gornik Zabrze	2-1	1970	Gornik Zabrze v Ruch Chorzow	3-1
1958	not held		1971	Gornik Zabrze v Zaglebie Sosnowiec	3-1
1959	not held		1972	Gornik Zabrze v Legia Warsaw	5-2
			1973	Legia Warsaw v Polonia Bytom	0-0 4-2 pens
1960	not held		1974	Ruch Chorzow v Gwardia Warsaw	2-0
1961	not held		1975	Stal Rzeszow v Row II Rybnik	0-0 3-2 pens

1976	Slask Wroclaw v Stal Mielec	2-0		1983	Lechia Gdansk v Piast Gleiwitz	2-1
1977	Zaglebie Sosnowiec v Polonia Bytom	1-0		1984	Lech Poznan v Wisla Krakow	3-0
1978	Zaglebie Sosnowiec v Piast Gliwice	2-0		1985	Widzew Lodz v GKS Katowice	0-0 3-1 pens
1979	Arka Gdynia v Wisla Krakow	2-1		1986	GKS Kotowice v Gornik Zabrze	4-1
				1987	Slask Wroclaw v GKS Katowice	0-0 4-3 pens
1980	Legia Warsaw v Lech Poznan	5-0		1988	Lech Poznan v Legia Warsaw	1-1 3-2 pens
1981	Legia Warsaw v Pogon Szczecin	1-0		1989	Legia Warsaw v GKS Katowice	5-2
1982	Lech Poznan v Pogon Szczecin	1-0				

POLISH SUPER CUP

1988	Gornik Zabrze v Lech Poznan	2-1
1989	Legia Warsaw v Ruch Chorzow	3-0

FEATURED CLUBS IN EUROPEAN COMPETITION

Legia Warsaw	Gornik Zabrze	Ruch Chorzow	Gwardia Warsaw
Widzew Lodz	Wisla Krakow	Slask Wroclaw	Stal Mielec
Lech Poznan	Polonia Bytom	Zaglebie Sosnowiec	LKS Lodz
GTS Katowice	GKS Tichy	Zaglebie Walbrzych	Odra Opole
Arka Gdynia	GKS Szombierki Bytom	Lechia Gdansk	Pogon Szczecin
Stal Rzeszow			

CWKS LEGIA WARSAW

Founded 1916 as WKS, 1920 Legia, 1930 CWKS, 1957 Legia, 1967 CWKS Legia
Colours white shirts with green sleeves, black shorts
Stadium Lazienkowska (25,000) ☎ 022-21 08 96
Champions 1955, 1956, 1969, 1970
Cup Winners 1955, 1956, 1964, 1966, 1973, 1980, 1981, 1989
Polish Super Cup Winners 1989

Season	Opponent	Home	Play off Result	Away	Rnd	Cup
as CWKS WARSAW						
1956-57	Slovan Bratislava, Czechoslovakia	2-0		0-4	pr	ECC
as LEGIA WARSAW						
1960-61	AGF Aarhus, Denmark	1-0		0-3	pr	ECC
1964-65	Admira Vienna, Austria	3-1		1-0	1	CWC
	Galatasaray, Turkey	2-1	1-0*	0-1	2	CWC
			* in Warsaw			
	TSV 1860 Munich, Germany	0-0		0-4	qf	CWC
1966-67	Chemie Leipzig, East Germany	2-2		0-3	pr	CWC
1968-69	TSV 1860 Munich, Germany	6-0		3-2	1	Fairs
	Waregem KSV, Belgium	2-0		0-1	2	Fairs
	Ujpest Dozsa, Hungary	0-1		2-2	3	Fairs
1969-70	UT Arad Flamurarosie, Romania	8-0		2-1	1	ECC
	St Etienne, France	2-1		1-0	2	ECC
	Galatasaray, Turkey	2-0		1-1	qf	ECC
	Feyenoord Rotterdam, Holland	0-0		0-2	sf	ECC
1970-71	IFK Gothenburg, Sweden	2-1		4-0	1	ECC
	Standard Liege, Belgium	2-0		0-1	2	ECC
	Atletico Madrid, Spain	2-1	lag	0-1	qf	ECC
1971-72	Lugano, Switzerland	0-0		3-1	1	UEFA
	Rapid Bucharest, Romania	2-0		0-4	2	UEFA
1972-73	Vikingur Reykjavik, Iceland	9-0		2-0*	1	CWC
				* in Reykjavik		
	AC Milan, Italy	1-1		1-2	2	CWC
1973-74	PAOK Salonika, Greece	1-1		0-1	1	CWC
1974-75	FC Nantes, France	0-1		2-2	1	UEFA
1980-81	Slavia Sofia, Bulgaria	1-0		1-3	1	CWC

227

POLAND

1981-82	Valerengens IF Oslo, Norway	4-1		2-2	1	CWC
	Lausanne Sport, Switzerland	2-1		1-1	2	CWC
	Dynamo Tbilisi, USSR	0-1		0-1	qf	CWC
1985-86	Viking Stavanger, Norway	3-0		1-1	1	UEFA
	Videoton Sekesfehervar, Hungary	1-1		1-0	2	UEFA
	Inter Milan, Italy	0-1		0-0	3	UEFA
1986-87	Dnepr Dnepropetrovsk, USSR	0-0		1-0	1	UEFA
	Inter Milan, Italy	3-2	lag	0-1	2	UEFA
1988-89	Bayern Munich, Germany	3-7		1-3	1	UEFA
1989-90	FC Barcelona, Spain	0-1		1-1	1	CWC

KS GORNIK ZABRZE

Founded 1948 by amalgamation of Concordia, Pogon, Skra, Zjednoczenie and Scaley
Colours red shirts, blue shorts
Stadium Roosevelta (20,000) ☎ 832-71 49 26/71 05 30
Champions 1957, 1959, 1961, 1963, 1964, 1965, 1966, 1967, 1971, 1972, 1985, 1986, 1987, 1988
Cup Winners 1965, 1968, 1969, 1970, 1971, 1972
Polish Super Cup Winners 1988
CWC Finalists 1970

Season	Opponent	Home	Play off Result	Away	Rnd	Cup
1961-62	Tottenham Hotspur, England	4-2		1-8	pr	ECC
1963-64	FK Austria Vienna, Austria	1-0	2-1*	0-1	pr	ECC
			* in Vienna			
	Dukla Prague, Czechoslovakia	2-0		1-4	1	ECC
1964-65	Dukla Prague, Czechoslovakia	3-0*	0-0 lot**	1-4	pr	ECC
			* in Warsaw, ** in Duisburg aet			
1965-66	Linzer ASK, Austria	2-1*		3-1	pr	ECC
			* in Krakow			
	Sparta Prague, Czechoslovakia	1-2		0-3	1	ECC
1966-67	ASK Vorwaerts Berlin, East Germany	2-1	3-1*	1-2	pr	ECC
			* in Budapest			
	CSKA Sofia, Bulgaria	3-0		0-4	1	ECC
1967-68	Djurgarden IF Stockholm, Sweden	3-0		1-0	1	ECC
	Dynamo Kiev, USSR	1-1		2-1	2	ECC
	Manchester United, England	1-0		0-2	qf	ECC
1968-69	Spartak Sofia, Bulgaria	withdrew			1	CWC
1969-70	Olympiakos Piraeus, Greece	5-0		2-2	1	CWC
	Glasgow Rangers, Scotland	3-1		3-1	2	CWC
	Levski Spartak Sofia, Bulgaria	2-1	wag	2-3	qf	CWC
	AS Roma, Italy	2-2	1-1* wot	1-1	sf	CWC
			* in Strasbourg			
	Manchester City, England	1-2	in Vienna		FINAL	CWC
1970-71	AB Aalborg, Denmark	8-1		1-0	1	CWC
	Goztepe Izmir, Turkey	3-0		1-0	2	CWC
	Manchester City, England	2-0	1-3*	0-2	qf	CWC
			* in Copenhagen			
1971-72	Olympique Marseille, France	1-1		1-2	1	ECC
1972-73	Sliema Wanderers, Malta	5-0		5-0	1	ECC
	Dynamo Kiev, USSR	2-1		0-2	2	ECC
1974-75	Partizan Belgrade, Yugoslavia	2-2		0-3	1	UEFA
1977-78	Valkeakoski Haka, Finland	5-3		0-0	1	UEFA
	Aston Villa, England	1-1		0-2	2	UEFA
1985-86	Bayern Munich, Germany	1-2*		1-4	1	ECC
			* in Chorzow			
1986-87	RSC Anderlecht, Belgium	1-1		0-2	1	ECC
1987-88	Olympiakos Piraeus, Greece	2-1		1-1	1	ECC
	Glasgow Rangers, Scotland	1-1		1-3	2	ECC
1988-89	Jeunesse Esch, Luxembourg	3-0		4-1	1	ECC
	Real Madrid, Spain	0-1		2-3	2	ECC
1989-90	Juventus, Italy	0-1		2-4	1	UEFA

KS RUCH CHORZOW

Founded 1920 as Ruch, 1950 Unia, 1955 Ruch
Colours blue and white striped shirts, white shorts
Stadium Ruch (40,000) or Slaski (93,000) ☎ 41 04 79/41 05 56
Champions 1933, 1934, 1935, 1936, 1938, 1951, 1952, 1953, 1960, 1968, 1974, 1975, 1979, 1989
Winners 1951, 1974

Season	Opponent	Home	Result	Away	Rnd	Cup
1968-69	withdrew				1	ECC
1969-70	Wiener Sport Club, Austria	4-1		2-4	1	Fairs
	Ajax Amsterdam, Holland	1-2		0-7	2	Fairs
1970-71	Fiorentina, Italy	1-1		0-2	1	Fairs
1972-73	Fenerbahce, Turkey	3-0		0-1	1	UEFA
	Dynamo Dresden, East Germany	0-1		0-3	2	UEFA
1973-74	Wuppertaler SV, Germany	4-1		4-5	1	UEFA
	Carl Zeiss Jena, East Germany	3-0		0-1	2	UEFA
	Honved Budapest, Hungary	5-0		0-2	3	UEFA
	Feyenoord Rotterdam, Holland	1-1		1-3	qf	UEFA
1974-75	Hvidovre IF, Denmark	2-1		0-0	1	ECC
	Fenerbahce, Turkey	2-1		2-0	2	ECC
	St Etienne, France	3-2		0-2	qf	ECC
1975-76	KuPS Kuopion Palloseura, Finland	5-0		2-2	1	ECC
	PSV Eindhoven, Holland	1-3		0-4	2	ECC
1979-80	BFC Dynamo Berlin, East Germany	0-0		1-4	1	ECC
1989-90	Sredets CFKA Sofia, Bulgaria	1-1		1-5	1	ECC

WKS GWARDIA WARSAW

Founded 1948
Colours blue shirts, white shorts
Stadium Raclawicka (12,000) ☎ 22-44 62 74
Champions 1949, 1950

Season	Opponent	Home	Play off Result	Away	Rnd	Cup
1955-56	Djurgarden IF Stockholm, Sweden	1-4		0-0	1	ECC
1957-58	SC Wismut Karl Marx Stadt, East Germany	3-1	1-1* lot	1-3	1	ECC
			* in East Berlin			
1969-70	Vojvodina Novi Sad, Yugoslavia	1-0		1-1	1	Fairs
	Dunfermline Athletic, Scotland	0-1		1-2	2	Fairs
1973-74	Ferencvarosi TC, Hungary	2-1		1-0	1	UEFA
	Feyenoord Rotterdam, Holland	1-0		1-3	2	UEFA
1974-75	Bologna, Italy	2-1	5-3p	1-2	1	CWC
	PSV Eindhoven, Holland	1-5		0-3	2	CWC

POLAND

RTS WIDZEW LODZ

Founded 1910
Colours white shirts, red shorts
Stadium Armii Czerwonej (25,000) ☎ 071-74 72 18/74 41 06
Champions 1981, 1982
Cup Winners 1985

Season	Opponent	Home	Result	Away	Rnd	Cup
1977-78	Manchester City, England	0-0	wag	2-2	1	UEFA
	PSV Eindhoven, Holland	3-5		0-1	2	UEFA
1979-80	St Etienne, France	2-1		0-3	1	UEFA
1980-81	Manchester United, England	0-0	wag	1-1	1	UEFA
	Juventus, Italy	3-1	4-1 pen	1-3	2	UEFA
	Ipswich Town, England	1-0		0-5	3	UEFA
1981-82	RSC Anderlecht, Belgium	1-4		1-2	1	ECC
1982-83	Hibernians, Malta	3-1		4-1	1	ECC
	Rapid Vienna, Austria	5-3		1-2	2	ECC
	Liverpool, England	2-0		2-3	qf	ECC
	Juventus, Italy	2-2		0-2	sf	ECC
1983-84	Elfsborg IF Boras, Sweden	0-0	wag	2-2	1	UEFA
	Sparta Prague, Czechoslovakia	1-0		0-3	2	UEFA
1984-85	AGF Aarhus, Denmark	2-0		0-1	1	UEFA
	Borussia Monchengladbach, Germany	1-0	wag	2-3	2	UEFA
	Dynamo Minsk, USSR	0-2		1-0	3	UEFA
1985-86	Galatasaray, Turkey	2-1	lag	0-1	1	CWC
1986-87	Linzer ASK, Austria	1-0		1-1	1	UEFA
	Bayer Uerdingen, Germany	0-0		0-2	2	UEFA

GTS WISLA KRAKOW

Founded 1906, 1949 Gwardia, 1955 Wisla
Colours blue and white striped shirts, white shorts
Stadium Wisla (40,000) ☎ 10 15 32/37 71 20
Champions 1927, 1928, 1949, 1950, 1951, 1978
Cup Winners 1967

Season	Opponent	Home	Result	Away	Rnd	Cup
1967-68	HJK Helsinki, Finland	4-0		4-1	1	CWC
	Hamburger SV, Germany	0-1		0-4	2	CWC
1976-77	Glasgow Celtic, Scotland	2-0		2-2	1	UEFA
	RWD Molenbeeck, Belgium	1-1	4-5 pen	1-1	2	UEFA
1978-79	Clube Bruges, Belgium	3-1		1-2	1	ECC
	Zbrojovka Brno, Czechoslovakia	1-1	wag	2-2	2	ECC
	Malmo FF, Sweden	2-1		1-4	3	ECC
1981-82	Malmo FF, Sweden	1-3		0-2	1	UEFA
1984-85	IBV Vestmannaeyjar, Iceland	4-2		3-1	1	CWC
	Fortuna Sittard, Holland	2-1		0-2	2	CWC

WKS SLASK WROCLAW

Founded 1947 as Slask, 1948 Ogniwo, 1956 Slask
Colours white shirts, green shorts or green shirts, white shorts
Stadium Wroclaw (15,000) or Olimpijski (45,000) ☎ 071-61 22 11/61 33 42
Champions 1977
Cup Winners 1976, 1987

Season	Opponent	Home	Result	Away	Rnd	Cup
1975-76	GAIS Gothenburg, Sweden	4-2		1-2	1	UEFA
	Royal Antwerp, Belgium	1-1		2-1	2	UEFA
	Liverpool, England	1-2		0-3	3	UEFA
1976-77	Floriana, Malta	2-0		4-1	1	CWC
	Bohemians Dublin, Eire	3-0		1-0	2	CWC
	Napoli, Italy	0-0		0-2	qf	CWC
1977-78	Levski Spartak Sofia, Bulgaria	2-2		0-3	1	ECC
1978-79	Pezoporikos Larnaca, Cyprus	5-1		2-2	1	UEFA
	IBV Vestmannaeyjar, Iceland	2-1		2-0*	2	UEFA
				* in Reykjavik		
	Borussia Monchengladbach, Germany	2-4		1-1	3	UEFA
1980-81	Dundee United, Scotland	0-0		2-7	1	UEFA
1982-83	Dynamo Moscow, USSR	2-2		1-0	1	UEFA
	Servette Geneva, Switzerland	0-2		1-5	2	UEFA
1987-88	Real Sociedad San Sebastian, Spain	0-2		0-0	1	CWC

FKS STAL MIELEC

Founded 1939
Colours blue shirts, white shorts
Stadium Solskiego (30,000) ☎ 3905/2426
Champions 1973, 1976

Season	Opponent	Home	Result	Away	Rnd	Cup
1973-74	Red Star Belgrade, Yugoslavia	0-1		1-2	1	ECC
1975-76	Holbaek BI, Denmark	2-1		1-0	1	UEFA
	Carl Zeiss Jena, East Germany	1-0	3-2 pen	0-1	2	UEFA
	Internacional Bratislava, Czechoslovakia	2-0		0-1	3	UEFA
	Hamburger SV, Germany	0-1		1-1	qf	UEFA
1976-77	Real Madrid, Spain	1-2		0-1	1	ECC
1979-80	AGF Aarhus, Denmark	0-1		1-1	1	UEFA
1982-83	KSC Lokeren, Belgium	1-1		0-0	1	UEFA

KKS LECH POZNAN

Founded 1922 as Lech, 1947 Kolejarz, 1956 Lech
Colours blue shirts, white shorts
Stadium Lech (24,000) ☎ 061-67 30 61/67 65 12
Champions 1983, 1984
Cup Winners 1982, 1984, 1988

Season	Opponent	Home	Result	Away	Rnd	Cup
1978-79	MSV Duisburg, Germany	2-5		0-5	1	UEFA
1982-83	IBV Vestmannaeyjar, Iceland	3-0		1-0*	1	CWC
				* in Kopavogur		
	Aberdeen, Scotland	0-1		0-2	2	CWC
1983-84	Athletic Bilbao, Spain	2-0		0-4	1	ECC
1984-85	Liverpool, England	0-1		0-4	1	ECC
1985-86	Borussia Monchengladbach, Germany	0-2		1-1	1	UEFA
1988-89	Flamurtari Vlore, Albania	1-0		3-2	1	CWC
	FC Barcelona, Spain	1-1 aet	4-5p	1-1	2	CWC

POLAND

KS POLONIA BYTOM

Founded 1920 as Polonia, 1948 Ogniwo, 1955 Polonia
Colours blue shirts, red shorts
Stadium Koniewa (36,000) ☎ 81 97 12/81 69 50
Champions 1954, 1962
Cup Winners 1952

Season	Opponent	Home	Result	Away	Rnd	Cup
1958-69	MTK Budapest, Hungary	0-3		0-3	pr	ECC
1962-63	Panathinaikos, Greece	2-1		4-1	1	ECC
	Galatasaray, Turkey	1-0		1-4	2	ECC

GKS ZAGLEBIE SOSNOWIEC

Founded 1906 as Milowice, 1908 Union, 1918 Sosnowiec, 1921 Victoria, 1931 Unia, 1939 RKV, 1948 Stal, 1963 Zaglebie
Colours red and white shirts, green shorts
Stadium Stad Ludowy (34,000) ☎ 66 18 02/66 34 28
Cup Winners 1962, 1963, 1977

Season	Opponent	Home	Play off Result	Away	Rnd	Cup
1962-63	Ujpest Dozsa, Hungary	0-0		0-5	1	CWC
1963-64	Olympiakos Piraeus, Greece	1-0	0-2* * in Piraeus	1-2	1	CWC
1971-72	Atvidaberg FF, Sweden	3-4		1-1	1	CWC
1972-73	Vitoria Setubal, Portugal	1-0		1-6	1	UEFA
1977-78	PAOK Salonika, Greece	0-2		0-2	1	CWC
1978-79	Wacker Innsbruck, Austria	2-3		1-1	1	CWC

LKS LODZ

Founded 1908 as Lodzianka, 1912 LKS Lodz, 1948 Wlokniarz, 1954 LKS Lodz, LKS=Lodzki Klub Sportowy
Colours red shirts, white shorts
Stadium Unii (30,000) ☎ 042-33 20 47/33 67 25
Champions 1958

Season	Opponent	Home	Result	Away	Rnd	Cup
1959-60	Jeunesse Esch, Luxembourg	2-1		0-5	pr	ECC

GKS KATOWICE

Founded 1964
Colours red shirts, white shorts
Stadium Bukowa (18,000) ☎ 832-51 12 71
Cup Winners 1986

Season	Opponent	Home	Result	Away	Rnd	Cup
1970-71	CF Barcelona, Spain	0-1		2-3	1	Fairs
1986-87	Fram Reykjavik, Iceland	1-0		3-0	1	CWC
	FC Sion, Switzerland	2-2* * in Chorzow		0-3	2	CWC
1987-88	Sportul Studentesc Bucharest, Romania	1-2		0-1	1	UEFA
1988-89	Glasgow Rangers, Scotland	2-4		0-1	1	UEFA
1989-90	RoPs Rovaniemen, Finland	0-1		1-1	1	UEFA

GKS TICHY

Founded 1971
Colours green and black striped shirts, red shorts
Stadium Engelsa (18,000) ☎ 27 42 70/27 64 41

Season	Opponent	Home	Result	Away	Rnd	Cup
1976-77	1.FC Koln, Germany	1-1		0-2	1	UEFA

GKS ZAGLEBIE WALBRZYCH

Founded 1946 as Thorez, 1967 Zaglebie
Colours green shirts, black shorts
Stadium Ratuszowa (25,000) ☎ 220 31

Season	Opponent	Home	Result	Away	Rnd	Cup
1971-72	Union Teplice, Czechoslovakia	1-0		3-2	1	UEFA
	UT Arad Flamurarosie, Romania	1-1		1-2	2	UEFA

OKS ODRA OPOLE

Founded 1945 Odra, 1948 Budowiani, 1956 Odra
Colours blue shirts, red shorts
Stadium Oleska (20,000) ☎ 285 77/285 95

Season	Opponent	Home	Result	Away	Rnd	Cup
1977-78	1.FC Magdeburg, Germany	1-2		1-1	1	UEFA

MZKS ARKA GDYNIA

Founded 1929
Colours yellow shirts, blue shorts
Stadium Ejsmonda (16,000) ☎ 20 47 55/20 13 97
Cup Winners 1979

Season	Opponent	Home	Result	Away	Rnd	Cup
1979-80	Beroe Stara Zagora, Bulgaria	3-2		0-2	1	CWC

GKS SZOMBIERKI BYTOM

Founded 1919 as Szombierki, 1948 Gornik, 1956 Szombierki
Colours green and white shirts, black shorts
Stadium Frycza Modrzewskiego (35,000) ☎ 832-81 70 53/86 15 44
Champions 1980

Season	Opponent	Home	Result	Away	Rnd	Cup
1980-81	Trabzonspor, Turkey	3-0		1-2	1	ECC
	CSKA Sofia, Bulgaria	0-1		0-4	2	ECC
1981-82	Feyenoord Rotterdam, Holland	1-1		0-2	1	UEFA

233

POLAND

BKS LECHIA GDANSK

Founded 1945 as Lechia, 1949 Budowlani, 1956 Lechia
Colours white shirts, green shorts
Stadium Tragutta (30,000) ☎ 058-41 25 70/41 92 93
Cup Winners 1983

Season	Opponent	Home	Result	Away	Rnd	Cup
1983-84	Juventus, Italy	2-3		0-7	1	CWC

MKS POGON SZCZECIN

Founded 1948
Colours light and dark blue striped shirts, red shorts
Stadium Pogon (17,000) ☎ 891-780 31/381 15

Season	Opponent	Home	Result	Away	Rnd	Cup
1984-85	1.FC Koln, Germany	0-1		1-2	1	UEFA
1987-88	Hellas-Verona, Italy	1-1		1-3	1	UEFA

STAL RZESZOW

Founded 1944
Colours white shirts, blue shorts
Stadium Stalingradu (25,000) ☎ 415 92/465 45
Cup Winners 1975

Season	Opponent	Home	Result	Away	Rnd	Cup
1975-76	Skeid Oslo, Norway	4-0		4-1	1	CWC
	Wrexham, Wales	1-1		0-2	2	CWC

PORTUGAL

Founded 1914 Federacao Portuguesa de Football, Corres ADD, Apartado 21 100,128 Lisboa Codex ☎ 32 82 07/08/09, 32 82 00 Telefax 346 7231
National colours red shirts, white shorts, red socks
Season September to July

CAMPEONATO DE PORTUGAL

1922	FC Porto v Sporting Lisbon	3-1	1930	Benfica v Barreirense	3-1
1923	Sporting Lisbon v Academica Coimbra	3-0	1931	Benfica v FC Porto	3-0
1924	Olhanese v FC Porto	4-2	1932	FC Porto v Belenenses	2-0
1925	FC Porto v Sporting Lisbon	2-1	1933	Belenenses v Sporting Lisbon	3-1
1926	Maritimo v Belenenses	2-0	1934	Sporting Lisbon v Barreirense	4-3
1927	Belenenses v Vitoria Setubal	3-0	1935	Benfica v Sporting Lisbon	2-1
1928	Carcavelinhos v Sporting Lisbon	3-1	1936	Sporting Lisbon v Belenenses	3-1
1929	Belenenses v Uniao de Tomar	2-1	1937	FC Porto v Sporting Lisbon	3-2
			1938	Sporting Lisbon v Benfica	3-1

LEAGUE CHAMPIONS

1935	FC Porto	1950	Benfica	1964	Benfica	1978	FC Porto
1936	Benfica	1951	Sporting Lisbon	1965	Benfica	1979	FC Porto
1937	Benfica	1952	Sporting Lisbon	1966	Sporting Lisbon		
1938	Benfica	1953	Sporting Lisbon	1967	Benfica	1980	Sporting Lisbon
1939	FC Porto	1954	Sporting Lisbon	1968	Benfica	1981	Benfica
		1955	Benfica	1969	Benfica	1982	Sporting Lisbon
1940	FC Porto	1956	FC Porto			1983	Benfica
1941	Sporting Lisbon	1957	Benfica	1970	Sporting Lisbon	1984	Benfica
1942	Benfica	1958	Sporting Lisbon	1971	Benfica	1985	Benfica
1943	Benfica	1959	FC Porto	1972	Benfica	1986	FC Porto
1944	Sporting Lisbon			1973	Benfica	1987	Benfica
1945	Benfica	1960	Benfica	1974	Sporting Lisbon	1988	FC Porto
1946	Belenenses	1961	Benfica	1975	Benfica	1989	Benfica
1947	Sporting Lisbon	1962	Sporting Lisbon	1976	Benfica		
1948	Sporting Lisbon	1963	Benfica	1977	Benfica		
1949	Sporting Lisbon						

PORTUGUESE SUPER CUP

1979	Boavista v FC Porto	2-1	1981	FC Porto v Benfica	4-1 0-2
			1982	Sporting Lisbon v Sporting Braga	6-1 1-2
1980	Benfica v Sporting Lisbon	2-1 2-2	1983	FC Porto v Benfica	0-0 2-1

235

PORTUGAL

1984 FC Porto v Benfica	1-0 0-1 3-0 1-0	**1987** Sporting Lisbon v Benfica	1-0 3-0
1985 Benfica v FC Porto	1-0 0-0	**1988** Vitoria Guimaraes v FC Porto	2-0 0-0
1986 FC Porto v Benfica	1-1 4-2	**1989** Benfica v Belenenses	2-0 2-0

FEATURED CLUBS IN EUROPEAN COMPETITION

Benfica Lisbon	**Vitoria Guimaraes**	**Vitoria Setubal**	**Sporting Lisbon**
FC Porto	**Sporting Clube Braga**	**OS Belenenses**	**Grupo Desportivo Quimigal**
Barreirense Barreiro	**Academica Coimbra**	**Boavista**	**Portimonense**
Leixoes	**Desportivo Chaves**		

SPORT LISBOA E BENFICA

Founded 28-2-1904
Colours red shirts, white shorts
Stadium Estadio Da Luz (120,000) ☎ 01-72 66 129/72 66 158
Champions 1930, 1931, 1936, 1937, 1938, 1942, 1943, 1945, 1950, 1955, 1957, 1960, 1961, 1963, 1964, 1965, 1967, 1968, 1969, 1971, 1972, 1973, 1975, 1976, 1977, 1981, 1983, 1984, 1987, 1989
Cup Winners 1940, 1943, 1944, 1949, 1951, 1952, 1953, 1955, 1957, 1959, 1962, 1964, 1969, 1970, 1972, 1980, 1981, 1983, 1985, 1986, 1987
Portuguese Super Cup Winners 1980, 1985, 1989
European Champions 1961, 1962
European Cup Finalists 1963, 1965, 1968, 1988
UEFA Cup Finalists 1983

Season	Opponent	Home	Play off Result	Away	Rnd	Cup
1957-58	Sevilla CF, Spain	0-0		1-3	pr	ECC
1960-61	Heart of Midlothian, Scotland	3-0		2-1	pr	ECC
	Ujpest Dozsa, Hungary	6-2		1-2	1	ECC
	AGF Aarhus, Denmark	3-1		4-1*	qf	ECC
				* in Copenhagen		
	Rapid Vienna, Austria	3-0		1-1	sf	ECC
	CF Barcelona, Spain	3-2	in Berne		FINAL	ECC
1961-62	bye				1	ECC
	FK Austria Vienna, Austria	5-1		1-1	2	ECC
	1.FC Nurnberg, Germany	6-0		1-3	qf	ECC
	Tottenham Hotspur, England	3-1		1-2	sf	ECC
	Real Madrid, Spain	5-3	in Amsterdam		FINAL	ECC
1962-63	bye				1	ECC
	IFK Norrkoping, Sweden	5-1		1-1	2	ECC
	Dukla Prague, Czechoslovakia	2-1		0-0	qf	ECC
	Feyenoord Rotterdam, Holland	3-1		0-0	sf	ECC
	AC Milan, Italy	1-2	at Wembley		FINAL	ECC
1963-64	Distillery, Ireland	5-0		3-3	pr	ECC
	Borussia Dortmund, Germany	2-1		0-5	1	ECC
1964-65	Aris Bonneweg, Luxembourg	5-1		5-1	1	ECC
	FC La Chaux de Fonds, Switzerland	5-0		1-1	2	ECC
	Real Madrid, Spain	5-1		1-2	qf	ECC
	Vasas Gyoer Eto, Hungary	4-0		1-0	sf	ECC
	Inter Milan, Italy	0-1	in Milan		FINAL	ECC
1965-66	Stade Dudelingen, Luxembourg	10-0		8-0	pr	ECC
	Levski Sofia, Bulgaria	3-2		2-2	1	ECC
	Manchester United, England	1-5		2-3	2	ECC
1966-67	bye				1	Fairs
	Spartak Plovdiv, Bulgaria	3-0		1-1	2	Fairs
	1.FC Lokomotive Leipzig, East Germany	2-1		1-3	3	Fairs
1967-68	Glentoran, Ireland	0-0	wag	1-1	1	ECC
	St Etienne, France	2-0		0-1	2	ECC
	Vasas Budapest, Hungary	3-0		0-0	qf	ECC
	Juventus, Italy	2-0		1-0	sf	ECC
	Manchester United, England	1-4	at Wembley		FINAL	ECC

236

Season	Opponent					
1968-69	Valur Reykjavik, Iceland	8-1		0-0	1	ECC
	bye				2	ECC
	Ajax Amsterdam, Holland	1-3	0-3 *aet * in Paris	3-1	qf	ECC
1969-70	KB Copenhagen, Denmark	2-0		3-2	1	ECC
	Glasgow Celtic, Scotland	3-0	lot	0-3	2	ECC
1970-71	Olimpia Llubljana, Yugoslavia	8-1		1-1	1	CWC
	FC Vorwaerts Berlin, East Germany	2-0	3-4 pen	0-2 aet	2	CWC
1971-72	Wacker Innsbruck, Austria	3-1		4-0	1	ECC
	CSKA Sofia, Bulgaria	2-1		0-0	2	ECC
	Feyenoord Rotterdam, Holland	5-1		0-1	qf	ECC
	Ajax Amsterdam, Holland	0-0		0-1	sf	ECC
1972-73	Malmo FF, Sweden	4-1		0-1	1	ECC
	Derby County, England	0-0		0-3	2	ECC
1973-74	Olympiakos Piraeus, Greece	1-0		1-0	1	ECC
	Ujpest Dozsa, Hungary	1-1		0-2	2	ECC
1974-75	Vanlose IF, Denmark	4-0		4-1	1	CWC
	Carl Zeiss Jena, East Germany	0-0	wag	1-1	2	CWC
	PSV Eindhoven, Holland	1-2		0-0	qf	CWC
1975-76	Fenerbahce, Turkey	7-0		0-1* * in Izmir	1	ECC
	Ujpest Dozsa, Hungary	5-2		1-3	2	ECC
	Bayern Munich, Germany	0-0		1-5	qf	ECC
1976-77	Dynamo Dresden, East Germany	0-0		0-2	1	ECC
1977-78	Torpedo Moscow, USSR	0-0	4-1 pen	0-0	1	ECC
	KB Copenhagen, Denmark	1-0		1-0	2	ECC
	Liverpool, England	1-2		1-4	qf	ECC
1978-79	FC Nantes, France	0-0		2-0	1	UEFA
	Borussia Monchengladbach, Germany	0-0		0-2	2	UEFA
1979-80	Aris Salonika, Greece	2-1		1-3	1	UEFA
1980-81	Altay Izmir, Turkey	4-0		0-0	pr	CWC
	Dinamo Zagreb, Yugoslavia	2-0		0-0	1	CWC
	Malmo FF, Sweden	2-0		0-1	2	CWC
	Fortuna Dusseldorf, Germany	1-0		2-2	qf	CWC
	Carl Zeiss Jena, East Germany	1-0		0-2	sf	CWC
1981-82	Omonia Nicosia, Cyprus	3-0		1-0	1	ECC
	Bayern Munich, Germany	0-0		1-4	2	ECC
1982-83	Real Betis, Spain	2-1		2-1	1	UEFA
	KSC Lokeren, Belgium	2-0		2-1	2	UEFA
	FC Zurich, Switzerland	4-0		1-1	3	UEFA
	AS Roma, Italy	1-1		2-1	qf	UEFA
	Universitatea Craiova, Romania	0-0	wag	1-1	sf	UEFA
	RSC Anderlecht, Belgium	1-1		0-1	FINAL	UEFA
1983-84	Linfield, Ireland	3-0		3-2	1	ECC
	Olympiakos Piraeus, Greece	3-0		0-1	2	ECC
	Liverpool, England	1-4		0-1	qf	ECC
1984-85	Red Star Belgrade, Yugoslavia	2-0		2-3	1	ECC
	Liverpool, England	1-0		1-3	2	ECC
1985-86	bye				1	CWC
	Sampdoria, Italy	2-0		0-1	2	CWC
	Dukla Prague, Czechoslovakia	2-1	lag	0-1	qf	CWC
1986-87	Lillestrom SK, Norway	2-0		2-1* * in Oslo	1	CWC
	Girondins Bordeaux, France	1-1		0-1	2	CWC
1987-88	Partizani Tirana, Albania	4-0	Partizani disq		1	ECC
	AGF Aarhus, Denmark	1-0		0-0	2	ECC
	RSC Anderlecht, Belgium	2-0		0-1	qf	ECC
	Steaua Bucharest, Romania	2-0		0-0	sf	ECC
	PSV Eindhoven, Holland	0-0	5-6 pens	in Stuttgart	FINAL	ECC
1988-89	Montpellier la Paillade, France	3-1		3-0	1	UEFA
	RFC Liege, Belgium	1-1		1-2	2	UEFA
1989-90	Derry City, Eire	4-0		2-1	1	ECC
	Honved Budapest, Hungary	7-0		2-0	2	ECC
	Dnepr Dnepropetrovsk, USSR	1-0		3-0	qf	ECC
	Olympique Marseille	1-0	wag	2-1	sf	ECC
	AC Milan, Italy	0-1	in Vienna		FINAL	ECC

PORTUGAL

VITORIA SPORT CLUBE

Founded 22-9-1922
Colours all white
Stadium Estadio Municipal de Guimaraes (28,000) ☎ 41 81 35/41 21 70
Portuguese Super Cup 1988

Season	Opponent	Home	Result	Away	Rnd	Cup
1969-70	Banik Ostrava, Czechoslovakia	1-0		1-1	1	Fairs
	Southampton, England	3-3		1-5	2	Fairs
1970-71	Angouleme, France	3-0		1-3	1	Fairs
	Hibernian, Scotland	2-1		0-2	2	Fairs
1983-84	Aston Villa, England	1-0		0-5	1	UEFA
1986-87	Sparta Prague, Czechoslovakia	2-1		1-1	1	UEFA
	Atletico Madrid, Spain	2-0		0-1	2	UEFA
	FC Groningen, Holland	3-0		0-1	3	UEFA
	Borussia Monchengladbach, Germany	2-2		0-3	qf	UEFA
1987-88	Tatabanya Banyasz, Hungary	1-0		1-1	1	UEFA
	Beveren Waas, Belgium	1-0	5-4 pen	0-1	2	UEFA
	TJ Vitkovice, Czechoslovakia	2-0	4-5 pen	0-2	3	UEFA
1988-89	Roda JC Kerkrade, Holland	1-0		0-2	1	CWC

VITORIA FUTEBOL CLUBE SETUBAL

Founded 20-11-1910
Colours green and white striped shirts, white shorts
Stadium Estadio do Bonfim Setubal (32,500) ☎ 065-22219/32991
Cup Winners 1965, 1967

Season	Opponent	Home	Result	Away	Rnd	Cup
1962-63	St Etienne, France	0-3		1-1	1	CWC
1965-66	AGF Aarhus, Denmark	1-2		1-2	1	CWC
1966-67	Juventus, Italy	0-2		1-3	2	Fairs
1967-68	Fredrikstad FK, Norway	2-1		5-1	1	CWC
	Bayern Munich, Germany	1-1		2-6	2	CWC
1968-69	Linfield, Ireland	3-0		3-1	1	Fairs
	Olympique Lyon, France	5-0		2-1	2	Fairs
	Fiorentina, Italy	3-0		1-2	3	Fairs
	Newcastle United, England	3-1*		1-5	qf	Fairs
		* in Lisbon, ground reconstruction				
1969-70	Rapid Bucharest, Romania	3-1*		4-1	1	Fairs
		* in Lisbon, ground reconstruction				
	Liverpool, England	1-0	wag	2-3	2	Fairs
	Hertha BSC Berlin, Germany	1-1		0-1	3	Fairs
1970-71	Lausanne Sport, Switzerland	2-1		2-0	1	Fairs
	Hajduk Split, Yugoslavia	2-0		1-2	2	Fairs
	RSC Anderlecht, Belgium	3-1		1-2	3	Fairs
	Leeds United, England	1-1		1-2	qf	Fairs
1971-72	Nimes, France	1-0	wag	1-2	1	UEFA
	Spartak Moscow, USSR	4-0		0-0	2	UEFA
	UT Arad Flamurarosie, Romania	1-0		0-3	3	UEFA
1972-73	Zaglebie Sosnowice, Poland	6-1		0-1	1	UEFA
	Fiorentina, Italy	1-0	wag	1-2	2	UEFA
	Inter Milan, Italy	2-0		0-1	3	UEFA
	Tottenham Hotspur, England	2-1	lag	0-1	qf	UEFA
1973-74	K Beerschot VAV Belgium	2-0		2-0	1	UEFA
	RWD Molenbeeck, Belgium	1-0	wag	1-2	2	UEFA
	Leeds United, England	3-1		0-1	3	UEFA
	VfB Stuttgart, Germany	2-2		0-1	qf	UEFA
1974-75	Real Zaragoza, Spain	1-1		0-4	1	UEFA
1988-89	Roda JC Kerkrade, Holland	1-0		0-2	1	CWC

SPORTING CLUBE DE PORTUGAL

Founded 1-6-1906
Colours green and white hooped shirts, black shorts
Stadium Estadio Jose de Alvalade (75,230) ☎ 01-758 90 21
Champions 1923, 1934, 1936, 1938,1941, 1944, 1947, 1948, 1949, 1951, 1952, 1953, 1954, 1958, 1962, 1966, 1970,
1974, 1980, 1982
Cup Winners 1941, 1945, 1946, 1948, 1954, 1963, 1971, 1973, 1974, 1978, 1982
Portuguese Super Cup Winners 1982, 1987
CWC Winners 1964

Season	Opponent	Home	Play off Result	Away	Rnd	Cup
1955-56	Partizan Belgrade, Yugoslavia	3-3		2-5	1	ECC
1958-59	DOS Utrecht, Holland	2-1		4-3	pr	ECC
	Standard Liege, Belgium	2-3		0-3	1	ECC
1961-62	Partizan Belgrade, Yugoslavia	1-1		0-2	pr	ECC
1962-63	Shelbourne, Eire	5-1		2-0	pr	ECC
	Dundee, Scotland	1-0		1-4	1	ECC
1963-64	Atalanta Bergamo, Italy	3-1	3-1*	0-2	1	CWC
			* in Barcelona			
	Apoel Nicosia, Cyprus	16-1*		2-0*	2	CWC
			* both in Lisbon			
	Manchester United, England	5-0		1-4	qf	CWC
	Olympique Lyon, France	1-1	1-0*	0-0	sf	CWC
			* in Madrid			
	MTK Budapest, Hungary	3-3	in Brussels		FINAL	CWC
	MTK Budapest, Hungary	1-0	in Antwerp		REPLAY	CWC
1964-65	bye	1				
	Cardiff City, Wales	1-2		0-0	2	CWC
1965-66	Girondins Bordeaux, France	6-1		4-0	1	Fairs
	Espanol Barcelona, Spain	2-1	1-2*	3-4	2	Fairs
			* in Barcelona			
1966-67	Vasas Budapest, Hungary	0-2		0-5	1	ECC
1967-68	Clube Bruges, Belgium	2-1		0-0	1	Fairs
	Fiorentina, Italy	2-1		1-1	2	Fairs
	FC Zurich, Switzerland	1-0		0-3	3	Fairs
1968-69	Valencia CF, Spain	4-0		1-4	1	Fairs
	Newcastle United, England	1-1		0-1	2	Fairs
1969-70	Linzer ASK, Austria	4-0		2-2	1	Fairs
	Arsenal, England	0-0		0-3	2	Fairs
1970-71	Floriana, Malta	5-0		4-0	1	ECC
	Carl Zeiss Jena, East Germany	1-2		1-2	2	ECC
1971-72	Lyn Oslo, Norway	4-0		3-0	1	CWC
	Glasgow Rangers, Scotland	4-3	lag	2-3	2	CWC
1972-73	Hibernian, Scotland	2-1		1-6	1	CWC
1973-74	Cardiff City, Wales	2-1		0-0	1	CWC
	Sunderland, England	2-0		1-2	2	CWC
	FC Zurich, Switzerland	3-0		1-1	qf	CWC
	1.FC Magdeburg, East Germany	1-1		1-2	sf	CWC
1974-75	St Etienne, France	1-1		0-2	1	ECC
1975-76	Sliema Wanderers, Malta	3-1		2-1	1	UEFA
	Vasas Budapest, Hungary	2-1		1-3	2	UEFA
1977-78	SEC Bastia Corsica, France	1-2		2-3	1	UEFA
1978-79	Banik Ostrava, Czechoslovakia	0-1		0-1	1	CWC
1979-80	Bohemians Dublin, Eire	2-0		0-0	1	UEFA
	1.FC Kaiserslautern, Germany	1-1		0-2	2	UEFA
1980-81	Honved Budapest, Hungary	0-2		0-1	1	ECC
1981-82	Red Boys Differdange, Luxembourg	4-0		7-0	1	UEFA
	Southampton, England	0-0		4-2	2	UEFA
	FC Neuchatel Xamax, Switzerland	0-0		0-1	3	UEFA
1982-83	Dinamo Zagreb, Yugoslavia	3-0		0-1	1	ECC
	CSKA Sofia, Bulgaria	0-0	wag	2-2	2	ECC
	Real Sociedad San Sebastian, Spain	1-0		0-2	qf	ECC

Season	Opponent	Home	Result	Away	Rnd	Cup
1983-84	Seville, Spain	3-2		1-1	1	UEFA
	Glasgow Celtic, Scotland	2-0		0-5	2	UEFA
1984-85	AJ Auxerre, France	2-0		2-2	1	UEFA
	Dynamo Minsk, USSR	2-0	3-5 pen	0-2	2	UEFA
1985-86	Feyenoord Rotterdam, Holland	3-1		1-2	1	UEFA
	Dinamo Tirana, Albania	1-0		0-0	2	UEFA
	Athletic Bilbao, Spain	3-0		1-2	3	UEFA
	1.FC Koln, Germany	1-1		0-2	qf	UEFA
1986-87	IA Akranes, Iceland	6-0		9-0*	1	UEFA
				* in Reykjavik		
	FC Barcelona, Spain	2-1	lag	0-1	2	UEFA
1987-88	FC Tirol, Austria	4-0		2-4	1	CWC
	Kalmar FF, Sweden	5-0		0-1	2	CWC
	Atalanta Bergamo, Italy	1-1		0-2	qf	CWC
1988-89	Ajax Amsterdam, Holland	4-2		2-1	1	UEFA
	Real Sociadad San Sebastian, Spain	1-2		0-0	2	UEFA
1989-90	Napoli, Italy	0-0	3-4p	0-0aet	1	UEFA

FUTEBOL CLUBE DO PORTO

Founded 2-8-1906
Colours blue and white striped shirts, blue shorts
Stadium Estadio das Antas (90,000) ☎ 40 02 61/40 02 36
Champions 1922, 1925, 1932, 1935, 1937, 1939, 1940, 1956, 1959, 1978, 1979, 1985, 1986
Cup Winners 1956, 1958, 1968, 1977, 1984
Portuguese Super Cup Winners 1981, 1983, 1984, 1986
World Club Champions 1987
European Cup Winners 1987
CWC Finalists 1984
European Supercup Winners 1987

Season	Opponent	Home	Result	Away	Rnd	Cup
1956-57	Atletico Bilbao, Spain	1-2		2-3	pr	ECC
1959-60	Red Star Bratislava, Czechoslovakia	0-2		1-2	pr	ECC
1962-63	Dinamo Zagreb, Yugoslavia	1-2		0-0	1	Fairs
1963-64	Atletico Madrid, Spain	0-0		1-2	1	Fairs
1964-65	Olympique Lyon, France	3-0		1-0	1	CWC
	TSV 1860 Munich, Germany	0-1		1-1	2	CWC
1965-66	Stade Francais, France	1-0		0-0	1	Fairs
	Hannover 96, Germany	2-1		0-5	2	Fairs
1966-67	Girondins Bordeaux, France	2-1	lot	1-2	1	Fairs
1967-68	Hibernian, Scotland	3-1		0-3	1	Fairs
1968-69	Cardiff City, Wales	2-1		2-2	1	CWC
	Slovan Bratislava, Czechoslovakia	1-0		0-4	2	CWC
1969-70	Hvidovre IF, Denmark	2-0		2-1	1	Fairs
	Newcastle United, England	0-0		0-1	2	Fairs
1971-72	FC Nantes, France	0-2		1-1	1	UEFA
1972-73	CF Barcelona, Spain	3-1		1-0	1	UEFA
	Clube Bruges, Belgium	3-0		2-3	2	UEFA
	Dynamo Dresden, East Germany	1-2		0-1	3	UEFA
1974-75	Wolverhampton Wanderers, England	4-1		1-3	1	UEFA
	Napoli, Italy	0-1		0-1	2	UEFA
1975-76	Avenir Beggen, Luxembourg	7-0		3-0	1	UEFA
	Dundee United, Scotland	1-1		2-1	2	UEFA
	Hamburger SV, Germany	2-1		0-2	3	UEFA
1976-77	FC Schalke 04 Gelsenkirchen, Germany	2-2*		2-3	1	UEFA
				* in Lisbon		
1977-78	1.FC Koln, Germany	1-0*		2-2	1	CWC
				* in Coimbra		
	Manchester United, England	4-0		2-5	2	CWC
	RSC Anderlecht, Belgium	1-0		0-3	qf	CWC
1978-79	AEK Athens, Greece	4-1		1-6	1	ECC
1979-80	AC Milan, Italy	0-0		1-0	1	ECC
	Real Madrid, Spain	2-1	lag	0-1	2	ECC

1980-81	Dundalk, Eire	1-0		0-0	1	UEFA
	Grasshoppers Zurich, Switzerland	2-0		0-3	2	UEFA
1981-82	Vejle BK, Denmark	3-0		1-2	1	CWC
	AS Roma, Italy	2-0		0-0	2	CWC
	Standard Liege, Belgium	2-2		0-2	qf	CWC
1982-83	FC Utrecht, Holland	2-0*		1-0**	1	UEFA
		* in Lisbon		** in Groningen		
	RSC Anderlecht, Belgium	3-2		0-4	2	UEFA
1983-84	Dinamo Zagreb, Yugoslavia	1-0	wag	1-2	1	CWC
	Glasgow Rangers, Scotland	1-0	wag	1-2	2	CWC
	Shakhtyor Donetsk, USSR	3-2		1-1	qf	CWC
	Aberdeen, Scotland	1-0		1-0	sf	CWC
	Juventus, Italy	1-2	in Basle		FINAL	CWC
1984-85	Wrexham, Wales	4-3	lag	0-1	1	CWC
1985-86	Ajax Amsterdam, Holland	2-0		0-0	1	ECC
	FC Barcelona, Spain	3-1	lag	0-2	2	ECC
1986-87	Rabat Ajax, Malta	9-0		1-0	1	ECC
	TJ Vitkovice, Czechoslovakia	3-0		0-1	2	ECC
	Brondbyernes IF, Denmark	1-0		1-1	qf	ECC
	Dynamo Kiev, USSR	2-1		2-1	sf	ECC
	Bayern Munich, Germany	2-1	in Vienna		FINAL	ECC
1987-88	Vardar Skopje, Yugoslavia	3-0		3-0	1	ECC
	Real Madrid, Spain	1-2		1-2*	2	ECC
				* in Valencia		
1988-89	HJK Helsinki, Finland	3-0		0-2	1	ECC
	PSV Eindhoven, Holland	2-0		0-5	2	ECC
1989-90	Flacara Moreni, Romania	2-0		2-1	1	UEFA
	Valencia CF, Spain	3-1		2-3	2	UEFA
	Hamburger SV, Germany	2-1	lag	0-1	3	UEFA

SPORTING CLUBE BRAGA

Founded 19-1-1921
Colours red shirts, white shorts ☎ 053-73924
Stadium Estadio 1 de Maio (40,000)
Cup Winners 1966

Season	Opponent	Home	Result	Away	Rnd	Cup
1966-67	AEK Athens, Greece	3-2		1-0	pr	CWC
	Vasas Gyoer Eto, Hungary	2-0		0-3	1	CWC
1978-79	Hibernians, Malta	5-0		2-3	1	UEFA
	West Bromwich Albion, England	0-2		0-1	2	UEFA
1982-83	Swansea City, Wales	1-0		0-3	pr	CWC
1984-85	Tottenham Hotspur, England	0-3		0-6	1	UEFA

PORTUGAL

CLUBE DE FUTEBOL "OS BELENENSES"

Founded 23-9-1919
Colours blue shirts, white shorts
Stadium Estadio do Restelo Lisbon (40,000) ☎ 61 04 61/61 29 14
Champions 1927, 1929, 1933, 1946
Cup Winners 1942, 1960, 1989

Season	Opponent	Home	Play off Result	Away	Rnd	Cup
1961-62	Hibernian, Scotland	1-3		3-3	1	Fairs
1962-63	CF Barcelona, Spain	1-1	2-3*	1-1	1	Fairs
			* in Barcelona			
1963-64	Tresnjevka Zagreb, Yugoslavia	2-1		2-0	1	Fairs
	AS Roma, Italy	0-1		1-2	2	Fairs
1964-65	Shelbourne, Eire	1-1	1-2*	0-0	pr	Fairs
			* in Dublin			
1973-74	Wolverhampton Wanderers, England	0-2		1-2	1	UEFA
1976-77	FC Barcelona, Spain	2-2		2-3	1	UEFA
1987-88	FC Barcelona, Spain	1-0		0-2	1	UEFA
1988-89	Bayer Leverkusan, Germany	1-0		1-0	1	UEFA
	Velez Mostar, Yugoslavia	0-0	3-4p	0-0	2	UEFA
1989-90	AS Monaco, France	1-1		0-3	1	CWC

GRUPO DESPORTIVO QUIMIGAL

Founded 1937 as CUF Barreiro, 1987 as Grupo Desportivo Quimigal
Colours green shirts, white shorts
Stadium Estadio Alfredo da Silva (25,000) ☎ 01 207 2566

Season	Opponent	Home	Play off Result	Away	Rnd	Cup
as CUF, BARREIRO						
1965-66	bye				1	Fairs
	AC Milan, Italy	2-0	0-1*	0-2	2	Fairs
			* in Milan			
1967-68	Vojvodina Novi Sad, Yugoslavia	1-3		0-1	1	Fairs
1972-73	Racing White Brussels, Belgium	2-0		1-0	1	UEFA
	1.FC Kaiserslautern, Germany	1-3		1-0	2	UEFA

FUTEBOL CLUBE BARREIRENSE

Founded 11-4-1911
Colours red and white striped shirts, white shorts
Stadium Campo D Manuel de Melo, Barreiro (10,535) ☎

Season	Opponent	Home	Result	Away	Rnd	Cup
1970-71	Dinamo Zagreb, Yugoslavia	2-0		1-6	1	Fairs

ASSOCIACAO ACADEMICA DE COIMBRA

Founded 1876, 1914 as Academica de Coimbra, 1974 as Clube Academico de Coimbra, 1984-5 as Associacao de Coimbra
Colours all black
Stadium Estadio Municipal de Coimbra (27,500) ☎ 039-26 689

Season	Opponent	Home	Result	Away	Rnd	Cup
1968-69	Olympique Lyon, France	1-0	lot	0-1	1	Fairs
1969-70	KuPS Kuopion Palloseura, Finland	0-0		1-0	1	CWC
	1.FC Magdeburg, East Germany	2-0		0-1	2	CWC
	Manchester City, England	0-0		0-1	qf	CWC
1971-72	Wolverhampton Wanderers, England	1-4		0-3	1	UEFA

BOAVISTA

Founded 1-8-1903
Colours black and white checked shirts, black shorts
Stadium Estadio do Bessa, Porto (28,000) ☎ 02-66 85 06/69 09 75/69 81 59
Cup Winners 1975, 1976, 1979
Portuguese Super Cup Winners 1979

Season	Opponent	Home	Result	Away	Rnd	Cup
1975-76	Spartak Trnava, Czechoslovakia	3-0		0-0	1	CWC
	Glasgow Celtic, Scotland	0-0		1-3	2	CWC
1976-77	CSU Galati, Romania	2-0		3-2	1	CWC
	Levski Spartak Sofia, Bulgaria	3-1	lag	0-2	2	CWC
1977-78	Lazio Rome, Italy	1-0		0-5	1	UEFA
1979-80	Sliema Wanderers, Malta	8-0		1-2	1	CWC
	Dynamo Moscow, USSR	1-1	lag	0-0	2	CWC
1980-81	Vasas Budapest, Hungary	0-1		2-0	1	UEFA
	Sochaux, France	0-1		2-2	2	UEFA
1981-82	Athletic Madrid, Spain	4-1		1-3	1	UEFA
	Valencia CF, Spain	1-0		0-2	2	UEFA
1985-86	Clube Bruges, Belgium	4-3		1-3	1	UEFA
1986-87	Fiorentina, Italy	1-0	3-1 pen	0-1	1	UEFA
	Glasgow Rangers, Scotland	0-1		1-2	2	UEFA
1989-90	Karl Marx Stadt, East Germany	2-2aet		0-1	1	UEFA

PORTIMONENSE SPORTING CLUBE

Founded 14-8-1914
Colours black and white striped shirts, black shorts
Stadium Estadio do Portimonense (17,300) ☎ 082-22 926/22 427

Season	Opponent	Home	Result	Away	Rnd	Cup
1985-86	Partizan Belgrade, Yugoslavia	1-0		0-4	1	UEFA

PORTUGAL

LEIXOES SPORT CLUB

Founded 28-11-1907
Colours red and white striped shirts, white shorts
Stadium Estadio do Mar, Matosinhos (24,000) ☎ 93 36 17
Cup Winners 1961

Season	Opponent	Home	Result	Away	Rnd	Cup
1961-62	FC La Chaux de Fonds, Switzerland	5-0		2-6	1	CWC
	Progresul Oradea, Romania	1-1*		1-0	2	CWC
		* in Lisbon				
	Motor Jena, East Germany	1-3*		1-1**	3	CWC
		* in Gera		** in Jena		
1964-65	Glasgow Celtic, Scotland	1-1		0-3	pr	Fairs
1968-69	Argesul Pitesti, Romania	1-1	lag	0-0	1	Fairs

GRUPO DESPORTIVO DE CHAVES

Founded 27-9-1949
Colours blue shirt with wide red centre panel, blue shorts
Stadium Estadio Municipal de Chaves (27,000) ☎ 24446/22353

Season	Opponent	Home	Result	Away	Rnd	Cup
1987-88	Universitatea Craiova, Romania	2-1	wag	2-3	1	UEFA
	Honved Budapest, Hungary	1-2		1-3	2	UEFA

ROMANIA

Founded 1908
Federatia Romina de Fotbal, Vasile Conta 16, Bucharest 6 ☎ 12 10 60/11 97 87 Fax 0-119 869
National colours yellow shirts, blue shorts, red socks

LEAGUE CHAMPIONS

1910	Olimpia Bucharest	1930	Juventus Bucharest	1953	CCA Bucharest	1973	Dinamo Bucharest
1911	Olimpia Bucharest	1931	SSUD Resita	1954	UT Arad Flamurarosie	1974	Universitatea Craiova
1912	United Ploesti	1932	Venus Bucharest	1955	Dinamo Bucharest	1975	Dinamo Bucharest
1913	CA Colentina Bucharest	1933	Ripensia Temesvar	1956	CCA Bucharest *	1976	Steaua Bucharest
1914	CA Colentina Bucharest	1934	Venus Bucharest	1957	CCA Bucharest	1977	Dinamo Bucharest
1915	Soc RA Bucharest	1935	Ripensia Bucharest	1958	Petrolui Ploesti	1978	Steaua Bucharest
1916	Prahova Ploesti	1936	Ripensia Bucharest	1959	Petrolui Ploesti	1979	Arges Pitesti
1917	not held	1937	Venus Bucharest			1980	Universitatea Craiova
1918	not held	1938	Ripensia Timisoara	1960	CCA Bucharest	1981	Universitatea Craiova
1919	not held	1939	Venus Bucharest	1961	CCA Bucharest	1982	Dinamo Bucharest
				1962	Dinamo Bucharest	1983	Dinamo Bucharest
1920	Venus Bucharest	1940	Venus Bucharest	1963	Dinamo Bucharest	1984	Dinamo Bucharest
1921	Venus Bucharest	1941	Unirea Tricolor Bucharest	1964	Dinamo Bucharest	1985	Steaua Bucharest
1922	CSC Temesvar	1942	Rapid Bucharest	1965	Dinamo Bucharest	1986	Steaua Bucharest
1923	CSC Temesvar	1943	Craiova Bucharest	1966	Petrolui Ploesti	1987	Steaua Bucharest
1924	CSC Temesvar	1947	UT Arad Flamurarosie	1967	Rapid Bucharest	1988	Steaua Bucharest
1925	CSC Temesvar	1948	UT Arad Flamurarosie	1968	Steaua Bucharest	1989	Steaua Bucharest
1926	CSC Temesvar	1949	Progresul Oradea	1969	UT Arad Flamuarosie		
1927	CSC Temesvar			1970	UT Arad Flamuarosie	* unofficial	
1928	CSC Brasov	1950	UT Arad Flamuarosie	1971	Dinamo Bucharest		
1929	Venus Bucharest	1951	CCA Bucharest	1972	Arges Pitesti		
		1952	CCA Bucharest				

CUP WINNERS

1934	Ripensia Timisoara v Universitatea Cluj	5-0
1935	CFR Bucharest v Ripensia Timisoara	6-5
1936	Ripensia Timisoara v Unirea Tricolor Buch	5-1
1937	Rapid Bucharest v Ripensia Timisoara	5-1
1938	Rapid Bucharest v CAMT Timisoara	3-2
1939	Rapid Bucharest v Sportul Studentesc Bucharest	2-0
1940	Rapid Bucharest v Venus Bucharest	2-2 4-4 2-2 2-1
1941	Rapid Bucharest v Unirea Tricolor Bucharest	4-3
1942	Rapid Bucharest v Universitatea Sibiu	7-1

1943	CFR Turnu Severin v Sportul Studentesc Bucharest	4-0
1948	UT Arad Flamurarosie v CFR Timisoara	3-2
1949	Steaua Bucharest v CSU Cluj	2-1 1-1 3-0
1950	Steaua Bucharest v UT Arad Flamurarosie	3-1
1951	Steaua Bucharest v Flacara Medias	3-1
1952	Steaua Bucharest v Flacara Poesti	2-0
1953	UT Arad Flamurarosie v Steaua Bucharest	1-0
1954	Metalul Resita v Dinamo Bucharest	2-0
1955	Steaua Bucharest v Progresul Oradea	6-3

ROMANIA

1956	Progresul Oradea v Metalul Turzii	2-0
1958	Stintza Timisoara v Progresul Bucharest	1-0
1959	Dinamo Bucharest v CSM Baia Mare	4-0
1960	Progresul Bucharest v Dinamo Obor Bucharest	2-0
1961	Progresul Bucharest v Rapid Bucharest	2-1
1962	Steaua Bucharest v Rapid Bucharest	5-1
1963	Petrolui Ploesti v Siderurgistul Galati	6-1
1964	Dinamo Bucharest v Steaua Bucharest	5-3
1965	Stintza Cluj Univ v Dinamo Pitesti	2-1
1966	Steaua Bucharest v UT Arad Flamurarosie	4-0
1967	Steaua Bucharest v Foresta Falticeni	6-0
1968	Dinamo Bucharest v Rapid Bucharest	3-1
1969	Steaua Bucharest v Dinamo Bucharest	2-1
1970	Steaua Bucharest v Dinamo Bucharest	2-1
1971	Steaua Bucharest v Dinamo Bucharest	3-2
1972	Rapid Bucharest v Jiul Petrosani	2-0
1973	Chimia Ramnicu Vilcea v Constructorul Galatzi	1-1 3-0

1974	Jiul Petrosani v Politehnica Timisoara	4-2
1975	Rapid Bucharest v Universitatea Craiova	2-1
1976	Steaua Bucharest v CSU Galati	1-0
1977	Universitatea Craiova v Steaua Bucharest	2-1
1978	Universitatea Craiova v Olympia Sathmar	3-1
1979	Steaua Bucharest v Sportul Studentesc Bucharest	3-0
1980	Politehnica Timisoara v Steaua Bucharest	2-1
1981	Universitatea Craiova v Politehnica Timisoara	6-0
1982	Dinamo Bucharest v Baia Mare	3-2
1983	Universitatea Craiova v Politechnica Timisoara	2-1
1984	Dinamo Bucharest v Steaua Bucharest	2-1
1985	Steaua Bucharest v Universitatea Craiova	2-1
1986	Dinamo Bucharest v Steaua Bucharest	1-0
1987	Steaua Bucharest v Dinamo Bucharest	1-0
1988	Steaua Bucharest v Dinamo Bucharest	1-1 abd
	later awarded to Steaua	
1989	Steaua Bucharest v Dinamo Bucharest	1-0

FEATURED CLUBS IN EUROPEAN COMPETITION

Unirea Tricolor (Dinamo Bucharest)		**Petrolui Ploesti**	**Rapid Bucharest**
UT Arad Flamurarosie	**Steaua Bucharest (CCA)**	**Bacau**	**Universitatea Stintza Cluj**
FC Arges Pitesti	**Universitatea Craiova**	**Politehnica Timisoara**	**Dunarea CSU Galati**
Corvinul Hunedoara	**FC Baia Mare**	**Steagul Rosu Brasov**	**Progresul Oradea**
Jiul Petrosani	**Chimia Ramnicu Valcea**	**AS Armata Tirgu Mures**	**Sportul Studentesc Bucharest**
Victoria Bucharest	**Otelul Galati**	**Flacara Moreni**	

UNIREA TRICOLOR

**Founded 1948 by amalgamation of Unirea Tricolour and Ciocanul, name changed from Dinamo Bucharest on 2-1-90
Colours all white
Stadium Narodni (18,000) or 23rd August (95,000) ☎ 90-105700
Champions 1955, 1962, 1963, 1964, 1965, 1971, 1973, 1975, 1977, 1982, 1983, 1984
Cup Winners 1959, 1964, 1968, 1982, 1984, 1986**

Season	Opponent	Home	Result	Away	Rnd	Cup
as DINAMO BUCHAREST						
1956-57	Galatasaray, Turkey	3-1		1-2	pr	ECC
	CDNA Sofia, Bulgaria	3-2		1-8	1	ECC
1962-63	Galatasaray, Turkey	1-1		0-3	1	ECC
1963-64	Motor Jena, East Germany	2-0		1-0	1	ECC
	Real Madrid, Spain	1-3		3-5	2	ECC
1964-65	Sliema Wanderers, Malta	5-0		2-0	pr	ECC
	Inter Milan, Italy	0-1		0-6	1	ECC
1965-66	B 1909 Odense, Denmark	4-0		3-2	pr	ECC
	Inter Milan, Italy	2-1		0-2	1	ECC
1968-69	Vasas Gyoer Eto, Hungary	withdrew			1	CWC
	West Bromwich Albion, England	1-1		0-4	2	CWC
1970-71	PAOK Salonika, Greece	5-0		0-1	1	Fairs
	Liverpool, England	1-1		0-3	2	Fairs
1971-72	Spartak Trnava, Czechoslovakia	0-0	lag	2-2	1	ECC
	Feyenoord Rotterdam, Holland	0-3		0-2	2	ECC
1973-74	Crusaders, Ireland	11-0		1-0	1	ECC
	Atletico Madrid, Spain	0-2		2-2	2	ECC
1974-75	Boluspor Bolu, Turkey	3-0		1-0	1	UEFA
	1.FC Koln, Germany	1-1		2-3	2	UEFA
1975-76	Real Madrid, Spain	1-0		1-4	1	ECC

1976-77	AC Milan, Italy	0-0		1-2	1	UEFA
1977-78	Atletico Madrid, Spain	2-1		0-2	1	ECC
1979-80	Alki Larnaca, Cyprus	3-0		9-0	1	UEFA
	Eintracht Frankfurt, Germany	2-0		0-3	2	UEFA
1981-82	Levski Spartak Sofia, Bulgaria	3-0		1-2	1	UEFA
	Inter Milan, Italy	3-2		1-1	2	UEFA
	IFK Gothenburg, Sweden	0-1		1-3	3	UEFA
1982-83	Valerengen IF Oslo, Norway	3-1		1-2	pr	ECC
	Dukla Prague, Czechoslovakia	2-0		1-2	1	ECC
	Aston Villa, England	0-2		2-4	2	ECC
1983-84	Kuusysi Lahti, Finland	3-0		1-0	1	ECC
	Hamburger SV, Germany	3-0		2-3	2	ECC
	Dynamo Minsk, USSR	1-0		1-1	qf	ECC
	Liverpool, England	1-2		0-1	sf	ECC
1984-85	Omonia Nicosia, Cyprus	4-1		1-2	1	ECC
	Girondins Bordeaux, France	1-1		0-1	2	ECC
1985-86	Vardar Skopje, Yugoslavia	2-1	lag	0-1	1	UEFA
1986-87	17 Nentori Tirana, Albania	1-2		0-1	1	CWC
1987-88	KV Mechelen, Belgium	0-2		0-1	1	CWC
1988-89	Kuusysi Lahti, Finland	3-0		3-0	1	CWC
	Dundee United, Scotland	1-1		1-0	2	CWC
	Sampdoria, Italy	1-1	lag	0-0*	qf	CWC
			* in Cremona, ground being renovated			
1989-90	Dinamo Tirana, Albania	2-0		0-1	1	CWC
	Panathinaikos, Greece	6-1		2-0	2	CWC
	Partizan Belgrade, Yugoslavia	2-1		2-0	qf	CWC
as UNIREA TRICOLOR						
	RSA Anderlecht, Belgium	0-1		0-1	sf	CWC

PETROLUI PLOESTI

Founded 1952 as Flacara, 1957 (Spring) Energia (Autumn) Petrolui
Colours yellow shirts, blue shorts
Stadium Petrolul (25,000) ☎ 971-22258
Champions 1958, 1959, 1966
Cup Winners 1963

Season	Opponent	Home	Playoff Result	Away	Rnd	Cup
1958-59	Wismut Karl Marx Stadt, East Germany	2-0	0-4* * in Kiev	2-4	pr	ECC
1959-60	Wiener Sport Club, Austria	1-2		0-0	pr	ECC
1962-63	Spartak Brno, Czechoslovakia	4-2		1-0	1	Fairs
	Leipzig City XI, East Germany	1-0	1-0* * in Budapest	0-1	2	Fairs
	Ferencvarosi TC, Hungary	1-0		0-2	3	Fairs
1963-64	Fenerbahce, Turkey	1-0		1-4	pr	CWC
1964-65	Goztepe Izmir, Turkey	2-1		1-0	1	Fairs
	Lokomotiv Plovdiv, Bulgaria	1-0		0-2	2	Fairs
1966-67	Liverpool, England	3-1	0-2* * in Brussels	0-2	pr	ECC
1967-68	Dinamo Zagreb, Yugoslavia	2-0		0-5	1	Fairs

247

ROMANIA

RAPID BUCHAREST

Founded 1923 as CFR, 1936 Rapid, 1946 CFR, 1950 Lokomotiva, 1958 Rapid
Colours white shirts, orange shorts
Stadium Republicii (30,000)☎ 90-170301
Champions 1942, 1967
Cup Winners 1935 as CFR, 1937, 1938, 1939, 1940, 1941, 1942, 1972, 1975

Season	Opponent	Home	Result	Away	Rnd	Cup
1967-68	Trakia Plovdiv, Bulgaria	3-0		0-2	1	ECC
	Juventus, Italy	0-0		0-1	2	ECC
1968-69	OFK Belgrade, Yugoslavia	3-1		1-6	1	Fairs
1969-70	Vitoria Setubal, Portugal	1-4		1-3*	1	Fairs
			* in Lisbon, ground reconstruction			
1971-72	Napoli, Italy	2-0		0-1	1	UEFA
	Legia Warsaw, Poland	4-0		0-2	2	UEFA
	Tottenham Hotspur, England	0-2		0-3	3	UEFA
1972-73	Landskrona BoIS, Sweden	3-0		0-1	1	CWC
	Rapid Vienna, Austria	3-1		1-1	2	CWC
	Leeds United, England	1-3		0-5	qf	CWC
1975-76	RSC Anderlceht, Belgium	1-0		0-2	1	CWC

UT ARAD FLAMURAROSIE

UT=Uzinelor Textile
Founded 1945 as ITA Arad, 1950 Flamura Rosie, 1958 UTA Arad
Colours red shirts, white shorts
Stadium UTA (17,000) ☎ ??????
Champions 1947, 1948, 1950, 1954, 1969, 1970
Cup Winners 1948, 1953

Season	Opponent	Home	Result	Away	Rnd	Cup
1969-70	Legia Warsaw, Poland	1-2		0-8	1	ECC
1970-71	Feyenoord Rotterdam, Holland	0-0	wag	1-1	1	ECC
	Red Star Belgrade, Yugoslavia	1-3		0-3	2	ECC
1971-72	Austria Salzburg, Austria	4-1		1-3	1	UEFA
	Zaglebie Walbrzych, Poland	2-1		1-1	2	UEFA
	Vitoria Setubal, Portugal	3-0		0-1	3	UEFA
	Tottenham Hotspur, England	0-2		1-1	qf	UEFA
1972-73	IFK Norrkoping, Sweden	1-2		0-2	1	UEFA

STEAUA BUCHAREST

Founded 1947 as Armata, 1948 CSCA, 1950 CCA, 1962 Steaua
CCA=Casa Central Army full name is now "Clubul sportiv al-amatai Steaua Bucharest
Colours all red or all white
Stadium Steaua, Ghencea (30,000) ☎ 90-493390
Champions 1951, 1952, 1953, 1956, 1957, 1960, 1961 As Steaua 1968, 1976, 1978, 1985, 1986, 1987, 1988, 1989
Cup Winners 1949, 1950, 1951, 1952, 1955, 1962, 1966, 1967, 1969, 1970, 1971, 1976, 1979, 1985, 1987, 1988, 1989
European Cup Winners 1986, European Cup Finalists 1989
World Club Cup Finalists 1986
European Super Cup Winners 1986

Season	Opponent	Home	Playoff Result	Away	Rnd	Cup
as CCA BUCHAREST						
1957-58	Borussia Dortmund, Germany	3-1	1-3*	2-4	1	ECC
			* in Bologna			

1960-61	Spartak Hradec Kralove, Czechoslovakia	withdrew				ECC
1961-62	FK Austria Vienna, Austria	0-0		0-2	pr	ECC
as STEAUA						
1962-63	Botev Plovdiv, Bulgaria	1-5		3-2	1	CWC
1964-65	Derry City, Ireland	3-0		2-0	pr	CWC
	Dinamo Zagreb, Yugoslavia	1-3		0-2	1	CWC
1966-67	RC Strasbourg, France	1-1		0-1	pr	CWC
1967-68	FK Austria Vienna, Austria	2-1		2-0	1	CWC
	Valencia CF, Spain	1-0		0-3	2	CWC
1968-69	Spartak Trnava, Czechoslovakia	3-1		0-4	1	ECC
1969-70	Glasgow Rangers, Scotland	0-0		0-2	1	CWC
1970-71	Carpath Lvov, USSR	3-3		1-0	1	CWC
	PSV Eindhoven, Holland	0-3		0-4	2	CWC
1971-72	Hibernians, Malta	1-0		0-0	1	CWC
	CF Barcelona, Spain	2-1		1-0	2	CWC
	Bayern Munich, Germany	1-1	lag	0-0	qf	CWC
1976-77	Clube Bruges, Belgium	1-1		1-2	1	ECC
1977-78	FC Barcelona, Spain	1-3		1-5	1	UEFA
1978-79	AS Monaco, France	2-0		0-3	pr	ECC
1979-80	Young Boys Bern, Switzerland	6-0		2-2	1	CWC
	FC Nantes, France	1-2		2-3	2	CWC
1980-81	Standard Liege, Belgium	1-2		1-1	1	UEFA
1984-85	AS Roma, Italy	0-0		0-1	1	CWC
	Barcelona, Spain	0-0	2-0 pens	in Seville	FINAL	ECC
1986-87	bye				1	ECC
	RSC Anderlecht, Belgium	1-0		0-3	2	ECC
1987-88	MTK/VM Budapest, Hungary	4-0		0-2	1	ECC
	Omonia Nicosia, Cyprus	3-1		2-0	2	ECC
	Glasgow Rangers, Scotland	2-0		1-2	qf	ECC
	Benfica, Portugal	0-0		0-2	sf	ECC
1988-89	Sparta Prague, Czechoslovakia	2-2		5-1	1	ECC
	Spartak Moscow, USSR	3-0		2-1	2	ECC
	IFK Gothenburg, Sweden	5-1		0-1	qf	ECC
	Galatasaray, Turkey	4-0		1-1	sf	ECC
	AC Milan, Italy	in Barcelona			FINAL	ECC
1989-90	Fram Reykjavik, Iceland	4-0		1-0	1	ECC
	PSV Eindhoven, Holland	1-0		1-5	2	ECC

BACAU

Founded 1950 as Dinamo
Colours blue shirts, red shorts
Stadium 23rd August (20,000) ☎ 931-41922

Season	Opponent	Home	Result	Away	Rnd	Cup
1969-70	Floriana, Malta	6-0		1-0	1	Fairs
	Skeid Oslo, Norway	2-0		0-0	2	Fairs
	Kilmarnock, Scotland	2-0		1-1	3	Fairs
	Arsenal, England	0-2		1-7	qf	Fairs

ROMANIA

UNIVERSITATEA CLUJ

Founded 1919 as Universitatea Cluj, 1940 Universitatea Sibiu, 1944 Universitatea Cluj, 1948 CSU Cluj,
1950 Stiinta Cluj, 1966 Universitatea Cluj
Colours white shirts, black shorts
Stadium Muncitoresc (28,000) ☎ 951-16181
Cup Winners 1965

Season	Opponent	Home	Result	Away	Rnd	Cup
as STINTA CLUJ						
1965-66	Wiener Neustadt, Austria	2-0		1-0	1	CWC
	Atletico Madrid, Spain	0-2		0-4	2	CWC
as UNIVERSTATEA CLUJ						
1972-73	Levski Spartak Sofia, Bulgaria	4-1		1-5	1	UEFA

FC ARGES PITESTI

Founded 1953 as Dynamo, 1967 Argesul, 1970 FC Arges
Stadium 1st May (15,000) ☎ 976-33642
Colours violet shirts, white shorts or all blue
Champions 1972, 1979

Season	Opponent	Home	Result	Away	Rnd	Cup
as DYNAMO PITESTI						
1966-67	Sevilla CF, Spain	2-0		2-2	1	Fairs
	Toulouse FC, France	5-1		0-3	2	Fairs
	Dinamo Zagreb, Yugoslavia	0-0		0-1	3	Fairs
as ARGESUL PITESTI						
1967-68	Ferencvarosi TC, Hungary	3-1		0-4	1	Fairs
1968-69	Leixoes Sporting, Portugal	0-0	wag	1-1	1	Fairs
	Goztepe Izmir, Turkey	3-2		0-3	2	Fairs
as FC ARGES						
1972-73	Aris Bonneweg, Luxembourg	4-0		2-0	1	ECC
	Real Madrid, Spain	2-1		1-3	2	ECC
1973-74	Fenerbahce, Turkey	1-1		1-5	1	UEFA
1978-79	Panathinaikos, Greece	3-0		2-1	1	UEFA
	Valencia CF, Spain	2-1		2-5	2	UEFA
1979-80	AEK Athens, Greece	3-0		0-2	1	ECC
	Nottingham Forest, England	1-2		0-2	2	ECC
1980-81	FC Utrecht, Holland	0-0		0-2	1	UEFA
1981-82	Apoel Nicosia, Cyprus	4-0		1-1	1	UEFA
	Aberdeen, Scotland	2-2		0-3	2	UEFA

UNIVERSITATEA CRAIOVA

Founded 1919 as CSR, 1923 Universitatea, 1948 CSU Cluj, 1950 Stiinta, 1966 Universitatea
Colours white shirts, blue shorts
Stadium Central (30,000) ☎ 941-32480
Champions 1943, 1974, 1980, 1981
Cup Winners 1977, 1978, 1981, 1983

Season	Opponent	Home	Result	Away	Rnd	Cup
1970-71	Pecsi Dozsa, Hungary	2-1		0-3	1	Fairs
1973-74	Fiorentina, Italy	1-0		0-0	1	UEFA
	Standard Liege, Belgium	1-1		0-2	2	UEFA
1974-75	Atvidaberg FF, Sweden	2-1		1-3	1	ECC
1975-76	Red Star Belgrade, Yugoslavia	1-3		1-1	1	UEFA
1977-78	Olympiakos Nicosia, Cyprus	2-0		6-1	1	CWC
	Dynamo Moscow, USSR	2-0	0-3 pen	0-2	2	CWC

1978-79	Fortuna Dusseldorf, Germany	3-4		1-1	1	CWC
1979-80	Wiener Sport Club, Austria	3-1		0-0	1	UEFA
	Leeds United, England	2-0		2-0	2	UEFA
	Borussia Monchengladbach, Germany	1-0		0-2	3	UEFA
1980-81	Inter Milan, Italy	1-1		0-2	1	ECC
1981-82	Olympiakos Piraeus, Greece	3-0		0-2	1	ECC
	KB Copenhagen, Denmark	4-1		0-1	2	ECC
	Bayern Munich, Germany	0-2		1-1	qf	ECC
1982-83	Fiorentina, Italy	3-1		0-1	1	UEFA
	Shamrock Rovers, Eire	3-0		2-0	2	UEFA
	Girondins Bordeaux, France	2-0		0-1	3	UEFA
	1.FC Kaiserslautern, Germany	1-0	wag	2-3	qf	UEFA
	Benfica, Portugal	1-1	lag	0-0	SF	UEFA
1983-84	Hajduk Split, Yugoslavia	1-0	1-3 pen	0-1	1	UEFA
1984-85	Real Betis Seville, Spain	1-0	5-3 pen	0-1	1	UEFA
	Olympiakos Piraeus, Greece	1-0		1-0	2	UEFA
	Zeljeznicar Sarajevo, Yugoslavia	2-0		0-4	3	UEFA
1985-86	AS Monaco, France	3-0		0-2	1	CWC
	Dynamo Kiev, USSR	2-2		0-3	2	CWC
1986-87	Galatasaray, Turkey	2-0		1-2	1	UEFA
	Dundee United, Scotland	1-0		0-3	2	UEFA
1987-88	Desportivo Chaves, Portugal	3-2		1-2	1	UEFA

POLITEHNICA TIMISOARA

Founded 1920 as UCAS Politechnica Timisoara, 1930 CSU Timisoara, 1950 Stiinta Timisoara,
1966 Politehnica Timisoara
Colours violet shirts, white shorts
Stadium 1st May (36,000) ☎ 961-35373
Cup Winners 1980

Season	Opponent	Home	Result	Away	Rnd	Cup
1978-79	MTK Budapest, Hungary	2-0		1-2	1	UEFA
	Honved Budapest, Hungary	2-0		0-4	2	UEFA
1980-81	Glasgow Celtic, Scotland	1-0	wag	1-2	1	CWC
	West Ham United, England	1-0		0-4	2	CWC
1981-82	1.FC Lokomotive Leipzig, East Germany	2-0		0-5	pr	CWC

DUNAREA CSU GALATI

CSU=Clubul Sportiv Univeisitar
Founded 1970 as FC Galati, 1982 amalgamation of CSU Galati and FCM Galati to become Dunarea CSU
Colours white shirts, blue shorts
Stadium Muncitoresc ☎

Season	Opponent	Home	Result	Away	Rnd	Cup
1976-77	Boavista, Portugal	2-3		0-2	1	CWC

CORVINUL (HUNEDOARA)

Founded 1921 as Corvinul, 1946 UF Hunedoara, 1948 IMS Hunedoara, 1952 Metalul, 1957 Corvinul,
1963 Siderurgistul, 1964 Metalul, 1970 Corvinul Hunedoara
Colours blue and white striped shirts, blue shorts
Stadium Corvinul (15,000) ☎ 957-14906

Season	Opponent	Home	Result	Away	Rnd	Cup
1982-83	Grazer ASK, Austria	3-0		1-1	1	UEFA
	FK Sarajevo, Yugoslavia	4-4		0-4	2	UEFA

ROMANIA

FC BAIA MARE

Founded 1930 as Phoenix, 1938 CSM Baia Mare, 1940 Carpati, 1956 Minerul, 1962 FC Baia Mare
Colours yellow shirts, blue shorts
Stadium 23rd August (13,000) ☎

Season	Opponent	Home	Result	Away	Rnd	Cup
1982-83	Real Madrid, Spain	0-0		2-5	1	CWC

STEAGUL ROSU BRASOV

Founded 1950 as Dinamo Brasov, 1957 Energia Brasov, 1959 Steagul Rosu Brasov
Colours red shirts, white shorts
Stadium Tineretului (17,000) ☎ 921-66020
Champions as CSC Brasov, 1928

Season	Opponent	Home	Playoff Result	Away	Rnd	Cup
1963-64	Lokomotiv Plovdiv, Bulgaria	1-2		1-3	1	Fairs
1965-66	bye				1	Fairs
	ZNK Zagreb, Yugoslavia	1-0		2-2	2	Fairs
	Espanol Barcelona, Spain	1-3	0-1*	4-2	3	Fairs
			* in Barcelona			
1974-75	Besiktas, Turkey	3-0		0-2	1	UEFA
	Hamburger SV, Germany	1-2		0-8	2	UEFA

PROGRESUL ORADEA

Founded 1911 as Libertatea, 1918 Nagyvarad, 1920 CAO Oradea, 1940 Nagyvard, 1944 Libertatea, 1948 ICO Oradea, 1951 Progresul, 1958 CSO Oradea, 1961 Crisana, 1972 FC Bihor
Colours blue and white striped shirts, white shorts
Stadium Josif Vulcan ☎
Champions 1949
Cup Winners 1956, 1960, 1961

Season	Opponent	Home	Result	Away	Rnd	Cup
1961-62	bye				1	CWC
	Leixoes Sport Club, Portugal	0-1		1-1*	2	CWC
				* in Lisbon		

JIUL PETROSANI

Founded 1919 as Minerilor, 1924 amalgamated with Vulcan to become UCAS, 1930 amalgamated with CS Lupeni to become Jiul, 1951 Partizanul, 1951 Flacara, 1953 Minerul, 1958 Jiul
Colours black and white striped shirts, black shorts
Stadium Jiul (20,000) ☎
Cup Winners 1974

Season	Opponent	Home	Result	Away	Rnd	Cup
1974-75	Dundee United, Scotland	2-0		0-3	1	CWC

CHIMIA RAMNICU VALCEA

Founded 1924 as Vilceana, 1944 CSM Vilcea, 1955 Flamura Rosie, 1957 Unirea, 1958 Santierul Govora, 1959 Chimia
1962 Unirea, 1966 Oltul, 1967 Chimia
Colours blue shirts, white shorts or white shirts, blue shorts
Stadium 1st May (13,000) ☎
Cup Winners 1973

Season	Opponent	Home	Result	Away	Rnd	Cup
1973-74	Glentoran, Ireland	2-2		0-2	1	CWC

AS ARMATA TIRGU MURES

Founded 1962, previous names CS Tirgu Mures, Monopol, CFR Tirgu Mures, Dinamo, Vointa, Alimentara,
Medizina and Viiturul
Colours red and blue striped shirts, red shorts
Stadium 23rd August ☎ 954-17624

Season	Opponent	Home	Result	Away	Rnd	Cup
1975-76	Dynamo Dresden, East Germany	2-2		1-4	1	UEFA
1976-77	Dinamo Zagreb, Yugoslavia	0-1		0-3	1	UEFA
1977-78	AEK Athens, Greece	1-0		0-3	1	UEFA

SPORTUL STUDENTESC BUCHAREST

Founded 1916 as Universitar, 1919 Sportul, 1944 Sparta, 1948 Central Universitar, 1954 Stiinta,
1967 Politehnica, 1969 Sportul
Colours white shirts, black shorts
Stadium Sportul Republicii (15,000) ☎ 90-497430

Season	Opponent	Home	Result	Away	Rnd	Cup
1976-77	Olympiakos Piraeus, Greece	3-0		1-2	1	UEFA
	FC Schalke 04 Gelsenkirchen, Germany	0-1		0-4	2	UEFA
1983-84	Sturm Graz, Austria	1-2		0-0	1	UEFA
1984-85	Inter Milan, Italy	1-0		0-2	1	UEFA
1985-86	FC Neuchatel Xamax, Switzerland	4-4		0-3	1	UEFA
1986-87	Omonia Nicosia, Cyprus	1-0		1-1	1	UEFA
	AA Ghent, Belgium	0-3		1-1	2	UEFA
1987-88	GKS Katowice, Poland	1-0		2-1	1	UEFA
	Brondbyernes IF, Denmark	3-0	3-0 pen	0-3	2	UEFA
	Hellas-Verona, Italy	0-1		0-3	3	UEFA

VICTORIA BUCHAREST

Founded 1971
Colours white shirts, red shorts
Stadium Metalul-Pantelimon (8,000) ☎ 90-593707

Season	Opponents	Home	Result	Away	Rnd	Cup
1987-88	Pezoporikos Larnaca, Cyprus	3-0		1-0	1	UEFA
	Dynamo Tbilisi, USSR	1-2		0-0	2	UEFA
1988-89	Sliema Wanderers, Malta	6-1		2-0	1	UEFA
	Dynamo Minsk, USSR	1-0	wag	1-2	2	UEFA
	TPS Palloseura Turun Turku, Finland	1-0	wag	2-3	3	UEFA
	Dynamo Dresden, East Germany	1-1		0-4	qf	UEFA
1989-90	Valencia CF, Spain	1-1		1-3	1	UEFA

ROMANIA

OTELUL GALATI

Founded 1964 as Metalosport Galati, 1982 Otelul Galati
Colours blue and red striped shirts, blue shorts or yellow shirts, red shorts
Stadium Valea Domanului (20,000) ☎ 934-30875

Season	Opponents	Home	Result	Away	Rnd	Cup
1988-89	Juventus, Italy	1-0		0-5	1	UEFA

FLACARA AUTOMECANICA MORENI

Founded 1922 as Imser, 1931 Astra Romana, 1950 Fiacara, 1977 amalgamated with Automecanica
Colours white shirts, black shorts
Stadium Flacara (10,000) ☎ 926-66054

Season	Opponents	Home	Result	Away	Rnd	Cup
1989-90	FC Porto, Portugal	1-2		0-2	1	UEFA

SAN MARINO

Colours all blue
Federazone, Via del Bando 28, Borgo Maggiore, RSM ☎ 549-90 22 28 Telex 910 123 fsgc so

LEAGUE CHAMPIONS

1986 Faetano
1987 La Fiorita
1988 Tre Fiori
1989

CUP WINNERS

1986	La Fiorita v Dogana	2-1
1987	Libertas v Tre Penne	1-1 2-0
1988	Domagnano v La Fiorita	2-1
1989		

SCOTLAND

Founded 1873
The Scottish Football Association, 6 Park Gardens, Glasgow C3 Fax 041 332 7559
National colours navy blue shirts, white shorts, red socks
Season August to May

LEAGUE CHAMPIONS

For Glasgow Celtic and Glasgow Rangers read Celtic and Rangers

1891	Dumbarton & Rangers	1910	Celtic	1930	Rangers	1957	Rangers
1892	Dumbarton	1911	Rangers	1931	Rangers	1958	Heart of Midlothian
1893	Celtic	1912	Rangers	1932	Motherwell	1959	Rangers
1894	Celtic	1913	Rangers	1933	Rangers		
1895	Heart of Midlothian	1914	Celtic	1934	Rangers	1960	Heart of Midlothian
1896	Celtic	1915	Celtic	1935	Rangers	1961	Rangers
1897	Heart of Midlothian	1916	Celtic	1936	Celtic	1962	Dundee
1898	Celtic	1917	Celtic	1937	Rangers	1963	Rangers
1899	Rangers	1918	Rangers	1938	Celtic	1964	Rangers
		1919	Celtic	1939	Rangers	1965	Kilmarnock
1900	Rangers					1966	Celtic
1901	Rangers	1920	Rangers	1947	Rangers	1967	Celtic
1902	Rangers	1921	Rangers	1948	Hibernians	1968	Celtic
1903	Hibernians	1922	Celtic	1949	Rangers	1969	Celtic
1904	Third Lanark	1923	Rangers				
1905	Celtic	1924	Rangers	1950	Rangers	1970	Celtic
1906	Celtic	1925	Rangers	1951	Hibernians	1971	Celtic
1907	Celtic	1926	Celtic	1952	Hibernians	1972	Celtic
1908	Celtic	1927	Rangers	1953	Rangers	1973	Celtic
1909	Celtic	1928	Rangers	1954	Celtic	1974	Celtic
		1929	Rangers	1955	Aberdeen	1975	Rangers
				1956	Rangers		

PREMIER LEAGUE

1976	Rangers	1980	Aberdeen	1984	Aberdeen	1988	Celtic
1977	Celtic	1981	Celtic	1985	Aberdeen	1989	Rangers
1978	Rangers	1982	Celtic	1986	Celtic	1990	Rangers
1979	Celtic	1983	Dundee United	1987	Rangers		

CUP WINNERS

1874	Queens Park v Clydesdale	2-0
1875	Queens Park v Renton	3-0
1876	Queens Park v Third Lanark	1-1 2-0
1877	Vale of Levan v Rangers	0-0 1-1 3-2
1878	Vale of Levan v Third Lanark	1-0
1879	Vale of Levan v Rangers	1-1 walkover
1880	Queens Park v Thornlibank	3-0
1881	Queens Park v Dumbarton	3-1
1882	Queens Park v Dumbarton	2-2 4-1
1883	Dumbarton v Vale of Levan	2-2 2-1
1884	Queens Park v Vale of Levan (didn't appear)	
1885	Renton v Vale of Levan	0-0 3-1
1886	Queens Park v Renton	3-1
1887	Hibernian v Dumbarton	2-1
1888	Renton v Cambuslang	6-1
1889	Third Lanark v Celtic	2-1
1890	Queens Park v Vale of Levan	1-1 2-1
1891	Heart of Midlothian v Dumbarton	1-0
1892	Celtic v Queens Park	5-1
1893	Queens Park v Celtic	2-1
1894	Rangers v Celtic	3-1
1895	St Bernards v Renton	2-1
1896	Heart of Midlothian v Hibernian	3-1
1897	Rangers v Dumbarton	5-1
1898	Rangers v Kilmarnock	2-0
1899	Celtic v Rangers	2-0
1900	Celtic v Queens Park	4-3
1901	Heart of Midlothian v Celtic	4-3
1902	Hibernian v Celtic	1-0
1903	Rangers v Heart of Midlothian	1-1 0-0 2-0
1904	Celtic v Rangers	3-2
1905	Third Lanark v Rangers	0-0 3-1
1906	Heart of Midlothian v Third Lanark	1-0
1907	Celtic v Heart of Midlothian	3-0
1908	Celtic v St Mirren	5-1
1909	cup witheld - riot, Celtic v Rangers	2-2 1-1
1910	Dundee v Clyde	2-2 0-0 2-1
1911	Celtic v Hamilton Academicals	0-0 2-0
1912	Celtic v Clyde	2-0
1913	Falkirk v Raith Rovers	2-0
1914	Celtic v Hibernian	0-0 4-1
1920	Kilmarnock v Albion Rovers	3-2
1921	Partick Thistle v Rangers	1-0
1922	Greenock Morton v Rangers	1-0
1923	Celtic v Hibernian	1-0
1924	Airdrieonians v Hibernian	2-0
1925	Celtic v Dundee	2-1
1926	St Mirren v Celtic	2-0
1927	Celtic v East Fife	3-1
1928	Rangers v Celtic	4-0
1929	Kilmarnock v Rangers	2-0
1930	Rangers v Partick Thistle	0-0 2-1
1931	Celtic v Motherwell	2-2 4-2
1932	Rangers v Kilmarnock	1-1 3-1
1933	Celtic v Motherwell	1-0
1934	Rangers v St Mirren	5-0
1935	Rangers v Hamilton Academicals	2-1
1936	Rangers v Third Lanark	1-0
1937	Celtic v Aberdeen	2-1
1938	East Fife v Kilmarnock	1-1 4-2
1939	Clyde v Motherwell	4-0
1947	Aberdeen v Hibernian	2-1
1948	Rangers v Greenock Morton	1-1 1-0
1949	Rangers v Clyde	4-1
1950	Rangers v East Fife	3-0
1951	Celtic v Motherwell	1-0
1952	Motherwell v Dundee	4-0
1953	Rangers v Aberdeen	1-1 1-0
1954	Celtic v Aberdeen	2-1
1955	Clyde v Celtic	1-1 1-0
1956	Heart of Midlothian v Celtic	3-1
1957	Falkirk v Kilmarnock	1-1 2-1
1958	Clyde v Hibernian	1-0
1959	St Mirren v Aberdeen	3-1
1960	Rangers v Kilmarnock	2-0
1961	Dunfermline Athletic v Celtic	0-0 2-0
1962	Rangers v St Mirren	2-0
1963	Rangers v Celtic	1-1 3-0
1964	Rangers v Dundee	3-1
1965	Celtic v Dunfermline Athletic	3-2
1966	Rangers v Celtic	0-0 1-0
1967	Celtic v Aberdeen	2-0
1968	Dunfermline Athletic v Heart of Midlothian	3-1
1969	Celtic v Rangers	4-0
1970	Aberdeen v Celtic	3-1
1971	Celtic v Rangers	1-1 2-1
1972	Celtic v Hibernian	6-1
1973	Rangers v Celtic	3-2
1974	Celtic v Dundee United	3-0
1975	Celtic v Airdrieonians	3-1
1976	Rangers v Heart of Midlothian	3-1
1977	Celtic v Rangers	1-0
1978	Rangers v Aberdeen	2-1
1979	Rangers v Hibernian	0-0 0-0 3-2
1980	Celtic v Rangers	1-0
1981	Rangers v Dundee United	0-0 4-1
1982	Aberdeen v Rangers	4-1
1983	Aberdeen v Rangers	1-0
1984	Aberdeen v Celtic	2-1
1985	Celtic v Dundee United	2-1
1986	Aberdeen v Heart of Midlothian	3-0
1987	St Mirren v Dundee United	1-0 aet
1988	Celtic v Dundee United	2-1
1989	Celtic v Rangers	1-0
1990	Celtic v Aberdeen	

SCOTLAND

LEAGUE CUP FINALS

1947	Rangers v Aberdeen	4-0		**1970**	Celtic v St Johnstone	1-0
1948	East Fife v Falkirk	0-0 4-1		**1971**	Rangers v Celtic	1-0
1949	Rangers v Raith Rovers	2-0		**1972**	Partick Thistle v Celtic	4-1
				1973	Hibernian v Celtic	2-1
1950	East Fife v Dunfermline Athletic	3-0		**1974**	Dundee v Celtic	1-0
1951	Motherwell v Hibernian	3-0		**1975**	Celtic v Hibernian	6-3
1952	Dundee v Rangers	3-2		**1976**	Rangers v Celtic	1-0
1953	Dundee v Kilmarnock	2-0		**1977**	Aberdeen v Celtic	2-1
1954	East Fife v Partick Thistle	3-2		**1978**	Rangers v Celtic	2-1
1955	Heart of Midlothian v Motherwell	4-2		**1979**	Rangers v Aberdeen	2-1
1956	Aberdeen v St Mirren	2-1				
1957	Celtic v Partick Thistle	0-0 3-0		**1980**	Dundee United v Aberdeen	0-0 3-0
1958	Celtic v Rangers	7-1		**1981**	Dundee United v Dundee	3-0
1959	Heart of Midlothian v Partick Thistle	5-1		**1982**	Rangers v Dundee United	2-1
				1983	Celtic v Rangers	2-1
1960	Heart of Midlothian v Third Lanark	2-1		**1984**	Rangers v Celtic	3-2
1961	Rangers v Kilmarnock	2-0		**1985**	Rangers v Dundee United	1-0
1962	Rangers v Heart of Midlothian	1-1 3-1		**1986**	Aberdeen v Hibernian	3-0
1963	Heart of Midlothian v Kilmarnock	1-0		**1987**	Rangers v Celtic	2-1
1964	Rangers v Greenock Morton	5-0		**1988**	Rangers v Aberdeen	1-1 5-3 pens
1965	Rangers v Celtic	2-1		**1989**	Rangers v Aberdeen	3-2
1966	Celtic v Rangers	2-1				
1967	Celtic v Rangers	1-0		**1990**	Aberdeen v Rangers	2-1
1968	Celtic v Dundee	5-3				
1969	Celtic v Hibernian	6-2				

BRITISH CHAMPIONS (UNOFFICIAL)

1989 Rangers v Arsenal   1-2 Glasgow

FEATURED CLUBS IN EUROPEAN COMPETITION

Glasgow Celtic	Glasgow Rangers	Hibernian	Dundee
Dunfermline Athletic	Kilmarnock	Heart of Midlothian	Aberdeen
Dundee United	Partick Thistle	St Mirren	St Johnstone
Greenock Morton			

GLASGOW CELTIC

Founded 1888
Colours green and white hooped shirts, white shorts
Stadium Parkhead (61,800) ☎ 041-554 8408
Champions 1893, 1894, 1896, 1898, 1905, 1906, 1907, 1908, 1909, 1910, 1914, 1915, 1916, 1917, 1919, 1922, 1926, 1936, 1938, 1954, 1966, 1967, 1968, 1969, 1970, 1971, 1972, 1973, 1974, 1977, 1979, 1981, 1982, 1986, 1988
Cup Winners 1892, 1899, 1900, 1904, 1907, 1908, 1911, 1912, 1914, 1923, 1925, 1927, 1931, 1933, 1937, 1951, 1954, 1965, 1967, 1969, 1971, 1972, 1974, 1975, 1977, 1980, 1985, 1988, 1989
League/Skol Cup Winners 1957, 1958, 1966, 1967, 1968, 1969, 1970, 1975, 1983
European Cup Winners 1967 **European Cup Finalists** 1970

Season	Opponents	Home	Playoff Result	Away	Rnd	Cup
1962-63	Valencia CF, Spain	2-2		2-4	1	Fairs
1963-64	FC Basle, Switzerland	5-0		5-1	1	CWC
	Dinamo Zagreb, Yugoslavia	3-0		1-2	2	CWC
	Slovan Bratislava, Czechoslovakia	1-0		1-0	qf	CWC
	MTK Budapest, Hungary	3-0		0-4	sf	CWC
1964-65	Leixoes Sport Club, Portugal	3-0		1-1	1	Fairs
	CF Barcelona, Spain	0-0		1-3	2	Fairs
1965-66	Go Ahead Deventer, Holland	1-0		6-0	1	CWC
	AGF Aarhus, Denmark	2-0		1-0	2	CWC
	Dynamo Kiev, USSR	3-0		1-1*	qf	CWC
				* in Tiblisi		
	Liverpool, England	1-0		0-2	sf	CWC
1966-67	FC Zurich, Switzerland	2-0		3-0	1	ECC
	FC Nantes, France	3-1		3-1	2	ECC
	Vojvodina Novi Sad, Yugoslavia	2-0		0-1	qf	ECC
	Dukla Prague, Czechoslovakia	3-1		0-0	sf	ECC
	Inter Milan, Italy	2-1	in Lisbon		FINAL	ECC
1967-68	Dynamo Kiev, USSR	1-2		1-1	1	ECC
1968-69	St Etienne, France	4-0		0-2	1	ECC
	Red Star Belgrade, Yugoslavia	5-1		1-1	2	ECC
	AC Milan, Italy	0-1		0-0	qf	ECC
1969-70	FC Basle, Switzerland	2-0		0-0	1	ECC
	Benfica, Portugal	3-0	wot	0-3	2	ECC
	Fiorentina, Italy	3-0		0-1	qf	ECC
	Leeds United, England	2-1*		1-0	sf	ECC
				* Hampden Park		
	Feyenoord Rotterdam, Holland	1-2	in Milan		FINAL	ECC
1970-71	KPV Kokkolan, Finland	9-0		5-0	1	ECC
	Waterford, Eire	3-2		7-0*	2	ECC
				* in Dublin		
	Ajax Amsterdam, Holland	1-0		0-3	qf	ECC
1971-72	B 1903 Copenhagen, Denmark	3-0		1-2	1	ECC
	Sliema Wanderers, Malta	5-0		2-1	2	ECC
	Ujpest Dozsa, Hungary	1-1		2-1	qf	ECC
	Inter Milan, Italy	0-0	4-5 pen	0-0	sf	ECC
1972-73	Rosenborg Trondheim, Norway	2-1		3-1	1	ECC
	Ujpest Dozsa, Hungary	2-1		0-3	2	ECC
1973-74	TPS Turku, Finland	3-0		6-1	1	ECC
	Velje BK, Denmark	0-0		1-0	2	ECC
	FC Basle, Switzerland	4-2		2-3	qf	ECC
	Atletico Madrid, Spain	0-0		0-2	sf	ECC

259

SCOTLAND

1974-75	Olympiakos Piraeus, Greece	1-1		0-2	1	ECC
1975-76	Valur Reykjavik, Iceland	7-0		2-0	1	CWC
	Boavista, Portugal	3-1		0-0	2	CWC
	Sachenring Zwichau, East Germany	1-1		0-1	qf	CWC
1976-77	Wisla Krakow, Poland	2-2		0-2	1	UEFA
1977-78	Jeunesse Esch, Luxembourg	5-0		6-1	1	ECC
	Wacker Innsbruck, Austria	2-1		0-3*	2	ECC
* in Salzburg						
1979-80	Partizani Tirana, Albania	4-1		0-1	1	ECC
	Dundalk, Eire	3-2		0-0	2	ECC
	Real Madrid, Spain	2-0		0-3	qf	ECC
1980-81	Diosgyoer Miskolc, Hungary	6-0		1-2	pr	CWC
	Politechnica Timisoara, Romania	2-1	lag	0-1	1	CWC
1981-82	Juventus, Italy	1-0		0-2	1	ECC
1982-83	Ajax Amsterdam, Holland	2-2		2-1	1	ECC
	Real Sociedad San Sebastien, Spain	2-1		0-2	2	ECC
1983-84	AGF Aarhus, Denmark	1-0		4-1	1	UEFA
	Sporting Lisbon, Portugal	5-0		0-2	2	UEFA
	Nottingham Forest, England	1-2		0-0	3	UEFA
1984-85	AA Ghent, Belgium	3-0		0-1	1	CWC
	Rapid Vienna, Austria	3-0*	0-1**	1-3	2	CWC
	* match declared void, ** in Manchester					
1985-86	Atletico Madrid, Spain	1-2		1-1	1	CWC
1986-87	Shamrock Rovers, Eire	2-0		1-0	1	ECC
	Dynamo Kiev, USSR	1-1		1-3	2	ECC
1987-88	Borussia Dortmund, Germany	2-1		0-2	1	UEFA
1988-89	Honved Budapest, Hungary	4-0		0-1	1	ECC
	Werder Bremen, Germany	0-1		0-0	2	ECC
1989-90	Partizan Belgrade, Yugoslavia	5-4	lag	1-2*	1	CWC
	* in Mostar					

GLASGOW RANGERS

Founded 1873
Colours royal blue shirts, white shorts
Stadium Ibrox Park (43,471) ☎ 041-427 5232/427 6641
Champions 1899(shared), 1900, 1901, 1902, 1911, 1912, 1913, 1918, 1920, 1921, 1923, 1924, 1925, 1927, 1928, 1929, 1930, 1931, 1933, 1934, 1935, 1937, 1939, 1947, 1949, 1950, 1953, 1956, 1957, 1959, 1961, 1963, 1964, 1975, 1976, 1978, 1987, 1989, 1990
Cup Winners 1894, 1897, 1898, 1903, 1928, 1930, 1932, 1934, 1935, 1936, 1948, 1949, 1950, 1953, 1960, 1962, 1963, 1964, 1966, 1973, 1976, 1978, 1979, 1981
League/Skol Cup Winners 1947, 1949, 1961, 1962, 1964, 1965, 1971, 1976, 1978, 1979, 1982, 1984, 1985, 1987, 1988, 1989
CWC Winners 1972 CWC Cup Finalists 1961, 1967

Season	Opponents	Home	Playoff Result	Away	Rnd	Cup
1956-57	OGC Nice, France	2-1	1-3*	1-2	1	ECC
			* in Paris			
1957-58	St Etienne, France	3-1		1-2	pr	ECC
	AC Milan, Italy	1-4		0-2	1	ECC
1959-60	RSC Anderlecht, Belgium	5-2		2-0	pr	ECC
	Red Star Bratislava, Czechoslovakia	4-3		1-1	1	ECC
	Sparta Rotterdam, Holland	0-1	3-2*	3-2	qf	ECC
			* at Arsenal			
	Eintracht Frankfurt, Germany	3-6		1-6	sf	ECC
1960-61	Ferencvarosi TC, Hungary	4-2		1-2	1	CWC
	Borussia Monchengladbach, Germany	8-0		3-0	qf	CWC
	Wolverhampton Wanderers, England	2-0		1-1	sf	CWC
	Fiorentina, Italy	0-2		1-2	FINAL	CWC
1961-62	AS Monaco, France	3-2		3-2	pr	ECC
	ASK Vorwaerts Berlin, East Germany	4-1*		2-1	1	ECC
			* in Malmo			
	Standard Liege, Belgium	2-0		1-4	2	ECC

1962-63	Seville, Spain	4-0		0-2	1	CWC
	Tottenham Hotspur, England	2-3		2-5	2	CWC
1963-64	Real Madrid, Spain	0-1		0-6	pr	ECC
1964-65	Red Star Belgrade, Yugoslavia	3-1	3-1*	2-4	pr	ECC
			* at Arsenal			
	Rapid Vienna, Austria	1-0		2-0	1	ECC
	Inter Milan, Italy	1-0		1-3	2	ECC
1966-67	Glentoran, Ireland	4-0		1-1	1	CWC
	Borussia Dortmund, Germany	2-1		0-0	2	CWC
	Real Zaragoza, Spain	2-0	wot	0-2	qf	CWC
	Slavia Sofia, Bulgaria	1-0		1-0	sf	CWC
	Bayern Munich, Germany	0-1	in Nurnburg		FINAL	CWC
1967-68	Dynamo Dresden, East Germany	2-1		1-1	1	Fairs
	1.FC Koln, Germany	3-0		1-3	2	Fairs
	bye				3	Fairs
	Leeds United, England	0-0		0-2	qf	Fairs
1968-69	Vojvodina Novi Sad, Yugoslavia	2-0		0-1	1	Fairs
	Dundalk, Eire	6-1		3-0	2	Fairs
	DWS Amsterdam, Holland	2-1		2-0	3	Fairs
	Atletico Bilbao, Spain	4-1		0-2	qf	Fairs
	Newcastle United, England	0-0		0-2	sf	Fairs
1969-70	Steaua Bucharest, Romania	2-0		0-0	1	CWC
	Gornik Zabrze, Poland	1-3		1-3	2	CWC
1970-71	Bayern Munich, Germany	1-1		0-1	1	Fairs
1971-72	Rennes, France	1-0		1-1	1	CWC
	Sporting Lisbon, Portugal	3-2	wag	3-4	2	CWC
	Torino, Italy	1-0		1-1	qf	CWC
	Bayern Munich, Germany	2-0		1-1	sf	CWC
	Dynamo Moscow, USSR	3-2	in Barcelona		FINAL	CWC
1973-74	Ankaragucu, Turkey	4-0		2-0	1	CWC
	Borussia Monchengladbach, Germany	3-2		0-3	2	CWC
1975-76	Bohemians Dublin, Eire	4-1		1-1	1	ECC
	St Etienne, France	1-2		0-2	2	ECC
1976-77	FC Zurich, Switzerland	1-1		0-1	1	ECC
1977-78	Young Boys Bern, Switzerland	1-0		2-2	pr	CWC
	Twente Enschede, Holland	0-0		0-3	1	CWC
1978-79	Juventus, Italy	2-0		0-1	1	ECC
	PSV Eindhoven, Holland	0-0		3-2	2	ECC
	1.FC Koln, Germany	1-1		0-1	qf	ECC
1979-80	Lillestrom SK, Norway	1-0		2-0	pr	CWC
	Fortuna Dusseldorf, Germany	2-1		0-0	1	CWC
	Valencia CF, Spain	1-3		1-1	2	CWC
1981-82	Dukla Prague, Czechoslovakia	2-1		0-3	1	CWC
1982-83	Borussia Dortmund, Germany	2-0		0-0	1	UEFA
	1.FC Koln, Germany	2-1		0-5	2	UEFA
1983-84	Valletta, Malta	10-0		8-0	1	CWC
	FC Porto, Portugal	2-1	lag	0-1	2	CWC
1984-85	Bohemians Dublin, Eire	2-0		2-3	1	UEFA
	Inter Milan, Italy	3-1		0-3	2	UEFA
1985-86	CA Osasuna, Spain	1-0		0-2	1	UEFA
1986-87	Ilves Tampere, Finland	4-0		0-2	1	UEFA
	Boavista, Portugal	2-1		1-0	2	UEFA
	Borussia Monchengladbach, Germany	1-1	lag	0-0	3	UEFA
1987-88	Dynamo Kiev, USSR	2-0		0-1	1	ECC
	Gornik Zabrze, Poland	3-1		1-1	2	ECC
	Steaua Bucharest, Romania	2-1		0-2	qf	ECC
1988-89	GKS Katowice, Poland	1-0		4-2	1	UEFA
	1.FC Koln, Germany	1-1		0-2	2	UEFA
1989-90	Bayern Munich, Germany	1-3		0-0	1	ECC

SCOTLAND

HIBERNIAN

Founded 1875
Colours green shirts with white sleeves, white shorts
Stadium Easter Road, Edinburgh (29,300) ☎ 031-661 2159
Champions 1903, 1948, 1951, 1952
Cup Winners 1887, 1902
League/Skol Cup Winners 1973

Season	Opponents	Home	Playoff Result	Away	Rnd	Cup
1955-56	Rot Weiss Essen, Germany	1-1		4-0	1	ECC
	Djurgarden IF Stockholm, Sweden	1-0		3-1*	qf	ECC
				* Firhill Park, Glasgow		
	Stade de Reims, France	0-1		0-2*	sf	ECC
				* in Paris		
1960-61	Lausanne Sport, Switzerland	2-0	withdrew		1	Fairs
	CF Barcelona, Spain	3-2		4-4	qf	Fairs
	AS Roma, Italy	3-3	0-6*	2-2	sf	Fairs
			* in Rome			
1961-62	Belenenses, Portugal	3-3		3-1	1	Fairs
	Red Star Belgrade, Yugoslavia	0-1		0-4	2	Fairs
1962-63	Copenhagen XI, Denmark	4-0		3-2	1	Fairs
	Utrecht City XI, Holland	2-1		1-0	2	Fairs
	Valencia CF, Spain	2-1		0-5	3	Fairs
1965-66	Valencia CF, Spain	2-0	0-3*	0-2	1	Fairs
			* in Valencia			
1967-68	FC Porto, Portugal	3-0		1-3	1	Fairs
	Napoli, Italy	5-0		1-4	2	Fairs
	Leeds United, England	1-1		0-1	3	Fairs
1968-69	Olimpia Ljubljana, Yugoslavia	2-1		3-0	1	Fairs
	1.FC Lokomotive Leipzig, East Germany	3-1		1-0	2	Fairs
	Hamburger SV, Germany	2-1	lag	0-1	3	Fairs
1970-71	Malmo FF, Sweden	6-0		3-2	1	Fairs
	Vitoria Guimaraes, Portugal	2-0		1-2	2	Fairs
	Liverpool, England	0-1		0-2	3	Fairs
1972-73	Sporting Lisbon, Portugal	6-1		1-2	1	CWC
	Besa Kavaja, Albania	7-1		1-1	2	CWC
	Hajduk Split, Yugoslavia	4-2		0-3	qf	CWC
1973-74	IBK Keflavik, Iceland	2-0		1-1*	1	UEFA
				* in Reykjavik		
	Leeds United, England	0-0	4-5 pen	0-0	2	UEFA
1974-75	Rosenborg Trondheim, Norway	9-1		3-2	1	UEFA
	Juventus, Italy	2-4		0-4	2	UEFA
1975-76	Liverpool, England	1-0		1-3	1	UEFA
1976-77	Sochaux, France	1-0		0-0	1	UEFA
	Osters IF Vaxjo, Sweden	2-0		1-4	2	UEFA
1978-79	IFK Norrkoping, Sweden	3-2		0-0	1	UEFA
	RC Strasbourg, France	1-0		0-2	2	UEFA
	Videoton Szekesfehervar, Hungary	1-0		3-0	1	UEFA
	RFC Liege, Belgium	0-0		0-1	2	UEFA
1989-90	Videoton Szekesfehervar, Hungary	1-0		3-0	1	UEFA
	RFC Liege, Belgium	0-0		0-1	2	UEFA

DUNDEE

Founded 1893
Colours dark blue shirts, white shorts
Stadium Dens Park (22,381) ☎ 0382-826 104
Champions 1962
Cup Winners 1910
League/Skol Cup Winners 1952, 1953, 1974

Season	Opponents	Home	Result	Away	Rnd	Cup
1962-63	1.FC Koln, Germany	8-1		0-4	1	ECC
	Sporting Lisbon, Portugal	4-1		0-1	2	ECC
	RSC Anderlecht, Belgium	2-1		4-1	qf	ECC
	AC Milan, Italy	1-0		1-5	sf	ECC
1964-65	Real Zaragoza, Spain	2-2		1-2	1	CWC
1967-68	DWS Amsterdam, Holland	3-0		1-2	1	Fairs
	RFC Liege, Belgium	3-1		4-1	2	Fairs
	bye				3	Fairs
	FC Zurich, Switzerland	1-0		1-0	qf	Fairs
	Leeds United, England	1-1		0-1	sf	Fairs
1971-72	AB Akademisk Copenhagen, Denmark	4-2		1-0	1	UEFA
	1.FC Koln, Germany	4-2		1-2	2	UEFA
	AC Milan, Italy	2-0		0-5	3	UEFA
1973-74	Twente Enschede, Holland	1-3		2-4	1	UEFA
1974-75	RWD Molenbeck, Belgium	2-4		0-1	1	UEFA

DUNFERMLINE ATHLETIC

Founded 1907
Colours blue and white striped shirts, black shorts
Stadium East End Park (19,320) ☎ 0383-724 295
Cup Winners 1961, 1968

Season	Opponents	Home	Playoff Result	Away	Rnd	Cup
1961-62	St Patrick's Athletic, Eire	4-1		4-0	1	CWC
	Varder Skopje, Yugoslavia	5-0		0-2	2	CWC
	Ujpest Dozsa, Hungary	0-1		3-4	qf	CWC
1962-63	Everton, England	2-0		0-1	1	Fairs
	Valencia CF, Spain	6-2	0-1*	0-4	2	Fairs
			* in Barcelona			
1964-65	Orgryte IS Gothenburg, Sweden	4-2		0-0	1	Fairs
	VfB Stuttgart, Germany	1-0		0-0	2	Fairs
	Atletico Bilbao, Spain	1-0	1-2*	0-1	3	Fairs
			* in Bilbao			
1965-66	bye				1	Fairs
	KB Copenhagen, Denmark	5-0		4-2	2	Fairs
	Spartak Brno, Czechoslovakia	2-0		0-0	3	Fair
	Real Zaragoza, Spain	1-0		2-4 aet	qf	Fairs
1966-67	Frigg Oslo, Norway	3-1		3-1	1	Fairs
	Dinamo Zagreb, Yugoslavia	4-2	lag	0-2	2	Fairs
1968-69	Apoel Nicosia, Cyprus	10-1		2-0	1	CWC
	Olympiakos Piraeus, Greece	4-0		0-3	2	CWC
	West Bromwich Albion, England	0-0		1-0	qf	CWC
	Slovan Bratislava, Czechoslovakia	1-1		0-1	sf	CWC
1969-70	Girondins Bordeaux, France	4-0		0-2	1	Fairs
	Gwardia Warsaw, Poland	2-1		1-0	2	Fairs
	RSC Anderlecht, Belgium	3-2	lag	0-1	3	Fairs

263

SCOTLAND

KILMARNOCK

Founded 1878
Colours blue and white hooped shirts, white shorts
Stadium Rugby Park (17,528) ☎ 0563-25184
Champions 1965
Cup Winners 1920, 1929

Season	Opponents	Home	Result	Away	Rnd	Cup
1964-65	Eintracht Frankfurt, Germany	5-1		0-3	pr	Fairs
	Everton, England	0-2		1-4	1	Fairs
1965-66	17 Nentori Tirana, Albania	1-0		0-0	pr	ECC
	Real Madrid, Spain	2-2		1-5	1	ECC
1966-67	bye				1	Fairs
	Royal Antwerp, Belgium	7-2		1-0	2	Fairs
	La Ghantoise, Belgium	1-0		2-1	3	Fairs
	1.FC Lokomotive Leipzig, East Germany	2-0		0-1	qf	Fairs
	Leeds United, England	0-0		2-4	sf	Fairs
1969-70	FC Zurich, Switzerland	3-1		2-3	1	Fairs
	Slavia Sofia, Bulgaria	4-1		0-2	2	Fairs
	Dynamo Bacau, Romania	1-1		0-2	3	Fairs
1970-71	Coleraine, Ireland	2-3		1-1	1	Fairs

HEART OF MIDLOTHIAN

Founded 1873
Colours maroon shirts, white shorts
Stadium Tynecastle Park (29,000) ☎ 031-337 6132
Champions 1895, 1897, 1958, 1960
Cup Winners 1891, 1896, 1901, 1906, 1956
League/Skol Cup Winners 1955, 1959, 1960, 1963

Season	Opponents	Home	Playoff Result	Away	Rnd	Cup
1958-59	Standard Liege, Belgium	2-1		1-5	pr	ECC
1960-61	Benfica, Portugal	1-2		0-3	1	ECC
1961-62	Union St Gilloise, Belgium	2-0		3-1	1	Fairs
	Inter Milan, Italy	0-1		0-4	2	Fairs
1963-64	Lausanne Sport, Switzerland	2-2	2-3*	4-4	1	Fairs
			* in Lausanne			
1965-66	bye				1	Fairs
	Valerengen IF Oslo, Norway	1-0		3-1	2	Fairs
	Real Zaragoza, Spain	3-3	0-1	2-2	3	Fairs
1976-77	1.FC Lokomotive Leipzig, East Germany	5-1		0-2	1	- CWC
	Hamburger SV, Germany	1-4		2-4	2	CWC
1984-85	Paris St Germain, France	2-2		0-4	1	UEFA
1986-87	Dukla Prague, Czechoslovakia	3-2	lag	0-1	1	UEFA
1988-89	St Patrick's Athletic, Eire	2-0		2-0	1	UEFA
	FK Austria Vienna, Austria	0-0		1-0	2	UEFA
	Velez Mostar, Yugoslavia	3-0		1-2	3	UEFA
	Bayern Munich, Germany	1-0		0-2	qf	UEFA

ABERDEEN

Founded 1903
Colours red shirts, white shorts
Stadium Pittodrie Park (22,568) all seated ☎ 0224-632 328
Champions 1955, 1980, 1984, 1985
Cup Winners 1947, 1970, 1982, 1983, 1984, 1986
League/Skol Cup Winners 1956, 1977, 1986, 1990
CWC Winners 1983
Super Cup Winners 1983

Season	Opponents	Home	Result	Away	Rnd	Cup
1967-68	KR Reykjavik, Iceland	10-0		4-1	1	CWC
	Standard Liege, Belgium	2-0		0-3	2	CWC
1968-69	Slavia Sofia, Bulgaria	2-0		0-0	1	Fairs
	Real Zaragoza, Spain	2-1		0-3	2	Fairs
1970-71	Honved Budapest, Hungary	3-1	4-5p	1-3	1	CWC
1971-72	Celta Vigo, Spain	1-0		2-0	1	UEFA
	Juventus, Italy	1-1		0-2	2	UEFA
1972-73	Borussia Monchengladbach, Germany	2-3		3-6*	1	UEFA
				* in Nurnburg		
1973-74	Finn Harps, Eire	4-1		3-1	1	UEFA
	Tottenham Hotspur, England	1-1		1-4	2	UEFA
1977-78	RWD Molenbeeck, Belgium	1-2		0-0	1	UEFA
1978-79	Marek Stanke Dimitrov, Bulgaria	3-0		2-3	1	CWC
	Fortuna Dusseldorf, Germany	2-0		0-3	2	CWC
1979-80	Eintracht Frankfurt, Germany	1-1		0-1	1	UEFA
1980-81	FK Austria Vienna, Austria	1-0		0-0	1	ECC
	Liverpool, England	0-1		0-4	2	ECC
1981-82	Ipswich Town, England	3-1		1-1	1	UEFA
	FC Arges Pitesti, Romania	3-0		2-2	2	UEFA
	Hamburger SV, Germany	3-2		1-3	3	UEFA
1982-83	FC Sion, Switzerland	7-0		4-1	pr	CWC
	Dynamo Tirana, Albania	1-0		0-0	1	CWC
	Lech Poznan, Poland	2-0		1-0	2	CWC
	Bayern Munich, Germany	3-2		0-0	qf	CWC
	Waterschei Thor Genk, Belgium	5-1		0-1	sf	CWC
	Real Madrid, Spain	2-1	in Gothenburg		FINAL	CWC
1983-84	IA Akranes, Iceland	1-1		2-1*	1	CWC
				* in Reykjavik		
	SK Beveren Waas, Belgium	4-1		0-0	2	CWC
	Ujpest Dozsa, Hungary	3-0		0-2	qf	CWC
	FC Porto, Portugal	0-1		0-1	sf	CWC
1984-85	BFC Dynamo Berlin, East Germany	2-1	4-5 pen	1-2	1	ECC
1985-86	IA Akranes, Iceland	4-1		3-1*	1	ECC
				* in Reykjavik		
	Servette Geneva, Switzerland	1-0		0-0	2	ECC
	IFK Gothenburg, Sweden	2-2	lag	0-0	qf	ECC
1986-87	FC Sion, Switzerland	2-1		0-3	1	CWC
1987-88	Bohemians Dublin, Eire	1-0		0-0	1	UEFA
	Feyenoord Rotterdam, Holland	2-1		0-1	2	UEFA
1988-89	Dynamo Dresden, East Germany	0-0		0-2	1	UEFA
1989-90	Rapid Vianna, Austria	2-1	lag	0-1	1	UEFA

SCOTLAND

DUNDEE UNITED

Founded 1909 as Dundee Hibs, changed name to Dundee United in 1923
Colours tangerine shirts with black trim, black shorts
Stadium Tannadice Park (22,310) ☎ 0383-826 289
Champions 1983
League/Skol Cup Winners 1980, 1981
UEFA Cup Finalists 1987

Season	Opponents	Home	Result	Away	Rnd	Cup
1966-67	bye				1	Fairs
	CF Barcelona, Spain	2-0		2-1	2	Fairs
	Juventus, Italy	1-0		0-3	3	Fairs
1969-70	Newcastle United, England	1-2		0-1	1	Fairs
1970-71	Grasshoppers Zurich, Switzerland	3-2		0-0	1	Fairs
	Sparta Prague, Czechoslovakia	1-0		1-3	2	Fairs
1974-75	Jiul Petrosani, Romania	3-0		0-2	1	CWC
	Bursaspor, Turkey	0-0		0-1	2	CWC
1975-76	IBK Keflavik, Iceland	4-0		2-0	1	UEFA
	FC Porto, Portugal	1-2		1-1	2	UEFA
1977-78	KB Copenhagen, Denmark	1-0		0-3	1	UEFA
1978-79	Standard Liege, Belgium	0-0		0-1*	1	UEFA
				* in Ghent		
1979-80	RSC Anderlecht, Belgium	0-0	wag	1-1	1	UEFA
	Diosgyoer, Hungary	0-1		1-3	2	UEFA
1980-81	Slask Wroclaw, Poland	7-2		0-0	1	UEFA
	KSC Lokeren, Belgium	1-1	lag	0-0	2	UEFA
1981-82	AS Monaco, France	1-2		5-2	1	UEFA
	Borussia Monchengladbach, Germany	5-0		0-2	2	UEFA
	KFC Winterslag, Belgium	5-0		0-0	3	UEFA
	Radnicki Nis, Yugoslavia	2-0		0-3	qf	UEFA
1982-83	PSV Eindhoven, Holland	1-1		2-0	1	UEFA
	Viking Stavanger, Norway	0-0		3-1	2	UEFA
	Werder Bremen, Germany	2-1		1-1	3	UEFA
	Bohemians Prague, Czechoslovakia	0-0		0-1	qf	UEFA
1983-84	Hamrun Spartan, Malta	3-0		3-0	1	ECC
	Standard Liege, Belgium	4-0		0-0	2	ECC
	Rapid Vienna, Austria	1-0	wag	1-2	qf	ECC
	AS Roma, Italy	2-0		0-3	sf	ECC
1984-85	AIK Stockholm, Sweden	3-0		0-1	1	UEFA
	Linzer ASK, Austria	5-1		2-1	2	UEFA
	Manchester United, England	2-3		2-2	3	UEFA
1985-86	Bohemians Dublin, Eire	2-2		5-2	1	UEFA
	Vardar Skopje, Yugoslavia	2-0		1-1	2	UEFA
	FC Neuchatel Xamax, Switzerland	2-1		1-3	3	UEFA
1986-87	Racing Lens, France	2-0		0-1	1	UEFA
	Universitatea Craiova, Romania	3-0		0-1	2	UEFA
	Hajduk Split, Yugoslavia	2-0		0-0	3	UEFA
	FC Barcelona, Spain	1-0		2-1	qf	UEFA
	Borussia Monchengladbach, Germany	0-0		2-0	sf	UEFA
	IFK Gothenburg, Sweden	1-1		0-1	FINAL	UEFA
1987-88	Coleraine, Ireland	3-1		1-0	1	UEFA
	TJ Vitkovice, Czechoslovakia	1-2		1-1	2	UEFA
1988-89	Floriana, Malta	1-0		0-0	1	CWC
	Dinamo Bucharest, Romania	0-1		1-1	2	CWC
1989-90	Glentoran, Ireland	2-0		3-1	1	UEFA
	Royal Antwerp, Belgium	3-2		0-4	2	UEFA

PARTICK THISTLE

Founded 1876
Colours red and yellow shirts with broad vertical stripe, white shorts
Stadium Firhill Park, Glasgow (19,950) ☎ 041-946 2673/1348
Cup Winners 1921
League/Skol Cup Winners 1972

Season	Opponents	Home	Result	Away	Rnd	Cup
1963-64	Glentoran, Ireland	3-0		4-1	1	Fairs
	Spartak Brno, Czechoslovakia	3-2		0-4	2	Fairs
1972-73	Honved Budapest, Hungary	0-3		0-1	1	UEFA

ST MIRREN

Founded 1877
Colours all white
Stadium Love Street, Glasgow (24,600) ☎ 041-889 2558/840 1337
Cup Winners 1959, 1987

Season	Opponents	Home	Result	Away	Rnd	Cup
1980-81	Elfsborg IF Boras, Sweden	0-0		2-1	1	UEFA
	St Etienne, France	0-0		0-2	2	UEFA
1983-84	Feyenoord Rotterdam, Holland	0-1		0-2	1	UEFA
1985-86	Slavia Prague, Czechoslovakia	3-0		0-1	1	UEFA
	Hammarby IF Stockholm, Sweden	1-2		3-3	2	UEFA
1987-88	Tromso IL, Norway	1-0		0-0	1	UEFA
	KV Mechelen, Belgium	0-2		0-0	2	UEFA

ST JOHNSTONE

Founded 1884
Colours blue shirts, white shorts
Stadium Muirton Park, Perth (10,000) ☎ 0738-26961

Season	Opponents	Home	Result	Away	Rnd	Cup
1971-72	Hamburger SV, Germany	3-0		1-2	1	UEFA
	Vasas Budapest, Hungary	2-0		0-1	2	UEFA
	Zeljeznicar Sarajevo, Yugoslavia	1-0		1-5	3	UEFA

GREENOCK MORTON

Founded 1896
Colours blue and white shirts, white shorts
Stadium Cappielow Park (16,577) ☎ 0475-23571/25594
Cup Winners 1922

Season	Opponents	Home	Result	Away	Rnd	Cup
1968-69	Chelsea, England	3-4		0-5	1	Fairs

SPAIN

Founded 1913
Real Federacion Espanola de Futbol, Calle Alberto Bosch 13, Madrid 14 ☎ 420 13 62/21/04 Fax 42020 94
National colours red shirts, dark blue shorts, black socks
Season September to June

LEAGUE CHAMPIONS

1929	Barcelona FC	1946	Sevilla CF	1962	Real Madrid	1978	Real Madrid
		1947	Valencia CF	1963	Real Madrid	1979	Real Madrid
1930	Athletic Bilbao	1948	CF Barcelona	1964	Real Madrid		
1931	Athletic Bilbao	1949	CF Barcelona	1965	Real Madrid	1980	Real Madrid
1932	Real Madrid			1966	Atletico Madrid	1981	Real Sociedad
1933	Real Madrid	1950	Atletico Madrid	1967	Real Madrid	1982	Real Sociedad
1934	Athletic Bilbao	1951	Atletico Madrid	1968	Real Madrid	1983	Athletic Bilbao
1935	Real Betis	1952	CF Barcelona	1969	Real Madrid	1984	Athletic Bilbao
1936	Athletic Bilbao	1953	CF Barcelona			1985	FC Barcelona
		1954	Real Madrid	1970	Atletico Madrid	1986	Real Madrid
1940	Aviacione	1955	Real Madrid	1971	Valencia CF	1987	Real Madrid
	(Atletico Madrid)	1956	Atletico Bilbao	1972	Real Madrid	1988	Real Madrid
1941	Aviacione	1957	Real Madrid	1973	Atletico Madrid	1989	Real Madrid
	(Atletico Madrid)	1958	Real Madrid	1974	CF Barcelona		
1942	Valencia CF	1959	CF Barcelona	1975	Real Madrid	1990	Real Madrid
1943	Atletico Bilbao			1976	Real Madrid		
1944	Valencia CF	1960	CF Barcelona	1977	Atletico Madrid		
1945	CF Barcelona	1961	Real Madrid				

CUP WINNERS

1902	Vizcaya v Barcelona FC	2-1	1913	Racing Club Irun v Athletic Bilbao	2-2 1-0
1903	Athletic Bilbao v Real Madrid	3-2	1914	Athletic Bilbao v Espanol Barcelona	2-1
1904	Athletic Bilbao	no finalist appeared	1915	Athletic Bilbao v Espanol Barcelona	5-0
1905	Real Madrid v Athletic Bilbao	1-0	1916	Athletic Bilbao v Real Madrid	4-0
1906	Real Madrid v Athletic Bilbao	4-1	1917	CF Madrid v Arenas Guecho Bilbao	0-0 2-1
1907	Real Madrid v Vizcaya	1-0	1918	Union Irun v Real Madrid	2-0
1908	Real Madrid v Vigo Sporting	2-1	1919	Arenas Guecho v Barcelona FC	5-2
1909	Ciclista San Sebastian v Espanol Madrid	3-1			
			1920	Barcelona FC v Athletic Bilbao	2-0
1910	Athletic Bilbao v Vasconia San Sebastian	1-0	1921	Athletic Bilbao v Atletico Madrid	4-1
1910	Barcelona FC v Espanol Madrid	3-2	1922	Barcelona FC v Union Irun	5-1
1911	Athletic Bilbao v Espanol Barcelona	3-1	1923	Athletic Bilbao v Europa Barcelona	1-0
1912	Barcelona FC v Gimnast Madrid	2-0	1924	Union Irun v Real Madrid	1-0
1913	CF Barcelona v Real Sociedad	2-1	1925	Barcelona FC v Arenas Guecho	2-0

268

Year	Match	Score		Year	Match	Score
1926	Barcelona FC v Atletico Madrid	3-2		1960	Atletico Madrid v Real Madrid	3-1
1927	Union Irun v Arenas Guecho	1-0		1961	Atletico Madrid v Real Madrid	3-2
1928	Barcelona FC v Real Sociedad	1-1 1-1 3-1		1962	Real Madrid v Sevilla CF	2-1
1929	Espanol Barcelona v Real Madrid	2-1		1963	CF Barcelona v Real Zaragoza	3-1
				1964	Real Zaragoza v Atletico Madrid	2-1
1930	Athletic Bilbao v Real Madrid	3-2		1965	Atletico Madrid v Real Zaragoza	1-0
1931	Athletic Bilbao v Real Betis	3-1		1966	Real Zaragoza v Atletico Madrid	2-0
1932	Athletic Bilbao v Barcelona FC	1-0		1967	Valencia CF v Atletico Bilbao	2-1
1933	Athletic Bilbao v Real Madrid	2-1		1968	CF Barcelona v Real Madrid	1-0
1934	Real Madrid v Valencia FC	2-1		1969	Atletico Bilbao v Elche	1-0
1935	Sevilla FC v CD Sabadell	3-0				
1936	Real Madrid v Barcelona FC	2-1		1970	Real Madrid v Valencia CF	3-1
1939	Sevilla FC v Racing Ferrol	6-2		1971	CF Barcelona v Valencia CF	4-3
				1972	Atletico Madrid v Valencia CF	2-1
1940	Espanol Barcelona v Real Madrid	3-2		1973	Athletic Bilbao v Castelion	2-0
1941	Valencia FC v Espanol Barcelona	3-1		1974	Real Madrid v CF Barcelona	4-0
1942	CF Barcelona v Atletico Bilbao	4-3		1975	Real Madrid v Atletico Madrid	0-0 4-3 pens
1943	Atletico Bilbao v Real Madrid	1-0		1976	Atletico Madrid v Real Zaragoza	1-0
1944	Atletico Bilbao v Valencia CF	2-0		1977	Real Betis v Athletic Bilbao	2-2 8-7 pens
1945	Atletico Bilbao v Valencia CF	3-2		1978	FC Barcelona v Las Palmas	3-1
1946	Real Madrid v Valencia CF	3-1		1979	Valencia CF v Real Madrid	2-0
1947	Real Madrid v Espanol Barcelona	2-0				
1948	Sevilla CF v Celta Vigo	4-1		1980	Real Madrid v Castilia CF	6-1
1949	Valencia CF v Atletico Bilbao	1-0		1981	FC Barcelona v RS Gijon	3-1
				1982	Real Madrid v RS Gijon	2-1
1950	Atletico Bilbao v Real Valladolid	4-1		1983	FC Barcelona v Real Madrid	2-1
1951	CF Barcelona v Real Sociedad	3-0		1984	Athletic Bilbao v FC Barcelona	1-0
1952	CF Barcelona v Valencia CF	4-2		1985	Atletico Madrid v Athletic Bilbao	2-1
1953	CF Barcelona v Atletico Bilbao	2-1		1986	Real Zaragoza v FC Barcelona	1-0
1954	Valencia CF v CF Barcelona	3-0		1987	Real Sociedad v Atletico Madrid	2-2 4-3 pens
1955	Atletico Bilbao v Sevilla CF	1-0		1988	FC Barcelona v Real Sociadad	1-0
1956	Atletico Bilbao v Atletico Madrid	2-1		1989	Real Madrid v Real Valladolid	1-0
1957	CF Barcelona v Espanol Barcelona	1-0				
1958	Atletico Bilbao v Real Madrid	2-0		1990	FC Barcelona v Real Madrid	2-0
1959	CF Barcelona v Granada	4-1				

LEAGUE CUP

Year	Match	Score
1983	FC Barcelona v Real Madrid	2-1 2-2
1984	Valladolid v Atletico Madrid	3-1 0-0
1985	Real Madrid v Atletico Madrid	2-0 2-3
1986	CF Barcelona v Real Betis Seville	2-0 0-1

SPANISH SUPER CUP

Year	Match	Score
1982	Real Sociadad v Real Madrid	4-1 0-1
1983	FC Barcelona v Athletic Bilbao	0-1 3-1
1984	not held Athletic Bilbao won the double	
1985	Atletico Madrid v FC Barcelona	3-1 0-1
1988	Real Madrid v FC Barcelona	2-0 1-2
1989	Real Madrid won League and Cup	

It was decided they would play FC Barcelona (League runners up) and Real Valladolid (Cup runners up) on triangular tournament. Real beat Valladolid 1-0, but no further dates could be agreed, the competition was abandoned

SPAIN

FEATURED CLUBS IN EUROPEAN COMPETITION

Real Madrid	FC Barcelona	Atletico Madrid	Real Zaragoza
Las Palmas	Real Betis Sevilla	Valencia CF	Athletic Bilbao
Espanol Barcelona	Sevilla FC	Real Sociedad San Sebastien	Valladolid
Sabadell Barcelona	Real Sporting Gijon	Celta de Vigo	Castilla Madrid
CA Osasuna			

REAL MADRID CF

Founded 1902
Colours all white
Stadium Santiago Bernabeu (90,200) formerly named Chamartin ☎ 91-250 06 00
Champions 1932, 1933, 1954, 1955, 1957, 1958, 1961, 1962, 1963, 1964, 1965, 1967, 1968, 1969, 1972, 1975, 1976, 1978, 1979, 1980, 1986, 1987, 1988, 1989, 1990
Cup Winners 1905, 1906, 1907, 1908, 1917, 1934, 1936, 1946, 1947, 1962, 1970, 1974, 1975, 1980, 1982, 1989
European Cup Winners 1956, 1957, 1958, 1959, 1960, 1966 European Cup Finalists 1962, 1964, 1981
CWC Finalists 1971, 1983
UEFA Cup Winners 1985, 1986
World Club Championship Winners 1960 World Club Championship Finalists 1966
League Cup Winners 1985
Spanish Super Cup Winners 1988

Season	Opponent	Home	Playoff Result	Away	Rnd	Cup
1955-56	Servette Geneva, Switzerland	5-0		2-0	1	ECC
	Partizan Belgrade, Yugoslavia	4-0		0-3	qf	ECC
	AC Milan, Italy	4-2		1-2	sf	ECC
	Stade de Reims, France	4-3	in Paris		FINAL	ECC
1956-57	Rapid Vienna, Austria	4-2	2-0* * in Madrid	1-3	1	ECC
	OGC Nice, France	3-0		3-2	qf	ECC
	Manchester United, England	3-1		2-2	sf	ECC
	Fiorentina, Italy	2-0	in Madrid		FINAL	ECC
1957-58	Royal Antwerp, Belgium	6-0		2-1	1	ECC
	Sevilla CF, Spain	8-0		2-2	qf	ECC
	Vasas Budapest, Hungary	4-0		0-2	sf	ECC
	AC Milan, Italy	3-2	in Brussels		FINAL	ECC
1958-59	Besiktas, Turkey	2-0		1-1	1	ECC
	Wiener Sport Club, Austria	7-1		0-0	qf	ECC
	Atletico Madrid, Spain	2-1	2-1* * in Zaragoza	0-1	sf	ECC
	Stade de Reims, France	2-0	in Stuttgart		FINAL	ECC
1959-60	Esch sur Alette, Luxembourg	7-0		5-2	1	ECC
	OGC Nice, France	4-0		2-3	qf	ECC
	CF Barcelona, Spain	3-1		3-1	sf	ECC
	Eintracht Frankfurt, Germany	7-3	in Glasgow		FINAL	ECC
1960-61	CF Barcelona, Spain	2-2		1-2	1	ECC
1961-62	Vasas Budapest, Hungary	3-1		2-0	pr	ECC
	B 1913 Odense, Denmark	9-0		3-0	1	ECC
	Juventus, Italy	0-1	3-1* * in Paris	1-0	qf	ECC
	Standard Liege, Belgium	4-0		2-0	sf	ECC
	Benfica, Portugal	3-5	in Amsterdam		FINAL	ECC
1962-63	SC Anderlecht, Belgium	3-3		0-1	pr	ECC
1963-64	Glasgow Rangers, Scotland	6-0		1-0	pr	ECC
	Dinamo Bucharest, Romania	5-3		3-1	1	ECC
	AC Milan, Italy	4-1		0-2	qf	ECC
	FC Zurich, Switzerland	6-0		2-1	sf	ECC
	Inter Milan, Italy	1-3	in Vienna		FINAL	ECC

1964-65	B 1909 Odense, Denmark	4-0		5-2	1	ECC
	Dukla Prague, Czechoslovakia	4-0		2-2	2	ECC
	Benfica, Portugal	2-1		1-5	qf	ECC
1965-66	Feyenoord Rotterdam, Holland	5-0		1-2	1	ECC
	Kilmarnock, Scotland	5-1		2-2	2	ECC
	RSC Anderlecht, Belgium	4-2		0-1	qf	ECC
	Inter Milan, Italy	1-0		1-1	sf	ECC
	Partizan Belgrade, Yugoslavia	2-1	in Brussels		FINAL	ECC
1966-67	bye				1	ECC
	TSV 1860 Munich, Germany	3-1		0-1	2	ECC
	Inter Milan, Italy	0-2		0-1	qf	ECC
1967-68	Ajax Amsterdam, Holland	2-1		1-1	1	ECC
	Hvidovre IF, Denmark	4-1		2-2	2	ECC
	Sparta Prague, Czechoslovakia	3-0		1-2	qf	ECC
	Manchester United, England	3-3		0-1	sf	ECC
1968-69	Apollon Limassol, Cyprus	6-0		6-0	1	ECC
	Rapid Vienna, Austria	2-1	lag	0-1	2	ECC
1969-70	Olympiakos Nicosia, Cyprus	6-1		8-0*	1	ECC
				* in Madrid		
	Standard Liege, Belgium	2-3		0-1	2	ECC
1970-71	Hibernian, Malta	5-0		0-0	1	CWC
	Wacker Innsbruck, Austria	0-1		2-0	2	CWC
	Cardiff City, Wales	2-0		0-1	qf	ECC
	PSV Eindhoven, Holland	2-1		0-0	sf	CWC
	Chelsea, England	1-1	both	1-2 in Athens FINAL		CWC
1971-72	FC Basle, Switzerland	2-1		2-1	1	UEFA
	PSV Eindhoven, Holland	3-1	wag	0-2	2	UEFA
1972-73	IBK Keflavik, Iceland	3-0		1-0*	1	ECC
				* in Reykjavik		
	FC Arges Pitesti, Romania	3-1		1-2	2	ECC
	Dynamo Kiev, USSR	3-0		0-0*	qf	ECC
				* in Odessa		
	Ajax Amsterdam, Holland	0-1		1-2	sf	ECC
1973-74	Ipswich Town, England	0-0		0-1	1	UEFA
1974-75	Fram Reykjavik, Iceland	6-0		2-0	1	CWC
	FK Austria Vienna, Austria	3-0		2-2	2	CWC
	Red Star Belgrade, Yugoslavia	2-0	5-6p	0-2	qf	CWC
1975-76	Dinamo Bucharest, Romania	4-1		0-1	1	ECC
	Derby County, England	5-1		1-4	2	ECC
	Borussia Monchengladbach, Germany	1-1	wag	2-2	qf	ECC
	Bayern Munich, Germany	1-1		0-2	sf	ECC
1976-77	Stal Mielec, Poland	1-0*		2-1	1	ECC
		* in Valencia				
	Clube Bruges, Belgium	0-0*		0-2	2	ECC
		* in Malaga				
1978-79	Progres Niedercorn, Luxembourg	5-0		7-0	1	ECC
	Grasshoppers Zurich, Switzerland	3-1	lag	0-2	2	ECC
1979-80	Levski Spartak Sofia, Bulgaria	2-0		1-0	1	ECC
	FC Porto, Portugal	1-0	wag	1-2	2	ECC
	Glasgow Celtic, Scotland	3-0		0-2	qf	ECC
	Hamburger SV, Germany	2-0		1-5	sf	ECC
1980-81	Limerick, Ireland	5-1		2-1*	1	ECC
				* in Dublin		
	Honved Budapest, Hungary	1-0		2-0	2	ECC
	Spartak Moscow, USSR	2-0		0-0*	qf	ECC
				* in Tbilisi		
	Inter Milan, Italy	2-0		0-1	sf	ECC
	Liverpool, England	0-1	in Paris		FINAL	ECC
1981-82	Tatabanya Banyasz, Hungary	1-0	wag	1-2	1	UEFA
	Carl Zeiss Jena, East Germany	3-2		0-0	2	UEFA
	Rapid Vienna, Austria	0-0		1-0	3	UEFA
	1.FC Kaiserslautrn, Germany	3-1		0-5	qf	UEFA
1982-83	FC Baia Mare, Romania	5-2		0-0	1	CWC
	Ujpest Dozsa, Hungary	3-1		1-0	2	CWC
	Inter Milan, Italy	2-1		1-1	qf	CWC

Season	Opponents	Home	Playoff Result	Away	Rnd	Cups
	FK Austria Vienna, Austria	3-1		2-2	sf	CWC
	Aberdeen, Scotland	1-2	in Gothenburg		FINAL	CWC
1983-84	Sparta Prague, Czechoslovakia	1-1		2-3	1	UEFA
1984-85	Wacker Innsbruck, Austria	5-0		0-2	1	UEFA
	NK Rijeka, Yugoslavia	3-0		1-3	2	UEFA
	RSC Anderlecht, Belgium	6-1		0-3	3	UEFA
	Tottenham Hotspur, England	0-0		1-0	qf	UEFA
	Inter Milan, Italy	3-0		0-2	sf	UEFA
	Videoton Sekesfehervar, Hungary	0-1		3-0	FINAL	UEFA
1985-86	AEK Athens, Greece	5-0		0-1	1	UEFA
	Chernomorets Odessa, USSR	2-1		0-0	2	UEFA
	Borussia Monchengladbach, Germany	4-0	wag	1-5*	3	UEFA
				* in Dusseldorf		
	FC Neuchatel Xamax, Switzerland	3-0		0-2	qf	UEFA
	Inter Milan, Italy	5-1		1-3	sf	UEFA
	1.FC Koln, Germany	5-1		0-2*	FINAL	UEFA
				* in West Berlin		
1986-87	Young Boys Bern, Switzerland	5-0		0-1	1	ECC
	Juventus, Italy	1-0	3-1 p	0-1	2	ECC
	Red Star Belgrade, Yugoslavia	2-0		2-4	qf	ECC
	Bayern Munich, Germany	1-0		1-4	sf	ECC
1987-88	Napoli, Italy	2-0 *		1-1	1	ECC
			* Played behind closed doors (no spectators)			
	FC Porto, Portugal	2-1 *	2-1		2	ECC
			* played in Valencia			
	Bayern Munich, Germany	2-1	wag	2-3	qf	ECC
	PSV Eindhoven, Holland	1-1	lag	0-0	sf	ECC
1988-89	FK Moss, Norway	3-0		1-0	1	ECC
	Gornik Zabrze, Poland	3-2		1-0	2	ECC
	PSV Eindhoven, Holland	2-1 aet		1-1	qf	ECC
	AC Milan, Italy	1-1		0-5	sf	ECC
1989-90	Spora, Luxembourg	6-0		3-0*	1	ECC
				in Saarbrucken		
	AC Milan, Italy	1-0		0-2	2	ECC

FC BARCELONA

Founded 1899 as Barcelona FC, 1940 CF Barcelona, 1975 FC Barcelona
Colours blue and red striped shirts, blue shorts
Stadium Nou Camp (115,000) ☎ 93-330 9411, previous ground Estadio Las Corts until 1957
Champions 1929, 1945, 1948, 1949, 1952, 1953, 1959, 1960, 1974, 1985
Cup Winners 1910, 1912, 1913, 1920, 1922, 1925, 1926, 1928, 1942, 1951, 1952, 1953, 1957, 1959, 1963, 1968, 1971, 1978, 1981, 1983, 1988, 1990
League Cup Winners 1983, 1986
Spanish Super Cup Winners 1983
European Cup Finalists 1961, 1986
CWC Winners 1979, 1982, 1989 Finalists 1969
Fairs/UEFA Cup Winners 1958, 1960, 1966 Finalists 1962
Super Cup Finalists 1979, 1982
Latin Cup Winners 1949, 1951

Season	Opponents	Home	Playoff Result	Away	Rnd	Cups
1955-58	Copenhagen XI, Denmark	6-2		1-1	1	Fairs
	Birmingham City, England	1-0	2-1*	3-4	sf	Fairs
			* in Basel			
	London XI, England	6-0		2-2	FINAL	Fairs
1958-60	Basel City XI, Switzerland	5-2		2-1	1	Fairs
	Inter Milan, Italy	4-0		4-2	qf	Fairs
	Belgrade City XI, Yugoslavia	3-1		1-1	sf	Fairs
	Birmingham City, England	4-1		0-0	FINAL	Fairs

Season	Opponent				Round	Comp
1959-60	CDNA Sofia, Bulgaria	6-2		2-2	pr	ECC
	AC Milan, Italy	5-1		2-0	1	ECC
	Wolverhampton Wanderers, England	4-0		5-2	qf	ECC
	Real Madrid, Spain	1-3		1-3	sf	ECC
1960-61	Lierse SK, Belgium	2-0		3-0	pr	ECC
	Real Madrid, Spain	2-1		2-2	1	ECC
	Spartak Hradec Kralove, Czechoslovakia	4-0		1-1	qf	ECC
	Hamburger SV, Germany	1-0	1-0*	1-2	SF	ECC
			* in Brussels			
	Benfica, Portugal	2-3	in Berne		FINAL	ECC
1960-61	Zagreb City XI, Yugoslavia	4-3		1-1	1	Fairs
	Hibernian, Scotland	4-4		2-3	qf	Fairs
1961-62	West Berlin City XI, Germany	3-0		0-1	1	Fairs
	Dinamo Zagreb, Yugoslavia	5-1		2-2	2	Fairs
	Sheffield Wednesday, England	2-0		2-3	qf	Fairs
	Red Star Belgrade, Yugoslavia	2-0		4-1	sf	Fairs
	Valencia CF, Spain	1-1		2-6	FINAL	Fairs
1962-63	Belenenses, Portugal	1-1	3-2*		1	Fairs
			* in Barcelona			
	Red Star Belgrade, Yugoslavia	1-0	0-1*	2-3	2	Fairs
			* in Nice			
1963-64	Shelbourne, Eire	3-1		2-0	1	CWC
	Hamburger SV, Germany	0-0	2-3*	4-4	2	CWC
			* in Lausanne			
1964-65	Fiorentina, Italy	0-1		2-0	1	Fairs
	Glasgow Celtic, Scotland	3-1		0-0	2	Fairs
	RC Strasbourg, France	2-2	0-0* lot	0-0	3	Fairs
			* in Barcelona			
	DOS Utrecht, Holland	7-1		0-0	1	Fairs
	Royal Antwerp, Belgium	2-0		1-2	2	Fairs
	Hanover 96, Germany	1-0	1-1 *wot	1-2	3	Fairs
			* in Barcelona aet			
	Espanol Barcelona, Spain	1-0		1-0	qf	Fairs
	Chelsea, England	2-0	5-0*	0-2	sf	Fairs
			* in Barcelona			
	Real Zaragoza, Spain	0-1		4-2	FINAL	Fairs
1966-67	bye				1	Fairs
	Dundee United, Scotland	1-2		0-2	2	Fairs
1967-68	FC Zurich, Switzerland	1-0		1-3	1	Fairs
1968-69	Lugano, Switzerland	3-0		1-0	1	CWC
	bye				2	CWC
	Lyn Oslo, Norway	3-2		2-2	qf	CWC
	1.FC Koln, Germany	4-1		2-2	sf	CWC
	Slovan Bratislava, Czechoslovakia	2-3	in Basle		FINAL	CWC
1969-70	B 1909 Odense, Denmark	4-0		2-0	1	Fairs
	Vasas Gyoer Eto, Hungary	2-0		3-2	2	Fairs
	Inter Milan, Italy	1-2		1-1	3	Fairs
1970-71	GKS Katowice, Poland	3-2		1-0	1	Fairs
	Juventus, Italy	1-2		1-2	2	Fairs
1971-72	Distillery, Ireland	4-0		3-1	1	CWC
	Steaua Bucharest, Romania	0-1		1-2	2	CWC
1972-73	FC Porto, Portugal	0-1		1-3	1	UEFA
1973-74	OGC Nice, France	2-0		0-3	1	UEFA
1974-75	SK VoEST Linz, Austria	5-0		0-0	1	ECC
	Feyenoord Rotterdam, Holland	3-0		0-0	2	ECC
	Atvidaberg FF, Sweden	2-0		3-0	qf	ECC
	Leeds United, England	1-1		1-2	sf	ECC
1975-76	PAOK Salonika, Greece	6-1		0-1	1	UEFA
	Lazio Rome, Italy	4-0	3-0*		2	UEFA
			* awarded to Barcelona			
	Vasas Budapest, Bulgaria	3-1		1-0	3	UEFA
	Levski Spartak Sofia, Bulgaria	4-0		4-5	qf	UEFA
	Liverpool, England	0-1		1-1	sf	UEFA

SPAIN

1976-77	Belenenses, Portugal	3-2		2-2	1	UEFA
	KSC Lokeren, Belgium	2-0		1-2	2	UEFA
	Osters IF Vaxjo, Sweden	5-1		3-0	3	UEFA
	Athletic Bilbao, Spain	2-2		1-2	qf	UEFA
1977-78	Steaua Bucharest, Romania	5-1		3-1	1	UEFA
	AZ 67 Alkmaar, Holland	1-1	5-4 pen	1-1	2	UEFA
	Ipswich Town, England	3-0	3-1 pen	0-3	3	UEFA
	Aston Villa, England	2-1		2-2	qf	UEFA
	PSV Eindhoven, Holland	3-1		0-3	sf	UEFA
1978-79	Shakhtyor Donetsk, USSR	3-0		1-1	1	CWC
	RSC Anderlecht, Belgium	3-0	4-1 pen	0-3	2	CWC
	Ipswich Town, England	1-0	wag	1-2	qf	CWC
	SK Beveren Waas, Belgium	1-0		1-0	sf	CWC
	Fortuna Dusseldorf, Germany	4-3	in Basel		FINAL	CWC
1979-80	IA Akranes, Iceland	5-0		1-0*	1	CWC
				* in Reykjavik		
	Aris Bonneweg, Luxembourg	7-1		4-1	2	CWC
	Valencia CF, Spain	0-1		3-4	qf	CWC
1980-81	Sliema Wanderers, Malta	1-0		2-0	1	UEFA
	1.FC Koln, Germany	0-4		1-0	2	UEFA
1981-82	Trakia Plovdiv, Bulgaria	4-1		0-1	1	CWC
	Dukla Prague, Czechoslovakia	4-0		0-1	2	CWC
	1.FC Lokomotive Leipzig, East Germany	1-2		3-0	qf	CWC
	Tottenham Hotspur, England	1-0		1-1	sf	CWC
	Standard Liege, Belgium	2-1	in Barcelona		FINAL	CWC
1982-83	Appollon Limassol, Cyprus	8-0		1-1	1	CWC
	Red Star Belgrade, Yugoslavia	2-1		4-2	2	CWC
	FK Austria Vienna, Austria	1-1	lag	0-0	qf	CWC
1983-84	1.FC Magdeburg, East Germany	2-0		5-1	1	CWC
	NEC Nijmegen, Holland	2-0		3-2	2	CWC
	Manchester United, England	2-0		0-3	qf	CWC
1984-85	FC Metz, France	1-4		4-2	1	CWC
1985-86	Sparta Prague, Czechoslovakia	0-1	wag	2-1	1	ECC
	FC Porto, Portugal	2-0	wag	1-3	2	ECC
	Juventus, Italy	1-0		1-1	qf	ECC
	IFK Gothenburg, Sweden	3-0	5-4p	0-3	sf	ECC
	Steaua Bucharest, Romania	0-0	0-2 pen	in Seville	FINAL	ECC
1986-87	Flamurtari Vlore, Albania	0-0	wag	1-1	1	UEFA
	Sporting Lisbon, Portugal	1-0	wag	1-2	2	UEFA
	Bayer Uerdingen, Germany	2-0		2-0	3	UEFA
	Dundee United, Scotland	1-2		0-1	qf	UEFA
1987-88	Belenenses, Portugal	2-0		0-1	1	UEFA
	Dynamo Moscow, USSR	2-0		0-0	2	UEFA
	Flamurtari Vlora, Albania	4-1		0-1	3	UEFA
	Bayer Leverkusen, Germany	0-1		0-1	qf	UEFA
1988-89	Fram Reykjavik, Iceland	5-0		2-0	1	CWC
	Lech Poznan, Poland	1-1	5-4p	1-1	2	CWC
	AGF Aarhus, Denmark	0-0		1-0	qf	CWC
	CFKA Sredets Sofia, Bulgaria	4-2		3-1	sf	CWC
	Sampdoria, Italy	2-0	in Bern		FINAL	CWC
1989-90	Legia Warsaw, Poland	1-1		1-0	1	CWC
	RSC Anderlecht, Belgium	2-1 aet		0-2	2	CWC

CLUB ATLETICO MADRID

Founded 26-4-1903 Athletic de Madrid, 1939 Atletico Aviacion (merger of Athletic Madrid and Aviacion Nacional, 1946 Atletico Madrid
Colours red and white striped shirts, light blue shorts
Stadium Vicente Calderon (70,000) ☎ 91-266 4707
Champions as Aviacione 1940, 1941, as Atletico Masdrid 1950, 1951, 1966, 1970, 1973, 1977
Cup Winners 1960, 1961, 1965, 1972, 1976, 1985
European Cup Finalists 1974
CWC Winners 1962 CWC Finalists 1963, 1986
Spanish Super Cup Winners 1985

Season	Opponents	Home	Playoff Result	Away	Rnd	Cups
1958-59	Drumcondra, Eire	8-0		5-1	pr	ECC
	CDNA Sofia, Bulgaria	2-1	3-1*	0-1	1	ECC
			* in Geneva			
	FC Schalke 04 Gelsenkirchen, Germany	3-0		1-1	qf	ECC
	Real Madrid, Spain	1-0	1-2*	1-2	sf	ECC
			* in Zaragoza			
1961-62	Sedan, France	4-1		3-2	1	CWC
	Leicester City, England	2-0		1-1	2	CWC
	Werder Bremen, Germany	3-1		1-1	qf	CWC
	SC Motor Jena, East Germany	4-0		1-0*	sf	CWC
				* in Malmo		
	Fiorentina, Italy	1-1	in Glasgow		FINAL	CWC
	Fiorentina, Italy	3-0	in Stuttgart		REPLAY	CWC
1962-63	bye				1	CWC
	Hibernians, Malta	4-0		1-0	2	CWC
	Botev Plovdiv, Bulgaria	1-1		4-0	qf	CWC
	1.FC Nurnburg, Germany	2-0		1-2	sf	CWC
	Tottenham Hotspur, England	1-5	in Amsterdam		FINAL	CWC
1963-64	FC Porto, Portugal	2-1		0-0	1	Fairs
	Juventus, Italy	1-2		0-1	2	Fairs
1964-65	Servette Geneva, Switzerland	6-1		2-2	1	Fairs
	Shelbourne Dublin, Eire	1-0		1-0	2	Fairs
	RFC Liege, Belgium	2-0		0-1	3	Fairs
	bye				qf	Fairs
	Juventus, Italy	3-1	1-3*	1-3	sf	Fairs
			* in Turin			
1965-66	Dinamo Zagreb, Yugoslavia	4-0		1-0	1	CWC
	Universitatea Stintza Cluj, Romania	4-0		2-0	2	CWC
	Borussia Dortmund, Germany	1-1		0-1	qf	CWC
1966-67	Malmo FF, Sweden	3-1		2-0	pr	ECC
	Vojvodina Novi Sad, Yugoslavia	2-0	2-3* aet	1-3	1	ECC
			* in Madrid			
1967-68	Wiener Sport Club, Austria	2-1		5-2	1	Fairs
	Goztepe Izmir, Turkey	2-0		0-3	2	Fairs
1968-69	KSV Weregem, Belgium	2-1	lag	0-1	1	Fairs
1970-71	FK Austria Vienna, Austria	2-0		2-1	1	ECC
	Cagliari Sardinia, Italy	3-0		1-2	2	ECC
	Legia Warsaw, Poland	1-0	wag	1-2	qf	ECC
	Ajax Amsterdam, Holland	1-0		0-3	sf	ECC
1971-72	Panionios, Greece	2-1	lag	0-1	1	UEFA
1972-73	SEC Bastia Corsica, France	2-1		0-0	1	CWC
	Spartak Moscow, USSR	3-4	lag	2-1	2	CWC
1973-74	Galatasaray, Turkey	0-0		1-0	1	ECC
	Dynamo Bucharest, Romania	2-2		2-0	2	ECC
	Red Star Belgrade, Yugoslavia	0-0		2-0	qf	ECC
	Glasgow Celtic, Scotland	2-0		0-0	sf	ECC
	Bayern Munich, Germany	1-1		0-4	FINAL	ECC
			both in Brussels			

275

SPAIN

1974-75	KB Copenhagen, Denmark	4-0		2-3	1	UEFA
	Derby County, England	2-2	6-7 pen	2-2	2	UEFA
1975-76	FC Basle, Switzerland	1-1		2-1	1	CWC
	Eintracht Frankfurt, Germany	1-2		0-1	2	CWC
1976-77	Rapid Vienna, Austria	1-1		2-1	1	CWC
	Hajduk Split, Yugoslavia	1-0		2-1	2	CWC
	Levski Spartak Sofia, Bulgaria	2-0		1-2	qf	CWC
	Hamburger SV, Germany	3-1		0-3	sf	CWC
1977-78	Dinamo Bucharest, Romania	2-0		1-2	1	ECC
	FC Nantes, France	2-1		1-1	2	ECC
	Clube Bruges, Belgium	3-2		0-2	qf	ECC
1979-80	Dynamo Dresden, East Germany	1-2		0-3	1	UEFA
1981-82	Boavista, Portugal	3-1		1-4	1	UEFA
1983-84	FC Groningen, Holland	2-1		0-3	1	UEFA
1984-85	FC Sion, Switzerland	2-3		0-1	1	UEFA
1985-86	Glasgow Celtic, Scotland	1-1		2-1	1	CWC
	Bangor City, Wales	1-0		2-0	2	CWC
	Red Star Belgrade, Yugoslavia	1-1		2-0	qf	CWC
	Bayer Uerdingen, Germany	1-0		3-2	sf	CWC
	Dynamo Kiev, USSR	0-3	in Lyon		FINAL	CWC
1986-87	Werder Bremen, Germany	2-0		1-2	1	UEFA
	Vitoria Guimaraes, Portugal	1-0		0-2	2 .	UEFA
1988-89	FC Groningen, Holland	2-1	lag	0-1	1	UEFA
1989-90	Fiorentina, Italy	1-0	1-3p	0-1aet* in Perugia	1	UEFA

REAL ZARAGOZA CLUB DEPORTIVO

Founded 28-3-1932
Colours white shirts with blue trim, blue shorts
Stadium La Romareda (45,000) ☎ 976-2341 92/2133 22
Cup Winners 1964, 1966, 1986
Fairs Cup Winners 1964 Finalists 1966

Season	Opponents	Home	Playoff Result	Away	Rnd	Cups
1962-63	Glentoran, Ireland	6-2		2-0	1	Fairs
	AS Roma, Italy	1-2		2-4	2	Fairs
1963-64	Iraklis Salonika, Greece	6-1		3-0	1	Fairs
	Lausanne Sport, Switzerland	3-0		2-1	2	Fairs
	Juventus, Italy	3-2		0-0	qf	Fairs
	RFC Liege, Belgium	2-1	2-0* * in Liege	0-1	sf	Fairs
	Valencia CF, Spain	2-1	in Barcelona		FINAL	Fairs
1964-65	Valletta, Malta	3-1		3-0	1	CWC
	Dundee, Scotland	2-1		2-2	2	CWC
	Cardiff City, Wales	2-2		1-0	qf	CWC
	West Ham United, England	1-1		1-2	sf	CWC
1965-66	bye				1	Fairs
	Shamrock Rovers, Eire	2-1		1-1	2	Fairs
	Heart of Midlothian, Scotland	2-2	1-0* * in Zaragoza	3-3	3	Fairs
	Dunfermline Athletic, Scotland	4-2	aet	0-1	qf	Fairs
	Leeds United, England	1-0	3-1* * in Zaragoza	1-2	sf	Fairs
	CF Barcelona, Spain	1-0		2-4	FINAL	Fairs
1966-67	Skeid Oslo, Norway	3-1		2-3	1	CWC
	Everton, England	2-0		0-1	2	CWC
	Glasgow Rangers, Scotland	2-0	lot	0-2	qf	CWC
1967-68	DOS Utrecht, Holland	3-1		2-3	1	Fairs
	Ferencvarosi TC, Hungary	2-1		0-3	2	Fairs

1968-69	Trakia Plovdiv, Bulgaria	2-0	wag	1-3	1	Fairs
	Aberdeen, Scotland	3-0		1-2	2	Fairs
	Newcastle United, England	3-2	lag	1-2	3	Fairs
1974-75	Vitoria Setubal, Portugal	4-0		1-1	1	UEFA
	Grasshoppers Zurich, Switzerland	5-0		1-2	2	UEFA
	Borussia Monchengladbach, Germany	2-4		0-5	3	UEFA
1975-76	Internacional Bratislava, Czechoslovakia	2-3		0-5	1	UEFA
1986-87	AS Roma, Italy	2-0	4-3 pen	0-2	1	CWC
	Wrexham, Wales	0-0	wag	2-2	2	CWC
	Vitosha Sofia, Bulgaria	2-0		2-0	qf	CWC
	Ajax Amsterdam, Holland	2-3		0-3	sf	CWC
1989-90	Apollon Limassol, Cyprus	1-1		2-0	1	UEFA
	Hamburger SV, Germany	1-0		0-2aet	2	UEFA

UNION DEPORTIVA LAS PALMAS

Founded 22-8-1949
Colours yellow shirts, sky blue shorts
Stadium Estadio Insular (20,000) ☎ 928-2413 42/43

Season	Opponents	Home	Result	Away	Rnd	Cups
1969-70	Hertha BSC Berlin, Germany	0-0		0-1	1	Fairs
1972-73	Torino, Italy	4-0		0-2	1	UEFA
	Slovan Bratislava, Czechoslovakia	2-2		1-0	2	UEFA
	Twente Enschede, Holland	2-1		0-3	3	UEFA
1977-78	Sloboda Tuzla, Yugoslavia	5-0		3-4	1	UEFA
	Ipswich Town, England	3-3		0-1	2	UEFA

REAL BETIS BALOMPIE

Founded 1907
Colours green and white striped shirts, white shorts
Stadium Benito Villamarin, Sevilla (50,000) ☎ 954-6103 40 formerly Estadio Heliopolis
Champions 1935
Cup Winners 1977

Season	Opponents	Home	Playoff Result	Away	Rnd	Cups
1964-65	Stade Francais, France	1-1		0-2	pr	Fairs
1977-78	AC Milan, Italy	2-0		1-2	1	CWC
	1.FC Lokomotive Leipzig, East Germany	2-1		1-1	2	CWC
	Dynamo Moscow, USSR	0-0		0-3*	qf	CWC
				* in Tbilisi		
1982-83	Benfica, Portugal	1-2		1-2	1	UEFA
1984-85	Universitatea Craiova, Romania	1-0	3-5 pen	0-1	1	UEFA

VALENCIA CF

Founded 18-3-1919 as Valencia Football Club, 1940 as Valencia Club de Futbol
Colours all white
Stadium Luis Casanova (49,291) ☎ 96-360 05 50
Champions 1942, 1944, 1947, 1971
Cup Winners 1941, 1949, 1954, 1967, 1979
CWC Winners 1980
Fairs Cup Winners 1962, 1963 Finalists 1964

277

SPAIN

Season	Opponents	Home	Playoff Result	Away	Rnd	Cups
1961-62	Nottingham Forest, England	5-1		2-0	1	Fairs
	Lausanne Sport, Switzerland	4-3	not played		2	Fairs
	Inter Milan, Italy	2-0		3-3	qf	Fairs
	MTK Budapest, Hungary	3-0		7-3	sf	Fairs
	CF Barcelona, Spain	6-2		1-1	FINAL	Fairs
1962-63	Glasgow Celtic, Scotland	4-2		2-2	1	Fairs
	Dunfermline Athletic, Scotland	4-0	1-0*	2-6	2	Fairs
			* in Barcelona			
	Hibernian, Scotland			5-0	1-2 qf	Fairs
	AS Roma, Italy	3-0		0-1	sf	Fairs
	Dinamo Zagreb, Yugoslavia	2-1		2-0	FINAL	Fairs
1963-64	Shamrock Rovers, Eire	1-0		2-2	1	Fairs
	Rapid Vienna, Austria	3-2		0-0	2	Fairs
	Ujpest Dozsa, Hungary	5-2		1-3	qf	Fairs
	1.FC Koln, Germany	4-1		0-2	sf	Fairs
	Real Zaragoza, Spain	1-2	in Barcelona		FINAL	Fairs
1964-65	RFC Liege, Belgium	1-1		1-3	pr	Fairs
1965-66	Hibernian, Scotland	2-0	3-0*	0-2	1	Fairs
			* in Valencia			
	FC Basle, Switzerland	5-1		3-1	2	Fairs
	Leeds United, England	0-1		1-1	qf	Fairs
1966-67	1.FC Nurnburg, Germany	2-0		2-1	1	Fairs
	Red Star Belgrade, Yugoslavia	1-0		2-1	2	Fairs
	Leeds United, England	0-2		1-1	qf	Fairs
1967-68	Crusaders, Ireland	4-0		4-2	1	CWC
	Steaua Bucharest, Romania	3-0		0-1	2	CWC
	Bayern Munich, Germany	1-1		0-1	qf	CWC
1968-69	Sporting Lisbon, Portugal	4-1		0-4	1	Fairs
1969-70	Slavia Sofia, Bulgaria	1-1		0-2	1	Fairs
1970-71	Cork Hibernians, Eire	3-1		3-0	1	Fairs
	SK Beveren Waas, Belgium	0-1		1-1	2	Fairs
1971-72	Union Spora, Luxembourg	3-1		1-0	pr	ECC
	Hajduk Split, Yugoslavia	0-0	wag	1-1	1	ECC
	Ujpest Dozsa, Hungary	0-1		1-2	2	ECC
1972-73	Manchester City, England	2-1		2-2	1	UEFA
	Red Star Belgrade, Yugoslavia	0-1		1-3	2	UEFA
1978-79	CSKA Sofia, Bulgaria	4-1		1-2	1	UEFA
	FC Arges Pitesti, Romania	5-2		1-2	2	UEFA
	West Bromwich Albion, England	1-1		0-2	3	UEFA
1979-80	BK 1903 Copenhagen, Denmark	4-0		2-2	1	CWC
	Glasgow Rangers, Scotland	1-1		3-1	2	CWC
	FC Barcelona, Spain	4-3		1-0	qf	CWC
	FC Nantes, France	4-0		1-2	sf	CWC
	Arsenal, England	0-0	5-4 pen	in Brussels	FINAL	CWC
1980-81	AS Monaco, France	2-0		3-3	1	CWC
	Carl Zeiss Jena, East Germany	1-0		1-3	2	CWC
1981-82	Bohemians Prague, Czechoslovakia	1-0		1-0	1	UEFA
	Boavista, Portugal	2-0		0-1	2	UEFA
	Hajduk Split, Yugoslavia	5-1		1-4	3	UEFA
	IFK Gothenburg, Sweden	2-2		0-2	qf	UEFA
1982-83	Manchester United, England	2-1		0-0	1	EFA
	Banik Ostrava, Czechoslovakia	1-0		0-0	2	UEFA
	Spartak Moscow, USSR	2-0		0-0	3	UEFA
	RSC Anderlecht, Belgium	1-2		1-3	qf	UEFA
1989-90	Victoria Bucharest, Romania	3-1		1-1	1	UEFA
	FC Porto, Portugal	3-2		1-3	2	UEFA

ATHLETIC CLUB DE BILBAO

Founded 1898 as Athletic Club de Bilbao, 1940 Atletico Club de Bilbao, 1970 Athletic Club de Bilbao
Colours red and white striped shirts, black shorts
Stadium San Mames (46,500) ☎ 94-424 08 77/8
Champions 1930, 1931, 1934, 1936, 1943, 1956, 1983, 1984
Cup Winners 1903, 1904, 1910, 1911, 1914, 1915, 1916, 1921, 1923, 1930, 1931, 1932, 1933, 1943, 1944, 1945, 1950, 1955, 1956, 1958, 1969, 1973, 1984
UEFA Cup Finalists 1977

Season	Opponents	Home	Playoff Result	Away	Rnd	Cups
1956-57	FC Porto, Portugal	3-2		2-1	1	ECC
	Honved Budapest, Hungary	3-2		3-3*	2	ECC
				* in Brussels		
	Manchester United, England	5-3		0-3	qf	ECC
1964-65	OFK Belgrade, Yugoslavia	2-2		2-0	1	Fairs
	Royal Antwerp, Belgium	2-0		1-0	2	Fairs
	Dunfermline Athletic, Scotland	1-0	2-1*	0-1	3	Fairs
			* in Bilbao			
	Ferencvarosi TC, Hungary	0-1	0-3*	2-1	qf	Fairs
			* in Budapest			
1966-67	Red Star Belgrade, Yugoslavia	2-0		0-5	1	Fairs
1967-68	Frem Copenhagen, Denmark	3-2		1-0	1	Fairs
	Girondins Bordeaux, France	1-0		3-1	2	Fairs
	bye				3	Fairs
	Ferencvarosi TC, Hungary	1-2		1-2	qf	Fairs
1968-69	Liverpool, England	2-1	wot	1-2	1	Fairs
	Panathinaikos, Greece	1-0		0-0	2	Fairs
	Eintracht Frankfurt, Germany	1-0		1-1	3	Fairs
	Glasgow Rangers, Scotland	2-0		1-4	qf	Fairs
1969-70	Manchester City, England	3-3		0-3	1	CWC
1970-71	Sparta Prague, Czechoslovakia	1-1		0-2	1	Fairs
1971-72	Southampton, England	2-0		1-2	1	UEFA
	Eintracht Braunschweig, Germany	2-2		1-2	2	UEFA
1973-74	Torpedo Moscow, USSR	2-0		0-0	1	CWC
	Beroe Stara Zagora, Bulgaria	1-0		0-3	2	CWC
1976-77	Ujpest Dozsa, Hungary	5-0		0-1	1	UEFA
	FC Basle, Switzerland	3-1		1-1	2	UEFA
	AC Milan, Italy	4-1		1-3	3	UEFA
	FC Barcelona, Spain	2-1		2-2	qf	UEFA
	RWD Molenbeeck, Belgium	0-0	wag	1-1	sf	UEFA
	Juventus, Italy	2-1	lag	0-1	FINAL	UEFA
1977-78	Servette Geneva, Switzerland	2-0		0-1	1	UEFA
	Ujpest Dozsa, Hungary	3-0		0-2	2	UEFA
	Aston Villa, England	1-1		0-2	3	UEFA
1978-79	Ajax Amsterdam, Holland	2-0		0-3	1	UEFA
1982-83	Ferencvarosi TC, Hungary	1-1		1-2	1	UEFA
1983-84	Lech Poznan, Poland	4-0		0-2	1	ECC
	Liverpool, England	0-1		0-0	2	ECC
1984-85	Girondins Bordeaux, France	0-0		2-3	1	ECC
1985-86	Besiktas, Turkey	4-1		1-0	1	UEFA
	RFC Liege, Belgium	3-1		1-0	2	UEFA
	Sporting Lisbon, Portugal	2-1		0-3	3	UEFA
1986-87	1.FC Magdeburg, East Germany	2-0		0-1	1	UEFA
	SK Beveren Waas, Belgium	2-1		1-3	2	UEFA
1988-89	AEK Athens, Greece	2-0		0-1	1	UEFA
	Juventus, Italy	3-2		1-5	2	UEFA

REAL CLUB DEPORTIVO ESPANOL BARCELONA

Founded 1900
Colours blue and white striped shirts, blue shorts
Stadium Sarria (41,000) ☎ 93-203 48 00
Cup Winners 1929, 1940
UEFA Finalists 1988

Season	Opponents	Home	Playoff Result	Away	Rnd	Cups
1961-62	Hannover 96, Germany	2-0		1-0	1	Fairs
	Birmingham City, England	5-2		0-1	2	Fairs
	Red Star Belgrade, Yugoslavia	2-1		0-5	3	Fairs
1965-66	bye				1	Fairs
	Sporting Lisbon, Portugal	4-3	2-1*	1-2	2	Fairs
			* in Barcelona			
	Steagul Rosu Brasov, Romania	2-4	1-0*	3-1	3	Fairs
			* in Barcelona			
	CF Barcelona, Spain	0-1		0-1	qf	Fairs
1973-74	RWD Molenbeeck, Belgium	0-3		2-1	1	UEFA
1976-77	OGC Nice, France	3-1		1-2	1	UEFA
	Eintracht Braunschweig, Germany	2-0		1-2	2	UEFA
	Feyenoord Rotterdam, Holland	0-1		0-2	3	UEFA
1987-88	Borussia Monchengladbach, Germany	4-1		1-0	1	UEFA
	AC Milan, Italy	0-0		2-0*	2	UEFA
				* in Lecce		
	Inter Milan, Italy	1-0		1-1	3	UEFA
	TJ Vitkovice, Czechoslovakia	2-0		0-0	qf	UEFA
	Clube Bruges, Belgium	3-0		0-2	sf	UEFA
	Bayer Leverkusen, Germany	3-0	2-3p	0-3	FINAL	UEFA

SEVILLA FUTBOL CLUB

Founded 14-10-1905 as Sevilla Football Club, 1940 Sevilla Club Futbol, 1980 Sevilla Futbol Club
Colours all white
Stadium Ramon Sanchez Pizjuan (70,410) formerly Nervion ☎ 954-575750
Champions 1946
Cup Winners 1935, 1939, 1948

Season	Opponents	Home	Result	Away	Rnd	Cups
1957-58	Benfica, Portugal	3-1		0-0	pr	ECC
	AGF Aarhus, Denmark	4-0		0-2	1	ECC
	Real Madrid, Spain	2-2		0-8	qf	ECC
1962-63	Glasgow Rangers, Scotland	2-0		0-4	1	CWC
1966-67	Dynamo Pitesti, Romania	2-2		0-2	1	Fairs
1970-71	Eskisehirspor, Turkey	1-0		1-3	1	Fairs
1982-83	Spartak Sofia, Bulgaria	3-1		3-0	1	UEFA
	PAOK Salonika, Greece	4-0		0-2	2	UEFA
	1.FC Kaiserslautern, Germany	1-0		0-4	3	UEFA
1983-84	Sporting Lisbon, Portugal	1-1		2-3	1	UEFA

REAL SOCIEDAD DE FUTBOL

Founded 7-9-1909 as Real Sociadad, 1931 Donostia FC, 1940 Real Sociadad
Colours blue and white striped shirts, white shorts
Stadium Atocha (Atoxa), San Sebastian (27,400) ☎ 943-451109
Champions 1981, 1982
Cup Winners 1987
Spanish Super Cup Winners 1982

Season	Opponents	Home	Result	Away	Rnd	Cups
1974-75	Banik Ostrava, Czechoslovakia	0-1		0-4	1	UEFA
1975-76	Grasshoppers Zurich, Switzerland	1-1	wag	3-3	1	UEFA
	Liverpool, England	1-3		0-6	2	UEFA
1979-80	Inter Milan, Italy	2-0		0-3	1	UEFA
1980-81	Ujpest Dozsa, Hungary	1-0		1-1	1	UEFA
	Zbrojovka Brno, Czechoslovakia	2-1		1-1	2	UEFA
	KSC Lokeren, Belgium	2-2		0-1	3	UEFA
1981-82	CSKA Sofia, Bulgaria	0-0		0-1	1	ECC
1982-83	Vikingur, Iceland	3-2		1-0*	1	ECC
				* in Reykjavik		
	Glasgow Celtic, Scotland	2-0		1-2	2	ECC
	Sporting Lisbon, Portugal	2-0		0-1	qf	ECC
	Hamburger SV, Germany	1-1		1-2	sf	ECC
1987-88	Slask Wroclaw, Poland	0-0		2-0	1	CWC
	Dynamo Minsk, USSR	1-1	lag	0-0	2	CWC
1988-89	Dukla Prague, Czechoslovakia	2-1	wag	2-3	1	UEFA
	Sporting Lisbon, Portugal	0-0		2-1	2	UEFA
	1.FC Koln, Germany	1-0		2-2	3	UEFA
	VfB Stuttgart, Germany	1-0aet	2-4p	0-1	qf	UEFA

REAL VALLADOLID DEPORTIVO

Founded 22-7-1928
Colours lilac/violet and white striped shirts, white shorts
Stadium Nuevo Jose Zorrilla, (33,046) ☎ 983-3064 22/3065 22/3065 33
League Cup 1984

Season	Opponents	Home	Result	Away	Rnd	Cups
1984-85	NK Rijeka, Yugoslavia	1-0		1-4	1	UEFA
1989-90	Hamrun Spartans, Malta	5-0		1-0	1	CWC
	Djurgarden IF Stockholm, Sweden	2-0		2-2	2	CWC
	AS Monaco, France	0-0	1-3p	0-0aet	qf	CWC

CENTRE D'ESPORTS SABADELL FUTBOL CLUB

Founded 1903
Colours blue and white halved shirts, blue shorts
Stadium Nova Creu Alta, Barcelona (20,000) ☎ 93-716 47 25, formerly Creu Alta in 1984

Season	Opponents	Home	Result	Away	Rnd	Cups
1969-70	Clube Bruges, Belgium	2-0		1-5	1	Fairs

SPAIN

REAL SPORTING GIJON

Founded 1905
Colours red and white striped shirts, blue shorts
Stadium El Molinon (45,000) ☎ 985-341457

Season	Opponents	Home	Result	Away	Rnd	Cups
1978-79	Torino, Italy	3-0		0-1	1	UEFA
	Red Star Belgrade, Yugoslavia	0-1		1-1	2	UEFA
1979-80	PSV Eindhoven, Holland	0-0		0-1	1	UEFA
1980-81	Bohemians Prague, Czechoslovakia	2-1		1-3	1	UEFA
1985-86	1.FC Koln, Germany	1-2		0-0	1	UEFA
1987-88	AC Milan, Italy	1-0		0-3	1	UEFA

REAL CLUB CELTA DE VIGO

Founded 10-8-1923
Colours pale blue shirts, white shorts
Stadium Balaidos (33,000) ☎ 986-292850/54

Season	Opponents	Home	Result	Away	Rnd	Cups
1971-72	Aberdeen, Scotland	0-2		0-1	1	UEFA

CASTILLA CLUB DE FUTBOL MADRID

Founded 1943 as Plus Ulta, 1962 Castilla CF (Real Madrid nursery club not allowed to play in the same Division)
Colours all white
Stadium Santiago Bernabeu (90,200) or Ciudad Deportiva

Season	Opponents	Home	Result	Away	Rnd	Cups
1980-81	West Ham United, England	3-1		1-5*	1	CWC

* behind closed doors

CLUB ATLETICO OSASUNA

Founded 20-11-1920
Colours red shirts, marine blue shorts
Stadium El Sadar (25,000) ☎ 948-212027

Season	Opponents	Home	Result	Away	Rnd	Cups
1985-86	Glasgow Rangers, Scotland	2-0		0-1	1	UEFA
	Waregem KSV, Belgium	2-1		0-2	2	UEFA

SWEDEN

Founded 1904 Svenska Fotbollforbundet, Fotbollstadion, Solna ☎ 08-7350900
National colours yellow shirts, blue shorts, yellow and blue socks
Season April to October (break in July)

CUP CHAMPIONS

From 1896 until 1925 Champions were decided on Cup basis

1896	Orgryte IS Gothenburg v "IV" Gothenburg	3-0
1897	Orgryte IS Gothenburg v Orgryte II Gothenburg	1-0
1898	Orgryte IS Gothenburg v AIK Stockholm	3-0
1899	Orgryte IS Gothenburg v Gothenburg FF	4-0
1900	AIK Stockholm v Orgryte IS Gothenburg	1-0
1901	AIK Stockholm v Orgryte IS Gothenburg	wo
1902	Orgryte IS Gothenburg v Jonkopings AIF	9-0
1903	Gothenburg IF v Gothenburg FF	5-2
1904	Orgryte IS Gothenburg v Djurgarden IF Stockholm	2-1
1905	Orgryte IS Gothenburg v IFK Stockholm	2-1
1906	Orgryte IS Gothenburg v Djurgarden IF Stockholm	4-3
1907	Orgryte IS Gothenburg v IFK Uppsala	4-1
1908	IFK Gothenburg v IFK Uppsala	4-3
1909	Orgryte IS Gothenburg v Djurgarden IF Stockholm	8-2
1910	IFK Gothenburg v Djurgarden IF Stockholm	3-0
1911	AIK Stockholm v IFK Uppsala	3-2

1912	Djurgarden IF Stockholm v Orgryte IS Gothenburg	3-1
1913	Orgryte IS Gothenburg v Djurgarden IF Stockholm	3-2
1914	AIK Stockholm v Helsingborgs IF	7-2
1915	Djurgarden IF Stockholm v Orgryte IS Gothenburg	4-1
1916	AIK Stockholm v Djurgarden IF Stockholm	3-1
1917	Djurgarden IF Stockholm v AIK Stockholm	3-1
1918	IFK Gothenburg v Helsingborgs IF	5-0
1919	GAIS Gothenburg v Djurgarden IF Stockholm	4-1
1920	Djurgarden IF Stockholm v Sleipner	1-0
1921	IFK Eskilstuna v Sleipner	2-1
1922	GAIS Gothenburg v Hammarby IF	3-1
1923	AIK Stockholm v IFK Eskilstuna	5-1
1924	Fassberg v Sirius	5-0
1925	Brynas v Derby	4-2

LEAGUE CHAMPIONS

1925 to 1930 Swedish League Championship, from 1931 Official Swedish Champions. 1924 to 1957 Autumn to Spring (22 matches), 1957-58 Autumn + Spring + Autumn (33 matches), 1959 onwards Spring to Autumn

1925	GAIS Gothenburg	1933	Helsingborgs IF	1941	Helsingborgs IF	1950	Malmo FF
1926	Orgryte IS Gothenburg	1934	Helsingborgs IF	1942	IFK Gothenburg	1951	Malmo FF
1927	GAIS Gothenburg	1935	IFK Gothenburg	1943	IFK Norrkoping	1952	IFK Norrkoping
1928	Orgryte IS Gothenburg	1936	IF Elfsborg Boras	1944	Malmo FF	1953	Malmo FF
1929	Helsingborgs IF	1937	AIK Stockholm	1945	IFK Norrkoping	1954	GAIS Gothenburg
		1938	IK Sleipner Norrkoping	1946	IFK Norrkoping	1955	Djurgardens IF
1930	Helsingborgs IF	1939	IF Elfsborg Boras	1947	IFK Norrkoping		Stockholm
1931	GAIS Gothenburg			1948	IFK Norrkoping	1956	IFK Norrkoping
1932	AIK Stockholm	1940	IF Elfsborg Boras	1949	Malmo FF	1957	IFK Norrkoping

283

SWEDEN

1958 IFK Gothenburg	**1962** IFK Norrkoping	**1969** IFK Gothenburg	**1977** Malmo FF
1959 Djurgardens IF Stockholm	**1963** IFK Norrkoping		**1978** Osters IF Vaxjo
	1964 Djurgardens IF Stockholm	**1970** Malmo FF	**1979** Halmstad BK
1960 IFK Norrkoping*		**1971** Malmo FF	
* IFK Malmo represented	**1965** Malmo FF	**1972** Atvidaberg FF	**1980** Osters IF Vaxjo
Sweden in the European Cup	**1966** Djurgardens IF Stockholm	**1973** Atvidaberg FF	**1981** Osters IF Vaxjo
in 1960-61 season as halfway		**1974** Malmo FF	
leaders Spring season	**1967** Malmo FF	**1975** Malmo FF	
1961 IF Elfsborg Boras	**1968** Osters IF Vaxjo	**1976** Halmstad BK	

LEAGUE CHAMPION PLAY-OFFS (Final)

From 1982 top group play off for Championship

1982 IFK Gothenburg v Hammarby IF	1-2 3-1	**1986** Malmo FF v AIK Stockholm	5-2 0-1
1983 IFK Gothenburg v Osters IF Vaxjo	3-0 1-1	**1987** IFK Gothenburg v Malmo FF	1-0 1-2 wag
1984 IFK Gothenburg v IFK Norrkoping	2-0 5-1	**1988** Malmo FF v Djurgarden IF	7-3 0-0
1985 Orgryte IS Gothenburg v IFK Gothenburg	4-2 2-3	**1989** IFK Norrkoping v Malmo FF	1-0 0-1 0-0 4-3p

CUP WINNERS

1941 Helsingborgs IF v IK Sleipner	3-1	**1972** Landskrona BoIS v IFK Norrkoping	0-0 3-2
1942 GAIS Gothenburg v IF Elfsborg Boras	2-1	**1973** Malmo FF v Atvidabergs IF	7-0
1943 IFK Norrkoping v AIK Stockholm	0-0 5-2	**1974** Malmo FF v Osters Vaxjo	2-0
1944 Malmo FF v IFK Norrkoping	4-3	**1975** Malmo FF v Djurgardens IF	1-0
1945 IFK Norrkoping v Malmo FF	4-1	**1976** AIK Stockholm v Landskrona BoIS	1-1 3-0
1946 Malmo FF v Atvidabergs FF	3-0	**1977** Osters IF Vaxjo v Hammarby IF	1-0
1947 Malmo FF v AIK Stockholm	3-2	**1978** Malmo FF v Kalmar FF	2-0
1948 * Raa IF v BK Kenty	6-0	**1979** IFK Gothenburg v Atvidabergs FF	6-1
* no First Division teams, best players in Olympic team			
1949 AIK Stockholm v Landskrona BoIS	1-0	**1980** Malmo FF v IK Brage	3-3 7-6 pens
		1981 Kalmar FF v IF Elfsborg Boras	4-0
1950 AIK Stockholm v Helsingborgs IF	3-2	**1982** IFK Gothenburg v Osters IF Vaxjo	3-2
1951 Malmo FF v Djurgardens IF	2-1	**1983** IFK Gothenburg v Hammarby IF	1-0
1952 no competition Olympic year		**1984** Malmo FF v Landskrona	1-0
1953 Malmo FF v IFK Norrkoping	3-2	**1985** AIK Stockholm v Oster IF Vaxjo	1-1 4-3 pens
1954-66 no competition		**1986** Malmo FF v IFK Gothenburg	2-1
		1987 Kalmar FF v GAIS Gothenburg	2-0
1967 Malmo FF v IFK Norrkoping	2-0	**1988** IFK Norrkoping v Orebro SK	3-1
1969 IFK Norrkoping v AIK Stockholm	1-0	**1989** Malmo FF v Djurgarden IF	3-0
1970 Atvidabergs FF v Sandvikens IF	2-0		
1971 Atvidabergs FF v Malmo FF	3-2		

FEATURED CLUBS IN EUROPEAN COMPETITION

IFK Gothenburg	Malmo FF	Osters IF Vaxjo	Atvidabergs FF
AIK Stockholm	IFK Norrkoping	Djurgarden IF Stockholm	Orgryte IS Gothenburg
IFK Malmo	IF Elfsborg Boras	Landskrona BoIS	Halmstads BK
Kalmar FF	IK Brage	Hammarby IF STK	GAIS Gothenburg

IFK GOTHENBURG

Founded 1904
Colours blue and white striped shirts, blue shorts
Stadium Nya Ullevi (50,000) ☎ 031-1005 65
Champions 1908, 1910, 1918, 1935, 1942, 1958, 1969, 1982, 1983, 1984, 1987
Cup Winners 1979, 1982, 1983
UEFA Cup Winners 1982, 1987

Season	Opponents	Home	Playoff Result	Away	Rnd	Cup
1958-59	Jeunesse Esch, Luxembourg	0-1	5-1*	2-1*	pr	ECC
			* both in Gothenburg			
	Wismut Karl Marx Stadt, East Germany	2-2		0-4	1	ECC
1959-60	Linfield, Ireland	6-1		1-2	pr	ECC
			(in ECC as Halfway leaders)			
	Sparta Rotterdam, Holland	3-1	1-3*	1-3	1	ECC
			* played in Bremen			
1961-62	Feyenoord Rotterdam, Holland	0-3		2-8	pr	ECC
			(in ECC as Halfway leaders)			
1970-71	Legia Warsaw, Poland	0-4		1-2	1	ECC
1979-80	Waterford, Eire	1-0		1-1aet	1	CWC
	Panionios, Greece	2-0		0-1	2	CWC
	Arsenal, England	0-0		1-5	qf	CWC
1980-81	Twente Enschede, Sweden	2-0		1-5	1	UEFA
1981-82	Haka Valkeakosken, Finland	4-0		3-2	1	UEFA
	Sturm Graz, Austria	3-2		2-2	2	UEFA
	Dinamo Bucharest, Romania	3-1		1-0	3	UEFA
	Valencia CF, Spain	2-0		2-2	qf	UEFA
	1.FC Kaiserslautern, Germany	2-1 aet		1-1	sf	UEFA
	Hamburger SV, Germany	1-0		3-0	FINAL	UEFA
1982-83	Ujpest Dozsa, Hungary	1-1		1-3	1	CWC
1983-84	AS Roma, Italy	2-1		0-3	1	ECC
1984-85	Avenir Beggen, Luxembourg	9-0		8-0	1	ECC
	SK Beveren Waas, Belgium	1-0	wag	1-2	2	ECC
	Panathinaikos, Greece	0-1		2-2	qf	ECC
1985-86	Trakia Plovdiv, Bulgaria	3-2		2-1	1	ECC
	Fenerbahce, Turkey	4-0		1-2	2	ECC
	Aberdeen, Scotland	0-0	wag	2-2	qf	ECC
	FC Barcelona, Spain	3-0	4-5 pens	0-3	sf	ECC
1986-87	Sigma Olumouc, Czechoslovakia	4-0		1-1	1	UEFA
	Stahl Brandenburg, East Germany	2-0		1-1	2	UEFA
	AA Ghent, Belgium	4-0		1-0	3	UEFA
	Inter Milan, Italy	0-0	wag	1-1	qf	UEFA
	FC Tirol, Austria	4-1		1-0	sf	UEFA
	Dundee United, Scotland	1-0		1-1	FINAL	UEFA
1987-88	Brondbyernes IF, Denmark	0-0		1-2	1	UEFA
1988-89	Pezoporikos Larnaca, Cyprus	5-1		2-1	1	ECC
	17 Nentori Tirana, Albania	1-0		3-0	2	ECC
	Steaua Bucharest, Romania	1-0		1-5	qf	ECC
1989-90	Zalgiris Vilnius, USSR	1-0		0-2	1	UEFA

SWEDEN

MALMO FF

Founded 1910
Colours sky blue shirts, white shorts
Stadium Malmo (30,000) ☎ 040-101765
Champions 1944, 1949, 1950, 1951, 1953, 1965, 1967, 1970, 1971, 1974, 1975, 1977, 1986, 1988
Cup Winners 1944, 1946, 1947, 1951, 1953, 1967, 1973, 1974, 1975, 1978, 1980, 1984, 1986, 1989
ECC Finalists 1979

Season	Opponents	Home	Result	Away	Rnd	Cup
1964-65	Lokomotiv Plovdiv, Bulgaria	2-0		3-8	pr	ECC
1965-66	TSV 1860 Munich, Germany	0-3		0-4	1	Fairs
1966-67	Atletico Madrid, Spain	0-2		1-3	pr	ECC
1967-68	Liverpool, England	0-2		1-2	1	Fairs
1968-69	AC Milan, Italy	2-1		1-4	1	ECC
1969-70	VfB Stuttgart, Germany	1-1		0-3	1	Fairs
1970-71	Hibernian, Scotland	2-3		0-6	1	Fairs
1971-72	Ujpest Dozsa, Hungary	1-0		0-4	1	ECC
1972-73	Benfica, Portugal	1-0		1-4	1	ECC
1973-74	Pezoporikos Larnaca, Cyprus	11-0		0-0	1	CWC
	FC Zurich, Switzerland	1-1	lag	0-0	2	CWC
1974-75	FC Sion, Switzerland	1-0	5-4p	0-1	1	CWC
	Reipas Lahti, Finland	3-1		0-0	2	CWC
	Ferencvarosi TC, Hungary	1-3		1-1	qf	CWC
1975-76	1.FC Magdeburg, East Germany	2-1	2-1 pen	1-2	1	ECC
	Bayern Munich, Germany	1-0		0-2	2	ECC
1976-77	Torino, Italy	1-1		1-2	1	ECC
1977-78	RC Lens, France	2-0		1-4	1	UEFA
1978-79	AS Monaco, France	0-0		1-0	1	ECC
	Dynamo Kiev, USSR	2-0		0-0	2	ECC
	Wisla Krakow, Poland	4-1		1-2	qf	ECC
	FK Austria/WAC Vienna, Austria	1-0		0-0	sf	ECC
	Nottingham Forest, England	0-1	in Munich		FINAL	ECC
1979-80	KuPS Kuopio Palloseura, Finland	2-0		1-2	1	UEFA
	Feyenoord Rotterdam, Holland	1-1		0-4	2	UEFA
1980-81	Partizani Tirana, Albania	1-0		0-0	1	CWC
	Benfica, Portugal	1-0		0-2	2	CWC
1981-82	Wisla Krakow, Poland	2-0		3-1	1	UEFA
	FC Neuchatel Xamax, Switzerland	0-1		0-1	2	UEFA
1983-84	Werder Bremen, Germany	1-2		1-1	1	UEFA
1984-85	Dynamo Dresden, East Germany	2-0		1-4	1	CWC
1985-86	Videoton Sekesfeheruar, Hungary	3-2	lag	0-1	1	UEFA
1986-87	Apollon Limassol, Cyprus	6-0		1-2	1	CWC
	17 Nentori Tirana, Albania	0-0		3-0	2	CWC
	Ajax Amsterdam, Holland	1-0		1-3	qf	CWC
1987-88	RSC Anderlecht, Belgium	0-1		1-1	1	ECC
1988-89	Torpedo Moscow, USSR	2-0		1-2aet	1	UEFA
	Inter Milan, Italy	0-1		1-1	2	UEFA
1989-90	Inter-Milan, Italy	1-0		1-1	1	ECC
	KV Mechelen, Belgium	0-0		1-4	2	ECC

OSTERS IF VAXJO

Founded 1930
Colours red shirts, blue shorts
Stadium Varendsvallen (22,000) ☎ 0470-19020/19021
Champions 1968, 1978, 1980, 1981
Cup Winners 1977

Season	Opponents	Home	Result	Away	Rnd	Cup
1969-70	Fiorentina, Italy	1-2		0-1	1	ECC
1973-74	Feyenoord Rotterdam, Holland	1-3		1-2	1	UEFA

1974-75	Dynamo Moscow, USSR	3-2	lag	1-2	1	UEFA
1975-76	Molde SK, Norway	6-0		0-1	1	UEFA
	AS Roma, Italy	1-0		0-2	2	UEFA
1976-77	Kuopion Palloseura KuPS, Finland	2-0		2-3	1	UEFA
	Hibernian, Scotland	4-1		0-2	2	UEFA
	FC Barcelona, Spain	0-3		1-5	3	UEFA
1977-78	Lokomotiva Kosice, Czechoslovakia	2-2	lag	0-0	1	CWC
1979-80	Nottingham Forest, England	1-1		0-2	1	ECC
1981-82	Bayern Munich, Germany	0-1		0-5	1	ECC
1982-83	Olympiakos Piraeus, Greece	1-0		0-2	1	ECC
1984-85	Linzer ASK, Austria	0-1		0-1	1	UEFA
1988-89	DAC Dunajska Streda, Czechoslovakia	2-0		0-6	1	UEFA

ATVIDABERGS FF

Founded 1907
Colours blue shirts, white shorts
Stadium Kopparvallen (11,500) ☎ 0120-12947
Champions 1972, 1973
Cup Winners 1970, 1971

Season	Opponents	Home	Result	Away	Rnd	Cup
1970-71	Partizani Tirana, Albania	1-1		0-2	pr	CWC
1971-72	Zaglebie Sosnowice, Poland	1-1		4-3	1	CWC
	Chelsea, England	0-0	wag	1-1	2	CWC
	BFC Dynamo Berlin, East Germany	0-2		2-2	qf	CWC
1972-73	Clube Bruges, Belgium	3-5		2-1	1	UEFA
1973-74	Bayern Munich, Germany	3-1	3-4p	1-3	1	ECC
1974-75	Universitatea Craiova, Romania	3-1		1-2	1	ECC
	HJK Helsinki, Finland	1-0		3-0	2	ECC
	CF Barcelona, Spain	0-3*		0-2	qf	ECC
	* both in Barcelona					

AIK STOCKHOLM

AIK=Allmanna Idrottsklubben
Founded 1891
Colours black shirts, white shorts
Stadium Rosunda Solna (45,000) ☎ 08-7358080
Champions 1900, 1901, 1911, 1914, 1916, 1923, 1932, 1937
Cup Winners 1949, 1950, 1976, 1985

Season	Opponents	Home	Result	Away	Rnd	Cup
1965-66	Daring, Belgium	0-0		3-1	1	Fairs
	Servette Geneva, Switzerland	2-1		1-4	2	Fairs
1968-69	Skeid Oslo, Norway	2-1		1-1	1	Fairs
	Hannover 96, Germany	4-2		2-5	2	Fairs
1973-74	B 1903 Copenhagen, Denmark	1-1		1-2	1	UEFA
1975-76	Spartak Moscow, USSR	1-1		0-1	1	UEFA
1976-77	Galatasaray, Turkey	1-2		1-1	1	CWC
1984-85	Dundee United, Scotland	1-0		0-3	1	UEFA
1985-86	Red Boys Differdange, Luxembourg	8-0		5-0	1	CWC
	Dukla Prague, Czechoslovakia	2-2		0-1	2	CWC
1987-88	TJ Vitkovice, Czechoslovakia	0-2		1-1	1	UEFA

SWEDEN

IFK NORRKOPING

Founded 1897
Colours white shirts, blue shorts
Stadium Idrottsparken (25,000) ☎ 011-132225/131771
Champions 1943, 1945, 1946, 1947, 1948, 1952, 1956, 1957, 1960, 1962, 1963, 1989
Cup Winners 1943, 1945, 1969, 1988

Season	Opponents	Home	Playoff Result	Away	Rnd	Cup
1956-57	Fiorentina, Italy	0-1*		1-1	1	ECC
		* in Rome				
1957-58	Red Star Belgrade, Yugoslavia	2-2		1-2	1	ECC
1962-63	Partizani Tirana, Albania	2-0		1-1	1	ECC
	Benfica, Portugal	1-1		1-5	2	ECC
1963-64	Standard Liege, Belgium	2-0		0-1	1	ECC
	AC Milan, Italy	1-1		2-5	2	ECC
1968-69	Crusaders, Ireland	4-1		2-2	1	CWC
	Lyn Oslo, Norway	3-2		0-2	2	CWC
1969-70	Sliema Wanderers, Malta	5-1		0-1	1	CWC
	FC Schalke 04 Gelsenkirchen, Germany	0-0		0-1	2	CWC
1972-73	UT Arad Flamurarosie, Romania	2-0		2-1	1	UEFA
	Inter Milan, Italy	0-2		2-2	2	UEFA
1978-79	Hibernian, Scotland	0-0		2-3	1	UEFA
1982-83	Southampton, England	0-0	wag	2-2	1	UEFA
	AS Roma, Italy	1-0	2-4 pen	0-1	2	UEFA
1988-89	Sampdoria, Italy	2-1		0-2	1	CWC

DJURGARDENS IF

Founded 1891
Colours light and dark blue striped shirts, blue shorts
Stadium Stockholm Stadion (23,000) ☎ 08-115711, most big matches at Solna
Champions 1912, 1915, 1917, 1920, 1955, 1959, 1964, 1966

Season	Opponents	Home	Result	Away	Rnd	Cup
1955-56	Gwardia Warsaw, Poland	0-0		4-1	1	ECC
	Hibernian, Scotland	1-3*		0-1	2	ECC
		* in Firhill Park, Glasgow				
1964-65	Manchester United, England	1-1		1-6	pr	Fairs
1965-66	Levski Spartak Sofia, Bulgaria	2-1		0-6	pr	ECC
1966-67	1.FC Lokomotive Leipzig, East Germany	1-3		1-2	1	Fairs
1967-68	Gornik Zabrze, Poland	0-1		0-3	1	ECC
1971-72	OFK Belgrade, Yugoslavia	2-2		1-4	1	UEFA
1974-75	IK Start Kristinsand, Norway	5-0		2-1	1	UEFA
	Dukla Prague, Czechoslovakia	0-2		1-3	2	UEFA
1975-76	Wrexham, Wales	1-1		1-2	1	CWC
1976-77	Feyenoord Rotterdam, Holland	2-1		0-3	1	UEFA
1989-90	US Luxembourg, Luxembourg	5-0		0-0	1	CWC
	Real Valladolid, Spain	2-2		0-2	2	CWC

ORGRYTE IS

Founded 1887
Colours red shirts, blue shorts
Stadium Nya Ullevi, Gothenburg (50,000) ☎ 031-801610
Champions 1896, 1897, 1898, 1899, 1902, 1904, 1905, 1906, 1907, 1909, 1913, 1926, 1928, 1985

Season	Opponents	Home	Result	Away	Rnd	Cup
1964-65	Dunfermline Athletic, Scotland	0-0		2-4	pr	Fairs

1966-67	OGC Nice, France	2-1		2-2	1	Fairs
	Ferencvarosi TC, Hungary	0-0		1-7	2	Fairs
1986-87	BFC Dynamo Berlin, East Germany	2-3		1-4	1	ECC
1989-90	Hamburger SV, Germany	1-2		1-5	1	UEFA

IFK MALMO

Founded 1899
Colours yellow shirts, white shorts
Stadium Malmo (23,000) ☎ 040-88 37 24
European Cup entrant as leading club after Spring Season 1960

Season	Opponents	Home	Result	Away	Rnd	Cup
1960-61	HIFK Kamraterna Helsinki, Finland	2-1		3-1	1	ECC
	CDNA Sofia, Bulgaria	1-0		1-1	2	ECC
	Rapid Vienna, Austria	0-2		0-2	qf	ECC

IF ELFSBORG BORAS

Founded 1904
Colours yellow shirts, black shorts
Stadium Ryavallen (18,526) ☎ 033-139191
Champions 1936, 1939, 1940, 1961 * entry to ECC was IFK Gothenburg as halfway leaders

Season	Opponents	Home	Result	Away	Rnd	Cup
1971-72	Hertha BSC Berlin, Germany	1-4		1-3	1	UEFA
1978-79	RC Strasbourg, France	2-0		1-4	1	UEFA
1980-81	St Mirren, Scotland	1-2		0-0	1	UEFA
1983-84	Widzew Lodz, Poland	2-2	lag	0-0	1	UEFA

LANDSKRONA BoIS

Founded 1915
Colours black and white striped shirts, black shorts
Stadium Landskrona IP (20,000) ☎ 0418-13898
Cup Winners 1972

Season	Opponents	Home	Result	Away	Rnd	Cup
1972-73	Rapid Bucharest, Romania	1-0		0-3	1	CWC
1977-78	Ipswich Town, England	0-1		0-5	1	UEFA

HALMSTADS BK

Founded 1914
Colours blue shirts, white shorts
Stadium Orjansvall (20,000) ☎ 035-103285
Champions 1976, 1979

Season	Opponents	Home	Result	Away	Rnd	Cup
1977-78	Dynamo Dresden, East Germany	2-1		0-2	1	ECC
1980-81	Esbjerg FB, Denmark	0-0		2-3	1	ECC

SWEDEN

KALMAR FF

Founded 1910
Colours all red
Stadium Fredriksskans (15,000) ☎ 0480-11477/88720
Cup Winners 1981, 1987

Season	Opponents	Home	Result	Away	Rnd	Cup
1978-79	Ferencvarosi TC, Hungary	2-2		0-2	1	CWC
1979-80	IFK Keflavik, Iceland	2-1	lag	0-1	1	UEFA
1981-82	Lausanne Sport, Switzerland	3-2	lag	1-2	1	CWC
1986-87	Bayer Leverkusen, Germany	1-4		0-3	1	UEFA
1987-88	IA Akranes, Iceland	1-0		0-0	1	CWC
	Sporting Lisbon, Portugal	1-0		0-5	2	CWC

IK BRAGE

Founded 1925
Colours green shirts, white shorts
Stadium Domnarvsvallen, Borlange (19,000) ☎ 0243-84100

Season	Opponents	Home	Result	Away	Rnd	Cup
1982-83	Lyngby BK, Denmark	2-2		2-1	1	UEFA
	Werder Bremen, Germany	2-6		0-2	2	UEFA
1988-89	Inter Milan, Italy	1-2		1-2	1	UEFA

HAMMARBY IF

Founded 1897
Colours white shirts, green shorts
Stadium Soderstadion, Stockholm (14,200) ☎ 08-413592

Season	Opponents	Home	Result	Away	Rnd	Cup
1983-84	17 Nentori Tirana, Albania	4-0		1-2	1	CWC
	Haka Valkeakosken, Finland	1-1		1-2	2	CWC
1985-86	Pirin Blagovograd, Bulgaria	4-0		3-1	1	UEFA
	St Mirren, Scotland	3-3		2-1	2	UEFA
	1.FC Koln, Germany	2-1		1-3	3	UEFA

GAIS GOTHENBURG

Founded 1894
Colours green and black striped shirts, white shorts
Stadium Nya Ullevi (50,000) ☎ 031-119090/112690
Champions 1919, 1922, 1925, 1927, 1931, 1954

Season	Opponents	Home	Result	Away	Rnd	Cup
1975-76	Slask Wroclaw, Poland	2-1		2-4	1	UEFA

SWITZERLAND

Founded 1895
Schweizerischer Fussballverbund, Laubeggstrasse 70 BP 24, 3000 Bern 32 ☎ (031) 44-62-23 Telefax 31-4350 81
National colours red shirts, white shorts, red socks
Season September to May

LEAGUE CHAMPIONS

1898	Grasshoppers Zurich	**1920**	Young Boys Bern	**1944**	Lausanne Sport	**1970**	FC Basel
1899	Anglo American FC Zurich	**1921**	Grasshoppers Zurich	**1945**	Grasshoppers Zurich	**1971**	Grasshoppers Zurich
		1922	Servette Geneva	**1946**	Servette Geneva	**1972**	FC Basel
		1923	FC Bern *	**1947**	Bienne	**1973**	FC Basel
1900	Grasshoppers Zurich	** no title awarded as FC Bern*		**1948**	Bellinzone	**1974**	FC Zurich
1901	Grasshoppers Zurich	*fielded ineligible players dur-*		**1949**	Lugano	**1975**	FC Zurich
1902	FC Zurich	*ing the season*				**1976**	FC Zurich
1903	Young Boys Bern	**1924**	FC Zurich	**1950**	Servette Geneva	**1977**	FC Basel
1904	FC St Gallen	**1925**	Servette Geneva	**1951**	Lausanne Sport	**1978**	Grasshoppers Zurich
1905	Grasshoppers Zurich	**1926**	Servette Geneva	**1952**	Grasshoppers Zurich	**1979**	Servette Geneva
1906	Winerthur	**1927**	Grasshoppers Zurich	**1953**	FC Basel		
1907	Servette Geneva	**1928**	Grasshoppers Zurich	**1954**	La Chaux De Fonds	**1980**	FC Basel
1908	Winterthur	**1929**	Young Boys Bern	**1955**	La Chaux De Fonds	**1981**	FC Zurich
1909	Young Boys Bern			**1956**	Grasshoppers Zurich	**1982**	Grasshoppers Zurich
		1930	Servette Geneva	**1957**	Young Boys Bern	**1983**	Grasshoppers Zurich
1910	Young Boys Bern	**1931**	Grasshoppers Zurich	**1958**	Young Boys Bern	**1984**	Grasshoppers Zurich
1911	Young Boys Bern	**1932**	Lausanne Sport	**1959**	Young Boys Bern	**1985**	Servette Geneva
1912	Aarau	**1933**	Servette Geneva			**1986**	Young Boys Bern
1913	Montriond Sport Lausanne	**1934**	Servette Geneva	**1960**	Young Boys Bern	**1987**	FC Neuchatel Xamax
		1935	Lausanne Sport	**1961**	Servette Geneva	**1988**	FC Neuchatel Xamax
1914	Aarau	**1936**	Lausanne Sport	**1962**	Servette Geneva	**1989**	FC Luzern
1915	FC Bruhl St Gallen	**1937**	Grasshoppers Zurich	**1963**	FC Zurich		
1916	FC Cantonal Neuchatel	**1938**	Lugano	**1964**	La Chaux De Fonds		
1917	Winterthur	**1939**	Grasshoppers Zurich	**1965**	Lausanne Sport		
1918	Servette Geneva			**1966**	FC Zurich		
1919	FC Etoile La Chaux De Fonds	**1940**	Servette Geneva	**1967**	FC Basel		
		1941	Lugano	**1968**	FC Zurich		
		1942	Grasshoppers Zurich	**1969**	FC Basel		
		1943	Grasshoppers Zurich				

OCH-CUP

Donated and sponsored by "Och" Company

1921	FC Bern (3 way Finals)	
1922	FC Concordia Basel v FC Etoile La Chaux de Fonds	1-0
1925	FC Bern v FC Concordia Basel	2-0

SWITZERLAND

CUP WINNERS

1926	Grasshoppers Zurich v FC Bern	2-1		**1960**	Luzern v Grenchen	1-0
1927	Grasshoppers Zurich v Young Fellows	3-1		**1961**	La Chaux De Fonds v Biel	1-0
1928	Servette Geneva v Grasshoppers Zurich	5-1		**1962**	Lausanne Sport v Bellinzona	4-0
1929	Urania Geneva v Young Boys Bern	1-0		**1963**	FC Basel v Grasshoppers Zurich	2-0
				1964	Lausanne Sport v La Chaux De Fonds	2-0
1930	Young Boys Berne v Aarau	1-0		**1965**	Sion v Servette Geneva	2-1
1931	Lugano v Grasshoppers Zurich	2-1		**1966**	FC Zurich v Servette Geneva	2-0
1932	Grasshoppers Zurich v Urania Geneva	5-1		**1967**	FC Basel v Lausanne Sport	2-1 *
1933	FC Basel v Grasshoppers Zurich	4-3		* game stopped and awarded to FC Basle 3-0 when score was		
1934	Grasshoppers Zurich v Servette Geneva	2-0		2-1 because of Lausanne protests.		
1935	Lausanne Sport v FC Nordstern Basel	10-0		**1968**	Lugano v Winterthur	2-1
1936	Young Fellows v Servette Geneva	2-0		**1969**	St Gallen v Bellinzona	2-0
1937	Grasshoppers Zurich v Lausanne Sport	10-0				
1938	Grasshoppers Zurich v Servette Geneva	2-2 5-1		**1970**	FC Zurich v FC Basel	4-1
1939	Lausanne Sport v FC Nordstern Basel	2-0		**1971**	Servette Geneva v Lugano	2-0
				1972	FC Zurich v FC Basel	1-0
1940	Grasshoppers Zurich v Grenchen	3-0		**1973**	FC Zurich v FC Basel	2-0
1941	Grasshoppers Zurich v Servette Geneva	1-1 2-0		**1974**	Sion v FC Neuchatel Xamax	3-2
1942	Grasshoppers Zurich v FC Basel	0-0 3-2		**1975**	FC Basel v Winterthur	2-1
1943	Grasshoppers Zurich v Lugano	2-1		**1976**	FC Zurich v Servette Geneva	1-0
1944	Lausanne Sport v FC Basel	3-0		**1977**	Young Boys Bern v St Gallen	1-0
1945	Young Boys Bern v St Gallen	2-0		**1978**	Servette Geneva v Grasshoppers Zurich	2-2 1-0
1946	Grasshoppers Zurich v Lausanne Sport	3-0		**1979**	Servette Geneva v Young Boys Bern	1-1 3-2
1947	FC Basel v Lausanne Sport	3-0				
1948	La Chaux De Fonds v Grenchen	2-2 2-2 4-0		**1980**	Sion v Young Boys Bern	2-1
1949	Servette Geneva v Grasshoppers Zurich	3-0		**1981**	Lausanne Sport v FC Zurich	4-3
				1982	Sion v FC Basel	1-0
1950	Lausanne Sport v Cantonal	1-1 4-0		**1983**	Grasshoppers Zurich v Servette Geneva	2-2 3-0
1951	La Chaux De Fonds v Locarno	3-2		**1984**	Servette Geneva v Lausanne Sport	1-0
1952	Grasshoppers Zurich v Lugano	2-0		**1985**	FC Aarau v FC Neuchatel Xamax	1-0
1953	Young Boys Bern v Grasshoppers Zurich	1-1 3-1		**1986**	Sion v Servette Geneva	3-1
1954	La Chaux De Fonds v Fribourg	2-0		**1987**	Young Boys Bern v Servette Geneva	4-2 aet
1955	La Chaux De Fonds v FC Thurn	3-1		**1988**	Grasshoppers Zurich v FC Schaffhausen	2-0
1956	Grasshoppers Zurich v Young Boys Bern	1-0		**1989**	Grasshoppers Zurich v FC Aarau	2-1
1957	La Chaux De Fonds v Lausanne Sport	3-1				
1958	Young Boys Bern v Grasshoppers Zurich	1-1 4-1				
1959	Grenchen v Servette Geneva	1-0				

ANGLO-SWISS CUP

1910	Young Boys Bern v FC St Gallen	1-1 7-0
1911	Young Boys Bern v Servette FC Geneva	3-1
1912	Young Boys Bern v FC Stella Fribourg	4-0
1913	FC Basel v FC Weissenbuhl Bern	5-0

LEAGUE CUP

1972	FC Basel v FC Winterthur	4-1		**1980**	Servette Geneva v Grasshoppers Zurich	2-0
1973	Grasshoppers Zurich v FC Winterthur	2-2 5-4p		**1981**	FC Zurich v Lausanne Sports	0-0 2-1
1975	Grasshoppers Zurich v FC Zurich	3-0		**1982**	FC Aarau v FC St Gallen	0-0 1-0
1976	Young Boys Bern v FC Zurich	4-2		**Discontinued due to lack of public interest**		
1977	Servette Geneva v FC Neuchatel Xamax	2-0				
1978	FC St Gallen v Grasshoppers Zurich	3-2				
1979	Servette Geneva v FC Basel	2-2 4-3p				

SWISS SUPER CUP

1986	Young Boys Bern v FC Sion	3-1
1987	FC Neuchatel Xamax v Young Boys Bern	3-0
1988	FC Neuchatel Xamax v	
	Grasshoppers Zurich	2-2 aet 3-0 pens
1989	Grasshoppers Zurich v FC Luzern	4-2

FEATURED CLUBS IN EUROPEAN COMPETITION

FC Zurich	FC Basle	Grasshoppers Zurich	Servette Geneva
Lausanne Sport	FC Aarau	Young Boys Bern	Sion
FC La Chaux De Fonds	Luzern	FC St Gallen	Lugano
FC Neuchatel Xamax	Basel City XI	FC Wettingen	

FC ZURICH

Founded 1896
Colours all white
Stadium Letzigrund (27,500) ☎ 01-492 74 74
Champions 1902, 1924, 1963, 1966, 1968, 1974, 1975, 1976, 1981
Cup Winners 1966, 1970, 1972, 1973, 1976
League Cup 1981

Season	Opponents	Home	Playoff Result	Away	Rnd	Cup
1963-64	Dundalk, Eire	1-2		3-0*	1	ECC
				* in Dublin		
	Galatasaray, Turkey	2-0	2-2 wot*	0-2	2	ECC
			* in Rome aet			
	PSV Eindhoven, Holland	3-1		0-1	qf	ECC
	Real Madrid, Spain	1-2		0-6	sf	ECC
1966-67	Glasgow Celtic, Scotland	0-3		0-2	pr	ECC
1967-68	CF Barcelona, Spain	3-1		0-1	1	Fairs
	Nottingham Forest, England	1-0	wag	1-2	2	Fairs
	Sporting Lisbon, Portugal	3-0		0-1	3	Fairs
	Dundee, Scotland	0-1		0-1	qf	Fairs
1968-69	AB Copenhagen, Denmark	1-3		2-1	1	ECC
1969-70	Kilmarnock, Scotland	3-2		1-3	1	Fairs
1970-71	IBA Akureri, Iceland	7-0		7-1*	1	CWC
				* in Switzerland		
	Clube Bruges, Belgium	3-2		0-2	2	CWC
1972-73	Wrexham, Wales	1-1		1-2	1	CWC
1973-74	RSC Anderlecht, Belgium	1-0	wag	2-3	1	CWC
	Malmo FF, Sweden	0-0	wag	1-1	2	CWC
	Sporting Lisbon, Portugal	1-1		0-3	qf	CWC
1974-75	Leeds United, England	2-1		1-4	1	ECC
1975-76	Ujpest Dozsa, Hungary	5-1	lag	0-4	1	ECC
1976-77	Glasgow Rangers, Scotland	1-0		1-1	1	ECC
	Turun Palloseura TPS Turku, Finland	2-0		1-0	2	ECC
	Dynamo Dresden, East Germany	2-1	wag	2-3	qf	ECC
	Liverpool, England	1-3		0-3	sf	ECC
1977-78	CSKA Sofia, Bulgaria	1-0		1-1	1	UEFA
	Eintracht Frankfurt, Germany	0-3		3-4	2	UEFA
1979-80	1.FC Kaiserslautern, Germany	1-3		1-5	1	UEFA
1981-82	BFC Dynamo Berlin, East Germany	3-1	lag	0-2	1	ECC
1982-83	Pezoporikos Larnaca, Cyprus	1-0		2-2	1	UEFA
	Ferencvarosi TC, Hungary	1-0		1-1	2	UEFA
	Benfica, Portugal	1-1		0-4	3	UEFA
1983-84	Royal Antwerp, Belgium	1-4		2-4	1	UEFA

SWITZERLAND

FC BASEL

Founded 1893
Colours red and black halved shirts, blue shorts
Stadium St Jakob (60,000) ☎ 061-32 40 84
Champions 1953, 1967, 1969, 1970, 1972, 1973, 1977, 1980
Cup Winners 1933, 1947, 1963, 1967, 1975
League Cup Winners 1973

Season	Opponents	Home	Result	Away	Rnd	Cup
1963-64	Glasgow Celtic, Scotland	1-5		0-5	1	CWC
1964-65	CA Spora, Luxembourg	2-0		1-0	pr	Fairs
	RC Strasbourg, France	0-1		2-5	1	Fairs
1965-66	bye		.		1	Fairs
	Valencia CF, Spain	1-3		1-5	2	Fairs
1966-67	DOS Utrecht, Holland	2-2		1-2	1	Fairs
1967-68	Hvidovre IF, Denmark	1-2		3-3	1	ECC
1968-69	Bologna, Italy	1-2		1-4	1	Fairs
1969-70	Glasgow Celtic, Scotland	0-0		0-2	1	ECC
1970-71	Spartak Moscow, USSR	2-1	wag	2-3	1	ECC
	Ajax Amsterdam, Holland	1-2		0-3	2	ECC
1971-72	Real Madrid, Spain	1-2		1-2	1	UEFA
1972-73	Ujpest Dozsa, Hungary	3-2		0-2	1	ECC
1973-74	Fram Reykjavik, Iceland	5-0		6-2*	1	ECC
				* in Olten, Swiss		
	Clube Bruges, Belgium	6-4		1-2	2	ECC
	Glasgow Celtic, Scotland	3-2		2-4	qf	ECC
1975-76	Atletico Madrid, Spain	1-2		1-1	1	CWC
1976-77	Glentoran, Ireland	3-0		2-3	1	UEFA
	Athletic Bilbao, Spain	1-1		1-3	2	UEFA
1977-78	Wacker Innsbruck, Austria	1-3		1-0	1	ECC
1978-79	VfB Stuttgart, Germany	2-3		1-4	1	UEFA
1980-81	Clube Bruges, Belgium	4-1		1-0	1	ECC
	Red Star Belgrade, Yugoslavia	1-0		0-2	2	ECC

GRASSHOPPER CLUB

Founded 1886
Colours blue and white halved shirts, white shorts
Stadium Hardturm, Zurich (36,500) ☎ 01-44 33 88
Champions 1898, 1900, 1901, 1905, 1921, 1927, 1928, 1931, 1937, 1939, 1942, 1943, 1945, 1952, 1956, 1971, 1978, 1982, 1983, 1984
League Cup Winners 1974, 1975
Cup Winners 1926, 1927, 1932, 1934, 1937, 1938, 1940, 1941, 1942, 1943, 1946, 1952, 1956, 1983, 1988, 1989
Swiss Super Cup Winners 1989

Season	Opponents	Home	Playoff Result	Away	Rnd	Cup
1956-57	Slovan Bratislava, Czechoslovakia	2-0		0-1*	1	ECC
				* in Munich		
	Fiorentina, Italy	2-2		1-3	2	ECC
1968-69	Napoli, Italy	1-0		1-3	1	Fairs
1970-71	Dundee United, Scotland	0-0		2-3	1	Fairs
1971-72	Reipas Lahti, Finland	8-0		1-1	1	ECC
	Arsenal, England	0-2		0-3	2	ECC
1972-73	Olympique Nimes, France	2-1		2-1	1	UEFA
	Ararat Yerevan, USSR	1-3		2-4	2	UEFA
1973-74	Tottenham Hotspur, England	1-5		1-4	1	UEFA
1974-75	Panathinaikos, Greece	2-0		1-2	1	UEFA
	Real Zaragoza, Spain	2-1		0-5	2	UEFA
1975-76	Real Sociedad San Sebastian, Spain	3-3	lag	1-1	1	UEFA

1976-77	Hibernians, Malta	7-0		2-0	1	UEFA
	1.FC Koln, Germany	2-3		0-2	2	UEFA
1977-78	Frem Copenhagen, Denmark	6-1		2-0	1	UEFA
	Internacional Bratislava, Czechoslovakia	5-1		0-1	2	UEFA
	Dynamo Tbilisi, USSR	4-0		0-1	3	UEFA
	Eintracht Frankfurt, Germany	1-0	wag	2-3	qf	UEFA
	SEC Bastia Corsica, France	3-2	lag	0-1	sf	UEFA
1978-79	Valletta, Malta	8-0		5-3	1	ECC
	Real Madrid, Spain	2-0	wag	1-3	2	ECC
	Nottingham Forest, England	1-1		1-4	qf	ECC
1979-80	Progres Niedercorn, Luxembourg	4-0		2-0	1	UEFA
	Ipswich Town, England	0-0	wag	1-1	2	UEFA
	VfB Stuttgart, Germany	0-2		0-3	3	UEFA
1980-81	KB Copenhagen, Denmark	3-1		5-2	1	UEFA
	FC Porto, Portugal	3-0		0-2	2	UEFA
	Torino, Italy	2-1	4-3 pen	1-2	3	UEFA
	Sochaux, France	0-0		1-2	qf	UEFA
1981-82	West Bromwich Albion, England	1-0		3-1	1	UEFA
	Radnicki Nis, Yugoslavia	2-0	0-3 pen	0-2	2	UEFA
1982-83	Dynamo Kiev, USSR	0-1		0-3	1	ECC
1983-84	Dynamo Minsk, USSR	2-2		0-1	1	ECC
1984-85	Honved Budapest, Hungary	3-1		1-2	1	ECC
	Juventus, Italy	2-4		0-2	2	ECC
1987-88	Dynamo Moscow, USSR	0-4		0-1	1	UEFA
1988-89	Eintracht Frankfurt, Germany	0-0		0-1	1	CWC
1989-90	Slovan Bratislava, Czechoslovakia	4-0aet		0-3	1	CWC
	Torpedo Moscow, USSR	3-0		1-1	2	CWC
	Sampdoria, Italy	1-2		0-2	qf	CWC

SERVETTE FC

Founded 1890
Colours claret shirts with white collars and cuffs, blue shorts
Stadium Charmillesm, Geneva (30,000) ☎ 022-2036 26/45 06 66
Champions 1907, 1918, 1922, 1925, 1926, 1930, 1933, 1934, 1940, 1946, 1950, 1961, 1962, 1979, 1985
Cup Winners 1928, 1949, 1971, 1978, 1979, 1984
League Cup Winners 1977, 1979, 1980

Season	Opponents	Home	Playoff Result	Away	Rnd	Cup
1955-56	Real Madrid, Spain	0-2		0-5	1	ECC
1961-62	Hibernians, Malta	5-0		2-1	pr	ECC
	Dukla Prague, Czechoslovakia	4-3		0-2	1	ECC
1962-63	Feyenoord Rotterdam, Holland	1-3	1-3*	3-1	1	ECC
			* in Dusseldorf			
1963-64	Spartak Brno, Czechoslovakia	1-2		0-5	1	Fairs
1964-65	Atletico Madrid, Spain	2-2		1-6	1	Fairs
1965-66	bye				1	Fairs
	AIK Stockholm, Sweden	4-1		1-2	2	Fairs
	TSV 1860 Munich, Germany	1-1		1-4	3	Fairs
1966-67	AIFK Kamraterna Abo, Finland	1-1		2-1	1	CWC
	Sparta Rotterdam, Holland	2-0		0-1	2	CWC
	Slavia Sofia, Bulgaria	1-0		0-3	qf	CWC
1967-68	TSV 1860 Munich, Germany	2-2		0-4	1	Fairs
1971-72	Liverpool, England	2-1		0-2	1	CWC
1974-75	Derby County, England	1-2		1-4	1	UEFA
1976-77	Cardiff City, Wales	2-1	lag	0-1	pr	CWC
1977-78	Athletic Bilbao, Spain	1-0		0-2	1	UEFA
1978-79	PAOK Salonika, Greece	4-0		0-2	1	CWC
	Nancy, France	2-1		2-2	2	CWC
	Fortuna Dusseldorf, Germany	1-1	lag	0-0	qf	CWC
1979-80	SK Beveren Waas, Belgium	3-1		1-1	1	ECC
	BFC Dynamo Berlin, East Germany	2-2		1-2	2	ECC

SWITZERLAND

1980-81	Sochaux, France	2-1		0-2	1	UEFA
1982-83	Progres Niedercorn, Luxembourg	3-0		1-0	1	UEFA
	Slask Wroclaw, Poland	5-1		2-0	2	UEFA
	Bohemians Prague, Czechoslovakia	2-2		1-2	3	UEFA
1983-84	Avenir Beggen, Luxembourg	4-0		5-1	1	CWC
	Shakhtyor Donetsk, USSR	1-2		0-1	2	CWC
1984-85	Apoel Nicosia, Cyprus	3-1		3-0	1	CWC
	Larissa, Greece	0-1		1-2	2	CWC
1985-86	Linfield, Ireland	2-1		2-2	1	ECC
	Aberdeen, Scotland	0-0		0-1	2	ECC
1988-89	Sturm Graz, Austria	1-0		0-0	1	UEFA
	FC Groningen, Holland	1-1		0-2	2	UEFA

LAUSANNE SPORT

Founded 1896 as FC Montrimond later changed to Montrimond Sports, 1920 merged with unimportant club and became Lausanne Sport
Colours blue shirts, white shorts
Stadium Olympic de la Pontaise (38,000) ☎ 021-36 13 41
Champions 1932, 1935, 1936, 1944, 1951, 1965
Cup Winners 1935, 1939, 1944, 1950, 1962, 1964, 1981

Season	Opponents	Home	Playoff Result	Away	Rnd	Cup
1955-58	Leipzig City XI, East Germany	7-3		3-6	pr	Fairs
	London XI, England	2-1		0-2	sf	Fairs
1958-60	Belgrade City XI, Yugoslavia	3-5		1-6	1	Fairs
1960-61	Hibernian, Scotland	withdrew		0-2	1	Fairs
1961-62	bye				1	Fairs
	Valencia CF, Spain	not played		3-4	2	Fairs
1962-63	Sparta Rotterdam, Holland	3-0		2-4	1	CWC
	Slovan Bratislava, Czechoslovakia	0-1		1-1	2	CWC
1963-64	Heart of Midlothian, Scotland	2-2	3-2*	4-4	1	Fairs
			* in Lausanne			
	Real Zaragoza, Spain	1-2		0-3	2	Fairs
1964-65	Honved Budapest, Hungary	2-0		0-1	1	CWC
	Slavia Sofia, Bulgaria	2-1	3-2*	0-1	2	CWC
			* in Rome			
	West Ham United, England	1-2		3-4	qf	CWC
1965-66	Sparta Prague, Czechoslovakia	0-0		0-4	pr	ECC
1966-67	bye				1	Fairs
	Burnley, England	1-3		0-5	2	Fairs
1967-68	Spartak Trnava, Czechoslovakia	3-2		0-2	1	CWC
1968-69	Juventus, Italy	0-2		0-2	1	Fairs
1969-70	Vasas Gyoer Eto, Hungary	1-2		1-2	1	Fairs
1970-71	Vitoria Setubal, Portugal	0-2		1-2	1	Fairs
1972-73	Red Star Belgrade, Yugoslavia	3-2		1-5	1	UEFA
1978-79	Jeunesse Esch, Luxembourg	2-0		0-0	1	UEFA
	Ajax Amsterdam, Holland	0-4		0-1	2	UEFA
1981-82	Kalmar FF, Sweden	2-1	wag	2-3	1	CWC
	Legia Warsaw, Poland	1-1		1-2	2	CWC

FC AARAU

Founded 1902
Colours red and white shirts, black shorts
Stadium Brugglifeld (14,000) ☎ 064-22 91 25
Champions 1912, 1914
Cup Winners 1985
League Cup Winners 1982

Season	Opponents	Home	Result	Away	Rnd	Cup
1985-86	Red Star Belgrade, Yugoslavia	2-2* * in Zurich		0-2	1	CWC
1988-89	1.FC Lokomotive Leipzig, East Germany	0-3		0-4	1	UEFA

YOUNG BOYS BERN

Founded 1898
Colours yellow shirts, black shorts
Stadium Wankdorf (58,500) ☎ 031-41 84 84
Champions 1903, 1909, 1910, 1911, 1920, 1929, 1957, 1958, 1959, 1960, 1986
Cup Winners 1930, 1945, 1953, 1958, 1977, 1987
League Cup Winners 1976
Swiss Super Cup Winners 1986

Season	Opponents	Home	Playoff Result	Away	Rnd	Cup
1957-58	Vasas Budapest, Hungary	1-1* * in Geneva		1-2	1	ECC
1958-59	Manchester United, England	withdrew			pr	ECC
	MTK Budapest, Hungary	4-1		2-1	1	ECC
	SC Wismut Karl Marx Stadt, East Germany	2-2	2-1* * in Amsterdam	0-0	qf	ECC
	Stade de Reims, France	1-0		0-3* * in Paris	sf	ECC
1959-60	Eintracht Frankfurt, Germany	1-4		1-1	1	ECC
1960-61	Limerick, Eire	4-2		5-0	1	ECC
	Hamburger SV, Germany	0-5		3-3	2	ECC
1975-76	Hamburger SV, Germany	0-0		2-4	1	UEFA
1977-78	Glasgow Rangers, Scotland	2-2		0-1	pr	CWC
1979-80	Steaua Bucharest, Romania	2-2		0-6	1	CWC
1986-87	Real Madrid, Spain	1-0		0-5	1	ECC
1987-88	Dunajska Streda, Czechoslovakia	3-1		1-2	1	CWC
	FC Den Haag, Holland	1-0		1-2	2	CWC
	Ajax Amsterdam, Holland				qf	CWC

FC SION

Founded 1909
Colours white shirts, red shorts
Stadium Stade de Tourbillon (13,000) ☎ 027-22 42 50
Cup Winners 1965, 1974, 1980, 1982, 1986

Season	Opponents	Home	Playoff Result	Away	Rnd	Cup
1965-66	Galatasaray, Turkey	5-1		1-2	1	CW
	1.FC Magdeburg, East Germany	2-2		1-8	2	CWC
1973-74	Lazio Rome, Italy	3-1		0-3	1	UEFA
1974-75	Malmo FF, Sweden	1-0	4-5p	0-1	1	CWC
1980-81	Haugar, Norway	1-1		0-2	1	CWC

297

SWITZERLAND

			Home	Result	Away	Rnd	Cup
1982-83	Aberdeen, Scotland		1-4		0-7	pr	CWC
1984-85	Atletico Madrid, Spain		1-0		3-2	1	UEFA
	Zeljeznicar Sarajevo, Yugoslavia		1-1		1-2	2	UEFA
1986-87	Aberdeen, Scotland		3-0		1-2	1	CWC
	GKS Katowice, Poland		3-0		2-2*	2	CWC
					* in Chorzow		
	1.FC Lokomotive Leipzig, East Germany		0-0		0-2	qf	CWC
1987-88	Velez Mostar, Yugoslavia		3-0		0-5	1	UEFA
1989-90	Iraklis Salonika, Greece		2-0		0-1	1	UEFA
	Karl Marx Stadt, East Germany		2-1		1-4	2	UEFA

FC LA CHAUX DE FONDS

Founded 1894
Colours yellow shirts, blue shorts
Stadium Parc des Sports la Charriere (14,450) ☎ 039-28 42 51
Champions 1954, 1955, 1964
Cup Winners 1948, 1951, 1954, 1955, 1957, 1961

Season	Opponents	Home	Result	Away	Rnd	Cup
1961-62	Leixoes Sport Club, Portugal	6-2		0-5	1	CWC
1964-65	St Etienne, France	2-1		2-2	pr	ECC
	Benfica, Portugal	1-1		0-5	1	ECC

LUZERN

Founded 1901
Colours blue and white
Stadium Allmend (23,300) ☎ 041-23 20 41
Cup Winners 1960
Champions 1989

Season	Opponents	Home	Result	Away	Rnd	Cup
1960-61	Fiorentina, Italy	0-3		2-6	1	CWC
1986-87	Spartak Moscow, USSR	0-1		0-0	1	UEFA
1989-90	PSV Eindhoven, Holland	0-2		0-3	1	ECC

FC ST GALLEN

Founded 1879
Colours green shirts, white shorts
Stadium Espenmoos (15,200) ☎ 071-25 67 65
Champions 1904
Cup Winners 1969
League Cup Winners 1978

Season	Opponents	Home	Playoff Result	Away	Rnd	Cup
1969-70	Frem Copenhagen, Denmark	1-0	wag	1-2	1	CWC
	Levski Spartak Sofia, Bulgaria	0-0		0-4	2	CWC
1983-84	Radnicki Nis, Yugoslavia	1-2		0-3	1	UEFA
1985-86	Inter Milan, Italy	0-0		1-5	1	UEFA

SWITZERLAND

LUGANO

Founded 1908
Colours black shirts with white V, white shorts
Stadium Comunale di Cornaredo (25,500) ☎ 091-51 94 47
Champions 1938, 1941, 1949
Cup Winners 1931, 1968

Season	Opponents	Home	Result	Away	Rnd	Cup
1968-69	CF Barcelona, Spain	0-1		0-3	1	CWC
1971-72	Legia Warsaw, Poland	1-3		0-0	1	UEFA

FC NEUCHATEL XAMAX

Founded 1954 as FC Xamax, merged in 1970 with Cantonal Neuchatel to form present club
Colours red and black striped shirts, black shorts
Stadium de la Maladiere (21,500) ☎ 038-25 44 28
Champions 1987, 1988
Swiss Super Cup Winners 1987, 1988

Season	Opponents	Home	Playoff Result	Away	Rnd	Cup
1981-82	Sparta Prague, Czechoslovakia	4-0		2-3	1	UEFA
	Malmo FF, Sweden	1-0		1-0	2	UEFA
	Sporting Lisbon, Portugal	1-0		0-0	3	UEFA
	Hamburger SV, Germany	0-0		2-3	qf	UEFA
1984-85	Olympiakos Piraeus, Greece	2-2		0-1	1	UEFA
1985-86	Sportul Studentesc Bucharest, Romania	3-0		4-4	1	UEFA
	Lokomotiv Sofia, Bulgaria	0-0	wag	1-1	2	UEFA
	Dundee United, Scotland	3-1		1-2	3	UEFA
	Real Madrid, Spain	2-0		0-3	qf	UEFA
1986-87	Lyngby BK, Denmark	2-0		3-1	1	UEFA
	FC Groningen, Holland	1-1	lag	0-0	2	UEFA
1987-88	Kuuysyi Lahti, Finland	5-0		1-2	1	ECC
	Bayern Munich, Germany	2-1		0-2	2	ECC
1988-89	Larissa, Cyprus	2-1	3-0p	1-2	1	ECC
	Galatasaray, Turkey	3-0		0-5	2	ECC

BASEL CITY XI

Season	Opponents	Home	Result	Away	Rnd	Cup
1955-58	London XI, England	0-5		0-1	pr	Fairs
	Eintracht Frankfurt, Germany	1-5		2-6	pr	Fairs
1958-60	CF Barcelona, Spain	1-2		2-5	1	Fairs
1960-61	Frem Copenhagen, Denmark	3-3		1-8	1	Fairs
1961-62	Red Star Belgrade, Yugoslavia	1-1		1-4	1	Fairs
1962-63	Bayern Munich, Germany	not played		0-3	pr	Fairs

FC WETTINGEN

Founded 1931
Colours all white
Stadium Altenburg (9,500) ☎ 056-261500

Season	Opponents	Home	Result	Away	Rnd	Cup
1989-90	Dundalk, Eire	3-0		2-0	1	UEFA
	Napoli, Italy	0-0*		1-2	2	UEFA

* in Zurich

TURKEY

Founded 1923
Federation Turque de Football, Ulus 15 Hani, A Blok Kat 4, Ankara ☎ 24 39 34/5
National colours all white
Season September to June

LEAGUE CHAMPIONS

League Championship started in 1959. In Istanbul, Ankara and Izmir regional Championships took place since 1922-23.

1959	Fenerbahce	1967	Besiktas	1975	Fenerbahce	1983	Fenerbahce
		1968	Fenerbahce	1976	Trabzonspor	1984	Trabzonspor
1960	Besiktas	1969	Galatasaray	1977	Trabzonspor	1985	Fenerbahce
1961	Fenerbahce			1978	Fenerbahce	1986	Besiktas
1962	Galatasaray	1970	Fenerbahce	1979	Trabzonspor	1987	Galatasaray
1963	Galatasaray	1971	Galatasaray			1988	Galatasaray
1964	Fenerbahce	1972	Galatasaray	1980	Trabzonspor	1988	Galatasaray
1965	Fenerbahce	1973	Galatasaray	1981	Trabzonspor	1989	Fenerbahce
1966	Besiktas	1974	Fenerbahce	1982	Besiktas		

CUP WINNERS

1963	Galatasaray v Fenerbahce	2-1 2-1	1977	Trabzonspor v Besiktas	1-0 0-0	
1964	Galatasaray v Altay Izmir	0-0 3-0	1978	Trabzonspor v Adana Demirspor	3-0 0-0	
1965	Galatasaray v Fenerbahce	0-0 0-0	1979	Fenerbahce v Altay Izmir	2-0 1-2	
1966	Galatasaray v Besiktas	0-0 1-0				
1967	Altay Izmir v Goztepe Izmir	2-2	1980	Altay Izmir v Galatasaray	1-0 1-1	
1968	Fenerbahce v Altay Izmir	2-0 0-1	1981	Ankaragucu v Boluspor	2-1 0-0	
1969	Goztepe Izmir v Galatsar	1-0 1-1	1982	Galatasaray v Ankaragucu	3-0 1-2	
			1983	Fenerbahce v Mersin Idmanyurdu	2-1 2-0	
1970	Goztepe Izmir v Eskisehirspor	3-1 1-2	1984	Trabzonspor v Besiktas	2-0	
1971	Eskisehirspor v Bursaspor	2-0 0-1	1985	Galatasaray v Trabzonspor	2-1 0-0	
1972	Ankaragucu v Altay Izmir	3-0 0-0	1986	Bursaspor v Altay Izmir	2-0	
1973	Galatasaray v Ankaragucu	3-1 1-1	1987	Genclerbirligi v Eskisehirspor	5-0 1-2	
1974	Fenerbahce v Bursaspor	0-1 3-0	1988	Sakaryaspor v Samsunspor	2-0 1-1	
1975	Besiktas v Trabzonspor	2-0 1-0	1989	Besiktas v Fenerbahce	1-0 2-1	
1976	Galatasaray v Trabzonspor	1-0 0-1 5-4 p				

TURKISH SUPER CUP

1966	Galatasaray v Besiktas	2-0
1967	Besiktas v Altay Izmir	1-0
1968	Fenerbahce won League and Cup	
1969	Galatasaray v Goztepe Izmir	2-0
1970	Goztepelzmir v Fenerbahce	3-1
1971	Eskisehirspor v Galatasaray	3-2
1972	Galatasaray v Ankaraguc	3-0
1973	Fenerbahce v Galatasaray	2-1
1974	Besiktas v Fenerbahce	3-0
1975	Fenerbahce v Besiktas	2-0
1976	Trabzonspor v Galatasaray	2-1
1977	Trabzonspor v Besiktas	1-1 3-1 pens
1978	Trabzonspor v Fenerbahce	1-0
1979	Trabzonspor v Fenerbahce	2-1

1980	Trabzonspor v Altay Izmir	3-0
1981	Ankaragucu v Trabzonspor	1-0
1982	Galatasaray v Besiktas	2-0
1983	Trabzonspor v Fenerbahce	2-0
1984	Fenerbahce v Trabzonspor	1-0
1985	Fenerbahce v Galatasaray	1-1 4-2 pens
1986	Besiktas v Bursaspor	2-1 aet
1987	Galatasaray v Genelerbirligi	
1988	Galatasaray v Sakaryaspor 2-0	
1989	Fenerbahce v Besiktas	

FEATURED CLUBS IN EUROPEAN COMPETITION

Fenerbahce Istanbul	**Galatasaray**	**Goztepe Izmir**	**Besiktas Istanbul**
Eskisehirspor Kuluebue	**Trabzonspor**	**Altay Izmir Gencik**	**Bursaspor**
Ankaragucu	**Boluspor Bolu**	**Orduspor**	**Adanaspor**
Mersin Idmanyurdu	**Genclerbirligi, Ankara**	**Sakaryaspor**	

FENERBAHCE

Founded 1907
Colours blue and yellow striped shirts, white shorts
Stadium Stade 19 Mayis, Istanbul (35,000) ☎ 1-337 8605/338 4084
Champions 1959, 1961, 1964, 1965, 1968, 1970, 1974, 1975, 1978, 1983, 1985, 1989
Cup Winners 1968, 1974, 1979, 1983
Turkish Super Cup Winners 1968, 1973, 1975, 1984, 1985

Season	Opponent	Home	Playoff Result	Away	Rnd	Cup
1959-60	Csepel Budapest, Hungary	1-1		3-2	pr	ECC
	OGC Nice, France	2-1	1-5*	1-2	1	ECC
			* played in Geneva			
1961-62	1.FC Nurnburg, Germany	1-2		0-1	1	ECC
1963-64	Petrolul Ploesti, Romania	4-1		0-1	1	CWC
	Linfield, Ireland	4-1		0-2	2	CWC
	MTK Budapest, Hungary	3-1	0-1*	0-2	qf	CWC
			* in Rome			
1964-65	DWS Amsterdam, Holland	0-1		1-3	pr	ECC
1965-66	RSC Anderlecht, Belgium	0-0		1-5	pr	ECC
1968-69	Manchester City, England	2-1		0-0	1	ECC
	Ajax Amsterdam, Holland	0-2		0-2	2	ECC
1970-71	Carl Zeiss Jena, East Germany	0-1		0-4	1	ECC
1971-72	Ferencvarosi TC, Hungary	1-1		1-3	1	UEFA
1972-73	Ruch Chorzow, Poland	1-0		0-3	1	UEFA
1973-74	FC Arges Pitesti, Romania	5-1		1-1	1	UEFA
	OGC Nice, France	2-0		0-4	2	UEFA
1974-75	Jeunesse Esch, Luxembourg	2-0		3-2	1	ECC
	Ruch Chorzow, Poland	0-2		1-2	2	ECC
1975-76	Benfica, Portugal	1-0		0-7	1	ECC
1976-77	Videoton Sekesfehervar, Hungary	2-1		0-4	1	UEFA
1977-78	Aston Villa, England	0-2		0-4	1	UEFA
1978-79	PSV Eindhoven, Holland	2-1		1-6	1	ECC
1979-80	Arsenal, England	0-0		0-2	1	CWC
1980-81	Beroe Stara Zagora, Bulgaria	0-1		1-2	1	UEFA
1983-84	Bohemians Prague, Czechoslovakia	0-1		0-4	1	ECC
1984-85	Fiorentina, Italy	0-1		0-2	1	UEFA

301

TURKEY

1985-86	Girondins Bordeaux, France	0-0		3-2	1	ECC
	IFK Gothenburg, Sweden	2-1		0-4	2	ECC
1989-90	Sparta Prague, Czechoslovakia	1-2		1-3	1	ECC

GALATASARAY

Founded 1905
Colours red and yellow striped shirts or red and yellow halved shirts, white shorts
Stadium Ali Sam Yen, Istanbul (40,000) ☎ 1-144 3980/579 3386
Champions 1962, 1963, 1969, 1971, 1972, 1973, 1987, 1988
Cup Winners 1963, 1964, 1965, 1966, 1973, 1976, 1982, 1985
Turkish Super Cup 1966, 1969, 1972, 1982, 1988

Season	Opponent	Home	Playoff Result	Away	Rnd	Cup
1956-57	Dinamo Bucharest, Romania	2-1		1-3	pr	ECC
1962-63	Dinamo Bucharest, Romania	3-0		1-1	1	ECC
	Polonia Bytom, Poland	4-1		0-1	2	ECC
	AC Milan, Italy	1-3		0-5	qf	ECC
1963-64	Ferencvarosi TC, Hungary	4-0		0-2	pr	ECC
	FC Zurich, Switzerland	2-0	2-2 lot* * in Rome aet	0-2	1	ECC
1964-65	Aufbau Magdeburg, East Germany	1-1	1-1 wot* * in Vienna	1-1	pr	CWC
	Legia Warsaw, Poland	1-0	1-2* * in Warsaw	0-1	1	CWC
1965-66	FC Sion, Switzerland	2-1		1-5	1	CWC
1966-67	Rapid Vienna, Austria	3-5		0-4	pr	CWC
1969-70	Waterford, Eire	2-0		3-2* * in Dublin	1	ECC
	Spartak Trnava, Czechoslovakia	1-0	wot	0-1	2	ECC
	Legia Warsaw, Poland	1-1		0-2	qf	ECC
1971-72	CSKA Moscow, USSR	1-1		0-3	1	ECC
1972-73	Bayern Munich, Germany	1-1		0-6	1	ECC
1973-74	Atletico Madrid, Spain	0-1		0-0	1	ECC
1975-76	Rapid Vienna, Austria	3-1		0-1	1	UEFA
	Torpedo Moscow, USSR	2-4		0-3	2	UEFA
1976-77	AIK Stockholm, Sweden	1-1		2-1	1	CWC
	RSC Anderlecht, Belgium	1-5		1-5	2	CWC
1978-79	West Bromwich Albion, England	1-3* * in Izmir		1-3	1	UEFA
1979-80	Red Star Belgrade, Yugoslavia	0-0		1-3	1	UEFA
1982-83	Kuusysi 69 Lahti, Finland	2-1		1-1	1	CWC
	FK Austria Vienna, Austria	2-4		1-0	2	CWC
1985-86	Widzew Lodz, Poland	1-0	wag	1-2	1	CWC
	Bayer Uerdingen, Germany	1-1		0-2	2	CWC
1986-87	Universitatea Craiova, Romania	2-1		0-2	1	UEFA
1987-88	PSV Eindhoven, Holland	2-0		0-3	1	ECC
1988-89	Rapid Vienna, Austria	2-0		1-2	1	ECC
	FC Neuchatel Xamax, Switzerland	5-0		0-3	2	ECC
	AS Monaco, France	1-1* * in Koln		1-0	qf	ECC
	Steaua Bucharest, Romania	1-1* * in Izmir		0-4	sf	ECC
1989-90	Red Star Belgrade, Yugoslavia	1-1		0-2	1	UEFA

GOZTEPE IZMIR

Founded 1925
Colours yellow and red striped shirts, white shorts
Stadium Stade d'Ataturk, Izmir (70,000) ☎ 154833/152472
Cup Winners 1969, 1970
Turkish Super Cup Winners 1970

Season	Opponent	Home	Result	Away	Rnd	Cup
1964-65	Petrolul Ploesti, Romania	0-1		1-2	pr	Fairs
1965-66	bye				1	Fairs
	TSV 1860 Munich, Germany	2-1		1-9	2	Fairs
1966-67	Bologna, Italy	1-2		1-3	1	Fairs
1967-68	Royal Antwerp, Belgium	0-0		2-1	1	Fairs
	Atletico Madrid, Spain	3-0		0-2	2	Fairs
	Vojvodina Novi Sad, Yugoslavia	0-1		0-1	3	Fairs
1968-69	Olympique Marseille, France	2-0	wot	0-2	1	Fairs
	Argesul Pitesti, Romania	3-0		2-3	2	Fairs
	OFK Belgrade, Yugoslavia	2-0	wag	1-3	3	Fairs
	Hamburger SV, Germany	withdrew			qf	Fairs
	Ujpest Dozsa, Hungary	1-4		0-4	sf	Fairs
1969-70	Union Sportive, Luxembourg	3-0		3-2	1	CWC
	Cardiff City, Wales	3-0		0-1	2	CWC
	AS Roma, Italy	0-0		0-2	qf	CWC
1970-71	Union Sportive, Luxembourg	5-0		0-1	1	CWC
	Gornik Zabrze, Poland	0-1		0-3	2	CWC

BESIKTAS

Founded 1903
Colours black and white striped shirts, black shorts
Stadium Stade Mithatpasat, Istanbul (40,000)
Champions 1958, 1960, 1966, 1967, 1982, 1986
Cup Winners 1975, 1989 ☎ 1-161 2454/161 8804
Turkish Super Cup Winners 1967, 1974, 1986

Season	Opponent	Home	Result	Away	Rnd	Cup
1958-59	Olympiakos Piraeus, Greece	withdrew			pr	ECC
	Real Madrid, Spain	1-1		0-2	1	ECC
1960-61	Rapid Vienna, Austria	1-0		0-4	1	ECC
1966-67	Ajax Amsterdam, Holland	1-2		0-2	pr	ECC
1967-68	Rapid Vienna, Austria	0-1		0-3	1	ECC
1974-75	Steagul Rosa Brasov, Romania	2-0		0-3	1	UEFA
1975-76	Fiorentina, Italy	0-3		0-3	1	CWC
1977-78	Diosgyoer, Hungary	2-0		0-5	1	CWC
1982-83	Aston Villa, England	0-0		1-3*	1	ECC
				* behind closed doors		
1984-85	Rapid Vienna, Austria	1-1		1-4	1	CWC
1985-86	Athletic Bilbao, Spain	0-1		1-4	1	UEFA
1986-87	Dinamo Tirana, Albania	2-0		1-0	1	ECC
	Apoel Nicosia, Cyprus	walkover			2	ECC
	Dynamo Kiev, USSR	0-5		0-2	qf	ECC
1987-88	Inter Milan, Italy	0-0		1-3	1	UEFA
1988-89	Dinamo Zagreb, Yugoslavia	1-0		0-2	1	UEFA
1989-90	Borussia Dortmund, Germany	0-1		1-2	1	CWC

TURKEY

ESKISEHIRSPOR KULUEBUE

Founded 1965
Colours red shirts with black trim, black shorts
Stadium Sade d'Ataturk (35,000) ☎ 221-13360
Cup Winners 1971
Turkish Super Cup Winners 1971

Season	Opponent	Home	Result	Away	Rnd	Cup
1970-71	Sevilla CF, Spain	3-1		0-1	1	Fairs
	Twente Enschede, Holland	3-2		1-6	2	Fairs
1971-72	MP Mikkelin, Finland	4-0		0-0	1	CWC
	Dynamo Moscow, USSR	0-1		0-1	2	CWC
1972-73	Fiorentina, Italy	1-2		0-3	1	UEFA
1973-74	1.FC Koln, Germany	0-0		0-2	1	UEFA
1975-76	Levski Spartak Sofia, Bulgaria	1-4		0-3	1	UEFA

TRABZONSPOR

Founded 1923
Colours maroon shirts, blue shorts
Stadium Avni Aker (25,000) ☎ 031-11292
Champions 1976, 1977, 1979, 1980, 1981, 1984
Cup Winners 1977, 1978, 1984
Turkish Super Cup Winners 1976, 1977, 1978, 1979, 1980, 1983

Season	Opponent	Home	Result	Away	Rnd	Cup
1976-77	IA Akranes, Iceland	3-2		3-1*	1	ECC
				* in Reykjavik		
	Liverpool, England	1-0		0-3	2	ECC
1977-78	B 1903 Copenhagen, Denmark	1-0		0-2	1	ECC
1979-80	Hajduk Split, Yugoslavia	0-1		0-1	1	ECC
1980-81	GKS Szombierki Bytom, Poland	2-1		0-3	1	ECC
1981-82	Dynamo Kiev, USSR	1-1		0-1	1	ECC
1982-83	1.FC Kaiserslautern, Germany	0-3		0-3	1	UEFA
1983-84	Inter Milan, Italy	1-0		0-2*	1	UEFA
				* in Cesena		
1984-85	Dnerp Dnerpopetrovsk, USSR	1-0		0-3*	1	ECC
				* in Krivoy Rog		

ALTAY IZMIR GENCIK

Founded 1914
Colours black and white striped shirts, black shorts
Stadium Stade Alsancak, Izmir (30,000) ☎ 51-210626
Cup Winners 1967, 1980

Season	Opponent	Home	Result	Away	Rnd	Cup
1962-63	AS Roma, Italy	2-3		1-10*	pr	Fairs
				* in Istanbul		
1967-68	Standard Liege, Belgium	2-3		0-0	1	CWC
1968-69	Lyn Oslo, Norway	3-1		1-4	1	CWC
1969-70	Carl Zeiss Jena, East Germany	0-1		0-0	1	Fairs
1977-78	Carl Zeiss Jena, East Germany	4-1		1-5	1	UEFA
1980-81	Benfica, Portugal	0-0		0-4	pr	CWC

BURSASPOR

Founded 1963
Colours green and white hooped shirts, white shorts
Stadium Ataturk (30,000) ☎ 24-113501
Cup Winners 1986

Season	Opponent	Home	Result	Away	Rnd	Cup
1974-75	Finn Harps, Eire	4-2		0-0	1	CWC
	Dundee United, Scotland	1-0		0-0	2	CWC
	Dynamo Kiev, USSR	0-1		0-2	qf	CWC
1986-87	Ajax Amsterdam, Holland	0-2		0-5	1	CWC

ANKARAGUCU

Founded 1910
Colours all blue with white trim
Stadium 19th May (35,000) ☎ 4-1220175
Cup Winners 1972, 1981
Turkish Super Cup Winners 1981

Season	Opponent	Home	Result	Away	Rnd	Cup
1972-73	Leeds United, England	1-1		0-1	1	CWC
1973-74	Glasgow Rangers, Scotland	0-2		0-4	1	CWC
1981-82	Rostov on Don SKA, USSR	0-2		0-3	1	CWC

BOLUSPOR

Founded 1965
Colours red shirts, white shorts or white shirts, red shorts
Stadium Sehir Stadi (18,000) ☎ 4611-1360

Season	Opponent	Home	Result	Away	Rnd	Cup
1974-75	Dinamo Bucharest, Romania	0-1		0-3	1	UEFA

ORDUSPOR

Founded 1967
Colours purple shirts, white shorts
Stadium 19 Eylul (20,000) ☎ 2585

Season	Opponent	Home	Result	Away	Rnd	Cup
1979-80	Banik Ostrava, Czechoslovakia	2-0		0-6	1	UEFA

TURKEY

ADANASPOR

Founded 1954
Colours orange and white striped shirts, white shorts
Stadium Adana Sehir (30,000) ☎ 71-134839

Season	Opponent	Home	Result	Away	Rnd	Cup
1976-77	Austria Salzburg, Austria	2-0		0-5	1	UEFA
1978-79	Honved Budapest, Hungary	2-2		0-6	1	UEFA
1981-82	Inter Milan, Italy	1-3		1-4	1	UEFA

MERSIN IDMANYURDU

Founded 1925
Colours red and black halved shirts, white shorts
Stadium Teveik Sirri Gur (15,000) ☎ 15317/17787

Season	Opponent	Home	Result	Away	Rnd	Cup
1983-84	Spartak Varna, Bulgaria	0-0		0-1	1	CWC

GENCLERBIRLIGI

Founded 1923
Colours black and red striped shirts, black shorts
Stadium 19 May Inonu, Ankara (30,000) ☎ 4-129 5852
Cup Winners 1987

Season	Opponents	Home	Result	Away	Rnd	Cup
1987-88	Dynamo Minsk, USSR	1-2		0-2	1	CWC

SAKARYASPOR

Founded 1965
Colours all white with black shoulders or green and black striped shirts, white shorts
Stadium Sehir Ataturk (15,000) ☎ 261-12900 Cup Winners 1988

Season	Opponents	Home	Result	Away	Rnd	Cup
1988-89	Bekescsaba Elore Spartacus, Hungary	2-0		0-1	1	CWC
	Eintracht Frankfurt, Germany	0-3		1-3	2	CWC

Union of Soviet Socialist Republics
Founded 1912 USSR Football Federation, Luzhnetskaya Naberezhnaja 8, 119270 Moscow ☎ 201 0834
National Colours red shirts, white shorts, red socks
Season: South - March to December, Central - April to October, North - May to Sept

LEAGUE CHAMPIONS

Before 1936 there was no official Championship, played as a Cup in 1922, 1923,1924, 1928, 1931, 1932 and as a
League in 1935 consisting of selected teams from big Cities

1936 Dynamo Moscow (Spring)	**1952** Spartak Moscow	**1967** Dynamo Kiev	**1980** Dynamo Kiev
1936 Spartak Moscow (Autumn)	**1953** Spartak Moscow	**1968** Dynamo Kiev	**1981** Dynamo Kiev
	1954 Dynamo Moscow	**1969** Spartak Moscow	**1982** Dynamo Minsk
	1955 Dynamo Moscow		**1983** Dnepr Dnepropetrovsk
1937 Dynamo Moscow	**1956** Spartak Moscow	**1970** CSKA Moscow	**1984** Zenit Leningrad
1938 Spartak Moscow	**1957** Dynamo Moscow	**1971** Dynamo Kiev	**1985** Dynamo Kiev
1939 Spartak Moscow	**1958** Spartak Moscow	**1972** Zarja Voroschilovgrad	**1986** Dynamo Kiev
	1959 Dynamo Moscow	**1973** Ararat Yerevan	**1987** Spartak Moscow
1940 Dynamo Moscow		**1974** Dynamo Kiev	**1988** Dnepr Dnepropetrovsk
1945 Dynamo Moscow	**1960** Torpedo Moscow	**1975** Dynamo Kiev	**1989** Spartak Moscow
1946 CDKA Moscow	**1961** Dynamo Kiev	**1976** Dynamo Moscow (Spring)	
1947 CDKA Moscow	**1962** Spartak Moscow	**1976** Torpedo Moscow (Autumn)	
1948 CDKA Moscow	**1963** Dynamo Moscow	**1977** Dynamo Kiev	
1949 Dynamo Moscow	**1964** Dynamo Tbilisi	**1978** Dynamo Tbilisi	
	1965 Torpedo Moscow	**1979** Spartak Moscow	
1950 CDKA Moscow	**1966** Dynamo Kiev		
1951 CDKA Moscow			

CUP WINNERS

1936 Lokomotic Moscow v Dynamo Tbilisi	2-0	
1937 Dynamo Moscow v Dynamo Tbilisi	3-2	
1938 Spartak Moscow v Krasnaya Zarya Leningrad	3-0	
1939 Spartak Moscow v Zenit Leningrad	3-1	
1944 Zenit Leningrad v CDKA Moscow	3-1	
1945 CDKA Moscow v Dynamo Moscow	2-1	
1946 Spartak Moscow v Dynamo Tbilisi	3-2	
1947 Spartak Moscow v Torpedo Moscow	2-0	
1948 CDKA Moscow v Spartak Moscow	3-0	
1949 Torpedo Moscow v Dynamo Moscow	2-1	

1950 Spartak Moscow v Dynamo Moscow	3-0	
1951 CDKA Moscow v Kalilin	2-1	
1952 Torpedo Moscow v Spartak Moscow	1-0	
1953 Dynamo Moscow v Kryla Kuibishev	1-0	
1954 Dynamo Kiev v Ararat Yerevan	2-1	
1955 CDSA Moscow v Dynamo Moscow	2-1	
1956 no competition		
1957 Lokomotiv Moscow v Spartak Moscow	1-0	
1958 Spartak Moscow v Torpedo Moscow	1-0	
1959 no competition		

USSR

1960	Torpedo Moscow v Dynamo Tbilisi	4-3
1961	Shakhtyor Donetsk v Torpedo Moscow	3-1
1962	Shakhtyor Donetsk v Znamia Truda	2-0
1963	Spartak Moscow v Shakhtyor Donetsk	2-1
1964	Dynamo Kiev v Kryla Kuibishev	1-0
1965	Spartak Moscow v Dynamo Minsk	2-1
1966	Dynamo Kiev v Torpedo Moscow	2-0
1967	Dynamo Moscow v CSKA Moscow	3-0
1968	Torpedo Moscow v Pakhator Tashkent	1-0
1969	Carpath Lvov v SKA Rostov	2-1
1970	Moscow Dynamo v Dynamo Tbilisi	2-1
1971	Spartak Moscow v SKA Rostov	1-0
1972	Torpedo Moscow v Spartak Moscow	0-0 1-1 4-1 pens
1973	Ararat Yerevan v Dynamo Kiev	2-1
1974	Dynamo Kiev v Zarja Voroschilovgrad	3-0

1975	Ararat Yerevan v Zarja Voroschilovgrad	2-1
1976	Dynamo Tbilisi v Ararat Yerevan	3-0
1977	Dynamo Kiev v Shakhtyor Donetsk	2-1 aet
1978	Dynamo Moscow v Shakhtyor Donetsk	2-1
1979	Dynamo Tbilisi v Dynamo Moscow	0-0 5-4 pens
1980	Shakhtyor Donetsk v Dynamo Tbilisi	2-1
1981	SKA Rostov on Don v Spartak Moscow	1-0
1982	Dynamo Kiev v Torpedo Moscow	1-0
1983	Shakhtyor Donetsk v Metellist Kharkov	1-0
1984	Dynamo Moscow v Zenit Leningrad	2-0
1985	Dynamo Kiev v Shakhtyor Donetsk	2-1
1986	Torpedo Moscow v Shakhtyor Donetsk	1-0
1987	Dynamo Kiev v Dynamo Minsk	3-3 4-2 pens
1988	Metallist Kharkov v Torpedo Moscow	2-0
1989	Dnepr Drepropetrovsk v Torpedo Moscow	1-0

FEATURED CLUBS IN EUROPEAN COMPETITION

Dynamo Moscow	Dynamo Kiev	Spartak Moscow	Torpedo Moscow
CSKA Moscow	Shakhtyor Donetsk	Cernomorez Odessa	Ararat Yerevan
Zaria Voroschilovgrad	Carpath Lvov	SKA Rostov on Don	Zenit Leningrad
Dynamo Tbilisi	Dynamo Minsk	Dnepr Dnepropetrovsk	Metallist Kharkov
Zhalgiris Vilnius (Lithuania)			

DYNAMO MOSCOW

Founded 1923
Colours white shirts, blue shorts with white hoop
Stadium Dynamo (51,000) ☎ 214 87 13
Champions 1936, 1937, 1940, 1945, 1949, 1954, 1955, 1957, 1959, 1963, 1976 (shared)
Cup Winners 1937, 1953, 1967, 1978, 1984
CWC Finalists 1972

Season	Opponents	Home	Result	Away	Rnd	Cup
1968-69	1.FC Union Berlin, East Germany	withdrew			1	CWC
1971-72	Olympiakos Piraeus, Greece	2-0		1-2	1	CWC
	Eskisehirspor, Turkey	1-0		1-0	2	CWC
	Red Star Belgrade, Yugoslavia	1-1		2-1	qf	CWC
	BFC Dynamo (Berlin), East Germany	1-1	4-1p	1-1	sf	CWC
	Glasgow Rangers, Scotland	2-3	in Barcelona		FINAL	CWC
1974-75	Osters IF Vaxjo, Sweden	2-1	wag	2-3	1	UEFA
	Dynamo Dresden, East Germany	1-0	3-4p	0-1	2	UEFA
1976-77	AEK Athens, Greece	2-1		0-2	1	UEFA
1977-78	Valletta, Malta	5-0		2-0	1	CWC
	Universitatea Craiova, Romania	2-0	3-0p	0-2	2	CWC
	Real Betis, Spain	3-0*		0-0	qf	CWC
		* in Tbilisi				
	FK Austria Vienna, Austria	2-1*	4-5p	1-2	sf	CWC
		* in Tbilisi				
1979-80	Vlaznia Shkodar, Albania	withdrew			1	CWC
	Boavista, Portugal	0-0	wag	1-1	2	CWC
	FC Nantes, France	0-2		3-2	qf	CWC
1980-81	KSC Lokeren, Belgium	0-1		1-1	1	UEFA
1982-83	Slask Wroclaw, Poland	0-1		2-2	1	UEFA
1984-85	Hajduk Split, Yugoslavia	1-0		5-2	1	CWC
	Hamrun Spartans, Malta	5-0		1-0	2	CWC
	Larissa, Greece	1-0*		0-0	qf	CWC
		* in Tbilisi				
	Rapid Vienna, Austria	1-1		1-3	sf	CWC
1987-88	Grasshoppers Zurich, Switzerland	1-0		4-0	1	UEFA
	FC Barcelona, Spain	0-0		0-2	2	UEFA

DYNAMO KIEV

Founded 1927
Colours all white or white shirts with blue sleeves, blue shorts
Stadium Dynamo (30,000) or Republic (100,000) ☎ 299520
Champions 1961, 1966, 1967, 1968, 1971, 1974, 1975, 1977, 1980, 1981
Cup Winners 1954, 1964, 1966, 1974, 1977, 1982, 1985
CWC Winners 1975
Super Cup Finalists 1987

Season	Opponents	Home	Result	Away	Rnd	Cup
1965-66	Coleraine, Ireland	4-0		6-1	1	CWC
	Rosenborg Trondheim, Norway	2-0		4-1	2	CWC
	Glasgow Celtic, Scotland	1-1*		0-3	qf	CWC
		* in Tbilisi				
1967-68	Glasgow Celtic, Scotland	1-1		2-1	1	ECC
	Gornik Zabrze, Poland	1-2		1-1	2	ECC
1968-69	withdrew					ECC
1969-70	FK Austria Vienna, Austria	3-1		2-1	1	ECC
	Fiorentina, Italy	1-2		0-0	2	ECC
1972-73	Wacker Innsbruck, Austria	2-0		1-0	1	ECC
	Gornik Zabrze, Poland	2-0		1-2	2	ECC
	Real Madrid, Spain	0-0*		0-3	qf	ECC
		* in Odessa				
1973-74	Fredrikstad FK, Norway	4-0		1-0	1	UEFA
	B 1903 Copenhagen, Denmark	1-0		2-1	2	UEFA
	VfB Stuttgart, Germany	2-0		0-3	3	UEFA
1974-75	CSKA Sofia, Bulgaria	1-0		1-0	1	CWC
	Eintracht Frankfurt, Germany	2-1		3-2	2	CWC
	Bursaspor, Turkey	2-0		1-0	qf	CWC
	PSV Eindhoven, Holland	3-0		1-2	sf	CWC
	Ferencvarosi TC, Hungary	3-0	in Basle		FINAL	CWC
1975-76	Olympiakos Piraeus, Greece	1-0		2-2	1	ECC
	IA Akranes, Iceland	3-0		2-0*	2	ECC
				* in Reykjavik		
	St Etienne, France	2-0		0-3	qf	ECC
1976-77	Partizan Belgrade, Yugoslavia	3-0		2-0	1	ECC
	PAOK Salonika, Greece	4-0		2-0	2	ECC
	Bayern Munich, Germany	2-0		0-1	qf	ECC
	Borussia Monchengladbach, Germany	1-0		0-2	sf	ECC
1977-78	Eintracht Braunschweig, Germany	1-1	lag	0-0	1	UEFA
1978-79	Haka Valkeakosken, Finland	3-1*		1-0	1	ECC
		* in Kharkov				
	Malmo FF, Sweden	0-0		0-2	2	ECC
1979-80	CSKA Sofia, Bulgaria	2-1		1-1	1	UEFA
	Banik Ostrava, Czechoslovakia	2-0		0-1	2	UEFA
	Lokomotiv Sofia, Bulgaria	2-1	lag	0-1	3	UEFA
1980-81	Levski Spartak Sofia, Bulgaria	1-1	lag	0-0	1	UEFA
1981-82	Trabzonspor, Turkey	1-0		1-1	1	ECC
	FK Austria Vienna, Austria	1-1		1-0	2	ECC
	Aston Villa, England	0-0*		0-2	qf	ECC
		* in Simferopol				
1982-83	Grasshoppers Zurich, Switzerland	3-0		1-0	1	ECC
	17 Nentori Tirana, Albania	withdrew			2	ECC
	Hamburger SV, Germany	0-3*		2-1	qf	ECC
		* in Tbilisi				
1983-84	Lavallois, France	0-0		0-1	1	UEFA
1985-86	FC Utrecht, Holland	4-1		1-2	1	CWC
	Universitatea Craiova, Romania	3-0		2-2	2	CWC
	Rapid Vienna, Austria	5-1		4-1	qf	CWC
	Dukla Prague, Czechoslovakia	3-0		1-1	sf	CWC
	Atletico Madrid, Spain	in Lyon			FINAL	CWC

1986-87	Beroe Stara Zagora, Bulgaria	2-0		1-1	1	ECC
	Glasgow Celtic, Scotland	3-1		1-1	2	ECC
	Besiktas Istanbul, Turkey	2-0		5-0	qf	ECC
	FC Porto, Portugal	1-2		1-2	sf	ECC
1987-88	Glasgow Rangers, Scotland	1-0		0-2	1	ECC
1989-90	MTK/VM Budapest, Hungary	4-0		2-1	1	UEFA
	Banik Ostrava, Czechoslovakia	3-0		1-1	2	UEFA
	Fiorentina, Italy	0-0		0-1*	3	UEFA

SPARTAK MOSCOW

Founded 1922 as MKS, 1926 Pishchevik, Dukat, Promkooperatzia, MSPK until 1935 then Spartak
Colours red shirts with white hoop, white shorts
Stadium Lenin "Luzhniki" (102,000) ☎ 264 6510
Champions 1936, 1938, 1939, 1952, 1953, 1956, 1958, 1962, 1969, 1979, 1987, 1989
Cup Winners 1938, 1939, 1946, 1947, 1950, 1958, 1963, 1965, 1971

Season	Opponents	Home	Result	Away	Rnd	Cup
1966-67	OFK Belgrade, Yugoslavia	3-0		3-1	pr	CWC
	Rapid Vienna, Austria	1-1		0-1	1	CWC
1970-71	FC Basle, Switzerland	3-2	lag	1-2	1	ECC
1971-72	VSS Kosice, Czechoslovakia	2-0		1-2	1	UEFA
	Vitoria Setubal, Portugal	0-0		0-4	2	UEFA
1972-73	FC Den Haag, Holland	1-0		0-0	1	CWC
	Atletico Madrid, Spain	1-2	wag	4-3	2	CWC
	AC Milan, Italy	0-1		1-1	qf	CWC
1974-75	Velez Mostar, Yugoslavia	3-1	lag	0-2	1	UEFA
1975-76	AIK Stockholm, Sweden	1-0		1-1	1	UEFA
	1.FC Koln, Germany	2-0		1-0	2	UEFA
	AC Milan, Italy	2-0		0-4	3	UEFA
1980-81	Jeunesse Esch, Luxembourg	4-0		5-0	1	ECC
	Esbjerg FB, Denmark	3-0		0-2	2	ECC
	Real Madrid, Spain	0-0*		0-2	qf	ECC
	* in Tbilisi					
1981-82	Clube Bruges, Belgium	3-1		3-1	1	UEFA
	1.FC Kaiserslautern, Germany	2-1		0-4	2	UEFA
1982-83	Arsenal, England	3-2		5-2	1	UEFA
	HFC Haarlem, Holland	2-0		3-1	2	UEFA
	Valencia CF, Spain	0-0		0-2	3	UEFA
1983-84	HJK Helsinki, Finland	2-0		5-0	1	UEFA
	Aston Villa, England	2-2		2-1	2	UEFA
	Sparta Rotterdam, Holland	2-0		1-1	3	UEFA
	RSC Anderlecht, Belgium	1-0		2-4	qf	UEFA
1984-85	OB 1913 Odense, Denmark	2-1		5-1	1	UEFA
	1.FC Lokomotive Leipzig, East Germany	2-0		1-1	2	UEFA
	1.FC Koln, Germany	1-0*		0-2	3	UEFA
	* in Tbilisi					
1985-86	TPS Turun Turku, Finland	1-0		3-1	1	UEFA
	Clube Bruges, Belgium	1-0		3-1	2	UEFA
	FC Nantes, France	0-1*		1-1	3	UEFA
	* in Tbilisi					
1986-87	FC Luzern, Switzerland	0-0		1-0	1	UEFA
	Toulouse FC, France	5-1		1-3	2	UEFA
	FC Tirol, Austria	1-0		0-2	3	UEFA
1987-88	Dynamo Dresden, East Germany	3-0		0-1	1	UEFA
	Werder Bremen, Germany	4-1		2-6	2	UEFA
1988-89	Glentoran, Ireland	2-0		1-1	1	ECC
	Steaua Bucharest, Romania	1-2		0-3	2	ECC
1989-90	Atalanta Bergamo, Italy	2-0		0-0	1	UEFA
	1.FC Koln, Germany	0-0		1-3	2	UEFA

TORPEDO MOSCOW

Founded 1924 as Proletarskaya Kuznitza, 1936 Torpedo
Colours white shirts, black shorts
Stadium Torpedo (16,000) ☎ 277 88 00
Champions 1960, 1965, 1976 (shared)
Cup Winners 1949, 1952, 1960, 1968, 1972, 1986

Season	Opponents	Home	Playoff Result	Away	Rnd	Cup
1966-67	Inter Milan, Italy	0-0		0-1	pr	ECC
1967-68	Motor Zwickau, East Germany	0-0		1-0	1	CWC
	Spartak Trnava, Czechoslovakia	3-0*		3-1	2	CWC
	* in Tashkent					
	Cardiff City, Wales	1-0*	0-1**	0-1	qf	WCC
	* in Tashkent, ** in Augsburg					
1969-70	Rapid Vienna, Austria	1-1	lag	0-0	pr	CWC
1973-74	Athletic Bilbao, Spain	0-0		0-2	1	CWC
1975-76	Napoli, Italy	4-1		1-1	1	UEFA
	Galatasaray, Turkey	3-0		4-2	2	UEFA
	Dynamo Dresden, East Germany	3-1		0-3	3	UEFA
1977-78	Benfica, Portugal	0-0	1-4 pen	0-0	1	ECC
1978-79	Molde FK, Norway	4-0		3-3	1	UEFA
	VfB Stuttgart, Germany	2-1		0-2	2	UEFA
1982-83	Bayern Munich, Germany	1-1	lag	0-0	1	CWC
1986-87	Valkeakosken Haka, Finland	3-1		2-2	1	CWC
	VfB Stuttgart, Germany	2-0		5-3	2	CWC
	Girondins Bordeaux, France	3-2*	lag	0-1	qf	CWC
	* in Tbilisi					
1988-89	Malmo FF, Sweden	2-1 aet		0-2	1	UEFA
1989-90	Cork City, Eire	5-0		1-0	1	CWC
	Grasshoppers Zurich, Switzerland	1-1		0-3	2	CWC

CSKA MOSCOW

Founded 29-4-1923 as O.L.L.S. 1923 O.P.P.V. 1928 CDKA, 1951 CDSA, 1957 CSK Mo, 1960 CSKA
Colours red shirts, white shorts
Stadium Dynamo (51,000) ☎ 213 69 63
Champions 1946, 1947, 1948, 1950, 1951, 1970
Cup Winners 1945, 1948, 1951, 1955

Season	Opponents	Home	Result	Away	Rnd	Cup
1971-72	Galatasaray, Turkey	3-0		1-1	1	ECC
	Standard Liege, Belgium	1-0		0-2	2	ECC
1981-82	Sturm Graz, Austria	2-1	lag	0-1	1	UEFA

USSR

SHAKHTYOR DONETSK

Founded 1935 as Stakhanovetz Stalino, 1947 Shakhtyor
Colours orange and black striped shirts, black shorts
Stadium Shakhtyor (43,000) or Lokomotiv (40,485) ☎ 340045
Cup Winners 1961, 1962, 1980, 1983

Season	Opponents	Home	Result	Away	Rnd	Cup
1976-77	BFC Dynamo (Berlin), East Germany	3-0		1-1	1	UEFA
	Honved Budapest, Hungary	3-0		3-2	2	UEFA
	Juventus, Italy	1-0		0-3	3	UEFA
1978-79	FC Barcelona, Spain	1-1		0-3	1	CWC
1979-80	AS Monaco, France	2-1		0-2	1	UEFA
1980-81	Eintracht Frankfurt, Germany	1-0		0-3	1	UEFA
1983-84	B 1901 Nykobing, Denmark	4-2		5-1	1	CWC
	Servette Geneva, Switzerland	1-0		2-1	2	CWC
	FC Porto, Portugal	1-1		2-3	qf	CWC

CERNOMOREIZ ODESSA

Founded 1958
Colours white and blue shirts, white shorts
Stadium Central (43,000)

Season	Opponents	Home	Result	Away	Rnd	Cup
1975-76	Lazio Rome, Italy	1-0		0-3	1	UEFA
1985-86	Werder Bremen, Germany	2-1	wag	2-3	1	UEFA
	Real Madrid, Spain	0-0		1-2	2	UEFA

ARARAT YEREVAN

Founded 1937 as Dynamo Yerevan, 1954 Spartak, 1963 Ararat
Colours all white
Stadium Rasdan (70,000) ☎ 58 26 01
Champions 1973
Cup Winners 1973, 1975

Season	Opponents	Home	Result	Away	Rnd	Cup
1972-73	EPA Larnaca, Cyprus	1-0		1-0	1	UEFA
	Grasshoppers Zurich, Switzerland	4-2		3-1	2	UEFA
	1.FC Kaiserslautern, Germany	2-0	4-5p	0-2	3	-UEFA
1974-75	Viking Stavanger, Norway	4-2		2-0	1	ECC
	Cork Celtic, Eire	5-0		2-1	2	ECC
	Bayern Munich, Germany	1-0		0-2	qf	ECC
1975-76	Anorthosis Famagusta, Cyprus	1-1		9-0	1	CWC
	West Ham United, England	1-1		1-3	2	CWC

ZARIA VOROSCHILOVGRAD

Founded 1938 as Trudovie Rezervior or Lugansk, 1964 Zaria
Colours all white
Stadium Avangard (40,000) formerly Metallurg, changed to Zaria 1964
Champions 1972

Season	Opponents	Home	Result	Away	Rnd	Cup
1973-74	Apoel Nicosia, Cyprus	2-0		1-0	1	ECC
	Spartak Trnava, Czechoslovakia	0-1		0-0	2	ECC

SKA CARPATH LVOV

Founded 1963 as Carpathy Lvov, 1982 SKA Carpathy Lvov
Colours green and white shirts, white shorts
Stadium Druzhba (40,000)
Cup Winners 1969

Season	Opponents	Home	Result	Away	Rnd	Cup
1970-71	Steaua Bucharest, Romania	0-1		3-3	1	CWC

SKA ROSTOV ON DON

Founded 1958 as SKVO, 1960 SKA Rostov on Don
Colours red shirts, dark blue or white shorts
SKA Stadion (50,000) or Rostselmar (35,000)
Cup Winners 1981

Season	Opponents	Home	Result	Away	Rnd	Cup
1981-82	Ankaragu, Turkey	3-0		2-0	1	CWC
	Eintracht Frankfurt, Germany	1-0		0-2	2	CWC

ZENIT LENINGRAD

Founded 1931 as Stalinetz, 1940 Zenit
Colours blue shirts, white shorts
Stadium Kirov (74,000) ☎ 234 58 34
Champions 1984
Cup Winners 1944

Season	Opponents	Home	Result	Away	Rnd	Cup
1981-82	Dynamo Dresden, East Germany	1-2		1-4	1	UEFA
1985-86	Valerengen IF Oslo, Norway	2-0		2-0	1	ECC
	Kuusysi Lahti, Finland	2-1		1-3	2	ECC
1987-88	Clube Bruges, Belgium	2-0		0-5	1	UEFA
1989-90	Naestved IF, Denmark	3-1		0-0	1	UEFA
	VfB Stuttgart, Germany	0-1		0-5	2	UEFA

DYNAMO TBILISI

Founded 1925
Colours blue and white shirts, white shorts
Stadium Lenin (75,000) ☎ 95 43 86
Champions 1964, 1978
Cup Winners 1976, 1979
CWC Winners 1981

Season	Opponents	Home	Result	Away	Rnd	Cup
1972-73	Twente Enschede, Holland	3-2		0-2	1	UEFA
1973-74	Slavia Sofia, Bulgaria	4-1		0-2	1	UEFA
	OFK Belgrade, Yugoslavia	3-0		5-1	2	UEFA
	Tottenham Hotspur, England	1-1		1-5	3	UEFA
1976-77	Cardiff City, Wales	3-0		0-1	1	CWC
	MTK/VM Budapest, Hungary	1-4		0-1	2	CWC
1977-78	Inter Milan, Italy	0-0		1-0	1	UEFA
	KB Copenhagen, Denmark	2-1		4-1	2	UEFA
	Grasshoppers Zurich, Switzerland	1-0		0-4	3	UEFA

313

1978-79	Napoli, Italy	2-0		1-1	1	UEFA
	Hertha BSC Berlin, Germany	1-0		0-2	2	UEFA
1979-80	Liverpool, England	3-0		1-2	1	ECC
	Hamburger SV, Germany	2-3		1-3	2	ECC
1980-81	Kastoria, Greece	2-0		0-0	1	CWC
	Waterford, Ireland	4-0		1-0	2	CWC
	West Ham United, England	0-1		4-1	qf	CWC
	Feyenoord Rotterdam, Holland	3-0		0-2	sf	CWC
	Carl Zeiss Jena, East Germany	2-1	in Dusseldorf		FINAL	CWC
1981-82	Grazer AK (GAK), Austria	2-0		2-2	1	CWC
	SEC Bastia Corsica, France	3-1		1-1	2	CWC
	Legia Warsaw, Poland	1-0		1-0	qf	CWC
	Standard Liege, Belgium	0-1		0-1	sf	CWC
1982-83	Napoli, Italy	2-1	lag	0-1	1	UEFA
1987-88	1.FC Lokomotive Leipzig, East Germany	3-0		1-3	1	UEFA
	Victoria Bucharest, Romania	0-0		2-1	2	UEFA
	Werder Bremen, Germany	1-1		1-2	3	UEFA

DYNAMO MINSK

Founded 1935 as Dynamo, 1954 Spartak, 1960 Beloruss, 1963 Dynamo
Colours blue shirts with white sleeves, white shorts
Stadium Dynamo (50,000) ☎ 22 11 33
Champions 1982

Season	Opponents	Home	Result	Away	Rnd	Cup
1983-84	Grasshoppers Zurich, Switzerland	1-0		2-2	1	ECC
	Raba Vasas Eto, Hungary	3-1		6-3	2	ECC
	Dinamo Bucharest, Romania	1-1		0-1	qf	ECC
1984-85	HJK Helsinki, Finland	4-0		6-0	1	UEFA
	Sporting Lisbon, Portugal	2-0	5-3 pen	0-2	2	UEFA
	Widzew Lodz, Poland	0-1		2-0	3	UEFA
	Zeljeznicar Sarajevo, Yugoslavia	1-1		0-2	qf	UEFA
1986-87	Rabo Vasas Eto, Hungary	2-4		1-0	1	UEFA
1987-88	Genclerbirligi Izmir, Turkey	2-0		2-1	1	CWC
	Real Sociadad San Sebastien, Spain	2-0		1-1	2	CWC
	KV Mechelen, Belgium	1-1		0-1	qf	CWC
1988-89	Trakia Plovdiv, Bulgaria	0-0		2-1	1	UEFA
	Victoria Bucharest, Romania	2-1	lag	0-1	2	UEFA

DNEPR DNEPROPETROVSK

Founded 1936 as Stal, 1949 Metallurg, 1962 Dniepr
Colours red shirts, white shorts
Stadium Meteor (34,000) ☎ 91 05 26
Champions 1983, 1988
Cup Winners 1989

Season	Opponents	*Home	Result	Away	Rnd	Cup
* all Home matches played in Krivoy Rog						
1984-85	Trabzonspor, Turkey	3-0		0-1	1	ECC
	Levski Spartak Sofia, Bulgaria	2-0	wag	1-3	2	ECC
	Girondins Bordeaux, France	1-1	3-5 pen	1-1	qf	ECC
1985-86	Wismut Aue, East Germany	2-1		3-1	1	UEFA
	PSV Eindhoven, Holland	1-0		2-2	2	UEFA
	Hajduk Split, Yugoslavia	0-1		0-2	3	UEFA
1986-87	Legia Warsaw, Poland	0-1		0-0	1	UEFA
1988-89	Girondins Bordeaux, France	1-1		1-2	1	UEFA
1989-90	Linfield, Ireland	1-0		2-1*	1	ECC
				*in Wrexham		
	FC Tirol, Austria	2-0		2-2	2	ECC
	Benfica, Portugal	0-3		0-1	qf	ECC

METALLIST KHARKOV

Founded 1944 as Lokomotiv, 1956 Avangard, 1967 Metallist
Colours red shirts, white shorts
Stadium Metallist (42,000) or Avangard (36,000) ☎ 23 10 36
Cup Winners 1988

Season	Opponents	Home	Result	Away	Rnd	Cup
1988-89	FK Borac Banja Luka, Yugoslavia	4-0		0-2	1	CWC
	Roda JC Kerkrade, Holland	0-0		0-1	2	CWC

ZHALGIRIS VILNIUS

Founded 1947 as Dynamo, 1948 Spartak, 1962 Zhalgiris
Colours green and white striped shirts, white shorts
Stadium Zhalgiris, Lithuania (15,000) ☎ 75 1693

Season	Opponents	Home	Result	Away	Rnd	Cup
1988-89	FK Austria, Austria	2-0		2-5	1	UEFA
1989-90	IFK Gothenburg, Sweden	2-0		0-0	1	UEFA
	1.FC Koln, Germany	0-0		1-4	2	UEFA

• Mungersdorf Koln

WALES

Founded 1875
The Football Association of Wales, 3 Fairy Road, Wrexham, Clwyd LL13 7PS
National colours red shirts, white shorts
Season (English League) August to May

As far as European Competitions are concerned the Welsh League are not eligable to enter for ECC or the UEFA Cups, only for the Cup Winners Cup. Most of the clubs from Wales who enter the CWC play in the English Football League

CUP WINNERS

Year	Match	Score
1878	Wrexham v Druids	1-0
1879	Newtown v Wrexham	1-0
1880	Druids v Ruthin	2-1
1881	Druids v Newtown White Stars	2-0
1882	Druids v Northwich	2-1
1883	Wrexham v Druids	1-0
1884	Oswestry v Druids	3-2
1885	Druids v Oswestry	2-0
1886	Druids v Newtown	5-2
1887	Chirk v Davenham	4-2
1888	Chirk v Newtown	5-0
1889	Bangor v Northwich	2-1
1890	Chirk v Wrexham	1-0
1891	Shrewsbury Town v Wrexham	5-2
1892	Chirk v Westminster Rovers	2-1
1893	Wrexham v Chirk	2-1
1894	Chirk v Westminster Rovers	2-0
1895	Newtown v Wrexham	3-2
1896	Bangor v Wrexham	3-1
1897	Wrexham v Newtown	2-0
1898	Druids v Wrexham	1-1 2-1
1899	Druids v Wrexham	2-2 1-0
1900	Aberystwyth v Druids	3-0
1901	Oswestry v Druids	1-0
1902	Wellington v Wrexham	1-0
1903	Wrexham v Aberaman	8-0
1904	Druids v Aberdare	3-2
1905	Wrexham v Aberdare	3-0
1906	Wellington v Whitchuch	3-2
1907	Oswestry v Whitchurch	2-0
1908	Chester v Connah's Quay	3-1
1909	Wrexham v Chester	1-0
1910	Wrexham v Chester	2-1
1911	Wrexham v Connah's Quay	6-1
1912	Cardiff City v Ponypridd	0-0 3-0
1913	Swansea v Pontypridd	0-0 1-0
1914	Wrexham v Llanelly	0-0 3-0
1915	Wrexham v Swansea Town	1-1 1-0
1920	Cardiff City v Wrexham	2-1
1921	Wrexham v Pontypridd	1-1 3-1
1922	Cardiff City v Ton Pentre	2-0
1923	Cardiff City v Aberdare	3-2
1924	Wrexham v Merythyr Tidfil	2-2 1-0
1925	Wrexham v Flint	3-1
1926	Ebbw Vale v Swansea Town	3-2
1927	Cardiff City v Rhyl	2-0
1928	Cardiff City v Bangor	2-0
1929	Connah's Quay v Cardiff City	3-0
1930	Cardiff City v Rhyl	0-0 4-2
1931	Wrexham v Shrewsbury	7-0
1932	Swansea v Wrexham	1-1 2-0
1933	Chester v Wrexham	2-0
1934	Bristol City v Tranmere Rovers	1-1 3-0
1935	Tranmere Rovers v Chester	1-0
1936	Crewe v Chester	2-0
1937	Crewe v Rhyl	1-1 3-1
1938	Shrewsbury v Swansea	2-1
1939	South Liverpool v Cardiff City	2-1
1940	Wellington Town v Swansea	4-0
1947	Chester v Merthyr Tydfil	0-0 5-1
1948	Lovell's Athletic v Shrewsbury Town	3-0
1949	Merthyr Tydfil v Swansea Town	2-0
1950	Swansea Town v Wrexham	4-1
1951	Merthyr Tydfil v Cardiff City	1-1 3-2
1952	Rhyl v Merthyr Tydfil	4-3
1953	Rhyl v Chester	2-1
1954	Flint Town United v Chester	2-0
1955	Barry Town v Chester	1-1 4-3

1956	Cardiff City v Swansea Town	3-2
1957	Wrexham v Swansea Town	2-1
1958	Wrexham City v Chester	1-1 2-0
1959	Cardiff City v Lovell's Athletic	2-0
1960	Wrexham v Cardiff City	1-1 1-0
1961	Swansea Town v Bangor City	3-1
1962	Bangor City v Wrexham	0-3 2-0 3-1
1963	Borough United v Newport County	2-1 0-0
1964	Cardiff City v Bangor City	0-2 3-1 2-0
1965	Cardiff City v Wrexham	5-1 0-1 3-0
1966	Swansea Town v Chester	3-0 0-1 2-1
1967	Cardiff City v Wrexham	2-2 2-1
1968	Cardiff City v Hereford United	2-0 4-1
1969	Cardiff City v Swansea Town	3-1 2-0
1970	Cardiff City v Chester	1-0 4-0
1971	Cardiff City v Wrexham	1-0 3-1
1972	Wrexham v Cardiff City	2-1 1-1

1973	Cardiff City v Bangor City	0-1 5-0
1974	Cardiff City v Stourbridge	1-0 1-0
1975	Wrexham v Cardiff City	2-1 3-1
1976	Cardiff City v Hereford United	3-3 3-2
1977	Shrewsbury Town v Cardiff City	1-2 3-0
1978	Wrexham v Bangor City	0-0 3-1
1979	Shrewsbury Town v Wrexham	1-0 1-1
1980	Newport County v Shrewsbury Town	2-1 3-0
1981	Swansea City v Hereford United	1-0 1-1
1982	Swansea City v Cardiff City	2-1 0-0
1983	Swansea City v Wrexham	2-0 2-1
1984	Shrewsbury Town v Wrexham	2-1 0-0
1985	Shrewsbury Town v Bangor City	3-1 2-0
1986	Wrexham v Kidderminster Harriers	1-1 2-1
1987	Merthyr Tydfil v Newport County	2-2 1-0
1988	Cardiff City v Wrexham	2-0 in Swansea
1989	Swansea City v Kidderminster Harriers	5-1 in Swansea

FEATURED CLUBS IN EUROPEAN COMPETITION

Cardiff City   **Bangor City**   **Borough United**   **Wrexham**
Swansea City   **Newport County**   **Merthyr Tydfil**

Shrewsbury Town do not play in Wales and are not eligible for the Cup Winners Cup

CARDIFF CITY

Founded 1899
Colours royal blue shirts, white shorts
Stadium Ninian Park (30,000) ☎ 0222-398636/7/8
Welsh Cup Winners 1912, 1920, 1922, 1923, 1927, 1928, 1930, 1956, 1959, 1964, 1965, 1967, 1968, 1969, 1970, 1971, 1973, 1974, 1976, 1988

Season	Opponent	Home	Playoff Result	Away	Rnd	Cup
1964-65	Esbjerg FB, Denmark	1-0		0-0	1	CWC
	Sporting Lisbon, Portugal	0-0		2-1	2	CWC
	Real Zaragoza, Spain	0-1		2-2	qf	CWC
1965-66	Standard Liege, Belgium	1-2		0-1	1	CWC
1967-68	Shamrock Rovers, Eire	2-0		1-1	1	CWC
	NAC Breda, Holland	4-1		1-1*	2	CWC
				* in Eindhoven		
	Torpedo Moscow, USSR	1-0	1-0*	0-1**	qf	CWC
			* in Augsburg, ** in Tashkent			
	Hamburger SV, Germany	2-3		1-1	sf	CWC
1968-69	FC Porto, Portugal	2-2		1-2	1	CWC
1969-70	Mjondalen IF, Norway	5-1		7-1	1	CWC
	Goztepe Izmir, Turkey	1-0		0-3	2	CWC
1970-71	Pezoporikos Larnaca, Cyprus	8-0		0-0	1	CWC
	FC Nantes, France	5-1		2-1	2	CWC
	Real Madrid, Spain	1-0		0-2	qf	CWC
1971-72	BFC Dynamo Berlin, East Germany	1-1	4-5 pen	1-1	1	CWC
1973-74	Sporting Lisbon, Portugal	0-0		1-2	1	CWC
1974-75	Ferencvarosi TC Hungary	1-4		0-2	1	CWC
1976-77	Servette Geneva, Switzerland	1-0	wag	1-2	pr	CWC
	Dynamo Tbilisi, USSR	1-0		0-3	1	CWC
1977-78	FK Austria Vienna, Austria	0-0		0-1	1	CWC
1988-89	Derry City, Eire	4-0		0-0	1	CWC
	AGF Aarhus, Denmark	1-2		0-4	2	CWC

WALES

BANGOR CITY

Founded 1876
Colours all blue
Stadium Farrar Road (10,000) ☎ 0248 712464
Welsh Cup Winners 1889, 1896, 1962

Season	Opponents	Home	Playoff Result	Away	Rnd	Cup
1962-63	Napoli, Italy	2-0	1-2*	1-3	1	CWC
			* at Arsenal			
1985-86	Fredrikstad FK, Norway	0-0	wag	1-1	1	CWC
	Atletico Madrid, Spain	0-2		0-1	2	CWC

BOROUGH UNITED

Founded late 1950's
Colours maroon shirts with white trim, white shorts
Stadium at Cyffordd Llandudno
Welsh Cup Winners 1963 disbanded in the mid 1960's

Season	Opponents	Home	Result	Away	Rnd	Cup
1963-64	Sliema Wanderers, Malta	2-0		0-0	1	CWC
	Slovan Bratislava, Czechoslovakia	0-1		0-3	2	CWC

WREXHAM

Founded 1873
Colours red shirts, white shorts
Stadium Racecourse (28,500) ☎ 0978-262129
Welsh Cup Winners 1878, 1883, 1893, 1897, 1903, 1905, 1909, 1910, 1911, 1914, 1915, 1921, 1924, 1925, 1931, 1957, 1958, 1960, 1972, 1975, 1978, 1986

Season	Opponents	Home	Result	Away	Rnd	Cup
1972-73	FC Zurich, Switzerland	2-1		1-1	1	CWC
	Hajduk Split, Yugoslavia	3-1	lag	0-2	2	CWC
1975-76	Djurgardens IF Stockholm, Sweden	2-1		1-1	1	CWC
	Stal Rzeszow, Poland	2-0		1-1	2	CWC
	RSC Anderlecht, Belgium	1-1		0-1	qf	CWC
1978-79	NK Rijeka, Yugoslavia	2-0		0-3	1	CWC
1979-80	1.FC Magdeburg, East Germany	3-2		2-5	1	CWC
1984-85	FC Porto, Portugal	1-0	wag	3-4	1	CWC
	AS Roma, Italy	0-1		0-2	2	CWC
1986-87	Zurrieq, Malta	4-0		3-0	1	CWC
	Real Zaragoza, Spain	2-2	lag	0-0	2	CWC

SWANSEA CITY

Founded 1900 as Swansea Town, February 1970 as Swansea City
Colours all white
Stadium Vetch Field (26,237) ☎ 0792-474114
Welsh Cup Winners 1913, 1932, 1950, 1961, 1966, 1981, 1982, 1983, 1989

Season	Opponents	Home	Result	Away	Rnd	Cup
1961-62	Motor Jena, East Germany	2-2		1-5	pr	CWC
1966-67	Slavia Sofia, Bulgaria	1-1		0-4	pr	CWC
1981-82	1.FC Lokomotive Leipzig, East Germany	0-1		1-2	1	CWC
1982-83	Sporting Braga, Portugal	3-0		0-1	pr	CWC
	Sliema Wanderers, Malta	12-0		5-0	1	CWC
	Paris St Germain, France	0-1		0-2	2	CWC
1983-84	1.FC Magdeburg, East Germany	1-1		0-1	pr	CWC
1989-90	Panathinakos, Greece	3-3		2-3	1	CWC

NEWPORT COUNTY

Founded 1912
Colours amber shirts, black shorts
Stadium Somerton Park (8,000) ☎ 0633-277543/277271/
Welsh Cup Winners 1980
Relegated out of the Football League at the end of 1987-88 Season, were dissolved on the 5th April 1989 for financial reasons

Season	Opponents	Home	Result	Away	Rnd	Cup
1980-81	Crusaders, Ireland	4-0		0-0	1	CWC
	Haugar, Norway	6-0		0-0	2	CWC
	Carl Zeiss Jena, East Germany	0-1		2-2	qf	CWC

MERTHYR TYDFIL

Founded 1945
Colours white shirts, black shorts
Stadium Penydarren Park (8,000) ☎ 0685-3884
Cup Winners 1987

Season	Opponent	Home	Result	Away	Rnd	Cup
1987-88	Atalanta Bergamo, Italy	2-1		0-2	1	CWC

YUGOSLAVIA

Founded 1919
Yugoslav Football Association, BP 263, Terazije No 35, 1100BP 263, Belgrade ☎ 33 34 33/47 Fax 11-333 433
National colours blue shirts, white shorts, red socks
Season August to June

LEAGUE CHAMPIONS

1923 Gradjanski Zagreb	1940 Gradjanski Zagreb	1962 Partizan Belgrade	1978 Partizan Belgrade
1924 Jugoslovija Belgrade	1947 Partizan Belgrade	1963 Partizan Belgrade	1979 Hajduk Split
1925 Jugoslovija Belgrade	1948 Dinamo Zagreb	1964 Red Star Belgrade	
1926 Gradjanski Zagreb	1949 Partizan Belgrade	1965 Partizan Belgrade	1980 Red Star Belgrade
1927 Hajduk Split		1966 Vojvodina Novi Sad	1981 Red Star Belgrade
1928 Gradjanski Zagreb	1950 Hajduk Split	1967 Sarajevo	1982 Dinamo Zagreb
1929 Hajduk Split	1951 Red Star Belgrade	1968 Red Star Belgrade	1983 Partizan Belgrade
	1952 Hajduk Split	1969 Red Star Belgrade	1984 Red Star Belgrade
1930 Concordia Zagreb	1953 Red Star Belgrade		1985 Sarajevo
1931 BSK Belgrade	1954 Dinamo Zagreb	1970 Red Star Belgrade	1986 Red Star Belgrade
1932 Concordia Zagreb	1955 Hajduk Split	1971 Hajduk Split	1987 Partizan Belgrade
1933 BSK Belgrade	1956 Red Star Belgrade	1972 Zeleznicar Sarajevo	1988 Red Star Belgrade
1934 not held	1957 Red Star Belgrade	1973 Red Star Belgrade	1989 Vojvodina Novi Sad
1935 BSK Belgrade	1958 Dinamo Zagreb	1974 Hajduk Split	
1936 BSK Belgrade	1959 Red Star Belgrade	1975 Hajduk Split	
1937 Gradjanski Zagreb		1976 Partizan Belgrade	
1938 HASK Zagreb	1960 Red Star Belgrade	1977 Red Star Belgrade	
1939 BSK Belgrade	1961 Partizan Belgrade		

CUP WINNERS

1947 Partizan Belgrade v Nasa Krila	2-0		1960 Dinamo Zagreb v Partizan Belgrade	3-2	
1948 Red Star Belgrade v Partizan Belgrade	3-0		1961 Vardar Skopje v Varteks Varazdin	2-1	
1949 Red Star Belgrade v Nasa Krila	3-2		1962 OFK Belgrade v Spartak Subotica	4-1	
			1963 Dinamo Zagreb v Hajduk Split	4-1	
1950 Red Star Belgrade v Dinamo Zagreb	1-1 3-0		1964 Red Star Belgrade v Dinamo Zagreb	3-0	
1951 Dinamo Zagreb v Vojvodina Novi Sad	2-0 2-0		1965 Dinamo Zagreb v Buducnost Titograd	2-1	
1952 Partizan Belgrade v Red Star Belgrade	6-0		1966 OFK Belgrade v Dinamo Zagreb	6-2	
1953 BSK Belgrade v Hajduk Split	2-0		1967 Hajduk Split v Sarajevo	2-1	
1954 Partizan Belgrade v Red Star Belgrade	4-1		1968 Red Star Belgrade v Bor FK	7-0	
1955 BSK Belgrade v Hajduk Split	2-0		1969 Dinamo Zagreb v Hajduk Split	3-0	
1956 not held			1970 Red Star Belgrade v Olimpia Llubljana	2-2 1-0	
1957 Partizan Belgrade v Radnicki Belgrade	5-3		1971 Red Star Belgrade v Sloboda Tuzla	2-0 4-0	
1958 Red Star Belgrade v Velez Mostar	4-0		1972 Hajduk Split v Dinamo Zagreb	2-1	
1959 Red Star Belgrade v Partizan Belgrade	3-1		1973 Hajduk Split v Red Star Belgrade	1-1 2-1	

1974	Hajduk Split v Borac Banja Luka	1-0		1982	Red Star Belgrade v Dinamo Zagreb	2-2 4-2
1975	not held			1983	Dinamo Zagreb v Sarajevo	3-2
1976	Hajduk Split v Dinamo Zagreb	1-0 aet		1984	Hajduk Split v Red Star Belgrade	0-0 2-1
1977	Hajduk Split v Buducnost Titograd	2-0 aet		1985	Red Star Belgrade v Dinamo Zagreb	1-1 2-1
1978	Rijeka v Trepca Mitrovica	1-0		1986	Velez Mostar v Dinamo Zagreb	3-1
1979	Rijeka v Partizan Belgrade	0-0 2-0		1987	Hajduk Split v Rijeka	1-1 9-8 pens
				1988	Borac Banja Luka v Red Star Belgrade	1-0
1980	Dinamo Zagreb v Red Star Belgrade	1-1 1-0		1989	Partizan Belgrade v Velez Mostar	6-1
1981	Velez Mostar v Zeljeznicar Sarajevo	3-2				

FEATURED CLUBS IN EUROPEAN COMPETITION

Red Star Belgrade	Dinamo Zagreb	Hajduk Split	OFK Belgrade
Partizan Belgrade	Vojvodina Novi Sad	NK Rijeka	ZNK Zagreb
Olimpia Llubljana	Borac Banja Luka	Bor FK	FK Sarajevo
Tresnjevka Zagreb	Vardar Skopje	Sloboda Tuzla	Radnicki Nis
Velez Mostar	Napredak Krusevac	FK Zeljeznicar Sarajevo	Zagreb City XI
Belgrade City XI	RAD Belgrade		

RED STAR BELGRADE

Belgrade University ☎ 011-668213/660216
Founded 1945
Colours red and white striped shirts, white shorts
Stadium Crvena Zvezda Marakana (110,000)
Champions 1951, 1953, 1956, 1957, 1959, 1960, 1964, 1968, 1969, 1970, 1973, 1977, 1980, 1981, 1984, 1986, 1988
Cup Winners 1948, 1949, 1950, 1958, 1959, 1964, 1968, 1970, 1971, 1982, 1985
UEFA Cup Finalists 1979
Mitropa Cup Winners 1968

Season	Opponent	Home	Playoff Result	Away	Rnd	Cup
1956-57	Rapid Haarlem, Holland	2-0		4-3	1	ECC
	CDNA Sofia, Bulgaria	3-1		1-2	qf	ECC
	Fiorentina, Italy	0-1		0-0	sf	ECC
1957-58	Stade Dudelingen, Luxembourg	9-1		5-0	pr	ECC
	IFK Norrkoping, Sweden	2-1		2-2	1	ECC
	Manchester United, England	3-3		1-2	2	ECC
1959-60	Wolverhampton Wanderers, England	1-1		0-3	1	ECC
1960-61	Ujpest Dozsa, Hungary	1-2		0-3	1	ECC
1961-62	Basel City XI, Switzerland	4-1		1-1	1	Fairs
	Hibernian, Scotland	4-0		1-0	2	Fairs
	Espanol Barcelona, Spain	5-0		1-2	qf	Fairs
	CF Barcelona, Spain	1-4		0-2	sf	Fairs
1962-63	Rapid Vienna, Austria	1-1		1-0	1	Fairs
	CF Barcelona, Spain	3-2	1-0*	0-1	2	Fairs
			* in Nice			
	AS Roma, Italy	2-0		0-3	qf	Fairs
1964-65	Glasgow Rangers, Scotland	4-2	1-3*	1-3	1	ECC
			* at Arsenal			
1965-66	Fiorentina, Italy	0-4		1-3	1	Fairs
1966-67	Atletico Bilbao, Spain	5-0		0-2	1	Fairs
	Valencia CF, Spain	1-2		0-1	2	Fairs
1968-69	Carl Zeiss Jena, East Germany	withdrew			1	ECC
	Glasgow Celtic, Scotland	1-1		1-5	2	ECC
1969-70	Linfield, Ireland	8-0		4-2	1	ECC
	FC Vorwaerts Berlin, East Germany	3-2	lag	1-2	2	ECC
1970-71	Ujpest Dozsa, Hungary	4-0		0-2	1	ECC
	UT Arad Flamurarosie, Romania	3-0		3-1	2	ECC
	Carl Zeiss Jena, East Germany	4-0		2-3	qf	ECC
	Panathinaiakos, Greece	4-1	lag	0-3	sf	ECC
1971-72	Komlo Banyasz, Hungary	1-2		7-2	1	CWC
	Sparta Rotterdam, Holland	2-1		1-1	2	CWC
	Dynamo Moscow, USSR	1-2		1-1	qf	CWC

321

YUGOSLAVIA

1972-73	Lausanne Sport, Switzerland	5-1		2-3	1	UEFA
	Valencia CF, Spain	3-1		1-0	2	UEFA
	Tottenham Hotspur, England	1-0		0-2	3	UEFA
1973-74	Stal Mielec, Poland	2-1		1-0	1	ECC
	Liverpool, England	2-1		2-1	2	ECC
	Atletico Madrid, Spain	0-2		0-0	qf	ECC
1974-75	PAOK Salonika, Greece	2-0	aet	0-1	1	CWC
	Avenir Beggen, Luxembourg	5-1		6-1	2	CWC
	Real Madrid, Spain	2-0	6-5p	0-2	qf	CWC
	Ferencvarosi TC, Hungary	2-2		1-2	sf	CWC
1975-76	Universitatea Craiova, Romania	1-1		3-1	1	UEFA
	Hamburger SV, Germany	1-1		0-4	2	UEFA
1976-77	Lokomotiv Plovdiv, Bulgaria	4-1		1-2	1	UEFA
	Austria Salzburg, Austria	1-0	wag	1-2	2	UEFA
	AEK Athens, Greece	3-1	lag	0-2	3	UEFA
1977-78	Sligo Rovers, Eire	3-0		3-0	1	ECC
	Borussia Monchengladbach, Germany	0-3		1-5	2	ECC
1978-79	BFC Dynamo Berlin, East Germany	4-1	wag	2-5	1	UEFA
	Real Sporting Gijon, Spain	1-1		1-0	2	UEFA
	Arsenal, England	1-0		1-1	3	UEFA
	West Bromwich Albion, England	1-0		1-1	qf	UEFA
	Hertha BSC Berlin, Germany	1-0	wag	1-2	sf	UEFA
	Borussia Monchengladbach, Germany	1-1		0-1*	FINAL	UEFA
	* in Dusseldorf					
1979-80	Galatasaray, Turkey	3-1		0-0	1	UEFA
	Carl Zeiss Jena, East Germany	3-2		3-2	2	UEFA
	Bayern Munich, Germany	3-2		0-2	3	UEFA
1980-81	Viking Stavanger, Norway	4-1		3-2	1	ECC
	FC Basle, Switzerland	2-0		0-1	2	ECC
	Inter Milan, Italy	0-1		1-1	qf	ECC
1981-82	Hibernians, Malta	8-1		2-1	1	ECC
	Banik Ostrava, Czechoslovakia	3-0		1-3	2	ECC
	RSC Anderlecht, Belgium	1-2		1-2	qf	ECC
1982-83	Lillestrom SK, Sweden	3-0		4-0	1	CWC
	FC Barcelona, Spain	2-4		1-2	2	CWC
1983-84	Hellas Verona, Italy	2-3		0-1	1	UEFA
1984-85	Benfica, Portugal	3-2		0-2	1	ECC
1985-86	FC Aarau, Switzerland	2-0		2-2*	1	CWC
	* in Zurich					
	Lyngby BK, Denmark	3-1		2-2	2	CWC
	Atletico Madrid, Spain	0-2		1-1	qf	CWC
1986-87	Panathinaikos, Greece	3-0		1-2	1	ECC
	Rosenborg Trondheim, Norway	4-1		3-0	2	ECC
	Real Madrid, Spain	4-2	lag	0-2	qf	ECC
1987-88	Trakia Plovdiv, Bulgaria	3-0		2-2	1	UEFA
	Clube Bruges, Belgium	3-1		0-4	1	UEFA
1988-89	Dundalk, Eire	3-0		5-0	1	ECC
	AC Milan, Italy	1-0* 1-1	2-4p	1-1	2	ECC
	* abandoned after 61 mins - fog					
1989-90	Galatasaray, Turkey	2-0		1-1	1	UEFA
	Zalgiris Vilnius, USSR	4-1		1-0	2	UEFA
	1.FC Koln, Germany	2-0		0-3	3	UEFA

DINAMO ZAGREB

Founded 1945
Colours all blue
Stadium Maksimir (55,000) ☏ 041-219900/223234
Champions 1948, 1954, 1958, 1982
Cup Winners 1951, 1960, 1963, 1965, 1969, 1980, 1983
Fairs Cup Winners 1967 Fairs Cup Finalists 1963

Season	Opponent	Home	Playoff Result	Away	Rnd	Cup
1958-59	Dukla Prague, Czechoslovakia	2-2		1-2	pr	ECC
1960-61	Red Star Brno, Czechoslovakia	2-0		0-0	qf	CWC
	Fiorentina, Italy	2-1		0-3	sf	CWC
1961-62	Copenhagen XI, Denmark	7-2		2-2	pr	Fairs
	CF Barcelona, Spain	2-2		1-5	1	Fairs
1962-63	FC Porto, Portugal	0-0		2-1	1	Fairs
	Union St Gilloise, Belgium	2-1	3-2*	0-1	2	Fairs
			* in Linz			
	Bayern Munich, Germany	4-1		0-0	qf	Fairs
	Ferencvarosi TC, Hungary	1-0		2-1	sf	Fairs
	Valencia CF, Spain	0-2		1-2	FINAL	Fairs
1963-64	Linzer ASK, Austria	1-0	1-1*wot	0-1	1	CWC
			* in Zagreb			
	Glasgow Celtic, Scotland	2-1		0-3	2	CWC
1964-65	AEK Athens, Greece	3-0		0-2	1	CWC
	Steaua Bucharest, Romania	2-0		3-1	2	CWC
	Torino, Italy	1-2		1-1	qf	CWC
1965-66	Atletico Madrid, Spain	0-1		0-4	1	CWC
1966-67	Spartak Brno, Czechoslovakia	2-0	wot	0-2	1	Fairs
	Dunfermline Athletic, Scotland	2-0	wag	2-4	2	Fairs
	Dynamo Pitesti, Romania	1-0		0-0	3	Fairs
	Juventus, Italy	3-0		2-2	qf	Fairs
	Eintracht Frankfurt, Germany	4-0		0-3	sf	Fairs
	Leeds United, England	2-0		0-0	FINAL	Fairs
1967-68	Petrolul Ploesti, Romania	5-0		0-2	1	Fairs
	Bologna, Italy	1-2		0-0	2	Fairs
1968-69	Fiorentina, Italy	1-1		1-2	1	Fairs
1969-70	Slovan Bratislava, Czechoslovakia	3-0		0-0	1	CWC
	Olympique Marseille, France	2-0		1-1	2	CWC
	FC Schalke 04 Gelsenkirchen, Germany	1-3		0-1	qf	CWC
1970-71	Barreirense, Portugal	6-1		0-2	1	Fairs
	Hamburger SV, Germany	4-0		0-1	2	Fairs
	Twente Enschede, Holland	2-2		0-1	3	Fairs
1971-72	Botev Vratza, Bulgaria	6-1		2-1	1	UEFA
	Rapid Vienna, Austria	2-2	lag	0-0	2	UEFA
1973-74	AC Milan, Italy	0-1		1-3	1	CWC
1976-77	Tirgu Armata Mures, Romania	3-0		1-0	1	UEFA
	1.FC Magdeburg, East Germany	2-2		0-2	2	UEFA
1977-78	Olympiakos Piraeus, Greece	5-1		1-3	1	UEFA
	Torino, Italy	1-0		1-3	2	UEFA
1979-80	Perugia, Italy	0-0		0-1	1	UEFA
1980-81	Benfica, Portugal	0-0		0-2	1	CWC
1982-83	Sporting Lisbon, Portugal	1-0		0-3	1	ECC
1983-84	FC Porto, Portugal	2-1	lag	0-1	1	CWC
1988-89	Besiktas, Turkey	2-0		0-1	1	UEFA
	VfB Stuttgart, Germany	1-3		1-1	2	UEFA
1989-90	AJ Auxerre, France	1-3		1-0	1	UEFA

YUGOSLAVIA

HAJDUK SPLIT

Founded 1911
Colours blue and red striped shirts, blue shorts
Stadium Poljud (50,000) ☎ 058-41755/45390
Champions 1927, 1929, 1950, 1952, 1955, 1971, 1974, 1975, 1979
Cup Winners 1967, 1972, 1973, 1974, 1975, 1976, 1977, 1984, 1987

Season	Opponent	Home	Playoff Result	Away	Rnd	Cup
1967-68	Tottenham Hotspur, England	0-2		3-4	1	CWC
1970-71	Slavia Sofia, Bulgaria	3-0		0-1	1	Fairs
	Vitoria Setubal, Portugal	2-1		0-2	2	Fairs
1971-72	Valencia CF, Spain	1-1	lag	0-0	1	ECC
1972-73	Fredrikstad FK, Norway	1-0		1-0	1	CWC
	Wrexham, Wales	2-0	wag	1-3	2	CWC
	Hibernian, Scotland	3-0		2-4	qf	CWC
	Leeds United, England	0-0		0-1	sf	CWC
1974-75	IBK Keflavik, Iceland	2-0		7-1*	1	ECC
				* in Split		
	St Etienne, France	4-1		1-5	2	ECC
1975-76	Floriana, Malta	3-0		5-0	1	ECC
	RWD Molenbeeck, Belgium	4-0		3-2	2	ECC
	PSV Eindhoven, Holland	2-0		0-3	qf	ECC
1976-77	Lierse SK, Belgium	3-0		0-1	1	CWC
	Atletico Madrid, Spain	1-2		0-1	2	CWC
1977-78	Dundalk, Eire	4-0		0-1	1	CWC
	Diosgyoer, Hungary	2-1	4-3 pen	1-2	2	CWC
	FK Austria Vienna, Austria	1-1	0-3 pen	1-1	qf	CWC
1978-79	Rapid Vienna, Austria	2-0		1-2	1	UEFA
	Arsenal, England	2-1	lag	0-1	2	UEFA
1979-80	Trabzonspor, Turkey	1-0		1-0	1	ECC
	Vejle BK, Denmark	3-0		1-2	2	ECC
	Hamburger SV, Germany	3-2	lag	0-1	qf	ECC
1981-82	VfB Stuttgart, Germany	3-1		2-2	1	UEFA
	SK Beveren Waas, Belgium	1-2	wag	3-2	2	UEFA
	Valencia CF, Spain	4-1		1-5	3	UEFA
1982-83	Zurrieq, Malta	4-0		4-1	1	UEFA
	Girondins Bordeaux, France	4-1		0-4	2	UEFA
1983-84	Universitatea Craiova, Romania	1-0	3-1 pen	0-1	1	UEFA
	Honved Budapest, Hungary	3-0		2-3	2	UEFA
	Radnicki Nis, Yugoslavia	2-0		2-0	3	UEFA
	Sparta Prague, Czechoslovakia	2-0		0-1	qf	UEFA
	Tottenham Hotspur, England	2-1	lag	0-1	sf	UEFA
1984-85	Dynamo Moscow, USSR	2-5		0-1	1	CWC
1985-86	FC Metz, France	5-1		2-2	1	UEFA
	Torino, Italy	3-1		1-1	2	UEFA
	Dnepr Dnepropetovsk, USSR	2-0		1-0*	3	UEFA
				* in Tbilisi		
	Waregem KSV, Belgium	1-0	4-5 pen	0-1	qf	UEFA
1986-87	OFI Crete, Cyprus	4-0		0-1	1	UEFA
	Traka Plovdiv, Bulgaria	3-1		2-2	2	UEFA
	Dundee United, Scotland	0-0		0-2	3	UEFA
1987-88	Aab Aalborg, Denmark	1-0	4-2 pen	0-1	1	CWC
	Olympique Marseille, France	2-0		0-4	2	CWC

OFK BELGRADE

Founded 1911 as BSK, 1940 Metalac, 1950 BSK, 1957 OFK
Colours blue and white striped shirts, blue shorts
Stadium Omladinski Karaburma (30,000) ☎ 011 765425
Cup Winners 1953, 1955 as BSK 1962, 1966

Season	Opponent	Home	Playoff Result	Away	Rnd	Cup
1962-63	SC Chemie Halle, East Germany	2-0		3-3*	1	CWC
	Portadown, Ireland	5-1		2-3*	2	CWC
				* in Belfast		
	Napoli, Italy	2-0	3-1*	1-3	qf	CWC
			* in Marseilles			
	Tottenham Hotspur, England	1-2		1-3	sf	CWC
1963-64	Juventus, Italy	2-1	0-1*	1-2	1	Fairs
			* in Trieste			
1964-65	Atletico Bilbao, Spain	0-2		2-2	1	Fairs
1966-67	Spartak Moscow, USSR	1-3		0-3	1	CWC
1968-69	Rapid Bucharest, Romania	6-1		1-3	1	Fairs
	Bologna, Italy	1-0		1-1	2	Fairs
	Goztepe Izmir, Turkey	3-1	lag	0-2	3	Fairs
1971-72	Djurgarden IF Stockholm, Sweden	4-1		2-2	1	UEFA
	Carl Zeiss Jena, East Germany	1-1		0-4	2	UEFA
1972-73	Dukla Prague, Czechoslovakia	3-1		2-2	1	UEFA
	Feyenoord Rotterdam, Holland	2-1	wag	3-4	2	UEFA
	Beroe Stara Zagora, Bulgaria	0-0		3-1	3	UEFA
	Twente Enschede, Holland	3-2		0-2	qf	UEFA
1973-74	Panathinaikos, Greece	0-1	wag	2-1	1	UEFA
	Dynamo Tbilisi, USSR	1-5		0-3	2	UEFA

PARTIZAN BELGRADE

Founded 1945
Colours black and white striped shirts, white shorts
Stadium Army Stadion JNA (60,000) ☎ 011 648158/648067
Champions 1947, 1949, 1961, 1962, 1963, 1965, 1976, 1978, 1983, 1987 (awarded title after dispute)
Cup Winners 1947, 1952, 1954, 1957, 1989
European Cup Finalists 1966
Mitropa Cup Winners 1978

Season	Opponent	Home	Result	Away	Rnd	Cup
1955-56	Sporting Lisbon, Portugal	5-2		3-3	1	ECC
	Real Madrid, Spain	3-0		0-4	2	ECC
1961-62	Sporting Lisbon, Portugal	2-0		1-1	1	ECC
	Juventus, Italy	1-2		0-5	2	ECC
1962-63	CDNA Sofia, Bulgaria	1-4		1-2	1	ECC
1963-64	Anorthosis Famagusta, Cyprus	3-0		3-1	1	ECC
	Jeunesse Esch, Luxembourg	6-2		1-2	2	ECC
	Inter Milan, Italy	0-2		1-2	qf	ECC
1965-66	FC Nantes, France	2-0		2-2	1	ECC
	Werder Bremen, Germany	3-0		0-1	2	ECC
	Sparta Prague, Czechoslovakia	5-0		1-4	qf	ECC
	Manchester United, England	2-0		0-1	sf	ECC
	Real Madrid, Spain	1-2	in Brussels		FINAL	ECC
1967-68	Lokomotiv Plovdiv, Bulgaria	5-1		1-1	1	Fairs
	Leeds United, England	1-2		1-1	2	Fairs
1969-70	Ujpest Dozsa, Hungary	2-1		0-2	1	Fairs
1970-71	Dynamo Dresden, East Germany	0-0		0-6	1	Fairs
1974-75	Gornik Zabrze, Poland	3-0		2-2	1	UEFA
	Portadown, Ireland	5-0		1-1	2	UEFA
	1.FC Koln, Germany	1-0		1-5	3	UEFA

YUGOSLAVIA

1976-77	Dynamo Kiev, USSR	0-2		0-3	1	ECC
1978-79	Dynamo Dresden, East Germany	2-0	4-5 pen	0-2	1	ECC
1983-84	Viking Stavanger, Norway	5-1		0-0	1	ECC
	BFC Dynamo Berlin, East Germany	1-0		0-2	2	ECC
1984-85	Rabat Ajax, Malta	2-0		2-0	1	UEFA
	Queens Park Rangers, England	4-0	wag	2-6	2	UEFA
	Videoton Sekesfehervar, Hungary	2-0		0-5	3	UEFA
1985-86	Portimonense, Portugal	4-0		0-1	1	UEFA
	FC Nantes, France	1-1		0-4	2	UEFA
1986-87	Borussia Monchengladbach, Germany	1-3		0-1	1	UEFA
1987-88	Flamutari Vlora, Albania	2-1		0-2	1	UEFA
1988-89	Slavia Sofia, Bulgaria	5-0		5-0	1	UEFA
	AS Roma, Italy	4-2	lag	0-2	2	UEFA
1989-90	Glasgow Celtic, Scotland	2-1*	wag	4-5	1	CWC
		* in Mostar				
	FC Groningen, Holland	3-1		3-4	2	CWC
	Dinamo Bucharest, Romania	0-2		1-2	qf	CWC

VOJVODINA NOVI SAD

Founded 1914 as Vojvodina, 1945 Sloga, 1951 Vojvodina
Colours red and white halved shirts, red shorts
Stadium Gradski (22,000) ☎ 021-25481
Champions 1966, 1989
Mitropa Cup Winners 1977

Season	Opponent	Home	Playoff Result	Away	Rnd	Cup
1961-62	AC Milan, Italy	2-0		0-0	1	Fairs
	Iraklis Salonika, Greece	9-1		1-2	2	Fairs
	MTK Budapest, Hungary	1-2		1-4	qf	Fairs
1962-63	Leipzig City XI, East Germany	0-2		1-0	1	Fairs
1964-65	Lokomotiv Plovdiv, Bulgaria	1-1	0-2*	1-1	pr	Fairs
			* in Sofia			
1966-67	Admira Vienna, Austria	0-0		1-0	1	ECC
	Atletico Madrid, Spain	3-1	3-2*aet	0-2	2	ECC
			* in Madrid			
	Glasgow Celtic, Scotland	1-0		0-2	qf	ECC
1967-68	CUF Barreiro, Portugal	1-0		3-1	1	Fairs
	1.FC Lokomotive Leipzig, East Germany	0-0		2-0	2	Fairs
	Goztepe Izmir, Turkey	1-0		1-0	3	Fairs
	Bologna, Italy	0-2		0-0	qf	Fairs
1968-69	Glasgow Rangers, Scotland	1-0		0-2	1	Fairs
1969-70	Gwardia Warsaw, Poland	1-1		0-1	1	Fairs
1972-73	Slovan Bratislava, Czechoslovakia	1-2		0-6	1	UEFA
1975-76	AEK Athens, Greece	0-0		1-3	1	UEFA
1989-90	Honved Budapest, Hungary	2-1	lag	0-1	1	ECC

NK RIJEKA NOGOMENTI

Founded 1945 as Kvarner, 1954 NK Rijeka
Colours all white with blue horizontal stripes
Stadium Kantrida (20,000) ☎ 051-611622/611003
Cup Winners 1978, 1979

Season	Opponent	Home	Result	Away	Rnd	Cup
1978-79	Wrexham, Wales	3-0		0-2	1	CWC
	SK Beveren Waas, Belgium	0-0		0-2	2	CWC
1979-80	Beerschot, Belgium	2-1		0-0	1	CWC
	Lokomotiva Kosice, Czechoslovakia	3-0		0-2	2	CWC
	Juventus, Italy	0-0		0-2	qf	CWC
1984-85	Real Valladolid, Spain	4-1		0-1	1	UEFA
	Real Madrid, Spain	3-1		0-3	2	UEFA
1986-87	Standard Liege, Belgium	0-1		1-1	1	UEFA

ZNK ZAGREB

Founded 1921 as Borac Zagreb, 1952 NK Zagreb
Colours blue and white
Stadium Kranjcevicevej (25,000) ☎ 041 311625

Season	Opponent	Home	result	Away	Rnd	Cup
1964-65	Grazer AK (GAK), Austria	3-2		6-0	1	Fairs
	AS Roma, Italy	1-1		0-1	2	Fairs
1965-66	RFC Liege, Belgium	2-0		0-1	1	Fairs
	Steagul Rosu Brasov, Romania	2-2		0-1	2	Fairs
1969-70	Sporting Charleroi SC, Belgium	1-3		1-2	1	Fairs

OLIMPIA LJUBLJANA

Founded 17-4-1946
Colours all green
Stadium Bezigrad (20,000) ☎ 061 210108

Season	Opponent	Home	Result	Away	Rnd	Cup
1966-67	Ferencvarosi TC, Hungary	3-3		0-3	1	Fairs
1968-69	Hibernian, Scotland	0-3		1-2	1	Fairs
1970-71	Benfica, Portugal	1-1		1-8	1	CWC

BORAC BANJA LUKA

Founded 1926
Colours red shirts with blue sleeves and shorts
Stadium Gradsa (25,000) ☎ 078-35614/35615
Cup Winners 1988

Season	Opponent	Home	Result	Away	Rnd	Cup
1975-76	US Rumelingen, Luxembourg	9-0		5-1*	1	CWC
				* in Esch		
	RSC Anderlecht, Belgium	1-0		0-3	2	CWC
1988-89	Metallist Kharkov, USSR	2-0		0-4	1	CWC

YUGOSLAVIA

FK BOR

Founded 1934
Colours black and white striped shirts, black shorts
Stadium Gradski (15,000) ☎ ??????

Season	Opponent	Home	Result	Away	Rnd	Cup
1968-69	Slovan Bratislava, Czechoslovakia	2-0		0-3	1	CWC

FK SARAJEVO

Founded 1946 by merger of Udarnik and Sloboda
Colours maroon shirts, white shorts
Stadium Kosevo (35,000) ☎ 071-39764/39599
Champions 1967, 1985

Season	Opponent	Home	Result	Away	Rnd	Cup
1967-68	Olympiakos Nicosia, Cyprus	3-1		2-2	1	ECC
	Manchester United, England	0-0		1-2	2	ECC
1980-81	Hamburger SV, Germany	3-3		2-4	1	UEFA
1982-83	Slavia Sofia, Bulgaria	4-2		2-2	1	UEFA
	Corvinul, Romania	4-0		4-4	2	UEFA
	RSC Anderlecht, Belgium	1-0		1-6	3	UEFA
1985-86	Kuusysi Lahti, Finland	1-2		1-2	1	ECC

TRESNJEVKA ZAGREB

Founded 1926
Colours red shirts, white shorts
Stadium Tresnjevka (10,000) ☎ ??????

Season	Opponent	Home	Result	Away	Rnd	Cup
1963-64	Belenenses, Portugal	0-2		1-2	1	Fairs

VARDAR SKOPJE

Founded 1947 by merger Pobeda and Mekedonijom
Colours blue and white shirts, blue shorts
Stadium Gradski-Vrt (28,200) ☎ 091-230455
Champions 1987 (played in ECC during dispute)
Cup Winners 1961

Season	Opponent	Home	Result	Away	Rnd	Cup
1961-62	bye				1	
	Dunfermline Athletic, Scotland	2-0		0-5	2	CWC
1985-86	Dinamo Bucharest, Romania	1-0	wag	1-2	1	UEFA
	Dundee United, Scotland	1-1		0-2	2	UEFA
1987-88	FC Porto, Portugal	0-3		0-3	1	ECC

SLOBODA TUZLA

Founded 1919
Colours red and black striped shirts, black shorts
Stadium Tusan (15,000) ☎ 075-32477/223160

Season	Opponent	Home	Result	Away	Rnd	Cup
1977-78	Las Palmas, Spain	4-3		0-5	1	UEFA

RADNICKI NIS

Founded 1923
Colours all blue with white shoulders
Stadium Cair (20,000) ☎ 018-22016/21336

Season	Opponent	Home	Result	Away	Rnd	Cup
1980-81	Linzer ASK, Austria	4-1		2-1	1	UEFA
	Beroe Stara Zagora, Bulgaria	2-1		1-0	2	UEFA
	AZ 67 Alkmaar, Holland	2-2		0-5	3	UEFA
1981-82	Napoli, Italy	0-0	wag	2-2	1	UEFA
	Grasshoppers Zurich, Switzerland	2-0	wop	0-2	2	UEFA
	Feyenoord Rotterdam, Holland	2-0		0-1	3	UEFA
	Dundee United, Scotland	3-0		0-2	qf	UEFA
	Hamburger SV, Germany	2-1		1-5	sf	UEFA
1983-84	St Gallen, Switzerland	3-0		2-1	1	UEFA
	Internacional Bratislava, Czechoslovakia	4-0		2-3	2	UEFA
	Hajduk Split, Yugoslavia	0-2		0-2	3	UEFA

VELEZ MOSTAR

Founded 1922
Colours all red
Stadium Pod Bijeci Brijegom (21,000) ☎ 088-54306/21985
Cup Winners 1981, 1986

Season	Opponent	Home	Result	Away	Rnd	Cup
1973-74	Tatran Presov, Czechoslovakia	1-1		2-4	1	UEFA
1974-75	Spartak Moscow, USSR	2-0	wag	1-3	1	UEFA
	Rapid Vienna, Austria	1-0		1-1	2	UEFA
	Derby County, England	4-1		1-3	3	UEFA
	Twente Enschede, Holland	1-0		0-2	qf	UEFA
1981-82	Jeunesse Esch, Luxembourg	6-1		1-1	1	CWC
	1.FC Lokomotive Leipzig, East Germany	1-1	0-3p	1-1	2	CWC
1986-87	Vasas Budapest, Hungary	3-2		2-2	1	CWC
	Vitosha Sofia, Bulgaria	4-3		0-2	2	CWC
1987-88	FC Sion, Switzerland	5-0		0-3	1	UEFA
	Borussia Dortmund, Germany	2-1		0-2	2	UEFA
1988-89	Apoel Nicosia, Cyprus	1-0		5-2	1	UEFA
	Belenenses, Portugal	0-0	4-3p	0-0	2	UEFA
	Heart of Midlothian, Scotland	2-1		0-3	3	UEFA

YUGOSLAVIA

NAPREDAK KRUSEVAC

Founded 1946
Colours white shirts, black shorts
Stadium Mlodost (25,000) ☎ 037-29432

Season	Opponent	Home	Result	Away	Rnd	Cup
1980-81	Dynamo Dresden, East Germany	0-1		0-1	1	UEFA

FK ZELJEZNICAR SARAJEVO

Founded 1921
Colours all sky blue
Stadium Grbavica (26,000) ☎ 071-523246
Champions 1972

Season	Opponent	Home	Result	Away	Rnd	Cup
1970-71	RSC Anderlecht, Belgium	3-4		4-5	1	Fairs
1971-72	Clube Bruges, Belgium	3-0		1-3	1	UEFA
	Bologna, Italy	1-1	wag	2-2	2	UEFA
	St Johnstone, Scotland	5-1		0-1	3	UEFA
	Ferencvarosi TC, Hungary	1-2	5-7 pen	2-1	qf	UEFA
1972-73	Derby County, England	1-2		0-2	1	ECC
1984-85	Sliven, Bulgaria	5-1		0-1	1	UEFA
	FC Sion, Switzerland	2-1		1-1	2	UEFA
	Universitatea Craiova, Romania	4-0		0-2	3	UEFA
	Dynamo Minsk, USSR	2-0		1-1	qf	UEFA
	Videoton Sekesfehervar, Hungary	2-1		1-3	sf	UEFA

ZAGREB CITY XI

Season	Opponent	Home	Result	Away	Rnd	Cup
1955-58	Birmingham City, England	0-1		0-3	pr	Fairs
	Inter Milan, Italy	0-1		0-4	pr	Fairs
1958-60	Ujpest Dozsa, Hungary	4-2		0-1	1	Fairs
	Birmingham City, England	3-3		0-1	2	Fairs
1960-61	CF Barcelona, Spain	1-1		3-4	1	Fairs

BELGRADE CITY XI

Colours white and blue
Entered the Fairs Cup as Ville de Beogradski

Season	Opponent	Home	Playoff Result	Away	Rnd	Cup
1958-60	Lausanne Sport, Switzerland	6-1		5-3	1	Fairs
	Chelsea, England	4-1		0-1	qf	Fairs
	CF Barcelona, Spain	1-1		1-3	sf	Fairs
1960-61	Leipzig City XI, East Germany	4-1	2-0*	2-5	1	Fairs
			* in Budapest			
	Inter Milan, Italy	1-0		0-5	2	Fairs

RAD BELGRADE

Founded 1958
Colours blue shirts, white shorts
Stadium FK Rad (13,000) ☎ 011-663039/666884

Season	Opponent	Home	Result	Away	Rnd	Cup
1989-90	Olympiakos Piraeus, Greece	2-1		0-2	1	UEFA

● Stade Louis II Nouveau, Monaco

CROATIA

Separate State 1941 to 1944, part of Yugoslavia

LEAGUE CHAMPIONS

1941 Gradjanska Agram
1942 Concordia Agram
1943 Gradjanska Agram
1944 Gradjanska Agram

332 ● Santiago Bernabeu, Madrid, Spain. Real Madrid, ECC Finals 1957, 1969, 1980

ESTONIA

EESTI JALGPALLI LIIT
Founded 14th December 1921, affiliated FIFA 20th May 1923, absorbed into the USSR in 1943
Tallinn, Jarju tan 48.6, PO Box 70, Takkubb as at 1935

LEAGUE CHAMPIONS

1921	V.s.Sport Tallinn v TJK Tallinn	5-3
1922	V.s.Sport Tallinn v Kalev Tallinn	4-2
1923	Kalev Tallinn v Tarku ASK	6-0
1924	V.s.Sport Tallinn v Kalev Tallinn	1-1 2-0
1925	V.s.Sport Tallinn v Kalev Tallinn	5-0
1926	TJK Tallinn v V.s.Sport Tallinn	4-1
1927	V.s.Sport Tallinn v TJK Tallinn	2-0
1928	TJK Tallinn v Tallinna Merkuur	4-1 1-4 2-0
1929	V.s.Sport Tallinn	

1930	Kalev Tallinn
1931	V.s.Sport Tallinn
1932	V.s.Sport Tallinn
1933	V.s.Sport Tallinn
1934	Estonia Tallinn
1935	Estonia Tallinn
1936	Estonia Tallinn
1937	Estonia Tallinn
1938	Estonia Tallinn
1939	Estonia Tallinn

1940	Tartu Olimpia
1941	not held
1942	SV Dorpat
1943	Estonia Tallinn

LEAGUE TABLES

1929
V.s.Sport Tallinn	15-1	10
TJK Tallinn	14-7	7
Kalev Tallinn	9-9	5
Estica	8-13	3
Merkuur Tallinna	7-15	3
Tarku JK	4-12	2

1930
Kalev Tallinn	13-1	5
V.s.Sport Tallinn	9-1	5
TJK Tallinn	7-6	2
Narva Voitleja	2-23	0

1931
V.s.Sport Tallinn	14-2	9
Kalev Tallinn	9-2	7
TJK Tallinn	9-5	7
Puhkekodu	10-10	3
Narva Voitleja	9-18	2
NTHK (Narva)	4-18	2

1932
V.s.Sport Tallinn	42-9	18
Puhkekodu	18-17	13
Kalev Tallinn	16-15	11
TJK Tallinn	22-21	9
NTHK (Narva)	14-21	7
Narva Voitleja	6-35	2

1933
V.s.Sport Tallinn	26-7	16
Estonia Tallinn	35-10	15
TJK Tallinn	28-15	14
Kalev Tallinn	15-30	8
Puhkekodu	12-27	5
NTHK (Narva)	10-37	2

1934
Estonia Tallinn	22-3	17
V.s.Sport Tallinn	23-5	15
Puhkekodu	19-11	11
TJK Tallinn	19-13	11
Kalev Tallinn	9-35	3
Tartu Olimpia	7-32	3

1935
Estonia Tallinn	26-3	13
TJK Tallinn	15-8	8
V.s.Sport Tallinn	7-8	8
Puhkekdou	11-14	8
Kalev Tallinn	16-13	6
Parnu Tervis	10-15	6
Narva Voitleja	10-15	5
Tartu Olimpia	5-24	2

1936
Estonia Tallinn	60-15	23
V.s.Sport Tallinn	36-19	18
Puhkekodu	35-21	17
Parnu Tervis	34-49	15
Kalev Tallinn	28-27	14
Esta	24-26	11
TJK Tallinn	19-35	9
Narva Voitleja	15-59	5

1937-38
Estonia Tallinn	51-17	22
Esta	32-22	19
Kalev Tallinn	43-26	18
V.s.Sport Tallinn	48-25	17
NTHK (Narva)	30-44	11
Parnu Tervis	29-54	9
UENUTO	26-50	8
Puhkekodu	18-39	8

1938-39
Estonia Tallinn	40-11	23
TJK Tallinn	43-26	17
V.s.Sport Tallinn	35-26	15
Esta	25-21	15
Kalev Tallinn	27-23	14
Tartu Olimpia	22-36	14
Parnu Tervis	21-42	9
NTHK (Narva)	18-46	5

1939-40
Tartu Olimpia	39-14	22
Estonia Tallinn	36-16	21
Esta	28-25	16
V.s.Sport Tallinn	34-23	14
Kalev Tallinn	18-21	14
TJK Tallinn	25-31	12
UENUTO	22-38	8
Parnu Tervis	18-52	5

LATVIA

LATVUAS FUTBOLA SAVIENIBA
Founded 28th May 1921, Affiliated FIFA 20th May 1923
Riga, Valdemara iela 65, PO Box 712 as in 1935
Now absorbed into the USSR

LEAGUE CHAMPIONS

1922	Kaiserwood Riga	1928	Olympia Libau	1933	Olympia Libau	1940	Rigaer FK
1923	Kaiserwood Riga	1929	Olympia Libau	1934	Rigaer FK	1941	not held
1924	Rigaer FK			1935	Rigaer FK	1942	ASK Riga
1925	Rigaer FK	1930	Rigaer FK	1936	Olympia Libau	1943	ASK Riga
1926	Rigaer FK	1931	Rigaer FK	1937	Olympia Libau		
1927	Olympia Libau	1932	ASK Riga	1938	Rigaer FK		
				1939	Olympia Libau		

LITHUANIA

LIETUVOS KAMUOLIO ZAIDIMU SAJUNGA
Founded 18th February 1923, affiliated FIFA 21st May 1923
Kaunas, Kuno Kultures Rumai PO, Box 188, address as in 1935
Absorbed by the USSR in 1943

LEAGUE CHAMPIONS

1922	Lietuvos Fizinio Lavinimosi, Sajunga, Kaunas (LFLS Kaunas)
1923	Lietuvos Fizinio Lavinimosi, Sajunga, Kaunas (LFLS Kaunas)
1924	Sporto Clubas Kovas, Kaunas (Kovas)
1925	Sporto Clubas Kovas, Kaunas (Kovas)
1926	Sporto Clubas Kovas, Kaunas (Kovas)
1927	Lietuvos Fizinio Lavinimosi, Sajunga, Kaunas (LFLS Kaunas)
1928	Klaipedos Sporto Sajunga, Klaipeda (KSS)
1929	Klaipedos Sporto Sajunga, Klaipeda (KSS)
1930	Klaipedos Sporto Sajunga, Klaipeda (KSS)
1931	Klaipedos Sporto Sajunga, Klaipeda (KSS)
1932	Lietuvos Fizinio Lavinimosi, Sajunga, Kaunas (LKLS Kaunas)

1933	sanciu sauliu Klubas Kovas, Kaunas
1934	Maisto Sporto Klubas, Kaunas (MSK)
1935	Klubas Sporto Kovas, Kaunas (KSK)
1936	Klubas Sporto Kovas, Kaunas (KSK)
1937	Klaipedos Sporto Sajunga, Klaipeda (KSS)
1938	Klaipedos Sporto Sajunga, Klaipeda (KSS)
1939	LGSF Kaunas (LGSF)
1939	LGSF Kaunas (LGSF)
1941	not held
1942	not held
1943	Tauras Kaven

LEAGUE POSITIONS/TABLES

Where known

1922	Points
LFLS Kaunas	26
LFLS Sanciu	18
Makabi Kaunas	14
LFLS II Kaunas	14
Aviacija	13
Balttgidziu	4

1923	
LFLS Kaunas	7
KSK Kaunas	5
Kovas Kaunas	4
Makabi Kaunas	2

1924
KAUNAS LEAGUE

Kovas	9
LFLS	8
KSK	4
Makabi	3

KLAIPEDA LEAGUE

Sportverein	8
MTV	6
Silutes MTV	6
Freya	6
Spielvereinigung	4
Sarunas	0

Final: Kovas v Sportverein 2-1

1925
KAUNAS LEAGUE

Kovas	10
LFLS	6
KSK	5
Makabi	3

KLAIPEDA LEAGUE

Freya	17
Spielvereinigung	15
MTV	11
Silutes Vorwarts	8
VfR	6
Sportverein	3

SIAULIU LEAGUE

LFLS	8
Ziezirba	4
Makabi	0

Final: Kovas v LFLS Siauliu 2-0

1926
KAUNAS LEAGUE

Kovas	9
LFLS	7
Makabi	5
KSK	3

SIAULIU LEAGUE

LFLS	11
Ziezirba	7
Hakabi	4
ZAK	2

Play off: Kovas v LFLS Siauliu 2-0

KLAIPEDA-SIAURES LEAGUE

KSS	18
Freya	14
Spielvereinigung	13
MTV	8
Silutes Vorwarts	5
VfR	2

GRUP LEAGUE

Pagegiu SV	7
Juknoviciu SV	3
Rambynu	2

Play off: KSS v Pagegiu 6-1
Final: Kovas v KSS 3-2

1927
KAUNAS LEAGUE

LFLS	16
KSK	9
Kovas	6
Makabi	5
Sparta	4

SIAULIU LEAGUE

LFLS	2
Makabi	2

Play off: LFLS Kaunas beat LFLS Siauliu

KLAIPEDA-SIAURES LEAGUE

Spielvereinigung I	13
KSS	12
Freya	7
Spielvereinigung II	7
Silutes Vorwarts	1

PIETU LEAGUE

Pagegiu SV	12
Oudu SV	6
Ouknoviciu SV	4
Stoniskiu SV	2

Play off: Pagegiu SV v Spielvereinigung I 2-1
Final: LFLS Kaunas v Pagegiu SV 3-1

1928
KAUNAS LEAGUE

LFLS	19
KSK	15
Kovas	10
Sparta	7
Makabi	6
Kultas	3

SIAULIU LEAGUE

LDS	
SSK	
Kraft	
Makabi	

Play off: LFLS Kaunas beat LDS Siauliu

KLAIPEDA-SIAURES LEAGUE

KSS	14
Spielvereinigung	8
SSK	8
Freya	6
Silutes Vorwarts	4

PIETU LEAGUE

Pagegiu SV	18
Stoniskiu SV	16
Pagegiu SV II	2
Stoniskiu SV II	2
Oudu SV	2

Play off: KSS beat Pagegiu SV
Final: KSS Kleipeda v LFLS Kaunas 3-1

1929
KAUNAS LEAGUE

LFLS	16
KSK Kultas	15
Tauras	12
Kovas	10
Sparta	6
Makabi	1

KLAIPEDA LEAGUE

KSS	15
Freya	10
Spielvereinigung	8
SSK	7
Silutes Vorwarts	0

Final: KSS Klaipeda v LFLS Kaunas 4-2

1936-37	P	W	D	L	F-A	Pts
KSS Kaunas	16	12	2	1	61-17	28
Kovas Kaunas	16	8	5	3	33-19	21
LFLS Kaunas	16	8	5	3	28-15	21
MSK Kaunas	16	8	4	4	17-12	20
CTSO Kaunas	16	6	6	2	16-17	18
LGSF Kaunas	16	6	1	9	23-24	13
Svyturys Klaipeda	16	4	2	10	18-30	10
Tauras Kaunas	16	3	2	11	20-37	8
Marij Saulys	16	0	0	16	10-55	0

1937-38	P	W	D	L	F-A	Pts
KSS Kaunas	18	12	2	4	54-20	26
LGSF Kaunas	18	12	2	4	43-18	26
Svyturys Klaipeda	18	11	2	5	34-20	24
Kovas Kaunas	18	9	5	4	44-24	23
MSK Kaunas	18	7	7	4	36-25	21
LFLS Kaunas	18	8	4	6	34-22	20
CTSO Kaunas	18	7	2	9	30-30	16
Makabi Kaunas	18	5	3	8	25-45	13
Kybartu TSO	18	2	2	14	15-60	6
Siauliu Sakalas	18	2	1	15	15-66	5

1938-39	P	W	D	L	F-A	Pts
LGSF Kaunas	13	8	1	4	31-20	17
Kovas Kaunas	13	8	0	5	28-18	16
KSS Klaipeda	13	8	0	5	34-31	16
Tauras Kaunas	13	5	3	5	21-17	13
CTSO Kaunas	13	5	3	5	23-24	13
LFLS Kaunas	13	4	3	6	20-25	11
MSK Kaunas	13	4	1	8	15-26	9
Svyturys Klaipeda	7	1	1	5	9-20	3

1939 (Autumn)	P	W	D	L	F-A	Pts
LGSF Kaunas	7	5	2	0	22-4	12
Tauras Kaunas	7	4	1	2	16-10	9
LFLS Kaunas	7	4	0	3	19-11	8
CTSO Kaunas	7	4	0	3	11-7	8
MSK Kaunas	7	3	1	3	8-10	7
KSS Telsiai	7	2	1	4	3-10	5
Siauliai Sakalas	7	2	0	5	6-17	4
Kovas Kaunas	7	0	1	6	8-24	1

335

SLOVAKIA

Seperate state from 9 March 1939 to 1944

LEAGUE CHAMPIONS

1940 SK Bratislava Pressburg
1941 SK Bratislava Pressburg
1942 SK Bratislava Pressburg
1943 Army Pressburg
1944 SK Bratislava Pressburg